386

# THE VIEW FROM CHRISTOPHER STREET

# THE VIEW FROM CHRISTOPHER STREET

Edited by

*Michael Denneny*

*Charles Ortleb*

*Thomas Steele*

CHATTO & WINDUS
THE HOGARTH PRESS
LONDON

Published in 1984 by
Chatto & Windus · The Hogarth Press
40 William IV Street
London WC2N 4DF

British Library Cataloguing in Publication Data

[The Christopher Street reader]. The view
   from Christopher Street.
   1. Homosexuals—United States
   I. Denneny, Michael    II. Ortleb, Charles
   III. Steele, Thomas    IV. The view from
   Christopher Street
   306.7'66'0973        HQ76.3.U5

   ISBN  0–7011–2906–9

Printed in Great Britain by
Redwood Burn Limited, Trowbridge, Wiltshire
and Bound by Pegasus Bookbinding, Melksham, Wiltshire

# Acknowledgments

The editors would like to express their gratitude to the following people: Patrick Merla, whose tireless and exacting editing is surpassed only by his love of words; Thomas Miller, whose cooperative genius brought this book together; and all the writers represented herein, whose kind consent made this book possible, and whose dedication to the literature of gay life sustains *Christopher Street* magazine. We'd also like to thank the people who helped get *Christopher Street* off the ground: Peter Anastos, Paul Baron, Dorianne Beyer, Blanche Boyd, Sharon DeLano, Kevin Fisher, Byrne Fone, Ron Gans, Ric Garcia, Bertha Harris, Doug Ireland, Tommy McCarthy, Frank Rose, Vito Russo, Isaaca Siegel, David Stein, and our founding art director, Rick Fiala. Special thanks are due to Stephen Temmer, without whom *Christopher Street* would not exist.

# *Contents*

# Introduction

Since the 17th century, magazines have been a peculiarly modern device for bringing a public space into existence. Like a town meeting, a magazine enables people to be in each other's company by sharing talk about matters that concern them. And it is through talking with others that most of us start to make some sense out of the world, and begin to discover who we are and what we think. Such talk usually does not lead toward general agreement but, paradoxically, to even greater diversity of opinion. Only people who don't talk to each other—or don't do it well—think they agree. In my experience, the better and longer the talk, the more you find yourself in disagreement with others, and, if the discussion has genuine quality, eventually in disagreement with yourself—at which point it gets interesting, for this is when change becomes possible and things begin to happen.

Publishing a magazine, writing for a magazine, subscribing to and supporting a magazine are all aspects of an activity whose final purpose is not general agreement, a party line, but rather a greater ease and sureness in moving in the world, a firmer grasp of who we are and what we think. *Christopher Street* has never tried to develop a party line; we always thought our task was to open a space, a forum, where the developing gay culture could manifest and experience itself. For people who have been excluded from the social world—gays, blacks, women, any minority group that has been colonized by a dominating culture—this access to public space is basic and urgent. Gays know, or should know, as well as blacks and colonized people the cost of being "invisible men." We're intimately aware of "the havoc wrought in the souls of people who aren't supposed to exist" (Ntozake Shange). This is no benign neglect, it is an active assault against our persons, a total public denial of the validity of our lives as we experience them. The gap between our inner lives and the socially acceptable version of reality is so wide it makes existence into a charade. It makes you dizzy. It makes you wonder if you're really there.

This experience of displacement and insubstantiality is common to all people society forces to be invisible. The dizziness of the dizzy queen not only expresses the inner confusion of finding oneself constantly forced to play in a charade—"Am I real, honey? Is this world for real?"—it is also a stubborn, insidious, perhaps unconscious but quite effective political assertion—"Don't you dare think I'm really here, that this is really real, that this is who I am." The celebrated ambiguity of camp is a psychological zap, guerrilla tactics for people who can't afford open warfare—not unlike the legendary laziness of blacks or stupidity of colonized people. Straights are irritated or uncomfortable with it because it's meant to make them irritated or uncomfortable—if you're going to press us down with those values, we're going to camp it up and undermine those values, ridicule them and expose them for the pretentions they are. Those reactionaries who in their heart of hearts *know* we're making a mockery of them are right on this point. You bet. When you can't afford to fight back openly, you ridicule, you undermine, you resist in the only way you can.

But the cost is too high. Living in the closet and putting on a mask when you go into the world does not leave your soul intact. Social invisibility reaches inward and causes a confusion of spirit. Our imaginations become closeted *internally*—a phenomenon feminists are pointing to when they discuss "male identified women." We are no longer able to imagine our own lives. It's well known that we come out sexually before we come out socially, that most of us have been screwing for years before we're willing to say to ourselves, never mind publicly, "I'm gay." After all, homosexuals were undoubtedly sexually active before Stonewall as well as after. But the assertion of gay liberation that started with the Stonewall riot is not enough. Pecs, track lighting, and brunch do not a soul make. We all know people who dress like clones—and whether they know it or not, this is a militant act, broadcasting the statement "I am gay" not only to gays (we could always recognize each other) but primarily to the straight world—but these same clones wouldn't be caught dead reading a gay book or subscribing to a gay magazine.

This seems to me an enormous strategic mistake. (Of course, being deeply involved in the business of gay books and magazines, I'm not exactly an impartial commentator—on the other hand, who is?) Put simply, I don't think it's possible to have a liberated gay world socially or a satisfying and fulfilling gay life individually without developing a gay culture. Over a decade ago, we found that a private gay life was not enough, that we required some kind of public and visible assertion of our gayness, that "coming out" was the path to liberation and the "closet" a repressive trap, not only politically but in terms of our immediate day-to-day lives. While we may be obscure about the precise nature of this connection, unable even to our own satisfaction to articulate why we feel the necessity of this public assertion—which, quite honestly, most straights and not a few gays still view as a perverse flaunting of our lifestyle—still, in our gut we knew it was necessary, and this obscure but quite powerful conviction is what has fueled the gay movement for the last ten years.

It is as if liberation proceeds in three stages. The first is the sheer exhilarating discovery of sex and same-sex emotional bonding, which becomes the true center of our lives and the ultimate excitement of our souls even if we remain socially in the closet. The second stage is the public and social assertion of our gayness; our demand for the rights and dignity that a decent respect for humanity in all its diversity would grant to everyone. To these, I suggest, should be added a third stage, the liberation of our imaginations from the closet of straight culture. We need to be able to imagine our own lives *as we live them* if we are to have any chance of living them well. To use a concrete example: for many years I used the term "ex-lover" to name relationships I thought had ended, had failed. It took forever before I woke up to the patent fact that I spent a substantial part of my social time with these "ex" lovers; that these were among the deepest, closest, most stable and rewarding relationships I had. When I looked around and saw this was increasingly the case with many of my friends, it began to dawn on me that we were in the process of redefining the family, or better still, that we were creating new structures—little tribes—that functioned in our lives in much the same way as, and perhaps in place of, the traditional family. For me this incident encapsulates a general phenomenon: we are in the odd position of having trouble seeing the very lives we lead because we still look at them through the lenses of straight culture, the same straight culture that has gone to such bizarre efforts to deny that we even exist.

Anyone today who thinks he can lead a free gay life without participating in the creation of gay culture is in the same position as those homosexuals of the fifties and sixties who thought they could have meaningful and significant intimate relationships while staying in the closet. It won't work. It didn't work then. Untold numbers of homosexuals were severely damaged or driven to distraction by this contradiction between their intimate and their public lives—a situation brilliantly captured by *The Boys in the Band*, an analysis of an emotional pre-revolutionary situation if I've ever seen one. The only way to consolidate the gains of the past decade of gay liberation is to forge a new imagination of our lives and the world, and this can only be done by a serious interaction with our writers and artists, for these after all are the people who have elected the task of reporting and imagining and celebrating and criticizing how we live now.

I suppose it's necessary to add that a commitment to a separate gay culture and identity in no way requires the rejection of straight culture. Does anybody think that a Jew who gains sustenance and identity from his people's heritage cannot also be an American; that someone deeply involved in the forging of an American black culture cannot love Shakespeare and Cezanne? The idea is absurd and is never raised with other groups; when it comes up in discussions of gay culture, in attacks on what's called gay separatism, it's a red herring.

The writings included in this book are among the most interesting and valuable attempts I know at imagining our lives anew. These writers do not agree with one another. They are pushing and probing, thinking and criticizing, celebrating and berating the new lives we find ourselves leading and the new people we have become. To the reader who takes them seriously, they offer invaluable and concrete assistance in the daily struggle we all face to invent ourselves anew, and to recognize ourselves when we've done it.

Any collection of articles from a magazine presents the opportunity for, in fact requires, a reflective interpretation of what exactly that magazine is all about. In re-reading five years of published material inevitably one begins to see the collective endeavor in the clearer light of hindsight. In the case of *Christopher Street*, my own experience of this massive re-reading left me—a bit to my surprise—with a new sense of a roughly coherent public discussion with its own logic and progression. It is this rough sense of the unfolding of an ongoing discussion that informs the present collection, its content and arrangement.

This coherence should not be overemphasized. A magazine publishes articles—glimpses of how we are, brief and tentative surveys of the geography of our lives, sudden clearings of self-awareness, reports from different corners of our world—and a collection of such articles could never offer a systematic and balanced overview. The vagaries of interest, accidents of timing and pressures of circumstance, financial and otherwise, see to that. Yet it did seem to us that an unusual number of articles retained their interest and vitality, that even this scattered record of the attempts of a large and open-ended group of people to make sense of their lives and confront the problems and paradoxes of establishing a gay culture was coherent enough to warrant the permanence of a book.

The final decisions on the contents and arrangement of this collection reflect our sense of the cultural evolution this magazine has recorded and reflected back to the public.

The most striking aspect of this book for regular readers of *Christopher Street* will undoubtedly be the absence of women. From the first issue until today, *Christopher Street* has not only published but gone out of its way to publish articles, fiction, art and poetry by and interviews with women writers, both lesbian and non-lesbian, including Bertha Harris, Kate Millett, Rita Mae Brown, Ntozake Shange, Audre Lord, Blanche Boyd, Mary Daly, Joan Baez, Sheila Ortiz Taylor, Noretta Koertge, Jane Rule, Olga Broumas, and Nicole Hollander among others. Yet in reading it all over, it became apparent that this was a secondary aspect of the magazine. The initial selection of material for this book included articles by some nine women and about sixty men which, sensibly enough, made us all nervous, especially since a third of those women were not gay. It would be easy to charge the magazine with tokenism and this collection with chauvinism—and we shall no doubt hear such charges—but I think the truth of the matter is more complex, less hostile, and ultimately promising.

*Christopher Street* started with a determined effort at gender parity which lasted about a year and a half. It would be superfluous to recount the demise of this effort—virtually everyone who has been active in any gay endeavor will be familiar with the scenario. What I personally remember with striking clarity was the time one of the women editors told me she actually didn't read any of the pieces by men. She preferred to concentrate her work, energy, and enthusiasm on developing women writers; she simply wasn't particularly interested in what men had to say, unless it touched on a feminist concern. I was startled because I generally found the writing of the women so interesting myself. In fact, we found it to be more or less the case that male readers were quite interested and enthusiastic about women writers, but that women had little interest in the work of the men. Their concern was so intensely engaged in the situation of women that reading the articles by men seemed irrelevant to them. So the magazine was, by and large, never able to win the loyalty of women readers, and the women on the staff slowly drifted away.

At the time all this led to some muttered sound and muted fury and hurt feelings on both sides, but it makes more sense to me now. The connection between gay men and gay women was only ideological; we did not really share a world in common. Women needed their own space, as the lesbian feminists correctly argued, and gay men were trying to create a cultural space to begin with (without the great initial advantage gay women had in the very fact of the feminist movement). The attempt at integration may or may not have been misguided, but it certainly came too soon. Both gay men and lesbians were still struggling to gain some sense of their own identity and apparently neither could afford the effort to try to make themselves acceptable to or even understood by the other.

Where it will all end up is another matter. The relation between lesbians and straight feminists may be changing, the relation between gay men and the feminist movement is certainly changing, and the relation between gay women and gay men seems to be in flux. We can all be good allies with anyone who is on our side, but we cannot be good allies, or even good friends, if we confuse ourselves with each other. We need our separate identities and we need to respect the differences between us.

Personally I think that gay men can greatly benefit from reading the several excellent collections like this one, consisting entirely of the work of gay women, which are now available. But to have a few women represented in a dominantly male collection does seem objectionable to me. *Christopher Street* simply has to accept the fact that at the moment it is a gay male magazine; as such, it will continue to publish the best women writers we can find who will interest our readers. Before I'm attacked in print for all this, I would urge people to consider whether any feminist or lesbian magazine has ever opened its pages to as many gay men as *Christopher Street* has consistently to gay women—much to its benefit.

Lesbians and gay men have a lot in common, but we're not the same folk. This would seem to be a very simple fact, one that has been abundantly clear for years. Yet confusion over this issue and the attempt to wring from the word "gay" a uniformity that would cover both men and women has led to unbelievable wrangling. It's time to accept our differences with good humor and a genuine interest in each other's lives and work. Lesbians and gay men are natural allies, if only because a generally hostile society sees us as the same—homosexuals. But only if we recognize our differences and can live with the same tolerance of diversity we're demanding of straight society will we be able to work together and enjoy each other's company.

—MICHAEL DENNENY

# I

---

## LIVING
## THE LIFE

## One Life, One Prom

*T*he simple, obvious thing would have been to go to the senior prom with a girl. But that would have been a lie—a lie to myself, to the girl, and to all the other students.

What I *wanted* to do was to take a male date. But as Paul Guilbert had shown the year before when he had attempted to take another man to the prom, such honesty is not always easy. There was an important difference between Paul's case and mine, though. Paul had not been able to fight for his rights because he was seventeen at the time. I was now eighteen and legally able to make my own decisions. If I wanted to go to the prom with a male escort and the school tried to stop me, I could take the case to court.

But should I do that? This would require a lot of thought if I was to make a decision without being selfish, uncaring, or irrational.

If I went to the prom with another guy, what would be the benefits? For myself, it would mean participating in an important social event and doing so with a clear conscience and a sense of wholeness. But how would it affect the rest of the people involved?

I believed that those who had themselves faced discrimination or prejudice would immediately understand what I was doing and its implications for human rights. There would be others who may never have had direct experiences with prejudice but who would recognize my right to the date of my choice. These people may have been misled to believe that homosexuality is wrong, but they could still understand that my rights were being denied.

At the opposite end of the spectrum were the homophobics who might react violently. But the example I set would be perfect for everyone. We would be just one more happy couple. Our happiness together would be something kids could relate to. I would be showing that my dignity and value as a human being was not affected by my sexual preference.

I concluded that taking a guy to the prom would be a strong positive statement about the existence of gay people. Any opposition to my case (and I anticipated a good bit) would show the negative side of society—not of homosexuality.

To attend the prom with a girl would not be unenjoyable, but it would be dishonest to my true feelings. Besides, most kids now knew I was gay. If I went with a female, I would probably have received more taunts than from going with a male. By going with a male I would win some respect from the more mature students, and I would keep my self-esteem.

I tried not to worry about the possibility of violence. Certainly I would face opposition. It was inevitable given the rampant prejudice against homosexuals today. But the threat of violence was not enough to change my mind, since I encountered that every day to some degree. Perhaps such threats would diminish in the future as people saw more homosexuals participating openly in everyday life.


My biggest concern was for my parents. Although the entire student body and administration of Cumberland High School knew or assumed I was gay, my family had remained blissfully blind to this reality. The news could be heartbreaking to them. Plus, it might get them ostracized by the neighbors, banned from town social gatherings . . . from church . . . from Tupperware parties! Was I willing to take this risk? No! As much as I believed in my rights, I valued my relationship with my parents too much to have it abruptly severed. After all, for years I had hidden my sexuality for fear of losing my parents' love. As a child it had been *the* most important thing to me. Now, as a man, it was just as important as before. I wanted to go to my prom, but it was not as important as eighteen years of love.

I decided to tell my parents of my homosexuality first, then ask them how they would feel about my going to the prom. If it seemed like too much for them to accept, I would forget the prom and just be happy that I no longer had to be secretive with my parents. But if they rejected me merely because I was gay, then I would still pursue my rights, even at the prom, realizing that my parents were good people but were horribly misled.

Until now, I had never spoken to them about my homosexuality. Like many adolescents I had drifted away from my parents lately. Now I had an impetus to improve my communication with them. I decided to approach my parents separately; a thousand times I rehearsed what I would say.

It began, "Ever since I was a kid . . ." and ended, "I hope you love me enough not to reject me." But when the moment of truth came, I felt more self-confident and said, "I don't know if you've had any suspicions, but I'm gay."

Long pause. My mother replied, "I'm so glad you were finally able to be honest with me." She had long suspected. My father had not; when I told him he broke down and cried. Yet they both loved me unconditionally. When I explained why I wanted to go to the prom, they were supportive. I was my own man, they each said, and I would have to make my own decisions.

It felt great to be able to talk to my parents about this. Their reaction was encouraging, and I decided to go ahead. I would invite Paul Guilbert to the prom.

Anne Guillet wrote me a note in environmental science class when I asked for her advice about the prom. She wrote:

Dear Aaron,
    Last year, Paul's attempt to bring a guy to the prom was seen by most people, in fact I think by all, as a grab at publicity. That was because no one knew Paul, he just showed up out of a clear blue sky (and raised a ruckus). Since you've been in Cumberland much

longer and have more close friends, people won't suspect you of such ill motives so easily, but this is what they will think.

1. Paul made you do it.
2. You're crazy.
3. You believe in gay rights.

In that order. Now *I* know you did it for reason 3, but you should think about how other people are going to react and I think you should make an effort to explain what you believe. I respect any decision you make, as long as you really think about it carefully.

Love,
Anne

I took her advice and painstakingly wrote a letter to the school newspaper, explaining why I decided to go to the prom with a male date. The letter said that I hoped no one would be hurt by what I was doing, that a victory in court would be a victory for every Cumberland High student because it would be a blow against prejudice. The next issue of the school paper had space for all sorts of trivia, but my letter never appeared.

Later in April, the school theater group took its annual bus trip to New York City. Our teacher, Miss Frappier, was an exceptionally warm and friendly person, and we were a tightly-knit bunch—one of those rare groups of thespians whose members had no pent-up distrust or jealousy toward each other. On the bus Miss Frappier gave out the spring awards; I received one of them for an outstanding performance in *A Thurber Carnival.*

In New York we went to the Guggenheim Museum and to the Broadway production of *They're Playing Our Song;* then when the group returned to Rhode Island, I stayed in New York to spend time with Paul, who had moved there from Cumberland.

Paul seemed to be getting happier in the city. Our friendship had not faded, although Paul and I had not seen each other in months. We took a long walk through the Village, bringing each other up to date on what we'd been doing, and enjoying the feeling of the trees in bloom and spring in the air.

By evening I had settled any doubts I still had about who I wanted to invite to the prom. And so, with sweaty palms and butterflies in my stomach, I finally asked Paul: "I was wondering, um, do you have a date for the Cumberland High prom this year?"

Paul began laughing. "I'd love to attend the senior prom with you," he finally said. My feeling of happiness lasted all the way back to Rhode Island.

In Cumberland, prom tickets were on sale. Rather than go through the motion of trying to buy tickets in the cafeteria, where they would want the name of my date and would refuse to sell me the tickets anyway, I went right to the main office and asked Mrs. Dunbarton to tell Mr. Lynch, the principal, that I wanted to speak with him. She courteously took my name, leaned over the intercom, and buzzed Mr. Lynch. I couldn't hear much of what she said, but my imagination filled in the silence: "Oh, Mr. Lynch, that little faggot is here to see you."

Mr. Lynch soon appeared and, on my insistence, granted me the privacy of his office to speak to him. His office was familiar to me by now. I'd sat in it the year before when Mr. Lynch gave me that in-house suspension for cutting gym. But this time things were different.

Without mentioning Paul by name, I explained that I wanted to take a male escort to the prom. Mr. Lynch listened politely, then did exactly what I had assumed he would do.

He said no.

[*Aaron Fricke appealed to the National Gay Task Force for help and got it. He was advised to sue his school in federal court; NGTF would cover legal fees.*

*After several weeks in court, Judge Pettine ruled in favor of Fricke, on the grounds that the social context of an act can represent a political statement, which is therefore protected by the First Amendment.*

*National media attention focused on Aaron Fricke, Paul Guilbert, and Cumberland High School.*]

When we arrived at the prom site on the night of May 30, 1980, we were greeted with a glare of television lights. Flash bulbs were popping and everybody was talking and trying to ask questions as we walked toward the building. The reporters broke down the velvet ropes that were supposed to hold them back. I was too full of anticipation and excitement to think of anything to say. So a second before walking in the door, in a grand gesture of looniness, camp, and high drama, I turned to the reporters, waved, and stuck out my tongue.

Once inside, Mr. Lynch quickly ushered Paul and me away from the door so that the reporters would be unable to see us. We were shown to an empty table, which neither of us enjoyed because there were no kids to talk to. My ninth-grade Spanish teacher, Mrs. Noelte, eventually sat with us.

Dinner was soon served. It was chicken cordon something or other and consisted of mushed chicken encased in oil. My piece looked like a monster from the film *Alien*. The salad looked better, but when I bit into the cherry tomato, it splattered right onto my pants. I did my best to ignore the stain, but it kept showing up in the pictures people took.

After dinner was cleared away, many students began coming by to offer us a few good words. There was more good feeling than I would ever have anticipated. One after another, students came by and expressed their happiness that we could share the prom with each other.

I wandered over to a big picture window and stared out. Several reporters were talking outside on the lawn. For a moment I thought of all the people who would have enjoyed going to their proms with the date of their choice, but were denied that right; of all the people in the past who wanted to live respectably with the person they loved but could not; of all the men and women who had been hurt or killed because they were gay; and of the rich history of lesbians and homosexual men that had so long been ignored. Gradually we were triumphing over ignorance. One day we would be free.

The dance music came on. Kelleen Driskell came over and asked me to dance the first song with her. I was happy to accept. I'd known Kelleen in elementary school, but I had drifted away from her, as from so many other people, during my fat years. We fast-danced for that song and just through our physical movements together, without exchanging words, it felt as if we were reestablishing a communication.

After the dance I had to use the bathroom. Throughout the evening, Paul and I would see all kinds of defense mechanisms from the other guys whenever we went to the bathroom. Some of them made a beeline for the door as soon as we walked in. Others stayed, their desire to escape temporarily overcome by their curiosity about how gay people go to the bathroom.

When I got back to the dance floor, Paul asked me if I wanted to slow-dance. I did. The next song was Bob Seger's "We've Got the Night," and we stepped out onto the dance floor.

The crowd receded. As I laid my head on Paul's shoulder, I saw a few students start to stare at us. I closed my eyes and listened to the music, my thoughts wandering over the events of that evening. When the song ended, I opened my eyes. A large crowd of students had formed a ring around us. Probably most of them had never before seen two happy men embracing in a slow dance. For a moment I was uncomfortable. Then I heard the sound that I knew so well as a B-52's fan. One of my favorite songs was coming up: "Rock Lobster."

Paul and I began dancing free-style. Everyone else was still staring at us, but by the end of the first stanza, several couples had also begun dancing. The song has a contagious enthusiasm to it, and with each bar, more dancers came onto the floor.

More students were coming onto the floor to dance. I doubt that any two people were dancing with the same movements: the dancing was an expression of our individuality, and no one felt bad about being different. Everyone was free to be themselves.

A quarter of the way into the song, thirty people were on the dance floor. "Down, Down, Down," commanded the lyrics. Everyone on the dance floor sank to their knees and crouched on the ground. I lifted my head slightly to look around. Dozens of intertwining bodies crouched on their knees as if praying. We were all one; we shared a unity of pure love. And those who did not want to share it sat on the sidelines.

> "Red snappers snappin'
> Clamshells clappin' "

Everyone jumped to their feet again and resumed dancing. Many more kids had joined us and there must have been sixty or eighty people on the dance floor now.

As Paul and I danced, we had gradually drifted from our original space on the floor. "Down, Down, Down," cried the B-52's again, and we all went down. The feeling of unity among us permeated the air again. There were at least a hundred people on the dance floor. The tempo became more frenetic and everyone danced faster.

"Let's Rock!!!" bellowed from the speakers, and to my surprise, when I looked up, I saw that Paul had disappeared. I looked around; several other guys were dancing with each other, and girls were dancing with girls. Everybody was rockin', everybody was fruggin'. Who cared why? Maybe they were doing it to mock me and Paul, maybe they were doing it because they wanted to, maybe one was an excuse for the other.... I didn't know and I didn't care. It was fun. Everyone was together. I danced with girls, I danced with guys, I danced with the entire group.

Then the music stopped. "Rock Lobster" has an abrupt ending, and no one was quite ready for it to stop. I had been having so much fun that I lost track of time; I had also lost track of Paul and had to look around the room for him.

I could see that everyone felt a sense of disorientation. For six minutes and forty-nine seconds, the students on the dance floor had forgotten about their defenses, forgotten about their shells. We just had fun.

... I do not blame my torments on heterosexuality. I have been friends with many loving, open-minded heterosexuals. The thing I blame has no sexuality. It is the nameless, faceless entity of prejudice and oppression. Often that oppression has taken a physical form in people who are straight; perhaps those people are themselves just pawns, trapped in a vicious cycle of oppression. I am only reporting their actions as I have experienced them.

The prom case brought about many good changes. It exposed people to the gay rights issue. It encouraged them to look at it more rationally than they might have otherwise. The hatred that many people feel when they hear the word *gay* must have diminished after the fourteenth time they heard it on the six o'clock news.

The media often handled this case well. The day Judge Pettine's ruling was announced, reporter Bob Blanchard came on the news and said, "Those who support equal rights for gay people say today's decision is a major victory.... In reality, however, it was not ... because the much larger question of rampant discrimination gay people face in housing and the job market remains."

Although the prom case is a bit more serious than the Village People's song "YMCA," its main value was to bring the issue to the attention of the public and make them aware that there *is* a problem, a problem that remains to be solved.

Parents sometimes teach their children that homosexuality is a disease, whereas homophobia is not. Actually, it is the contrary. Homophobia is a degeneration of respect for humans, and it is contagious. One person exhibits hatred toward a gay person, impressionable people see it, and they recreate those actions. Parents who teach their children to hate or fear homosexuals do not realize that *their* children could be homosexuals. Prejudiced attitudes serve only to confuse the children, whether they have homosexual tendencies or not.

My last day at Cumberland High School ended on a particularly sad note. As I walked off the football field after commencement, now escorted by several uniformed policemen, two children approached me before I stepped into my car. "Faggot!" one said. "You queer," said the other. I had never felt so defenseless. They were only about ten years old, and I felt no hostility toward them. But I pity the society that sits back and encourages children to feel bitterness and hatred toward anything.

I live with pride every day of my life now—pride in the idea that my openness can set an example for all people about the benefits of being open. My memories of the oppression I felt will not be forgotten, nor will my awareness that people continue to experience these emotional deprivations. But I am now confident that I *can* overcome the barriers that heterosexual prejudice will present.

Even so, I will be reminded *daily* of the torments gay people face. My writing will hopefully serve as a vehicle to make others more actively aware. I will remind heterosexuals that we are human. And I will remind gay people struggling for a positive identity that, in the words of Andre Gide, "it is better to be hated for what one is than loved for what one is not."

# ARTHUR BELL

## The Sixties

*I* don't remember the sixties. Quite frankly, they were mostly lousy years and I have a tendency to block out dreck. So this "memoir" is nostalgia through hypnosis via the wonder of Olivetti.

Part of my block is because of two long affairs I had then. The first began almost the minute I hit town. Rather than live with my grandparents in Coney Island, I rented a studio apartment on East Eighty-eighth Street. Each night I would visit Carl Schurz Park, gaze at the Pearl Wick Hamper sign across the bay and pray that love would find Andy Hardy. Love came in the form of an interior decorator from Texas. Along with love came Bobby Short, Parsons tables, Brooks Brothers, Unitarianism, sleepless nights, endless fights, Louis XIV chairs, and lectures on taste. I guess it was bad taste on his part to kick down the front door one night, especially since we were living in Lenox Hill, and great taste when he moved out and into the Sixty-third Street Y. That was in June 1964, long before the baths were tasteful.

During those days one wasn't supposed to cheat. So, naturally, one did: in the balcony of the Symphony, the rear of the Thalia, and a wonderful little cinema on Pineapple Street in Brooklyn Heights. *Paris Blues* was playing. When the decorator and I went to the movies together, it was always Cinema I.

Neither of us was honest enough to go to bars. Bars spelled infidelity, and infidelity spelled the death of gay marriage. The day John Kennedy died, however, I stopped into a gay bar. I question now—for the first time—whether that gesture meant I wanted to be with my own people during a time of crisis. Fortunately, none of our mutual friends saw me. Friends, in those days, were always offering advice to lovers—"for your own good." It was always bad.

I went back to the bars as soon as love went out the window. Back then, there weren't many to go to. I have vague memories of a suit-and-tie spot called the Arctic on Fifty-third near Third. There was Julius', of course. And the Café Cino, which wasn't really gay, but was an off-off-Broadway theater hangout and a terrific antidote to Billy Baldwin, William Paley, and the *Vogue Book of Etiquette*. At the Cino I first met Helen Hanft, John Matthews, Tom Eyen, and Jackie Curtis—people who were to weave in and out of my life during the rest of the sixties and through the seventies. They exemplified the freedom that was to come to many more gay people in 1969 when the Stonewall riots broke out. The Cino group made me want to assert my own gayness to the world, no matter what the world said was wrong. Their effect was evident in the fall of 1965 when I kissed a man goodbye on the subway to work—a spontaneous gesture, perhaps iconoclastic considering the times. Anyway, a co-worker caught the kiss and word got back to the office, but quick, that little Arthur was a faggot. After the high-falutin' years with the interior decorator, the stigma was a blessing.

On December 7, 1964, John Matthews introduced me to a young philosophy student who was a radical, a brain, a hunk, and an innocent. He lived in a dump on Avenue C, and taste, to him, was something that was not taught in books but was what one felt was inherently right.

We fell in love. I read *The Brothers Karamazov*, learned a few words in Greek, listened to Lenny Bruce records, saw Czechoslovakian and Ukrainian films, marched with Ginsberg, learned to read the front page of the *Times*, learned that capitalists were pigs, cops were pigs, but pigs weren't pigs—they were poor oppressed animals, dependent on humans for care and feeding.

Learning was something we did in between fucking. During the Columbia riots, I visited the campus with homemade grapefruit pies, which I fed to the students who had blockaded themselves in the philosophy building. During the 1968 campaign, I stayed at home and cried at the injustices perpetrated on us by the pigs while my philosopher was out in Chicago, shouting obscenities at Mayor Daley's stormtroopers.

Eventually, I began to feel left out. I started to resent the man I loved. Subliminally, I became aware of our role-playing. Sure, it was my own fault. I could have locked myself in a building at Columbia. I could have had my head bashed in by one of Chicago's finest. But one of us had to keep the home fires burning. Although I didn't knit and haven't yet learned how to sew or iron, I felt like Marmie in *Little Women*. Soon, what had first attracted me to this man made me loathe him. One night, we saw *Who's Afraid of Virginia Woolf*. I related to the film; he wrote a ten-page thesis on Albee and history. I began looking for thrills and adventure elsewhere. Dancing was good. I went into group therapy at the Karen Horney Clinic for six months and learned how to interpret dreams, took courses at the New School in the psychology of the horror film, learned to string prayer beads, allowed my hair to grow, and saw *Hair*.

Oddly enough, I related to the women's movement, which had sprung up about the time that I first started feeling disenchantment. I was working at Random House then, and our editorial offices were drop-in spots for Robin Morgan and Ti-Grace Atkinson. My secretary would talk about how she demanded equal rights and I'd think to myself, "Baby, you are not alone."

When Stonewall happened in the summer of 1969, the philosopher and I were in Paris. When we came back, a Little Orphan Annie–haired kid on Christopher Street told us about a gay meeting at Washington Methodist Church. For kicks, we went.

At first, I thought gay liberation would mean freedom from sexual bondage, leaving your mate, the women's liberation stuff that nightclub comics make fun of. Later, I discovered that the most important part was finding yourself.

I can't say I've found myself yet, but I have freed myself. As we entered the seventies, I said goodbye to the philosopher and to my old ideas of love.

The sixties were conception years, prelude years to the seventies. As such, they were necessary. As a free gay man, I was really born in 1970.

# *Fantasia on the Seventies*

$F$or me New York gay life in the seventies came as a completely new beginning. In January 1970 I moved to Rome after having lived in the Village for eight years. When I returned ten months later to the United States, an old friend met me at the airport, popped an "up" in my mouth, and took me on a tour of the back-room bars. In Rome there had been only one bar, the St. James, where hustlers stood around in fitted velvet jackets; the only sex scenes had been two movie theaters, where a businessman with a raincoat in his lap might tolerate a handjob, and the Colosseum, where in winter a few vacationing foreigners would cluster in nervous, shadowy groups. For real sex in bed I had to rely on other Americans and upper-class Italians, the only ones who didn't regard love between men as ludicrous. (I had an affair with an impoverished Florentine baron who was writing his dissertation on William Blake.) On the streets, even when shopping or going to lunch, I dressed in a fitted velvet jacket and kept my eyes neutral, uninquisitive. Today, of course, Italy has an active gay-liberation party, large annual gay congresses that choke on Marxist rhetoric, and articles in *Uomo* about gay fashions that purport to be without *any* historical precedent (actually they're just overalls or unironed shirts). But when I lived there Rome was still a bastion of the *piccolo borghese* and miniskirts were considered scandalous.

I have a disturbing knack for doing what used to be called "conforming," and by the end of my Roman holiday I was hiding my laundry in a suitcase (to avoid the disgrace of being seen—a man!—carrying dirty shirts through the streets), and I was even drifting into the national sport of cruising women. My assimilation of heterosexuality and respectability made the new New York all the more shocking to me. My friend took me to Christopher's End, where a go-go boy with a pretty body and bad skin stripped down to his jockey shorts and then peeled those off and tossed them at us. A burly man in the audience clambered up onto the dais and tried to fuck the performer but was, apparently, too drunk to get an erection. After a while we drifted into the back room, which was so dark I never received a sense of its dimensions, although I do remember standing on a platform and staring through the slowly revolving blades of a fan at one naked man fucking another in a cubbyhole. A flickering candle illuminated them. It was never clear whether they were customers or hired entertainment; the fan did give them the look of actors in a silent movie. All this was new.

At another bar, called the Zoo or the Zodiac (both existed, I've just confused them), a go-go boy did so well with a white towel under black light that I waited around till he got off—at 8 A.M. In the daylight he turned out to be a bleached blond with chipped teeth who lived in remotest Brooklyn with the bouncer, a three-hundred-pound man who had just lost fifty pounds. I was too polite to back out and was driven all the way to their apartment, which was decorated with a huge blackamoor lamp from Castro Convertible.

For the longest time everyone kept saying the seventies hadn't started yet. There was no distinctive style for the decade, no flair, no slogans. The mistake we made was that we were all looking for something as startling as the Beatles, acid, Pop Art, hippies and radical politics. What actually set in was a painful and unexpected working-out of the terms the sixties had so blithely tossed off. Sexual permissiveness became a form of numbness, as rigidly codified as the old morality. Street cruising gave way to half-clothed quickies; recently I overheard someone say, "It's been months since I've had sex in bed." Drugs, once billed as an aid to self-discovery through heightened perception, became a way of injecting lust into anonymous encounters at the baths. At the baths everyone seemed to be lying face down on a cot beside a can of Crisco; fistfucking, as one French savant has pointed out, is our century's only brand-new contribution to the sexual armamentarium. Fantasy costumes (gauze robes, beaded headache bands, mirrored vests) were replaced by the new brutalism: work boots, denim, beards and mustaches, the only concession to the old androgyny being a discreet gold earbob or ivory figa. Today nothing looks more forlorn than the faded sign in a suburban barber shop that reads "Unisex."

Indeed, the unisex of the sixties has been supplanted by heavy sex in the seventies, and the urge toward fantasy has come out of the clothes closet and entered the bedroom or back room. The end to role-playing that feminism and gay liberation promised has not occurred. Quite the reverse. Gay pride has come to mean the worship of machismo. No longer is sex confused with sentiment. Although many gay people in New York may be happily living in other, less rigorous decades, the gay male couple inhabiting the seventies is composed of two men who love each other, share the same friends and interests, and fuck each other almost inadvertently once every six months during a particularly stoned, impromptu three-way. The rest of the time they get laid with strangers in a context that bears all the stylistic marks and some of the reality of S and M. Inflicting and receiving excruciating physical pain may still be something of a rarity, but the sex rap whispered in a stranger's ear conjures up nothing but violence. The other day someone said to me, "Are you into fantasies? I *do* five." "Oh?" "Yes, five: rookie-coach; older brother–younger brother; sailor-slut; slave-master; and father-son." I picked older brother–younger brother, although it kept lapsing into a pastoral fantasy of identical twins.

The temptation, of course, is to lament our lost innocence, but my Christian Science training as a child has made me into a permanent Pollyanna. What *good* is coming out of the seventies? I keep wondering.

Well, perhaps sex and sentiment *should* be separated. Isn't sex, shadowed as it always is by jealousy and ruled by caprice, a rather risky basis for a sustained, important relationship? Perhaps our marriages should be sexless, or "white," as the French used to say. And then, perhaps violence, or at least domination, is the true subtext of all sex, straight or gay; just recently I was reading an article in *Time* about a psychiatrist who has taped the erotic fantasies of lots of people and discovered to his dismay that most of them depend on a sadomasochistic scenario. Even Rosemary Rogers, the author of such gothic potboilers as *The Wildest Heart* and *Sweet Savage Love*, is getting rich feeding her women readers tales of unrelenting S and M. The gay leather scene may simply be more honest—and because it is explicit, less nasty—than more conventional sex, straight or gay.

As for the jeans, cowboy shirts and work boots, they at least have the virtue of being cheap. The uniform conceals the rise of what strikes me as a whole new class of gay indigents. Sometimes I have the impression every fourth man on Christopher Street is out of work, but the poverty is hidden by the costume. Whether this appalling situation should be disguised is another question altogether; is it somehow egalitarian to have both the rich and the poor dressed up as Paul Bunyan?

Finally, the adoration of machismo is intermittent, interchangeable, between parentheses. Tonight's top is tomorrow's bottom. We're all like characters in a Genet play and more interested that the ritual be enacted than concerned about which particular role we assume. The sadist barking commands at his slave in bed is, ten minutes after climax, thoughtfully drawing him a bubble bath or giving him hints about how to keep those ankle restraints brightly polished.

The characteristic face in New York these days is seasoned, wry, weathered by drama and farce. Drugs, heavy sex, and the ironic, highly concentrated experience (so like that of actors everywhere) of leading uneventful, homebodyish lives when not on stage for those two searing hours each night—this reality, or release from it, has humbled us all. It has even broken the former tyranny youth and beauty held over us. Suddenly it's okay to be thirty, forty, even fifty, to have a streak of white crazing your beard, to have a deviated septum or eyes set too close together. All the looks anyone needs can be bought—at the army-navy store, at the gym, and from the local pusher; the lisped shriek of "Miss Thing!" has faded into the passing, over-the-shoulder offer of "loose joints." And we do in fact seem looser, easier in the joints, and if we must lace ourselves nightly into chaps and rough up more men than seems quite coherent with our soft-spoken, gentle personalities, at least we need no longer be relentlessly witty or elegant, nor need we stand around gilded pianos bawling out choruses from *Hello, Dolly*, our slender bodies embalmed in youth, bedecked with signature scarves, and soaked in eau de cologne.

My enthusiasm for the seventies, as might be guessed, is not uninflected. Politically, the war will not take place. Although Anita Bryant has given us the temporary illusion of solidarity, gay liberation as a militant program has turned out to be ineffectual, perhaps impossible; I suspect individual gays will remain more loyal to their different social classes than to their sexual colleagues. The rapport between gay men and lesbians, still strong in small communities, has collapsed in the city, and this rupture has also weakened militancy. A general American rejection of the high stakes of shared social goals for the small change of personal life (study of the self has turned out to be a form of escapism) has left the movement bankrupt.

But in the post-Stonewall decade there is a new quality to New York gay life. We don't hate ourselves so much (although I do wish everyone would stop picking on drag queens; I at least continue to see them as the Saints of Bleecker Street). In general we're kinder to our friends. Discovering that a celebrity is gay does not automatically lower him now in our eyes; once it was enough to say such-and-such a conductor or pop singer was gay for him to seem to us a fake, as inauthentic as we perceived ourselves to be. The self-acceptance of the seventies might just give us the courage to experiment with new forms of love and camaraderie, including the *mariage blanc,* the three- or four-way marriage, bi- or trisexuality, a community of artists or craftsmen or citizens from which tiresome heterosexual competitiveness will be banished—a community of tested *seaworthy* New Yorkers.

# MICHAEL DENNENY

## *Interview with Felice Picano*

*A*t thirty-five, Felice Picano is a successful writer, one who has actually been able to live on the earnings of his novels (*Smart as the Devil* [Arbor House, 1975], *Eyes* [Arbor House, 1976], and *The Mesmerist* [Delacorte, 1977]). He has also managed to publish a volume of gay poems, *The Deformity Lover,* and to establish a small gay publishing house, the Seahorse Press.

The following interview-conversation took place on the Fire Island Pines and was occasioned by the publication of his novel, *The Lure* (Delacorte), which has a gay setting and story remarkably similar to the movie *Cruising* in everything but politics and attitude.

Given the book and the times, the conversation raised a number of intriguing and puzzling issues about gay literature and culture. Like political matters, these are not really questions to be answered by specialists but issues to be confronted by all of us. Everybody will, of course, find their own answers as we each become clear about who we are and what we are doing. For us, the discussion raised rather than answered questions; we hope it will stimulate and provoke further thought.

*The world portrayed in your new novel,* The Lure, *is the same scene that's covered in* Cruising, *the movie that's causing so much agitation*

*right now, and also, for that matter, the world of* Faggots *and* Dancer
from the Dance. *But it seems to me there's a real difference in the way you
see it and the way it's been depicted in those novels, and probably in the
movie, from what I've heard. Yours seems both a more sympathetic and a
much more accurate version of this . . . seamier side of the gay world.*

Well, I don't know if it's seamy. But I tried to make it as authentic as
possible. A lot depends on how I narrate my point of view, how my *character* sees it. For example, I see Fire Island in various ways, having spent a
lot of time here. When *he* sees it, he sees it from one particular point of
view . . . that is, as somebody who's frustrated, confused and unsure. To
him it appears very different than it appears to me. And I specifically chose
a different type of character to go into this world, in order to bring out
some objective points about it—because he's a sociologist, essentially. And,
of course, he's straight at the beginning of the novel and completely ignorant of the gay world.

*Why choose to set it in the sexual demimonde, as it were?*

You want to hear what this book grew out of? Because there really was
one factual occurrence which set me going. In the early seventies there was
a series of murders of gays in the West Village, murders that were connected with bars and bar owners and clubs. Arthur Bell did some articles
on them and then he stopped and nothing more was heard about it. At that
time I was living on Jane Street. A good friend and neighbor of mine was
working for the Jane Street Block Association, which was very aggressive
in neighborhood relations, and they met with police liaison units, etc. etc.
At that time, he told me that the police had set up a very hush-hush organization in the Village that was going around trying to find out what these
murders were all about, what the links were to the mob and whatever else.
This went on for about two years. Later, from friends of mine who were
connected with bars or tricks who knew bartenders or people—it's a floating type of world—from them I heard that this special police unit was disbanded, and I wasn't able to find out why. I began speculating, trying to
find out what had happened. It was something that interested me, it was
right there in my neighborhood and I wanted to know what was going on.

About the same time that I was putting together the proposal for this
book, there was an article in the *New York Times* which talked about how
this police unit which had been set up to investigate these murders, was
now being revealed for the first time and only then because it was being
disbanded, and there was an investigation into corruption within the
unit—none of which was terribly clear. When I called up the reporter who
had done the story, he said all the information was in his article and that
was all I could find out. At that point I decided that a little bit more was
going on than what we had been told. And so that was the basis of my
novel. I said let's speculate on what the police did, on what this unit was
and why it was disbanded, and why there was an investigation into it. That
was how my idea developed.

What I liked about the idea was that it struck a really fascinating metaphor for what being homosexual in our time and place means. Because
instead of a gay man pretending to be straight in every aspect of his life,
having to build up a second life, what I was interested in was a straight
man who had to build up a gay life. The idea of reversing the metaphor for

the way gay men live in this country is what actually appealed to me. And the story that worked was all predicated on the fact that this man had to develop—something would have to happen to him *internally* as a result of what happened in his dealings with the world.

*Do you think you're taking a big risk, as a successful mainline novelist, to turn to this subject matter in your fourth novel?*

Yes.

*And especially to try to portray in a popular novel a straight man who essentially becomes converted to gay by the end of the novel?*

Well, if I hadn't had the support of my agent and editor, I don't know whether I would have done it. I felt I had to address the issue at some point. I had done a book of gay poems, and I've been doing some gay short stories, but I had to address the issue of homosexuality in a novel. To my mind, there are a lot of really fine writers in their fifties, sixties and seventies who are homosexual and who could have really taken off if they had addressed the issue. The only one who seems to have done that is Christopher Isherwood, and I think, more and more, that he's going to be the one who stands out. I felt that as a novelist who claimed to be a reporter—which is one of the duties of the novelist, to report on certain aspects of life around us—I had to deal with the subject, which is really close to me. So even at this point of risk, I decided to do it.

*But it seems to me you also directed it toward the straight audience without compromising yourself in any way, which is really quite an accomplishment.*

Well, there are a certain number of people who have bought books by Felice Picano who expect a kind of book, a book that is going to take them into an area they have not necessarily gone into before. And so in that sense I felt that I was being true to the readership I already had. They were going to get another Picano mind-trip into some new area of life today.

*Have you had any response? Any idea of knowing how the straight audience will respond to it so far?*

Well, there are a certain number of people who have bought books by Felice, books that I write. But straight men also seem to like it a lot! And I think one reason is that it's like escapist literature for straight men, it provides them with what is, after all, a masculine, rather bold and courageous, if sometimes impulsive and sometimes stupid, hero. Someone they can identify with, who goes through an adventurous period of time. He gets to try out all sorts of things that they are forbidden to do by their position in society, by their position as family men and by their self-image.

*And your publishing house has been totally supportive?*

Dell/Delacorte?

*Yeah. I hear a lot about the difficulty gay writers have because a lot of publishing houses are homophobic, and I'm not sure if that's true or not. I have to say I haven't run into that.*

Well, here's the situation. Believe it or not, I originally intended this as a film. I had been talking to a film producer who'd read some of my work and wanted to do a film set in the gay area. When I was out in Los Angeles, we discussed it, but this was in 1976 and I really felt that they were not interested in going as far or as deeply as I wanted to go with the material. So we agreed to disagree at that point and I came back to New York. I was handing a completely different proposal to my publisher, and my editor said, "I understand you were out in Hollywood doing something with a scenario." And I said, "Yes, they didn't accept it," and she said, "Well, I'd like to take a look at it." As soon as I showed it to her, she said, "I really think this is your next book." So the support came real fast. When I did hand in the final draft, I think they were a little surprised by the authenticity and the eroticism and the violence that I portrayed, and I think they were unsure about who would read this book. But everyone at Dell/Delacorte liked the book, so that seemed to change real fast.

*Well, they seem to be building up the book in a very big way. They seem very much behind it from everything I've seen. Are they going to run this also as a gay book, advertise in the gay press and all that?*

Absolutely. We discussed that. Since I had experience with advertising as a gay publisher, we got together and discussed what proportion of the advertising budget would go to the gay media. And it's a good portion. So it's being run simultaneously as a mainline book and as a gay book.

*I think you have this interesting position, because you're working both in mainline publishing through your novels and simultaneously in the gay subculture through your volume of poetry, and now as publisher of Seahorse Press, which does only gay books.*

Yes, only gay stuff. And to my knowledge, it's the only gay book publisher in New York. Ashley is out of town. . . .

*What else has Seahorse published?*

Doric Wilson's book, the two plays that are running at the Spike, *The West Street Gang* and *A Perfect Relationship*, and we're publishing a book of poetry by Dennis Cooper.

*Called what?*

*Idols.* A wonderful book.

*What's interesting is that you can work simultaneously and evidently extremely well in both the mainstream and in the gay subculture.*

I'm hoping that this book is the one that pulls it together. (Laughs) Because I'm going to continue splitting it apart from here on. I've just started another novel, which is not in any way gay, because that's . . . one of my concerns, but not my *only* concern as a writer. And I'm probably going to be publishing a book of my short stories, in a year or two, which *are* all gay. It's nice to be able to do both. I don't know who else is doing it. I'd like to try to get more people interested.

*Ed White, in a way.*

Ed White, definitely.

*. . . not as commercially successful yet as you, but he seems to be able to do both of those things. It's interesting: I'm always trying to figure out whether there is in fact a gay literature, a separate and distinct cultural identity.*

Well, would you consider *Myra Breckinridge* part of gay literature?

*I don't know.*

Because I think I would. And if that's so, then Gore Vidal is an example of somebody who's done it before but has done it rather coyly and very carefully because of what happened to him. But he's hiding a great deal, and I don't really see that as necessary from where I am.

*That's the feeling I have. But it's odd in terms of other cultural movements. If there's a separate gay cultural identity that would justify these institutions, like magazines, newspapers, small presses, and a separate literature, you'd expect people to get exclusively into that. Look at the black movement. But it does seem possible that gays can work in both simultaneously, which I think is a peculiarity. Like there are all these discussions about ghettoization. And I must admit a few years ago I was totally against it, and now ... I mean, here we are in the Pines.*

What a ghetto! (Laughs)

*And I like it. And it's real odd, but it doesn't seem to me in any way to contradict the fact that I work in the mainline world. It seems that "straight" publishing houses, for instance, can serve the gay community perfectly well. Provided the books have sufficient commercial potential, of course.*

But I think the real problem is what's happening with gay books that *are* being published: they're coming under an incredible amount of attack, for any and all reasons. Especially from political radicals.

*More from the gay press than the straight press.*

Much more, much more.

*That's what's so disturbing. For all the gay books I've published, we get much better reviews in the straight press than in the gay press. I really don't understand it. I realize there are issues ... I don't think we should only puff stuff that's gay.*

Right.

*But somehow I feel that's not the question. The books really are attacked in the gay press. ...*

For not presenting what some people feel is a true picture. If I were to present a true picture of gay life around me, it would be Marvin and his lover of ten years finding a new recipe for tuna noodle casserole and inviting their friends over for an evening, and perhaps there's a genius somewhere who can pull that off in a novel, but to me that's not what novels are all about. ... *Novel* means new, and it's supposed to bring something that's new to you, a new viewpoint, a new look at the world, or just new places, new people, new characters. And so, to a large extent I feel that criticism of gay literature is misplaced. The gay critics are claiming everything that's being done by gay writers now is, in one way or another, sensational. *Lovers* is sensational because it's a failed love affair. And *Dancer from the Dance* is sensational because it overromanticizes everything. And *Faggots* because it overcriticizes everything. But art is not reality; it's a distortion. And I think you have to choose whether you're going to read something as a document and accept it only as a document, or whether you're going to read it as a work of art. One of the problems may be that the gay audience is, in a real deep sense, illiterate. By that I mean that ever since they have come to gay consciousness they have been fed on pornography, on one hand, and gay political rhetoric, on the other. And between the two of them there's no space for anything that's judgment or value or setting up standards or criteria. To my mind, that's a really disturbing type of illiteracy. I'm hoping it changes.

*It's also happening at a very dangerous time, because this attitude is*

*opposite of nurturing at a time when we're just starting to get a certain
number of gay writers and the audience is so acerbic and so critical. You
know, we'll go back to the Gore Vidals and Truman Capotes.*

I don't think that's going to happen though. I'll tell you why. My feeling is that the whole 'coming out' idea as a metaphor is so strong and so
variable—it's like Sophocles' 'Know Yourself'—it can support a huge
amount of fictional and non-fictional work and that is going to continue to
interest people. It's too good an idea to die. And I think as long as it exists,
there are going to be writers who say, "Hey, I can really take this idea and
do something fabulous with it."

*But there seems to be such a lag. What I seem to see, increasingly, is a
greater self-awareness of gay personal identity, which has to do with how
people clothe themselves, how they look, what they . . . I mean, all of gay
New York has reshaped its body in the last four years. People are not at all
closeted, or much less so. There's a very assertive experiment to establish a
new type of masculinity as an alternative to the old straight version. But
there's such a lag in the literary response to that. If you see how people deal
with clothing and life-style and everything else, how come their taste in
fiction doesn't keep pace? I don't quite understand that. Most of these people do read. And, of course, they'd want to read about their own life, so
why don't they?*

Right. But look who's doing the criticism. One of the problems that gay
writers have at this stage—and I think Andrew Holleran said this first—is
that we have to *describe* gay life because it's never been described before.
And it's crystallizing around us, it's happening around us, so we have to
describe—almost minute by minute—what the changes are, what the various points of concentration are. We have to describe what people dress like,
what they do, where they go out, how they use their drugs or their alcohol,
or what they do for entertainment. A lot of what we're doing is taken up
with the description of what gay life looks like and feels like and what it's
like to live it. We can only deal with particular areas in *one* book, you
know, between two covers. A lot of people are complaining and saying,
"You're not describing *my* life, you're describing some New York queen's
life." And I do think that's a problem, I really do.

*Except that in literature, nobody sets out simply to describe somebody's
life—I mean, that's sociology. Artists, writers use certain material. . . . The
point you or Andrew or anybody else is finally making is not just to describe a certain segment of life, but to use it as a concrete metaphor, like
you would any other material. Well, I suppose not knowing that is the illiteracy you were talking about.*

Yes, exactly.

*It really is true. Illiteracy is not knowing what the function of litera-
ture is in relation to your life; in the most basic way, it's not knowing how
to read. And it does seem that we don't. At least the gay critics don't. It's
just astonishing.*

Well, Pablo Neruda once said that a book is a letter that's written to the
world. Some people receive it; some people answer it. And to my mind a
lot of the gay critics are like people who've lost their mailbox keys. I mean,
I don't think they *want* to receive these letters, these books. I don't think
they're really that interested.

One of the problems is that a writer, no matter what he's doing, is going to be a rebel. You can't trust a writer, basically. The writer is the gadfly, the outsider, the observer. I think that's the writer's strength, especially in gay society, which is forming itself right before our eyes. I mean the movement is only ten years old. Everything is only ten years old. If the gay writer comes under attack, as he does so much these days, it's a sort of self-criticism. People are seeing what they don't want to see about themselves. And he's pointing it out rather fearlessly and saying, "Hey, look at what you're doing, jerks." I think that's a lot of what's being responded to. Then again, there are some real puritans in the movement. I sort of distrust politics the way I distrust religion. And a lot of the gay criticism that's coming to books is coming from a political point of view. I don't see how the two mix at all. It's sort of a shame.

*It's like the literary Stalinism in the late thirties. It is on such an appallingly low level of political censorship, actually.*

That's right. Also there is the big question of our enormous heterogeneity. What do I have in common with a gay steelworker in Flint, for example? Very little. And because of that, there are people who are bound to have completely different ideas of how to lead what they consider a gay life. I know people whose only way of looking at gay life is to have a single partner for the rest of their lives. Something like that is naturally going to color the way they see almost everything that's important in gay life. And they're going to criticize the way we live our lives, the way we party, the way we dress, the way we spend our money, the way we have sex, from that viewpoint; whereas someone who is promiscuous or someone who decides to have a life that is a series of short and perhaps not terribly meaningful relationships, but which are very pleasant—because people *have* reached decisions like that, too—he's going to lead as free and independent a life as possible, and he's going to look down on that other person and say, "Hey, I think you're just stuck in straight-world conventionality." And so we're going at it from all sorts of different angles. There's a great variety of life-styles *within* this life-style . . . and a critic should be able to say where he comes from. He should provide his credentials before he reviews and criticizes a book. (Laughs) It's a terrible thing to have to say.

*It's funny. We could make a checklist; all critics would have to reveal their positions on certain questions.*

Right! Because I think that's where their criticisms are coming from a lot; they're coming from really root questions of how you define yourself as gay.

*Precisely. But this is extremely interesting and, as far as I know, there's no parallel. Take the difference between you and the steelworker. What do you have in common? You're both gay. You could try to make analogies, like between an intellectual Jew on the Upper West Side of Manhattan and a Jewish steelworker in Flint. But they'll have something in common eventually, because they've inherited this Jewishness, which may . . . I mean there are questions about it, but there is some kind of cultural identity there. And they will fight over the portrayal of the "black experience." But again, they have an identity that can't be walked away from. Now, our identity is very odd, because in a way, it's freely accepted. I mean, you could go out and fuck men without making a* culture *of it. Obviously, that's what most people have done for . . .*

*. . . hundreds of years.*

*Right. And now we seem to want to make a culture of an act that doesn't necessarily lead to a culture, to have a certain form of cultural identity. I mean, you see that here at the Pines. I think the Pines is really a source of values, in a certain way, or an experiment in values.*

To my mind, it's a crucible of values, because to a large extent they get tested here.

*Right. But I can't think of any parallel for that. Andrew Kopkind pointed out recently in his* Village Voice *article that what we're seeing is the creation of an artificial culture, in the sense that it's not necessary. We're not stuck with the Old Testament and three thousand years of persecution like the Jews. We don't have black skin. You know, we wouldn't have to be gay. We might have to be homosexual, or not; that's a psychological and/or biological question. But being a homosexual—having sex with men—does not necessarily lead to being gay—that is, having a gay culture, shopping at Bloomingdale's, reading gay novels, etc. It really is extraordinarily odd. Kopkind was the first person who made that clear to me—the enormous peculiarity of the idea of the gay culture or gay identity. And it still seems to me very problematic, but I feel it very strongly.*

Right. Another problem I think we're dealing with is that there really is a difference between the political critics and what people refer to as style queens, who have in fact shaped all the visible aspects of gay culture and have done it almost intuitively. They've done it because it looked good, it felt good. The people who are doing the thinking around it, who are trying to formulate an ideology that will work, not only politically but sociologically and psychologically, are quite different. That's where the real split is. The culture's being formed by people who are not necessarily thinking about it, but who *are* doing it because it feels good or looks good or will make a nice effect. And, in fact, if you take a New York or San Francisco or Houston man who looks gay and lives a gay life and you strip away the accouterments, you have just an ordinary man. It's all been put in, it's all styled on top, all surface—the man's haircut, clothing, where he goes dancing, the choice of drugs he takes, and what he will try out in bed.

*But what else would there* be *to an identity, to a cultural identity but those things—how one looks, how one chooses to move in the world?*

The difficulty with people who are trying to build up an ideological framework is that there *isn't* any ideological framework. It really *is* surface, it really is a series of attributes, and it seems to work. As you said, we're not stuck with a skin color or a genetic difference, or a religious difference that sets us apart. So gay culture is a distinctive setting apart of ourselves, by a whole stylistic framework. And political people criticize that stylistic framework. Part of that is just the distrust of artists, whether they're hairdressers, or interior decorators, or writers, or painters, or whatever.

*You're saying the basic division is between what you call style queens and the intellectuals and writers.*

Well, my point is that the intellectuals are not necessarily the writers. I think that's where the problem is. The so-called gay intellectuals that I know of are involved in formulating an ideology they hope everyone lives up to. Most gay writers haven't fallen into that camp. They're on their own. They're somewhere between the two, and if they seem closer to the intuitive-style gay people, it's because there's more to be seen, more to be commented on—the way people behave, manners, social customs. That's where a writer's real material is; it's not in the idea. Writers hope to sometimes expose the ideology. But they're not sitting in the intellectual's camp, and I think that's a problem.

*Well, it gets us very far afield, but it's interesting. If there is an ideology for being gay, more to it than an aesthetic way of being in the world . . . and I think you could dredge one up, I think you could even make a fairly high-falutin' argument where metaphysically the gay condition seems to me—unless I just have blinders on—to coincide with the essential position of "modern man." In a very odd way, in the sense of making it anew, in the sense of not having traditions, in the sense of dealing with a great deal of self-consciousness. Other people are encumbered by cultures that seem to be a weight from the past. But it certainly means nothing to me that I'm Irish. You know. Any of that tradition is absolutely . . .*

*. . .* gone, yeah.

*Gone. It has no impact on me whatsoever. I don't know what it means to someone else if they're Polish or if they're German, or Italian or something like that.*

I was approached by an Italian-American magazine to do something for them, and I told them I didn't know what I could do for them. That's not an identity I feel in any way connected with. I didn't grow up in an Italian neighborhood; I learned my Italian when I went to Florence. That isn't one of the ways I identify myself. Whereas as soon as I got in contact with gay magazines I said, "Yes, I can do it. This is realistic." So okay, I'll grant you that: being gay is one of the most basic ways of defining ourselves.

*Okay, then that would mean there's a great deal of cultural content in being gay, that it is not simply a parochial identity crisis or whatever, the formation of a small group.*

That's right.

*A gay culture would have a great deal of relevant significance to the community at large, because the gay situation does seem to coincide with where, on the whole, we are as . . . whatever you want to call us . . . postmodern people.*

Well, as soon as we can get mainstream readers for our books, then we'll see whether straight people feel that something is being illuminated for them in a gay writer's works. I think that would make the difference. But, you know, this line of thought makes me a bit nervous, just as it makes me nervous when people claim that literature has a function. I don't know if literature does have a function except to continue. For me that seems to be such a large thing for literature to do in the face of all the demands on people's attention today. I don't know. There are people who really claim that literature, and especially gay literature, should have a meaning beyond its own existence. I don't know if that's true. Someone complained, after seeing one of Doric Wilson's plays that I published, and said, "Well, it does nothing more than mirror our lives." I said, "As far as I'm concerned, that's enough." It would be fabulous if you could see that his play did something more, but the fact that it *does* mirror our lives is important to me, because it hasn't been done before.

*Yeah, it's also a question of how far beyond that you could go. I mean, poets are not supposed to be legislators. We don't want them to tell us how we're supposed to live. Ideological novels are horribly dull, as a rule.*

Exactly. But that seems to be what most gay critics are demanding. And you'd better agree with them, too!

*I've only read one good ideological book, which was* Coming Out *by Wallace Hamilton. I think it was badly misjudged, because nobody considered it as a political book, which it basically was. I mean, it's a very systematic progay novel. You have to go back to Jack London, or some of the Red Chinese writers, or some of the powerful proletarian writers of the thirties, to really compare it within the framework of literature as a political tract. And I think it compares quite favorably. But I do think you can only go so far with that. And I think probably in the long-term seriously literary and nonpolitical fiction about the gay world will attract general readers who aren't gay. I'm sure general readers are going to respond to your book. I hope so. I wish they were making the movie from your book rather than* Cruising.

Yeah, although I really didn't mind that we got no film interest at the time, I'm sort of annoyed now that the producers that I'd originally talked to about it didn't take it on. Just because *Cruising is* being made now, and *The Lure* would have presented what I think is a more accurate version of the same material. So it's sort of a shame.

*Because politically it would have been much more—how do we say?— progressive.*

Yes, but also because my book asks more questions. Because it goes beyond politics or sexuality and asks people . . . my character asks himself, "What am I doing? Who and what am I living for?" I think that's something a lot of gay people have to ask . . . and a lot of straight people, too. And we can't help them out too much more than that. But I think people go to a film with a different attitude than they go to a book. I know I do. I don't think people expect to see reality on the silver screen, after all this time. I think they expect to see a distortion. Whereas when they go to a book they seem to want to know more of what is actually going on and will accept more reality in that form, because it's a private and not a communal experience.

*But I do think films have traditionally functioned to show people how to be American. Wave after wave of immigrants have learned what it means to be American, even learned the language, from Hollywood. That's why I think . . . I guess I do think it's legit to use muscle to try to get our own point of view there. Because movies do somehow still reflect and help create the popular consciousness of the whole nation.*

Absolutely. But it's a *public* consciousness. I'm not sure whether private attitudes are as affected by films.

*Okay, but Hollywood's public attitude is incredibly homophobic. And a gayer industry you can't imagine. But everyone's really closeted.*

Yeah. I know from experience.

*Well, I suppose we have no more bitch than black people do, in this country. . . .*

Whose culture has been misused for years.

*And probably never filmed decently except for* Stormy Weather, *the only film I know which was totally black. I don't know if it was black-directed.*

Lady Sings the Blues was, to my mind, a black film, inside and out.

*Well, if it's taken blacks so long, and they've gotten so little, I guess we shouldn't despair.*

Well, on the other hand, we should be angry because unlike blacks and women there are gays who are wealthy and powerful and in important positions in this country, including—even especially—in the film industry. And it sort of behooves them, since they're in these extraresponsible positions with all this extra clout that other minorities don't have, to do something a little extra. And I say it's a great shame if people in those positions aren't doing anything. You know, it's really irresponsible. That irresponsibility is really more deplorable than the irresponsibility of a Billy Friedkin, who seems to be simply after commercial success.

*I agree. Do you have something else you want to talk about? Or do you want to go back to the pool . . . an appropriate way to end an interview in the Pines.*

The pool is heaven. It really is.

# Tim Dlugos

◇◆◇◆◇◆◇◆◇◆◇◆◇◆◇◆◇◆◇

## Gay Widows

*W*hen Stanley Saul received the phone call that changed his life, he was in his Manhattan apartment. It was Labor Day weekend 1978, and he could have been at Egg Harbor, New Jersey, in the summer house he shared with his lover, Philip Perl. But Stanley had decided not to take time off that weekend, so Perl had gone to the country without him, bringing along a couple of house guests. When Stanley picked up the phone on Saturday morning, one of those guests was on the other end of the line.

"Stanley, I have bad news. It's Phil. I think he may have died. I called an ambulance, but he's lying very still."

Numbly, Stanley dialed a friend. Together, they borrowed a car and sped to the hospital nearest Egg Harbor. Phil was not there. They found him half an hour later in the local morgue.

Philip Perl was fifty-two years old when a sudden heart attack ended his life that holiday weekend. He left behind a devoted lover, both parents, four siblings, and an estate valued at more than half a million dollars. He did not leave behind a will. That crucial lapse has plunged Stanley Saul into a complicated, frustrating, heartbreaking legal battle with implications for every gay couple in the United States.

Today, Stanley Saul's court fight has made him as familiar to talk-show audiences and newspaper readers as to the judges who have heard his case. The dispute is not over any gain Saul seeks to realize from his lover's estate. In the absence of a will, Saul has no discernible claim to most of Philip Perl's property—the stocks, the bonds, or the shares of family-owned apartment buildings in Manhattan. Relatives by blood or matrimony are the only persons entitled to inherit property in a legal system that does as much as any religious dictum to sanctify the institution of heterosexual marriage.

Saul's legal action, which has cost him thousands of dollars, is a last-ditch attempt to prevent the loss of his home: the cooperative apartment he shared with Philip Perl for eleven years. In this effort, Saul is opposed not only by the Perl family but by the legal machinery of the City of New York, which administers the co-op and claims that Saul must leave because he and Perl did not constitute a "family."

Saul's attorney Marvin Lerman calls his client's case the "Son of *Marvin*," referring to the Lee Marvin–Michelle Triolla "palimony" decision in California in 1979. "What's the difference if a man and a woman live together for ten years, or two men?" he asks. "I don't see it as a homosexual issue. It's more a matter of the legal definition of a family." Nevertheless, Lerman readily admits that Saul's predicament is made bleaker by his homosexuality. A heterosexual couple living together has the option of entering a legally sanctioned marriage—a choice unavailable to gay couples. In some states (though not New York), the recognition of common-law marriages can benefit the survivor of a long-term heterosexual relationship. That recognition is not extended to gay people, no matter how long they live together. Finally, Saul has been hurt by the absence of a gay antidiscrimination law in New York City or State, a law that Lerman says would "improve his chances" of winning in court.

Stanley Saul's case will be a litmus test of the actual progress gay Americans have made toward equal protection under the law. So far, the results of that test are discouragingly negative: Saul has lost in New York Housing Court and on his first appeal of that decision.

Beyond the new legal ground he is attempting to stake out and the symbolic significance of his case, a single simple question haunts Stanley Saul. When he asks it, his voice is filled with hurt: "If you give eleven years of your life to somebody, is it right that their family can come in and clean you out?"

Stanley Saul met the man who was to be his "life-partner" while waiting in line at the Public Health Center in Chelsea. "We were both getting shots to go to Europe," he remembers. "We started talking, and I told him it was my first trip to Europe. So he invited me to have dinner with him and talk about things to see." At their first meal together, Perl confided to Saul that he was homosexual.

"I told him I was, too," recalls Saul. "Remember, this was in the mid-sixties. Phil was in the closet. He was terrified about people finding out he was gay. Phil was older than me, and I was more interested in younger people then, so I began to set him up on dates with friends of mine at MGM, where I worked. Our friendship grew gradually. I didn't start sleeping with him until a year after we met. Finally, I realized I was in love with him."

Shortly thereafter, Saul moved into the co-op that Perl had bought four years before. On Ninth Avenue in Manhattan, the apartment is part of Mutual Redevelopment Houses, one of the first joint ventures in housing between a labor union and the federal, state, and city governments. From the first day he lived with Perl, Saul paid half of the apartment's maintenance. Nevertheless, Perl steadfastly refused to include Saul's income on the annual statement he submitted to the co-op's governing board. "It wasn't required that he list both our incomes," explains Saul, "and Phil was afraid that if he did, they'd know we were gay."

Perl was a writer and fact-checker for the *New Yorker* during most of his years with Saul. "He was the sophisticated New Yorker, I was the country bumpkin," says Saul of their early days together. "Before I met Phil, I didn't know where the Hamptons were. I didn't know what an East Side restaurant was."

Both men came from protective Jewish families, but that was the only similarity in their upbringings. Saul's background was more modest: a lower-middle-class life in northern New Jersey. Perl grew up in Sands Point on Long Island's "Gold Coast," the pampered son of an enormously wealthy family.

"Phil was rich, but he didn't have a rich person's mentality," reminisces Saul. "He was very frugal; the only nice clothes he had I bought for him. Mostly he shopped in thrift shops. If I bought him a shirt that cost $40, I'd have to say it cost $20. He couldn't enjoy expensive things. When we fought, it was over things like the cost of cleaning or of a haircut. I'd say, 'Did you get a haircut? We're going to a party,' and he'd get mad and tell me I wasn't his mother. The apartment was always cluttered, the apartment of a writer—there were stacks of magazines and newspapers everywhere. It didn't get painted for ten years."

Initially, Perl was leery of introducing his lover to his parents. "In the beginning, I wanted to go and visit them, but he didn't want me to," says Saul. "Eventually, I was going out there every holiday and most weekends. I was the only person Phil ever took to his family's house. I'd go fishing with his father. At the end, I didn't want to go out there so much, but Phil wanted me to."

In the first weeks after Philip Perl's death, Saul's relations with his lover's family continued to be smooth. "They gave me the honor of carrying his casket," he recalls. "I sat shibah with the family for seven days. And I was there when the vault with Phil's papers was opened. Let me tell you, when you see every bond and bankbook of the man you've lived with for eleven years, and the only other name on them is his mother's, you feel like shit."

Saul was in a state of shock in the months after Perl's death; only recently, he claims, has he begun to recover. When Perl's family began removing things from the apartment, Saul was too upset to raise any objection. "They wanted Phil's old clothes," he says. "Now this man *bought* old clothes, so he didn't have anything worth much, but they took them all anyway. I ended up having to fight for my own clothes—Phil and I wore the same size. Then they accused me of buying old clothes to give to them so I could keep the good ones for myself.

"His mother took the pillows and pillowcases off the bed. One night, she called me at three in the morning and said, 'I have a snapshot of my son in this sports jacket—where's the sports jacket?'"

When Philip's executor, his brother Irving Perl, asked when the family could come in to take the furniture, it dawned on Stanley Saul that his home of more than ten years was in jeopardy. So he made a verbal agreement with the Perls to purchase the co-op from Philip's estate, to gain legal title to the apartment he had already paid thousands of dollars to live in.

At this juncture, however, the co-op administration stepped in. Mutual Redevelopment Houses has a long waiting list of prospective tenants. Although the Perl family agreed to sell Saul his own home, the city's Department of Housing Preservation and Development forbade it. The apartment had been sold to Philip Perl and his family, they ruled; since Saul was not related by blood, marriage, or adoption, the next person on the waiting list was entitled to purchase the co-op.

Marvin Lerman asserts that the city's ruling is far too narrow. "If Saul had been Phil Perl's fourth cousin and had lived there for two weeks, he'd have the apartment," he explains. "Saul and Perl lived together as intimately as any married couple for ten years—and now they tell Saul he has to go? It's absurd."

Lerman says that the city is afraid that by bending its strict definition of *family*, they would "open Pandora's box; there'd be lots of challenges." The attorney insists, however, that a more important issue than bureaucrats' headaches must be considered. "A person's rights shouldn't be jeopardized because it costs a few extra bucks to administer."

The city agency's ruling seems to have been as capricious as it was arbitrary. According to Saul, another man in the same cooperative was able to retain possession of his home upon his lover's demise, with no questions asked by the Department of Housing Preservation.

On Saul's behalf, Lerman has filed suit before the Supreme Court of the State of New York, challenging the grounds of the city's decision to dispossess. In the suit, which has not yet come to trial, Saul is claiming that the co-op administrators violated his civil rights, as well as Mayor Edward Koch's 1978 proclamation forbidding city agencies to discriminate against gay people. If the suit is settled in Saul's favor, it will be a milestone in the legal protection of gay rights in New York. But by the time the case comes before the bench, Saul may be forced out of his home by a separate suit filed by the Perl family, in which he is the defendant.

As soon as they learned that Saul would be prohibited from staying in the co-op he shared with their son, the Perls asked the New York City Housing Court to force him off the premises. For Saul, this legal action converted the ominous possibility of losing his home into an imminent peril. Even worse, the nature of the suit placed Saul in a classic Catch-22 situation: the Perl family could use the Department of Housing Preservation's decision as a weapon against Saul, but Saul could not challenge or even address that decision, because the City of New York was not a party in the trial.

In preparing his defense against the Perl estate, Saul learned exactly what a crazy-quilt of legal contradictions gay couples face. Although homosexuals living together are not considered a "family" by city housing administrators, they *are* considered a "family" in certain cases by the U.S. Department of Housing and Urban Development (HUD) and the state Crime Victims Compensation Board. Thus, if Philip Perl had become incapacitated or died as the result of violent crime, Stanley Saul could receive compensation from New York State as Perl's "family"—although he would still have to fight New York City if he wanted to keep their apartment.

In March 1979, Saul lost the first round of his fight for his home when Judge Ferdinand M. Pellegrino of the New York City Housing Court was "unable to find any authority that holds homosexuals living together constitute a family unit." Months later, Saul lost again when the Appellate Term of New York State unanimously upheld Pellegrino's verdict, claiming "we are not prepared to state that . . . unmarried or otherwise unrelated persons constitute a family unit." Both decisions are remarkable for what they did *not* say (the appellate decision was also remarkable for its brevity—the court did not even bother to address four of the six legal arguments Saul presented to overturn the original decision). The city court found no precedent; the state court was indisposed to make any substantive judgment at all. Neither court made a firm ruling either for or against the notion that a gay couple can be considered a family.

"Ten or twenty years from now, there would be no problem with that case," says one attorney who has been following the court battle closely. "By that time, there will probably have been a number of decisions about the rights of unmarried persons living together, and the legal precedents will have developed along the way. After all, the whole trend in our society is for unmarried people to live together. But right now, those three appeals judges—all of whom are over seventy—just didn't want to deal with it. Frankly, I don't think that at this point in legal history Saul has much chance of winning."

Stanley Saul must now await permission from the courts to proceed up the next step of the appeals ladder. If the court agrees to his request, there will be many more months of wading through a defense that has already cost Saul many thousands of dollars. If the court refuses permission, he will have to pack his possessions and move out of his home.

"This has been a real struggle for me," he says sadly. "I had a rich lover. We had a house outside Atlantic City. I never felt threatened by being gay. Most of the people I knew lived in beautiful houses. They spent summers on Fire Island, and winters they flew to the Caribbean. I had no idea we needed gay rights or any kind of protection. It seemed to me that gay people didn't have too much to complain about.

"Now it seems like Germany in the thirties. Gay people are social, not political. We're at the bars every night; we're real party people. That's fine if you're very young or if you're settled down. But the minute things change and you have to go to society at large for help, watch out."

Oddly enough, Stanley Saul's best friend—the person with whom he drove to New Jersey on the day of Phil Perl's death—is another "gay widow." John Vincent lost his lover in 1967, two years before gay liberation was born at the Stonewall Tavern. A French exchange student working on his graduate degree at New York University, Vincent had lived for nearly three years with "Tom Bates," a TWA purser. One weekend at Jones Beach, Bates drowned. He was forty years old. Five days later, John came home from classes to find that the lock on his apartment door had been changed.

"It was Tom's brother, the executor of his estate," Vincent remembers. "All my clothes, my books, my skis—everything I had in the world was in that apartment. But his family refused to let me in.

"Tom had outsmarted them in one way: I was the beneficiary of his life-insurance policy. Even so, his brother tried to get me to sign that over to the estate. He threatened to report me as a homosexual to the Immigration and Naturalization Service. 'We don't need no French faggots in this country,' he told me. 'We've got enough American ones as it is.' "

Vincent resisted the pressure and eventually collected the insurance money, which enabled him to make a new start in his life. Today, the events of thirteen years ago are just a bitter memory. Nevertheless, if the same set of circumstances were to occur in 1980, John Vincent's legal rights—or lack of them—would be exactly the same as they were in 1967. After eleven years of gay liberation, the legal prejudices against gay survivors are just as strong as they were before the movement.

"I always told Stanley to be sure he had a will, to remember what happened to me," says Vincent. "And Stanley listened to me; he made a very detailed will. It was Phil who didn't listen."

In the process of writing this story, I discovered that dozens of people I know could tell me a horror story about an acquaintance of theirs who faced the loss of home or property when his or her lover suddenly died. There is Dick G. from Buffalo, prettiest boy in the city and the lover of a rich doctor, who found himself penniless and in the street when his lover's family zeroed in after the doctor's death in a car accident. There is Mary H., a lesbian from Iowa who lost the nursery business that she and her lover had built when the lover died in a plane crash. There is the elderly novelist who worried over having to leave his place of retirement when his wealthy lover died before him. And there are many more.

The argument against legal recognition of gay relationships is usually made on moral or ethical grounds. When Anita Bryant or Scoop Jackson or John Connally oppose the legalization of gay unions, they invoke "our Judeo-Christian tradition," "America's moral climate," or "the sanctity of the family" to defend their position.

Stanley Saul, John Vincent, and thousands of other gay men and women whose lives have been changed because of that prohibition don't suffer in their moral lives. Their traditions aren't wounded. They lose their homes, their possessions, the cherished proofs of a shared life which the law, the codifier of society's values, has as yet found no need to protect.

The traditionalists are right, however: the issue is at its heart a moral one. It has to do with the value and validity of human experience and human love. Throughout history, affirming one's humanity has often been a struggle. Stanley Saul, who, against his will, finds himself in the forefront of that struggle, expresses that affirmation very simply. "We're part of the human race," he says. "We're people. We do enter into relationships. That should be recognized."

## Holding Your Own

*With his partner George A. Terzian, Manhattan attorney Daniel Pinello conducts a weekly clinic, "The Law Stop," for gay women and men in need of legal advice. Here are four legal tools which Pinello advises gay people to use to protect what happens to their property in case of death or incapacity.*

*1. Joint tenancy with the right of survivorship.* When lovers are "joint tenants," all shared property (usually bank accounts or real estate) automatically belongs to one upon the death of the other. This arrangement is different from the more usual "tenancy in common," under which a decedent's share in common property becomes part of his or her estate to be divided among heirs. When property is shared, the law *presumes* tenancy in common, unless the property deed or bank account title specifically states otherwise.

Each state has its own formula for establishing joint tenancy. In New York, the property deed must read that A and B are "joint tenants with a right of survivorship." A shared bank account should be titled "A or B or Either Survivor." Remember, unless the exact wording for joint tenancy appears on the deed or bankbook, the property will be regarded as commonly held and will be divided among heirs when one of the owners dies.

To transfer jointly held property from two names to one name after one of the owners dies, all that is needed is a valid death certificate. The automatic transfer can prevent your home or joint savings from becoming part of any inheritance—for legal purposes, it is not even considered part of an estate.

*2. The power of attorney.* If your lover becomes incapacitated, who is legally empowered to act on his or her behalf? You are not—unless you have obtained that right by receiving the "power of attorney" to handle your beloved's affairs.

The power of attorney is a legal form through which you may share your right to sign checks or sell your home to another party. The power operates only during the lives of the participants in the agreements, so it is not a substitute for estate planning. It is a way of guaranteeing that your financial interests are in each other's hands throughout your life together.

Problems with this method of mutual responsibility can occur when you and your lover are no longer together—if you split up before one dies or is seriously disabled. Pinello knows of one case in which a vindictive ex-lover raided his former partner's bank accounts years after they had exchanged their powers of attorney. Since the original agreement was not time-limited, there was no legal impediment to such a sneak attack. The only way the power of attorney could be ended was for the victimized party to obtain and destroy the original piece of paper on which he had signed away his rights.

3. *A will*. A will is generally the most effective method of disposing of one's property after death. It can make three important decisions:

*The disposition of bodily remains.* If you want your ashes scattered from the Morton Street Pier but your siblings want you buried in the family plot at Fort Smith . . . if you are a militant atheist whose parents would demand a Mass of the Angels at your funeral . . . then a will is your best bet for controlling what will happen to your earthly shell when your spirit has departed.

*Naming an executor.* An executor is the person who acts on the legal behalf of a dead person. If a will is contested, the executor leads the fight to defend the decedent's wishes. Unless you have a will, the court will appoint an "administrator" to execute your estate. A next-of-kin is a likely choice—and by "next-of-kin," they do not mean your lover.

*Disposition of property.* If you die without a will, all your property goes to your "distributees"—that is, your relatives by blood or marriage. None of your property can be legally given to your lover without the distributees' consent. Through a will, you can leave your fortune to your lover, your ten best friends, or the animal shelter down the block. The point is, it is *your* choice.

Even with a will, however, there can still be trouble. Distributees have the right to contest any will in court. If a will is contested, for whatever reason, the legal fees of both parties to the dispute are usually taken out of the estate. "If a will is drafted and executed properly," says Pinello, "it will be upheld by a court 90 to 95 percent of the time. But a distributee can substantially reduce an estate through years of legal challenges to a will." This gives distributees a strong bargaining position with a legatee who might be tempted to pay off the family to avoid draining the estate's assets.

Regardless of *anything* in your will, if you were married and have no formal separation agreement or divorce, your spouse has an absolute right to half your estate (one-third, if there were children by the union). By "spouse," the law does not mean lover, either.

4. *Insurance.* Gay lovers can name each other as beneficiaries of their life-insurance policies. But this can only be done by changing the name of the beneficiary on an already existing policy from your parent or next-of-kin to your current beloved. Insurance companies will only issue a new policy when the new beneficiary has what they call an "insurable interest" in the life of the policy's owner; that's usually interpreted to mean your family, not your lover. Once a policy has been issued, however, there is

nothing to prevent you from changing the beneficiary to your lover or to anyone else.

## T. P. N. DODGE

## Lancaster, Pennsylvania

*A*mong the Amish in Lancaster County ("The Heart of the Pennsylvania Dutch Country," paper placemats everywhere tell you), "to go gay" means to leave the fold and become "worldly." In the past four or five years, the city of Lancaster has indeed "gone gay": its gay community has come out into public—if only at night—and Lancaster, coincidentally, has been treated to a revival of a "worldliness" it had forgotten.

Lancaster lies in the middle of the County, which is dotted with small villages such as Bird-In-Hand, Blue Ball, Gap, Intercourse, Paradise, and Peach Bottom. The soil is rich, the vegetation lush; the farms are neat and immaculate. Solid industries, like Armstrong Cork, Alcoa, Donnelly Printing (the Manhattan White and Yellow Pages are printed here), New Holland Machine, Hamilton Watch, Schick, and RCA, bolster the general prosperity of the area. But not too many years ago, it often seemed to me as though Lancaster was isolated by impassable mountains and miles of ice and that nothing could ever inject a wild strain into its stagnant gene pool.

It was not always this way: Lancaster, an old and seemingly respectable dowager, had a *past*. It was the home of Robert Fulton, inventor of the steamship, and of James Buchanan, the only lifelong bachelor president of the United States. Congress convened in Lancaster for one day during the Revolution, making the town one of the nation's historic capitals. Benjamin Franklin founded the esteemed Franklin and Marshall College here in the late 1700s. The Fulton Opera House, now a national landmark, was once a major theater in the East, the likes of Sarah Bernhardt, W. C. Fields, and Helen Hayes having performed on its stage. The Conestoga wagon, the sturdy vehicle in which most pioneers made their way west, and the so-called Kentucky rifle were both manufactured here. The nation's oldest watchmakers' school, Bowman Tech, thrives even today. There were speakeasies during Prohibition, and for years the Hotel Brunswick gave natives and visitors alike a taste of Plaza-like elegance. In spite of these credits, Lancaster ultimately succumbed to the all-plastic ambiance of one of its last claims to fame—Woolworth's, which was founded here.

The story of Lancaster's loss of history-makers (and worldliness) has never been chronicled. But by the 1950s the Fulton Opera House—the central symbol of the town's cultural life—was all but shut down and in the 1960s narrowly saved from being demolished for a projected parking lot. The Hotel Brunswick *was* demolished to make way for a new hotel—a monstrous rectangle of orange brick filled with hanging plastic plants. Much of the town's scar tissue is in the form of parking lots. Where there are parking lots, there are cars, and it was the new availability of the automobile and the ensuing flight to the suburbs that was, in part, responsible for the town's decline. Another problem was the decades-long lack of émigrés from other parts of the country, a lack that made possible the osmotic seepage of ignorant and conservative attitudes from the area's extreme religious groups—the Amish, the Mennonites, and, most bothersome and vocal of all, the nondenominational fundamentalists.

Even the wealthy community did little to bring culture and education into Lancaster as they once had. The rich now hightailed it to Philadelphia, New York, or Europe for their pleasures and returned home as unobtrusive and quietly respectable citizens. For instance, the three newspapers of the city, the *Intelligencer Journal,* the Lancaster *New Era,* and the *Sunday News,* and the main TV station, WGAL (an NBC affiliate), are all owned by one woman, a Mrs. Hess, the richest of the rich Steinman family. Mrs. Hess is well traveled and well educated, but her papers and TV station are lowbrow mirrors on Lancaster life. (If an article is well written or a show well produced, it is because of the work of an unusual staff member, rather than any directive from Mrs. Hess.) The attitude that "the people don't want or need anything better" prevails even in the local media, potentially the most elevating force in the area.

By the early 1970s, however, there was a new influx of "outsiders." Many came from large cities and moved into town, where they bought handsome, but in-need-of-renovation, townhouses. But the downtown shopping district was dying, a result of suburban shopping centers, the most repulsive of which is the huge Park City (*Park* here referring to what one does with a car, not to a green haven).

In the meantime, Lancaster's gays were blithely having secret parties. There were "clubs" and "families" to which gay people belonged, but all activities were behind barred doors and draped windows. There was no place to go in Lancaster for gays, so private parties were numerous and raucous—a reaction from having to live out a day in a town where, as one person put it, "homosexuals are something you read about in health books." Gay people needed each other's company, and as a further result of being closeted, they formed long, close friendships and secure, loyal, "family" groups.

The "family" to which I belonged was called the Dodge family. Due to the senility of the founding member, we joked, the origin of the name was lost. The family consisted mainly of Franklin and Marshall students, but nonstudents were admitted on close inspection. Each member was given a Dodge name. It was decided, for instance, that I was very likely to end my life in some spectacular and messy way, so I was dubbed Tosca. (After my national heritage was revealed, Pola Negri was added as a middle name.) We had men and women members and even some straight members. The family had parties—large, loud, and frequent. Dancing was de rigueur, and dishing was prized as an art form (Dennis to Michael: "I'm not saying you're old, my dear, but you could have modeled for the Sphinx." Michael to Dennis: "And *you* could have modeled for the base.") But the group was made up of some very talented and well-educated people. Our everyday conversations were at times seminars in music, art, politics, and literature. Toward the end, there were about seventy-five members, some of whom are close friends even today, although no longer in Lancaster. The feeling within the family was very much akin to that of brothers and sisters who reveled in their own incest.

One summer, through the efforts of a few people from Armstrong Cork Company and Franklin and Marshall's theater department, the Fulton Opera House was renovated and revived as a live theater (it had languished for years as a movie house)—and herein lies the story of Lancaster's "going gay."

As the Fulton's new summer season went into rehearsals, it was evident that much of the talent and energy in the new theater came from gays. Gays and straights in the theater have always mixed, and the Fulton's company was no exception. After rehearsals, a number of the actors and stage-hands would stop in at a neighborhood bar, the Tally-Ho. It was seedy, if not downright hoody, but it was close to the theater, and the owner seemed to cater to the newcomers.

One evening, the owner was serving drinks to a particularly large and noisy theatrical contingent. He told the troupe that their patronage was welcome and, in fact, heartily encouraged. It turned out that the owner of the bar was gay himself, and in a short time, the Tally-Ho became *officially* gay, dance floor and all.

In the following years, gays became more open, and Lancaster was going through new birth pangs of renovation. Tourism boomed; museums were opened; a nearby town, Marietta, turned into a Pennsylvania Provincetown. Today, Lancaster's newfound "worldliness"—in the form of several permanent theater groups, new restaurants (two of the best are gay-owned), Big Name concerts, festivals and special exhibits, the constant tourist traffic—coincides with the new openness of its gay community. In fact, the Tally-Ho has competition now: a gay disco, called The Fiddler (named after *Fiddler on the Roof*, the musical playing at the Fulton at the time of the bar's opening). Both places are filled to capacity on weekends.

The gays themselves changed as a result of the new openness. When the Tally-Ho first opened, the men were "queens," and the lesbians were "bull-dykes"—in appearance and behavior. Now both men and women seem to have largely dropped these stereotypic roles. The scene at The Fiddler is particularly low-key: the men have done away with their coiffures, donned jeans or "college" clothes, and assumed unaffected walks; the women have let their DA haircuts grow out and take pleasure in makeup and stylish clothes.

In both the town itself and its gay community, however, something has been lost in the course of what has been gained. Lancaster can now offer its citizens and tourists a rather varied array of worldly pursuits, but some of the delights of small-town living are gone forever. Gays are more open, less frightened, and socialize more with the community at large, but the magic of "forbidden fruit" (no pun intended!) is lost, close-knit groups are non-existent, long-term friendships are rarer, and private parties—still the best way to get to *know* new people—are infrequent. Parties have been replaced by "going to the bars"—nights are more vaporous in texture, memories harder to savor.

Just how far Lancaster will continue to go gay remains to be seen. In the meantime, Amish parents will continue to worry about their children's attraction to the ever more worldly world just beyond their fields. For, as the Amish say, once you go gay, there is no turning back.

# GREGG KILDAY

## *Hollywood*

To understand Hollywood, recall if you will those Walt Disney nature films that use stop-action camera techniques to hop up the life of a plant. *Pnnggg*, a tiny periscope of green, *strumm*, the stalk lurches into life, *blamm*, the flower explodes like a biological A-bomb. Most people marvel at the obvious illusion of it all. Not here in Hollywood. In Hollywood such an effect would probably be mistaken for life itself. Hollywood has no respect for anything unless it happens very big and very fast.

At the moment Studio One, a discotheque-cum-nightclub, is enjoying the kind of glitzy, neon-glazed success that Hollywood finds so irresistible. Elizabeth Taylor dropped by the other night to catch Frances Faye's act in the Backlot, as the showroom at Studio One styles itself. Whenever he is in town, Elton John will be rumored to have been seen on the dance floor just the other night. (In truth it is Paul Lynde who is more likely to have been there.) If you prefer *real* gossip, though, you should know that it was Suzanne Pleshette who was turned away at the door for lack of proper ID. Her chauffeur had the only driver's license.

But to repeat the local chatter about "the Studio" is to oversell the club. By all objective standards, the Studio is just another loud, crowded, flashy gay dance bar. Out-of-town visitors, however, are invariably enthralled by the Studio's passing charms; they leave convinced that nowhere on the North American continent are the boys so presentable. And why not? The Southern California sun has done its bit for narcissism.

Disappointingly, though, sexual energies almost never run high at Studio One. There is convivial socializing, and there is dancing. (The LA Hustle—basically a group Busby Berkeley routine—still comes and goes in dismaying variations.) And there is inevitably a good deal of posing. But cruising per se is kept to a minimum. It is considered almost rude. Perhaps the regulars have invested too much into cultivating a self-contained attractiveness to admit to being on the sexual make. Or it may be, as one disenchanted witness decided one night, that everyone is simply afraid of fucking below himself.

So then what distinguishes Studio One? Not its waiters' tight basketball shorts—copied from New York's Le Jardin. Nor its California Deco interior (that is, an excess of silver on redwood)—that was seen a year or so earlier in San Francisco's Cabaret and L.A.'s own After Dark. What makes the Studio a continuing hit is that it is the first gay bar in Los Angeles to have gone public in a big, jazzy way.

Studio One opened two years ago, a lifetime by Hollywood standards, and it is still going strong. Of course, given Hollywood's pretended sexual laissez-faire, if this particular club hadn't arrived on the scene when it did some other bar would have been pressed into service to amuse the restless and the young. But none could have been more appropriate than Studio One, because Studio One is the old Factory gone gay.

The Factory, housed in a two-story hangarlike building where munitions once were made, was a private club concocted by Peter Lawford and a few of his pals in the late sixties. Membership, alas, was more coveted than exercised, and after a couple of years the enterprise folded. It is said that Barbra Streisand became too much the star to mix with her old Factory friends, who were then lured to Pips in Beverly Hills with the promise of a never-ending game of backgammon, and, show business folk being cavalier about such things, unpaid bills were all that was left behind.

In the stars' tracks followed a string of entrepreneurs. Nobody could figure out how to turn the old Factory into a paying proposition. It was successively re-outfitted as a meeting place for neohippie craftsmen, a spaghetti restaurant, and, under con man Bernie Cornfeld, an abortive discotheque. Then Scott Forbes, a Boston-born optometrist, came along. While the Factory was still in operation Forbes had rented it on Sunday evenings, called it the Odyssey Club, and opened it to a private, gay membership. (On Sunday nights, cognoscenti remarked, the Factory became the Faggotry.) Citing his past success and backed by a small group of gay professionals, Forbes convinced the building's owner to allow him to open a full-scale, seven-nights-a-week gay discotheque, complete with showroom and restaurant, electronic pong, jewelry concession, and random laser beams.

Forbes, a personably tanned young man who wears nothing more calculated than jeans and an official Studio One T-shirt, is very much a businessman, even if at times he seems to be affecting the sentiments of a social reformer. "I opened this place so that the gay kids would have a nice place to go," he insists, rather as if he were a latter-day Father Flanagan and the Studio a new-age Boys' Town. The club, Forbes points out, is a source of employment for gays. It has also become Hollywood's major point of contact with the Los Angeles gay community.

Let L.A.'s gay leadership squabble among themselves about who is to attend the intermittent gripe sessions staged by the studios and networks to exorcise gay complaints. All that adds up to is three or four column inches in the trades, the daily entertainment journals that spoonfeed a diet of gossip, stock indexes, and fantasies about the outside world into the entertainment industry's consciousness. In contrast, Studio One takes out prominent ads every other week to trumpet the performers appearing in its showroom.

Studio One is becoming as much a part of the Hollywood scene as the Polo Lounge. For the L.A. premiere of *Tommy*, professional party-giver Allan Carr took over the club for a night of elbow-wrenching slumming that was videotaped by David Frost for replay as an ABC late-night special. Don Kirshner followed suit by staging a disco special starring Tommy Tune. And when Kaye Ballard, just released from New York's Persian Room, opened recently, producer Ross Hunter threw a party for a Rolodex sampling of his friends—Zsa Zsa, Martha Raye, Debbie Reynolds, Rona Barrett, Rod McKuen, et al. This precipitated some cultural confusion. In what was misguidedly intended as a salute "to our newest minority, the gays," Kaye belted out a novelty number about "Bruce, the Gay Policeman" complete with jokes about Gucci handbags and lavender patrol cars. The Hunter party applauded loudly.

Leaving aside the question of whether such celebrities lend their prestige to the club or whether they are just on hand for a little voyeuristic titillation (one only suspected the latter somehow, when David Janssen and Dani Greco came parading through the club), there is still some unpleasant confusion about Studio One. While it craves respectability, it is unsure of how to handle its success.

Take the problem of the Door. There are two doors actually. One feeds into the showroom, allowing celebrities to enter without having to brave the dance floor's crush. The other, the main door, is for general admission, except that admission isn't necessarily all that general.

Forbes knows he has a problem with the Door. It is his single biggest headache. But you have to understand his position, he explains, this is a club for gay kids, and if straights invade the place, they'll drive the gays away. It has happened before. Straights catch on to what's happening, they take over a club, are rowdy, drunk, and, worst of all, since they only come out on weekends, they leave the place empty during the week. "This is a club for gay kids," Forbes repeats, "and I'm going to keep it that way. We don't discriminate. We just ask for a driver's license. The gay kids know enough to bring it. The straight kids don't always have it with them."

The argument sounds tenable until one realizes that when Forbes speaks of gay kids he is speaking only of white male gay kids. Studio One has become notorious for hassling women, Chicanos, and blacks who want in. It is following a pattern established by the city's other, smaller dance bars, but Studio One's status as the Gay Bar of the Moment only makes the practice all the more annoying.

Forbes refuses to admit that any discrimination has ever taken place, even though a sign above the door used to call for *three* pieces of age and picture-bearing ID, a requirement from which only gay white males could be sure of being exempted. Last summer, after monitoring the situation, a small group of gay leftists occasionally picketed the bar. Some patrons waiting in line to enter found the constant arguments at the door distasteful enough to send them off to less fashionable alternatives. Most simply paid their cover charge and joined the dance.

With time tension has lessened and the entrance requirement has been reduced to a California driver's license (specifically prohibited are such substitutes as school ID's and library cards). Undesirables appear to have gotten the message, and the line now inches forward without complaint. "I'm much more upset by the fact that they don't allow large hats or open-toed shoes," sighs one of the men on line.

So what's a poor boy to do? Women's bars often discourage men from entering; why should men's bars be more generous? And nobody wants a lot of heterosexual sightseers from Orange County trouping two by two through the hall. But then what do you do with your college roommate and his girlfriend who arrive from the East and want to see L.A.'s idea of a night on the town? It's super that the club stepped in to fill the vacuum, establishing itself as Hollywood's premier boîte, presenting everyone from Gotham, Craig Russell, and Wayland Flowers to Chita Rivera, Bernadette Peters, and Alexis Smith. But how does one respond to a dinosaur like Kaye Ballard, who really should be performing in some staider establishment where jokes about poodles still pass for wit?

There is something about LA, something in the way the natives tend to fade as soon as the sun dissolves into the Pacific, that inhibits the town's night life and reduces the possibility of effective competition. And as long as Studio One is the only game in town it will be forced to cater to a confusing jumble of patrons. The club can be applauded for forthrightly implementing gay capitalism, a relief after years of syndicated franchises. And one can thrill to its wall-to-wall sound and its beautifully bronzed boys. But Hollywood success stories are heady, hyper numbers, so one shouldn't be surprised if this one doesn't bear up well under frame-by-frame analysis.

# FELICE PICANO

◇◆◇◆◇◆◇◆◇◆◇◆◇◆◇◆◇◆◇◆◇◆◇

## Imitation of Life: Interview with Vito Russo

*W*hen I arrive at Vito Russo's Chelsea apartment, the place is mostly chaos. The living room floor is covered by stacks of boards, and cardboard boxes cover the shrouded furniture. The repainting is completed: gray walls, pale blue ceiling; Russo tells me that it will resemble the interior of a Christian Dior perfume box, but it looks pretty masculine to me. His study is also in shambles: a closet is being built there to hold his film library. "My first closet ever," he admits. "And my father is helping me to build it." We finally find and clear a space on the bed to place the cassette deck. During the interview we will be disturbed dozens of times—by urgently needed advice on the rebuilding, by numerous telephone calls, by the arrival of Clovis Ruffin with sandwich makings—before he collapses into slumber on the bed.

All this says much about Vito Russo: his mercurial temper, his charm and mischievous humor, his apparent calm in the midst of a real whirlwind of activity, of people, of news, gossip and hard information. As one of the country's better-known gay free-lance writers (he does a column for the San Francisco *Sentinel*, one with Arthur Bell for the *New York Native*, plus features for the *Village Voice*, *Soho News*, etc.) he seems to be one of the epicenters of communication in the gay world (I received a phone call there, even though I hadn't told anyone I was coming). The unlikely center is a slender, medium-sized man in his early thirties with glasses and short hair, who can be completely elfin one minute, and a serious Gay Academic Union intellectual the very next.

Films dominate Russo's life, and his decor, from posters to photo stills of his favorite films to his collection of Disneyana. And it is this devotion to films—and to the gay community—which makes his first book, *The Celluloid Closet* (Harper and Row, June 1981) one of the most knowledgeable, informative, and compelling gay books to be published this year.

*A lot of readers of* The Celluloid Closet *may not know your background. How did you get your start? I mean, besides going to the movies. When did you start writing about film, and why? Did you study film in college?*

The very first time I started writing about film was in the seventies. I always wanted to be a writer, ever since I was in grammar school. I've also loved movies since I was six years old, so when I got out of college, I went to graduate school at NYU and I got a masters degree in cinema studies in 1971. And that was at the same time that I joined the Gay Activists Alliance. I began writing for *GAY*, a newspaper which was an offshoot of *Screw*, owned by Al Goldstein, and my editors were Jack Nichols and Lige

Clark. That lasted—the paper—about a year. I reviewed films for them, and suddenly it occurred to me that I was a writer. Simultaneously, I got a job in the film department at the Museum of Modern Art. Since then I've written for a variety of magazines and newspapers.

*Have you made your living as a freelance writer?*

No. Until a year ago, I always had another job. Always. In a gay restaurant or a gay bathhouse. In fact, in the introduction to my book, I say, "Thank God for the ghetto." I don't think I would have survived as a freelance writer. Then about a year ago, I went to London to work for *Gay News*. I reviewed for them, I did features, I did anything you can think of related to America, because I was sort of their visiting American.

*When did you come up with the idea to do a book on the treatment of gays in American film? It's international in scope, really, isn't it?*

Well, international . . . it's mostly American. I talked about important foreign influences on American filmmaking attitudes. The idea first came to me in 1973. I was working at the Museum of Modern Art, and there was a symposium on minorities in film at the University of New Hampshire. I was openly gay at the museum; I was also in GAA. I was approached by Willard Van Dyke, who was the head of the film department at the Museum, and he said, "We're all going up to New Hampshire to do this symposium on minorities in film, and how would you like to put together an hour on gays and films for us?" First time it ever occurred to me. So I put together twenty-five or thirty minutes of film clips and a rap. . . .

*Film clips and an accompanying lecture, which you continue to do in theaters and colleges across the country.*

Hundreds of colleges . . . sometimes in enormous theaters, like the Fox Venice in L.A., where there were thousands of people—amazing.

*So it was out of this series that the book grew?*

Right. I knew that Parker Tyler had published, in 1971, *Screening the Sexes: Homosexuality in Cinema* (Holt, Rinehart, and Winston). That was the first and only book of this kind, other than the small book *Gays and Films*, edited by Richard Dyer, which was published by the British Film Institute, but essentially it's not a book; it's three essays. There's an essay on lesbians in film, gay stereotypes in film, and on camp.

*Were you able to find a publisher for* The Celluloid Closet *right away?*

It took a year. Two dozen publishers turned it down before Harper and Row took it.

*With what kinds of comments?*

Like, there's no market for this book . . . which I think is terribly short-sighted. Other people said Parker Tyler had already written this book, which is also very short-sighted, because if anybody ever read Parker Tyler's book, it was very esoteric. Parker Tyler was difficult to read to begin with. I have not found a dozen people who will admit to having gotten through that book. Also it's been out of print for five years, and the man is dead. I saw that there was no cohesive statement—broad, commercial statement—about this subject. I didn't sign with Harper and Row until 1976, and then I spent two years traveling around the country and the world. I saw films everywhere—I spent months watching films in Washington at the Library of Congress.

*Can you give me some figures, like how many films did you see?*

I saw a little over four hundred films.

*And then you also had people searching for you. How did that work?*

I just called up everybody I knew, everybody I'd ever talked to, and I said, "I'm doing this book, and if you can think of any gay character in American film, write it down or call me up. If you see a film on television, call me up and tell me to turn it on—anything." And people would do that constantly. I would get little slips of paper that would say, "For your book, I saw this, I saw that." Sometimes they would see gays where there weren't any. Andrew Sarris sent me a note and told me to see *My Son John*, which was a Leo McCarey film about Communism, and I saw it. There was no homosexuality in it. But it was a good thing, because once I saw the film, I realized there was a parallel between Communism and homosexuality in it. The way John's parents reacted to him when they found out he was a Communist was just the way parents react to having a gay child. A perfect gay analogy: the film worked on that level. Maybe that's what Sarris meant, for all I know.

*You portray an age of innocence in film, early film, regarding homosexuality. In the films that were made in the teens and twenties in America, something occurred which you call the sissification of films, right? Do you believe that this corresponds to a general sociological, ideological age of innocence in this country? Was it a direct reflection? Were films conveying exactly what people were thinking at that time?*

Yes. Well, maybe. Let's put it this way: in the sense that Americans in the teens really believed the myth of America, the conquering of the wilderness, our pioneer heritage. . . .

*But there was still room in all that, in the macho image, for the sissy. As a character.*

Yes, a sissy, but not a homosexual.

*How are they different?*

Because there was no threat in the teens.

*Because nobody spoke of it.*

First, because it wasn't discussed in polite society. But also because it was reflected in the cinema as asexual. Sissies were not homosexuals; they were simply Momma's boys.

*Are you familiar with the Blackwood gang? I did some research into New York City and Boston and a couple of other cities around the turn of the century for a previous novel, and I discovered that there were groups of Irish-American gangs—actual gangs—who lived in the ghetto areas of each of the three largest cities in the country at that time—Philadelphia, Boston, and New York City. And these were the toughs, you know, the Puerto Rican–black toughs of their time, and yet they were all gay hustlers, too. And that was at the turn of the century.*

If you go, today, to Greece or a Mediterranean country, every straight, married man has a boyfriend, and he's not considered queer.

*Where does the sissy fit into this, and why was it picked up so easily by film?*

I think it's part of the legacy of vaudeville, where men played women's roles. Part of our theatrical tradition in general is that the roles were reversed very often on the stage. I think that female impersonation was just *that* in the early cinema. It gave us clues. Watching men impersonate women in the teens, like Wallace Beery and Fatty Arbuckle (a classic example), watching that, one could do what Richard Dyer talks about in *Gays and Film*. He uses a term coined by Claude Levi-Strauss: *bricolage*, playing around with the cinematic elements of a film in order to bend its meaning to your own purpose. You could sit in an audience and from what you saw on the screen, you could make your own calculations, you could come up with your own version of what was happening.

*There were no gays in cinema? There were no references to it?*

Not until the twenties. Then it changed, in Europe.

*But in this country, too, didn't it? Various books have dealt with the rapprochement among theater people and literary people and Hollywood. Many theater people—Ben Hecht, Moss Hart, and Dorothy Parker, William Faulkner, Hemingway, Fitzgerald—all went out to Hollywood and got involved in films. That seems to correspond with what was, until recently, the most open period of any kind of exploration of sexuality in films. Do you think one thing had to do with the other?*

The filmmakers on the West Coast were actually pretty unsophisticated at that time. They were people like Harry Cohen. It wasn't until Nazimova and Lillian Hellman went out there that they started picking up on these things as ideas. And they were attacked as eastern sissy intellectuals. When Lillian Hellman first came to Hollywood and suggested that the production code be suspended in order that the screen might treat lesbianism with taste, they went crazy. They said, "With taste? How could that possibly be?"

*On the other hand, these folks—Mae West and so forth—got a lot accomplished out there.*

That's right. She was a Brooklyn girl.

*And it was in reaction to them and what they did that the Hays office began its code.*

That's right. It was sort of like an attack on the eastern establishment that was ensconced in Hollywood by the early thirties. But they were arresting Mae West on Broadway in 1926, and then she went out to Hollywood and, until the Hays office caught up with her, she got away with murder.

*So that's the second period in the treatment of gays in cinema, isn't it?*

The period between 1929 and 1933 is really the heyday. By 1934, the Hays office was the law. At that point, films were cleaned up, and there weren't even references to gays any longer. And that sort of changed in the fifties with Otto Preminger.

*I think it's wonderful the way you show how he broke down every single aspect, every single barrier of the Hays office code.*

His trick was to announce publicly that he was about to make a film that would break the production code, and he would defy the code.

*And they would extend it.*

The first one was *The Moon is Blue*. That was adultery, the use of the word *virgin*, which had never been used on the screen. Then drug addiction in *The Man with the Golden Arm*. And as Preminger made those films, he released them without a seal, which was unheard of. What he did was prove that a film released without a seal could make money.

*So that really opened up what was happening in films. On the other hand, even in the fifties and sixties, homosexuality was still taboo, and it was not until Boys in the Band. . . .*

The code was changed in 1961, and homosexuality was allowed. In 1959, you had *Suddenly, Last Summer.* For that there was a special dispensation by the code and the Catholic church.

*But even so, homosexuality is never mentioned in that film.*

Only indirectly. The only line in the script is when Elizabeth Taylor says, "Don't you understand? He used us for bait." And then you got the idea that they were bait for young boys. But they never said the word homosexual. And Mercedes McCambridge said, "Oh, I used to love Sebastian. . . . His friends were always so well-dressed and so arty."

*So meanwhile, during that whole period, right through the early sixties, there was an entire code of how to refer to a character as either a lesbian or as a gay man.*

Well, it became explicit pretty quickly. By 1961, Otto Preminger had made *Advise and Consent,* William Wyler had done *The Children's Hour, Walk on the Wild Side* with Barbara Stanwyck—all those films at once broke the code. I mean, it was just a flood, and suddenly gay topics were allowed.

*Up until the independent films of five or six years ago, there's been nothing but stereotypical treatment.*

It was unheard of until 1973, when Christopher Larkin made *A Very Natural Thing,* for an openly gay director to make an openly gay film about a gay subject. I mean, there was no such thing on film—ever—as an openly gay filmmaker telling a story from the inside of gay life. I still don't see that anything has changed. There's still no balls in Hollywood. All the balls are in the balcony.

*A gay film is being made now, isn't it?*

This is very interesting. The gay film that is being made right now, by Twentieth Century-Fox, is called *Making Love.* The fascinating thing about *Making Love* is that in *every way* it is the next logical step for the movie industry to take at this point in history. It is what Stanley Kramer's *Guess Who's Coming to Dinner?* was to black civil rights—ten years behind the times. By the time *Guess Who's Coming to Dinner?* came out, people were so aware of the issues that if it hadn't been for Katharine Hepburn and Spencer Tracy, that film wouldn't have made any money. People laughed at the politics. And in a certain sense, they're trying to avoid that structurally in *Making Love.* What I hated most about *Guess Who's Coming to Dinner?* was that you had every single confrontation. It was written so that first the black mother and the white mother get together, and then the black father and the white father get together, and then the daughter got together with the mother and the son got together with the father, and you had a string of all these confrontation scenes so that everybody got together with everybody else before the film was over. That's the way *Making Love* was originally written.

*What about the politics of Making Love?*

The politics of the film are, number one, it's being produced by a man named Dan Melnick, who produced *Altered States* and *All That Jazz* and is known in Hollywood for taking a chance. I don't think anybody else would have produced *All That Jazz* or *Altered States.* He's the kind of person who has the time and money and wants to do what he calls risky or courageous projects. And on his own terms, and in Hollywood's terms, that's perfectly true: he's done well and he has taken risks, and *Making Love* is a risk for Hollywood in the sense that if it doesn't do well, it's going to be another ten years before they make another picture like this.

*Well, you know that they optioned my* Late in the Season. *Do you think that will ever be made into a movie?*

I think that Hollywood is watching *Making Love*. I really do. It's a big-budget, Hollywood movie, and it's about a man who leaves his wife because he discovers that he's gay. He's young, attractive—

*That's twenty years behind its time!*

Right, right. I mean, I know scripts like this that were written ten or fifteen years ago that couldn't get produced, but now they've decided that Hollywood has come along to the point where they can take this step. The step is a small one. This film is not going to offend a soul, except maybe Jerry Falwell.

*Is anyone going to see it?*

Well, on paper, it's going to be worth seeing. Who knows how it's going to work out? It's being directed by Arthur Hiller, who did *Love Story* and *Airport* and *Hospital*—which wasn't bad, actually—but the thing about *Making Love* is that it has the whitest hero—if we can make that analogy—the safest, most nonthreatening hero to the American family. He's a nongay gay. He's a heterosexually identified male who has lived with a woman all his life and has discovered that he's gay, and the first thing he can think of to do is to find a lover and settle down the way he was with his wife, to imitate a heterosexual. Essentially, *Making Love* is—I hate to say it's a heterosexual view of homosexuality, because it's written by an openly gay man.

*Who?*

Barry Sandler. And by coming out with *Making Love,* he becomes the first screenwriter in the history of Hollywood to come out of the closet. Which is no small thing. He's written four films before; he's well established. And I think that's a big step, no matter what, even if you hate the film you have to say, "Bravo, Barry Sandler," because the point is that it has a gay character who is committed to a gay life-style, and he's played by Harry Hamlin. In some ways the screenplay is very pejorative toward that character because it said that he couldn't settle down and make a commitment. The truth about that character is that he didn't want to make a commitment. As I understand it, that is presented *now* in the film as not being such a loathesome thing, but an option. And Harry Hamlin and Michael Ontkean just weren't right for each other. Michael Ontkean eventually finds himself a lover he can settle down with at the end of the film. And *he's* the model son, daddy's little boy....

*So we're being asked to be good husbands whether we have a wife or a husband for a husband or a wife.*

And people have no argument with a statement like that, because realistically one could not ask Hollywood to make a radical statement on film about gay life. It's just not going to happen.

*Do you really believe that films have as profound an effect on our values and ways of life as, say, books do? Isn't film essentially a passive experience in which all you do is sit back and get hit by it, whereas when you're reading, you have to physically turn a page and move your eyes from top to bottom?*

Absolutely. But that answers your question. Films reach more people, but I don't think they reach people more. I think you're talking about the difference between millions and millions of people and a select few thousand who read and get something from it. You're talking about the intellectuals in this country as opposed to the masses.

*But given the fact that generally intellectuals are the people who do things in this country—99 percent of the people don't do anything—a book affecting an intellectual can make a large difference.*

Yes, but in the context that we're talking about, in a social context, I think that film, to a much, much greater degree than books, has shaped American values about social issues.

*The only way I've seen film ever make a difference is by providing totally unrealistic fantasies, romantic fantasies, to Americans.*

But I don't think that Americans have viewed what they've come away from a film with *as* fantasy. They've come away from it as a reality. It's unfortunate, I agree, but for instance, motion pictures have taught the majority of Americans what they know about homosexuals. Most people have never read a book about a homosexual in their lives. I would go even further and say that most people's attitudes in this country about blacks have not come from books but more from the cinema and from television.

*Rather than from contact.*

Yeah. Absolutely. Think about this: think about the fact that before there were major black actors in movies, people were comfortable in their illusion that the world was white.

*But also remember that in 1940 when they had Lena Horne in a movie with white people, she was completely by herself. They never had her in a scene with whites.*

Not only that, they whited her out. In the South, her scenes were cut. When she sang alone, they could take that sequence right out of the film and release it in South Carolina, so people wouldn't be offended by it. It was real easy.

*Gay people have been able to change TV people—TV directors, producers' attitudes toward gays, because of the FCC ruling. Is there any way that that can be done by groups which target change in films?*

No, because it's a completely different system. The airways belong to the people. It's not a "private" industry, so there's no way to interfere. You could go and picket Twentieth Century-Fox, and it wouldn't do any good, really. But if you boycott the advertisers on CBS—an economic boycott—there's real clout there.

*Do you know of any attempt by gays and lesbians to set up film programs in the American Film Institute or in other large film companies—NYU film schools—like those programs which were set up at the American Film Institute for women filmmakers, and which came up with films by Lee Grant and other women directors?*

No, all I know is that student filmmakers who happen to be gay at places like UCLA, NYU, and UFC have made, as their student projects, gay films. There is not, that I know of, any formalized program for gay filmmakers.

*Do you see any future for that?*

Oh, sure.

*Isn't that changing attitudes right where they begin?*

Oh, absolutely, because essentially you change the entire environment. That's what women did in film. First, it was only a few women making films about women's lib. Now it's gotten to the point where any woman, whether she's a feminist or not, can get a camera and make a movie.

*And not have to dress butch and smoke cigars like Dorothy Arzner. What can gays do when they're watching a movie in a movie theater that has knee-jerk homophobic stereotypes? Hiss? Boo? What can you suggest?*

They can do anything but stop the proceedings, as far as I'm concerned.

*Have you seen people do that?*

I've done it.

*Has it worked?*

Well, it's worked rather badly. If I hiss or boo at a screening because I find something homophobic, the only thing that happens is that the people who held the screening are pissed off at me for a couple of weeks.

*What about in movie theaters?*

I've done it in movie theaters too, but—

*Doesn't it raise consciousness?*

Sure, suddenly people are aware that they're sitting in an audience where there are some homosexuals. It shocks them. You'll find that after you hiss or boo there's the most incredible silence. It's a great guerrilla action. But what else can you do?

*What about film's current critical establishment? Have they been of any help to you in stopping homophobia in films?*

Yes, but it's been people, individuals. There are a lot of critics who are fascinated by learning about the society they live in through film. While other critics, like Richard Schickel and Pauline Kael and John Simon (although he's brighter than most of them), have set attitudes that never change. You find people like Richard Schickel yelling, "Why do we have to have all of this homosexuality in our movies?" As if they were *his* movies.

*What other films are being made that will be of interest to gay people?*

Well, I don't think *The Front Runner* is ever going to be made. The financial success of *La Cage aux Folles, I* and *II*, is catching the eye of Hollywood. *Partners*, for instance, is a gay cop and straight cop film. John Hurt will play the gay cop, and Ryan O'Neal the straight one. O'Neal is one of the most homophobic actors in Hollywood, you know. All this is as of this morning, and according to Rona Barrett. From what I understand, the script is a real travesty. The gay cop drives a pink Volkswagen and gets coffee for all the other cops. Paramount is doing it, and it's being produced by Bette Midler's former manager, Aaron Russo. Suddenly straight actors are doing gay roles. I mean, John Hurt, who played Quentin Crisp, is identified with effeminate gay roles. The point is that the Gay Actors Alliance—a new organization, I don't think anyone famous is in it—got ahold of the script and went up to Russo's office to protest. Russo met them wearing a leather harness—his idea of a joke. Tony Randall is doing a TV movie about a man who's been gay all his life and is having his first affair with a woman. And there's going to be a new TV series called *The Boys Next Door* about two gay lovers who live next door to the usual heterosexual couples.

*That's funny. Six years ago I was trying to sell exactly such an idea to TV. I was calling it* Lust for Tomorrow, *and it was about this gay couple, former high-school sweethearts, and all of their very bizarre heterosexual family and neighbors. They even gave each other matching cockrings on their anniversary. My lawyer, who's straight, loved it and thought it was terrifically funny. No one wanted it.*

The bottom line on all this is that Hollywood is in no shape to take on the real issues of our time, straight or gay.

*On the other hand, if they're losing money on big films and going into smaller films . . .*

Like *Ordinary People* and *Kramer vs. Kramer. . . .*

*. . . then it seems really likely that they're going to take on these other projects.*

What we used to call "problem films." Yes. But if you'll notice, Hollywood is not in the process of redefining the family. It's in the process of strengthening the American family. Look at *Ordinary People.* It's not redefining anything. Even in the twenties and thirties there were films dealing with bad, uncaring mothers, mothers who left the family. Any radical view of sexuality is out! But I think Hollywood will, in the words of Noel Purdon, continue its boring shuffle toward sexual liberation. And we'll all just go on with our lives. I don't think that Hollywood is in any shape to give credence to new ideas, to the idea of open relationships or of a promiscuous life as an acceptable life-style. Maybe they'll get to that point with straights. But we're last on the list.

*Do you want to tell me something about the basic structure of* The Celluloid Closet?

It's in four parts. The first part is called "Who's a Sissy?" and it deals with the genesis of the sissy through the teens, the twenties, and thirties. How Americans' ideas of masculinity and femininity have determined what is to be gay on the screen. The second part is the forties and fifties, and it's called "The Way We Weren't." The period in which the production code—the Hays office and all the rest—came in. It deals with a lot of things. Homosexuality removed from original source material—the laundering of homosexuality, such as in *The Children's Hour* and Charles Jackson's *Lost Weekend.* He was a gay writer in the book. It was originally about an alcoholic who drank because he was queer. In the film, it became about an alcoholic writer who drank because he had a writer's block. The funniest part about that was that Ray Milland keeps his typewriter in the *closet.* The best part of the movie. This section of my book also deals with men's relationships with each other in films—what has come to be called "buddy films." There's a real legacy of buddy films, starting with *The Flesh and the Devil,* because the film industry is a masculine industry. All the business of the industry is owned and operated by men, and these films were considered masculine dreams. The most valuable, significant relationships in many films of this era are between men—covertly, not only because the audience wasn't aware of it, but the filmmakers were often unaware of it.

The third section of *The Celluloid Closet* is about the sixties, when the code was finally smashed. It's called "Frightening the Horses," and it's about the emerging of the subject from the closet—its emergence as a dirty secret, as I write in the book. The last chapter is called "Struggle," and it's about the seventies, about films by gays outside the industry, and the first visibility of gays: the era from *The Boys in the Band* to *Cruising*—ironically by the same director. I don't want to go into the pros and cons of the demonstrations against *Cruising*, but it was important because it was the very first time that the consciousness of the industry was brought to the point where they realized they had another *Birth of a Nation* on their hands. For that film, blacks went into the streets. Now gays did too. And I think that the industry has gotten so embarrassed by it—if you talk to any Hollywood producer, they're embarrassed by it, ashamed of themselves for having had that happen. Even with the Moral Majority around, people in Hollywood like to think of themselves as just the opposite—as the more liberal types.

*Well, with all these gay projects for film and TV, is it going to last? Are we merely in the era of gaysploitation in film?*

Yes. It's not going to last. Just as the blaxploitation films didn't last. This seems to be the year of the gay in film. So we'd better enjoy it while it lasts.

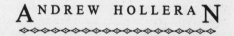

ANDREW HOLLERAN

# Four by Andrew Holleran

### Nostalgia for the Mud

New York, that accidental city, whose pleasures vanish sometimes without your ever having known they were there, had, from October 3 to December 3 at the Whitney Museum, a piece of environmental art by Michael McMillen called *Inner City:* a room-sized reconstruction of three entire blocks of a warehouse district in Los Angeles (it might well have been Manhattan). Large enough to walk around, and even, at one point, *through*, *Inner City* was complete with scaled-down neon signs, fire escapes, window shades, and even a squalid little poolroom with metal folding chairs strewn about, cues on the table, and a miniature ceiling fan rotating overhead. Like the rest of *Inner City* the poolroom was empty; but then, what city isn't empty, late at night in that part of town?

"It is only by directly experiencing the entire installation," states McMillen in the museum flyer, "that the position/concept of art as experience [may] be realized." But what *Inner City* actually amounts to, I think, is an extraordinary doll's house. (And a very evocative doll's house for anyone who has haunted such bleak, decaying blocks in reality. Consider: surely we would never have come to the purlieus of the Lower West Side but for the fact that they are the hunting grounds of other men looking for a certain style of sex. Who else knows this inner city? The poor, the recently arrived, the Hispanic.) How lovingly McMillen has recreated each detail of his urban doll's house: a hotel hallway, one-thousandth the size of its original, evokes precisely the erotic longing you feel walking home late at night in a run-down neighborhood, when physical loneliness corresponds exactly to psychic isolation, and you think—passing an abandoned truck, an empty lot screened by shrubbery or garbage under an open moon—wouldn't that be a wonderful place to make love? Just a few doors down from the tiny poolroom is a little bar, its door (no bigger than your thumb) half open; through the door come the sounds of the Village People singing "San Francisco," and the joyous hooting and screaming of (invisible) people within.

You stand back to gaze at the door, the darkness, the neon sign in the window. You say to yourself, "This is the door, the darkness, the music to which I have been drawn, irresistibly, so many winter nights; this the ruined neighborhood, the lonely street, the crumbling building (its shades drawn or half drawn); this the sordid, deserted, *poignant* place so many of us have wandered in for years. Look at it: a piece of art, life reconstructed to give you a feeling of distance from what embroils you."

"I was there last night," muttered one of two friends at my side.

Women, children, and grandmothers stood beside us, exclaiming over the tiny chairs and cues in the poolroom. ("Harry, why don't you take this up? You need a hobby.") Then they moved on, around the corner, in the faint and lurid light. But we three remained rooted; there was no way we were going to leave the little doorway with the music pouring out. We waited (as we had waited so many nights when the Eagle had the best jukebox in town) to hear what song came next. And we looked at the other museum patrons, wondering if they understood, if they *felt* the peculiar magic of this place, its romantic significance. For this was the bar of the past ten years of our lives. It was Love Among the Ruins.

"Don't touch!" one mother commanded her daughter, slapping the child's wrist as she reached out to fondle a tiny fire escape. "Look at the fan, Mom!" cried her son. And the Nuclear Family bent down to peer into a room where, in real life, young Chicanos or Puerto Ricans would surely cluster around the table, their transistor radio on a windowsill blaring salsa.

You imagine the empty streets of McMillen's papier-maché *Inner City* filled: outside the dark half-open door of this tiny bar should be a tiny man in chains; and ten feet (or, rather, half an inch) away, standing broken-hearted on the corner, another little man, wondering if the man in chains will follow him out of the bar. There should be miniature motorcycles, minute beards, and sweatshirts peeking out of little leather jackets, a min-uscule cop car out of which miniature police with flashlights scramble to clear men out of the crevices where they are having sex with one another's miniature cocks; and a gang of tiny teenage boys waiting for a solitary man to walk by so they can beat him up.

There were no cops or thugs, no bare-chested man lounging in his doorway as you walked past, wondering if he could really be that available; no one slowly masturbated in an upstairs window for all the world to see. But there was one advantage: late winter nights on West Street, passing the lit windows of otherwise deserted buildings, I often wonder what goes on inside and who could, who would, possibly live there; I needed only to peer through the tiny window of McMillen's Hotel Norton to see the pool-room, the bar. I was huge in relation to the cardboard-and-paint city blocks on the table before me, Gulliver among the Lilliputians, a Jolly Green Giant of a voyeur. I was free of the oppressive gloom I usually felt wan-dering the streets in real life.

But "San Francisco" is a long song; eventually we took our leave, with-out ever knowing what followed, and walked away from the Inner City.

"Why do gays love ruins?" I said to my friends when we emerged into the crisp autumn sunlight of a Sunday afternoon. "The Lower West Side, the docks. Why do we love slums so much?"

"One can hardly suck cock on Madison Avenue, darling," said the alumnus of the Mineshaft, curling his lip as we strolled down that very street: the *arrondissement* of gentility, so tasteful that coming uptown from his own street was truly traveling into another country. Nannies pushed strollers filled with fortunate heirs; adolescents in blazers, slacks, and Topsiders, young men in Rugby shirts passed by. "If Westway is ever built," continued my friend, "and the shoreline made pretty by city plan-ners—when the city is totally renovated, when gays have restored all the tenements, garden restaurants have sprouted on the Lower East Side, and the meatpacking district is given over entirely to boutiques and cardshops—then we'll build an island in New York Harbor composed entirely of rot-ting piers, blocks of collapsed walls, and litter-strewn lots. Ruins become decor, nostalgia for the mud. We all want to escape; you escaped to the city. Would you ever have ended up in the ruins had you not been gay?"

"If I weren't gay, I don't think I'd be in the city at all."

"Especially on a day like this."

We looked up at the hard blue sky, the brilliant autumn light, and rounded a corner to see the trees along Fifth Avenue already starting to change color.

"Soon New York will be occupied by no one but the rich and the per-verted," observed my friend, and at that moment we spotted a mutual friend who embodied both those traits standing in a worn leather jacket, faded, torn blue jeans, and scuffed engineer boots, hailing a cab.

"There's a perfect example," I said. "Why is there that strange axis between the extremely aesthetic"—the man getting into the cab possessed an encyclopedic knowledge of European culture and the history of ormolu—"and the extremely sleazy?"

"God only knows," sighed my other companion, whose neighborhood this was and who left it only to backpack in Vermont.

"Well," said my first friend, "ask yourself. Why could Brahms make love only in brothels? Why did Proust, the most sensitive and considerate of men, torture rats with pins? Why did he donate the furniture he inherited from his parents to a male brothel he frequented? What pleasure did he get from seeing a nude trolley-car conductor sitting on the sofa his grandmother had no doubt sat on to do needlepoint? Why did one of his characters, the lesbian daughter of a famous composer, spit on her father's photograph while making love? Why do we rush out to trick after talking to our mothers on the telephone? Why do we find graduate students from Princeton lying facedown in the Mineshaft?"—here he burst into laughter at some memory of the previous night. "Why our desire to grovel, to wallow in the slime? Why the beauty of those neighborhoods? Why is there a truck without a chassis on the eighth floor of the baths so that people may do the curious thing of going to the baths to make love in a truck (or a jail cell, or a cheap hotel room)? Why the trucks at all? Why did Huck Finn flee Aunt Sally? Why does great politeness produce a strain that often can only be relieved by cruelty? Why did Marie Antoinette play shepherdess? Why do gays wear ripped clothing and congregate in ruins? Why do I feel a strange sense of freedom the moment I enter a decaying neighborhood? Why do I imagine, when I pass a tenement with a collapsed wall on Avenue B, giving a party there—or better yet, conjure up a slender fellow, half hidden by the rusted doorframe, inviting me into the rubble to make love, entirely in ruins?"

"I hate to say this," said our third friend, "but I don't know what you mean."

"Pretentious prig!" we gasped.

And so we entered the sunny glade of Central Park and, watching children play with sailboats, forgot about these questions until later that evening. Just after sunset, we found ourselves drifting inevitably downtown to the very region whose simulacrum we had marveled at that afternoon. The shore, once lined with ships sailing for Le Havre and Cherbourg, was now (but for the new terminal at Forty-second Street) a series of rotting piers and empty lots from which isolated families fished; further south, behind the shattered windows of erstwhile shipping firms, moved silhouettes of men in search of another kind of nourishment. The warehouse, the bars, the cheap hotels pulled us into their shadows, into their peculiar mood. The detachment afforded by art at the Whitney Museum was gone. The bar was life-sized now and stood on a cobblestone corner. We went through the door into its dark room to find a frieze of bearded faces regarding us like stone visages in the jungle: blank, cold, and waiting. Whatever their attraction, whatever their meaning, these ruins were real.

## Fast-Food Sex

Most dinner parties have two lives: the dinner itself, at which you gather with others, and the remembered dinner, which is far more delicious, actually. Just as Wordsworth savored the beauty of his jocund daffodils while lying at home afterward in a reverie, so a dinner party fulfills itself as recollection, when the dish on the table gives way to the dish on the telephone. I just learned, for example, that a recent visitor from San Francisco—a cherubic journalist—told our host at a dinner we attended together that he found the other guests cerebral, New Yorkish, and antisexual. He got this impression when someone remarked that he'd had sex only three times in the past year and I said, "How civilized, how discreet!"—half ironic, half in earnest. The San Franciscan thought I was completely serious, and it confirmed his worst suspicions. "You look so weary, all of you in New York," he told our host the next morning. "Well," said the host sweetly, "that's because we *are* weary."

Weary of sex even—yes, I'm not afraid to admit it: I *was* congratulating that man for having sex only three times in the past year. The last time I had been intrigued by a sexual confession (such a staple in gay life, one would almost prefer a companion discuss nuclear fission) was when a friend told me of a fellow he had had to date nineteen times before he could kiss him. How marvelous that in 1979 someone would still refuse his person to another! For people aren't refusing their persons much any more. In fact, grabbing a body is about as easy as going downstairs and buying a hamburger—which is why in San Francisco they call it "fast-food sex."

When I first arrived in New York, friends would walk past buildings and say, "Oh, that was the Triangle, that was the Stud, that was . . . ," and I'd listen to tales of back-room bars as exotic as palaces of the Ming dynasty. In those days you would be ejected for blowing someone in a certain bar, but history has come round. Now that bar sports closed-circuit TVs on which pornographic films unfold; slides of Colt models appear on another wall, and the live men at your side have sex right there. The city has more baths and discotheques than ever before, and more homosexuals to have sex with. Visiting Sheridan Square has become an almost frightening experience: they come down Christopher Street like an army, in ranks and ranks, and (here's the nightmare) all of them are handsome, all of them your physical ideal. It's the doom of Don Juan: must I go to bed with *all* of them? A friend looking at this homogeneous mob one Sunday afternoon moaned, "It's like an invasion of the body snatchers."

And that's just what we all want, isn't it, kiddo: to snatch a body, to use someone's genitals and get off on his smooth, flat stomach.

I was delighted later to run into the man my friend had dated nineteen times before kissing. I was crossing Washington Square on a snowy Friday dusk, and he was out walking his dog. A handsome man in a gray topcoat whose collie was romping with some other dogs around a tree, he seemed embarrassed when I introduced myself and said how rare a species I considered him.

"It's not what I want, believe me," he said, blushing slightly. "But yes, it's true. In the old days I loved the very things I loathe today—like that fellow there" (he nodded at a young man crossing the square in torn jeans, engineer boots, hooded sweatshirt, and leather jacket). "Five years ago, the gayer the outfit the better. Someone like that struck me as a soldier of sex—devoted, in uniform, solely at the service of the only thing I lived for, sex with another man. Now" (the young man was disappearing into the trees) "I look at him and think: how ghastly, to extinguish one's individuality, to dress as a human dildo. . . . Everything that attracted me five years ago now seems totally stupid. Getting blown is so easy now, and so meaningless, that it's about as significant an event as a sneeze!" He turned to watch his collie hurl itself against an imperturbable Great Dane, then continued.

"My friend says that men are like dogs, they should screw every day, but," he sighed, "I'm afraid I've lost that talent. Last week in the baths I was sitting in a corner waiting for Mister Right when I saw two men go into an even darker nook and run through the entire gamut of sexual acts. And when they were finished—after all these *kisses*" (he was suddenly agitated) "and *moans* and *gasps*, things that caused scandals in the nineteenth century, toppled families, drove Anna Karenina to suicide—" (he raised his eyebrows) "after all that, they each went to a separate bedroom to wash up. Now, you may view this as the glory of the zipless fuck, but I found it suddenly—and it surprised me, for I'd always adored this event before—the most reductive, barren version of sex a man could devise. Barbarella was more human pressing her fingertips against the angel!"

"Fast-food sex," I said.

"Fast-food, twentieth-century, American sex!" he said, his face excited in the soft light of the descending sun.

"Well," I said, half ironic, half in earnest (that New York vice), "we've destroyed many aspects of the previous century, you know: luxury liners, formality, long lunches, handmade lace, leisure, and court balls. I guess we'll destroy sex, too."

"We already have! My orgasms don't interest me any more! Why do these assholes praise promiscuous sex, say there's nothing wrong with it, that because we're gay we're leaders in a brave new world who will set new patterns of behavior, and all that crap, when even sex, on that basis, ceases to be erotic? Do they really think that because we're gay, young, and urban we don't have the same need for fidelity and intimacy that any other human beings do? When sex is as easy to get as a burger at McDonald's, it ain't too mysterious or marvelous, believe me.

"Oh, I'm sorry," he said, lowering his eyes and then raising them to fix me with a desperate stare, "but you can't imagine how awful it is. To be gay, yet no longer able to respond to other gay men because you know it will only be an exchange as profound as eating an Egg McMuffin—I feel as if I've developed a disease or something, and I'm doomed to wander as a ghost, alienated from my own kind."

A man in a blue wool hat sauntered up to us: "Loose joynts, man, Valium, methadone, Black Beauties, anything that turns you on."

"Go fuck yourself," muttered the man my friend had dated nineteen times, and he began to walk westward with his dog. "I'm in a terrible mood lately," he said, "because I'm just as lonely as ever, and just as horny too, and yet I won't, I can't do it just for sex any more, it has to be with some kind of interest in the human personality connected to the genital," and he gave a deprecating little laugh.

We walked in silence in the gathering darkness till we were at the tiny park that gives onto Sheridan Square, where, as on every Friday night, the piazza was filled with faces shining beneath the streetlights. "Don't you think," the man who had dated nineteen times said with a shudder, echoing my own unease, "that there are more gay men in the West Village than ever before? And more attractive gay men! Look at them!" he exclaimed, staring wildly at the sea of black-eyed, mustached fellows coming toward us like the children in *The Village of the Damned*. "Quick, let's go down Grove Street!"

Running to catch up with him, I followed the man who had dated nineteen times down the short street that parallels Christopher Street but bears none of its gorgeous traffic.

"You see, sex is simpler than love," he said. "It doesn't interrupt your workout, or burden you with another person's ego, or with the fear that one day he'll cease to care. Do you suppose that's why we're all having sex instead of making love? Or is it because we hate ourselves? Or maybe because love is simply—as a matter of fact—a very rare thing we cannot beckon or search for but that simply happens to us if we're lucky. My best friend says he likes fast-food sex because he's tired of getting burnt, he no longer trusts people; so now he goes to the baths every Sunday night and comes back, his face aglow, after three ejaculations, and he's ready for the workweek. And I guess that's important in New York. But really! That's sex as a massage, sex as a face mask!

"How kind of you to listen to all this madness," he said. "It sounds like the sour grapes of someone who can't get laid—and yet I'm handsomer now, if you'll pardon me, than I ever was, and I'm cruised ten times a day; but my eyes lock with theirs and I think, 'Oh, what's the point?' And really" (he sighed again) "what *is* the point?" He looked at me through the falling snow. "I wrote a letter to Anna Karenina," he said and handed me an envelope before disappearing into a courtyard.

I sat down and read his letter to Anna K. later that night. "Dear Anna," it said, "Why so upset over Vronsky? If he is beginning to tire of you, to cease to love you, so what? Commit suicide over love? Get real! Instead of going into the street and driving to the train station in that *down* mood, dump the jerk! Take a Valium, dear, and play some paddle ball. You'll feel better, and tonight we'll go to the Ramrod; you'll meet someone new. Years ago, Anna, I used to get butterflies in my stomach at the baths before I approached someone I really wanted, sex meant that much to me. Now I rub my body against another the way you rub sticks to start a fire, curious to see if lust will develop. As the Marvelettes said, there are too many fish in the sea. Get *out*, girl, and remember: you've got to survive!"

But Anna still goes rattling off across the streets of Moscow to her inevitable doom, a hundred years too early. Certainly today she would know that we don't feel the pain of love any more, even if we don't feel much of anything else either (dry skin is about our most serious discomfort); certainly she would know that, the way we offer ourselves to each other today, kisses are not a surrender of the soul but mean very little—about as much (the man who dated nineteen times would say) as an Egg McMuffin.

## Dark Disco: A Lament

There's a new accessory in New York now: the large transistor radio cradled gracefully in one arm or hanging from a shoulder strap like a huge metallic communications purse. Like much fashion it started on the street and, as of this writing, is confined to adolescents of the Third World. They take their radios everywhere they go. If you love music, you may find yourself in the curious position of following a young man not because he is sexually interesting (or even sexually possible) but because the radio he carries is playing "Do or Die."

This phenomenon may hit you in one of two ways: either you find the boy on the subway with his blaring radio inconsiderate or you applaud him for wishing to have music beside him every step he takes through life (and which of these two responses you feel often depends on whether you like the song or not).

And if you do like the song and he gets off at the wrong stop, no matter—chances are the radios on the street when you come up will be playing the same song, not to mention the stores on Eighth Street, which you can now traverse from Sixth Avenue to Astor Place without ever completely losing the strains of "Boogie Woogie Woogie," if that's what WKTU-FM is playing. WKTU-FM shocked us all one morning when we got up to turn on "The Mellow Sound" to get us through that first hazy hour of consciousness (John Denver, Cream of Wheat) and found it playing instead the song we had danced to the night before: sometime in the night it had become twenty-four-hour disco Muzak.

Well, all of this—the twenty-four-hour disco station, the radios carried down the street, the music played in shoe stores and gymnasiums—is a tribute to how far disco has come ... or gone, if you feel that way about its rise from obscure dark rooms to the sunny sidewalk and the shag carpeting of The Athlete's Foot in the Village.

But other things too have changed in that time. When I first came to New York, the radio station we listened to for the music that eventually became disco, WBLS, dispensed positive thinking to its ghetto audience; now that audience tends to drive Porsches. In those days, when you went out to dance, disco had no uniform sound. There was no one word to describe the variegated music we spent the night with. It was distinct enough for the discaire to begin a set quietly, build gradually to a climax, then let you down to start all over again. Do you remember that vanished custom? It happened three or four times a night if you stayed long enough, and you could follow the tantalizing process by which the discaire laid a solid foundation of slow songs and then subtly (if he was good, as they all seemed to be in those days) built you up to the catharsis, say, of Deodato's "2001."

One thing for sure: disco was different then. The music was darker, sexual, troubled. Today the dark has vanished and the light is everywhere.

Two winters ago I walked into a discothèque and realized with a mixture of horror and disgust how far things had gone in this business. That was when I heard in the same night disco versions of "I Could Have Danced All Night" and (the mind reels) "The Little Drummer Boy." Why didn't the crowd stampede for the fire exits? Was I the only one who found these songs drivel? I went home that night in a terrible funk: I had seen the death of disco, I felt sure. That winter I let my membership in several clubs lapse and began asking everyone I knew, "What will we be doing *after* disco?" For I was certain that that form of diversion was kaput. The disco beat, which devotees of rock and jazz detest, suddenly seemed idiotic even to me, a certified disco maven.

A terrible uniformity of beat and style had come to dominate all disco music that year, so that when we went out we were never taken up, dropped, and taken up again several times in the course of a night. No, we entered the discothèque and stepped, as it were, on a moving jet of air that never slowed down until we ourselves stepped out of it—by simply leaving the room. Gloria Gaynor got faster with each song. By the time she did "How High the Moon" there was nothing left, said one acerbic friend, but the tarantella. Stepping onto the floor then was an occasion of apprehension, like gathering your energies to run the hundred-yard dash, for the music, and the discaire playing it seemed part of a conspiracy to keep me hopping against my will. (What were we to *do* to "How High the Moon"? Use roller skates? Pogo sticks?) But by then disco was big business. What I used to think was as wonderful and mysterious as the dancing madness of the Middle Ages or the rites of Dionysus was now a page in the annual corporate report of Gulf & Western.

There was nothing wrong with Gloria Gaynor, of course—there is nothing wrong with light disco. Some nights you arrive in tennis sneakers and your only regret is that you're not *allowed* roller skates or a pogo stick. Some nights you *do* want to float very lightly. You're feeling fast and cool and breezy, and light disco is just what you need. The wonderful lightness of "Spring Affair" (with its odd tinges of dark disco) is almost ethereal, and you rise and dip with it like a bird coasting on wind. But the dreck that falls in between, the Muzak of disco (which is clearly light), the fast, mechanical, monotonous, shallow stuff that is being produced for a mass market now, the kind of music one imagines hearing poolside at the Acapulco Hilton, beating against the brains of the guests as they squint into the sun looking for the pesky waiter who's bringing them their Margaritas—that is light years away from the old dark disco, which did not *know* it was disco, which was simply a song played in a room where we gathered to dance.

Deep in a funk the night I decided disco was dead, I began to wonder about the songs we heard no more that, it seemed to me, had created another feeling altogether in those early days. But each time I named a song, I asked myself, Was *that* dark disco? If we were to buy that record and play it, would it really be different? Or was it the time and place and atmosphere, not the music at all? The songs I remembered vaguely, if at all, were not fast and sassy and full of androgynous choral effects. They were not—I was sure—invitations to visit Rio or disco versions of songs from *My Fair Lady*. They were songs you could dance to for a long time, because they concentrated energy rather than evaporated it, songs that went inside you, rather than lodging in your feet and joints the way light disco does. You hardly moved, but suddenly you were closer—ever so slightly—to the person dancing with you, and you became conscious of your limbs, which even, as I remember, became heavier. You lowered your eyes. You closed them finally. It was gripping, real dancing, and the atmosphere in the room was one of surrender. Dark disco was our *fado*, our flamenco, our blues; it spoke of things in a voice partly melancholic, partly bemused by life, and wholly sexual. Dark disco was the song you sang to yourself on the first night of winter in New York walking down one of those long, dark, deserted blocks in Chelsea, when you realized anew that New York is also a winter city, a city where for one long season life turns indoors and we pursue freely our darker desires.

That was dark disco: late nights and love affairs and empty streets, and the sound of Al Green singing "Love and Happiness," and the version of that song by First Choice. It was B. B. King at the Tenth Floor singing "To Know You Is to Love You." It was the "Masterpiece" album of the Temptations, the sinister authority of those opening bars of "Papa Was a Rolling Stone," or "In the Ghetto," or the triumphant gloom of "Law of the Land." It was, finally, a song whose singer I cannot even remember but which is played occasionally today and contains a line that goes: "So you grow up and start a family. . . ." There was nothing strained or inconsequential about those songs. The last was even soft-spoken, exhausted, a song perhaps by a man on downs—not the downs we take as pills but rather the downs we take in life. It told me a little story (and how irrelevant to anything are the lyrics of light disco) of the whole sad progression of a life—the mundane pattern we all follow—but it told it in the most vulnerable mode, and we could all share it. We communed. The music wasn't being done to us; it was being done with us. And that song, so casual, so low-key and easygoing, had in it ten times the power of the fastest show-stopper. It was sexual, bluesy, and what can only be called dark. It was not an invitation to fly away or a mad whirl about the room. Oh, give me a slow song any day, one as melancholy as "Love and Happiness," which makes us dance from the pits of our stomachs (the solar plexus, if you will, where a French friend assures me all the major emotions are located) instead of the joints of our arms, the tips of our toes.

A friend who knows this business far better than I do told me yesterday that there will always be dancers in this city—that they were there before disco and they'll be there after disco. Still, wherever I go, I look for what comes next. The roller-skating disco in Flatbush? (The music now is so appropriate to roller-skating, the fast, monotonous, sexless disco that fills WKTU-FM.) Or will we abandon even that and just roller-skate through Central Park, as gay men are starting to do now on sunny weekends? Will we give dinner parties again? Stay home and form book clubs? When I arrived in New York, there were no back rooms and no discothèques; now there are many of each. In five years perhaps they will both have vanished, and we will have what in their place: Betamax societies? Will we all go to bed again at eleven, and do something in the morning? What? Not having been awake before noon in seven years myself, I am at a loss to say.

There is a solution, devotees of dance: dark disco still survives, in a curious way. It is this: To hear it once more, to enter that communion of the blood, don't go out this Saturday night. Eat early, go to bed at ten and set your alarm for five; and then, having showered before you sleep, having chosen your T-shirt and jeans, get up with the bell and dress as quickly as any fireman going to a fire, hail a cab, and go down to the disco of your choice around five-thirty. You will pass the wondering faces of the dancers coming out—pale, white, sweaty, on their way home. You may have to hammer on the door to get the man lurking in the back to come forward and let you in. But do it. Pay your money and go upstairs and you will travel back in time to the days of dark disco. The place will have emptied slightly—depending on the quality of what has gone before—and you, fresh as the morning star, will step onto the floor and find a friend, and start to get the very best of the night. For the best disco is saved (who knows why) for last, as if, under this new regime, the old, dark disco is played covertly, in secret. Then you'll hear "So you grow up and start a family," and maybe "Love and Happiness" or whatever else does that to you. You'll dance till seven, or eight, and when you come out you'll have captured what you've missed for so many years now in this tyranny of light disco. Tap dancing went, and the cakewalk, too, and one day our disco will be as quaint as Glenn Miller. But could we not detain its evaporation a bit? That, at any rate, is my plea for dark disco.

## Male Nudes and Nude Males

I went to see the exhibit of photography at the Pfeifer Gallery called "The Male Nude" for two reasons: I love the nude male, and someone said the reviews had decried what they perceived as art served up for the homosexual and feminist audience. The reviews were pinned up on a door to the proprietor's office. Looking at the photographs before I'd read the reviews, I found myself thinking two things: first, the people photographed were not particularly pretty, not even distant cousins of the boys in *Blueboy* or *GQ*, and, second, it was utterly elusive to me what makes a photograph a work of art as opposed to a mere photograph.

This second issue I still do not understand, but having been in the company of serious photographers, I realize there is a world there, with its own vocabulary, options, referents, and ironies—a world, quite frankly, closed to me. The simplest explanation perhaps lies in a lesson learned at a poetry seminar I attended years ago that came back to me at the exhibit. That first session our teacher distributed mimeographed copies of a poem, which we discussed heatedly for over an hour before he revealed at the close of the class that this "poem" was merely a paragraph chosen at random from his son's chemistry textbook and broken into lines by his secretary at the typewriter that morning. His answer to the question What is a poem? was simply that which is offered to us as a poem.

So here I was in a room on Madison Avenue perusing something I loved in life—the male body—extracted from life, selected, presented for the contemplation we bring to art, a contemplation different from that we would bring, for example, to the young man in the red polo shirt standing next to me perusing the same photographs. The photographs were black and white and studiously unglamorous; there were androgynes, transsexuals in midpassage, ordinary folk at home in the nude, soccer players soaping up in shower rooms, and, in a brief historical survey, aborigines, nineteenth-century boxers, and the Sicilian youths beloved of Baron von Gloeden. It seemed the one thing the various photos had in common, if anything, was that none of the figures had a prepossessing penis, whereas the reverse is the rule in those magazines that now festoon our newsstands.

In selecting these drab folk with ordinary genitals, the photographers seemed to be announcing very clearly that their studies were not beefcake, were not of the male body as an erotic object. What were they then? Were these drab bodies expressing something more worthy of my attention than a *Blueboy* centerfold? The *Times*'s critic (whom I read before perusing them a second time) claimed that while the male body may be used to express fear, power, effort, and the like, it is not successful as an erotic object. Yet a current exhibit at the Metropolitan Museum offers us "Images of Woman" as seen in the master drawings of several artists. This curious, absurd attitude—that a female body is erotic but not the male—is hardly limited to the *Times*'s critic. A close friend of mine has an extremely muscular body (which he works hard two hours a day to maintain) and yet feels a certain contempt for people who are attracted merely to his tits. Our attitude toward the nude male seems ambivalent indeed.

It was finally time, standing there in that hushed room, to ask what I had hoped to see in this collection, what the very words *the male nude* had in them to draw me uptown to see these photographs. The Elgin Marbles at the British Museum, a painting of St. Sebastian by Antonio Mor in an obscure corner of the Alte Pinakotek in Munich, the *David* in Florence had all brought me, a youth traveling through Europe, to a dead, awestruck halt: astonished by beauty. These photographs, in contrast, seemed to be pointedly unbeautiful, mundane, cerebral, and antisensual. At the same time, I reminded myself, there is also nothing less stirring in the end than the bodies that crowd the pages of the soft-core gay slicks. What was the male body I was searching for?

The question was complicated, I realized as I glanced at the fellow in the red polo shirt moving around the room (nagged by the question, even as I studied reproductions, of whether I should try to pick this real one up), by something curious that has happened in New York over the past two or three years, not to the male nude in art so much as to the nude male in life. It is simply this: the attractive body is no longer the exception it used to be. It's becoming, as a friend of mine would put it, as common as pig tracks. We are all Pygmalions to our own Galateas, fashioning, an hour each Monday, Wednesday, and Friday, the sculpture of our own bodies. And what have we chosen?

You see it in ranks and ranks on Fire Island, coming at you down the boardwalk or the water's edge, or on the Morton Street pier on sunny Sundays of spring, or in the hallways of the baths. You see it even in London, which is, if we can believe a friend's recent post card from that city, infiltrated by "a thousand clones all sprung from a single sperm cell at the West Sixty-third Street Y."

What is going on here? Four years ago in New York one knew the famous bodies, whose they were, and where you'd be likely to find them. I remember the day we sat up on our blanket on Fire Island and said of a figure coming toward us, "Now *that's* an important stomach." Well, it was. Now it is one of countless many. Now they all go to a gym and they've all got tits 'n' ass. My friend joined the Big Gym downtown and told the proprietor he wanted a chest and shoulders; the man said he'd give him a chest and shoulders, and a V-shape, too. "Just what I want," my friend replied. "A chest and shoulders and a V-shape. My dear," he told me later, "it was like shopping at Saks."

Well, this *is* the age of the department store; why shouldn't everyone be allowed to go in and buy a body too? Ah, there's the rub, I thought, as the handsome young man in the red polo shirt revealed his own trim torso passing before me: people wear bodies now the way they wore plaid shirts four years ago. (Burn those plaid shirts, darling.) And if a body is something people can just put on—the way we chose our favorite plaid—then isn't it just one more accoutrement? It finally becomes, like so much else in our culture, an item of merchandising and therefore worthless to those of us looking for something else. It was this, the calculated use of the body, that had caused these photographers to demonstrate the purity of their intentions by presenting us with the most unvoluptuous of males.

And it was just then, as I came to this understanding, that I saw the photograph, which no review had mentioned, that caused me to forget these irritating issues. It was a picture of a naked youth on crutches, with a cast on one leg, standing in the creaky hallway of one of those old, narrow houses (in Philadelphia, I imagined) whose floors slant. His astonished, open face, the grace of his body immobilized momentarily on the crutches by this accident one did not know the story of, the glow of light around his hair, the contrast between the power of his form and its temporary helplessness, supported by crutches, all seemed fraught with the original reason we gape before a work of art—as I'd done years ago beneath the Elgin Marbles, the *David* of Michelangelo—the quality absent from our plain reactions to the beefcake centerfolds, the perfect torsos of Fire Island, a quality one can hardly name but often tries to with the words beauty, grace, proportion. Were those slanted floors reminiscent of a house I'd been happy in, in Philadelphia or East Hampton, one week? Was it the vaguely academic air of the book-lined room behind him, or his youth, or white smoothness? Wasn't it all a mystery, in point of fact?

He was like water on a hot day, silence after relentless music, reassurance to the spirit when the intellect is helpless.

And so, having got what I came for—in a sense—I went down into the street, where I found a film crew shooting a scene with Desi Arnaz, Jr. I asked a cameraman what the movie was, and he replied, *How to Pick Up Girls.*

# EDMUND WHITE

# Texas: Sissies, Cowboys, and Good School Citizens

*T*he day I flew to Houston last July I was hung over and exhausted. I had had too much stimulation and too little sleep during a hectic week in New York and was looking forward to hiring a car, heading toward some sedate Texas hotel or other, and curling up for the night; I thought vaguely of buying cool summer pajamas and ordering toast and tea from room service. I was a bit surprised to notice that the plane was packed at one in the afternoon on a Tuesday, but I didn't become alarmed until the French engineer beside me said that a room might be hard to come by. "We're flying in from all over the world for a petro-chemical conference. There are eighty of us. My assistant has been on the phone for a week searching for rooms somewhere, anywhere, but as of now we still have three vice-presidents on cots in a single."

Fraternal and amusing as those arrangements sounded, they didn't augur well for me; I have always, when traveling, counted on fate to play the resourceful concierge. "But Houston is like that," my engineer said. "Always overcrowded, the whole world standing, hat in hand, at the door, wanting in. We may laugh at it—it *is* frightfully vulgar—but we are its clients." He turned back to his copy of Voltaire's *Micromegas.* A bit later he explained that he was "really" a writer; though he'd been working for thirty years as an engineer, that was just a curtain-raiser to the main piece, his upcoming career as an author and thinker. Having myself been a teacher, truck driver, editor, and PR man, I understood the delay.

In the airport I was cruised by two men and asked them where I should stay. One of them recommended a motel where he had lived for a few months after first arriving in Houston. It was, he said, near the action, only somewhat "infested," and quite cheap. The other man expressed mild surprise that I was visiting Houston for "pleasure." None of the rental services had a car; the attendants smiled wearily at the naive request. Nor could I find a taxi. At last I resorted to the bus—fortunately, since the airport is a costly hour and a half away from the city. (The optimistic Houstonians expect that one day the city will reach out to the airport. Certainly most of them are predicting that by the twenty-first century their city will outstrip all others in size, wealth, and power.)

As I rode in I observed through the tinted panes empty fields out of which erupted, here and there, not the expected house or store but an imposing bronze skyscraper, jutting up like a bold exclamation point following a bland, run-on sentence. Past me flew miles of mobile homes for sale, those shingled and windowed rectangular boxes longing to lose their mobility and sink peacefully into a plot and join their pipes to those in the raw earth. Fields of weeds, dusty trees, the odd skyscraper, and then a motel; its raised billboard proclaimed not "Welcome Engineers" but "Waitress Wanted—Top Pay—Bellboys, Too." We swept past an extensive development of what I believe are called "town houses" (terraces of row houses), all crunched under top-heavy mansard roofs. One ambitious design had even managed to pull the mansarding down nearly to the ground, turning the top three floors into stacked garrets peeking out at the weeds and skyscrapers through dormer windows; only the ground floor had a clapboard siding, painted the pale orange of an unlicked popsicle. The odd proportions reminded me of a little boy half hidden by his father's giant sombrero. But all buildings in Texas give an overall sense of prefabricated units that have been *landed* on the terrain. They are pure expressions of will and bear no relationship to the surroundings. Even the most modern space capsule, however, is awarded a name out of history. If there is a restaurant in the building, it too will have a historical name, though not necessarily of the same period. Thus, we will have Bluebeard's Dungeon in the Queen Victoria, or the Old West Saloon in the Forbidden Palace.

Finally the city itself materialized. My first glimpse of it was blurred by the sudden, cloacal collapse of a searing, five-minute rain. It was as though the devil had decided the infernal heat needed just a soupçon more of humidity to become the sort of torture he had had in mind. The buildings were indifferent to the miasma; with their spotless white mullions and smoked glass or blue, mirrored skins or long, tall merlons flanking windows no wider than a medieval archer's crenel, they were as alien as space stations deposited on hostile Mars. One suspected they were self-sufficient, tenantless (there were no pedestrians in sight), and fully computerized, that if they retained windows at all, they did so only as a courtesy nod to the past.

Later, when I toured the business district, I discovered why no one was visible: all the buildings are interconnected by air-conditioned second-story covered walkways or underground tunnels. The major buildings are the headquarters of oil companies, and all but one of them had been erected since 1968. The latest development is the Houston Center, which will comprise twelve buildings (including five thousand apartments). The architecture is so advanced that it was used with no modification as the set of the sci-fi movie *Logan's Run*. The floors and walls here are pink Texas granite; on a balcony one sees a bent aluminum tube (sculpture? exhaust?); the escalators are outlined in cold white neon. One glimpses into a restaurant filled with foliage and twinkling lights and sees flirtatious couples huddled over little tables—no, it's a bank, and those are desks. I kept thinking that there's no reason Houston should have skyscrapers at all; land isn't *that* valuable here yet. But of course, for Houstonians the buildings are their Tinker Toys. They contemplate the business district from a distance and say, pointing, "Now you need another black one over there—maybe a trapezoid. And then square that corner off with a nice silver one."

The bus deposited me at a terminal where a long row of brightly colored telephones promised to connect me instantly with a wide assortment of hostelries (there are, it turns out, few hotels, and they are listed in the Yellow Pages under "motels"). Every place was full, including the motel the guys at the airport had recommended. In a panic I decided to apply in person to their motel. I ordered a taxi and after a long wait obtained one. At the motel office I was for some reason accepted; I was directed to the sixth and last building of the complex, a good half-mile down a blinding gravel service road. Behind the motel were parked several semis; hanging over the balcony railing were trim black women in microskirts, plastic boots, and bouffant wigs. The rather dour whites I passed kept addressing one another as "Brother This" and "Sister That." Saudis in turbans were streaming into the restaurant. Dazed by the heat and feeble to begin with, I had difficulty reconciling these elements with one another. Was I feverish?

As it turned out, the motel was notorious as a hangout for hookers who serviced truckers. They and their stylish pimps occupied half the rooms; all night long men were tapping on my door and imploring Judi to "open up." The rest of the place had been rented by Jehovah's Witnesses; there were fifty-five thousand of them convening in Houston for a powwow at the Astrodome. Hookers and Witnesses rubbed shoulders all week in the coffee shop, which was also popular with Arab students who'd come to Houston to master the mysteries of petroleum technology. To add to the fun, Barnum and Bailey (the six o'clock news reported) had also descended on Houston—elephants, like overheated tanks, had rumbled through the empty streets that afternoon, their massive bulks hosed down with cold water every block or so to keep their radiators from boiling over. Agitated by so much that was *mal assorti*, I left my room, with its moderate infestation of roaches and water beetles and its *two* double beds, both their backs broken, and sallied forth for a walk—only to discover that the town fathers had neglected to give sidewalks to this neighborhood. There I stood, far from a bus route and unable to walk or rent a car or hail a taxi, and watched the traffic hurtle merrily by. I contented myself with an overdone steerburger, a rather sweet little covered basket of biscuits, and a large milk as I eavesdropped on Arabs, whores, and the religious, those poor souls subscribing to a regimen of no smoking and only light drinking in a city where Mexican grass sells for $12 an ounce and more beer than water is consumed in the summer months, a place that has the third highest rate of alcoholism in the nation and a crime rate that rose 12 percent in the first six months of the year. Houston also has no zoning laws, and as a consequence a church can be squeezed in between a shopping center and an adult bookstore and peep show (it is a city of unlikely company). Although one group is campaigning to keep the porn shops at least two thousand feet away from the churches and schools, the proposal for such a *cordon sanitaire* violates the Houston charter, which grants every microbe the run of the city.

Unsteady though I may have been, at ten in the evening I summoned a taxi and headed to the best leather bar in town, the Locker. There I stood in the back patio, propping myself up against a corral fence and looking out at a withered, spotlit tree. Its small leaves weren't stirring. Along one wall was painted a large mural of cacti on the moonlit mesas, looking like disembodied rabbit ears out for a midnight stroll. At one end of the yard rose the false front of an Old West hotel, a Potemkin set where pairs of men nursed funny cigarettes. The air was sweating, dreamless, more in a faint than asleep. The men around me, conserving their energies, weren't talking; the only vital sign was an occasional shift from foot to foot, unless that was an illusion performed by the warping heat waves.

And then, interrupting this saurian torpor, someone entered who was very much in motion. He hovered up to me, engaged me in conversation, and permitted me to buy him a beer. He was twenty-two and chubby and was experimenting with a mustache (it looked like a caterpillar paralyzed by stage fright halfway across a winter melon). All the little movements he produced (and he was as active, as rippling, as the draperies of an Ascending Virgin) arose from inner turmoil—the familiar conflict, for instance, between a desire to establish contact and a fear of being snubbed.

As he talked on, I turned my lidless eyes toward him, unscrolled my sticky tongue in a trial run, and watched my fly buzzing around another contradiction—his inclination to be flamboyant and his resolve to be reserved (one imagined him wearing a gold anklet under his cowboy boot). And then it wasn't clear whether he wanted to seduce me or himself, for though half his talk was about sex and the possibility of having it, the rest was devoted to his Past, a plot by Dreiser written in the vivid style of Georgette Heyer. Apparently even his life, his novel, was tremulously ambiguous, as was his recital of it; he had a trick of saying something sad about himself, which elicited sympathy—and then springing on me, out of nowhere, a big, disconcerting, shit-eating grin. When he spoke, he kept himself in modest profile, but when he produced that grin, he turned toward me with shocking intimacy. He seemed to be a writer who enjoyed torturing both his reader and his protagonist, despite the fact that the reader, in this case was a potential pickup and the protagonist his own immortal soul. My only fear is that I make him sound sinister; have I made it clear he was, despite the boots and mustache, that perennially endearing figure, the Southern Sissy?

"My father," he said, "liked me, but my mother never did. She didn't want us kids, didn't want to cook for us—heck, didn't even want to talk to us. My dad liked me"—and then the grin unleashed—"because he was gay.

I found that out by going into his closet (no pun intended) and discovering all these dirty magazines. When I was eighteen, he died from lung cancer, and he wasn't the smoker; my mother smokes and is still going strong. She threw me out of the house as soon as he was under the ground." (Southern speech, no matter how casual, always lilts with little literary touches: the parallelism of "out of the house" and "under the ground," even the old-fashioned periphrasis of "under the ground.")

"I got a job and some credit cards. And then I just charged and charged"—the "charged" is drawn out, sung first on a high note, then on a low—"until I'd run up a bill of $15,000. I didn't know what to do. So I fled town and came to Houston with nothing but a bag and a $5 bill."

"And *then?*" I asked anxiously; I am not one of those people who believes, as Rilke did, that the world will take care of you, that its hands are under you and will catch your fall.

"It's very easy to succeed in Houston," he said. "In one night at a bar you can make four or five friends and they will put you up one after another. Everyone's new here."

"And *then?*"

"I went into a beauty-supply store and asked for a job. I lied and told them I had a degree in cosmetology. They put me to work that very day. Now it's a year and three months later and I was just named the store manager."

"How," I asked, already suspecting the answer, "did you fake a knowledge of cosmetics?"

He seemed caught in another crosscurrent of uncertainty. His hand flew up to pat an invisible but palpable chignon, the chic saleswoman's bun, pierced *ukiyo-e*-style with several pencils at odd angles, while simultaneously his voice dropped into a lower register: "I know all about *that;* I had a lot of . . . uh . . . *friends* in drag." (The well-known "friend" strategy: "Doctor, I have this friend who's homosexual and needs advice.") "And what do you do?" he asked. It was his first acknowledgment that I, too, might have a life, might be more than a reader, though I suspect he was more eager to get away from the subject of drag than curious to explore my story.

"Write," I said.

"So do I!" he exclaimed, more delighted by the coincidence than I, since I had already been perusing his work. "I'm a writer, too. I loved English in school. My favorite period of poetry was the Romantic, and my favorite poet Percy Bysshe Shelley." Naturally. If Americans, as Gore Vidal says, are both Puritans and Romantics, then the Romance must begin in the South. Shelley is the South's favorite poet; Southerners name their sons Shelley.

Now if you're a Yankee I can hear you grumbling, "Texas isn't in the South; it's in the Southwest, which is something else entirely." Or more up-to-date Yankees will refer to the "Sunbelt" stretching from Florida around the Gulf to Houston and on west. I must confess I find these to be distinctions without differences. The Southwest was a fiction Lyndon Johnson invented when it became clear he would not win the South; the

Sunbelt, where Nixon liked to say his cronies came from, is a cultural fiction, if an economic fact. Northerners choose to refigure the map, I suspect, because the revision places the energy and industrial wealth of Texas in exemplary contrast to the racism and supposed rural character of the "true" South. Puritans demand a moral and hold that riches reward virtue; they are discontent with the prospect of unreconstructed rednecks becoming the most prosperous element of the population.

But Texas is Southern in the good sense and the bad, and it can never be understood if it is seceded from the Confederacy. Take the racism. In small towns and among older people it persists unchanged. Among the Houston young, the racism may be disguised by lighthearted "nigger" jokes told on the understanding that, of course, we're both liberals, we all know better—and isn't it fun to say "nigger," to use the real down-home word, the very word *they* use?

And so it might be if integration were more secure, equality more fully achieved, and the past more distant. As things stand, the jokes betray anxiety at best and conceal bigotry at worst.

Or take the rural character of Texas life. Although four out of five Texans live in cities, they are often from farms and dream of returning to them. The big, raw countryside—the fly-blown Nehi sign, the glass of ice tea on the porch swing in the sweltering evening heat, the shriveled grapes in the arbor in the back yard, the "bauking" of chickens, the rust-speckled blades of the creaking windmill, the trail of dust behind the pickup truck—this desolate countryside is both literally and spiritually close to the booming metropolises.

"What are you doing here in Houston?" my friend asked. "Business?"

"No, just looking around."

"You came *here* for *fun?* To Houston?"

Texans may be chauvinists, but few of them are loyal to Houston (though some transplanted Northerners defend it). It is only a place to run away to, a town where you can make a fast buck and then get out without regret—a sort of cloverleaf in the American Route to Riches.

My friend, sensing I was more chatty than randy and confident that I'd studied his text with care, hailed a waiter he knew and started giggling with him. Perhaps we'd understood each other too well to be mutually attracted. There were no occlusions in communication, those breaks in apprehension that awaken desire. Sex with strangers is an alternative to language, the code that replaces speech.

Inside the Locker things were picking up. It was midnight and the dance floor was crowded, as was the pool room. The prevailing "heavy" look for this malarial climate seems to be a black, sleeveless T-shirt, black or blue denims, and cowboy boots. Here and there, however, were ensembles that seemed ill-sorted. A tall, lanky man ambled past decked out in a ten-gallon hat, a faded workshirt, patched jeans—and sneakers. Home on the range in sneakers? Or the forty-year-old standing beside me wearing engineer boots, a black leather vest, chaps—and a cowboy hat. Yet another man had on an S-and-M top (chains, leather, tattoos)—and shorts.

These are expressions of individual taste in a state where personal flair is still regarded with nostalgic approval. By day, as one walks through the miles of air-conditioned corridors below the business district, one sees mostly fresh-faced executives in three-piece summer suits. But every once in a while one encounters an old, unbowed Buffalo Bill, his white locks flowing out from under his weathered Stetson, his $300 boots worn but polished, and a string tie around his neck—he is the magnate who grumbles about how the Yankees have turned Houston into a damn dude ranch.

Despite its architectural splendors and its hospitality to the arts, its influx of Northerners and its go-go economy (a survey revealed that young executives in Houston regarded a 10 percent annual raise as the minimum they would accept), the city remains raw. One talks to a tall twenty-year-old with an Adam's apple that rises and falls obscenely along his taut neck. His voice is too loud, given the social distance, but it goes with the depthless eyes that seem focused on a distant figure. "My damn dad," he drawls rapidly—that is a trick of the Texas accent, a Southern intonation speeded up—"tried to stop me going with guys. Ha! I beat that son of a bitch up. I slugged my goddamn brother, too, till he was a bloody pulp. My mom was screaming so I chased her around the house. See"—here he lowers his voice a bit—"I'd gotten this damn bitch I knew in high school pregnant, so the old man was hollering about that, too. But I'm bigger than him, I'll knock out his fuckin' teeth. I told the bitch to get her cunt scraped—then I moved in with Joey." He told me more—of night rides in old cars with six buddies heehawing and gulping down a carton of beer, of straight guys from high school he lured home and then fucked (using cooperative girls as bait), of parents howling around the house trying to shut down a late pot-and-disco party—but I withdrew from him. I didn't want to hear any more. Sure, I like tough guys, but only if the toughness is undermined by warmth and experience, only if I sense that in this man's head there is somewhere a court of higher appeal. I felt awed and overpowered—was this the gay liberation we had had in mind?—and headed home to my motel, at last to sleep.

This rawness crops up everywhere. Houston is a city where businessmen chew gum, sport long ginger sideburns and Baptist pins on their lapels, smoke cigars, dangle calculators from their belts, carry pens above their hearts in aqua plastic inserts, and choose beige summer suits with dark brown stitching to match their dark brown shirts underneath. It is the place where, during the fuel shortage in the North, a block-long Cadillac carried a bumper sticker that read, "Let Them Freeze In the Dark."

It is also the town where I met Harv. He approached me at the big disco, Numbers, with an opening line so contrived it was winning: "I'm doing a survey for the *New York Times*. Do you like blonds? How do you feel about blue eyes? And how would you like the best blow job in Houston?" We never got to the blow-job stage, but we did have a couple of drinks together in the glassed-in booth upstairs. Downstairs, lights strafed the crowded floor and glowed behind white silk curtains billowing inside tall, fancy scrollwork frames (I was reminded of the decor of a 1920s movie palace). Harv was a computer expert; he had been working late all week unscrambling a lousy program written by someone else. The pride he took in his work was all the greater because he was a self-made man. He had always fought with his parents, he told me—dark, murderous fights—and they fought with each other. When he was eight he begged them to send him away to boarding school. They complied, but when he came home for holidays he found them even more intolerable. The old hostility flared up again. After a particularly tormented, tormenting session his parents kicked him out. He was fourteen and had only $3 to his name. He worked in stores around his little Texas town until he finished high school. He then joined the Navy and was assigned a job in intelligence. At night he took more and more courses, determined to make something of himself—until one night, during a calculus exam, the numbers swam before his eyes and he could not read the questions. He had been, he told me, "overcome by nervous exhaustion."

After the Navy, Harv obtained a position in Houston with a computer-programming firm and rose rapidly. Now he was just twenty-four and owned a 1972 Oldsmobile and a two-bedroom suburban house complete with a game room—and a wet bar and fireplace he had installed himself. Harv assured me this was just the beginning; his goal was to make $200 million. His taste in men was correspondingly ambitious: his first lover had won a major muscle-building contest. The only problem was the lover's laziness. He was thirty-one and refused to work. "I did everything for him. I moved his mother into my house and took care of her. I bought him a new car and kept the old one for myself. But he kept pushing me. He didn't come home for four days, so I went after him. I entered that bar and ordered him out. He said, 'I ain't going.' I cleared the bar right out. I hit him, I ripped his shirt off, I lifted him by the seat of his pants and hauled him out. Then I asked him, 'You wanna come home or you wanna go back in the bar?' He said, 'The bar, but I'm too bloody.' So I said, 'Well, I'll drive you home and you can change and drive your car back, 'cause I don't want to fool with you no more.' I got him and the old lady out of my house. Now I live alone."

I've omitted to say that Harv is a boxer and presses three hundred pounds but is short and baby-faced and sprays his hair and drenches himself in cologne. We necked for a while and he was soft, yielding. I had the impression of being in the plush grip of a powerful androgyne; beneath the hairless skin lethal muscles lay coiled. On the dance floor four guys were passing poppers, stomping fast and hard, and ripping out rebel yells. Given the heat, the humidity, the darkness outside, the feeble porchlights streaked with worrying mosquitoes, the disco seemed all the more improbable, an overnight Klondike improvisation. If the electricity being piped in were to fail, the lights would dim and cease their arbitrary but assured revolutions, the air would warm and thicken, the tape would grumble into silence—and we would be left in a hot tin shack somewhere in the middle of the bayous.

The gaudy stereotype of American machismo is the Texas cowboy, but a visit to a gay cowboy bar forces one to recut that worn old plate and to print from it in fainter, more somber inks. The Brasos River Bottom is on a quiet side street but looks out toward the glowing spires of the business district. Inside are well-mannered couples sitting around the bar. A few people are playing pool. Most of the men are in their forties or fifties. A jukebox plays sad country-and-Western tunes while cowboys dance cheek to cheek. They sway to the strains of "Waltzing Across Texas" or do the two-step, or they perform a brisk fox trot to an upbeat song like "Big Ball's in Cowtown Tonight" (the title always draws a smile). Over the polished wood floor hangs a sign, "Get Hot or Get Out." That is the only modern note, though the redneck belligerence neutralizes the up-to-date vocabulary.

The etiquette is formal, almost severe. A brief nod of the head has taken the place of the dance-class bow from the waist. If both men are the same height, one of them (usually the one who leads) removes his 10V Ranch cowboy hat and holds it in his hand behind his partner's back. Since it is summer most of the hats are straw. The shirts, however, are long-sleeved; cowboys are frugal people who wear the same clothes year in and year out. As the men danced to the impassioned strains of Tammy Wynette singing Johnny Paycheck's "You Hurt the Love Right Out of Me," their faces were unsmiling. I was reminded of a story an Argentine once told me of a tango contest on the pampas: as the gauchos glided back and forth to heartbreaking lyrics about jealousy, great tears streamed down their stoic faces. It was the same here, except the words also covered divorce and the Pill.

When a city slicker has a jerk-off fantasy about cowboys, he usually forgets their true distinguishing marks—the air of detachment and the polite, old-fashioned decorum. He ignores the fact that cowboys are low in perceived status, suspicious of outsiders, grave, insecure, a bit touching—and quite conventional sex (they would be appalled by rough stuff, for instance). At the Brasos River Bottom, smoking grass (so common in all the other Houston bars) is forbidden, as is pissing in the patio (a curt sign reads, "Rest Rooms Are Inside"). The spirit that reigns is respectable and cozy—a few old friends getting together for a beer.

Only about half of the customers are genuine cowboys or farm people; they are the ones most reluctant to discuss their origins and work, as though they are afraid you might laugh at them. But for all Texans the emergence of the Western look has come as a relief. Ten years ago most Texans were uncomfortable in their alligator shirts, chinos, and Topsiders; now they have received permission to slip back into the clothes they wore as teenagers.

For most Northerners, Texas is the home of the real men. The cowboys, the rednecks, the outspoken self-made right-wing millionaires strike us as either the best or worst examples of American manliness. The metal-drilling voice; the flashes of canniness and dry humor; the loping walk and the rangy gestures; the readiness to offer help and the reluctance to accept it; the unspoken code of personal honor; the physical courage and the unexpected grace in combat—all these are aspects of the Man, and for most of us He is a Texan.

This is, obviously, the movie version, but it is based on fact. The ideal is not an illusion, nor is it contemptible, no matter what damage it may have done. Many people who scorn it in conversation want to submit to it in bed. Those who believe machismo reeks of violence choose to forget that it once stood for honor as well. Until recently, as a Houston lawyer told me, Texas businessmen could conclude staggering transactions with just a handshake. Today, the invasion of Yankees has meant that all deals must be firmed up with written contracts. The gentleman might have been more tough than gentle, but he was at least honest.

Nor are courage, strength, a touchy pride, and a muted range of emotions without their usefulness. They are the traits of the pioneer, quick to defend what he has won and slow to complain about what he has lost. Nor is the frontier a mythical past in Texas. Both my parents are Texans and most of my relatives still live there. My paternal grandfather came to Texas from Louisiana in a covered wagon. My maternal grandmother's parents were homesteaders, and my mother remembers vividly her girlhood on that farm with its smokehouse, its cool dugout under the pump house, its pecan trees along the creek, its rooms tacked on to the original cabin, its tribe of twelve uncles and aunts ruled by a mother who presided from an oak rocker where she read the Bible, chewed tobacco, and concocted herbal cures. Her husband was silent, hardworking, and strong.

When my mother returned to her home town for a reunion a few years ago and stepped breezily out of her Cadillac, an ancient woman wearing a bonnet approached her and asked her name. The name was given and the woman said, "Then I am the first person who kissed you. I was the midwife. As soon as you were born, I said to your mother, 'I'm going to kiss her.' Your mother said, 'Don't kiss that nasty old thing till you've washed her,' but I didn't wait. I was afraid someone would beat me to it." My mother is seventy-five; the midwife must be in her nineties.

I mention all this only to remind the reader that the day of early settlers is within living memory for Texans and that the frontier ideal of manliness was until recently functional, needed. My own father worked as a cowboy when he was young, before he moved North and became a businessman. My childhood was a battlefield on which two opposing Texas forces fought it out—the strictures of manliness and the aspirations toward culture. My parents divorced when I was seven, and I was shunted back and forth between them. What my mother wanted me to be was artistic, creative, someone who "contributed" to society; her father had been a math prof in a rural junior college and she herself had taught grade school. (Texas has always spent large sums on education. The school teacher remains the beacon of culture; and many a modest home has a good library of the classics, headed by the Harvard Five-foot Shelf. Even today a dedication to culture is maintained in Texas; after all, Houston is the only American city aside from New York to have a full complement of resident opera, ballet, theater, and symphony. No matter that old oilmen snore through a Handel revival; they have at least done their bit for uplift.)

My father subscribed to my mother's values in passing, though they struck him as more appropriate to a girl than a growing boy. What he wanted in a son was someone brave, quiet, hardworking, unemotional, modest. I can remember traveling to Mexico with him once after I'd spent a year with my mother. I embarrassed him by being a know-it-all and by admiring the cathedrals with too much enthusiasm. He drew me aside and

said, "A man doesn't say 'I love that building,' he says 'I like it.' Don't talk
with your hands. And you shouldn't correct older people, but if you must,
say 'In my opinion' or 'I believe' or 'I may be wrong, but I've heard. . . .' "
He also told me that I should never wear a wristwatch, smoke cigarettes, or
use cologne—all sissy things. Men have pocket watches, smoke cigars, and
use witch hazel. These are principles, alas, that I have failed to observe.

I've talked with many Texas men about the way machismo was in-
stilled in them, and they all agree it was done indirectly. I've never heard
one male Texan say of another, "He's a real man" or "He's not very masculine" or anything of the sort, though I have heard a few women say of a
child such things as "You'll like him. He's all boy." (Usually the comment
is repeated: "*All* boy.") But manliness is never mentioned by men in
Texas. I suppose the subject is too momentous and too tender to be voiced.
What is talked about is sissiness. The shape of the unspoken province of
manliness can easily be inferred from the explicit, exact, and surrounding
contours of sissiness, much as Canada might be deduced as a potent
shadow from the glittering boundaries of Alaska and our northern border.
If there were only two choices facing Texas WASPs—manliness or sissiness—then most of them would resemble the Chicanos, who are usually
either fiercely butch or extravagantly nelly. But there is a third option
available to white, middle-class men in Texas: the good school citizen. He
cannot talk in a high voice or *love* the arts (though he may like them), lest
he descend into sissiness. But he need not play contact sports or drink or
brawl in order to ascend into manliness. The good school citizen can run
for the student council, earn excellent grades, do charitable work, and lead
his church group. He may date an equally serious, upright girl and "respect" her virginity. This option is the one most of the gay men I met in
Texas took as teenagers. They may have experienced themselves as sissies,
but they were not taken as such by their friends and neighbors.
There's one last thing that should be said on this subject—the extraordinary naiveté among rural people about homosexuality, at least in years
gone by. Today television talk shows and the antics of Anita Bryant have
made the word *gay* part of everyone's vocabulary, but when I was a boy, I
never heard homosexuality mentioned once. When I was twelve, my
mother, sister, and I visited my grandparents in the village where they
lived, formerly "the oil capital of the world" (as a tattered banner over the
main street proclaimed) but by then virtually a ghost town (the wells had
run dry). My grandmother let me bunk with my grandfather and he and I
made passionate, nonstop love all night. So far so good, but in the morning
I heard him in the living room telling the others, "That Eddie is such a
sweet boy, we just hugged and kissed all night long." My grandmother
cooed with affection, "Well, isn't he the sweetest *thang*," but my mother
and sister subsided into ominous silence. I slid out of bed and turned on the
gas burner in the corner without lighting it; it was one of those free-stand-
ing grills, blue flames reddening bone-colored asbestos, fed by a hose out
of the floor. Though I intended to kill myself, I chickened out, turned off
the tap, and at last crept sheepishly into the living room. My mother was
clearly alarmed, my sister derisive, but my grandparents beamed at me

with all the charity of their innocent hearts. So gay love must have been in the nineteenth century. Other Texas boys have told me their own tales of gay idylls on farms and in small towns where general ignorance assured them personal immunity. I do not want to romanticize rural life, nor do I long for a return to Arcadia. I am simply suggesting that in the old Texas what could not be named was unknowingly tolerated—a far cry from the half-informed but well-indoctrinated Baptist bigotry of today.

The young man who took me to the Brasos River Bottom fell into the category of the good school citizen. He was not a cowboy, though he felt more comfortable there than in the other bars and had even, for a while, lived next door to it. He grew up in a small town in Oklahoma as one of three children out of four who eventually became gay (the others are a grown sister now in Austin and a teenage brother—a whiz at macramé— still at home with his folks). An older, straight sister lives in Houston but doesn't see Bill because she's "hurt" that he's homosexual. His parents know about their children's sexual orientation, but the gay kids dare not say too much to their mother because she too becomes "hurt." The word reminded me of the way some Southern women control their families by displaying a conspicuous wound—the wound of pouting, of a long face and swollen eyes, of meals eaten in silence and dishes washed in martyred solitude, of unusual afternoon naps taken restlessly behind a half-closed door to the tune of resigned sighs. This is the mother who tells her gay son, "I don't care what folks say about me, but it breaks my heart that they should laugh at you."

As an adolescent Bill weighed a mirthful 230 pounds (he loved eating and didn't mind the consequences). He was proficient on the tuba, the trumpet, the piano, and the organ; his parents even bought him an organ. As he explains without a trace of irony, "My older sister wanted an organ, too, but she was too skeered to ask for one. Me? I just upped and asked and got me a big old organ."

True enough.

During grade school and high school Bill saved $10 a month for college (he was guided to this goal by an aunt who taught in Denton, Texas). As an undergraduate he slimmed down to 160 pounds by eating nothing but tuna and swimming daily. He became so talented in the water that he was asked to join the swim team. He gained local renown by singing show tunes in a silvery falsetto voice. After graduation he moved to Houston and became—well, I don't want to reveal his identity, so I'll say a repairman of expensive European equipment. He likes this blue-collar work that brings him into contact with the carriage trade and earns him a handsome salary. His friends, however, regard him as "unsettled"—a polite way of saying "low-class."

I met Bill at an interesting moment in his life. He is just twenty-two, blond, handsome, and naturally trusting, though newly skeptical about other men's interest in him ("I know I'm good-looking and don't want to be liked just for that. Everyone is after me"). His attachment to the cowboy bar and the repair shop keeps him within a safe, small-town milieu. Yet that familiar circle is evaporating around him, a mist burning off to reveal larger but more perilous vistas. He dreams of knowing educated and civilized people and hopes he may find them in Texas but suspects they all live in the Northeast. He has just abandoned his old apartment, two rooms in a frame house where he kept comfortable family furniture and surrounded himself with images of his totemic animal, the tiger—tigers painted on black velvet, photos of tigers, stuffed toy tigers. His new place is in the Heights, the only hilly residential district of Houston, an area of big trees and houses that have porches, back doors, even attics. Here someone gay might buy his first house before moving on to a more modern and costly neighborhood.

Bill has purchased his house with an older friend, Chuck, a native of Houston (that rare species). It is a nice, slightly run-down place built in 1915, which they are restoring and improving. They've already installed central air conditioning and assembled one of those kitchens that foreigners and New Yorkers first envy and then laugh at (a cause-and-effect relationship). Wood cabinets, reaching all the way up to the twelve-foot ceiling, fill in the spaces left vacant by the microwave oven, the electric range, the dishwasher, the washing machine, and the garbage compactor. On one high shelf sit antique toy cars—a crude Dusenberg in painted balsa wood and a Hudson in gilded tin. Concealing the toaster in her skirts is an Aunt Jemima doll. In the window hangs an etched-glass reproduction of a Mucha poster of Bernhardt. No wonder Bill left his tigers on velvet behind; he is being inducted into the new art of Art Nouveau and camp memorabilia.

The living room is less resolutely up to date. Though an impressively thick Houston house-and-garden magazine lies open on a chair, the decor here has not yet emulated those coordinated pastels, those careless conversational islands stranded in a sea of beige carpet under an abstract, palette-knife daub. No, in this room the presence of the old Texas can be detected in the facing, matched couches covered in brown gingham, each paired with its own symmetrically placed mahogany coffee table, a place for dull visits from company rather than animated little chats. Inside a covered glass dish, tinted a delicate pink, rises a mound of miniature Tootsie Rolls and foil-wrapped candy kisses; one pictures relatives passing the dish around while discussing the route they took and the mileage they got. The curtains are drawn and the Venetian blinds tilted to screen out the afternoon glare. Here devolves that tedious Southern ritual called "visiting" (as in "Don't do the dishes right now; sit down and we'll visit for an hour"). Visiting is a long, ambling account of the births, marriages, and deaths of every person ever known by anyone, especially kin, no matter how remote.

Chuck tells me that he runs his own business, a pesticide service. For $100 a client's house is sprayed four times a year. He needs to work only five hours a day; afternoons he devotes to soap operas on television. He is enthralled by one program and proudly tells me he once met two of its stars when they visited Houston to perform in a dinner theater. He longs to travel to New York in order to see the studio where the show is taped.

He explained to me the gay social life of Houston. "The men in the A group are well-to-do, over thirty-five, and very exclusive. They have lots of parties. You have to remember that Houston is a big party town. We party long and hard. Last year the A group had the Mother's Party—everyone who *dared* brought his mom, so there were just hundreds of gay men and these nice old ladies. It was supposedly a great success. I wasn't there. I'm not a socialite. They also had the Bicycle Party. About six hundred men rode from house to house on their bikes, and at each place they were given drinks and joints. It went on all Saturday until everyone fell off his bike. Or so I've heard tell. Now, the other group—"

"The B group?"

"No, we've got A's but no B's. The other group, which is younger, puts on the Miss Camp America contest to coincide with the real pageant in Atlantic City. It's held in a hotel ballroom and more than a thousand guests attend. Each of the ten finalists displays his talent and presents himself in swimsuit and gown. I was Miss Hawaii, but they ruled me out for smoking my grass skirt." He pauses; only a second too late do I realize I've been told a joke. "When the contestants are presented, they're introduced with a dish."

"A what?"

"A dish. You know, an embarrassing story about something they did during the last year. Like: on the big cookout your steaks weren't rare; or on the freeway last October you got an attack of diarrhea all over yourself; or you're known to have sucked a nigger dick—no, they wouldn't say that, since blacks are present. They'd refer to dark meat or something."

Lavish entertainments do comprise a large part of Houston gay life. Members of the A group throw patio parties for more than a hundred men and decorate the grounds with cabanas and parachutes stretched from the trees. Last spring's big event was the "Mardi Gras Madness." During the holiday invitations were handed out in New Orleans to attractive strangers; as they passed back through Houston on their way home, about a thousand congregated for the party. Houstonians stand in friendly opposition to Dallas. Whereas Dallas is characterized as snobbish, pissy, phony elegant, and uptight, Houston sees itself as down-to-earth, butch, rowdy, and egalitarian. The rivalry is amiable, and gay men from the one city are perpetually racing to the other to attend parties. In Houston jeans, crew cuts, and S and M are in vogue; in Dallas designer slacks, styled coiffures, and social climbing rather than lovemaking are preferred ... or so the Houstonians would have it.

Chuck mentioned to me that he was interested in gay liberation but was unaware of anyone active in it. He was grateful when I passed on the phone number of someone I was planning to visit next. This young man, the perfect school citizen, was one of the organizers of Houston Town Meeting I, held in the Astroarena in May and June [1978]. The meeting, an open forum at which all members of the homosexual community could vote on major resolutions, was the first grass-roots political event for gays in the country. Despite the fact that homosexuals in Houston tend to be socially conservative, the meeting attracted some thirty-five hundred women and men. It provided Houston gays with a badly needed sense of community. There is no gay center. Until now the Wilde 'n' Stein bookshop and the

Unitarian Church have functioned as the only meeting places aside from bars.

The forum covered such topics as religion, mental health, the police, and the military. Before the meeting the Houston papers and television stations had ignored gay rights altogether, but the forum generated two front-page stories and several talk-show discussions. One of the newspaper stories concerned the attempt of the Harris County Commissioners Court to refuse the use of the Astroarena to a gay organization. In the article, one commissioner expressed his fear that a "nudist colony" would be asking for the arena next; another official, a Methodist, said, "My religious beliefs don't go along with this." The remaining three commissioners, who decided in favor of the gays, were equally squeamish, but their libertarianism overcame their distaste. One of them said, "As a conservative and advocate of limited government, I feel the constitutional protection of free speech must always take precedence over personal opinions of government officials."

The chairperson of the meeting was Ginny Apuzzo, a professor at Brooklyn College and leader of the Gay Rights National Lobby; the keynote speaker was Sissy Farenthold, a Texas feminist and political reformer. Forty-two Texas gay organizations were present. One of these was an engineers' group that has about a hundred members. As one of them told me, "You'd never believe those fellows are gay. They talk about nothing but oil drilling, offshore rigs, and freight forwarding. I guess we're deliberate, rational, macho. But we want to be freer."

Perhaps the biggest problem facing Houston gays is violence in the streets. The gay ghetto is Montrose (once pronounced "Mont Rose" but now said, Yankee-style, "Mon Trose"). In May and June alone there were three stabbings and eight beatings in Montrose. The victims were gay men and the muggers teenage Chicanos. The police ignore the danger; if they do respond to a call for help, they often arrest the gay victim on the charge of public intoxication, a vague measure that permits officers to harass anyone they choose to. The Town Meeting called for the formation of a citizens' police assistance group to patrol Montrose. It also asked for a civilian police-review board.

Police brutality remains troublesome. Last year five policemen beat a Chicano named Joe Torres and drowned him in the Buffalo Bayou (two of the cops were convicted of a misdemeanor). Two years ago a gay bartender, Gary Wayne Stock, made an illegal left turn and was shot to death by a Houston policeman, who was cleared of blame. The cop claims that Stock refused to pull over and was gunned down during a high-speed chase. But only eight minutes elapsed between Stock's departure from work and the moment he was killed. Since he was shot only a few blocks away from the bar, he could scarcely have been speeding. The court failed to subpoena any gay witnesses.

Police raids on bars and adult bookstores are a familiar part of Houston gay life. A year ago the cops raided the Locker and made sure TV cameramen were there to expose the identities of the arrested patrons. There used to be a back room at the Locker where customers had sex on a dark balcony; plainclothesmen infiltrated the crowd and picked up one person after another by whispering "You're under arrest." Last January the police entered the bar with guns drawn, turned off the jukebox, and ordered the customers to put their hands above their heads against the wall. A new mayor and a new police chief seem to be less hostile, but gays have no legal assurance against further harrassment.

The Town Meeting also called for the repeal of Section 21:06 of the Texas penal code, the sodomy law. Finally, the meeting censured discrimination within the gay community. The formation of a gay Chicano organization was especially welcomed—in recognition of the pressures exerted on gay Chicanos by their straight compatriots.

When the Town Meeting is held next year, it will undoubtedly discuss the problems of housing and employment. As things stand, two men or two women usually cannot rent a one-bedroom apartment in Houston, and if someone takes an apartment on his or her own and then moves a lover in, both of them can be (and usually are) evicted. Since houses sell for about $80,000 in Montrose, most gays are forced to rent and are thus clearly victimized by this form of legal discrimination. As for job discrimination, four of the men who organized the Town Meeting were fired from their jobs because of their activism. One of the co-chairs of the meeting wrote his name simply as "X," explaining that his "lifetime career would be imperiled by openly signing this decree." When photos were taken at the Town Meeting, many of those attending panicked. The fuss was still going on a month later when I visited Houston. One gay group had gone so far as to steal the photos from the archives.

Oppressive as this situation sounds, Houston gays stand a real chance of gaining power within the Texas Democratic Party. In a city of newcomers, where there is no Italian vote or Jewish bloc or labor vote, where everyone is young, materialistic, and indifferent to politics, a hardworking gay organization could become a force, especially since gays are so highly concentrated in the Montrose district. Similarly, gays in Dallas are sending delegates to the Democratic state convention, where they almost passed a resolution against the sodomy law. If only more gays would vote. . . .

Despite the emerging gay clout, Texas will probably soon be faced with a version of California's Briggs initiative barring gays from teaching positions. An educator at Texas A&M, who fought to integrate the University of Texas in 1969, is now trying to ban gay student organizations from his new campus. He is working hand in hand with a conservative black state legislator from Dallas who wants gay organizations routed out of all state schools and will undoubtedly introduce a Briggs-type initiative. Few legislators want to vote on a civil-rights issue, much less vote *against* such rights, but if they're forced to express a yea or a nay on an open roll call, they will surely vote against gays or abstain. Obviously Texas gays must organize even more vigorously than they have already.

The young man I met who is high up in the Town Meeting and the Houston Gay Political Caucus is in his twenties and from what Texans would call a "fine family." Prematurely balding, he has only a tuft of silky hair to indicate where his forehead once stopped. His dimples are so deep that in an overhead light his mouth appears to be a slim dash between thick parentheses. His eyebrows grow together but do not suggest jealousy, rather wistful earnestness. Yet when the phone rings this shy man sounds jocular, back-slapping—a good ole boy. It is a manner that works wonders with older Southern businessmen. Houston gays are lucky to have Tom (as I'll call him) as a spokesman.

The story of his coming-out is a tribute to his tenacity. As early as the seventh grade he knew he was gay, but like many truly queer boys he did not engage in the normal homosexual romps of puberty. In high school in Louisiana he was the first-chair flutist and became friendly with the first-chair oboist, who was notorious as the school fag. Because of their friendship Tom was kept out of the prestigious junior Kiwanis Club, so he turned around and started an American Field Service Club (the school-citizen strategy initiated dangerously late in the day). This office catapulted him into the president's council. His reputation as a homosexual, undeserved up to this point, continued to haunt him; anonymous teenage boys called him and threatened to reveal his queerness to his parents, and two guys in the band asked him outright for blow jobs. When Tom demurred, they started a whisper campaign against him.

The oboist had by this time discovered a gay bar. Tom went along one night. When someone asked him how long he'd been gay, he didn't answer—he didn't know what the word meant. The oboist was dating an older man. When the affair cooled off, the oboist hanged himself from a tree. The police grilled Tom for hours about a possible motive. Tom kept silent, but he was so upset he nailed the closet door shut. In college he majored in marketing, became an officer of his fraternity, and went to bed with women. But the cure didn't take. One of his school friends was making gasoline money as a hustler. Tom went with him to a gay bar and ran into a fraternity brother who said, "It's about time you came out, Miss Thing."

Tom did come out—and immediately came down with hepatitis. When he returned to school his fraternity brothers began to harass him; they hounded him out of the house. When he told his parents he was gay, they were outraged. Rich and prominent in politics, his father said, "We don't want to consort with your kind." His sister, an admirer of Anita Bryant, dropped him. Ridiculed and disowned, Tom could do nothing but leave town. Like so many other gay Southerners, he was attracted to Houston, the Ithaca of so many adventurers.

College graduates like Tom go to Houston to find good jobs in industry; working-class teenage runaways become hustlers. Recently Houston TV ran a five-part program on hustlers that "embarrassed" the gay community. The program did ignore the efforts of gay organizations to help runaways. Nevertheless, I'm not convinced that embarrassment is appropriate. Houston is, after all, the site of the "Houston murders," those grisly slayings of homeless youths. There is no use pretending the gay community is free of psychopaths. This problem must be dealt with openly and interpreted lucidly to the public. Considering the way in which oppression deforms us, the miracle is that more of us aren't mad.

In Houston Tom has found independence and freedom. He has a good position with a corporation that knows about his activism and accepts it. He owns a small apartment building, a brick four-family structure on a pretty street, and he lives there himself. His participation in gay politics has turned him into a sane, steady man, the very sort of upstanding type his parents would embrace if they had sufficient wit to do so. Tom confirmed me in my belief that activism is not only valuable for the community but also essential for one's own mental health. Being gay in a straight world, even in a hypothetically permissive straight world, is so alienating that the only way to avoid depression is through the assertion of one's own gay identity. Anger can take three forms—self-hatred, uncontrollable rage, and calm but constant self-assertion. The first solution is tiresome, the second useless, the third wise; Tom has chosen wisely.

Hank and Eddie, as I'll call them, invited me to dinner one night. They live in a Montrose apartment complex that is 70 percent gay and subject to the usual Houston rapid turnover of tenants. Hank has been there longer than anyone else—three years. He is twenty-nine, a handsome Floridian who is as smooth as a public-relations man; he knows how to project his considerable charms, but quietly, quietly. Eddie is twenty-five but looks seventeen, a small, perfect, exquisitely made animal so endearing that the desire or envy he might awaken is instantly tranquilized into friendship for him—the only recourse for an admirer, since his beauty is the kind that would otherwise inspire frustration. He is lapis-eyed and wears his black hair slicked back in a d.a., a quaint "period" touch that lends poignancy to his slender neck and small head. His youthfulness embarrasses him and on the job he smokes cigarettes, drinks coffee, and wears a tie to appear older.

Eddie grew up in a small Texas town but is now quite the sophisticate. He works for a shipping broker (Houston is one of the country's busiest ports), and most of the 250 people in his office know he is gay and accept it, even relish it. Women ask him to explain the fine points of fellatio, which he does; recently they've moved on to more serious questions about back rooms and fistfucking. They also feel free to pat him on the ass ("because I'm a man *and* gay," he observes with a trace of irritation). He's called the "token gay" to his face; that's a standing joke. When Hank sends him flowers, Eddie can put them on his desk and everyone beams. What they can't grasp, Eddie tells me, is that he's not Hank's "wife." Any suggestion that their roles are reversible will puzzle, even vex his straight co-workers.

Just as the Saturnalia, that grotesque mirror of society, confirmed the Romans in their belief that the world was hierarchical and proved (through its temporary elevation of slaves to freemen) that slavery and freedom must be enduring categories, so the perpetuation of traditional masculine and feminine roles by homosexual couples serves to demonstrate the inevitability and "naturalness" of such roles. The only threat of anarchy that homosexuality poses is in its openness to new relationships immune from the ancient corruption of the subjugation of one partner by another. If Eddie is not Hank's wife, then marriage itself is challenged and heterosexuals are no longer able to find in gay life fun-house distortions of their own unsatisfactory arrangements. I am not, mind you, opposed to gay role playing; that would be impertinent and display an ignorance of our moment in history. I'm simply noticing that the new gay ethic, which pairs equals and attempts to dismiss jealousy and possessiveness as leftovers from an era when marriage was primarily an economic transaction rather than an affectional tie—that this new ethic distresses even well-disposed heterosexuals.

When I arrived in Dallas it was suffering from the seventeenth straight day in the hundreds. It was, as Texans say, one of those days when chickens lay fried eggs. No rain had fallen for more than a month and the trees were turning brown. At night the temperature dropped only into the eighties. People were buying four-hundred-pound blocks of ice and dumping them into their swimming pools, with no appreciable effect. Everyone was pale; it was too hot to take the sun. Six people had died in the last week from heat prostration. The incidence of crimes of passion had increased, but the number of robberies had declined; it was too hot to go out and steal. The city was crazy with cabin fever.

The mood of Dallas also struck me as near the riot stage. Down the street from my hotel a crowd of Chicanos in the park was protesting the slaying of a twelve-year-old boy. The child had stolen eight dollars' worth of goods. When he was arrested a cop interrogated him while playing Russian roulette with a pistol aimed at the boy's head. This game resulted in the boy's death—and a very short sentence for the officer, who was convicted only of involuntary manslaughter.

Dallas is surer of itself than Houston, more rigid and smug. Whereas Houston is a young town, Dallas is the usual gerontocracy. Dallas is richer than Houston (it has one thousand million-dollar companies, as opposed to Houston's six hundred). Houston has new oil money, Dallas old banking wealth. In Houston gay circles, money counts for little and family for nothing; Dallas, by contrast, is status conscious.

Dallas is the design center of the Southwest, and I was pleased to spend an evening with a successful decorator. His tenth-floor apartment was in Turtle Creek, the most expensive gay neighborhood (Oaklawn is the less expensive ghetto). His apartment was decorated in taupes, browns, and grays and commanded a full view of the city. On one wall was a painting of the archangel Lucifer falling from heaven, a wing catching fire. On the facing wall hung an eventless Barbizon landscape, the thick gold frame alone certifying the significance of its frowsy pastoral inanities. There were bookcases, but they were filled with untouched matching sets with good bindings—"book furniture," as they say in the trade, ordered by the yard. A copy of Donatello's wicked David smiled in at me from the glassed-in balcony garden. The fur throws hurled everywhere would have seemed oppressive had one remembered the temperature, but one does not remember it in Texas. Just as Houston sells more sables in July than New York does in December, in the same way Dallas decorators ignore the climate, the terrain, and our century and concoct their fantasies of a polar Paris of the Belle Epoque and seal them in air-conditioned cubes.

Steve wore a white, short-sleeved Egyptian cotton shirt into which had been sewn blue panels. Around his neck dangled a silver bauble. His slacks were pocketless, revealing his trim figure; though he is in his mid-forties he still weighs just 145 pounds, lean for his height (five-foot-nine). Under his arm he carries a purse shaped like a dop kit. He drove us in his Cadillac to the Bronx, a restaurant for straights and gays with a friendly atmosphere. In Texas coffee is served throughout the meal. Over our first cup, Steve told me, "I've been wanting to have plastic surgery for some time now, but my daughter wouldn't let me. She said, 'People already think you're my brother or boyfriend.' We went on a Caribbean cruise together and folks did make that mistake. 'Wait till I'm married,' she said. Well, I just gave her away to a nice boy and now I'm going to have my eyes tightened, my nose thinned, my chin made stronger. The whole thing will cost only $3,000. I never get a chance to visit with my mother; she'll come to Dallas and take care of me for two weeks while I recuperate. The doctor's here in Dallas. I like his attitude. He considers a face-lift preventive and says the second and third operations are always easier. Some of my friends, I fear, waited too long."

I ask him how he happens to have a daughter. "I'm from a town in the Panhandle," he says. "My father was a deacon in the Baptist church, my wife's father was a deacon, and I became a deacon. My wife and I met at a Baptist college, married young, and had a boy and a girl. Although I fooled around with guys, it never occurred to me that two men could love each other. We were married happily for ten years and then I met a handsome guy from California and fell for him. I told my wife the next day I wanted a divorce, but I never confided in her that I was gay.

"Her parents were astounded; we were considered the ideal couple. Her father hired a private eye to investigate me. The detective found out everything. My father-in-law confronted me with the dirt and invited me to pray for strength to overcome this terrible sin. I refused the offer. A week later he tempted me with a tremendous sum of money. When I rejected it, he said, 'We're going to ruin you, take every penny you've got. Boy, a year from now you'll be in the gutter.' In court my wife demanded a million dollars, half of my net worth, but she asked for it in *cash*. I was given three years to come up with the money; to do so I had to sell my holdings at a big loss. My ex-wife has remarried, this time to a man whose first wife left him for another woman. Well, they have something in common.

"My lover and I bought a twelve-room Victorian house for the price of the lot, $30,000. We spent twice that fixing it up, of course."

"You stayed in that same town?"

"Yes. For *two years* no one would speak to us, just whisper behind our backs. But we hung in there. One day, I've heard, four important ladies were playing bridge and one of them said, 'You *know* what they are,' and the *grande dame* of our town replied, 'I don't care. They're the only interesting men in town and I'd sleep with either of them.' Everybody laughed and had to agree. It was a very dull place. Eventually we joined a country club as a couple and were invited to all the parties."

"Did you live in an entirely straight world?"

"Lord, no," he said. "We'd have big weekend parties of fifty men or so. They'd drive in from Dallas, Fort Worth, Houston, Austin. In the attic we'd set up an orgy room, twelve mattresses on the floor, and show fuck films. On the second floor people would get high and eat. On the ground floor they'd dance. Our maid would prepare several big meals in advance, but even so, it kept us busy—people wouldn't drive all that way just for one night.

"My children would visit and they loved my friend as much as me. We never discussed our homosexuality with them. Then, when my daughter was going to college, her mother wanted her to attend Baylor, the Baptist school. My daughter refused and I backed her up. My wife was so furious she sent a letter to my daughter telling her everything about me in the ugliest terms. When my daughter phoned me, I said, 'Well, it's all true. I'm glad your mother wrote that. Maybe she'll calm down now.' We had a good laugh."

"And are you still with your lover?" I asked.

"No," he said. "He wouldn't work. I set him up in several businesses, but they all failed. Finally he blamed me for his failures and left me. I've moved to Dallas and started a whole new life. It's very exciting."

"Are you still a Baptist?"

"I no longer go to church, but I still worship God. I just assume He will reward me for the good things I've done and ignore the bad."

"The bad?"

"My homosexuality."

The odd thing was that two days later I met someone at the baths who was from the very same small town in the Panhandle, though he didn't know Steve. Although he had been in Dallas for four years working as a clerk, he hadn't made any friends. He was intensely shy; his cheeks were cicatrized by deep acne scars. His eyes were an eerie blue, so pale he appeared blind. He had a lovely body and whispered to me with a sad smile, "Why don't you lick me all over?"

He hadn't come out till he was twenty-seven. Before that, the great event of his life had taken place in high school. A football player had awakened a grand passion in him, but they didn't know each other. In the fall my friend had prayed for the athlete to be in one of his classes and was intensely disappointed not to see him. "So I just *wished* him there. I knew that would work. I became calm and sure enough he came in the door. He'd decided to take Spanish after all. We didn't speak, but after class he grabbed my arm, the same way he took his girlfriend's, and steered me down the hall. Nobody laughed. When we got to the cafeteria, he went his way and I went mine. One other time he touched me. We were riding in a car to a church affair and he put his leg next to mine."

Suddenly my friend looked at me with genuine fear. "Do you own this place?" he asked.

"No," I said.

"Sure?"

"I'm certain." I have no idea what he feared or why that idea popped into his head. He seemed a naive country boy, though he was thirty-three years old. I had the impression he had never talked about these things before.

He went on with his story. He had never had sex until, when he was twenty-seven, a married man at work went down on him. "I felt real bad and the next day I said to him, 'Why'd you do *that?*'" (*That* comes out as "thigh-yat.") "'I don't never want you doing that again.'"

My friend laughed. "Two days later I was horny. His wife had gone to work and he called me and asked me over for breakfast. When I got there, he was nekkid. He was prancing around nekkid and I said, 'You look real comfortable.' He stretched out and said, 'Why don't you get comfortable, too, if you want to.' So I did and that went on for three years. He took care of me; I never did anything. He looked like Chad Everett on TV. Then he moved to Dallas and I visited him. His wife came downstairs and said, 'Why don't you go on up there and sleep with him?' I said, 'Heck, no. I can stay on this here couch,' but she insisted. I guess he must have told her. But then he got religion and was saved and we broke up."

"What religion?"

"Baptist."

The Baptists in Dallas, as elsewhere, are the storm troopers of the anti-gay offensive. The zealous, if not over scholarly, minister of the First Baptist Church in Dallas (the world's largest, as Texans say) thunders against homosexuals regularly from his television pulpit. In interpreting a passage from the scriptures about who will not be admitted into heaven, the minister identified "effeminates" as lesbians and the "philanderers" as gay men. The rest of his sermon was on that level. As a teacher used to handing out grades, I couldn't help feeling that this minister was himself the big D in Dallas.

Across the street from his church one finds the Baptist Book Store—the usual outlines for sermons, a section for teenage missionaries, and many tracts designed to prevent Baptists from lapsing into astrology, the occult, Buddhism, and Mormonism. Quite a few volumes were devoted to the "Biblical way to pray away pounds." Others ranged from the folksy (*Ain't God Good?*) to Colson's and Magruder's confessions, inspirational volumes (the tale of a famous star's blue baby told from the blue baby's point of view), and books for teens in their own language ("I hear where you're coming from, Lord"). For those who find reading a nuisance, much of this literature has been transferred onto cassettes; there is a whole battery of tapes on how to save your marriage.

Glancing through a Baptist encyclopedia of psychiatric disorders, I found a long, seemingly confused entry on homosexuality. The genetic argument was rejected (you're not born gay); I suppose the doctrine of free will would insist on that. The causes of homosexuality that were cited included faulty glands (aren't they genetic?), a domineering mother, and a shadowy or overcompetitive father (such a mother and father have always struck me as sounding like Italians, and I wonder why so few Italian men turn out to be gay). Fear of women was listed as another possible cause, for which the cure is—no, not man-woman sex, but mixed group therapy. Lesbians were ignored altogether. The entry concluded by saying that many practicing heterosexual men have psychological profiles that indicate they *should* be gay. The reason they're not is that they've heard the call to God. In repression lies salvation.

My cousin's son is studying to become a minister at this very Baptist center. Two years ago I visited his family in West Texas. At first I resisted discussing religion, but then I joined in the debates. For these people religion is the only form of intellectuality. They rise at six in the morning in order to spend an hour alone with their Bibles before breakfast. They have examined every aspect of the scriptures, and my cousin's son is learning Greek, Hebrew, and Aramaic in order to plumb the Bible's depths. Not only is religion an exciting intellectual sport, it also establishes decency within the family. (I think it might be hard for some of my readers to understand that for many households that are perilously close to alcoholism, shiftlessness, and violence, religion represents an opposing urge toward sobriety, industry, and order.) Finally, I became aware that in order to raise their four children and send them to college, the parents had to make big sacrifices, never larger than now, when inflation is squeezing out the middle class. Daily sacrifice requires a rigorous regime, and the Baptist church provides that discipline.

To understand the vehemence of Baptists one must recognize what they are fighting: the broken home; the drunk father; the philandering mother; the meals eaten alone standing in front of the refrigerator; the arbitrary beatings of wife and children; the straying of teenagers into truancy and drug addiction. What we must bear in mind is that what we gay people have been saying defiantly and polemically is in fact objectively true: the family doesn't work, especially not in the United States, the only nation in the industrial world that has no guaranteed family income program. Since the United States is also one of the few advanced countries with no public health system and very little free higher education, these expenses must be borne by the parents. Having children in a city is economically useless, a drain rather than a benefit, and the advantages of raising a family today are only spiritual or conventional, never practical. Religion is a last attempt to keep the institution afloat. Nor are any alternatives to the family visible, not even literally.

When I was with my relatives, I flew above their town in a private plane; below me were nothing but family houses, one after another. I met not one person who was over twenty-five and single. There are no apartment buildings, no singles' bars, no discos. For someone living there, it must seem that there are only good families and bad families. The good families all go to church, and religion indicates not only piety but also education and a commitment to decency. What can sexual freedom mean to such people? In a real sense they can't *afford* it.

Southern Baptists dislike homosexuals because they perceive gay men (they seldom think about lesbians) as hedonistic, selfish, dissolute—the very qualities they observe in families that have gone to seed. Some of the animosity must also be envy. Self-sacrifice doesn't come easily to anyone, nor does fidelity. If gays are seen as both rich and promiscuous, as capable of indulging their every whim as consumers and Don Juans, then they represent a temptation, an affront, which must be condemned. Moreover, the very *perversity* (as they see it) of homosexuality must seem like a first step toward abandoning *all* moral strictures; if someone can face the ridicule of being branded queer, then he is *egregious*—literally, "outside the flock." He has broken the social contract.

Of course, gay men and women don't really give up the harmonic principles of their youth; they simply transpose them into a new key. That was made clear to me one evening I spent in Dallas with a group of young professionals—a lawyer, an architect, and an executive. One of them, brought up in the Church of Christ, had come out in college with his "little brother" in the fraternity. The lover was a local rock star, and between them they dominated campus life. In college in the late sixties he did not defend gays—he didn't know anyone else who was gay—but in 1969 as a high officer in the student council he worked to integrate the school and ease blacks into fraternities. Today he is a bit closety on the job but busy in gay politics. He is an attractive, liberal, thoroughly decent man. One of the other two men had been a Methodist minister before he came out. He is in an awkward position, since he is a feeling person sensitive to the slightest sign of pain or unhappiness in someone else—and also the leader of the most snobbish gay clique in Dallas. Proust once observed that snobbishness is a deep but narrow vice that cannot be extirpated—but that need not infect the rest of the character. Ted, nevertheless, feels the strain between his universal compassion and his exclusive tastes. Naturally enough he denied that there were cliques in Dallas and would admit to nothing more definite than "overlapping circles." Once that distinction was established, he proceeded to tell me about last spring's Easter Bonnet Party (some men wore feathered hats larger than those seen at the Folies-Bergère), about camping weekends by a lake in Oklahoma where some people ("not *our* circle," which is too butch and sensible) hung chandeliers in the trees above their tents and ate off silver service on damask, and about the big Texas-OK (Oklahoma) football weekend in October when gays swarm in the streets as though it were Mardi Gras and Dallas hosts throw open their doors to five hundred guests at a time. Servants, stereos, drugs, open bars. . . .

It was easy to see how Ted had climbed to his social pinnacle. He had dark, almost Indian features, a solid white crescent of teeth worthy of a Wrigley's ad, an imposing build, and the nervous attentiveness of the professional host who nods and grins through one conversation while devising a plan to rescue Henry from the bore in the corner. When he left, he kissed his friends and murmured, "Well, good night, Sugar Booger." My mother would like him; wouldn't yours? The energy these men would have injected in another, heterosexual life into church clubs and country clubs is now diverted into gay social life and politics.

After Ted left, we all discussed cliques and the differences between Northern and Southern manners. In the South a host introduces a newcomer to everyone and says the guest's name at least twice to make sure it has sunk in; in the North the host, sprawled and stoned on the couch, might confer a chilly nod on a new arrival. In the South people have a distinct party style quite different from their tête-à-tête manner. At a party people joke and clown, keep it light, and seldom disagree. In the North people don't know how to behave in groups. They isolate one other person and argue with him. In the South, touching signifies friendliness, nothing more; in the North, it is invariably a sexual innuendo. Northerners consider Southerners to be "phony"; Southerners think of Yankees as "rude." These differences are so subtle and yet so divisive that a Texas university is offering a course for Yankees in how to get along with Texans.

What irritates Texans the most is Yankee condescension. It is surely a mistake to regard Texans as jejune, fun-loving braggarts or to expect them to rustle up grits or rope a bronco at the drop of a Stetson. They are proud, complex people who do eat black-eyed peas on occasion but who also fuss over French wine; they do own ranches, but they also buy villas on the Riviera. No state has been more satirized than Texas, and Texans, accordingly, have become wary of outsiders. Even their own accent troubles them. They remember bitterly how LBJ was made fun of by Yankees long before he had done anything to merit their ridicule. In some contexts Texans think of their accent as the way people should talk; it is the sound of sociability and sincerity. But they also know it is considered comical, substandard. Many educated Texans speak like Yankees at work and like Southerners at home and with friends.

My favorite city in Texas—indeed, one of my favorite cities in America—is Austin, the state capital and the home of the University of Texas. My paternal grandfather retired there, and as a boy I would promenade with him past storefronts where old farmers sat in straightbacked chairs in the shade. They would tip their hats and we would tip ours. The brown capitol building dwarfed the one-story blocks of feed stores and five-and-dimes surrounding it.

This time I stayed with a friend up in the hills west of town. He has twelve acres and a house that was built of field stones by two lesbians fifty years ago. They positioned it on a promontory so that it would catch any breeze that might be stirring. In the living room four sets of double doors are flung open to the elements, since this house is conditioned by the air alone. At night one sleeps under a tent of mosquito netting and listens to a fountain splashing in the courtyard. We ate our dinners outside, looking out at candles in glass-and-metal cages suspended from the trees. We listened to the music of Keith Jarrett, the sound of ice thawing if ice were silver. During the day, when I became too hot, I would wander down a winding pebble path to the swimming pool, circled by low gnarled live oaks and cedars hazy with gray-blue aromatic berries. The house would have pleased Matisse, with its blue-and-white striped deck chairs, its rough whitewashed walls, its straw mats, its fireplaces shaped like beehives, its marble washstands, its huge cacti—even the dead wasp crushed on the bleached wall.

One day an old Austin couple came out to visit. She was expressionless behind her dark glasses. She wore a large hat and sandals over white socks. Her husband had pulled his graying hair back into a pigtail and when he spoke his gold teeth flashed. They lived in town because they couldn't bear to part company with a particular ancient tree in their yard. The conversation ranged from Conrad's introduction to *The Nigger of the Narcissus* (they've memorized long passages) to a turn-of-the-century music critic to Ken Russell's films to a Texas painter living in New York ("his works look like *jewels*"). The woman told me that she had visited her husband one day and sat down to read books from his library. "I didn't get up till twenty years later."

One night my host and I drove into town and saw a production of *Sa-*

*lome* in Richard Howard's translation from Oscar Wilde's French. (Howard, who has always been known for his dramatic readings, played Herod, revealing new if expected talents as an actor.) After the play, which filled the stuffy old movie palace where it was presented with a continuous *basso obbligato* of desire, I went home with a big hunk of a man who had jug ears, meat-packing hands, and slightly overlapping teeth. We got stoned in his "town house" and entered a fantasy in which—oh, I dare not spell it out. Suffice it to say that he was the handsome stud, I his twelve-year-old son, and at one point he was in nothing but boots and hat.

His was the consummate Texas rap, complete with the expression, at the moment of climax, "I'm fixin' to come." Everything one could desire. And of course it had all been learned in New York.

My companion had grown up in West Texas in a town of thirty-four hundred people. His father, he said, was "a good provider but definitely of the laboring class." He was one of seven kids, a grinning, happy-go-lucky teenager who used to hang around the Frigid Queen drive-in and bang the carhops after they got off. A year of college was followed by a rapid montage of events—Navy service, coming out in Germany, a job in Dallas as a medic, a brief, bitter affair of one month in Oklahoma—that culminated with our hero in Manhattan. He'd come to New York to play the part of an escaped Texas convict in a play, but when the production didn't material-ize, he earned a lavish living as a hustler. His madam packaged and sold him as a Texas oil driller. After six months he returned to Texas. Now he starts and stops school, dashes off to L.A., returns to Dallas. He wants to be an actor. Of course, he already is. Not only does he have his stud rap down to a T (for Texas), he also amuses his friends at the bars with a slow-talk-ing Will Rogers routine: "I had a dream last night about a dog. I'm sick, I should see a doctor. [Pause]. I love dogs. [Pause]. He was a beautiful Dal-matian. We were dancing. He said [bass voice], 'You dance real nice.' I said [high voice], 'Thank you, so do you.' " The *you* is pronounced as though there were an umlaut over the *u*.

This young man has become an image broker. He has made himself into a sexual wish fulfillment for other people, and in doing so he has pre-served, with great sophistication, his own real-life teenage naiveté. "I'm fixin' to come," which he once said with the panting urgency of youth, he now introduces inauthentically at the critical moment of the well-rehearsed play. Method actors may do well on opening night, but it is the technical performers who can sustain a role through a long run.

I would contend that most Texans experience themselves from the same quizzical, difficult, uncomfortable angle. If Texas had been poor, it might never have lost its innocence. But since its people are rich and travel everywhere, since hungry Yankees are descending on them in daily hordes, a new, ever more complex society is evolving. If you want to meet simple, hospitable, relaxed people try the Northwest. Texas is a moiré of old and new, Northern and Southern, pristine and jaded. For that reason it inter-ests me; I'm an aficionado of the provisional.

# II

STATE OF
THE TRIBE

◇◇◇◇◇◇◇◇◇◇◇◇◇◇◇◇◇◇◇◇

## *Modern Arrangements: Careless Love*

*I* met Michael and David at the home of a friend who had invited me for tea on a late afternoon in July 1979. Teatime was a specialty of Wade's; it was novel, it was economical, and it was short. Tea meant tea (iced for the season) and nibbles, camp and chatter, and out before dinnertime. Wade's budget was close, but scarcer than money was time. Of the writers I know, Wade alone works full-time at a job which has nothing to do with writing or, for that matter, with the rest of his life. The evenings are his time for writing, and the leisure of the nights is spent disco-dancing rather than squandered on long dinners.

Wade is different in ways more peculiar than his rigid schedule. He is not interested in finding anything that would pay more or use more of his qualifications than his job of glorified receptionist/switchboard-operator. Yet he is also the most ambitious of young writers, determined for success, and if fame could be willed, it would be his. He has written plays, short stories, a novel, many pieces of criticism, essays on literature, and interviews, yet his constant work and publication, his carefully spent time at the typewriter have brought so far mostly promises. They have also brought him a wide range of friends, and he knows more of New York's gay literati than nearly anyone else so relatively unacknowledged.

I always count on meeting interesting and unexpected people at his Washington Square apartment. That late July afternoon, in his shaded cool living room, serene except for the incessant sounds of street life from the park, there were David and Michael.

At first, it was only Michael; David was arriving after work. Meanwhile, Michael barely interrupted his amusing anecdotes of tearoom adventures for our introduction. Michael looked younger than twenty-nine; the image was your basic bright graduate student in scholarly tortoise-shell glasses, carefully groomed beard, an orchestrated casualness to his simple, expensive, chic shirt with funky tie, and just-right khaki pants. He was animated, witty, and eager to please; I felt older than usual and a trifle wilted by his vigorous charm.

When David arrived, it was soon clear that the men were lovers. So here was one of those modern open relationships among younger men I had heard of so often, with equal parts of curiosity and skepticism. After David's introduction, the conversation shifted. Michael performed less as my attention divided between the men. David eschewed smartness for frank sexual heat; a plain T-shirt and jeans showed him off amply as he splayed on the couch more from the humidity than for sexual provocation.

Wade grew restless. The changing light in the apartment, glowing with a spectacular New York summer sunset, meant it was time for work. The three of us dawdled our good-byes, and walking westward through the park, we were mostly quiet. At Sixth Avenue, I said I was taking a cab and offered them a lift, but they were returning home to Brooklyn Heights. Then Michael made the gesture: he would like to meet again. I said I was delighted as we exchanged telephone numbers.

After I had talked to Wade about them, I called them to ask if they would be interviewed about their relationship. Michael agreed immediately, and David agreed some two days later. I could understand that David might be wary, since I was a stranger, but it turned out to be less a matter of trust than of time. Three months later, the demands of his time continued to make our taping erratic; the importance of his trusting me was never articulated.

Michael brought up trust immediately as we began our first session and laid down ground rules. I said I would not presume with the other what I had been told by one. Of course, I could not help raising questions with one man provoked by my talk with the other, but I would not act as if I already knew the answers. They were free to do as they wished: discuss the tapings between themselves, ask any questions, omit what they wanted to. For whatever reasons, they did little or none of that. They only discussed the tapings in the beginning, when they were novel; they asked no questions; and they seemed to omit nothing in their answers.

Michael was verbose, helpful, precise about sexual matters, and flatteringly unreserved about himself. David thought about every answer before he spoke, was always opaque during the interviews, and would only tell me about what I asked. He was equally frank, and I came to understand that his reticence was more his character than the momentary nervousness in an interview. Both men had been in couple therapy for some months before our meeting, and they hoped the taping would clarify for them some of the explosive issues that had arisen there. The analogy with therapy came up often, mostly with Michael. To some degree it was inevitable that I would assume the air of a therapist as I asked questions and probed their responses while trying to reveal little of my own. This was balanced in two ways: I would clarify questions that were painful or difficult by personal examples that were as honest and forthright as I could make them, and thus leaven the psychological imbalance, and as I found I liked both men, the possibility of genuine friendship emerged.

I wanted most of all to know how they managed love in an eight-year relationship, given that from the inception it was presumed that their sexual lives were open. How had they sustained romantic intimacy and promiscuity, domestic coherence and casual infidelity, the priority of the lover and the vagrance of erotic desire? Perhaps all the terms were foreign: *promiscuity, infidelity, priority;* perhaps those were terms relevant only to men of my generation. Had sexual liberation and gay liberation in fact freed the psyche and changed the quality of the intimate life, or was liberation more libertine than liberty?

For men my age, the choices seem to have broadened, but if the quality of sexual life has changed, it is more a product of age than of new values and new feelings. Some men in their late forties truly wish to embrace the autonomy promised by this new life-style, and they struggle vehemently with their own reactionary pasts, with the old wish to be coupled in an identity that is as psychically bound as it is socially.

Here were two men for whom homosexuality and enduring love were assumed as "free," whose consciousness had never needed raising, since they were created by sexual revolution. What had they found to replace the old foundations of romance? What had new definitions of masculinity and role done for them in love? How did they manage to sleep with others and forgo guilt, and if monogamy were irrelevant, what had they found instead to define their loyalty?

In the beginning, when the men were barely out of their teens, Michael discovered that he could be intensely jealous, but he could not be monogamous himself.

"I fucked around because I could not command monogamy; for me, monogamy is the *last* demand." The first demand was, of course, commitment, but even that evolved slowly, and it took four years for the men to decide to live together. They met at Cornell in 1970. Michael was an undergraduate in the School of Architecture; David was majoring in English and planning to earn the doctorate, having assumed that an academic career was his calling. They were the entering class of 1968, the most politically violent and sexually radical generation in American history. Neither man was particularly interested in social change, although they took sexual politics for granted. When they talk of those days, neither remembers the upheaval at Cornell caused by the black students who took over a dormitory to demand separate facilities—part of the inauguration of separatism and black militance that was front-page news nationwide. David was living communally with men and women in a house off campus; Michael was absorbed by the snobberies of the architecture students who regarded themselves as the most urbane group in Ithaca, bohemian and sophisticated, but elegant as well.

Michael had grown up in a small country town, a second-generation Italian-American whose immigrant grandfather had left New York City after years as a bricklayer for a better life as the owner of a small grocery store in upstate New York and then a prosperous bowling alley. His father worked for the state prison system, from which he retired last year when he turned sixty. There is a younger sister who is married, but Michael is the first to have entered a university.

David is the child of comfortable suburban middle-class Jews; he has a brother and sister. Michael sees his family only on holidays, and usually they argue; David is in touch with his family much more regularly, and his relationships are outwardly serene. Neither is explicit about his homosexuality or the relationship with his family, but it is clear to everyone that they are lovers. When they attend the weddings or bar mitzvahs of their families, they are treated as a couple.

Both men were always bookish, smart in school, and led relatively untraumatic lives until the dramatic upheavals in college, where values, ambitions, and sexual orientation were redefined.

Michael has never regarded himself as unattractive, but he has no great investment in his appearance, which he claims to be ordinary, "except maybe once or twice a month all pulled together, it's striking." He discovered the gay world during his freshman year. He was confused and excited when he understood that his feelings were the basis of a new identity rather than furtive impulse. A psychologist he consulted diagnosed his state as "homosexual panic" and advised treatment. Michael decided that therapy had little to tell him. He was not interested in women; "I'm a pure Kinsey Six," he says. His first sexual experience was somewhat typical of his boldness and naivete: he answered an ad in the *Advocate*. His respondent was a man in his forties who flew up from Baltimore to spend the weekend with him. Michael was not attracted to him, but he felt it was too late to back out and, determined to satisfy his curiosity, went to a motel anyway. The sex was perfunctory: he was blown, they slept in separate beds, and the man left the next day. Nothing else happened. Michael was not sure what else *should* happen, but he knew enough to judge the night as insufficient. Soon after, he met Stuart, who became his closest friend. Stuart was "gorgeous and rich," a clothes horse and a camp with whom Michael cruised the bars of Ithaca and sometimes Syracuse. He became a familiar in the bar circuit, he had a crowd of gay friends on campus, he was picking men up easily and often, and then he met Jonathan, a working-class man some ten years older. They had a brief affair; Jonathan drank too much but was experienced and flattering if not emotionally engaging.

When Michael met David through a mutual friend, he found him attractive but not overwhelming. David considered himself heterosexual, but he thought Michael would make an interesting friend. Michael found David "kind, good, and sweet" and began to court him gently. Gradually, they held hands on walks, slept together to cuddle and hug, and tentatively explored further. It was David who was ambivalent, but it was also David who initiated the first kiss. They saw themselves as close friends, but they were also very romantic about each other, "very turned on." It was intensely erotic and, compared to the behavior of their peers, entirely innocent. Sex progressed to frottage, but it was harder for Michael to be with David than with other men because his feelings were so intense. He was sure he was in love, but he also became avidly promiscuous.

For David, there were no other men, and he was unsure what his feelings were. Michael was his first homosexual experience as well as his first glimpse of gay life. He did not know what it meant to him; it might only have been some specific if peculiar feelings for Michael. He did not have a revelation about his sexuality: he was not curious about other men, and he continued to explore his feelings about women. Verbally, he remained noncommittal. In fact, not until four years later, when Michael moved into David's apartment in Brooklyn Heights, did David use the word *lover*; until then, he "preferred" Michael to others.

After David graduated, he went to Chapel Hill in North Carolina for his master's degree, while Michael dropped out of school temporarily and took a job in the university library in Ithaca. During their separation, the men wrote, but it seemed the relationship was waning. David found the change emotionally distancing; Michael had an affair.

At the end of the year, David decided that academia was a mistake: "the poverty of the academic environment, the dull library grinds" who were his typical fellow students showed him that be belonged elsewhere. He decided to go to New York to try his luck, and he wanted to resolve the "issue" of Michael, whom he began to see on weekends. Perhaps provoked by Michael's affair and clearly missing him, he finally asked him to come live with him in the city. Michael came almost at once. Since their separation, he had pursued David by letter and still assumed that it was only a question of time before David would come around. Michael wanted them both to be in love, in that unreasonable idealized devotion he has still not quite given up. David wanted to see what would happen to them if they lived together.

During their separation, David had written a novel with Michael as the central character, and as he became more involved with the character, he "incorporated" Michael into himself in a way that enabled him to discover that he wanted—and could have—Michael in his life. Until that discovery, David was not certain that he was gay. He had always wanted a romantic heterosexual affair, and when he had thought of love, he had thought of women. It took fully two years for David to conceive of himself as gay. He explains that he came out very late sexually with both women and men; he was twenty before he acted on any sexual impulse, and his courting days with Michael were counterpointed by passionate experiments with women.

Initially, living together only posed the usual problems of sudden familiarity. David is somewhat careless domestically; Michael is obsessively neat and clean. If David leaves five cookie crumbs on the coffee table, it is because he does not notice them; Michael notices that there are exactly five.

But their shared enthusiasm for New York, the discoveries of work, spending money, and most of all travel, made domestic friction seem trivial. David is a Francophile, and Paris is his favorite place. After their first year in New York, David took Michael to Europe for his first trip abroad. David paid for the trip; he had made more money during the year, and he wanted to show off the city he loved so much. It was a very romantic time, a belated honeymoon, yet it was in Paris that they began to dabble sexually with others. Together, they cruised the Tuileries, and one night David went home with someone. For both men, this was "okay." They had always said they had no pretenses about monogamy, "except as a discipline to get off a neurotic jag of casual sex."

Since then, casual sex has been constant, and David has grown to need it for reasons he calls emotional rather than just sexual. Michael had never really stopped the tearoom cruising that he began at Cornell. But a year ago, David met a man in a porno bookstore and began to see him regularly. Until then, tricking had meant one-night stands.

"It was a time in the relationship when I needed more attention and wasn't getting it, and I wanted to follow through on all my feelings." The relationship with Michael had gradually become tenser and more difficult and neither of them knew why. David dated the new man, who also had a lover, for a period of some months. During that time, the man's relationship with his lover fell apart while David began to sense a new domestic solidity. Initially, Michael was nonchalant, but as David continued to see his friend, Michael grew uneasy, sensing more than a dalliance if not yet a threat, despite David's argument that he felt less pressured and more committed. Michael asked David to end the dates; when he refused, Michael grew bitchy, so David stopped talking about it and Michael stopped asking questions. David thought that Michael should have an equally "mild" affair, that it would reduce the pressure on them, and that it would be vicariously exciting.

David likes the feedback from casual sex, the compliments on his skill as a lover, the ease with which he makes out. He does not feel it is much more than vanity, nor does he think his vanity dangerous to Michael or a great personal vulnerability. It really means little to him; what means more is fulfilling a sexual appetite that he now regards as larger than Michael's.

The open nature of their sexual lives has recently created the tiresome problem of venereal disease: David contracted amebiasis and gave it to Michael. Now, Michael no longer wants to perform those sexual acts which make him so vulnerable to David's promiscuity. In his own sexual forays, Michael is physically circumspect and sexual performance is limited to masturbation. The real excitement is the adventure of merging fantasy and real danger; the haste and the anonymity enthrall him; sexual action is secondary. Michael regards these adventures as "fooling around," another kind of leisure or sport, merely a part of his self-image that is peripheral to what is important in his life. Occasionally, he thinks that perhaps monogamy would alleviate some of the abrasiveness in their relationship; it would certainly simplify it. But he is not sure that their conflicts are really aggravated by dalliance, and, more realistically, he is sure that David would not accept a closed relationship. Nevertheless, he now insists that David at least be more discriminating, restraining himself in places and situations where he is likely to get diseased.

Midway through the interviews, Michael showed up for a session excited and angry. He and David had had a major quarrel, and Michael was filled with outrage, pain, and ultimatums. His lab tests confirmed that he had two kinds of amebiasis, both benign but needing treatment, while David had four different strains, one of which is dangerous to the liver. The medication for both of them is expensive—the first batch of pills came to fifty dollars—and since David originally contracted the disease, he has offered to pay all the expenses including the tests and the doctor's bills. Both men are particularly short of money at this time, and more discouraging is the news of reinfection.

"David seemed shocked about all this, and I tried to comfort him and give him sympathy when we left the doctor's office, but he refused—he wanted diversion, not compassion." Michael wanted them to go out for coffee and talk about their responses and their situation. David wanted to get back to work, where assignments had piled up. Michael knew that David was deeply upset but that comfort could be found in confronting their economic privation, their promiscuity, and their gratingly different responses to dilemmas. He felt that it was important to clear the air, to restore intimacy with talk, since they were forbidden to nurture it with sexual closeness. David told him that the effort was "bullshit," that Michael just wanted discussion to manipulate him, and that compassion was irrelevant and unnecessary. By the time they reached the office—Michael works part-time for David—the quarrel erupted into violence, and they were bashing each other about. Michael stormed out and cut their therapy appointment. He feels his anger is very just. They have not spoken to each other for four days.

The quarrel seems to have touched almost every aspect of their relationship: their sexual styles, their responses to illness, work, money, therapy, talk, change, even to intimacy and their ideas about the nature of love. Michael is adamant: "David has attributed bad motivation to me, and I want an apology. This hating is no game like ones we've played in the past. I won't make up; I always make up when David comes in and acts stupid, which means we should make up." The doctor has ordered complete abstinence for at least a month, so the pattern of hot anger leading to hot sex that once worked for them is impossible, and tricking, which let off much domestic steam, is equally unavailable. In terms of the intensity of anger and hardness of attitude, the quarrel is unusual. The misunderstanding about Michael's motives looms large.

"He has to subscribe to my terms about this, or I've reached the limit. He's just not in touch with himself. If he can't see or accept what I was offering, it may be hopeless." When I ask if he is really willing to break up if his terms are not met (not only an apology but a recognition by David of his own emotional evasiveness), he insists he is, even if he is not quite as ready as he is willing. The power of the animosity comes from the moral outrage about questioned goodwill and motivation, but it also draws on wounding issues about tenderness and their sexual contract. The casual sex they both talk of so offhandedly seems a sacrifice for David but not for Michael. Is he perhaps welcoming this respite while David is furious about it? Michael does not disagree, but he does not think he has hidden yearnings for monogamy.

"No. David must be less careless about the consequences. I wanted to comfort him, to fulfill that need, to help him acknowledge his feelings, despite the fact that he may not want to." As Michael goes over his anger, it begins to lessen and other feelings about the relationship color his argument. He enjoys the social "strokes" of being part of a couple, especially the peer approval of his "nice" relationship.

"But anyone else would have left David long ago, like when he said, 'Get lost, fuck off, get out, I'm looking for another lover—', but I believed he needed me. And I was right; who else would have put up with such shit?"

Michael's psychological analysis of David is quite sophisticated, although neither he nor I am sure he is right. David's unwillingness to accept comfort and his evasiveness about admitting it because he wanted to get back to the office seems a weak alibi: how can there be no time for intimacy at such a time?

"I guess I'm intimidated by David's difference," Michael confesses sadly. "My man is more complicated than anything Sartre has written about. It scares me that I don't understand him. I'm much easier about figuring out the world than I am about figuring out David." The reference to Sartre is not an allusion; it is an example of Michael's fondness for metaphysical speculation about himself and his life and the world, which he is as prone to dwell on as he is to psychologize about his lover. What he does not do unless prodded or reminded is dwell as carefully on his own psychology. His sessions are fulsome and interesting—he never stops talking—but one gets twice as much from David in half the time.

Michael worries at the end of this session about my response, which has been veiled, what little there is of it. Am I taking sides? I am naturally curious to hear David's version of this next week.

"There's so many benefits-of-the-doubt that I may not get when you write this," Michael says after he has assured me that he trusts me not to distort. Despite my sphinxlike neutrality, he has rightly sensed doubts, noticing that between the initial session and the present one, during which time I have seen David twice, my attitude has shifted not so imperceptibly. I am less patient, prone to suggest another version, another motive—in short, to defend David, who is far more often under attack than Michael is.

At first, I was disarmed by Michael's flattering openness, a forthright generosity frankly offered as a gesture toward friendship. But David is seductive; without seeming to care if he pleases, chary if not wary, and very clear about his irritation with questions or responses of mine that he finds presumptuous, he nevertheless has evoked more sympathy. Partly, David is cleverer. He does not attack much, and when he does, he describes some outrage of Michael's that undeniably speaks for itself. He is a good storyteller and does not moralize. And he is poised, taking for granted all the things Michael is socially unsure of.

When I replay the tape some hours later to take notes, my feelings shift dramatically. All my suspicions that Michael was overdifficult, touchy, too demanding, and intrusive toward David disappear. David has had my sympathy, but he has not earned it. I gave it to him because he is handsome and because he emits some erotic aura that works for him. I feel guilty about Michael and want to give him the benefit of my doubts. My struggle for patience with him is grounded on the recognition that he and I are much alike, while David and I have little in common, especially in terms of temperament. Oddly, that has worked for David and not for Michael, whatever that says about me.

The catalyst for this recognition is a memory of a parallel pain in my own former relationship with a lover. Early in my affair with R (not too early for deeply felt pledges and romantically optimistic promises of lifelong endurance), one such crisis arose for me, if not for him, in the same terms.

I met R the night before I flew to Miami to visit my mother on one of my semiannual jaunts. During that five-day stay, I learned (though she did not) that the anemia she was bothered with was Hodgkin's disease. Her doctor was my cousin, and he assured me that at seventy-three, with her heart history, she was as likely to die of a heart attack as of lymphatic cancer. The disease in the elderly progresses slowly; she might have two years, maybe more. When I returned to New York, the burden of this knowledge somehow made me more vulnerable than I ordinarily would have been, and I found I was quite unexpectedly falling in love with a man I did not know very well.

Three months later, R's mother, until then a hale and hearty woman in her seventies, had a stroke while playing golf. She lingered barely a month. The night of her death, R and I had just finished a romantic candlelit dinner in my apartment when the phone rang. It was a relative of R's in Cleveland to whom he had given my number as well as his own, since he was just as likely to be one place as the other. The other place was a deluxe apartment in Greenwich Village that he shared with his former lover of eighteen years in a relationship that was far from over or emotionally sedate. In fact, R had made clear that while we might be lovers the rest of our lives, his living arrangements were quite as decidedly settled. I had accepted that we would not live together: I was not sure it did not suit me better.

When I answered the call, I knew what it must be, though I thought with irony that R had just flown back from Ohio the day before. His grief was intense and violent. I understood everything; how could I not? I loved him now without reservations, and this was a foreshadowing of some future night when the telephone would ring long-distance from Florida. But he would not even pause in my arms, he had to return to be home with S; only there could he find whatever comfort he needed. It was hardly the time for a jealous scene, but more painful than jealousy was the revelation of my importance: my priority may have been high, but not that high. What I had to give was not enough, and that I wanted to give it so much was quite irrelevant.

At that moment of unbidden memory, I fully understood Michael and David and comforting one's lover. They had so much going for them, and yet they were so careless. But Michael was in pain; David avoided that inefficiency. In the long run, I suspect David will cope better with everything; he does already.

The source of strife between David and Michael is similar to what it is among most couples: the relation of work and ambitiousness to domestic life, the demands for and resistance to change, the enigma of intimacy, the fragility of reconciliation after anger, the ogre of anger itself. These men, like others who have undertaken to create a home in a bond of love, have psychically recreated the family in terms equivalent to those accepted by heterosexual couples. But such a relationship, unrecognized in law, unfettered and unsupported by children, rests on material much more volatile than, say, friendship. Not only do they live out the psychic past, sometimes as if in oracularly fated drama, but they are held together exclusively by convenience and desire. Love rests reliably on neither of those pillars. Michael and David have the added complication of a modern sexual arrangement, as well as the traditional tangles of contrary temperaments, different values concerning the importance of language to intimacy, indeed, quite different ideas about the nature of love altogether.

Sexual heat is fed by difference, but domestic tranquility requires concurrence. There is much they agree on, including the recognition that they need help from others, that in therapy may lie discoveries about the self to sustain their relationship. They are both ambitious about the same work, writing, and they share an immense excitement about the world of culture, especially literature and opera.

When David comes to our next session, he is charming and casual. I ask how things are going; I draw a blank. I do not want to push him, since he objects to intrusiveness, which is difficult to determine in an endeavor like this, so I ask if everything is all right, and he says yes. Finally, I am blunt: does that mean you and Michael have made up? Is the quarrel over?

"Oh, the fight," he says sheepishly with a sweet grin. "Erase the last tape. Everything's fine."

Well, everything may be back to normal, but I do not get David's version of the crisis. According to him, there was no crisis. David is not callous, nor is he unserious about the relationship. On the contrary, if anything, his demeanor is too serious. He does not laugh or smile often. There is a wary sexiness to his common exchanges that is unusual because he is truly not flirtatious. Perhaps it is a combination of his undeniable physicality and well-developed body, his general handsomeness, and a discreet aloofness and boyishness that create such an odd chemistry. He is one of those men who makes an immediately interesting impression; compactly built, on the short side, smooth-shaven and close-cropped, he presents an image of vigor contradicted by a somewhat languid manner. He responds rather than initiates, and after many hours with him, one senses his subtle control. He is intelligent rather than witty, and his mind seems always turning, and if not judging, visibly thinking. Those thoughts are not entirely to be had for the asking. For David, the quarrel, which he has reduced to a fight, is completely over because the anger between himself and Michael is gone. He says he hates anger, especially Michael's, and his tolerance of hostility is only slightly less.

"Michael says extreme, hurtful things when he's angry. I just shut off. He can reconcile five minutes later, but it takes me time to get over it." That reticence is a lifelong pattern that may once have been defensive or withholding but now seems very much his character. His outbursts are occasional, the result of Michael's goading.

"I want the allowance of being upset. I get into bad moods. I would like Michael to accept it, to allow it. I expect him not to make it worse. He gets resentful that I'm cutting myself off, and that gets me more anxious. I overcommit myself—to appointments, for example—and try to jam it all in, so I'm always fifteen minutes late, and Michael gets my brusqueness. He initiates reconciliation, and I succumb. But I don't like it. I'm slower to respond, to understand—emotionally, intellectually, chemically. We have an argument and suddenly he wants to be affectionate, and that becomes a confrontation. He doesn't allow me to hold onto my anger, and it gets submerged into annoyance, sulkiness. I feel my anger has been taken from me." David says that the real difference about this argument was that Michael did not even want to be civil afterward. They just functioned, very busy in their own schedules, without time to explore a reconciliation, so the emotional distance was protracted. But David did not find the coldness nearly as frightening as Michael's emotional intensity.

"When we reconciled, it wasn't sudden, and the time used to get over it was good." It took a series of little things—for example, shopping that had to be done together—to initiate civility, and from there they gradually returned to sweetness.

"It was 'I love you, I hate you, I love you, I hate you.'" He says the sudden switching from anger to affection makes him take Michael's responses less seriously, but this time he became angry himself with Michael's self-righteousness.

"Michael thought he was absolutely right, but he was *involved* and abdicating responsibility for his contribution to the tension." David admits that the amebiasis was a blow, compounded by the expense, but that he had the right to refuse to discuss it because he simply did not want to. He also admits that he is depressed by the prospect of giving up quick sex in porno stores and recognizes that he will have to restrict himself at least to one-to-one contacts; he can no longer risk being the fiftieth trick of the hour. He is upset by being sick, broke, and having put Michael in jeopardy, but the significance of the quarrel is that it has revealed how threatening the tension between them really is.

"I want things from Michael, some of which are unreasonable, and some of which are reasonable, but not from him." Separating those two sets of unfulfilled needs is important because the frustration with vagueness threads David's days. He knows he fears dependency (perhaps Michael's on him more than the other way around), and despite the unanswered needs, David resists the idea of change.

"I don't want to change in order to make room for him. I want him to be there. I want him to be more supportive and less nagging and sexually more open to me: more available and more responsive." That sounds reasonable, and it sounds like Michael's complaint. The arguments arise because the words mean different things to each of them. David wants Michael to end the friction which in fact is a demand for serious change. Nagging and sexual politics are always divisive, and everyone should object to being subjected to them. But what exactly is "nagging" between these two, and what is happening—or rather not happening—in the bedroom?

Nagging and sex, the kitchen and the bedroom, are ever the battlefields where intimacy struggles with the contempt of familiarity for its survival. David agrees with Michael that they are long past hot quarrels that lead to hot reconciliations. The issues that engage them and irritate them are really the same ones, and are nearer the surface than before, when a steadier passion submerged them. David thinks that Michael does not take him seriously as a person in the world, and sometimes he does not take himself seriously at home. Both objections are painful, although they do not mean the same thing. David's place in the world is so far undetermined, although it would seem proper to expect one's lover to care about what it is becoming. However, such sympathy is negotiable; for some it may be necessary for love, for others, a luxury. But home is another story, not negotiable at all.

"Sometimes if I don't want to have sex, Michael will persist and that makes me angry. He'll arouse me—it isn't difficult—but I'd rather he didn't. It gets us into a pattern where I get coy and leave the initiative to him, just signaling when I'm available, and while it's better than it was, sexual action means different things to each of us. It's very exciting, and Michael certainly takes me seriously there, but I'm not clear if sex with Michael is as varied and full as I'd like. I don't know if that has anything to do with my outside sex either." David does not trace the anger of these occasions to Michael's wilfullness or to his disbelief in David's preference for not having sex, nor is it at all clear to what degree his own easy arousal is fuel for that anger, but the questions are left behind the less complex discomfort of responding with inappropriate coyness and the sense that their sexual lives with each other are not all they should be.

Michael agrees that David is more erotically innovative, that he himself would keep to the same sexual routine. For him, the event of sexuality is more important than sexual action even with his lover. Before their present work schedules, lovemaking was erratic, in the morning, afternoon, or anytime, and its very unpredictability was a kind of variety. Now it happens at night when they get into bed. Michael misses the spontaneity, but it cannot be helped. He emphasizes instead how natural it feels to be physically close to David, to be in touch with him, how they seem literally to fit together: their bodies, their mouths, their chemistry.

"We used to fuck a lot, but David got anal warts so we stopped. Like we stopped rimming after the first bout of amebiasis. I also am not into blowing David right now; it's not a health issue like the others are, it's more complicated: something is going on, and I can't get into it." The frequency of lovemaking has also diminished to an average of once a week even when they are not contagious, but Michael insists that neither the quantity of sexual contact nor the use of specific sexual techniques is important. He feels he is versatile enough, and he is willing to try anything David wants, since he is the one who *needs* change or variety—"doing it this way, that way, in the bathroom, with the mirror," he says somewhat patronizingly. For him, even when the action is most static (as in their fondness for mutual masturbation, which was their earliest satisfactory way of making love), it is the long romantic foreplay and the deep kissing that are more important. Michael knows that he can seduce David, who is "always erect," but he does not really see it as seduction, still less coercion. Rather, their involvement with sexuality differs more importantly then their capacities. David is easier to arouse, but Michael is the one blessed with easy orgasm, who can come whenever he wants to and who can feel satisfied even without orgasm. David is less predictable. For him, orgasm is necessary to defuse the sexuality, and he is frustrated without it. Michael likes to remain aroused and psychologically excited. He says somewhat judgmentally that David needs orgasm more to end sex than to fulfill it. Despite such differences, both agree that sex itself is the least of their problems. Their sexual selves are still evolving; they can go in any direction, and between them there is a genuine flexibility about new ideas and feelings to nurture their mutual erotic life. Even when sex is awkward or unsatisfactory, that does not loom large, nor have they wanted to repair to drugs, which neither uses (although David admits that he recently tried poppers with a number, but only for the novelty).

Michael laughs when he says that he used to think that words were forbidden, that you had to intuit everything or you were a failure. Now he believes that sexual communication is something that they have just begun to master. They rarely have postmortems or ask for what they want during sex, but Michael thinks it might be a good thing to try. Only recently has he discovered a darker side to his own sexual feelings, and he wonders if they will appear in his life with David.

"I came out gay and proud. Stonewall and the GAU [the Gay Academic Union] at Cornell and all that were perfectly okay. But recently I've had fantasies where shame or humiliation seem exotic. It's my own suppressed homophobia coming out." He clarifies that to mean sexual guilt, and this darker excitement he acts out mostly in anonymous sex with third-world men, preferably young Puerto Ricans. He is only now beginning to remember how sexual shame shadowed his adolescence, which was forgotten in the liberated days at Cornell. Now those memories are erotic fodder. David has no such legacy. He is not inhibited by gayness because he grew up thinking he was heterosexual. It took two years for him to decide that he was really homosexual, and then coming to terms with it was not difficult, intellectually or emotionally.

One difference in the value of sexual experience for them lies in how it is used: sex as reconciliation was unsatisfactory for David; the heat borrowed from arguments siphoned out the energy in the anger but did not resolve it. During the last quarrel when they did not talk for four days, the reconciliation was finally *real:* "I didn't have to carry the anger around any more."

As with so many other couples, large areas of the sexual landscape are unexplored. For both men, to ask for something sexual is an act loaded with uncomfortable overtones of sexual politics. Instead, they feel that what they decide to do is negotiable, and recently in couple therapy, even discussable. If they are too far apart in what they want, they do not have sex and they are not resentful; if they want sex, they find a common ground. They assume their sexual responses are protean. David says he always assumed that it was natural to be sexually flexible, to take any role, try out new notions.

"That's the way I am. I took it for granted, I was always that way. I didn't have to learn anything. When I meet people who are into something very specific, I don't find that odd—just restricted." David makes an important distinction about himself and Michael when he says, slowly and intensely, that he can feel more secure and loved more deeply in sexual than in nonsexual situations.

"I am more comfortable with being dependent, with acknowledging difference and imbalance and hierarchy in bed than outside it. If Michael is dominant or I'm submissive, it doesn't scare me sexually, but it does in the kitchen or at a party. I rarely need to reverse the need, to dominate Michael in bed, but I often have the need outside the bedroom. Sex is the least verbal or intellectual thing I do, and it is there that I am somehow expressive in a profoundly different way." He welcomes the diffusion of consciousness in sexuality.

When I ask about the nature of that intensity—whether he loses focus on Michael as a person, does it alter his usual sense of self, and is that a loss or a gain? does he pursue a surrender to his own pleasure? when Michael is lost in his pleasure, is that regarded as some achievement he's helped to create, or does he feel blotted out?—David says those are not his choices. He doesn't experience the difference between cock in his mouth and Michael's cock in his mouth. When the "you" and the "me" disappear and the egos are temporarily obliterated, sometimes that's wonderful, but it's not necessary.

"That's making love, but it's not love. When it's a verb, when 'I love,' that's a definite me and other person. All that depends on trust." For him, only in making love with Michael is there that fallout of tenderness, that afterglow. With strangers, something like it appears to happen, but it is really a memory of it, a nostalgia of tenderness.

I think David's distinctions are very appropriate if somewhat evasive, but it is hard to return to the questions I want answered about self-consciousness and nonconsciousness, for which there are no definitions and about which words have been so inadequate except in the mouths of poets. But neither David nor I am poetic, and I sense this is the limit beyond which he will not go.

It was not sexual matters that brought the men to couple therapy a year ago; it was debilitating tensions in their daily life, bickering and irritation. They had already agreed that if they were breaking up, it was not because of other men but because of something between them. They considered a trial separation. Both were seriously depressed and began to talk of looking for new apartments. David decided if he could afford to live by himself, he could certainly afford therapy. If they were going to split, it should be amicably, without ugliness. He says that whatever he seeks outside the relationship, it is not really another lover.

But in certain areas he simply does not understand what troubles Michael; intellectually he can accept what Michael says, but emotionally it does not make sense. For example, Michael has an acute sense of smell. When they were traveling in France, they arrived exhausted in Arles late one night, and it was difficult to find a hotel room. They finally did, and even before they unpacked, Michael complained of a smell, a dankness that suggested the sewer, and he wanted to leave. For David it was more important to have a room they could afford for the night; besides, he did not detect the odor, nor, he insists, would most people. Michael agreed to stay, coerced by the issue of money, since the trip was largely paid for by David, but he was upset that David could not understand what bothered him.

Taking each other seriously is rivaled only by money as the most popular occasion for argument. Money is always complicated in its connections, and its ties to work, domestic life, dominance, and nurture are not exceptional here. Like other relationships where the earning power of the two people differs widely and where money is short and tastes are expensive, with David and Michael money expresses many less tangible issues. If they had more money, some of the tension would be alleviated, fuzzed over but left unresolved.

When they returned from their last trip to Europe, Michael decided that he did not want to work full-time; he wanted time to write, and he wanted David to help him by paying more than half of the household expenses. David says he was badgered into the agreement.

"I paid, but I resented it. Michael retaliated by buying a $200 raincoat and lying about the price—he said he paid $130—but he left his checkbook open on the desk so I couldn't miss it." David resolved the problem by deciding to work free-lance himself. Once he left his regular job, the budget was again divided fifty-fifty. David thinks it is much better this way. When he paid the larger share of the expenses, he could not help judging Michael as extravagant, nor did he like the position of being the generous one. Around this time, their relationship grew worse and finally forced them into therapy. David is sympathetic to Michael's need for time to write, but he thinks there is more to it than that.

"After a wonderful trip to Europe, when we returned Michael just wouldn't look for work. He procrastinated and the money situation worsened, and I got more hostile. I felt so much that I was being ripped off, taken advantage of, and the more I pressured, the less he responded. It's not a question of whether I need the money; it's a question of Michael's sense of responsibility. If I lay out for ballet tickets and he doesn't pay me back for months, it then becomes something else besides my being generous. Michael must be responsible enough to try to pay me back as soon as he can. I don't want him to depend on me that way."

Michael disagrees strongly about the accusation. He wants lovely things; David wants his meal on the table.

"David wants Armani shirts for himself, and that's really why he's so moralistic about money. I don't have anything after I pay for half the household expenses, except money for carfare and lunches. He should treat me to the ballet because I can't afford it and because I can't say no when he asks me three weeks in advance if I want to go. I admit I have a fuzzy conception of finances. I say yes to the ballet because I can't remember that in three weeks some bill I'm in debt for will be due."

They were planning a trip to Peru, but David, who was to pay for it, discovered he had underestimated his self-employment taxes, and now the trip looks very dubious. They had been very eager to travel again because they both love it so much and because their trips have always been successful: exciting, romantic, healing. For such an occasion, David does not mind paying more than his share, nor does he feel Michael's extravagance or irresponsibility is relevant.

Michael does not understand his own extreme disappointment about the trip; it is as if some solemn promise had been broken, and the disappointment resonates with childhood memories. He senses that his reaction is deeply colored by the past and by some troubling mysterious presence of his father, which he is exploring in therapy. He wants David to deal with his own father in the same way, to try to discover how his past and his family figure into his attitude about money.

"If I ask for money, I want greenbacks, not a whole psycho-complex. I want us to talk about money in the same way. I think it's completely inadequate when the therapist suggests that I use money as a request for nurturing. When I want nurturing, I mean a lot more than money. Oh, it can mean generosity. David can be very generous. He celebrates my birthday that way, and he's very imaginative about it. Last year, he bought me a gift for every sense: oatmeal soap for smell, Eliot Porter's book of photographs of Antarctica, a place we both want to see, a recording of *Don Giovanni*, some French wafers we loved when we were over there as well as a splendid cake from a fancy patisserie, and a cock ring for touch. So when he wants to, money isn't just a budget issue. When I discover that maybe it's my father operating somewhere in there, I want the right to say to David that maybe it's his father too."

David challenges the right to speak about it, and they are soon in a quarrel.

"I want to say anything and everything I want to," Michael insists. "And I don't want it to be threatening. I expect a shared language where I can say anything I want. That has been and is my expectation."

I suggest, thinking of my own relationships, that it is an extraordinary expectation and no insignificant demand. Michael thinks my reaction is novel and asks me if he is responsible for his thoughts. I then see that Michael expects to be able to say anything he's *thinking*, another matter entirely. Of course he is not "responsible" for thoughts, but he certainly is responsible for censoring them. He is genuinely surprised by my observation that I know of no relationship that allows one person to *say* everything he thinks. Later, he speculates that there might be an aggressive edge to his psychological probing, for David has complained how hurtful it is. David is not interested in the psychological like Michael, who cannot come to terms with that difference and is unable to accept it. He even sees his unwillingness to compromise as good, as he sees that same unwillingness at work in the world or in his social life as ennobling, perhaps heroic. It is part of his sense that he is right, that his metaphysical and psychological interests validate his sternness. He does not believe that David's feelings about money are characterological, that he is selfish, preferring fancy clothes to his lover's need for time to write. If that were so, he would leave him.

"So it must be personal, some psychodrama of subconscious reasons—like his father, for example—and he has to try to get in touch with that and change."

This subject of talking, of what Michael calls repeatedly "a common language," relates to much more than money. It is the touchstone upon which are grounded notions of decorum, of privacy and familiarity, of what love entitles one to and what it does not. Most of all, it is used by Michael as the argument for change. When it is, David grows more resistant than usual.

"I have accepted Michael for what he is; it's enough for me. There's no need to leave. But he is still interested in changing me in particular ways, some of which I can't be and some of which I don't want to be. I admit he may be more sensitive to things like smells or how the apartment looks, but then he gets angry with me when I don't share his sensitivity. I usually give in on aesthetic issues. I have input, but the apartment basically reflects his taste, his very definite ideas. We bought a red bedspread that Michael wanted and I agreed to. Two weeks later, he changed his mind, it was a mistake. I tried to convince him it wasn't, or to live with it, but the spread ended up in the closet." Michael has more authority about things mostly because they matter more to him. David is sensitive but not particular; he is not very observant about the visual.

"Michael is much more spiritual, concerned with issues of philosophy, his existence in the world. I just do it. A lot of questions that are important to him are irrelevant to me." David is agnostic, but he does not mean that the question of meaning is irrelevant to his life; he thinks his life *is* meaningful, that the question is answered every day, and that his life is a good one.

Michael has no such assurance. He deeply fears death and is appalled that David does not worry about what is going to happen to him when he dies, that David will not take the fears seriously, and thinks he is really defensive about the matter. Michael's fears are partly Catholic, partly Freudian, and mostly his own. Sometimes ideas like the tortures of Hell worry him, and he feels lonely when he cannot discuss that with David, who at best tolerates Michael's anxiety. If David had his own system of belief, it would be easier for Michael to accept. Michael does not see himself as old-fashioned or religious in the conventional sense, but he is concerned with ideas of good and evil, of morality.

"I'm scared that it's a whole plane where we don't exist for each other. I need to communicate my fears to David, to discuss them, but he's just not interested. If I wake up in the middle of the night or if I can't sleep, David says not to wake him up unless it's panic. I'm too needy and he's too withholding."

When I suggest that sleep disturbance is no minor matter, that people can be irrational about it and that perhaps it is a demand that David can't handle, Michael clarifies the anxiety about death that comes to him before sleep or in the middle of the night, the images of coldness, distance, deprivation, oblivion. David's refusal to listen makes him lonelier than ever. He needs to discuss his ideas before the anxiety will dissipate. Are they ideas or are they feelings he is talking about? Michael says he confuses the two, but I am quibbling. After a pause, he concedes that sometimes David understands, sometimes "he allows it."

In therapy, Michael is beginning to accept the idea that a lover is less available for many things that he thought he needed and that he may have to turn inward for comforts David calls unreasonable claims. Michael has begun to look elsewhere for the intellectual rapport missing at home. He has initiated an informal discussion group of gay men who meet weekly to discuss serious subjects about which they try to be more than merely clever or chatty. They present papers to each other and regard their sessions as seminars. Michael knows he risks looking fanatic about spiritual questions, but that is less potentially wounding than it would be with David. And they are a companionable group who are not at all somber. Occasionally, they call themselves "The Society for the Previously Butch" and meet for a pajama party to gossip about sex, clothes, and the best facials.

He is also coming to terms with David's lousy housekeeping. He has decided to clean "quietly," to do most of the work himself because he likes to do it and it only meets his expectations when he does it himself. For example, on the anniversary of their eighth year together, a Sunday, they began the day with a thorough housecleaning. When Michael inspected the bathroom sink, he showed David that it was nowhere near his idea of clean, which meant using elbow grease and Comet to scrub out the stains, as he proceeded to demonstrate. Ten minutes later when he found David scrubbing Comet into the enamel refrigerator door, he was exasperated. He does not swear that David unconsciously fucked up the job so that he would not be expected to do it again, but he strongly suspects it. After eight years he believes his intuitions about David are true. They fought anyway. The spat was over by dinnertime, but Michael thought it would be nicer to stay home and bring in Chinese food, which they both love, although they had done that the night before. David wanted to go out to a fancy restaurant. Every other anniversary they had had reservations at restaurants, but ended up fighting instead; this year they had done the quarreling early. Over expensive French food, they acknowledged their intractability, the strong contrast of David's efficiency, orientation, and drive with Michael's dreaminess, his artistic nature. They reaffirmed that they love each other but also understood that it would not immediately help in the next argument.

After eight years of demands and capitulations, David seems to have called a halt to it. Perhaps when Michael stopped working, he decided to stop capitulating. Michael knows he has to be more patient and tolerant, but he does not know how. Since couple therapy began, words like *power*, *masculinity*, and *competitiveness* have entered their vocabulary when they discuss themselves. Before, Michael was more prone to think of the relationship as a marriage rather than as two men bound together; now he is beginning to wonder how other men talk of their relationships and what terms they use.

He still thinks a lover is someone who takes care of you, your closest friend, an uncritical and supportive reader of your work, someone you often share dinner with, and, most of all, someone you sleep with every night, "snuggling up like kittens." He already seems to have most of that. After a depressing therapy session, they drew up a list, half-jokingly, of what they agreed and disagreed about. One side read: the cat, Chinese food, oatmeal cookies, travel and France, Henry James, the opera. The other side was shorter: cleaning the house, money, the nature of love. On the cusp was "sex."

Michael can tolerate longer periods without sexual heat as long as there is cuddling, represented on the list by the cat, their gorgeous shy tomcat who is the symbol of their domestic life together and whom they adopted when they were still at Cornell. And they both are sustained by parallel if not mutual interests in the world of culture (Henry James and the opera), where they mean to realize their ambitions. They have hearty appetites for pleasure that each other's company enhances, and they have found an untroubled way to realize their need for warmth and closeness in their nightly intimacy.

With so much, David is less troubled about the future, but that is partly because he has less invested in love than Michael. A large share of his sense of well-being comes from achievement and recognition. If he has a sense of "incompleteness" at home, he can live with it because what he gets is enough.

"Overall, that'll continue to be true: I'm getting more good out of it than bad." He sounds phlegmatic when he is reflective, talking soberly about how fragile the sense of closeness is, how ephemeral that connectedness, and I glimpse in his opacity what keeps Michael off balance. "It's not that I need to get away from closeness as Michael says I do, but what I need to acknowledge and accept and learn to be comfortable with." For him, the closeness in bed, filial or passionate, is often sufficient. He does not envy other couples whose relationships are less "fluid, provocative, or developing." He would like to learn how to tolerate tension better. Compared to last year, when they thought they were at the breaking point, he sees them now as at a much more positive, if quarrelsome, stage. The confusion remains about what he has to offer, what he wants, and how much these intersect.

"I'm *beginning* to understand what he wants from me, and I'm not sure whether I want to or can give them, or whether the person I am right now can." In the rhetoric of therapy, Michael wants more attention, more energy invested in their relationship, more consistence: simply, he wants David not to pull away.

"I do and don't do all those things. Sometimes, I think I'd prefer a less intense relationship, fewer highs for fewer lows; more of a partnership with fewer confrontations and more tranquility." He wonders if it is not more valid, more suitable to have more separate sexual and emotional lives than Michael visualizes for them. It is not that responsiveness and feeling are not the bedrock of their living together, but a question of degree: to what degree is his resistance to more intense commitment neurotic stubbornness rather than adult recognition and honest appraisal of limitation? He hopes therapy will help them evolve an answer that will satisfy Michael and let him recover the parts of himself he feels he has given up in order to be Michael's lover.

"I want Michael to love me unconditionally, and he doesn't. I always have perceived criticism as aggressive, an attack or threat, and from Michael it's worse. If I leave crumbs, I want to feel he loves me anyway, and then I can *listen* to him and be motivated not to leave crumbs. Once there's a threat, I don't hear the content; I only hear Michael kvetching." It is not clear whether Michael really threatens to withdraw love or whether David's feeling is defensive. On the day-to-day level, he is more conflicted about himself, more vulnerable and "neurotic" than Michael, who at some other level is much more seriously in pain. He says he takes Michael's anxiety seriously, but not the issues he is anxious about. In contrast, he does not think Michael takes seriously how much of David he demands be left outside.

"Right now, to be me is to be refused by Michael. A lot of his intensity and brilliance frightens and intimidates me. It's hard for me to be proud of it when it swamps me and I feel lessened by it." For him there is an important difference between the demand that he take God seriously (which he can dismiss) and Michael's being frighteningly intense about it (which he cannot). Much more personal, and therefore important, to him is that Michael allow him to handle anger his own way, to express his own taste even if it is less well developed, to be less demonstrative and calmer, to let his intuitiveness count, if only second, to Michael's intellectuality. He wants therapy to help them both define the boundaries of self. Michael places David inside himself too often, asking and answering what he is really thinking and feeling. David cannot decide if it is empathy or hostility when Michael tells him what he himself is *really* thinking.

"He's not speaking *to* me, but *for* me, so he's really talking to himself. Whether he's right or wrong, I feel unnecessary and resent what's happening. I turn it all off. He's playing both parts, so why bother? I can't stop him from imagining what's going on inside of me. I say my motive is X and he says it's really Y, but I don't know it." Michael agrees he does this, but he also says that he knows David better than he knows himself.

David does not know how to cope with that, how to stop Michael from acting on his intuitions. It is an oddity, and I wonder if these days it is a problem more peculiar to homosexual than heterosexual couples. It was conventional for women to say to their husbands that they knew them better than they knew themselves, but what heterosexual couple, each twenty-nine years old in 1980, would presume that now? What straight man would dare say he really knows better than his lover or wife what she is really thinking and feeling?

It seems more than a lack of decorum, more than merely the price of long familiarity. In the novels of Henry James that both men so admire, it would be a major moral issue. When David visits Michael's parents upstate at Christmas or Thanksgiving and he is told not to be effusive with them, when Michael offhandedly tells him to shut up or not talk too much or be more discreet in his demeanor, Michael does not think he is being offensive, despite the fact that David is indeed well liked by these relatives. What Michael considers moral is not manners, not even behavior, but a system of values and the strong rapport he needs so much.

For Michael, it is partly the vocabulary, for it is always a matter of words. Words are his world; he loves their power and importance, he describes how their "resonance" is overwhelming, yet when he is forced to pin this down, those words become a "cloud." He has less surety with David than anywhere else in his life, and he is less sure of his judgments about David when he talks of them with me.

At our final taping, Michael tells me that he has felt younger, more naive with me than anywhere else, playing the ingenue, the "twitching adolescent." On his good days, despite being nearly thirty, he looks somewhat adolescent, his clothes so casual, his pockets barely holding more than carfare, the perpetual student in the elegant funky tie. That image is supported by his ambivalent status in the workaday world. His part-time job requires sophisticated skills, but he does not take it or the skills seriously; they are commercial, like David's work. His journal entries are serious work, such as his ruminative piece about the meaning of recitative in opera, what is behind the convention when the trio, for example, turns to the audience to sing. He thinks his ideas are brilliant, but he makes no attempt to publish them. He has not really connected his confidence in his own brilliance with success. "Someday perhaps," he says; meanwhile, he is singularly unambitious.

David is very ambitious. He now thinks of himself as a professional writer. He is very efficient; he writes clearly, in a straightforward, very structured manner. He begins slowly, letting the ideas gestate in his head, and as deadlines approach, he does a first outline, a revision, a detailed version, a first draft, and a final draft.

The men used to show each other their work, but criticism was hurtful.

David no longer shows Michael work in progress, and sometimes Michael does not even read what David writes after it is published. That used to be annoying, but it no longer is. The world's recognition of his professionalism has inured David to Michael's disdain of "commercial stuff," although since he has been forced to do some of that himself, he is now a bit more respectful.

David's ambitions are not grandiose. He wants enough money to travel, to buy the clothes he loves, to lead a nice, bourgeois life. He wants recognition, not fame; he has no dreams of going on the Johnny Carson show. He wants people to acknowledge and respect him as a critical voice in the performing arts; being a writer is not a state of mind for him the way Michael conceives it. Michael is often not sympathetic about David's professional disappointments and his depression about them. When an article he wrote on speculation for the *New York Times* was rejected, he felt crushed, but Michael tried to minimize it. In contrast, his friend Fred was immediately constructive, suggesting other places to send the piece (to *Christopher Street,* as it happens, which eventually printed it).

When I ask them about their future, whether they can envision themselves alone, Michael says he can, but the image is melodramatic and self-pitying. He has told David that, whatever happens, David is his last lover, that he does not want more from someone *else.* He certainly could not accept less, and he does not know if he can be different. The man whose words are so fulsome and often so expressive, half-jokingly and half-seriously asks for compassion "for poor me, locked in my feelings, burbling out that cloud of words."

David muses that people not in relationships have such misguided notions about what relationships are for. Now, more than ever before, he can acknowledge that he loves Michael, that he is more deeply in love than he has ever been.

"I don't predict, but we'll be together a long time. Despite the flux, it'll abide."

## The Male Southern Belle

*I have changed almost all the names, even though it should not matter any more. But there are those in the South who could not deal with homosexuality then and apparently still cannot fathom it today.*

*L*ake-tripping one night, we took Runaway's battered VW deep into the sharp, craggy hills just north of Tuscaloosa, where large reservoirs and deep lakes have been created by man-made dams. In good weather, Runaway invariably insisted we go there to skinny-dip. Earlier that night, Richard Weaver, the brilliant, young, straight poet, had thrown a party in the back yard of his Tuscaloosa house. Runaway and I had gotten wired out and needed the lakes to unwind.

I'd met Runaway a year before at a large party thrown for his twenty-first birthday. I had heard of him, this guy who had been a star athlete in high school, a halfback who sprinted for touchdowns with such deceptive speed and agility his coaches and teammates dubbed him Runaway, and I had no trouble identifying him the moment I walked into the crowded room. Barefoot, wearing cutoff jeans and a faded, torn polo shirt, he was an unkempt mess of boyish arrogance, the center of attention. His long dark hair fell in curls about his forehead as he perched in a highbacked chair, a joint in one hand, a beer in the other.

I said, "You must be Runaway."

He lifted his head and grinned. I gave him a bottle of champagne I'd bought to give someone else. He examined it carefully, but his blue eyes were drugged to impassivity. Then suddenly he came to life and said something I could never have anticipated—a move as adroit and skillfully disarming as any he might have made on the playing field.

"Thanks, man. Want to have a duel with Roman candles?"

We had our duel, just as we were to do everything else Runaway suggested, and always at the frantic pace he set. He moved me into his tight, straight clique with that same awesome speed. I loved him at once, but from a safe distance. And that distance remained intact until the night of Weaver's party.

Runaway and I sat beside each other, atop a wooden table in the yard. I felt him stir beside me, pat his bare feet on the table, ready to bolt. He was exhausted from the strain of hiding his shyness around men and women who were already legends within the region.

Throughout the evening, I had watched an almost stately procession of friends I had known for years. Most of us had been white Southern radicals, veterans of the civil rights movement, committed outsiders in our homeland. We were bound to one another by years spent on the battlefields of Dixie—the stinging dust of day-long marches, the sweltering heat of rural Alabama summer nights in black churches where we sang our hymns of freedom, the long lines in which we walked as if dazed behind mule-drawn wagons bearing the coffins of too many friends.

To Runaway and his clique, our work in the late sixties and early seventies might as well have been on another planet. While we invested our days in marathon political-strategy sessions and gave our evenings over to bleary, beer-soaked escapism in Tuscaloosa's radical Chukker Bar, Runaway devoted *his* idle mornings to hallucinogenic mushrooms and his evenings to *mano a mano* duels with Roman candles. The immediacy of our protest was to him only a curious historical abstraction, far less dangerous than the Roman-candle flares that disintegrated seconds before they could explode across our faces.

Now as I felt him fidget beside me I said, "It's up to you and the others."

Runaway said, "I don't want to get drunk here. Beat me at pinball and I'll buy you a beer."

We left the party and made a pit-stop at the house to load the car with beer and collect our supply of grass and pills. Runaway immediately shotgunned two joints, leaving us gagging, stoned.

They were handsome young men: Runaway perpetually unkempt, as if deliberately to distract attention from his boyish beauty; Wellington IV tall and languid with lazy, long hair and deep-set brown eyes; Phillip in a navy crew sweater and penny loafers, his face constantly animated by a steady stream of questions about the consequences of total nuclear war.

Coughing from the overkill of Runaway's two joints, we bounded from the house and made for the Chukker Bar. Runaway liked to go there because, he said, the spirit of its defiant years still prevailed. To some extent he was right. The clientele had not really changed, just grown older. Each time we went to the bar, Runaway or someone else asked me to recount in exact detail the nights I had been one of those who went wild in the Chukker.

Phillip and Wellington IV flipped coins to see who would buy the first round. Runaway and I joined in the toss. Runaway lost, and he scowled as he reached into the empty pockets of his ragged jeans, until Phillip loaned him the beer money that he would never repay.

Runaway said, "The pinball machines weren't here back then, were they?"

My machine lit up: TILT.

I said, "You just cost me a bonus game."

Runaway gave me a smile of exuberant tease. Then he rang up bonus games. Laughing, he danced a barefoot shuffle to the music of the pinball-machine bells.

Runaway said, "Got you. Buy the beer."

Wellington IV said, "Why don't you look around first?"

A guy with hair bleached to an orange tint sat like an orangutan on a table behind us. He wore an ill-fitting tank top, overalls, and dimestore flip-flops. I recognized him as a Chukker regular, a harmless although ex-

tremely vain and excessively effeminate male Southern belle. Another guy
stood beside him and addressed him by a woman's name. They appeared to
be talking amicably, making their usual loud, high-pitched observations
about the sexual availability of the straight "trade" at the pinball machines
and pool tables. Then suddenly they were yelling, "You cunt!" and "Dirty
bitch!" at each other. I braced myself to face a hair-pulling, eye-scratching,
kicking-and-screaming cat fight. It was a scene I especially did not want
Runaway or the boys to witness.

Such cat fights had taken place before in the Chukker. These Southern
bar queens were taking out their frustrations, the petty jealousies and ri-
valries of living together in a small, repressive town, on one another. But
each time they chose to behave in public like the spoiled Southern women
they unsuccessfully imitated, they exposed all Southern gay males to ridicule and derision.

We did not play any more pinball. For a few moments we watched the
fight, which fortunately remained only a screaming match. But Runaway
appeared rattled. He tucked himself tightly against my shoulder, pressed
against me as if he were afraid.

Runaway said, "The lakes."

We left in a hurry. Inside the car, Wellington IV tore open cans of beer
and Phillip dispensed marijuana and pills.

Runaway said, "Any particular lake?"

Phillip said, "Drive, man. Who cares?"

As he drove, Runaway stared ahead as if transfixed by the pavement.
We were frequently on the wrong side of the road, but it was late and the
Tuscaloosa streets were deserted. No one in the car mentioned the scene in
the bar. As we sped through town, the late-night quiet of the city was broken by intermittent explosions from the VW's engine.

I felt as if I were riding in a car without a windshield and the lawns and
houses of Tuscaloosa were being thrown up before me on a giant screen.
We made our way through the campus of the University of Alabama, past
the neocolonial apartment complex where Susan and I lived when we were
students, and turned onto the long, open stretch of highway that would
take us across the Warrior River to the lakes.

We crossed the high river bridge. Below, a tugboat pushed barges
downstream, its steering light flashing from riverbank to riverbank, its
pilot holding the boat and barges in center stream. Runaway flipped
the car's high beams on and off several times. The tug pilot responded
with a low, rumbling blast from the boat's whistle that shook the night.
Phillip and Wellington cheered from the back seat and popped open
beers. I leaned out of the car window as the river and the city lights disappeared behind us and we made, relentlessly, for the craggy molehills
and lakes.

Sitting beside Runaway in the VW, I thought about those flailing
queens who had erupted in the bar. I was a gay man in a region that historically allowed only one category of gay males, effeminate queens, and reduced those to the most wretched life-style imaginable—the second-class
citizenship of the male Southern belle.

It was a life-style I had never accepted for myself. I had gone to desperate, often haughty lengths not only to avoid it but to spurn those who did not. I had spent a year loving Runaway from a distance because I did not want to influence his decision whether to be gay in the South. If he made that decision, I wasn't sure he had the stamina to retain his masculinity, his innocence, his persona, to survive in the South as a gay male rather than a male Southern belle. Runaway's innocence deserved a better option.

Runaway cackled now as he drove the VW. He pounded the steering wheel with the palms of his hands and sang a repetitive ditty he had made up about "this black stinking hole of Alabama."

From the back seat, Wellington yelled, "Slow down before you waste us."

It was too late. I had already seen the blind turn Runaway had missed. He hit the brakes, and the VW skidded, throbbed and thudded as if all four tires had blown. I watched a solid wall of trees coming toward me and figured there was probably no quicker, happier way to go. Then the trees stopped. There was a slurp-gulp sound beneath us. We were thrown forward, then rocked back. The car started to sink. I was climbing out of the window, prepared to swim, when the VW came gently to rest.

Phillip said, in a mock whisper, "What'd we hit this time?"

Runaway screamed, joyously, "We're back in the mud flat."

Phillip said, "He never misses. The only mud flat between Tuscaloosa and Birmingham, and Runaway always hits it."

I said, "You bastard. You planned this all along."

We left the car. The mud was over my ankles, swallowing my shoes. Phillip made it to hard ground, not forgetting to bring the beer. He was dancing there, giggling.

Runaway took two sleeping bags from the trunk of the car. Wellington and Phillip sauntered down the road, walking toward town.

I said, "Where the hell are they going?"

Runaway said, "To call Charlie, the wrecker-man."

"But it's after three in the morning."

"Doesn't make any difference to the wrecker-man."

"The whole world has gone crazy."

"Every time I hit the mud flat, Charlie asks me to ball his wife while he watches."

Runaway left the pavement and climbed a hill. I followed. I did not tell him I had been here before. Not to this place, the short hill we climbed. Not to the spot where we spread the sleeping bags and undressed in the now-chilling night air. But I had been here before, all across Dixie, along a hundred obscure Southern highways, trying to find a place where men could love one another in a region that denies them that love.

I remember little more than the whispers, the caresses and kisses, and our skeletal-white bodies against the darkness. There was a great expanse of territory on the sleeping bags, and we used every inch of it. Then we held each other and listened to the spitting, whining wrecker speeding along the road to pull the VW out of Runaway's favorite quagmire.

Runaway said, "I never do."

I said, "Do what?"

"Screw his ugly wife."

"I could tell by the way you moved your ass."

"Wake up. You're talking in your sleep."

"No, I'm not. This has happened before, all over these hills."

"I've never been here before."

"I know. That's not what I meant. There's only a few places in the South where men can call their own tunes. The woods, for instance. But the price is pretty steep."

"At least we did it, finally."

As we dressed and made our way down the hill to the road, I thought, but did not say again, *I could tell by the way you moved your ass.* It was a fragment of a conversation I had had three years earlier with a biker in an almost identical setting. I remembered him and another biker Susan and I had shared five years before him. The memories were rolling down on me fast when Runaway caught my elbow, put his arms around me, and squeezed me tightly. He kissed me, told me he loved me, and said we would be together that summer in London.

I said, "Why not London? At least no one will know us or care what we do."

Runaway said, "No. It's a place we can be together outside this black stinking hole of Alabama."

*"I could tell by the way you moved your ass."*

*"But how did you know I liked cock?"*

*"I didn't. I just knew what I wanted."*

The biker was about a mile ahead of me when I first spotted him. He looked like an ant from that distance. I was doing eighty on the flat mega-highway, and North Carolina shacks, Protestant churches, and discount cigarette stands were bumming me out.

Sunday morning. The sides of the highway were lush with early-summer green. I was picking up on the church traffic—men in starched white shirts and double-knits, women with hair piled like beehives or dunce caps. I took my beer can off the dash. Most of them wouldn't notice, but I didn't want to invite trouble from people I didn't trust.

My car was a maroon, rental Camaro. All my belongings were stuffed inside—treasures and refuse from three years in graduate school were piled on top of the two rear bucket seats. An Andy Warhol poster of Mick Jagger in bluejeans and tight underwear was flush against the back window. I had taken off my shirt and was listening to gospel music when I whizzed up alongside the biker.

He was ugly as hell and beautiful. Leather jacket. Leather gloves. Dark mustache. Pitch-black sunglasses. I liked the shape of his face beneath his helmet, the gopher-grin on his lips. I decided that behind his sunglasses were the hot eyes of a water rat, ready for anything.

I sucked on my beer and dropped back behind him. He was awesome, a hunk from a dirty book who would tie your hands behind you and fuck you raw.

I was out of my mind. I had driven all night from New York City, heading into this remote bog of dismal North Carolina because I had impulsively accepted a reporter's job there for lack of anything better to do to relieve a fit of pique. I drank another beer, put the can on the dash, settled in behind the biker at seventy.

He preened his ass just an inch or so over the hump of the bike seat. I almost totaled the car into a highway marker. Then I settled down and put my plan into operation. First, a conspicuous sign. I reached for my kit-bag and took out pen and paper. I could feel his gloves as he ran his hands over my body.

I had to time my move cautiously. Otherwise, I might fuck up and he might cut my throat. That can happen if you land some sick number whose idea of enchantment is to expose your guts with a can opener.

I pulled out from behind, came even with him, sucked the beer, caught his sunglasses once, then twice so I could be at ease, shot past him to ninety, fishtailed the car when I pulled back into the lane, and watched him coming forward, chewing up all the asphalt, light, air, and distance between us when I slowed back down to seventy.

Now he preened his ass again over the hump of the bike seat as he gunned past.

I scrawled my message, holding the beer can in my crotch to support the pad, steering the car with my kneecaps.

Stomping the accelerator, I drove past him and waited. He came up looking mean as a hornet and stared at me as he whipped past. I knew he was ready. I hit the accelerator and left him in a holding pattern between two strips. Then I heard his bike whining behind me, spitting forward. When he shot up alongside and gave me his gopher-grin, I showed him my scrawled sign: WANT A BLOW JOB?

He read it for what seemed an interminably long time at eighty miles an hour on a North Carolina megastrip. And as he read the sign a kind of dumb, blank expression covered his face. He dropped back and out of sight, behind the car. Holy shit. I checked the gas level—over half a tank. The ultimate fuck-up. You don't fool around with bikers. You leave them alone. Passing him was bad enough, but now he's gonna snap my neck when he catches me, clean like a twig in a storm. I sped up and watched for an exit. None. Not on this stretch, anyway. And I couldn't very well spin around and try to run over him. That would kill us both. I couldn't cross over the median; I'd get stuck in the bottom and he'd trap me there and club me to death with a bike chain. I watched the rearview mirrors for him to whip back into sight, pistol in hand, aimed at my left ear. Even if I'd found an exit in time, he'd follow me off, ram his bike over the ass of my car, and kill us both.

I grabbed another beer, tore off the snap-top, nicked my finger, and sucked the beer. Might as well smoke one last cigarette, I decided, and pushed the accelerator for life's great G-force spinout. But my foot wouldn't cooperate and I almost hit the brake instead, and now he was beside me and I could sense his eyes hard on me.

He was directly beside the car window, those pitch-black sunglasses gunning me down, the mustache a fine, thin line over his tight lips. His face was tanned and smooth, youthful. I held up the beer, toasted him with it, drank, and watched his bike spit forward and slow down. I figured he'd lunge through the car windshield to kill me.

But as I came up beside him he was running his left hand up and down and around his crotch and he nodded his head an inch once, then a second time. I slipped way down on my seat, relaxed with a glorious scream, and turned the gospel music as loud as it would go.

We took the first exit we reached. It was a rest area, and as we went into frantic dust-spiraling, brake-pedal-stomping, cuss-and-hollering stops, we found ourselves smack up next to a busload of Baptist church kids at the cement picnic tables. The Sunday-school cadets froze, staring at us.

I handed the biker a beer through the car window and he drank it in huge gulps. Then he shook his head.

He said, "This won't do," and handed back the can.

The Baptist cadets were all eyes now, watching the two crazed vehicles that had roared like Calvin's Angel of Death Himself into their on-the-way-home-from-church pit stop. The bus driver and two Sunday-school matrons, Bibles in hand, glared at us.

I said, "I'm going to a motel in Charlotte. Thirty miles away. Follow me there and we can fuck like dogs."

He stared at my bare chest, nodded his head, and revved his bike. We left the rest area at the speed we had arrived and were back on the mega-strip, busting balls to Charlotte.

I had never driven to Charlotte before, and knowing only the address and not the location of the motel I took the wrong exit. The biker and I wasted time riding in circles along deserted streets while my guts raged for the fuck I was already visualizing in the motel room.

The streets and sidewalks were empty except for police cars and motorcycle cops who swirled about as we passed. The cops crept up at intersections, checking the license tag on the car and the big, bulging cock in the Jagger poster. Idling beside my car window, they glowered at my naked chest.

I found the motel, and I almost killed us both when I slammed on the brakes without giving the biker enough time to swerve around me. He parked his bike against a post and checked for damage. No damage.

He said, "Hurry up."

The desk clerk grumbled when I walked inside. He pitched down his newspaper and sashayed over to the desk. Immediately, I felt something inside me turn bitter and angry and sour. The desk clerk was the image of every Southern queen I could remember. He prissed, he lisped, he crooked his little fingers as he made change. He wore tacky double-knit. I tried not to look at him, to pretend he wasn't there. I had not put myself through megahighway sexual gymnastics and hyperfantasies with an anonymous biker in order to reach this. Outside, the sunlight was hot and white on the pavement around my horny, impatient biker.

For the second time, the clerk said, "A room for one, sir?"

"Yeah. A room for one. I told you that before."

"Identification, please."

"Identification? I don't need any identification. I already told you who I am. I'm moving to this town to write for that newspaper you just put down."

The clerk shrugged, grew more snippy. He counted out my change bill by bill, coin by coin.

"What about your friend?" he said and gestured like a bird with a broken wing toward the biker.

I looked over my shoulder. The pitch-black sunglasses intoxicated me. I wanted the biker to wear them in bed. His gloved hand covered his crotch.

"You mean him?"

"Yes."

"He's just gonna wash his hands before heading on."

Our room smelled like the inside of an undefrosted refrigerator. We flipped on the air conditioning and jumped for the shower. When we left the shower, the room was cool and we were like grappling hooks snagging each other across the bed, on the floor, on top of one of the chairs, in front of the bureau mirror, back in the bathroom on top of the toilet, in the shower again, and in front of the bathroom mirror. I was awkward and shakier than I'd thought I'd be, the fatigue of the drive from New York befuddling my head and movements. And then as he got down on his knees and took me and said what he wanted most in the world was to be fucked in the mouth by ten cocks at the same time, I asked him what he'd do about breathing, and we cracked up, laughing, and spilled onto the bed, and we were for that split-second as free as we had been on the highway.

He was a navy pilot, stationed in Florida, driving back after a week at the Pentagon. I wanted to know more about him. I wanted to visualize him at work in the Pentagon or flying a navy jet across the Florida gulf, and he wanted to know more of me. Although most of our conversations were short-circuited by sex, his voice, soft and firm, gave me the masculine comfort and reassurance I needed after the ride, the craziness on the highway, and the effeminate clerk in the motel office.

I went from the bed to the shower and rubbed off with a towel. I drank a beer while he dressed, watched him pull on his tight jeans and wished I hadn't forgotten in our haste to ask him to rub my ass with his gloves on and to wear his sunglasses while we made love. I sat on the bed. He leaned over and nuzzled my hair.

He said, "How did you know?"

I said, "What?"

"Out there, on the highway. How did you know?"

I didn't know how to tell him I hadn't known, that I was back in the South now and I'd done it because that's the way I do things in Dixie.

I sucked on my beer and said, "I could tell by the way you moved your ass."

"My ass?"

"Yes. Your ass. Every time you passed me you shifted your ass on the bike seat."

"I did?"

"Yes. The cock in my poster turned you on."

He sat on the bed and we kissed. Then he was standing in the door, holding his helmet, shaking his head, asking me again how I'd known he liked cock.

I lay on the bed and listened to his bike roar off. I could see him thirty minutes later barreling down I-85 through the flat of North Carolina, baking in the unrelenting Southern sun, tooling his bike toward his naval base in Florida, and I was instantly pissed off with myself for not leaving everything I owned right there in that motel room, climbing on behind him, my arms around his waist, going along for the ride.

My anger hit so hard I tore the Charlotte telephone book in half, then went to sleep and woke to the ringing of the telephone hours later. A can of beer had spilled all over me and the bed, and I was dizzy, lost in the sterility of a highway motel room, unable to locate the phone.

A newspaper editor, one of my future employers, was on the end of the line, inviting me over to supper with his wife and kids. He termed it a real down-to-earth home-cooked Southern supper with vegetables out of their back-yard garden and no alcoholic beverages. I almost puked.

I was back in the world I loved more than any other, the South, but I could not live there. I realized I had to find a way out, fast. I jumped for the motel-room door and pulled it open to relieve the claustrophobia. But the late-afternoon air was so hot I wondered if the earth had somehow been drawn closer to the sun and scorched while I was asleep.

I couldn't see myself in one of Charlotte's three abysmal gay-ghetto bars tepid with lisping hair-burners and leisure-suited motel clerks who snapped their fingers while they danced. My head jangled with music and visual images from hot New York bars and chic discothèques. I sat down and steadied myself. It was time to clear my head. I had to be ready to face Dixie again, to step willingly into the vacuum of its ageless time warp. Here on this one arid plain on the planet where time seems drained by the heat and everything can stand perfectly still, I had to move forward. Tonight I would listen to different music clocked at a different pace—the sad, sullen songs of a Southern gay bar, the songs of the male Southern belle.

Snapping their fingers as they moved, they danced as if to avoid hearing the lyrics of the songs they loved. Their steps were often out of sync, their rhythm only slightly faster than that of the region they survived. Nightly they gathered, hovering to drink and dance and stare with blank, self-protective eyes in the bars that were their only meeting places.

They filled every night of staring and waiting with identical songs, tunes that spoke to them of loneliness and isolation and the nonanswer to both: "Strangers in the Night," "People," "I'd Do It All Again." Leaving the bars at night, only a few of them would have been caught dead together in the daylight hours. Elbow-to-elbow, they drank and stared and waited. In this region where time never ran out, only drained away, they waited inert and patient, as if they were inmates in forlorn, self-imposed jails.

The floor space in each bar-jail was carefully defined—uneven wooden ovals or squares or hexagons nailed to the barroom floors of Dixie. And it was from these ovals and squares and hexagons that I first heard the jittery, tribal, primitive snapping of fingers when they turned their struck faces away from the lyrics of their music.

These male Southern belles were totally familiar to one another and hopelessly trapped by that familiarity. Living in Memphis and driving to Birmingham, a male Southern belle found the same bar he had left the night before. Memphis to Birmingham, Birmingham to Jackson, Jackson to Mobile, Mobile to Macon: the roads were jammed with the dashed hopes of

Southern gays. The roads were like lines on a graph, lines setting the limits and boundaries of their fragile existence and survival. There were not enough roads that led out of the South, away from their finite options.

The South was a region in which there was nothing gay about being homosexual. The male Southern belle was a victim of the South's ruthless, snickering petulance, a survivor in a land of belligerent, latter-day Confederate cadets. And if the effeminacy of the male Southern belle was overt, it was also his only protection, as Darwinian as the fluid skin colors of a lizard.

These male Southern belles chattered and gossiped incessantly. To them, innuendo was fact: effeminacy and flirtatious selfishness were a way of life. They had inherited from their female precursors—the classic Southern belles—a seemingly irresistible infatuation with family trees, as if the status denied to them by Southern society because they were gay would somehow be conferred by the accident of birth. Isolated within their region, these were the men who snapped their fingers while dancing in poorly lit bars, stared in their own dulled irony at barroom doors, and dreamed of some apocryphal date when strangers would arrive out of the night and they could make of their long, lonely waits for morning the fantasy-memories of gallantry, heroism, and grandeur.

Susan leaned against the headboard of the bed in our Tuscaloosa apartment. We shared four unkempt rooms near the university campus. She was reading aloud the postcard a biker had sent us from Phoenix. She wore a low-cut black dress and two strands of pearls. Her laughter filled the room.

When Susan and I met, she was trapped by the South as I was, and like me, she preferred to live on the edge. We lived together on the sexual periphery of Dixie—she was straight, I was gay, and our sexual life was built around making it in threesomes with masculine, straight men. I brought some of them home, Susan found others, and together we picked up dozens. She enjoyed watching me make love with other men.

The biker wrote us that even though his ass hurt like hell, he'd made it to Arizona and he'd look us up someday on his way back through. Susan laughed again as she read the message aloud a second time. I stood at the bureau mirror, parted my hair down the middle, switched the part to the side, and then asked her what the hell I should do. We were already over an hour late for a party her parents were giving at the country club.

Susan said, "I wonder when he's coming back through."

"Never. Do I have to part my hair for tonight's massacre?"

"They never come back."

"After what we do to them, they think they're lucky to be alive."

I brushed my hair flat and pulled on a jacket. Susan brought her drink to her lips. Her blue eyes stared at me over the rim of the glass.

I said, "I wish we could screw before we go to the club."

"We don't have time to call anybody. And knowing us, we'll probably do it right there."

"You pick him out tonight. I'm the one who found the biker."

"What if you don't like the one I pick out?"

"You know the rules."

"No sissies."

She drank from her glass. Then, imitating my accent, she said, "When I want a man, I want a man. When I want a woman, I'll let you know."

"Right. Get your ass in gear. Your mother's gonna kill us."

We left the apartment. Susan clinked her glass against the iron railing of the balcony as she walked to the steps. I stood watching her for a moment from the door.

We had watched our biker leave for Phoenix, standing on this balcony early one morning. He snapped on his silver helmet, preened his ass just above the bike seat, and revved away. I remembered the way the light from the bathroom had caught his shoulders and narrow waist the night before as the three of us lay in bed. And I recalled his sweat-drenched, determined face the afternoon I first found him in front of the Old Union building on campus.

I had parked my bicycle there to check my mail. I hadn't seen him when I stopped and didn't hear him until he moved toward me.

He said, in a foreign accent, "Do you know any pad around here where I can crash?"

His face was stained and grimy with sweat, his eyes hidden by sunglasses. He was a slender six feet and must have understood my confusion. Politely, he removed his sunglasses and smiled.

"A place to crash. Know any place I can crash?"

For some reason I was not up on slang. "Crash" was new to me that day and my first thought was that he was crazy if he was looking for a place to have an accident.

He said, "I've driven a long way, man. I'm tired."

Then I saw a motorcycle parked at the curb. I decided he was high on some new drug floating through Tuscaloosa, and I was ready to say, "Sorry, can't help you."

He said, "I need a place *to sleep*, man."

We had not taken our eyes off each other for several seconds.

I said, "Let's go in and drink a Coke."

He followed me into the Old Union building cafeteria. It was an ugly room with comfortable booths. I left him spinning his fountain Coke in his hands and went to a pay telephone.

I said, "Icarus is joining us for the night."

Susan said, "My god, where did you find him?"

"I didn't. He found me. I think he speaks Portuguese or something, too. He's definitely one of us."

He went with me to the apartment, and the three of us made a dash for the shower. Susan and I were more versatile that night than we had ever been, freed from any of the inhibitions or cautiousness we sometimes felt with local straight tricks. And when the three of us were finished, Susan leaned against the headboard and drank a Scotch. Our biker lay with his cheek against Susan's breast. I searched the stack of records for *Sgt. Pepper*.

I slapped the record onto the turntable and jumped on the bed for another round. The next morning I stood on the balcony beside Susan and watched him ride away.

\* \* \*

Susan clinked her glass against the balcony railing as she went to the stairs. I waited on the balcony until she was in the parking lot below.

She said, "I hope tonight he's somebody who'll stick around for a while."

We went to the party at the country club and then to a second, smaller party. At the second party, we both spotted the guy we wanted at the same time. He was tall and trim with brown curly hair, brown eyes, and a brown mustache that turned Susan and me on instantly. Susan made her moves; he left the party to go home to bed with us.

As we lay on the bed, smoking and drinking, the first round completed, he said to me, "I always heard you were heavily into politics."

"I am. You've just been behind the barricades."

"Well, I'd never kissed another man before tonight."

Susan said, "Neither have most of the guys who walk through that door."

"If you dig three-ways so much, why don't you get another guy who's gay?"

I said, "Because the only gays in this town are queens."

He didn't understand.

Susan said, "We only go to bed with men, not women."

He appeared more confused than ever. We made love again, he dressed, kissed us both, and left.

Susan said, "I wish they were all that easy."

"Assholes."

"What?"

"He's an asshole because the only way he'll have sex with another guy is with a woman present."

"But that's what we're all about."

I got out of bed and pulled on my jeans.

"Where are you going?"

"I'm horny. I want to fuck with a guy without you present."

"Where will you find one?"

"The Union building bathroom."

"That's disgusting."

"It's the dirtiest place in town, but the only place to pick up tricks."

Susan had never been one to cry in front of me, but tonight as she lay there I saw the tears she tried to hide, and the hurt that I couldn't care about now because I was stinging inside myself. I turned my back to avoid seeing.

Susan said, "We're never gonna win like this."

Now my anger flared out against a world that had created a whole race of straight assholes I wanted to get down with and make love to and could only reach sexually through Susan, which made it all a manipulative deal that shamed both of us.

"If you leave me tonight, then don't come back."

"Shut up. You're only talking like they want you to talk."

I couldn't wait now to plug up the vacuum inside me the guy had just left. And I know that Susan cried then, not because she could not satisfy me but because she saw we could not continue to afford, emotionally, these terms of coexistence.

"I'll be back in an hour."

But I knew as I closed the apartment door, hearing the first choked sobs coming from the bathroom where she'd run to hide them, that the guy I was sprinting toward now—any guy anywhere who would put his arms around me and hold me—would be no better, would be no different from the guy who had left us at the apartment. And I stopped on the balcony and squeezed the railing with all the strength I had to keep from crying myself because I knew it was over and because I did not want it to come back.

Susan and I remained together for months after that night. I was dreaming of the day I could put the South behind me and find a place where men can be together and make love.

I do not want to write about my years in New York. But I learned there my first tolerance for the queens who had made me skittish in the South. The New York queens were sassy, brassy, and tough, a cut above their Southern sisters. They had not been stuck with female Southern belles as role models. As I think of them now, I see men who had Lauren Bacall as a role model rather than the likes of LaBelle Lance. And my mind fills with the music and images of hundreds of nights, in half as many gay bars and restaurants and bathhouses, when it was not only easy and fun to stand with them, side by side, it gave the hours a sassy, wacky zaniness that made every morning seem like Christmas Day.

I stopped in London en route home to the United States from the North Sea and went to the good, cheap hotel I had found near Harrod's, anxious to spend this last weekend with a guy I'd met several weeks earlier. But there was a note waiting for me at the hotel.

A good friend of mine had called. He kept houses in New York and London and divided the year between them.

He answered the phone and said, "Your little brother has arrived."

"You know I don't have any little brothers."

"You do now. He's barefoot and everything he owns is in a pack on his back."

"You poor baby. I hope he doesn't have any Roman candles."

"No. But he's already sampled every pill in the house and wants cocaine."

"I'm on the way over."

Barefoot, wearing jeans and a white shirt with the sleeves torn off at the elbows, his dark hair a wonderful, unkempt mess, Runaway met me at the door of the house.

He said, "We're out of the black stinking hole of Alabama."

I ran my hand through his shaggy hair. We hugged each other, and I felt all the love I had ever wanted to give a wild, younger brother. I got a lump in my throat. It stayed there the entire weekend Runaway and I were together in London, for the two days he wore my sneakers until he tore them off to go barefoot again, throughout the long walks we took, the naps we shared in my hotel, and the parties my friends in London threw for this kid from Alabama who insisted that all new faces battle him with Roman candles.

In Hyde Park, Runaway said, "Thanks for keeping them away from me long enough to decide."

"Keeping who away? Decide what?"

"They didn't like the idea of going up against you to get to me."

"What the hell are you talking about?"

"The black stinking hole of Alabama."

"You make it sound like a sport."

"It was. I was fair game to them until you came along."

Then he tore off the sneakers and sprinted through the park. He turned cartwheels and somersaults and walked on his hands. I lay on the grass and watched him run. He took off his white shirt and held it in his hand like a banner while he ran. I hoped he would not do the same with his jeans. He ran back to where I lay and sprawled on the grass beside me.

"You make a great big brother."

"You scare the hell out of me."

"I'm not gonna hurt myself."

"That's not what I mean. If you decide to be gay, I don't want you to get hurt."

"You mean you don't want me to be like one of them back in the stinking hole?"

"That's a good way to put it."

"I don't like sissies either."

"I don't dislike sissies or anyone else. It just took me a long time to adjust."

"All these guys I've been meeting over here seem pretty elegant."

"That's because they're British and they think they can't be anything else."

"They seem to like me all right."

"Like you? You've taken them by storm. They've never met anyone like you in their lives, and probably never will again."

"Neither had you. Let's get a Frisbee."

We never got the Frisbee, because I had a plane to catch, and because Runaway had already decided he could take care of himself. He had come to London to tell me that. And he proved it to me when—either wearing my sneakers or barefoot—he did not need my protective cover at the parties we attended, with the people he termed "elegant" but who would have made the bar queens in Tuscaloosa appear butch.

Runaway and I met in Tuscaloosa six weeks later. Late at night after we returned, we went lake-tripping two or three times. But the lakes had lost some of the appeal that had once drawn us to them almost nightly. We gathered mushrooms before dawn some mornings, crawling through a cow pasture on our bellies, hiding from the dairy farmer whose cattle we were stalking. We picked the mushrooms directly from the still-moist cow turds and then slithered back to the car where Wellington and Phillip were our lookouts. Then we washed our hands and faces and the mushrooms with beer, chewed the mushrooms, swallowed their juice, spit them out, and waited for the trip to hit when we reached the city limits.

One evening I went to the Chukker. We were to meet there to drink beer and shoot pinball. No one else of our group had arrived yet. I drank a beer at the bar, sucking it down fast and ordering a second.

A university professor, middle-aged, recently divorced from his wife, stood next to me and told me he was coming out of the closet. I told him I'd never believed in closets, anyway.

He said, "I hear you and Runaway were together in London."

He smiled impishly. He was rapidly adopting the flirtatious, gossipy mannerisms of the Southern belle. It was a transformation I didn't want to witness, and he was asking for information I had no intention of feeding into the gossip-mill.

I said, "He's a nice kid with a great future."

He gave me another impish smile.

*Innuendo is fact to them.* I did not want him to take my answer as a double entendre, so I added, "He told me he had a very good time in London."

I hurried away, to the rear of the bar. A male Southern belle I knew was holding court at a round table, which I joined. He bought me a beer. He was a witty guy, full of long anecdotes based on innuendo, one of the resident spinners of apocryphal Chukker tall tales. He also taught at the university—his classes were famous, the loyalty of his students legendary.

Runaway and Phillip arrived. Phillip was asking Runaway questions about Russian ICBMs and whether or not he had felt safe in Europe where you have only a three-minute warning before doomsday. Runaway was telling Phillip he didn't give a fuck about doomsday, any more, and asking Phillip why he didn't go to Europe and see what it felt like for himself. Then they headed for the pinball machines. The loser would buy beer. Runaway was a better shot, and he was in a hurry to drink beer.

Elliott, the tale-spinning professor, said to me across the table, "Last summer you kept him all to yourself."

"Kept who where?"

"That boy. No one could go near him."

"I don't know what you're talking about, and I don't like the way it sounds."

"Then why aren't all of you living together this summer?"

"Because we've been scattered in different directions."

*Innuendo is fact.* I again felt protective of Runaway.

Elliott said, "Then you don't have your little boys to pal around with anymore."

"Even in the heat, every summer is different."

He wanted to draw out of me as much as he could. I wanted him to know nothing he could shape into a story for a table of local gossips.

Runaway and Phillip returned from the pinball machines. Runaway looked like a kid who has done something wrong and is afraid to mention it. He sat down beside me and nudged up close.

Runaway whispered, "I just lost. Can you lend me some money to buy the beer?"

He got the beer and sat down again at the table. We drank for a very long time. Elliott asked other questions, some directed at Runaway, all of them loaded with sexual implications. Runaway tossed them off as jokes.

*"Your little brother has arrived. He's barefoot and everything he owns is in a pack on his back."*

Elliott said, "Well, it's time for me to get my stylish cunt out of here."

Phillip audibly gasped, pleasing Elliott.

Elliott said, "I can't stay out like I used to. Old age is catching up with me fast."

Runaway laughed and said, "You're not old."

Elliott said, "Young man, I'm old enough to be your grandmother."

Runaway said, "Come on. How old are you?"

"Sixty-three-and-a-half," he said and drank from his beer bottle.

Runaway said, "You're younger than a lot of the people I met in Europe."

Elliott put down his beer and said, "Time to go. Must not keep Sarah Anne waiting."

I knew he shared a house with his sister Sarah Anne, who was perhaps twenty years older than Elliott. I had also heard about, but always discounted as gossip, his passion for rough trade. I had a quick, silent laugh at this contradiction. This guy was a self-styled, walking, talking Art Deco fixture on the Tuscaloosa gay landscape. But how did he ever explain to his older sister the unexpected overnight guests whose eight-wheel semis took up half the block in front of their house? I knew the answer immediately: he simply never explained anything to her, and he bottled up his own guilt or anxieties until he reached the Chukker.

Elliott left the bar. He spoke to almost every patron as he made his way to the open front door.

Phillip snickered and said, "That old fairy never gives up, does he?"

Runaway appeared to be searching the room, the faces in the bar. He seemed remote and intense and distant from us.

Runaway said, "It's not his fault the way he is."

Phillip said, "Then whose fault is it?"

Runaway said, "Your parents and my parents and you and me and everybody else in this black stinking hole of Alabama."

I said, "Let's go. We're too drunk to stay here."

Runaway drove slowly through the steamy, sticky heat of the Tuscaloosa night, communicating in silence as he made the turns that would take us to the bridge and the lakes.

For over a year I had been afraid for Runaway—fearing he would enter the limited, restricted world of the male Southern belle. But I had also wondered if I had been right in protecting him from that world, in shielding him as best I could from its vacuous, insidious web. What difference would it make if Runaway donned a woman's dress and danced in drag, instead of dueling with his futile Roman candles? What did it matter if one night he ran from a screaming-queen cat fight and another defended an innocuous, curious older fairy? What difference is it if one man sees right and tries to do it and another doesn't? With Runaway I had seen what I thought was right and tried to do it. He had given me a mirror-image of myself that told me I was right. He had run toward his goal lines, I had run away from the helpless victims of the South's past. And now the two of us were together, speeding across the high river bridge, with no intention of landing ever again in Runaway's favorite quagmire.

# MICHAEL DENNENY

## Blue Moves: Conversation with a Male Porn Dancer

> *In dancing one keeps taking a step and recovering one's balance.*
> —Edwin Denby

*How did it come about that you were dancing in a male porn theater?*
Well. . . .
*You're a professional dancer?*
Yes, I make my living as a dancer. I was very hard pressed for money and this seemed to be an easy way of making money fast, you know, without taking too much of my time and . . . staying in New York.
*What type of dancing had you done before?*
Just about everything: classical ballet and contemporary and musical comedy—mainly, though, ballet.
*What was the audition like?*
Well, what they do is, in the course of the day, if anyone wants to audition, they just put them into one of the shows as if you were part of the show, so the regular audience is there. They just add you on. And that's how you audition. The manager watches and if he likes what he sees or he thinks you're good enough or whatever, you're hired.
*Were you nervous?*
Yeah. The first time I was very nervous. And it was a strange feeling because I didn't think I would be. You know, having been on the stage before, and being a professional dancer, I didn't expect at all that I would be nervous. But having to strip—it was hard at the audition, it was hard to separate myself from the audience.

*Had you been to a porno theater before?*

No, I hadn't, so it was a totally different experience for me.

*What was the management like?*

Very nice. In fact, I probably wouldn't have stayed there as long as I did, or wouldn't have even taken the job, if the management wasn't as nice as they were. The manager was very up-front and seemed very honest to me. After my audition, I said, "Did you watch the whole thing?" And he said, "Yes," and I said, "I didn't think that I was going to be as nervous as I was." And he said, "Well, you know, it's different taking your clothes off at home and dancing around nude than doing it in front of a roomful of people."

*Was this guy straight, gay, young, old?*

Young. Young and gay. I'd say he was in his early thirties. Everyone who worked there, with the exception of maybe one or two people, everyone was gay.

*Was it owned by gay people?*

No, the theater was owned by straight people. I never met the man who owned it, but he was sort of an older man. He wasn't around very much.

*How many hours did you work and what did you get paid?*

I worked from about two in the afternoon till one in the morning. The thing is that I was at the theater during that time but I wasn't always working. We did seven shows, and each show lasted forty-five minutes. My individual number was anywhere from eight to ten minutes. So the actual time that I was working wasn't much, but you had to stay around the theater and be there for each show. There really wasn't enough time to go out and do anything. And I got $35 a night.

*What did you do between sets?*

Well, sometimes I would go out and go shopping, just window shopping, or . . . go out and eat . . . sometimes just hang out in the lobby and talk with customers. The customers were always—with me, it was a little different because I tried to really dance, so there were people who would talk to me and compliment me. And some of them were totally honest in their compliments, and they obviously saw that I had training, so they were surprised to see someone, you know, present themselves in a theater of that nature. I don't know why, because if more theaters—male theaters—had really good performers, it would add a different dimension. Erotic theater is really what it is, you know.

*Like a male burlesque?*

Right. So I would have conversations with people. And it was interesting: some of them were really turned on to the fact that I did a good act. And others sort of used that to try and proposition me. But I found that . . . that end of it hard to get into.

There were people who would just assume that the prices they paid to get into the theater gave them the right to proposition dancers or to have sex with them, or anything. And I found it insulting, in a way, that they assumed that all of the dancers would hustle.

*Did many of the other dancers hustle?*

A number of them did, yeah, but not *all* of them.

*What were the other guys like?*

All different backgrounds. I think two others had had dance training and had worked as dancers legitimately. There was one that was a male model.

*Legit male model or porn male model?*

Legitimate. And they're from all different backgrounds, and they were all really nice, and it was interesting because they were all at different stages in their lives.

*What age range, mostly young?*

Not necessarily. I would say the youngest was about nineteen, the oldest forty. A wide range.

*Could they dance? Did they take it seriously?*

Oh, yeah. Most of them worked hard at trying to come up with something. They worked on what they should wear, the music they should use—everything down to at what point they should take off what individual piece of clothing. It definitely was a form of expression for most of them—the way they chose their music and how they moved to it. They were expressing different things, but it was definitely something coming from them.

*When you started, what was your attitude toward the dancing?*

Well, like I said, I was really nervous at the audition, but once I started working there it totally reversed. I really enjoyed it . . . for the most part. It was hard, because being in that atmosphere for that many hours can be very difficult, but I found that if I really worked at what I was doing, like anything else, the audience would appreciate it.

*Didn't you feel you'd come down in the world? I mean, you'd done classical ballet, you'd done Broadway shows, and then you worked for the porn theater. Did that bother you?*

Not really, because my preconceived thought of it was all wrong. It bothered me before I even worked there, the thought of it. But then, as I said, the management was so up-front and so nice to me, plus everyone seemed to acknowledge me, all the other dancers. They realized that, wow, here was someone who was really a dancer; they were very complimentary and very supportive of what I was doing. So in that respect it made me feel good, because it wasn't like—sometimes in the theater there's less of that; it's a little more cutthroat and they weren't cutthroat at all, at this particular theater. I found that I could work on things, I could do almost what I've always done, and do it for myself and get enjoyment out of that. Sometimes I would do something, and it just didn't work or it didn't work out the way I wanted it to, but when it did, it was a good feeling. When you're a performer—any kind of a performer—you want to please the audience, otherwise you probably wouldn't be in front of an audience. But when you don't feel that you've pleased them or it hasn't worked out the way you wanted it to, it can be a little frustrating.

*So for you it was a legitimate mode of expression?*

Yeah, yeah, very much so. At times it seemed almost more honest—you know? Because I was expressing my sexuality and expressing myself emotionally at the same time, but it wasn't like the legitimate theater where sometimes something sexual is sort of glossed over and presented in such a way that it's almost dishonest . . . not as real.

*Did that feel hard at first, to present your sexuality so directly on stage and, in addition, to an audience of men?*

Ummmm ... it felt a little ... ah ... yeah, strange at first. But once I got over the initial shock of having to, of being in front of so many people and being so, I mean, totally naked....

*And sexual, not just naked but also sexual.*

Well, yeah, but aren't we all? I mean, we're all sexual beings, so it wasn't....

*But we don't get a chance to express it that much, especially if you're gay.*

Oh, to express it publicly, you mean? In front of an audience? Ah ... but, see, I always approached it like more of an affirmation of my sexuality, you know? It was a fine line.... I didn't want to exploit the audience either. There's a certain amount of tease that you put in, but I didn't want to ... ah ... sort of shove my sexuality in their face, so to speak. I always tried to enjoy what I was doing, to at least *look* like I was enjoying what I was doing so that, hopefully, people in the audience would connect with that feeling of enjoying their own sexuality, their own bodies, their own homosexuality. And that's what I tried to do. It didn't always work.

*Can you describe your act for me or—maybe that's not the right word—your pieces, or whatever you called them?*

Well, when I first started working, my costumes were very sort of everyday clothes. See, I always tried to get two different feelings in a number. I would go from soft to hard: I would come out with a white Yves St. Laurent shirt and black pants—right?—and then I would take the shirt off and eventually strip off the pants, but underneath I would have maybe, these black stretch bikini briefs and a stretch tank top that was cut, so it just went over my chest ... ummm ... just over the nipple, and a collar—a dog collar—and then eventually I would take off the top and underneath the briefs I would have maybe either a jock strap—I had this really neat green jock strap—or a black see-through G-string. And musically also, most of the time I would try to start with something slow and my movements would be slow and erotic, and direct it very much toward the audience. More of a soft kind of love thing. But then I would like to go into a harder type—either a rock type music or into faster, harder movement and music.

*Did you take the G-string off?*

Yeah. That was one of the requirements, actually, of the management.

*Was that hard to do at first?*

Yeah, it was. And also I noticed that nine times out of ten even the kids that worked there—I mean that's what they do for a living, they strip other places, too—when it came to the point of taking the G-string off, they would be with their backs to the audience. Which I thought was sort of interesting. Lots of times I would do the same thing too, except after a while I got so comfortable that it didn't bother me. But the first few weeks, it was very hard for me to work off the stage. I wouldn't get off the stage; I would work on the stage.

*You mean go into the audience?*

Yeah, it was hard for me to go into the audience. But then after a while

I even worked that into a number where I did my final strip. I took the G-string off . . . it was to Donna Summer and it was from her *Alive and More* album, and it was a fabulous number because it just worked out perfectly. I had one of those, like a jock strap but without two back straps? And a G-string underneath that and I would go from the stage onto the seats and do a whole strip on the seats. Standing on the armrests. Because then it went from a fast part to a very slow part . . . sometimes that was a little touchy, though.

*I was going to ask if people ever tried touching you and. . . .*

Yeah—well, the reactions were interesting because there were people who had fear written across their faces—just really afraid to touch you. I mean I don't know what they thought was going to happen if they touched you, but it's like they just did *not* want to have any contact. And there were other people who were grabbing, I mean, they couldn't keep their hands off of you. And there were some people you'd go to and they could enjoy the fun of it, they could just take it for what it was, you know, smile at you and be having a good time.

*What did you do about the people who were grabbing?*

At first that bothered me a lot, because I just felt that wasn't supposed to be part of the number and also like I was up for grabs. Like they felt that was what I was there for, and . . . you know, for me the whole thing is you wanted to feel some kind of warmth and sometimes that grabbing was. . . . There's nothing, no emotion involved with it, they just think you're a body and it's like going to the grocery and feeling the fruit or something. Suddenly you become a commodity or something.

*How did you handle it when it happened?*

I learned to play to it, more or less. Because I didn't want to become antagonistic toward the audience, but usually if that happened, if someone was that aggressive, I would just move to another part of the audience. I learned to take it to a point where it looked like I might reciprocate, because that also was a big turn-on. It's like anything else: it's not what actually happens but what people think might happen. That's what excites them, you know. So you can use that, if somebody was in the audience and they were touching you, you could use that to get across that feeling that something might happen. But just as it looks like it might, then you move on. And I found that was the best turn-on for the entire audience. That feeling. Because there were times when things actually did happen. Not so much with me, but with other people. And I think that sort of alienated the audience because it isolated them more.

*You told me once about an incident when someone was actually rimming you while you were dancing on the seats?*

Oh, yeah, that happened toward the end. . . .

*Of your career?*

Career? Yes—what about it?

*How did that feel? I mean. . . .*

Felt good!—no . . . it's very strange. . . . You know what it was, it was—on that particular day, I was very depressed for some reason. After a while, working there, I didn't find it terribly erotic. I mean, it's different for the customer who comes in for a couple of hours, sees a show, watches some of the movie, and maybe connects with a trick or whatever. But the dancer who has to be there for so many hours and who has to get up and turn on, it's like a sex machine or something and suddenly you have to come out with all this ... sexuality, sexual feelings. You have to come across with this total erotic feeling and, you know, you don't always feel that way. You *don't* always feel, at every moment of the day, you don't always feel sexual.

*So this day you were depressed. . . .*

This particular day—I don't know why—I felt depressed or something. And of course, the theater's dark, and it doesn't particularly help to lift your spirits. So I was doing the shows—it was about the second or third show—and there weren't that many people in the audience, and there was this man sitting in the very first row. From the very beginning it didn't matter what I did, or what anybody did, really—maybe he was stoned—he just wanted a good time and he was out to get whatever he could. So I got up to do that number and there was no one really, except sitting way back in the theater, except for this one man, and it was very hard. . . .

*How many people in the audience, five, ten, twenty?*

Like maybe five or ten total. There was no one really to play to, except this one man who was close enough. And I think it was more out of anger, on my part, than anything. I was dancing on the seats and he was just sitting there grabbing and making obscene gestures with his mouth and it was one of those things where I mentally said, "All right, if that's what you want, that's what you're going to get." So I did everything to him, I directed everything to him, and I did the strip. He kept motioning to me to come closer, to stand over him, so I did and I did the whole strip over him, and he started to go down on me and everything. But I did it. . . .

*What's everything?*

Well, rim me and, you know. . . . But I did it more out of anger because I wasn't really attracted to him, and it wasn't a sexual feeling at all for me. I don't know what it was for him. But it was more out of anger, because I wasn't getting anything from the audience, you know, emotionally. I was trying to put out something and nothing was coming back to me except this man. But it was not a good feeling at all. Having him that close. . . .

*It didn't feel good, you were saying, having him that close?*

No. It didn't, and I think it broke an illusion. I don't think it helped create any kind of feeling with the people who were watching, the people in the back of the theater. And I realized later that the whole thing took place really out of my anger of trying to get through to them. But it didn't help matters at all.

*Was that the only time? Or did that happen occasionally?*

Ah ... yeah, that's the only time it happened while I was there, that it was that graphic. Other times—there were times when people would grab your cock or they would feel your ass, but, you know, sometimes that felt fine because it was a different kind of touch. I mean, they really want you, and that, I suppose, is what it's all about. That feeling of being wanted and you're up there and you're creating that feeling of having every man in the audience want you.

*That must be a terrific rush.*

Yeah, when it happens it is. It is—it's beautiful. But it's a fantasy. It's a beautiful fantasy, you know, because realistically there's a lot more involved with it.

*Did you ever meet anyone in the audience or see anyone in the audience that you were attracted to?*

Yeah. Yeah, there were a number of times I did.

*Did that ever lead to anything?*

Ah . . . a couple of times it did, yes. I tried to—which was difficult—but I tried to, as a rule, not do that much in the theater. But I would meet people that I was turned on to and who were turned on to me and. . . .

*Go home with them?*

Yeah. Or we would exchange numbers and eventually get together. It only happened a couple of times, though.

The thing is that I found when you meet someone under those circumstances, it's very difficult because you don't know whether what they're attracted to really is the illusion or you. I found it's true in the legitimate theater, too. I mean I've done things. . . . I happened to have gotten letters, you know. Once I answered a letter—this was when I was doing something legitimate, dancing—and I was written a letter, and I answered it. But it was a mistake, and I find that this can so easily happen, because I was creating an illusion on the stage and the audience or that person might confuse that with the real me. It's one of the reasons I didn't get together with people. But the people that I did get together with were people that I was very attracted to.

*And you did it just for sex, not for money?*

Oh, yeah, yeah.

*How come you never hustled?*

I couldn't get into it. I think because—I don't know. Really I don't know. Except I think I figured out that my emotional needs are just too great. I can't separate my feelings from the sexual activity or the sexual being—I can't. I couldn't pretend. Like one of the kids who did hustle said he just put himself in another place or would think of someone else, and that was very hard for me to do. I couldn't—which, when I think of it, might be strange because it's just the reverse when I'm on stage. But then, that's maybe why I'm a performer. You know, when I'm on stage, I feel I can do almost anything. But it was too real for me—hustling—being that intimate, being with one other person, and having sex with them, for money. I guess the money just wasn't that important to me. I don't know. I did question myself because—I mean, I had never thought of hustling before, and in some sense people in the theater hustle all the time. You know, it's not a sexual thing, but in the same sense they're hustling. They're selling themselves all the time—they'll do almost anything to get parts—it's the same thing in a sense. But I just could not get myself to do it. It's funny because after a while I suppose I felt guilty about it.

*About* not *hustling?*

Yeah. But . . . I mean it wasn't—I didn't think anything was wrong with hustling. I don't think I'm someone to judge those things. But I guess I feel that you have to have a certain mentality or background or whatever or feelings, in order to allow yourself to do it. I mean, I tried a couple of times.

*You tried?*

Sure.

*What does that mean?*

Well, people offered me money a couple times, and . . . I went with them . . . but in fact, in one case, I even gave the guy back his money—but he demanded it back—he was very demanding. Because I just couldn't.

*It didn't work out physically; you couldn't get into it?*

No. I couldn't get into it. But I found out later on that there's a whole number that you do in hustling. First of all, people who are going to pay for it, I suppose either feel they have to for some reason, or they do have to for some reason, or they just get off on it—it's part of the fantasy, you know. I found out from someone who did hustle that there are all sorts of tricks you can do, like being aggressive and if someone wants something that you don't particularly do or don't like to do, you just tell them, and nine times out of ten they're still going to pay you. They're really—this is my head, again, but I guess I would like to think this—but I think in the end what they're paying for has nothing to do with, ah . . . the superficiality of it, the body. It has more to do with feelings. They just want something to touch and someone to feel a certain kind of love for. Even if it is for ten minutes or whatever.

*When you were on the stage performing, did you fantasize? I'm curious about what it would feel like to feel that erotic publicly.*

I . . . there were only a couple of times I fantasized, but when I did fantasize, it had nothing to do with the audience.

*What did it have to do with?*

It had to do with someone that I knew who was in my own head. I mean thoughts that I had—in fact, there probably were only two occasions that I can remember that I really fantasized to the extent of, you know, practically getting a hard-on. But in both cases it was about someone that I was seeing, and I think both times I had just come from being with him. So I was turned on, mentally, and therefore the audience was tuned into that, and turned on. Now, other times—obviously there were people in the audience who were really turning on to me, to my number, and sometimes, you know, I would go into the audience and I would see a fairly good-looking person, who was turning on to me. And I would play that, I would play up to that.

*Did you get turned on by turning him on?*

Ah . . . yes and no, because it was more of a mental turn-on. I mean, I didn't get a hard-on, necessarily, most of the time. I don't think I ever did, really, when I went to the audience. But the thought that I was turning them on that much and that they were attracted to me . . . ah . . . made me turn on mentally. I think when I was performing—especially in the audience—it was very hard to forget that there were people watching you, you know. In that sense, legitimate theater can be very different, because there's always the wall there, you know, the stage. But working at this theater—and maybe it's just an aspect of myself that came up—but it was very hard for me to forget the audience was there.

*Did you know that you could turn men on sexually, easily, before this?*

Yeah.

*So it didn't change your feeling about your own sexuality?*

Well, it did in a sense, because I don't think I was as open or as ready to admit it before. And I don't know why, except maybe I just thought that that would make me sound terribly vain, or something. Since I was ... since my teens, at least, I've always known that I was attracted to men and that I was attractive to men, that men turned on to me sexually. But I wasn't as ready to admit it, as much as now. I know, psychologically, doing this work has really helped me tremendously. It's opened me up a lot to my own sexuality.

*Did you ever go onto the stage feeling totally nonerotic, like used dishwater, not able to get turned on in the slightest and what did you do about it? Could you fake it?*

Fake what?

*Sexiness, being turned on.*

Yeah, because, as I said, it was like an act with me. Like some of the kids, I have to say, they didn't all approach it the same way I did. There were a couple who went on stage, like they could have felt like dishwater—I don't know what they felt like, but they looked like they might have felt like that—I mean they didn't express themselves, either because they were too young, or maybe too old, I don't know. I'm thinking of individual people, but they would get up on stage and they would just flaunt themselves. And I found that in most cases it was perhaps the ones with the big cocks, or the better-endowed ones who really weren't expressing anything sexual up on stage. Now, whether it was because they felt that they really didn't have to because all the men were there only to see a big cock, or whether they really didn't know how to express themselves, who knows? But I know, personally, watching them did not particularly turn me on.

*You said you tried not to be a cock-tease to the audience, not to exploit them. What did you try to do with the audience?*

Well ... there's a difference between assaulting someone and making love to someone. I tried to make love to the audience. I wanted them to feel that they were being loved. And not to feel that someone was forcing themselves upon them, sexually or any other way.

I think many times when a person got up with an arrogant attitude, it alienated the audience. But then there were people in the audience who, perhaps, wanted that. I mean, they may have had such a low opinion of themselves and that was their need for going to this theater, that, in a sense, turned them on. Someone getting up there and saying, "I'm it; you look at this big cock, and you know you want it"—this kind of dominant put-down. I'm sure there were people in the audience, at different times, that probably wanted that.

*Who was the audience? What type of people go there?*

All different types. There's no way you could stereotype the people who went there, because they were all different types. Straight-looking men, aggressive-looking men, effeminate-looking, total macho, old men, young men.

*There was no particular age; it wasn't older?*

A lot ... well ... I would say not most of the customers, but the most consistent customers were the older men. But there were all types and ages.

*Why do you think they went to the theater?*

Well, there were all different reasons. There was a man I had a long conversation with who was married; he was an older man, middle-class—you know, lives in a house with his wife, had a male lover. . . .

*Had a male lover?*

Uh huh. . . .

*But still came to the theater?*

But still came to the theater. He was totally—and he admitted he was—totally sexual. He had to have sex constantly. Just really hot, I guess. I don't know. Yeah, so he would come to the theater and try to pick up a trick or whatever, but a really nice man. We had a long talk, you know, he propositioned me. . . . And there was a young boy, one day, who came in.

*What do you mean young?*

High school age . . . happened to be off on vacation and . . . really a nice kid, and shy. He lived in the suburbs, was obviously isolated . . . probably it wasn't easy for him to meet gay people, and so this was the answer for now, anyway.

*Did he proposition you?*

No, but he was . . . he obviously wanted to get together with me, but I just . . . I don't know, you have to feel something—I do, anyway. And I didn't feel it for him. But I thought he was sweet and I like to get to know people, too. Then there was a man that same day who was dying to have this boy, and he was totally opposite from this young boy. From the minute he came into the theater until he left, it was like he expected to come into the theater and to find someone, connect with someone, and have sex. I mean, from the minute he walked in the door. And he couldn't understand why he wasn't getting any feedback from anybody. But it obviously was the vibes that he was putting out himself, you know. He was just so uptight about it. It's like for him this theater, because they showed pornographic movies and because they had a live show, was synonymous with sex. But this particular man, he didn't have a realistic view of himself.

*What were some of the other people like?*

There were some—well, I think I told you about him. There was an old man, one day, in the front row. I mean, he was *old;* he was in his eighties at least, and he was just moving to the music and making all these obscene gestures to different dancers, and he took his cock out and had a hard-on and was just jerking off and everything. It was incredible. This old man.

*What was your reaction to that?*

Well, it was funny. I laughed. But also, there was something about it that was almost an inspiration, to think that someone—this man, who was really up in his years—was still so full of energy, but even more, his sexual being was still so alive. It's incredible.

*What was your general feeling about the audience? I mean, did you like them, did you pity them?*

Ah . . . well . . . that's a hard question to answer. I think I had a lot of different feelings. I don't think I pitied them. I think my main feeling was wanting them to want me, or to acknowledge me, you know, that's my own personal hang-up—where my head is at, I guess. I don't know what some of them might have seen in the show, what it gave them. . . . That's why my act—I tried to do an act and a couple of other kids did an act, which was at least entertaining. But there were other people who were not. The younger guys saw that, and they would either walk out or they just turned off. But the older guys, I think, were more apt to accept just the nudity and the chance to see the male body. You know, it's a hard audience—a body of people—each one there for a different reason; each one has different psychological hang-ups or needs. So it really was hard to feel something for the audience as a whole. I suppose it's why, lots of times, I tried to connect with one individual or a couple of individuals within the audience, playing off of them.

*You said when you were doing this you were seeing someone?*

I was seeing a couple of people.

*Did any of the people you were seeing ever come to watch you at the theater?*

One—yes, one did. One I met at the theater, actually. The other one I was seeing had been to the theater but hadn't seen me. We met somewhere else. And he couldn't come to terms with what I was doing *at all.*

*I wondered about that—whether they were jealous or sort of freaked by it?*

Well, the one guy who I still see at times, since I met him there, it didn't bother him. I think he's into me as a person, so I think nothing would bother him, but the other guy didn't. I don't think he thought less of me, though I have to admit that the fact that he didn't understand what I was doing or really approve of it, bothered me because I was afraid that he was turned on to me only sexually and that he didn't really feel something for me as a person. But, I'm not sure—I mean, that's just a feeling that I had, because it was hard for him to come to terms with the fact that I was working in a porno movie house. But he was honest enough to admit that his whole upbringing and way of thinking had a lot to do with it. He . . . he was totally different from me anyway. He is very into material things, and he was doing a job that he didn't particularly enjoy, but he was doing it because it brought him enough money to live the way he wanted to live. Whereas I'm totally opposite. I'm not into material things. I'm more into doing what I want to do and trying to be happy doing it.

*How about you? Your upbringing was fairly conservative, right? How were you brought up?*

Yeah, middle-class, lower-middle-class.

*What did your father do?*

My father's dead. But both of them worked. My father was an accountant, and my mother still works. She's a combination housekeeper and nanny.

*And you were brought up Catholic?*

Uh huh.

*Was it a large family?*

Five kids.

*In Jersey?*

Yeah.

*So it was pretty conservative?*

Yeah.

*Italian Catholic?*

Italian and Irish.

*So you're an Irish Catholic. If this guy had trouble dealing with it because of his background, whatever it was, you must have had some trouble dealing with it, because of your background.*

Yeah.

*You said that working in the porn theater, dancing, had helped you a lot, had given you a lot of insights. In what way?*

Well . . . it made me feel . . . like I had never been able to admit that I might be attractive to men or turn men on a lot, because somehow I always felt that—I don't know—that was being like a real egotist or being terribly vain. But, being able to openly express my sexuality, which, for a long part of my life, I couldn't. I guess this gave me an opportunity to just bare all, so to speak. And also I think it was not only the feeling of identifying the audience as my family and saying, "Here I am; this is me," but seeing it myself. Being able to get up there and just be a sexual male, to enjoy my own sexuality. Which I think a lot of straight men miss out on. It's changing a lot, but—I can't picture my brothers really being aware of their bodies—really being into their bodies, really into looking good . . . the shape of their bodies. I just can't picture them. In fact, a lot of straight men just totally let themselves go physically, I think more so than gay men. I think it's because they're not into acknowledgment of the male body—to them it's admitting feelings that they're not allowed to be in touch with.

*Do you ever imagine what your mother would think if she walked into the theater? I mean, forgetting why your mother would ever walk into such a theater. Did you ever think of that, or your brothers?*

Yeah.

*How did you deal with it?*

Well, I'm not really that close to my family. My mother, perhaps, but my brothers, no. I've always done what I wanted to do, and I've always felt separate from them, so . . . you know, the thought did come into my mind, what if they found out, but . . . I have to live my own life also.

*Do they know you're gay, your family?*

Not officially. I'm sure they're . . . aware . . . but they wouldn't admit it, I don't think.

*Does that bother you?*

Yeah, 'cause I'm . . . I'm trying to be honest with myself, so . . . but, at the same time, it's very difficult. . . . I can't play with other people's emotions.

*Is it a number they're pulling, their not knowing? Do you think a number's been done on you?*

Oh, yeah, definitely. Quite a bit of a number's been done on me. But . . . but see, I'm dealing with that. I mean I . . . I've been dealing with that all my life, I guess.

*When did you come out as gay?*

Uh . . . I guess my early twenties. . . . But . . . I knew before then, all through my teens, and I had had experiences, but I don't think I admitted it until my twenties.

*Was it hard?*

It was hard . . . coming from the family that I did . . . where sex was something that really wasn't openly discussed . . . being in a household full of men.

*All five of you were boys?*

I have a sister, but she was out of the house when I was a baby. So here are all these straight, conservative, macho types, and me . . . with my feelings, but not really knowing how to express them. Feeling different, you know, and not knowing what exactly that difference was. So that . . . having this . . . having a feeling that there was something wrong with me or wrong with being gay, but yet knowing that those feelings existed, so that it was terribly difficult for me to admit it. I finally did. Of course, it opened a lot of doors. But that's why it was so hard to admit. Because of my environment.

*Were you going to a shrink during this time?*

Uh huh.

*Did you discuss this with him or her?*

Uh huh, yes I did.

*What was their reaction? A him or her?*

Her.

*Her—what was her reaction?*

Actually, one of the conclusions she came to was that it probably was good for me because I was getting something there I needed, which I wasn't getting anywhere else. The feeling that I was being acknowledged and accepted.

*As a kid did you feel nonacknowledged or just nonacknowledged as gay?*

As a kid, I did feel unacknowledged in my family. And this theater was an all-male audience and I come from a household of all males, with the exception of my mother. So I guess I always was looking for that acceptance from my family. And I was getting it at this theater.

*Do you think it had any direct impact on your sex life?*

Yes, I do.

*In what way? Let's be specific.*

Well . . . I don't know. It's made my sexual life better. . . . It's made me appreciate, I think, someone who is turned on to me. It's made me turn on to them more. It's somehow made me more flexible, more open to a sex partner.

*So, are you glad you did it?*

Yes. Work at the theater, you mean? Of course. Yeah, definitely. I don't know how much longer I would have been able to do it, but I am glad I did it.

*Just for the tape, tell us what you're doing now.*

Just for the tape?

*I mean, with the Yiddish theater. I think that's so funny.*

What, that I'm dancing with the Yiddish theater in Brooklyn?

*Yeah. To go from one to the other.*

Well. . . .

*That's showbiz, right?*

It is. You never know where you'll be next.

# Interview with a Fetishist

The "new homosexuals"—that's what John Rechy in his 1979 novel, *Rushes,* calls the cowboys and leathermen who frequent the heavy cruising bars from New York to Los Angeles. He sees them as the principal actors in an exclusively macho world where women and sissies have no place. Although Rechy exposes the internalized hostility he often finds in their attitudes and practices, he also acknowledges his fascination for these men—for their rituals, their clothes, their sexual style. *Rushes* is, in fact, an attempt to describe the poetry of that world, however forbidding it may seem to outsiders.

The man in this interview did not like *Rushes* and thinks that Rechy has failed to understand the deeper sources of masculine desire. He also dislikes the word *homosexual* and finds nothing "new" in his own fascination with the power and beauty of masculinity. It has been present in his life since childhood and present also, he claims, in Western culture from its beginnings. Despite these reservations he has accepted the designation "new homosexual" because it does mark his position within the current sexual and political spectrum of gay life.

If his position is different from Rechy's, it is even more different from that of thinkers like Seymour Kleinberg, who, in *Alienated Affections,* strongly condemns the "new masculinity" of gay men because it eroticizes, he says, the very values of straight society that have tyrannized our lives. Curiously, the man in this interview also condemns today's macho style and the facile sexuality it supports, but he does so from a perspective that is opposed to Kleinberg's and in the name of values that many, straight or gay, would find difficult to accept.

This man is a purist, a true believer in the myths and fetishes of male sexuality, for whom compromise is corruption and fellow travelers are more dangerous than outright antagonists. He is an elitist, convinced of the superiority of his world and determined to remain anonymous. He is an eroticist in the sense that his thoughts are already sexual acts and his acts are always intensified and scrutinized by thought. In a tradition that has historically included many homosexual men, he is also an artist of life, a man who has succeeded in perfecting his person and his style to the point where they have become, as he will say, "supernatural." Finally, he is an intelligent and articulate spokesman for a world that has seldom been heard in its own voice. This articulateness explains why my questions and remarks have been kept to a minimum. This man is speaking less to me than to the reader.

Among other things, coming out means speaking out, even anonymously. It also means affirming the extraordinary diversity of gay life, which includes, together with individuals, distinct patterns of human relations. Although it contains elements that tempt me, this man's world is not mine and probably never will be. But it is a world that exists and works in that it satisfies the desires of those who inhabit it. This world will doubtless continue to exist in one guise or another as long as those desires do.

*How would you define yourself sexually?*

I'd have to define myself as homosexual, first—with gay experience but not gay attitudes; a fetishist, second; and a sadomasochist, third.

*Let's start with the first. What distinction are you making between* homosexual *and* gay?

*Gay* comes from the demimonde, from the world of "gay ladies," and suggests something promiscuous, public, semiprofessional. Today it refers to men who define themselves as gay, live in a gay neighborhood, have gay friends, go to gay bars, and have a kind of specialized ghetto mentality with a lot of sexual experience. That all makes them slightly jaded and gives them an almost professional attitude about their tits and their dick. "Gay" is also the upfront social element out of which all the public energy and all the public spokesmen come.

As for *homosexual*, it's a terrible term, but I can tell you what I mean this way: I spent the night before last in a truck with a guy who had come from California and who certainly likes men but who's hardly ever been in a bar. What he really likes are truckers, because he understands them. He has a girlfriend, but when he gets into the truck and on the road, it's all male. Truckers live in a world where they couldn't be exposed as cocksuckers, and they are very careful about each other, and very supportive and loyal. The gay world seems to operate on the expendability of the other men. "So many men, so little time"—that's gay. To talk about "tricking" or somebody's "trick" always gives me the creeps. It's a professional prostitute's word. Oh, I experiment a lot and with a lot of different men, but when it clicks, I hold onto these guys. I pull them back into my life.

*Give me a description of your kind of man.*

He has qualities of strength, of character, of self-sufficiency. He's got enough nobility in him to let go or to give some of it away. He's magnanimous and open-hearted. He has a strong feeling of loyalty to what he cares about. Sure, I also have some favorite body types; I've always liked Italian men. They've got that *noyau* behind them; they've got that super family. Family, neighborhood, Italianness—that's irrisistible to me because I'm an Episcopalian WASP with a family that makes very few demands on me, and that doesn't expect me to conform, because they don't conform. So I've had to create my own family, and it's more precious to me.

*Is fetishism one of the things that creates special ties for you?*

Yes. A fetish is an object, not the man himself, but so closely associated with him that it takes on sexual value because of that connection. Clothes, tools, and even some environments like locker rooms, ruins, and construction sites become eroticized. The classic fetishes are dick and ass coverers and extremity coverers—jockstraps, underpants, shoes, gloves. And there's protective equipment like rubber boots or a superheavy training jock that goes over your shorts when you're sparring in the ring. It's a transference of the passion for the vulnerable human skin and body to the equipment that protects that vulnerability. It's like kissing a man's armor.

*But isn't it important for what's inside or underneath to show through—the vulnerability, the body, the sweat?*

Absolutely. For me use and condition have so much to do with it. I like things that are salty, smoky, that have already seen some service. There's a beautiful line in *Let Us Now Praise Famous Men* where James Agee talks about Levis, and how they are a blueprint when they are brand new and how beautiful they are when they become worn and punched out.

*When I think of clothes as fetishes, their magical power, and the worship they command, the writer who comes to my mind immediately is Genet. It's one of the great obsessive themes in his novels and plays. But what is your explanation for this sexual power of clothes, particularly for men?*

I realized something once with a kind of flash when a man said to me in the course of a scene, "I love your boots." I realized that he couldn't say, "I love you." That was too intense, too much of a commitment, too dangerous to say. So the transference moves the attention away from what is frightening or taboo. It cools it, so that the attention can be poured out and lavished through the fetish. Look at all the guys who take a part of the body, your nipple, your dick, or a tattoo, and go at it in a way that they couldn't get into you, all of you, so intensely.

*And that attention is a form of worship?*

Yes, but it's also a feeling of service. Worship is a kind of service.

*What about leather and uniforms? How do they focus erotic attention?*

Leather is not a uniform. It's a material and a strong fetish in itself, and it can be authoritative or real pig-raunchy. The basic uniforms break down into military, law enforcement, industrial, and civil service uniforms. For uniform men, there is a hierarchy among them that has to do with authority. Those that are less authoritative tend to be more sensual to me.

*Let's take the men we see on the streets and in the bars—the gay cowboys, bikers, loggers, and construction workers. Some certainly look hot, but many others don't. What causes the difference?*

Take the Christopher Street clone. What he does is to assemble various individual items together in a fashion-dictated way that doesn't have any soul. The uniforms, the fetish pieces he wears are insufficiently eroticized because they don't form a totality that expresses his own personality. He takes the elements, the symbols of masculinity and combines them in a musical comedy way. The fact that eight-year-old kids want to go out on Halloween dressed like the Village People shows how desexualized those images can become. It's not hot when a man wears a white construction helmet because it's going to glow in the black light in the bars. And that helmet is just as undented and unmarred as a toilet bowl, and there's none of his sweat in the sweat band. But it is hot when a guy is so into his boots that he wears them all the time, so that after a while they collapse around his toes and take on the shape of his foot. He hasn't just selected them out of his wardrobe.

*How do you see the judgment of others and the influence it has on what we wear?*

I remember a guy I saw once in a bar in Boston who was dressed pretty well in full cowboy regalia, but with sneakers to show the rest of the guys in the bar what a good sport he was and that actually it was all a joke. So the sneakers desexualized the whole trip and gave the lie to everything else. The difference between gay life in the centers as opposed to the provinces—and even some uptown bars in New York are provincial bars—is that the social organization of the provincial bar is run by the bitches, by the two queens who sit at different ends of the bar and make a commentary on everyone who comes in. And that guy in Boston was avoiding the possibility that one of them was going to say to him, "Well, Mary, where do you get off dressing as a cowboy, when we all know you work in Filene's?" Another problem is that gay men in those safe places we call "leather 'n' Levi's" bars take their cues from each other only, without ever referring back to real life. Those are the clones.

*But what turns you on is not necessarily authenticity, at least not in the strictest sense.*

I don't care if they're not authentic, but they have to be supernatural. If you want an authentic construction worker, he'll be dancing with his shirt open to the navel in a disco, probably looking for female chicken. He certainly won't be dressed the way he is in the daytime.

*What's it like to be supernatural in New York?*

It was very hard five years ago to walk into the bar in the full uniform of the New York Police Department and have a quiet beer and field the dumb questions that ran from "Are you a real cop?" to "Officer, please arrest me."

*Do you still get some of those reactions?*

Sure, but less now. It's an acceptable authority trip in that world today. But perhaps in a way it's less hot than it was when I used to roll around the West Village in a sanitation man's uniform and beckon a guy into a doorway and tell him I only had three minutes.

*To be done for trade.*

Yes, but supertrade! Very enthusiastic, very encouraging!

*And unlike a real sanitation man, you were in control; you were creating the scene.*

Right. I always say, if you can't find the man you want, *be* the man you want, and get off on the electricity you can create with it.

*And in fact you were better at it than any real sanitation man could be.*

That's what *supernatural* means. A real sanitation man would always have his eye out for the boss or for the other two men on his detail. He would be nervous about the whole situation. But then, if you get out on the highway right now and into those truck stops, you'll see a lot of different kinds of truckers. The hot ones are the ones in a recognizable trucking uniform. They want truckers to recognize them as truckers, and that's especially true of those gay truckers who are after truckers and who gave up some other life they were being groomed for when they realized they were entitled to *be* truckers.

*I think in any group those who are into the particular clothes and gestures of that group will see it as a kind of theater. After all, we all know that there are real policemen who loved getting dressed up in policemen's uniforms and playing the part of real policemen.*

I belong to a uniform buffs association that's 100 percent gay but discreet because some of the men are married. There's also a solid base of guys who have to be discreet because they are working as auxiliaries or professionals in uniform, and there is a lot of homophobia in those areas. These are guys who, because of their enjoyment of their roles, are often very good cops, sheriff's deputies, or firemen.

*Are you comfortable wearing all uniforms?*

There comes a time when I'm not wholly satisfied with wearing the uniform of the NYPD because I'm not a New York cop. It may be more "authentic" to wear that uniform, but I would much rather dress in uniform without adopting another persona. I'd rather do it with my own club patch on my arm. It's something that I've earned just as the New York cop has earned his. But you can wear a NYPD uniform in a bar because it's understood that it's a kind of theater. Of course, there are nights when you're dressed wrong for expressing what you're after, and it affects your whole ability to satisfy yourself or someone else.

*Aren't there straight uniform collectors and clubs?*

Yes, but they have a real problem accepting or fulfilling the erotic fantasies inherent in a uniform. Also, the truth about most straight men is that in the background there is their mother or wife or girlfriend saying, "That's not nice." They want to be "nice" in a way that a lot of guys in my world are really free of being "nice." Your sanitation man knows that it's not nice to put his armpit into your face or push your head onto his greasy boots. He doesn't have a pigging-out feeling because always in the back are the women in his life saying, "Be nice, act nice, smell nice."

*That's also precisely what many women say—that without them we'd be much more brutal and uncivilized.*

Women do have a very civilizing effect.

*So is the world of men and uniforms a way to escape that influence?*

Think of Rome at the end of the third century, where the sign of a civilized man was that he wore a toga, and the sign of a Gothic barbarian was that he wore trousers because he rode all the time, and think of the Romans who affected Gothic clothes. Think of James Boswell, the nephew of a Scottish aristocrat, creating a whole fantasy persona for himself by getting dressed as a highwayman and going to roadhouses and getting girls to sit on his lap. Think of the Mohawks, a group of young bucks in the 1770s, who used to dress up as fantasy frontiersmen and hang out in the woods of St. James's Park and hassle people. There's a fascination of the city man for the country man that goes back to fifth-century Athens. There's a fascination of the civilized man for the barbarian. Man is divided into two basic types initially. He is either a hunter and a killer, or he is a planter and a creator; he is either a cowboy or a settler.

*And you would like to be among the hunters and cowboys.*

Of course I would, because I'm a man of civilization by my nature and background. And the more civilized the world becomes the less place there is for the nomadic hunter-killers on horseback or on motorcycles. Civilization weighs heavily on the thoughtful man, and so much of consciousness is painful that the man who doesn't carry the burden of civilization and who seems to run only on instincts seems a free man. There must have been Greeks who dreamed of getting pushed around by a couple of Scythians and soaked down in horse piss and fucked. That must have been a crazy, forbidden desire. I'm not talking about the realities of any of this. I'm talking about myth.

*But we're also talking about fantasies that are often acted out and become real in that sense. It then becomes a question of how this particular reality is viewed and controlled. Many people see such fantasies as fascistic and sexist.*

Sure they're sexist and also antidomestic. Men all alone together in a barracks situation is the material of homosexual fantasy. The uniform ideal has to do with those locker rooms and barracks, and the bonds that form between men who are part of the team together.

*How is S and M related to your fetishism?*

Both S and M and fetishism came into my life at the same time when I was eighteen. I had had plenty of sex since I was fifteen, but I was missing the mythic, the bigger-than-life thing. For everybody who's into S and M, and for many who aren't, what counts is Dionysian sex as opposed to Apollonian sex, which is love, warmth, domesticity, civilization, marriage. But Dionysian sex is not just another human function like shitting or eating. It is orgiastic, an escape, a special situation that is higher somehow. An orgasm is a shaking release that is not like any other satisfaction. Many Americans know that, and that's what makes them so sex-crazy and such good sex.

*Does this desire connect with particular fantasies you wanted to fulfill when you were young?*

Well, one of the earliest ones I remember started when I was old enough to know that those holes in the street were called manholes. Maybe I was four or three. I didn't know what was under the streets, but I could see that men went down the hole and came out and did something down there, and that was clearly why it was called a manhole. I was a child, and it was not a childhole. By the time I was ten, I felt I was trapped in the body of a child, and it was a humiliating experience. I yearned for all the signs and changes of puberty. I didn't know anything about sex, but I wanted to be a man because it was the only way to get to men, who would take me in and make a man out of me. I still like the kind of men who go down manholes.

*That's interesting because the manhole is an entrance and also an "asshole." Your fantasy shows how persistent certain situations are in our dreams and in our history. It's like a tribal initiation rite where the men go off to a secret place to perform mysterious acts related to puberty. Anthropologists and psychologists who have written on these situations have remarked that by fucking someone you could humiliate him and show his subordination, but by fucking a pubescent boy a man could inject his semen into him, his male essence, and allow the boy to become a man.*

Right! Of course, if they are important, initiations have to be repeated until you feel you are inside the group of all the men in the tribe who have gone through the ceremony. It has to be repeated because it wears off, as it were. That's why you don't just suck a dick once.

*Those times when sex is truly satisfying, is it like another initiation, getting in contact again with some special mystery?*

Yes, that's one basic experience. Another is reinforcing the mutual feeling that you and the other guy are both of it, in it, part of it. For example, if you like your Levis greased—what they call "naturals" in California—and you see, among all the men who are wearing Levis because they're supposed to, another man who has got his ass in his pants that way, there's a special recognition. S and M is not such an important part of it. That's why I've come through and beyond S and M in some ways, because the most satisfying experience for me is the mutual service on the inside, the barracks secrets that never get passed on to the captain. Of course, there are conventions that take over when a man in uniform meets another who isn't in uniform.

*The one who is out of uniform is automatically put in a subordinate position?*

That's right. Uniform has an inhibiting quality. And it's just wrong, or a very special "inverted" situation, for the trooper to stop you, make you get out of the car, pull down your pants, and blow you. It might even be disappointing to you.

*Do you like playing all the different roles, in or out of uniform, whether the roles show dominance, submission, or whatever?*

Yes, all of them. I even like the situation where two men in uniform can't find a satisfactory way for either of them to submit to the other. So you work as a team and get a civilian to do the things for each of you that you cannot do directly to each other. With some men, that's one way to get over the barrier. With other men the act of leaping the barrier is part of a kind of initiatory thing and also part of that demonstration of service and command that is S and M.

*You seem particularly fascinated by this idea of a barrier.*

I think you have to make a leap of the imagination to realize that you are entitled to get together with another man, and once you've made that jump, then there are a lot of jumps you can make. That's why homosexual S and M is so far advanced and so subtle and sophisticated compared to heterosexual S and M. Once you've taken the big hurdle and freed yourself, then all the other things become relative.

*But you're also suggesting that the essential push takes place in childhood.*

Right. If it doesn't go back to your childhood, forget it. All you can do is jump on a popular bandwagon. There must have been a pair of man's boots in daddy's closet when you were four years old, and you touched them once and thought you shouldn't. You can smack a man's ass, or grip his arm, or put your arm around his shoulder, but you're not supposed to touch his face or his shoes. So these things become eroticized because they're forbidden.

*You said that S and M and fetishism came into your life together when you were eighteen. How?*

It happened at an all-male Thanksgiving cocktail party in the early sixties. There was one man in a black T-shirt, khaki pants, and black Wellington boots. He carried himself differently. He seemed reserved and self-confident. He had some kind of male secret, and I had to know what it was. The guy I was seeing was at this party, but when this man went into the bathroom, I was drawn in after him. He pulled his cock out and made me suck it, and it was easy to suck it. I saw him later, and a third guy tied me to him so that we were strapped together face to face. That was the first time anybody had tied me up. It was very hot to be forced into this intimacy that you wanted so much.

*I assume you saw this man several times and that he was always in charge.*

I was a pretty eighteen-year-old hungry for an initiation. It was the natural way for us to come together. He was rough with me, and if he showed affection, it was in a very gruff way. More important than affection, he showed approval—I'd done well, I'd been courageous, I had performed well.

*Do you think there was something of the classic Greek pattern in your relationship with this man?*

K. J. Dover in *Greek Homosexuality* says that the boy was the passive one in that he was not to experience any pleasure. He was to submit out of a sense of the worth and the power of the older man who brought him gifts.

*At least he wasn't supposed to show he was having pleasure.*

We're not talking about the actual facts of the situation. We're talking about the basic ritual. That was how it was supposed to be. In my relationship, I was to submit and take care of his desires. What he knew and what I couldn't help showing was that it excited me enormously.

*Do you believe that the gay world you reject lacks true rituals and conventions, or even a sense of erotic barriers?*

Yes. One gay attitude is that because I'm gay and in a gay situation, I've got a free ticket to everything, that just because this is your apartment doesn't mean I can't take your lover into the bedroom and suck him off if I want to.

*That's not so.*

Maybe the conventions I respond to are heterosexual or even WASP conventions, but they don't seem to apply in the specifically gay world. For example, one of the most important conventions in a leather bar as opposed to a regular gay bar is that you don't ask someone what he does for a living. It's a totally inappropriate and ridiculous question.

*Doesn't every society or group have its rules and codes? There's a code in the baths and in the disco, and there's a code among street queens. I agree that for some groups rules are more important than for others, and they are elaborated and followed more consciously. But it's also true that outsiders often fail to see or understand the code of a particular group and conclude that none exists.*

Fair enough. But in public gay life I feel the absence of mutual responsibility and mutual respect. The respect that a real S and M pair have for each other is ineffable. I lived with a guy for a year and a half, and I absolutely ran his life and gave him stability. His name for me was "boss." I liked the confidence he had in me, and I was determined never to betray it.

Even if I sent him into a bedroom to present himself to a guest as available, I would never do it to the wrong guest or to someone who would not understand the offer or not take it in the way that was best for my friend, for me, and for himself.

*I think you're also talking about a real passion for order and for perfection, whether it be perfecting a sexual practice, a way of dressing, or an image of the self. If that's so, how does it all relate to the barbarian?*

For the civilized man, the barbarian is the man who invents his own order and then, perhaps, imposes this order on you. He creates his own nobility—the barbaric nobility of the Scythian, the Goth, the Hun, the Vandal.

*You remind me of the hero in Gide's* The Immoralist, *who is also fascinated by those barbarians, partly because he is a highly civilized man who begins to find the order of his society too rigid and deadening instead of creative. Some of us might feel a somewhat similar frustration with the prison of a nine-to-five job.*

Right. That's the real order whose limitations and imperfections we know so well. It's the oppressive order that we kick out against because we too would like to create our own order out of ourselves, create our own code. The sadist has done that, and perhaps he can initiate us into his order. Again, I'm not talking about the reality of individual situations and human frailties, but about the image and the myth. That's what is so misunderstood by the outsider who sees a man in a police uniform and is sure that if that guy really had the balls, he'd be wearing a Nazi uniform.

*I'll agree with you that accusations of fascism are often made too quickly and unthinkingly in such matters, but I also think there are important differences between creating your own order or having one imposed on you, or even just accepting one ready-made. As for images and myths, people live, die, and kill for them all the time, including saints and Nazis. But people also learn from them. What do you learn from the myths and rituals of S and M?*

We use them to achieve gnosis, a mystic understanding and strength in ourselves. We gain an understanding of violence and the uses of power in the world. We also learn about male bonding and about the natural human instinct that develops cohesiveness in any group.

*Right, and I'd like to see more cohesiveness develop among all gay men and women, which is somewhat contradictory because I also like the fact that there are "homosexualities," different gay tribes wearing different clothes and sending out different signals. So it seems that we face the same dilemmas as other societies—how to have diversity and unity at the same time, or at least diversity without hierarchy, without the feeling that one group is not only different but better.*

Anybody who feels like an insider feels smug about it. It's a natural human pattern—our tribe is better than the tribe on the other side of the mountain. Also, I don't think there is any single fundamental bond in homosexuality except homosexuality itself, and that's not enough to bring people together who have absolutely nothing else in common. Personally, I don't have a strong ecumenical outlook. I like the group feeling inside my world, and I like guys who are highly specialized.

# This Time Around I Belong to Him

*T*his interview is a portrait of an individual. It is not an attempt to characterize an entire group of gay men, or to describe a form of sexuality which, like any other, is subject to wide variation. What attracted me to this man was less his "masochism" than the intensity of his efforts to realize his desires.

*Would you define yourself as a masochist?*

I hadn't until we talked about doing this piece. Before, I could never admit that I was, and I didn't want to be classified under such a name. I guess I didn't want to see myself as one. Well, now I am, and I accept the fact that I am.

*Was it as difficult for you to accept this as it was to accept your homosexuality?*

I never had a problem accepting myself as a homosexual. I knew I liked men since I was thirteen.

*Do you think your masochism was there from the beginning?*

Oh, I think it must have always been there. I had fantasies of a kind of hidden, forbidden excitement, and I read stories and magazine articles, and I would look at certain pictures. But it never came out. I never met anybody I wanted to practice it with until I met the man I'm involved with now, who kind of took my fantasies and made them real. It's really with him that this life began for me.

*Can you talk about that beginning?*

I don't know where to start. Right from the first time I dug him. I thought he was really hot sexually, physically. I was going through a long, difficult period in my life. I was breaking up with a lover and kind of feeling lost. I met him, and we did it, and I found it very hot and very exciting. It's even more exciting now, because it's grown. We both put a lot of energy into it.

*How long have you been together?*

Almost two and a half years. We know what each one likes, and there's a challenge.

*What kind of challenge?*

Sexual, mental . . . to increase the pleasure and to increase our involvement with one another.

*How? Do you spend a lot of time together?*

Yes and no. Most of it is sexual, but we do meet a lot for lunch, and he calls me at night on the phone. We talk about sex, but I also help him sometimes with his problems. For example, I encourage him when he's troubled about his job. . . . He has a lover. He's involved emotionally with the man he lives with. That takes a lot of his time.

*That must disturb you.*

Of course it does, but I think that's part of my masochism also. I can't see him when I want. I don't call him that often at home. I have to wait for his call. Waiting, sitting around, is also masochistic.

*Would you say you enjoyed that?*

I must, because I do it.

*Somebody has actually defined masochism as "waiting in its pure form." But haven't we all gone through that at some time?*

I find it frustrating. I enjoy getting those calls. I don't enjoy it when he doesn't come through. I used to get very upset when I expected him to call and he didn't. But he never said he would call, so by getting upset I created some kind of trauma within myself. He also likes the idea of me sitting around waiting for his calls and being on call twenty-four hours a day.

*And that pleases you, the fact that it pleases him?*

Yes, but we're going a little too fast here. In the beginning I wasn't so devoted, and I wasn't always around. But then it grew to the point where I wouldn't do anything until I found out exactly what his plans were. I would arrange to have my free time around the time he was allotting me.

*So what makes that necessarily masochistic in your vision of it?*

Because I don't think that on his part it was waiting. Because it was one-sided. He was always in control. He would have the time; he wanted to see me. He wasn't around when I was free.

*Have you ever confronted him with this situation?*

That was my role, and I wanted it. That was the role of being the slave, the servant, being there for him twenty-four hours a day to fill any and all needs he had; and his needs were first, and by pleasing his needs, my needs would be taken care of.

*Does he use those words too?*

Yes, they came from his mouth, too, but not in the very beginning.

*Do you use the word* master *in reference to him?*

Yes, but more often I use *sir*.

*Has being designated a slave ever bothered you in any way?*

Yes and no. I have read about slaves in history. I know what that means. But for me it's different. There's a sexual excitement, a sexual stimulation about it that turns me on. I'm not living it 100 percent of the time like the historical slave. I do have to go out into the world and deal with it on another level. What I do with him is just one level, one fantasy.

*I know that you've had a very successful business career to the point where you don't have to work right now. We could say, in fact, that in the outside world you are one of the masters.*

True. In that sense my slavery is a fantasy. I haven't given up my life to be any person's slave or servant. I haven't given up my own self and personality to the extent of the historical thing, where somebody buys you, owns you, and tells you exactly what to do all the time. But I am a slave to him and to our sex, yes. I can't get out of it. I don't want to.

*But you are frustrated.*

Yes, because I can't have what I want when I want it.

*Isn't there something of the master in what you just said, a desire to call some of the shots? Would that be an accurate description?*

Yes, I'd say so. Yes.

*Have you played the role of master with someone else?*

Yes, but not with him. And as I said, in the last two and a half years I haven't fooled around with many other people at all.

*Have you acted toward other people the way you would like them to act toward you, were they the master?*

I have not been someone else's slave.

*No, we're talking about your role as master.*

I've done it with one or two other men. I'm not into following certain defined roles. I go to bed with them and take it as it comes. If I find they need to be tremendously dominated, I take that role. I enjoy and have desires to bind men and be stronger than them. But I haven't seen any other men for a good year now. I want to say again that my relationship with my man did not start out as slave and master. In the beginning things were basically equal, with one person being more dominant, so-called, in bed, and the other one not being so much passive as taking on the passive role. From there certain things were brought into the sexual field as we got to know each other better. One thing I found very exciting about him was that I never had to tell him what my fantasies were and to please do them to me. I don't go for setting up rules ahead of time. Little by little he kept doing certain things and saw that I responded very well. And of course, one thing led to another—bondage, water sports, we talked about fisting. Little by little things were tried. I was very excited by them. I did have fantasies about them and built up a certain confidence each time certain things were done to me. At first, if he bound me, I would always try to keep a certain amount of movement so I could get out. Of course, now it's gotten to the point where I trust him, and it doesn't matter. But this was all built up, since I was not into this kind of scene before and never did trust anybody to that degree. I never let myself go.

*When you met him, you were somewhat of a novice?*

A complete novice.

*But he wasn't.*

No, he's been doing it for years.

*And this is what you've been looking for?*

Right. What I'm looking for is a relationship. I'm not looking to go to a bar and be bound or beat or fisted and then left. I am looking to build a foundation with someone.

*Do you think that all relationships or even sexual encounters are governed by a dominant-submissive pattern?*

To an extent, yes. But with certain people it's not important to put what they do under categories, S or M or whatever. But certain people also need to have that feeling of dominance or that feeling of submissiveness.

*Have you thought about why you have this need?*

Actually, I've become aware of something only very recently, and I haven't really thought it out completely. I find Carl similar to—I associate him with—my father and certain ways my father used to treat me. When he would finally get mad at me, he would show his anger, and then right away he would reward me. He'd feel guilty for showing his anger.

*Would he strike you?*

No, he would never hit me. I always wanted him to. My mother would always hit us. He would just yell and scream. I really wanted my father to hold me, love me, kiss me, but he never did.

*So hitting you would have at least been a substitute for that?*

Right. The same thing is true here, with Carl.

*He just hits you? He never holds you and hugs you?*

Oh yes. Afterward.

*Is that one of the ways you relate pleasure to pain?*

I think it's more complex than that. I find pain more of a challenge. I see it more like two men in combat, two men in an arena fighting. One of course is giving it and one is taking it. I've learned to take pain and to build my tolerance up to it. I never give in. I always ask for more, which excites him. I've learned to take a lot, a tremendous amount.

*How is the pain inflicted?*

With a wide leather belt. I can take it to a point where I think I can't take it any more, and then I can switch it off. I seem to have no feeling.

*So, like some mystics, you've learned to master your body through your mind.*

Yes, I have done that.

*And you do this because it gives him pleasure, and because you prove your ...*

... masculinity.

*To him and to yourself?*

Yes, to both of us.

*And this is what you wanted to do with your father—to prove your masculinity to him and to be worthy of his love?*

Yes. Also, I know that Carl cares for me and loves me. I know there's a certain limit that he is aware of, and that he will stop when he reaches it. But I try to push him further, to challenge him.... You see, there's something very important to me here. This is the first time that I have a man who finds me extremely sexually exciting. I never had that in my life before. I've always either groveled after men or tried to seduce them to get my pleasure. I have a man now who can look at me and get excited. It turns me on, and I'll do anything for that feeling, to keep it. And I want him to beat me harder because I don't want him to look anywhere else to find that satisfaction. And that's answering the question about pain and pleasure. I'm taking my pain because I'm getting pleasure out of it.

*So each time he beats you, he expresses his need for you and affirms your own value to him.*

Right, and I also need him very much.

*And when he beats you, you feel more attractive?*

Yes, and I want to work on my body and make sure it's kept healthy.

*You're more satisfied now when you look at yourself in the mirror than you were before?*

Sure.

*What about the other big question—humiliation?*

That is a very interesting subject and has come out in our sexual response to each other. I think—how can I put this?—I think that in the outside world he has been humiliated and has very strong hostile feelings toward it. I, on the other hand, grew up in an atmosphere of prejudice directed at others. I saw people abused and had to stand by and could not react, could not change those events. I've had tremendous feelings of guilt because of it. We have gotten into certain sexual areas where those hostilities on his part have come out, and he has called me names and abused me, and that's related to my guilt. Am I making sense?

*Not completely. You have to be more specific.*

Well, he's a member of a minority group that has been abused. He's Puerto Rican.

*He's Puerto Rican, and you're . . .*

Jewish.

*And have you experienced humiliation in your life because you're Jewish?*

Very rarely.

*Not to the extent that he has felt it as a Puerto Rican?*

Right.

*And you have seen Puerto Ricans being abused?*

Yes, by Jews, by my father, in the garment industry.

*So, your father's presence in your relationship with Carl is even greater than what you acknowledged before.*

I guess it is.

*And when Carl abuses you, are you somehow taking the place of those Puerto Ricans and also expiating for the sins of your fellow Jews?*

No—for myself, for my own guilt.

*Because you weren't able to do anything about it?*

Right. We've gotten into name-calling. He calls me names, and I provoke him. I want that. It's very sexual and very exciting. It all came about spontaneously. We never planned it. It just worked that way. It has not been as important recently as when we first started, but it's still there.

*And afterward he shows you affection?*

Well, he's not a man who's very affectionate. It doesn't happen very often. It's not something that's consistent, that I know I'm going to get.

*Do you think that if he were more consistently affectionate that that would diminish the sexual excitement?*

No. I honestly believe that. I mean, the most exciting thing about him, what I love most, is that he can be totally sadistic while beating me and then just pick me up in his arms and carry me all the way down the hallway to the bedroom and make love to me.

*Do you like feeling like a child sometimes with him?*

Lately more than ever. I'm conscious of that, extremely so.

*Wasn't your last lover also Puerto Rican?*

Yes. My former lover and all my important affairs have been Puerto Ricans.

*So this man is about as close to the ideal as one could be for you.*

Yes. As I said, when I met him I was in a very down period. He came along, and it was like a shock and it was like a challenge to me. And I decided to write about it. I had almost never written anything before, but this time I kept writing and writing. I have four notebooks full.

*Could you pick out something you like, or that you consider particularly significant?*

Well, there is a poem that I wrote after the first weekend we spent together. It was the weekend that I was working for my man, taking care of him in every way possible. That's what I wanted to write about—those three days of total submission, of total selfless service. I know that one of my needs is a need to please and to do for somebody, and I get tremendous pleasure from doing for him. That includes cooking, cleaning, and all the rest. But I couldn't have done it for anybody else, because he was fulfilling my sexual needs as well.

*What I'm reading here is not about cooking.*

No, it's about what happened one night at about nine or ten o'clock. I was told to follow him. I was taken onto the beach, which he had already surveyed earlier that day without my knowing it. He had found this very big, long log, about eight feet long, with a large spike coming out of the top of it. He always carried a chain, which he sometimes put around my neck or around my crotch. This time, when we reached the log, he tightened the chain around one wrist then around the other, and then wrapped the chain around the spike. There was a hole in the log, and he put the chain through that, too. I had absolutely no way of freeing myself without the help of somebody else. I was bound face down with hands and legs spread out in front of him. This was the first time that I was beaten, whipped, with a tremendous amount of pain, pleasure.

*Were you frightened?*

Yes, very frightened. It was the first time that I felt completely helpless and completely within his control. I did not scream, as I remember. And since then, as I said, I've learned to take pain like a man.

*Let's read the passage from the poem that deals with that scene:*

> I rebelled the first afternoon.
> Not until evening did the heavens open up
> to allow lightning to strike its savage blows.
> Chains ripped through wrists
> in ice cold flashes of intolerance.
> There was no escape from the thick blackness
> that came crashing down through the night.
> Its shadow struck heavy blows
> of passion from every side.
> All oxygen was smashed out of my lungs
> till I was unconscious and death was approaching.
>
> Just in time my executioner
> reached down,
> wrapping his arms and body
> tightly around mine.
> I was gasping for life.
> He opened my mouth and gave
> life back to me.
>
> I've been reborn.
> This time around I belong to him.
> I'm born in his image.

*This says a lot.*

Yes, it says more than I could have said then, or now. That's why I wrote it.

*You describe coming close to a limit, to crossing a line.*

Yes, but I don't think I wanted to die. I think it was more the idea of giving up something of myself to be reborn or take on a new identity.

*Do you see it now as a kind of initiation rite?*

I never thought of it that way.

*Do you still like to think of him as a god, as your creator, your father?*

Yes and no. I have looked at him as my father, my god, a creator, but every time I've tried to turn that fantasy into something real, I've always found out that he is also a man.

*Was that a disappointment?*

Yes.

*But you were saying before that you want his affection and warmth. Well, those are human qualities.*

Yes, I want that too.

*But you're disappointed when you see his weaknesses, his fears, and limitations?*

Yes.

*And you want him to be perfect?*

As much as he wants me to be perfect.

*Don't you find that perfection somewhat inhuman?*

Yes. There are a lot of contradictions in what I'm saying. My disappointment comes when I've lost reality and tried to live his dream as reality. I love the man and want the relationship with the man, not with the god. Deep down, it's very exciting to have these fantasies and lose this reality, but deep down, too, I want to hold on to my man. I want that love. I want that affection.

*So, ultimately, his perfection should appear only at certain moments.*

Yes, and I want to be the man he wants me to be.

*That keeps coming back in what you say, the idea of proving your manhood.*

I never seemed to have to prove it before. Now I do. I have to prove it to him.

*Do you think that has any relation to your being gay? Nobody has called you names or humiliated you about that?*

It could have happened. It probably has, but nothing that was very traumatic in my life. There could be something unconscious, of course.

*Do you still feel reborn?*

At that time I did, and afterward too.

*I detect some disillusionment in your voice. Have you tired of the scene in any way?*

I can't say that I've been disillusioned, because I have not really been involved in the S-and-M scene outside my own scene. I've only seen a bit of it with him. He's more involved in it than I am.

*Have you been out to the bars together?*

Yes. We have gotten into exhibitionism in certain clubs in the city. He wanted it, and I went along, but I've had mixed feelings about it.

*You're into leather.*

Yes, yes. He's very interested in leather, the proper use of it, where to use it, the care of it.

*There's a fairly rigid code associated with leather.*

Right. A lot of people don't know that, are not aware of it, as I was not. There's a whole formal set of rules about what to wear and what not to wear, how to wear it. Then, of course, each person's standards are different, as with everything else.

*Do you also like uniforms?*

Yes. What I feel most comfortable in and enjoy is a policeman's uniform, especially riot police or motorcycle police, with helmet, high boots, and breeches. He gets excited seeing me dressed like that.

*I can understand why—a policeman in the role of a slave. But what about you? Does that also connect with the guilt feelings you mentioned before?*

I don't know if I can get into that right now. But there are other things. I mean, what I like best is the fact that you can't just walk into a store, into Bloomingdale's or Macy's, and say, I'd like one policeman's uniform. It takes time, unless you want to buy a uniform off of somebody. But to put together all the little pieces and the different shirts and the emblems, you have to do a lot of investigation; you have to be a little bit humiliated in trying to find out how you can buy these items. So what I enjoyed most was putting it all together, which took me a year, and then seeing his face when he walked in and saw me in it, and having him so sexually turned on by it.

*Are you turned on by policemen?*

Most policemen in the city I don't find sexually attractive, although I could get into a whole thing with Carl in that police context. And then, I have had fantasies about having sex with policemen—in the plural. Sucking them off in the barracks or something like that. . . . When I was growing up, the first man who talked to me about sex was a motorcycle policeman.

*Well!*

I was about fourteen or fifteen. My father was too embarrassed to talk about it, so he asked this man who was a close friend to do it. He was very attractive and used to come to the house a lot in uniform. So one day he talked to me and a friend and asked us what we did together.

*Were you doing something together?*

Yes, but I don't remember what we told him.

*So you were frightened and excited at the same time.*

It's very interesting that this relationship with Carl has a lot to do with feelings and experiences I had when I was growing up in my teens. In fact, I was arrested in lovers' lane with a kid when I was eighteen. We were picked up by the police, but they were plainclothesmen. At the time, when they came over to the car, I didn't think they were policemen. One of them had alcohol on his breath. I had just finished reading *The Sixth Man*, which was very popular at the time, and so I became kind of a know-it-all and started asking for their identification. But the kid I was with got very "yes sir, no sir," you know—very frightened and submissive. And so we were taken down to the police station. First, they questioned us in separate rooms. I had read in the book that you never admit to anything, so I said absolutely nothing. They told me that the other kid had said everything about what we did. So they called our parents, but of course only my parents came down. They said they couldn't get in touch with his. They had called mine because I was the wise guy.

*Your parents must have been very upset.*

True. They didn't know how to handle it at first. What I was wearing was kind of gay—tight pants and a short jacket. When I got home, my parents told me to throw the clothes out because I looked like a queer. So I just ripped them up into shreds and threw them to the bottom of the stairs in front of their bedroom. When my younger sister came down and asked my parents why my clothes were ripped up, they said that I looked too much like a hood, not that I looked queer.

*So, in a sense, you've put those clothes back together again.*

Yes.

*And you've reshaped the past.*

Yes, and I made something special.

*And that wasn't easy.*

No. One thing I thought I would never be able to do was to have a fist inside of me. It was very painful and took a long time to get into. But recently, this man, my master, has brought me to the height of passion, of total release, total giving, and has brought me to orgasms just by the manipulation of his hand. The pleasure has been unbelievable. I've never had such pleasure as that.

*What about him?*

It seems to be a very important part of our relationship, especially for him. He seems to have a great need for it, and he has said so. He has not said 100 percent that it has to be with me.

*What do you mean?*

He said that if I could not fulfill that need for him, it could be done with a third person.

*Where does that put you?*

I would watch.

*And you would enjoy that?*

No, I would not. I'd rather have it done to me. But things have changed. There's a problem now. I mean, I had an accident a few months ago. I ruptured my intestine with a large dildo.

*Ruptured it?*

Yes.

*Were you with him when it happened?*

No, I was alone. It was the day after we had had a wild scene, and I was thinking about it. I didn't realize what I had done until many hours later. Then I waited a few more hours, not wanting to do anything, until I had to be rushed to emergency. I had a four-hour operation.

*A very dangerous one.*

Oh, yes. Peritonitis had set in.

*Are you back in shape now?*

No. They performed a colostomy, so I have to return for a second operation in another few days.

*What about Carl? Have you seen him?*

Yes.

*Have you had sex with him?*

Mildly, yes. But what's important is that I reached the point where I told him I didn't want to see him any more.

*What was his reaction to that?*

If that was what I wished, he would abide by it.

*Doesn't his suggestion about a third person represent an effort to make an accommodation?*

I suppose it does.

*But you're afraid.*

There are several things. During the last few weeks before the accident happened it seemed that I was giving my whole self up, that I was becoming totally obsessed with him and was wanting more than I was getting. But I couldn't get it, and I couldn't get out of it.

*You wanted more of him and more pleasure?*

Yes, both those things. I also thought that when I came to the point of wanting more or of being frightened, he would be there to help me.

*That's assuming there's another point to go to.*

Well, I did have death wishes, death fantasies. They came very close in those last few weeks. I thought of the chain around my neck and having him pull it tighter and tighter until we reached orgasm. It was never tight enough. But now I want to live, and I want to associate him with living, not with death. Still, I want to give him the opportunity to get out of it. . . . What I'm trying to say is that I'm scared of the future. Before I had no fear of dying, and now I'm frightened of myself.

*And of what you still desire?*

Right. I know what I want. I do want it again. I do want to feel those feelings. But I also don't want to get hurt again, and if I do, I want him to look after me next time.

*Didn't he look after you this time?*

Yes, but I think—I know—that his first commitment is to his lover. What's funny is that the night it happened, it was my ex-lover who came for me and took me to the hospital. I've learned that you can't rely on anybody, that there's no one you can truly trust except yourself and some old friends, like my ex-lover. But when it comes to love and passion, you really have to pull yourself together and get it from within. That's where the ultimate power is.

*Earlier you said that things were better now than ever, but "now" must have been then, before the accident.*

Yes, I guess that's what I meant.

*So, in that respect, you seem to be in a kind of limbo, somewhere between the past and the future, or as you said, between fear and desire.*

That's right. That's where I am. I'm waiting to see what will happen—with him and with myself. But I do want a relationship, a relationship that grows, and a little ease.

*What?*

A little ease. Ease.

# SEYMOUR KLEINBERG

❖❖❖❖❖❖❖❖❖❖❖❖❖❖❖

## *Those Dying Generations: Harry and His Friends*

> *That is no country for old men. The young*
> *In one another's arms, birds in the trees*
> *—Those dying generations—at their song,*
> *The salmon falls, the mackerel-crowded seas,*
> *Fish, flesh, or fowl, commend all summer long*
> *Whatever is begotten, born, and dies.*
> *Caught in that sensual music all neglect*
> *Monuments of unageing intellect.*
>
> —William Butler Yeats
> "Sailing to Byzantium"

*P*oets see things earlier than ordinary men; poets like Yeats see them more clearly and tell us more movingly what we may expect from the present. In 1928, when he published his tragic lyric about the expendability of old men, Western society had not grown as callous and phobic toward old age as it has become in the last decades. One cliché claims that old age is more difficult in youth-mad America than elsewhere. True, America is the advance guard of all those forces which seem to provoke and promote social decline, but the condition of the aged is as bad in Europe and in socialist societies as it is here—if the old men or women happen to be gay.

When one is old and gay, one acquires a universal burden of social indifference or contempt to add to a lifelong oppression as a homosexual man or lesbian. In exploring the subject with the men I interviewed, one question was central: Has being gay made aging more difficult? Hearteningly, the answer seems to be, "No, not especially," even given the notoriously exaggerated investment in youthfulness among gays. In some cases it has made it easier. For men in their late sixties and seventies, living gay in this century and surviving those miseries has alleviated the traumas of aging. The long closeted life has often hardened the men; some are even more fortunate than their heterosexual counterparts, for whom widowhood and loneliness and loss of social place are terminal griefs. The men I interviewed, despite the diversity of their lives, are more than literal survivors.

I began to explore this subject accidentally. I intended to write about the instability of romantic sexuality—having recently been rejected by my lover of three years for a passing, pretty face. Depressed and obsessive, I hoped to exorcise the bitterness by documenting similar injustices among acquaintances, since sources for this particular sad story are everywhere. When I found that the bars and baths and organizations I had once been active in were dead ends as far as finding someone to be serious about is concerned, I decided to join a small consciousness-raising group and answered an ad in *Gay Community News* directed to men forty or older. Although, as one friend later put it, "You should have known that any fag admitting to forty is really sixty," I was not prepared for the group I entered: Ted is sixty-seven, Bert sixty-nine, Michael seventy-two, Harry seventy-five, Rudi seventy-nine, and Alex eighty-two. Six other men were in their fifties, but at forty-four, I was the baby.

When that day's leader calmly announced that the subject of the session was "Attitudes Toward Dying," I felt slammed with a double wave of anxiety. I had recently been experiencing some totally irrational fears and fantasies about dying and was generally eager to avoid a serious look at the subject (promising myself every day to stop smoking). But the idea of discussing death with men who possibly might keel over from natural causes during the hour was more than I'd bargained for.

As one might expect, only the younger men in the group seemed burdened by the subject, because the issue for them was not dying but its corollary: not living. Those men in their old age who had "lived," whether their lives were shadowed with regrets or not, regarded the subject as somehow irrelevant. They were going to die; none really denied that or seemed to find the idea horrifying, although all were concerned with the manner of their deaths and hoped they would not be cursed with senility or agony. But all of the men, including one presently in remission from cancer, agreed that they lived almost exclusively in the present. Tomorrow is Monday or Tuesday; the fantasy future of younger people had finally disappeared.

As I listened, I was struck with the richness of their collective pasts. These men had been homosexual in the twenties' and the Depression, in libertine New York of World War II; their pasts were an invaluable document of my history as a gay man. Like others who are working to record that past, I understood that here was a subject of great immediacy. At the next meeting I asked if I could interview them. They seemed surprised at the idea and consented with varying degrees of willingness, since I was a stranger. This, then, is about how two of those men live now. One day the fuller story of their lives should be told.

## Harry

No one would believe that Harry is nearly seventy-six. Not only is his face almost unlined, but he moves with vigor and ease; he is tanned and firm, sweet and outgoing. An Englishman, he has an accent, which does not define his class (it is neither Cockney nor Oxbridge). When Harry agrees to an interview, he gives me a small card from his wallet identifying his career field as industrial electronics, which I later translate to mean he is a highly skilled electrician. The card is a bit stained and yellow; the business address is inked out and in one corner he has pasted his home address. Harry retired at sixty-four, a year earlier than necessary, because he feared losing his pension when his union voted to strike. When I suggested this was a strike-breaking tactic, he looked pained and agreed that perhaps it was, but he chose to exercise his accumulated sick days to retire early.

Harry attributes his physical fitness to a "lucky" constitution, but he is also an avid hiker and walker, a nature lover, and a devotee of nude sunbathing. He spends as much time as he can with old friends in the country, where he combines his taste for nature and exercise with what he calls "having a party." When I ask him if that is a euphemism for fucking, he pauses and admits that he and his friends have always described casual sex as "having a party." Since I recently edited an anthology of gay short stories that included Tennessee Williams's "Two on a Party" without paying particular attention to the title, I got my first hint of how unexpectedly informative my research was going to be.

Harry's English background also comes out in his small, trimmed, gray moustache and in the Bermuda shorts he wears daily in the summer—with forest-green knee socks, sensible wing-tip shoes that I haven't seen outside Brooks Brothers for twenty years, and freshly pressed button-down shirts. It only takes a moment to figure out that the shoes and shirts *are* twenty years old, still meticulously polished and darned.

Harry is special in other ways: his mother was a lesbian. He is not sure when he learned this, but by his teens he seems to have been certain. Harry says his mother knew *he* was gay, although the subject was not discussed openly. His father and mother separated before World War I. When Harry was seventeen, he had his first love affair, in the Boy Scouts with a twenty-three-year-old Swiss living in England. When his lover left, Harry confided his grief to his scoutmaster, who counseled discretion and then seduced him.

In 1922, Harry's mother sent him to New York City to live with his father, a jeweler who had emigrated here earlier. Whether she desired her freedom or thought he would do better professionally under his father's care is not clear. At first, Harry lived in the East Fifties, then a working-class neighborhood, and in the 1930s on West Ninety-seventh Street. His sexual adventures were sporadic, limited mostly to pickups in Central and Riverside parks. Harry sometimes cruised the West Seventies, which he claims was the gayest neighborhood in the city, although not as bohemian as the Village. It was not until the Depression that Harry discovered gay bars and baths.

Early in the interview he confesses that he is beginning to worry about sex: he is having too much and perhaps it isn't good for his health.

"What is 'too much' at seventy-five, Harry?"

"Well, since my lover died, I've been having some wild parties. I feel I'm oversexed. But perhaps it's good for my longevity?"

I hope so also. Harry usually has sex twice a week, almost always with men he knows well. Dave, a librarian in New Haven, Connecticut, is a boyfriend of fifty-eight whom Harry visits twice a month for long weekends. He also pays a monthly visit to Norman, a long-standing friend whom he most enjoys sleeping with, now retired from active service in the Mattachine Society and living in the country. His friend Rudi, who lives in Queens, is seventy-nine, and he visits him weekly for dinner and partying.

Then there is the young thirty-eight-year-old hospital worker whom Harry describes as "hard of hearing, and he slurs when he speaks. He's very self-conscious, but he feels comfortable with me. He's very affectionate." He drops by regularly at Harry's North Bronx apartment on his way home. Finally, there is the occasional adventure that develops from an early evening at Carr's Bar or an afternoon at the baths.

Harry has not merely blurted out his erotic schedule. He does not brag about his virility, although he knows he is unusual. As I solicit answers, I wonder how coarse I can get, for I am consumed with curiosity. Harry appears forthright and he talks easily, but he is also decorous, unflirtatious, and genuinely friendly. His sex life seems extravagant for a man of seventy-five; perhaps he and his friends simply cuddle a lot. But as we talk it is apparent that he enjoys discussing it, even if he is unused to doing so with a stranger. Our terms have to be clarified. Harry doesn't say "fuck"; he says "brown" or "up the back." When he says he has sex, he takes for granted that we mean oral sex and that being affectionate implies oral reciprocation. Although my vocabulary is blunter, Harry doesn't shy when I say fuck or suck or rim; he simply responds in his own idiom.

Later, I understand that while Harry has no sexual prudery, the subject is just not as fascinating to him as it is to me. It wasn't sleeping with Dave but going to the Trolley Museum that he relishes from his recent weekend in New Haven. It is not the party with Norman that is memorable but sunbathing nude in Norman's isolated back yard with only an occasional cow meandering by. Harry's need for civilized, affectionate sexuality is not rare, but as he talks about the erotic life, it is clear he finds sexual encounters disassociated from friendliness and emotional responsiveness less exciting. Even when he speaks of the young man of thirty-eight who drops by occasionally, whom he describes as somewhat clumsy and inexperienced, he denies that the man is selfish or unemotional.

"Yes, it's true, I usually blow him, or sometimes be browns me, although I don't particularly care for that, but he's not a quickie. He likes to stay in bed a long time. Once, he stayed overnight."

Although Harry is no stranger to the baths, having discovered them forty years ago, he finds men his own age more satisfying, even if their activities are less exotic. What they do—mutual masturbation, oral sex, or dry fucking—is not an important issue. When I ask if there are things he does not do or disapproves of, he says, surprisingly, that he never enjoyed 69-ing. "It's too distracting." Concerning the apparent sexual excesses and novel tastes of the younger generation, Harry showed a puzzled disinterest, confessing that he could not understand the blatant interest in scatology or sadism. However, he admitted, giggling, to "perhaps a slight fetish you might call sadistic—I love to have my thighs bit. Norman bites me and it turns me on. I guess I love men's thighs. I go to soccer games to watch the players with their muscular thighs. A few years ago, when I was seventy-three, my lover had just died and I went to Everard's. I came four times! It never happened before, but this young fellow knew just what to do. My legs were very red the next day."

Harry draws the line at drugs. He says they seem alien to him, and he won't sleep with anyone who uses poppers. He sometimes feels self-conscious about his age at the baths, since it's obvious people want younger men, but it doesn't bother him terribly. He also thinks himself more fastidious than younger men. He has never had any form of VD, never contracted a sexually related disease, never experienced impotence. For a moment, the expression on my face must be peculiar, for he hastens to add, "Well, it takes me longer to come now ... sometimes."

Harry's lover Bob died in 1973 when he was sixty-one, of diabetic complications. Talking of his lover, he loses his customary cheer, but otherwise betrays little of what that loss means. Harry and Bob were together twenty-seven years. During World War II, both men were employed in essential industries (and were thus draft-exempt). Bob was the dispatcher for a fleet of trucks. They had known each other nearly a year before they became friends and waited almost as long before they became lovers. At first, they would meet at Riverside Drive near the George Washington Bridge to make love: "We did it on the rocks, but we never *went* on the rocks." When they could afford it, they'd rent a room in one of the small hotels in the West Thirties, since they both lived at home with parents. Although they made their emotional commitment gradually, it was solid enough to exclude jealousy and accommodate a mutual, if mild, promiscuity. Both would go together to the tiny, raunchy, very wild steamroom in the basement of the Penn Post Hotel (now a parking lot). Occasionally Harry would spend the night with Norman or another man, and although Bob clearly did not like this very much, it was not a serious issue.

It was Bob who first interested Harry in gay issues, in Mattachine, and in a community of gay friends. Bob wrote as an avocation; his special interest was vaudeville, which they went to regularly. Harry, in turn, introduced Bob to the ballet, which he'd always liked. He tells of seeing Martha Graham in the 1932 American premier of Stravinsky's *Le Sacre du Printemps*, for which "I squandered all my money."

Bob's other interest was drag. He wrote about American vaudeville for British trade journals and about drag for some early homosexual newspapers. Drag was one of Bob's delights even though photographs show him to have been wiry and craggy faced, and by the late 1950s he had grown a beard. The pictures of Bob in drag, with blond teased hair, sequin shift, long white gloves, gold purse, and so on, grinning broadly, indicate that for him drag was mostly a lark. Harry said that no matter how carefully *he* tried, in drag he always looked like Mrs. Roosevelt, so he gave it up.

When the men traveled to Europe, Bob got in touch with the newspaper correspondent Oscar Weibel, founder of Der Kreis ("The Circle"), a homophile organization in Zurich that dated from the thirties. Through him and Bob's interest in drag, they became friends of Quentin Crisp, whose autobiography, *The Naked Civil Servant*, has just been printed here. Bob was planning to write a book about drag that he had been researching for years when he became diabetic, and Harry still has the notes carefully stored in his apartment.

Harry assures me that while there were squabbles and ups and downs, it was a very "smooth" relationship and essentially monogamous. Only when Bob's health began to fail and emotional stress forced a kind of permanent withdrawal from an active social life did he become possessive or jealous. In the early years, Bob worked nights and Harry days, so they saw each other only on weekends, and in the hectic last year of the war, they worked even then. When they would meet, their favorite places were Beckman's Bar on Third Avenue and Thirty-fourth Street or the Pepper Pot on West Fourth, where, I gather, a McDonald's now stands.

In the seventh year of their relationship, they decided to live together. Bob's parents had died, his father of cancer and his mother a suicide, and he asked Harry to live with him. They then became "officially" a couple, sharing household duties, entertaining, meeting other couples, both gay men and lesbians. Bob's fondnes for drag and his hobby of writing about it brought occasional glitter to their Washington Heights home. After a piece on Francis Renault, Bob and the famous female impersonator became friends. Renault would turn up at their gatherings with exotic celebrities like Nita Naldi in tow.

They became close friends with another gay couple, especially Eddie, a Puerto Rican. Eddie introduced them to gay life in New Jersey and to bars that catered to working-class couples like themselves. In the 1960s, however, Bob became mysteriously withdrawn and despondent. "He was always touchy, but now he began to lose his friends." Easily offended by them, he became more reclusive and decided to stop working. "He suddenly became a housewife." Their sexual life diminished and became more role-defined, Bob insisting that Harry always be dominant. Gradually, they stopped seeing Eddie and lost contact with their other friends. They gave up working for the Mattachine library and stopped helping with the mail and newsletter.

Bob became an insomniac, and so they stopped sleeping in the same bed. In the middle of the night, Harry would discover Bob eating bread and butter thickly spread with sugar. Increasingly, Bob turned to masturbation, "to help him sleep, he said." Then he collapsed and was rushed to Fordham Hospital, where he was diagnosed as diabetic. After being under observation in a public ward for a month, he begged Harry to take him home. But once he was released and housebound, Harry discovered he was alcoholic. He would drink till he became sick and rage if he could not drink. Two months later, Bob collapsed again and died in the emergency room. I suggested that Bob's reclusiveness might mean that he had been drinking far longer than Harry suspected; although the idea seemed plausible, Harry regards Bob's behavior in his last months as an ugly mystery.

Bob died intestate. His only surviving relative, a sister who had cut off all communications when he and Harry began living together, took all Bob's assets, some $10,000—"though she paid the funeral expenses," Harry adds generously. However, there was a complication. Harry had bonds in Bob's safe deposit box that he was able to claim only after much red tape cluttered his life and his mourning for his lover of twenty-seven years. Since Harry had named Bob *his* beneficiary, he thought it strange that Bob never made out a will, but inasmuch as he was ten years the elder, it had seemed an academic, as well as a tactless, issue.

After Bob's death, Harry tried to find Eddie, but his only lead was a straight brother who refused him any information. Mattachine was finished. It was at the West Side Discussion Group the following year that

Harry met Dave and through West Side last fall that he heard of the CR group where I met him. Dave has invited Harry to live with him in New Haven, but Harry is ambivalent about such a move. He likes the freedom his pension and Social Security give him to travel, usually returning to Europe every year. He likes his inveterate walks all over the city or sunning at Orchard Beach when he can't get to the country. He likes meeting friends at Carr's, where the clientele is friendly and older than those at the usual Village bar. He does not cruise: "If I go to a bar, I'm not so concerned with meeting someone. I just like to be with gay people and talk." His complaint about the CR group is that it is too unsocial. He needs sociability; his consciousness is already raised. Like most men his age, he admires the openness of younger men and women but fears we are heading for a "backlash; things are going too fast, too quick." He means, of course, for straight people.

I ask him finally if he has serious regrets about the past, about never marrying or having children as some gay men in his generation have done. "I guess I once did seriously consider it, but no—I never have regrets about the past. And I don't look back, I'm not nostalgic."

## Rudi

Rudi, one of Harry's steadies, is seventy-nine. He came out when he was sixty-four. Married for over thirty years, he became a widower with a grown son when he was sixty-three. The following year at the racetrack, one of his favorite haunts, he struck up an acquaintance with a Cuban refugee, John, a man of his own age. For the next fourteen years they were lovers, until John died in 1976. John was not only Rudi's first gay lover but also his first gay experience. Rudi did not think of himself as homosexual nor did he experience closeted yearnings before he met John.

Rudi was obviously a beauty; photographs of him over the years document his sustained handsomeness. He is still goodlooking, a small man with an innocent smile and a well-shaped youthful body. His health is still remarkably intact. In the pictures, especially those from the 1920s and 1930s, he looks very dapper, sporting boutonnieres in his well-cut lapels. He shows me a pair of white kid gloves folded in a fine yellowing silk handkerchief that he wore on his wedding day. He is fond of looking fashionable. A recent snapshot of him at Acapulco in a bikini shows he has little to be self-conscious about and not much to hide. It isn't clear what Rudi looks like ethnically, although somehow he does not look American. In fact, he was born—to "real illiterate peasants," he says with some contempt—one of fourteen children, somewhere near Zemplin in modern Czechoslovakia. When he was nine, with eleven surviving siblings living in near serfdom, he left home with his parents' indifferent blessing. He was hired as a servant by a middle-class couple who took charge of his welfare and schooling, virtually adopting him.

At fifteen, he went to work as a clerk for the railroads, where his adoptive father held a somewhat important position. When World War I broke out, sixteen-year-old Rudi volunteered to serve the Hapsburg Empire. He became a hero accidentally when he and another cavalryman captured a hundred Russian deserters lost in the Carpathian Mountains. Although they were outnumbered nearly fifty to one, their offer of bread induced the starving, freezing, practically unarmed Russians to surrender.

Shortly after the war, in Budapest, he struck up an acquaintance with a captain in the Imperial Horse Guards—"such a beautiful man," he sighs. Rudi says he was not aware of any sexual attraction on either of their parts; he was just struck by the beauty of the man, who, it seems, had other intentions. He took Rudi into his home and soon arranged an engagement with his unmarried daughter.

Rudi decided to work in America for a few years to save a nest egg, and through Hungarian émigrés he became a waiter in one of the posh beach-front hotels in Atlantic City. Two years later, on the night of his departure for Europe, he was mugged, robbed of everything including his passport, and left unconscious in the streets of New York while his ship sailed. He was taken to a hospital, and the police found a translator (after fifty years, Rudi still speaks English with a thick accent) and located his boss. When he returned to work, the staff and guests had raised $1,000 for him. Ironically, an anonymous letter he wouldn't have received had he sailed earlier informed him that his bride-to-be had just given birth to an illegitimate child. Rudi returned to Europe to hire a detective and confront his handsome Hussar would-be father-in-law, a story he tells with a mixture of scorn and mild incredulity. Soon after, he met the woman he married and emigrated permanently.

Rudi describes his marriage as uneventful. He praises his wife as a good woman. Rudi's son, a bachelor in his early forties who teaches in New Jersey, keeps a room in his father's house, but owns a house somewhere in the Hamptons. Naturally, I ask if his son is gay and if he knows that Rudi is. Emphatic and politely outraged denials follow both questions.

Rudi's son and John seem to have tolerated each other, but there was little affection between them. When John came to live with Rudi, he ostensibly rented a studio apartment in the basement of the small two-family house Rudi owns in Astoria. They did not decide to live together immediately; Rudi was cautious, if not suspicious. From their initial meeting, John was aggressively ardent. At first, Rudi refused to give him his last name or telephone number, thinking him a racetrack sort, someone to be wary of. When they met again a few days later, John invited Rudi to visit him at his rooming house on West Fourteenth Street. Rudi describes his seduction laconically. John, who was experienced, was active, Rudi passive. The sex was exclusively oral.

Rudi is a pragmatic and compassionate man. Working forty years as a waiter (he retired as headwaiter from a prominent midtown hotel), he is careful about money. After two years of meeting at John's shabby, expensive room, the move was made. Rudi says he needed that length of time to accommodate himself to being gay. By the time of the move, the sexual adjustment had also been made. When I ask Rudi to describe the experience of learning to be homosexual after sixty-four years as a heterosexual man, he brushes aside the question; he was awkward at first but always responsive to John's tenderness. As he grew more adept, he found he could reciprocate fully. John slept in his own room, but the rest of their routine was spent together. Both liked to bet on horses or play cards and dominoes at a Spanish club in Manhattan that John belonged to. Their gambling was petty; Rudi's prudence and John's small income, if nothing else, kept it a reasonable pastime.

John was born in Spain; when his parents emigrated to Cuba, he became a grocer. In New York, he found work as a pants-cutter in the garment district. He met an interior decorator from New Jersey, a younger man, who became very smitten with him. After the gift of an expensive diamond ring (which Rudi now wears), John considered himself engaged, quit his job and kept house near Monmouth while his lover ran a successful antique and decorating business. Two years later when the lover died suddenly of a heart attack at the age of forty-five, also intestate, John returned penniless to the garment industry, from which he retired with Social Security and some small savings.

As Rudi neared seventy, he found the northern winters too trying and decided to spend the harshest months in Acapulco. John, who was unable to swing such a vacation financially, agreed to stay in New York to take care of Rudi's house. Although consistently jealous and possessive, he succumbed to Rudi's plea: "John, if you love me, you want me to live longer, to stretch my life, so I must get away from the winter." For nearly ten years now, Rudi has taken a small apartment where he is free to bring boys at night and enjoy the Mexican sun all day.

In the winter of 1975-76, John fell ill and went to relatives in Miami to recuperate. He was a poor letter writer, but as the winter drew on, his silence from Florida grew foreboding. Rudi cut short his vacation; at Kennedy Airport his son met him, and he demanded to know what was happening to John. His son evaded answering until Rudi made a scene. He then learned that John was dead, had in fact died six weeks earlier. Rudi says his son kept silent fearing that the news would shock his father, endangering his health. All Rudi's unopened letters to John had been forwarded to New York at his son's request to sustain the conspiracy. I suggest that this behavior indicates that his son was aware of the nature of the relationship, but Rudi again impatiently denies it. John died of cirrhosis of the liver. He had always been a heavy drinker, and in Rudi's absence he'd return to his boozing buddies at the club. When Rudi speaks of John, he shows much feeling. The grief is still fresh, and he is not sure he will return to Mexico this winter. There are complications, including his fear of leaving his house empty.

Just last spring, it seemed that there might be a solution. At the Church of the Beloved Disciple on Fourteenth Street, he met Bill. They hit it off, and Bill moved in with Rudi almost immediately, sharing Rudi's bedroom rather than the old studio. At fifty-nine, Bill was just coming out. Aside from one furtive experience in a porno movie house, Rudi is his first gay relationship.

Bill is still married, although his wife threw him out, after thirty-five years of marriage, in the fall of 1976. She simply said it was over for her, their two daughters and son were on their own, and she wished to be free. Bill claims he was totally unprepared for her decision; he thought he had a good marriage. His wife's behavior is inexplicable to him. Even more puzzling to me is Bill's response: he signed away his house and all his assets to her for one dollar and then had what he describes as a slight nervous breakdown. He resigned his position as music teacher in the New Jersey high school where he had worked for many years (but not long enough for him to retire).

Bill is a medium-sized man, well-built and cordial, eager to talk about his many problems; but he is also what most people would call homely. He looks his fifty-nine years, and his face and eyes are ravaged with sadness. When I said he was overgenerous to his wife and that he might have suggested she leave instead of him, he said that he wanted to leave the way open for a reconciliation. Rudi looked at me skeptically. When we are alone, he tells me he thinks he can love Bill, if only he will forget the past and face where he is. I cannot discover why Bill went to the Ramrod immediately upon arriving in New York, since he insists that he was straight until the breakup.

At this point, Rudi and I, who have been sitting on his porch, go inside the house, where a third man is quietly watching the evening news. He is Ernie, who worked under Rudi for thirty years. He is recovering from a severe heart attack and looks it. He now lives in John's old studio apartment, and Rudi nurses him, cooks his meals, shops for him, and generally shares his life with his old friend. Ernie wants me to see his room; he is proud of his collection of pinups of Hispanic wrestlers and his pornography.

Ernie is also seventy-nine. He was born in New Zealand, but his mother left for Australia when her husband deserted her. Like Harry, Ernie has a British accent, a typical Australian drawl to which he adds his own campy intonations. I would like to interview Ernie at length, but his illness, which has left him infirm, pallid, and slow to speak and move, has also jumbled his memory. He listens carefully and answers slowly but seems perpetually preoccupied. He prefers to show me his collection of pictures and chatter, and I decide to postpone the interview.

I revisit Rudi and Ernie and Bill a week later. At the first visit, Rudi would not let me use my tape recorder and showed alarm every time I took notes, but now I am invited to dinner along with Harry, allowed to use my tape, and kissed paternally when I enter. Rudi takes time from his cooking to talk to me, and Ernie is contentedly watching an old movie with Harry, but Bill is absent. He has packed up and returned to New Jersey. Rudi is saddened but not overwhelmed when he tells me that Bill has decided that the gay life is too difficult and that returning to his married daughter promises the best chance of resuming his own marriage. He has taken temporary work and promises to keep in touch. Rudi shakes his head pessimistically and asks if I think Bill was truthful. He confides that Bill was impotent. "He would get hard in a minute, but he would never come! I even asked Harry, who's so good, you know, to . . . see if he could help Bill, but, well, it didn't work out. He said to me, 'Rudi, I'm still young, I have to try.'" I agree that Bill is relatively young and that I do not think we got the whole picture.

Rudi is cooking goulash, which Ernie tells me is one of his specialties. While I sip a rum and Coke, bringing back memories of Cherry Grove in 1950, Rudi calmly chats about his daily routine. He likes to bet if there's a race. During the four months that Bill was there, they would drive to Riis

Park if the weather was good. Rudi had arranged to leave Bill in the apartment when he went to Acapulco, but now his winter plans are uncertain. He is also worried about Ernie. Just yesterday, Ernie foolishly went to Manhattan to visit an old trick whom Rudi dislikes. Ernie has always favored proletarian Hispanics and black men who mistreat him. Rudi has patiently listened to stories of Ernie's affairs of stolen money, beatings, scenes, neglect, and he is impatient with his friend's lack of self-esteem.

"John never liked Ernie. He was antigay. He would say, 'How can you walk down the street with him? He's such a fairy, aren't you ashamed to be seen with him?' " John never could tolerate effeminacy, and while Ernie is not flamboyant, he is soft-spoken, mild, a bit limp and campy. The contrast between John's Hispanic machismo and Ernie's willowiness amused Rudi, who would always defend Ernie against John's antipathy, which he thought peculiar. While he has known that Ernie was gay for thirty years, he had not known that Ernie was effeminate until he was told.

Rudi sighs again over Bill's departure; he is hurt but by no means distraught. He thinks of John more than Bill. We talk of the contemporary world, which Rudi regards as a great mistake. "We need another flood—wipe out everything and start again." Rudi finds conventional religious beliefs ridiculous. "If there's a heaven, it's not up there on the moon." I ask him to suppose there is; what will he do if both John and his wife are waiting for him when he dies? "Introduce them, of course. I'll explain to her that she left me first, so I had to console myself." John apparently has the stronger, more recent claim.

Impatient to attend his goulash, Rudi says he will send Ernie to me but warns me that Ernie has had a bad week: his black friend was unfriendly, he has been feeling sick, and, worst of all, his brother arrived from California at Rudi's behest and the reconciliation flopped. Ernie has not seen or had much contact with his brother in the twenty-two years since their mother died. Rudi felt that Ernie's poor health called for the family reunion, and he phoned the brother, who is eighty-four. I ask Ernie about the meeting.

"Oh, he was so nasty. All he said was 'Why do you have pictures of those men all over your walls? It's disgusting.' " Ernie and his brother, neither of whom have ever married, never discuss their private lives.

I ask him when he came out, and he laughs as his memory is jogged. "It was awful really, then. I was waiting tables in Australia, and I had just moved to this boarding house. The lady gave me a room for the night; it was very crowded in the city, and rooms were scarce. This was 1915, and Australia wasn't so built up then. Well, in the middle of the night, this man comes into my room and says, 'What are you doing here? This is my room.' I told him the landlady put me here and it was *my* room, but he was drunk and big, and I didn't want to argue; I was only seventeen. 'All right, we'll straighten it out in the morning. Shove over.' Well, when he got into bed, he suddenly said to me, 'I'm gonna fuck you.' I didn't know men even did that."

"Well, what happened?"

"Oh, he fucked me. I didn't like it at first," he smiles. Harry announces that dinner is on the table. It is 5:30, and I'm glad I skipped lunch. The kitchen table is carefully set. Rudi has cut long stems of Rose of Sharon from his back yard and arrayed them all over the tablecloth. When he pours Cherry Kijafa for us all, Ernie winks at me, remarking that it is indeed a special occasion. The goulash is good, but Rudi takes very little. He explains that for some years now he has been a vegetarian, and I note his plate contains only stew vegetables. Dinner proceeds amiably and quietly. I am a little sloshed on rum and Coke and worried about how cherry liqueur mixes with paprika. But as I watch Harry eating heartily, Ernie secure in his friend's beneficence, and Rudi serenely mothering us all, I am reminded of the calm of my own childhood meals. It seems there are kitchen tables to gather round again.

Recently, over after-dinner drinks, Carol, a lesbian-feminist lawyer, asked me what I thought of an idea she had about retirement homes for gays. "It would be complicated, buying land in Florida or the Hamptons or Hawaii; it would have to be covered by a single individual's name. But it's the coming thing. Now is the time to start." Her motives are certainly as pragmatic as they at least acknowledge that old men and women are alive and in need. Perhaps West Side tries to do too much, but I doubt it. It is what it is, and one should be glad it is still there and able to continue in times when the life span of most gay organizations keeps shrinking. When there was practically nothing, Mattachine and Daughters of Bilitis tenaciously held on. Militancy made them superfluous, with its contempt for the old styles and ideas of the closeted timidities. Now there are enough gay organizations in America to fill a telephone book (albeit a thin one), but it can hardly be called an embarrassment of riches. As I write this, I feel the subject of gay aging slipping away. I notice I am beginning to focus on my dissatisfaction with the movement, remembering the high hopes of the early GAA and the Gay Academic Union and my cynical relief when I no longer needed them, cocooned for a moment in a happy love affair.

Is it that one simply cannot imagine what it is like to live so exclusively in the present, with fantasies and rage alike burnt out? Perhaps the prejudices are more potent than one suspects, cutting one off from empathy and understanding. When I told a friend, a reasonably intelligent woman, what I was writing about, she grimaced.

"Why? It's disgusting."

"What is?"

"The whole thing. Dirty old men." She is a professor of humanities, no youngster herself, and generally concerned about social oppression. But for her, these issues are not real; they have no priority. Tacitly, it is understood that death will resolve the problems sooner than later. My colleague hastens to clarify that her response has nothing to do with the fact that the men are gay; she would feel the same way if they were straight.

Some of the difficulties are identical for people of whatever sexual persuasion. On August 8, 1977, the *New York Times* devoted two thirds of its Op-Ed page to "How Old Is Old?" by an enraged woman of sixty-six forced to retire last year. She catalogs her dismay and anger, the stupidity of wasting her professionalism when it is still invested with the authority of experience but without the bias of ambition. She is physically fit and has been educated to use her leisure in the richest possible ways; she has the money to do so. But she is immobilized with depression, with a sense of being unfit, rejected, subhuman. When she taught and had five sets of papers to mark over the weekend, she still found the time to tend to her family, bake bread, do a host of things: her energy was limitless. Now, completely free, she is imprisoned in fatigue and lassitude.

For those deprived of work "to make room for younger people," there may be no adequate compensation unless they find other work. Signs in Congress indicate that the extension of mandatory retirement is not far off. But those who would work longer if they could are a small minority, less than 10 percent of the elderly. Most welcome retirement. The quality of work in America is not so ideal that forty-five years on the job are insufficient.

More universal is the sense of being useless, whether one is active or not. In the July 16, 1977 issue of *Gay Community News*, the cover story was "Older Gays: Our Neglected Roots." Since Jonathan Katz's *Gay American History* appeared (Volume II is on the way), writers in gay journals everywhere have understood the need to become amateur historians of the past before it is irrevocably gone. Well and good. While I was interviewing Harry and Rudi, no doubt they were flattered to enter gay history. Perhaps they'll enjoy reading the article, and that will be another fleeting moment of esteem. However, the articles are *not* written for old men and women but for the forty-four-year-old babies who don't want to be old and peripheral in twenty years and who frankly doubt they'll arrive at seventy-five virile and healthy.

When I asked the men what they would want *now* that they don't have, the question was too vague. Of course, they would like a gay center devoted primarily to social needs, a place to be comfortable in where sexual issues are secondary but sexual opportunities still viable. They would like a place to go where they are the majority. But most would also like to leave such places at the end of the evening and return to their own lives. When I said earlier that I thought gays coped better with being old, I certainly had in mind the anonymous *Times* writer, who seems self-indulgent compared to those men and women who are old and never had a decent job in their lives. These gay men cope better because deprivation has been their daily fare: social contempt is such an old story. Like New York's bad weather, you just live with it. Unlike their heterosexual contemporaries, few expected relationships to last. Those like Harry and Rudi who were deeply involved for long periods are in the minority. Ironically, it is Harry and Rudi who seem the most self-reliant, the most vigorous, the least likely to want a retirement home.

When I compare these men to my relatives of the same age, I understand that Harry and his friends had no wider choices than my father and mother did. Foremost was a job, sometimes any job in a Depression that marred their entire adult lives and made material values paramount. Then there was political survival in the forties when the anxieties were even more nightmarish. But they have come to be who they are despite the bitterness and injustice and limitations they testify to. They are dignified, mostly serene, and remarkably free of self-pity. I think of my aunts and uncles lushly retired in Miami, still enmeshed in their lifelong hysterias, still trapped in their children's lives, and I am certain that the strength these men have is special. It is not like the fortitude of old black matriarchs whose lives were worse, harder and more bitter, filled with far greater injustices than lovers dying intestate. It is not like the strength of Jews I know who have survived the Holocaust only to relive it endlessly.

But these men, and lesbians like them, lived their lives as something else, as heterosexuals, and that duplicity created for them a sense of self and privacy that no interviewer and no loneliness can readily violate. Their experience is still typical for the majority of gays. No matter how many come out, one is not *born* out. One lives two lives until it is no longer tolerable. For many, "intolerable" is a luxury they can't yet afford. For some of the men, the duplicity was very expensive, but I think for all of them it was the foundation of a stoicism that sustains them. Without any help from straight society and with precious little from gay society today, they survive decently. If they ask little, it is because their experience tells them it is wisest to ask for no more than what one can expect.

## JOHN PRESTON

◇◇◇◇◇◇◇◇◇◇◇◇◇

# *Brothers and Fathers and Sons*

*I*n the late sixties and early seventies I was intensely involved with the gay liberation movement. I shared many of the early escapades and explorations with a group of fellow travelers in Minneapolis, which was one of the first centers of gay activism in the country. Our politics were deadly earnest, adamant, and self-righteous.

We especially focused on semantics. We were certain that a revolution could occur through changes in the English language, a point of view that certainly reflected our college graduate status. One of our targets was the term *sister*, which was used, we determined, in a deprecatory manner by gay men (there were no homosexuals anymore) to refer to one another and to insult women at the same time. We were convinced that it was necessary to substitute the revolutionary *brother* in its place—not quite conscious of the (at least) equally antifeminist emphasis we placed on that word.

*Brother* in that context was not a familial term. It was a euphemism for *comrade-in-arms*. There was seldom any emotional connotation to the word. It was not said softly with arms around shoulders; it was yelled, paraded, announced with clenched fist.

An equally powerful phrase was *gay community*. We determined that it existed. Therefore, it did. Our insistence on the fact of community made it difficult for us to understand how and why the observable gay population in Minnesota refused to function the way we thought a community should. Of course, the reality was that we were only dealing with a collection of individuals who were not at all sure that they had that much in common with one another. In fact, only those reactionary queens who called one another "sister" were experiencing anything close to community.

That's not quite true: we were blinded by our rhetoric to the true reason for our coming together. We said we were forming a vanguard, a leadership, a political force. We were actually constructing our own sense of community with one another. I now see that those of us who were involved with the first gay organizations were acting out of our own personal needs for companionship and support as we went through our not-very-unique process of coming out.

Such observations do not negate the importance of what was accomplished by those early organizations—or, for that matter, the political structures that function today. They're only useful to point out a new trend that seems to be developing in gay America.

Fashions in popular music are seldom accidental. I don't think it's a coincidence that the Richie Family's hit "We Are Family" swept gay discos with such a powerful impact recently. There is a growing sense of *family* among gay people, a trend that holds some of the most positive implications yet for our future.

I have to rely on my personal experience at this point. I don't apologize for that; my personal history isn't really one of a leader of an elite in terms of shaping the larger society or the gay subculture, but I do have to acknowledge that when I find myself attracted to a concept, a vogue, or an idea, it is usually an indication that there are other people doing the same thing in a way that just hasn't been publicized yet. My coming out publicly wasn't a revolutionary act but a move for self-preservation in the late sixties; it just so happens that a lot of other people were beginning to sense the same need for the same kind of survival at the same time.

My sense that there is a growing family is not only very difficult to document; it flies in the face of the reports we're hearing from suffering gay political organizations today. They're still wondering why all those people refuse to be organized the way they should be. The laments of groups in the eighties aren't really that different from our complaints in the sixties. There are plenty of bodies, they just won't do what they're supposed to do.

It seems to me that the entire gay movement leaped eagerly beyond enormous building blocks when we announced our status as community. Any anthropological or sociological definition of community assumes the preexistence of a family or clan subgroup. A population is only a population. If it does not have networks of primary association or allegiance, it cannot evolve into a true society.

I don't want to digress into theory. My claim is that there are certain bondings occurring in the gay world that lead me to believe we're moving in a progressive direction.

One element has to be the new and tender use of the word *brother*.

*Friend* no longer communicates the intensity of my relationship with one man for the last ten years. He has never been a lover, and even the label "best friend" is somehow insufficient. Time alone—those ten long years of mutual growth and change—makes it necessary for us to acknowledge a deeper relationship, a firmer commitment, a longer sense of expectation and involvement.

I am not devaluing the word *friend* by saying this. That category has a certain undeniable importance. But there is an emotional level of relationship that is more than friend. It is, in this world of masculinely attired clones and pro–feminist liberation, something akin to the sisterhood those gay men in Minnesota were so comfortable in declaring.

As we all become more relaxed about our homosexuality and our gayness, we are more able to extend to one another a type of relationship, a brotherhood, that is our own creation, at least in the contemporary world. I can sleep with my brother without sexual intent and without self-consciousness. I can put my arm around his shoulders in an expression of comradeship that isn't a denial of homosexuality but a statement of gayness.

It does seem to me that these brother relationships are more prevalent and more valued than they were when I first began to explore the gay world fifteen years ago, when communication between people and especially peers was so hurtfully hindered.

The existence of brothers (I am able to use the term to describe perhaps five men in my life) is a crucial need for us if we hope to approach the reality of community. Too often our networks have been either a group of tricks or political and social allies. There is no community possible among people who have only sex or ideas in common.

The formation of these gay relationships is especially important because it is a witness to the foundation of our identities. If, in fact, being gay is limited to sexual activity, then it is trivial. That was the whole purpose of the change in terms from *homosexual* to *gay*. I don't mean that to be an antisexual statement. It is also true for me and the people I know that most of the brothers we have are men we met through sex. The mutual and supportive ability to take that otherwise anonymous sexual encounter and use the intimacy it offered to produce a more lasting attachment helps make gay brotherhood a fact in our lives.

Brotherhood is not the only area in which familial structures are being activated. There is a fascinating tendency on the part of more experienced gay men to "adopt" young, less knowledgeable gay men in startlingly large numbers. I recently entered into two such adoptions without conscious thought. I don't know if I would even have noticed if a close friend hadn't done precisely the same thing at nearly the same time.

My age, thirty-five, isn't old enough to indicate a parenting relationship to two twenty-four-year-old men. But that sense of parenting may be explained by the experience represented by my twenty years of living as a gay man compared to their recent entries into this existence.

Again, it's difficult to define the lines beyond which friendship no longer adequately describes relationships. There is a mutually acknowledged point at which one is simply more aware. There's a jointly manufactured right on my part to intrude on actions and behavior that a friend might not presume to judge. I cajole G. because he's late in filing his application to law school; I don't think even that many other gay people know about his goal of a legal career. I insist that R. get his own apartment and stop bellyaching about things he could change. They call to find out what I think about a new lover, the color they want to paint their apartments, money problems, a night class. Part of the difference between this and another friendship is that explicit right to intrude. I find myself taking G. out to lunch to tell him that something's out of balance. I give R. a book and tell him he must read it.

These are not the benign S-and-M relationships they may appear to be. The mutuality of both roles alone prevents that interpretation. It is at least as common for G. to call to use my shoulder to cry on. And R. has a symbol for his need to be a younger person who is taken care of: he arrives at my apartment and asks for a bowl of cream of celery soup. Somehow that's become his way of telling me he needs to talk, he needs support, he needs comfort.

I feel vulnerable speaking about these relationships. For one thing, they are so precious to me it seems strange to share them on paper. I also know they're open to misinterpretation. I don't have the usual confidence in my writing to tell me that I will sound any different from any man talking about any friendship. The other part of this dilemma is that I suppose some of it sounds like a rationalization of a dirty old man—and I will be the first to celebrate the lustful "older man" role I perform with G. The significance of sex—or the lack of it—in these relationships is still a very open question.

I would feel differently about these matters if another component hadn't been brought to bear on the whole set of experiences: in the past year I have not only adopted two sons; I found a father for myself.

I have long admired two men: Samuel Steward, a member of Gertrude Stein's Charmed Circle and author of *Dear Sammy* and a pair of literary novels in the thirties, and Phil Sparrow, one of the first tattoo artists in the country whose work was consciously homoerotic. A third man I held in near hero status: I am not the only gay writer to claim Phil Andros as one of the major sources of inspiration for my work. Not too long ago I discovered, to my amazement, that all three men were, in fact, the same individual.

Sam Steward lives in a small cottage that he bought with his savings in Berkeley, California. There, among the collected mementos of his seventy-odd years, he holds court with a growing number of gay men who come to talk to Sam, Gertrude's friend, Phil Sparrow, or Phil Andros, the navigator of countless gay lives. My own pilgrimage—and I must use that word to convey some of the emotional weight that I gave to that transcontinental journey—was to all three men.

Sam doesn't begrudge friendship, nor does he squander it. There was a period of learning about one another that preceded the mutual acceptance which has come about between us—and a great deal of exploration before I requested the symbol of continuity that has come to be so important to me. I don't think I would ever have sought out a tattoo for its own sake. But my connection with a man who had already had so much impact on my life through his work and example made me anxious to have some manifestation of him and who he was in my mythology. Today, I wear a writer's mark on my chest, a tattoo wheedled out of Sam, who was scarcely anxious to abandon seven years of retirement to pick up his tools once more.

Much of my relationship with Sam *is* my mythology. By placing myself alongside him, I have enriched and revalued much of my own experience. Like most gay men I know, I have never really had the complete father-son relationship that we were led to expect. There hasn't been a figure in our lives who could bring his experience to bear to help us sift through our own encounters. There is so much about gay life that is rebellion that we haven't had the luxury of learning lovingly from older people. All of this has been intensified by the don't-trust-anyone-over-thirty, me-generation era in which many of us live.

Determining the ideals we will live by without credible examples from a previous generation may well have been a tremendously valuable experience for many of us. But I find myself adding Sam's learnings to my own with increasing frequency as I try to structure my integrity and my values—small things, perhaps, things I should have learned by myself but which now have more resonance. Sam wasted seventeen years of his life as an alcoholic. Now, whenever I reach for a second drink or hear an invitation to go to a bar, I am not just hesitating on my own; I remember him telling me about those wasted years and those unfinished manuscripts. When I worry about writing porn for money, I remember Sam giggling and reminding me that it's fun . . . and reminding me that there are ways to make it worthwhile. None of Phil Andros's books were published without a warning to the reader about sexually transmitted diseases or a guide to safe places to visit in the city in which they took place.

I also *use* Sam—and I use him in a way that I know G. and R. use me. He is a silent judge of my actions. Today, G. told me he had stayed home and accomplished a great deal of work even when there was a much more appealing invitation to a party. He claimed he did it because he knew how I would have reacted to an impetuous or irresponsible action on his part. G. is a perfectly competent worker, a college graduate and far from anchorless. He didn't *need* me to make his decision—and it was obviously his decision—but I helped him. He used me. I shamelessly use Sam. If there haven't been enough hours of productive writing, I worry about what he'll think if he calls this evening and asks what I've been up to. (Sam has a terminal case of what he terms "telephonitis" and is prone to picking up the instrument whenever the mood for contact strikes him.)

Sam provides another important role in my life. I have this sense (and it may sound trite in the telling, although I hope not) that every kindness from Sam is a debt I owe to a younger person. G. and R. probably would have entered my life in any event. I probably would have adopted them in my own way. But my relationship with Sam models a kind of responsibility I feel for them, a sense of caring that must be honored.

One of the facts of gay life has always been the alienation most of us feel from our genetic families. Some of us have been able to secure a vehicle for family membership; more of us have made the necessary accommodations. Our separations from our families and our denial of the basic values of the larger society have most often placed us in situations where we have a minimal sense of *context*. My personal relationships with R., G., and Sam are not the whole of a society, by any means, but remember that I am presenting them only as examples of something that may well be happening in the larger gay world.

There are other indications: Senior Actions in a Gay Environment (SAGE), a group of older gay people in New York, have formed for mutual support and have recently published a book of their oral histories that enriches the whole fabric of gay life (*Sage Writings*, edited by Barbara Baracks and Keith Jarratt, Teachers and Writers Collaborative). There has been a significant increase in the chronicled history of gay people. Jonathan Katz's remarkable, depressing volume *Gay American History*, didn't attract many readers a few years back, but more recently a play, *Bent*, and a book, *The Men with the Pink Triangle*, have documented the crisis of gay people under Hitler. Older gay novels have been reprinted (*The Way It Was*, Radclyffe Hall's works, and so forth).

All of these combine to give our relationships a context of continuity. They merge to make our sense of identity more than the fad that the media would have it appear to be, but the stuff of personal existence that we share with one another and that spares us—if we only pay attention—the profound isolation of history that we would have had to endure only ten years ago.

But the world of literature is not the whole of what I'm witnessing here. I know of a pair of older gay men who have their own business in a large city. They are often ridiculed for their tendency to hire much younger men to work in their small manufacturing shop. Everyone seems quick to insist on a genital cause for every action they take. But when I visit their plant (and I have more than once), I don't see any sexual exploitation. (I seriously doubt that the younger men in question—all in their twenties—are so naive that much overt exploitation could occur in any event.) What I do see is a place where their "sons," young gay men, complete with pierced and bejeweled ears and gay-themed T-shirts, are learning a trade and receiving careful instruction; a work situation in which they are decently paid and honestly trained. If you interrogate the proprietors, they'll talk about their own experiences decades ago when they lived in fear for their jobs every day, and they'll admit their pledge to one another to hire only obviously gay men who might be mysteriously turned away elsewhere. They also pledged to spend totally disproportionate amounts of their budget on education.

It must be apparent that one of the immutable elements of a parenting relationship is the mutual assumption of responsibility. That same responsibility is inherent in brother relationships. The crosspatching of these freely accepted obligations is the hallmark of family. Acceptance, self-sufficiency, and all the other terminology which the seventies brought us may well have deprived us of the richness of a cross-generational and historical weaving. The emergence of our respect for the people who came before us and those who will follow us is the most profoundly positive direction the gay world could ever take. It may finally produce our community.

# III

WORD
FROM ABROAD

# " G "

## The Secret Life of Moscow

$M$ikhail Aleksandrov was recently summoned by telephone to the Petrovka, the central Moscow office of the Soviet Ministry of Internal Affairs. There he listened, with a sense of foreboding, as an agent read him a list of names that included several of his friends and acquaintances.

"Do you know these people?" asked the agent. Aleksandrov made a noncommittal reply, realizing that any information he gave could be used against him and those named on the list. "We know that you know them," said the agent finally. "And do you know they are homosexuals?" Aleksandrov answered that he wasn't interested in the personal lives of his friends and acquaintances. "We know they are homosexuals," continued the agent, warming up to his task. "And we know you are too. We'd like to know more about how you meet such friends."

Aleksandrov's experience at the Petrovka is not a unique one. In recent months, as Moscow has been gearing up to impress the world during the 1980 Summer Olympics, police surveillance of gay life in the city, intense even in the best of times, has accelerated in an attempt to "clean up" the city before the foreigners arrive. Drunks, petty criminals, troublemakers of any sort—which, in the Soviet view of things, includes gay people—are being rounded up and harassed. Many are being threatened with exile to the city's outskirts during the summer, so they will be conveniently out of sight.

But the recent crackdown on Moscow's gays, who are more numerous than one might expect in such adverse circumstances, is only one more incident in the continuous police campaign against Soviet dissidents of all sorts—political or sexual. Homosexuality, like the "dissemination of anti-Soviet propaganda" that recently sent Andrei Sakharov into exile in the provincial town of Gorky, is strictly and completely illegal in the Soviet Union, punishable by a long prison sentence. There are no gay bars, or even cafes, in Moscow; there is no gay press. There is virtually no political consciousness among gay people: fear keeps them apart from each other—fear that their sexual partners are in fact police informers, fear of discovery and imprisonment, fear of losing jobs and becoming nonpersons. Since the Soviet government ultimately controls all employment and education, once a person is on the wrong side of the law, once his name gets on the wrong lists, he has nowhere to escape to.

In the face of these overwhelming obstacles, it is all the more surprising that a lively, diverse community of gay men stubbornly survives in Moscow. As in many other aspects of Soviet life, beneath the orderly monolithic concrete exterior presented to the outside world lies a thriving unofficial social network, as alien to the sacred tenets of Leninism as the black marketeers who hustle for blue jeans along Gorky Street.

The center of Moscow's tenacious gay culture lies in the very shadow of the massive brick Kremlin walls, a mere stone's throw from the marble tomb that preserves Lenin in his unchanged waxen state. There are no Castro or Christopher Streets here, no neon bars or mirrored discos—just a large, dank cellar toilet, washed out nightly by a muttering old woman with a straw broom. Toilets are a meeting place for gay men in virtually every country; the difference here is that they are almost the only meeting place outside private homes.

A short walk down toward the Bolshoi Theater through the Square of the Revolution (jammed with ice-cream vendors and ticket-sellers by day, deserted by night) leads to what Muscovites jokingly call "the Pleshka," which literally means the bald spot on a man's head, an open space in front of the theater where every evening scores of gay men circulate in search of partners, even in the dead of winter when they are bundled warmly in scarves and high fur hats. The Pleshka is also a favorite hunting ground for undercover police agents, who study the body language of Moscow's gays and then use it to attract and entrap them.

One reliable source described an incident in which one unsuspecting man struck up a conversation with another on the Pleshka. They agreed to go off to the first man's apartment. But as they descended into the subway station nearby, four heavy policemen—tipped off by the second man— surrounded the first man on the platform and escorted him to the police station. There they questioned him for hours about his sexual life and partners, threatening to ruin his career if he didn't cooperate.

Another meeting place—slightly less dangerous—is Moscow's public baths. The one most frequented by Moscow's gay community is the Central Baths on Marx Prospect, in an alleyway behind Children's World, a department store. The Russian bathhouse (*banya*) is a unique institution, a chaotic and lusty place where men gather to swear and joke at the end of the day. Getting into the baths, like getting into Moscow's stores or theaters or buses, is in itself a major ordeal. At the Central Baths, one waits in line for at least an hour, defending one's place in line with the ferocity of a lioness protecting her young.

An old woman collects your valuables as you enter, since inside there are no lockers, only long open benches with hooks for hanging clothes. Inside, the scene is a Slavic Inferno: robust fellows wrapped in long white sheets curse loudly as they swill down beer. The bath room itself is a nineteenth-century relic, a wide-open space crowded with bathers, with low marble benches on cracking tile floors. Friends scrub each other with hard sponges that leave the skin red and raw.

The lowest circle of the Inferno is the steam bath, a wet sauna kept at suffocatingly high temperatures. Here, on a raised platform (whose height further exaggerates the heat), men beat each other with birch branches; supposedly this cleans out the pores. There is a strong smell of sweat, birch, and burning wood.

Obviously, this is hardly the kind of gay bathhouse found in San Francisco or New York. Rarely do men have sex at the Central Baths, since, unlike its American counterparts, the clientele is definitely mixed. As in the toilets, furtive glances and sidelong looks pass between the gay customers, who, having found each other, get acquainted and go elsewhere for consummation.

Actually, the main problem with gay life in Moscow is not *how* to meet people—besides the toilets and the baths, there is a lot of cruising in the streets and in the gleaming subway—but where to go with them when you do. Apartments are hard to come by even for a respectable married couple; for a single person or for two lovers—or even friends—of the same sex to get their own apartment is extremely difficult. Another possible alternative, hotels, are, like meat and sausage, always in short supply and are strictly reserved for foreigners (who pay nearly $100 a night) or influential out-of-town Soviet citizens. Hotel entrances are patrolled by guards who are very dedicated to their job of keeping out all those who don't belong there. But scarcity breeds ingenuity, and more often than not, even this problem can be overcome. Friends make arrangements to borrow apartments for a morning or afternoon. (Even heterosexual couples do that.) In the summertime, when the pace of cruising activity in Moscow accelerates, there are forests and parks with soft green grass.

The situation is somewhat more open at certain summer resorts, especially in Sochi, on the Black Sea, and at some beaches on the Baltic. Hordes of Muscovites, many of them gay, descend on these overcrowded spas from June to August.

And yet winter, and the imperiled social and political position in which Moscow's gay population finds itself, has unexpected positive results as well. The combination of those long winter evenings and the pervasive mistrust that reigns in Soviet society—even among heterosexuals—creates a tendency to form small, close groups of friends. Such groups gather several times a week to spend hours conversing and perhaps listening to music, in lieu of the hours spent in bars and discos in San Francisco or New York. A strong sense of camaraderie results from the peculiar situation of Soviet gay people, a loyalty and devotion not only to one's lover but to one's circle of friends (*kruzhok,* or "salon"). Most often, gay people meet other gay people through their friends and acquaintances; this is true, of course, outside Russia, but due to the lack of alternatives, it is much more important in Moscow.

I went to Russia fearful and cautious, prepared for celibacy. Although I discovered there is certainly ample reason for fear and caution, I was also surprised to find an enormously wide range of gay people: restaurant waiters and research physicists, editors and mechanics, doctors and hotel managers. The spectrum does not reach the wild external extremes of Polk Street Halloween or New York leather bars; the differences are more subtle, like the small day-to-day changes in a winter landscape.

Boris is a handsome, blond, twenty-three-year-old Siberian whose ancestors served in the retinue of the czar—a fact of which he is obviously proud, despite his strong loyalty to the Soviet way of life. A journalist from Leningrad, he was in Moscow on a business trip. When we met, he was on his way to a hockey match, so I accompanied him to meet his friend, another blond, husky Siberian, who strangely resembled Robert Redford. I was the first American whom Boris had ever met—I was to be the first American for others as well. For some, the news of my nationality was almost paralyzing; to meet an American was no less strange than to meet a man from the moon.

When we first made love in my room, Boris was timid. Afterward, as he lit one cigarette after another, he said, "I don't know how to be with an American. I was afraid someone was looking in the window or listening on a microphone." He insisted on turning on my radio to create noise. (The radio was plugged into the wall and could receive just one station, on which glorious news of production victories in the steel plants and on the collective farms was interspersed with condemnations of American aggression in Iran and Afghanistan.)

Boris is a loyal Soviet citizen who has great faith in his future, knows little of the West, and has no desire to emigrate—unlike many of the gay people I met in Moscow. He came to Moscow to write a story about a factory worker famous for overfilling his production quota. Boris has been married for several years to a woman journalist, but they do not live together ("It's more romantic that way") because they've been unable to get their own apartment. Occasionally, they borrow a friend's apartment for a weekend and set up temporary housekeeping.

There are many gay men who, like Boris, marry, since it is virtually impossible for an unmarried person to get an apartment that would enable him to live away from his family. Boris said he had been afraid that if he didn't marry young, he never would. When I asked him if there were many gay people in Russia, he replied, "There are gays in every city, in every small town. They were in my village in Siberia. They always find each other."

Boris was filled with questions about America, and he asked them with a naivete and curiosity that transcended his strong, suspicious nationalism. What was the weather like in San Francisco? How did the Russians live there? Did I have a car? Who were the most popular American writers now? Did Americans read Soviet literature? We set up another meeting, and when I jokingly said, "Just be sure you come" (it was in an out-of-the-way place for me), he said, "Of course, I'll come. What would you think of me as a Soviet if I didn't come?"

And yet Boris *didn't* appear at the appointed time. It was my first—and not last—no-show experience in Moscow. Of course, I felt wounded and offended, but later on, after I had met more Soviet people, I came to understand how Russian society works and realized that such disappearances are the rule rather than the exception. It takes an extraordinary person to overcome the instinctive fear and caution that motivate Soviet behavior, especially in gay people and especially when a foreigner is involved—most of all an American. I pined over Boris for a few days, walking around the place where we first met, as overloaded buses sputtered by on the Marx Prospect. But he never reappeared. He faded into the crushing masses that covered the autumn streets.

Viktor, a thirty-five-year-old photographer from Sukhumi also on a business trip to Moscow, with whom I had a long conversation one day in

September in a rain-green park, was afraid to come to my room at all. He told me why. One summer, he met an American on the beach of the Black Sea at Sukhumi. While the American stayed, they saw each other, and when the American returned to the United States, Viktor began to correspond with him. Not long after, he was called into the director's office of his professional union and asked why he was corresponding with someone in America and who that someone was. Viktor stopped writing to his friend. Like Boris, Viktor is married, and he has several children. He gets together with his gay friends at his summer house outside Sukhumi.

Slava, thirty-two, was not so scared of discovery—in fact, for a Soviet citizen, he was remarkably free of fear. The reason may well have been that Slava's father is a party official who earns 700 rubles a month (the average income is about 150 rubles a month), and Slava lives in one of Moscow's most prestigious apartment buildings. He was the first single man I met who had his own apartment, but through him I met more. He only uses his two-room place for sexual encounters and occasional privacy, preferring to live with his family, where Mama cooks and washes for him. He, too, had been married but was divorced after five years, and he helps to support a small daughter. Slava's job is a good one, an editor in a publishing house. He is definitely one of the "haves" of Soviet society, accustomed to frequent trips abroad (if only to Eastern Europe), preferential treatment in Moscow's best restaurants and theaters, and imported clothing and shoes obtained through influence.

And yet Slava wants to leave all that behind. Slava is a Jew, which is more important in Russia than in many countries because in the past Jews have been mistreated (and still are) and because today Jews can emigrate. Tens of thousands of Jews have emigrated to the West through Israel during the last ten years, not a few of them gay. But Slava doesn't want to use his ethnic identity to leave, except as a last resort. His parents are strongly opposed to the idea, and if he emigrates as a Jew, he will never be able to return to Russia, not even for a visit.

A better course, in Slava's view, would be to marry a foreigner in Moscow and emigrate to her country as her spouse. This would enable him to visit Russia and would cause his family fewer problems than if he left as a Jew. Over a glass of vodka in his apartment cluttered with expensive art books and the books of the Russian poets, he told me of a gay friend who had met an American man in Moscow. They fell in love, and the American, after returning home, arranged for the Russian to marry an American woman so that he could leave the country. Most of Slava's friends had already emigrated, and others, including his own lover-friend of some years, were about to. He felt increasingly isolated and abandoned.

"Why should I hide what I am?" he asked me. Most of his close friends didn't know he was gay, except those in his *kruzhok*. "It's true I have everything I could want here—my life is good. But I know it would be better for me in America." Slava was especially concerned with emigration when I met him, because he believes that after the 1980 Olympics, when the international spotlight turns away from the Soviet Union, it will become very difficult to emigrate, and the official policy toward gays, which has relaxed somewhat in recent years, will tighten again.

* * *

Oleg, Slava's lover-friend, younger by about seven years, has decided to use his Jewish nationality to emigrate. His family comes from the Carpathians, in the Ukraine on the Hungarian border; his native language is Hungarian, although he speaks Russian with only the slightest trace of an accent. He works as a research economist and, like Slava, is used to a luxurious standard of living accessible to only a handful of Soviet citizens. Some years ago, Oleg's uncle emigrated to Paris, where he has set himself up comfortably as the owner of a restaurant catering to the burgeoning community of Russian Jewish émigrés in the city. Once, when his uncle visited Moscow, he promised Oleg that he would take care of him if he came to France. The hope of this new life has been the main motivating fact in Oleg's life ever since.

In order to leave the Soviet Union, Oleg needs an invitation to Israel, so he arranged to receive one from some distant relatives now living in Israel. (Soviet Jewish émigrés must obtain sponsorship in the West before they can get visas. When they reach Vienna, the entry point to the West from Russia, they can simply fly on to other cities instead of proceeding to Tel Aviv.) When I met Oleg, he was hurrying to submit his emigration papers before November 1, the rumored cutoff date for emigration before the Olympics. Because of his impending emigration, Oleg was less intimidated by dealing with a foreigner like me, since he felt he had very little to lose. It was very likely, he explained, that he would lose his job once he filed his emigration papers anyway. Then, deprived of Soviet rights and not yet entitled to Israeli or French rights, he would have to wait in limbo until approval came—a process that can sometimes take years.

One night over a dinner that began with canned crab, a delicacy obtainable in Moscow only through connections (*po znakomstvu*), Oleg told me why he wanted to emigrate. It wasn't so much that he felt oppressed as a gay person; as I began meeting his other friends, I understood why. They certainly had no problem finding new partners, and within their small circle they are entirely open. (Outside this circle, they are decidedly less open, however, as I discovered when Oleg introduced me to a less intimate acquaintance as a visitor from Estonia.) Oleg wants to leave primarily for material gain and also to realize his professional potential more fully. "I can't live here the way I want to without financial help from my family," he said. "Every month they send me money. I want to go abroad so I can be independent, so I can be rewarded for my initiative. Here in Russia there is no reason to excel."

Many Soviet people believe that the latest wave of emigration to the West has been motivated by purely material considerations like Oleg's, as opposed to the first wave right after the 1917 Revolution and the second wave after World War II, which were inspired by political convictions or the need to escape brutal oppression or execution. Most of the new émigrés are Soviet professionals who have had solid careers and the connections necessary to obtain the best that Soviet life can offer. But it is perhaps this very position of privilege and access to information that shows them the limitations of their life. The phenomenon of rising expectations has reached Soviet professionals, and since many gay men here are professionals, they have obviously been affected. Gay men, too, are frequently free from the family responsibilities that make emigration difficult. This is obviously analogous to the position of gay men in America, who are statistically one of the most mobile and financially successful groups.

Fedya, another friend of Slava and Oleg, is a thirty-three-year-old musician. Like his friends, Fedya is unusually cosmopolitan for a Russian; his father is a professor who has lived for long periods abroad, and Fedya himself has traveled several times with tourist groups to Paris. When he applied to travel there for a third visit, his request was denied because, he says, "they are afraid that I will make too many contacts there, that I will stay the next time." Fedya makes only 110 rubles a month. His parents give him financial assistance and were instrumental in getting him the pleasant, spacious studio in which he lives. (Rents are very low in the Soviet Union, usually around 15 rubles a month. The real problem is getting an apartment in the first place.)

"I am not Russian in temperament," Fedya told me one day as we listened to French *chansons* on his record player. "I love France and, oh, Paris." (I didn't have the heart to tell him that the French *chansons* were actually recycled American pop tunes.) Outside the window, a few dead, dry leaves clung stubbornly to the bare trees, shivering in the chill of approaching winter. "I am tired, tired of how difficult life is here. You see all these books?" he asked, pointing to the shelves that lined one wall from floor to ceiling, overloaded with poetry, novels, and plays, including twentieth-century Russian literature unobtainable in Moscow's bookstores. "I would give them all up—gladly—if I could go to the West. But how? My parents are Jewish, but they strongly object to my emigrating—they can't even understand why I would want to leave. And how could I leave, knowing I could never come back? For all that I hate about Russia, it is my country, my culture, and I love it. I couldn't leave it forever."

Fedya, too, was sharp on the lookout for a foreign woman to marry. Every time I introduced him to an American female friend, I watched him look for a wedding ring, sizing her up as a marriage prospect. "I think about this problem all the time now—how to leave," he said late one night as we stood in a damp mist, waiting for a taxi on the deserted slick streets. "I have thought of it always, but now it seems to me the time has come to do something." I fear that Fedya, like Hamlet, is still trying to figure out what to do, sitting in his apartment listening to *chansons*.

The only regular member of Slava, Oleg, and Fedya's *kruzhok* who didn't talk about leaving was Vanya, a blond, cheerful lawyer who could become quite outrageous in intimate company. He seemed to be the father confessor of the group, the one to whom the others turned for advice and consolation. His record collection included *Saturday Night Fever*—a gift from a foreigner—and other disco hits, and the parties in his apartment lasted late, invariably ending in a drunken haze. But Vanya, too, was cautious, as I discovered one evening when, in the midst of a heated argument on the respective merits of Soviet Communism and American democracy, he gingerly closed the kitchen door and pointed to the ceiling with his finger at his lips.

Fear and concealment are so much a part of the Soviet system that after a time I even began to forget that there was anything unusual about not discussing significant topics over the telephone or not revealing the fact that I was a foreigner in unknown company (which meant keeping my mouth closed). In Russia, one doesn't talk about one circle of friends with another circle: the less known, the less that can be reported. Fedya always became anxious when we left his apartment together, for the old lady sitting at the doorway always gave me a penetrating once-over. "You know, they've probably noticed that you've been here a few times, and they wonder who you are," Fedya mumbled, trying unsuccessfully to make light of it as we stepped out onto the sidewalk. I was careful not to say a word as we passed out the door, lest my American accent give me away.

After a few months in Moscow, I began to realize how the small gay circles intersected, that almost everyone knew everyone else. This, too, is certainly a phenomenon that can be encountered elsewhere, but not on the suffocating scale that prevails in Moscow. One day I met a research scientist. After a few minutes of conversation, I could guess that he knew many of the people I had met.

The obvious limitations on Russian gay life—and on Russian life in general—combined with the fact that it is very difficult for people to move (and no one living in Moscow would dream of moving anyway, since it is in almost every respect the most interesting and the freest city in Russia), do provide a certain stability and sanity to friendships and love relationships. In America there is always escape: from New York to California or from California to New York. There is no escaping in Moscow; you are there for life.

I was also surprised to learn that there is sex for money in Moscow. I met a handsome young Georgian, we walked for awhile, I invited him back to my room, and he said: "People usually give me things—jeans, shirts, sweaters. What do you have?" He told me there were more than a few hustlers in Moscow. He pined, however, for his native Georgia, where, he said, "Men are men—not like these *baby* ['females'] in Moscow."

Several sources told me that the legal position of gays in Russia, while hardly enviable, has improved somewhat in recent years—at least until the pre-Olympic crackdown began. In the past, gay people were openly provoked and harassed; consenting adults are now generally ignored even when their relationships and sexual orientations become known to the authorities—including the KGB, which most actively keeps track of that sort of thing. I was told of several instances in which men were called in by the KGB and informed that they were known to be homosexuals but that, for the moment, nothing would be done about it. Only when these men get in trouble for some other reason, or when minors are involved, or when crimes committed involve homosexuality, does the government prosecute.

There is also evidence that even though the Soviet ideology has traditionally conceived of homosexuality as a social maladjustment unconnected to individual psychological factors, a certain amount of Freudian theory is creeping into official Soviet attitudes. One psychiatrist I met by chance—not gay himself—has been involved for the last five years in treating self-described gay people and persons who have had sex-change operations. (The whole field of sex-change and sex therapy is very new in Russia and still extremely limited in scope. The psychiatrist told me that he was virtually the only professional involved in such therapy and his position was politically insecure.) Originally, he was asked to treat the numerous gay students in the Moscow Conservatory, including some world-famous musicians. He explained that he has only treated those who came to him for help in changing their sexual orientation to heterosexuality. Many of his patients, he says, are the sons of powerful official figures.

The alleged relaxation must not be exaggerated, however. Another acquaintance told me an unconfirmed story of a KGB raid on a group of gay students from Moscow State University. According to this story, an instructor at the university had gathered a large group of students who regularly participated in group sex at the instructor's apartment. Finally one of the participants informed the KGB, arranged a raid with them, and let them in the door so they could photograph the unclothed participants for proof. Twenty-four people were arrested, he told me, and seven were eventually sentenced.

Under Brezhnev, Soviet society has become relatively more tolerant of various forms of dissent—and homosexuality, in the official view, qualifies as a certain kind of dissent. Gay people, if discovered or if insistent upon advertising their sexual orientation, are likely to lose their jobs and respectability, but they are not executed, as was the case in the days of Stalinist terror in the late 1930s, when *homosexual* meant *traitor* and *spy*. Soviet society changes with glacial speed; the enormous advances in gay rights during the 1970s in America and Western Europe have not begun to happen here, nor are they likely to happen for generations to come. More important, even the small improvements that have occurred are not necessarily permanent. Who knows what will happen after Brezhnev? As one friend said philosophically, shaking his head, "We all know that everything could change for the worse any time—like tomorrow."

# Simon Karlinsky

## The Case of Gennady Trifonov

Gennady Trifonov is a young Leningrad poet who is currently serving a four-year sentence in a Soviet labor camp situated in the northern part of the Ural Mountains. He was tried and sentenced at a closed trial in November 1976. At the time of his trial his mother and friends were unable to learn the exact nature of the charges against him. His transgression? He circulated privately a series of master-fully written poems about his love for another man.

After Trifonov's case was mentioned in several gay publications in the West last spring (Richard Sylvester, "Gennady Trifonov," *Gay Sunshine* No. 32, Spring 1977; "From Russia with Love," *Christopher Street*, March 1977; Peter Burton, "Gennady Trifonov," *Gay News* No. 119, May 19–June 1, 1977), the mass-circulation Soviet illustrated magazine *Ogon-yok* responded with an official version of what had happened to Trifonov. In a vitriolic article about a Dutch divinity student who was expelled from the Soviet Union for gathering information about the dissident movement, Gennady Trifonov was mentioned as someone the Dutchman had met but did not try to recruit for espionage activities and who was subsequently convicted for serving liquor to a minor, theft, hooliganism, and "violating still another article of the criminal code, one that has a direct bearing on his miserable homosexual doggerel" (A. Kostrov, "The Second Face of Theo-dore Voort," *Ogonyok* No. 27, July, 1977).

Establishing guilt by association (Trifonov's name is brought up even though the article says he hardly knew Theodore Voort and passed no in-formation to him) and piling up trumped-up charges of petty crime are quite usual when the Soviet press writes of anyone considered a dissident. What was new in the *Ogonyok* piece was the previously unmentionable topic of homosexuality. The subject came up in the Soviet press several more times in 1977–78, always in contexts that equated homosexuality with crime (or insanity) and with anti-Soviet attitudes. Among these in-stances were the articles in *Sovetsky Sport* that denounced body-building as allegedly leading to both homosexuality and murder and the account in the *Literary Gazette* of the one-man demonstration for gay rights staged in Moscow on November 15, 1977, by the Italian gay liberationist Angelo Pezzano (V. Valentinov, "Signor Pezzano's Inalienable Right," *Literary Gazette*, Nov. 23, 1977). The article described Pezzano as an emissary from the Biennale of Dissent that was about to open at the time in Venice and implied that the Biennale of Dissent was organized by homosexuals and madmen.

After he had read in the labor camp the *Ogonyok* and the *Literary Ga-zette* pieces, Gennady Trifonov sent his friends in Leningrad a vehement "Open Letter" addressed to the *Literary Gazette* (where it does not have the slightest chance of getting printed). In his letter, Trifonov protested against the tendency to slander homosexuals in the Soviet press and docu-mented the brutal and inhuman treatment of homosexuals by both the administration and the other inmates of the labor camps that he has had occasion to observe since he began serving his sentence. The letter men-tioned that his food and his treatment by the camp authorities had im-proved somewhat after his case was publicized in the West.

Gennady Trifonov's friends are apprehensive about his ability to sur-vive the four years of harsh labor-camp regime. One of them has conveyed to the West the epistle in verse that Trifonov sent to his Leningrad friends in February 1978 (printed below in my translation). Trifonov's mother and his friends in the Soviet Union feel that the only way to help him is to give his case the greatest possible publicity in the West. To achieve this end, *The Body Politic* (Toronto), *Christopher Street*, *Gay News* (London), *Gay Sunshine* (San Francisco), and *Revolt* (Sweden) have agreed to publish Gennady Trifonov's "Letter from Prison" and David Dar's essay about him. Letters on Gennady Trifonov's behalf from private individuals to Soviet embassies and consulates, to Amnesty International, and to writers' organizations such as the PEN Club may also help to bring an end to the ugly and senseless persecution of this gifted poet.

## LETTER FROM PRISON

I get your letters, telling me
that I'm a poet, which is dazzling,
that this is why my lofty star
is not extinguished in the dark.

All of you write me that my voice
has been absorbed by wintry groves
which are obedient to my hand,
obedient like my own handwriting.

All of you tell me: I alone
sang—as no one's allowed to sing—
of how we love without response
him who's our sole necessity,

Him who gives shape to all our lives
the way the branches form a garden
when God will kiss us on the lips
the way the snowfall kisses earth;

The one for whom I shout at night,
for whom I call, a wounded bird;
One who no longer haunts my dreams,
One about whom my verse is silent.

You write, responding in advance.
You plead with me: "Do not give up,
Endure it all and stay alive."
And I live on. And there's no life.

—*Gennady Trifonov*
*North Urals, February 1978*

*Update, August 1982:*
Gennady Trifonov was released after serving four years in labor camps. He now lives in Leningrad and writes poetry and essays that cannot be published in the Soviet Union. He has received several invitations to teach or do graduate work in American and Western European universities, but the Soviet authorities have repeatedly refused to grant him an exit visa. He

desperately wants to leave and thinks that his only hope of getting out is to further publicize his case in the West. A collection of his poetry in English translation is being prepared by Mary Giles.

—S.K.

# DAVID DAR

## About Gennady Trifonov's Poetry

The poetry of my favorite poets does not live outside of me; it lives within me. If a poet failed to awaken my own mute voice, my own unwritten and even undreamt-of poetry, then such a poet, no matter how widely recognized, will never find a way into my heart. Gennady Trifonov has wrenched out of its captivity in my muteness the purest melody of all, one that had perhaps sounded inaudibly in my heart in rare moments of sublime infatuation. I would like for others to hear this melody. I think of it as quiet, gentle, and tinted a pale blue hue.

I once wrote about a young man in love. He did not sleep all night, and I listened to his beating heart.

"What is it beating against?" I asked.

"Can't you hear?" said the young man. "It is doing battle with my reason."

It beat as if against the walls of a dungeon, this little, inexperienced, desperate human heart.

"Have trust in me," it implored the young man. "Have trust in me! Your reason has been taught physics and chemistry, geography and history, it knows how to generalize and compare, to draw conclusions and foresee the future. But I remained illiterate, I can be taught nothing, just as one can teach nothing to a flower, a cloud, a star. So have trust in me, have trust!"

Gennady Trifonov's poetry is the poetry of someone who decided to trust his heart. Reason—solid, respectable, universally esteemed—had to retreat before the desperately defenseless, reckless little heart, naked and irresponsible. David vanquished Goliath. The young David, naked as a flower, is playing his songful reed flute. "I am the one," sings the flute, "who's most affectionate of all."

who falls to the ground from
    the heights
without breaking his neck or
    windpipe,
who opens his mouth wide to
    rhymes.

I'm music. Take me. Play me.
I am the reed flute of the
    steppes.
I know all there's to know of
    this life,
both when I laugh and when
    I moan
and that is my entire truth.

The greater part of Gennady Trifonov's poems is addressed to the one he loves. His poems plead for the least fleeting touch, express gratitude for brief encounters, voice a timid hope to be understood, vouchsafe total devotion. But the loved one is always elusive. He exists only in the past, never in the present. In the present there are only poems. They are of the utmost candor, protected by neither reason nor the accepted emotional norms, suggestively whispered by the naked, quivering heart.

It is a fragile reed flute. It can be broken, flung away, trampled underfoot. But it keeps on singing—tender, quiet, passionate, and pure:

My hands are cautious,
My lips are still slightly hot,
So touch them once more.
    All's permitted
By the light of the last candle.

But the entreaties are useless, they are not heard or not understood, or it could be that they are addressed not to a living person of flesh, but to a longing, a dream, a phantom. And the poet returns again and again to his only reality—a blank piece of paper:

No, I don't weep, I don't,
nor do I crumple my drafts
when I hasten to lend a
    successful line
the movement of a river.

I can feel this movement—the current of a singing river—in every line of Trifonov's. At times this current is a gently lulling one, one that barely ripples the bewitching transparency and clarity of his emotions:

We were as yet remote
from each other, and the
    names

> of your verbs were still easy
> when silence drew us close.

At other times this current becomes precipitous, foamy, ungovernable, and imperiously demanding:

> Everything can still come
>     to me:
> both life and death, but you—
>     I doubt it.
> This is why I long for your
>     sworn promise
> before the next winter sets in.
> I want the snow of Christmas
>     eve
> to promise me in advance
> the evening meaning of your
>     verbs—
> my swoon or my delight.

Among Gennady Trifonov's poems, not a single one can be found that is not inspired by tenderness, love, or sensuality. Now, there are different ways of speaking about sensuality. Philistine jokes degrade it to the level of something base or shameful. Genuine poetry elevates sensuality, cleanses it from everything that is base, informs it with beauty and nobility, adorns both the one who loves and the one who is loved. This is probably why all those to whom Trifonov's poems are addressed are bewitchingly beautiful:

> Oh Ghivi, say to me
> that it's a dream, a lie.
> Look, now your silver knife
> is bathed in my blood.
>
> I have not yet been killed—
> it is a surface wound
> from Georgian lips and cheeks
> that cast a shade on me.

The poet depicts his protagonist with a total of three strokes: the silver knife of the inhabitant of the Causasus and his "Georgian" (i.e., probably swarthy) lips and cheeks. The sketch is light and inspired. Together with the poet I experience admiration and an aching feeling of infatuation; the fact that he is infatuated not with a young girl enhances the sweetness of what is forbidden and the longing for what cannot be realized.

All of Trifonov's love lyrics are addressed not to women but to men. This aspect of his poetry, not understood by everyone, is perhaps the source of its special dramatic quality and purity. After all, man's love for woman or woman's love for man is in its essence always pragmatic and purposeful. It adorns, enriches, and covers up the starkness of the instinct for perpetuating the species. Same-sex love, however, is utterly aimless. It represents a sensual attraction that has no other purpose except satisfying the emotion which is without fail spiritualized by those who love. It is a pure play of emotions and is as contrary to nature, whimsical, incomprehensible and inexplicable as the equally unnatural desire of people to speak in rhymes or depict on a canvas objects and events of our surrounding world or extract from musical instruments sounds that do not exist in nature.

But then, every disinterested act of artistic creation is also tinged with drama. Each artist must, after all, sense the discrepancy between his ephemeral playing with words, colors, or sounds and the world of useful, practical activity. With equal inevitability he senses that he is unable to fuse the games he is playing fully with life, to embody his feelings totally in his rhymed lines, or to depict on canvas objects that would totally correspond to their essence.

This tragedy of inapplicability, of practical uselessness, of the impossibility of attaining the full reality of love is what renders the same-sex love akin to selfless and pure art. And this is probably why this love itself can become pure and sublime, just as the art of Beethoven and Bach, of Michelangelo and Petrarch, which has no application in practical life, is pure and sublime. It goes without saying that Trifonov's poems are not about sexual fun and games but always about the powerful and irresistible attraction of one human being for another.

This powerful attraction is imbued in Gennady Trifonov's poetry with a divine grandeur, as are also nature (forest, sky, rain, river) and poetry (line, pipes of Pan, rhyme, reed flute). Against this background of the always majestic eternal nature, lit up by the always majestic eternal poetry, in bewitching verbal and sonorous harmonies and clear-cut strokes that show their fidelity to the austere classical poetry of Europe, there unfolds in Trifonov's poetry, and in his life, the tragedy of his love—majestic, inapplicable, but irresistible as fate itself.

This is the reason I am bold enough to place the handwritten volume of the virtually unknown Russian poet, who is now paying for the defenseless unity of his poetry and his life by serving a sentence in the labor camps of the northern Urals, on my bookshelf next to the immortal sonnets of Petrarch and Michelangelo, not wishing to think about whether the justice of my judgment will or will not be confirmed by that unbribable and implacable judge of poets, time.—*Leningrad, 1978*

# DENNIS ALTMAN

## Down Rio Way

Rio de Janeiro is one of those cities that exist in the imagination even before we arrive. The famous view of Sugarloaf Mountain and Botafogo Bay (where in reality it is too polluted to swim) is one of those international postcard/travel-poster scenes we carry around in our heads, along with a whole wave of 1940s and 1950s movies set in Rio (or, in the case of *Flying Down to Rio*, set above it). In *Now, Voyager*, Bette Davis possibly lost her virginity on the road to Christ (the statue, that is, that looms above the city), and throughout the 1940s and 1950s Carmen Miranda fed the legend of the sexy Brazilian. My own desire to see Rio was originally kindled by the French film *Black Orpheus* and was kept alive by a continual succession of images of Rio as a magical city of beaches, mountains, samba music, carnival madness, and beautiful boys.

It is all of these, especially the last, but it is also a huge aggregation of urban problems in which most people live in sprawling, ugly, inland suburbs and suffer from one of the world's worst transport systems. Despite the *favellas*, homemade shanty towns that spring up wherever middle-class housing has left a crack, most people in Rio live in warm-weather tenements or stucco-and-concrete houses. The picture-book Rio, with its famous beaches (above all Copacabana and Ipanema) is in the southern zone, which all together holds about a fifth of the five? six? seven? million people who constitute greater Rio.

In some ways, Rio is like a tropical Chicago; the drive along the bay, from Copacabana to downtown, is remarkably like Lake Shore Drive. (São Paulo, now the biggest city and the commercial center of South America, is also like Chicago but without the lake.) Yet even in Copacabana, the seemingly luxurious apartment houses that stretch for several miles along the seafront, each with doorman and elevators, are really overcrowded rabbit warrens; from inside the apartments you can see laundry hanging from poles over the courtyards, like in the poorer quarters of Marseilles or Naples. To be middle-class in Rio (and that is perhaps 30 percent of the population) is to aspire to a North American level of consumption on a much lower income and with an inflation rate reaching 50 percent this year.

Of course, to be poor in Rio is to exist on the same level of misery as in the other great cities of the Third World; but even if the poverty is greater, it is not clear that life is more miserable in Rio than in the worst slums of Buffalo, Cleveland, and the South Bronx. That I will write no more of this is not to deny its importance but rather to recognize that a middle-class white foreigner will inevitably fail to see or understand the life of the poor during a touristic foray into Brazil. Giving money to beggars, of whom there are remarkably few (probably due more to police efficiency than adequate social services), is as close as one tends to come to the misery of the great majority of Brazilians.

Rio—and, even more, São Paulo—are First World cities as much as Third World cities, and the size and strength of their middle class are significantly greater than in poor countries in Africa and most of Asia. This is reflected in the press (one of the freer in Latin America—democratization is proceeding here, however cautiously), which consists of the same kinds of journals and periodicals found in Western Europe or North America (that is, the United States and Canada). If it is a mistake to believe that middle-class Rio and São Paulo exemplify Brazil, it is also a mistake to ignore them; the starvation and misery of the northeast do not necessarily make the country ripe for successful revolution.

Yet, as in prerevolutionary Russia, class divisions are all-pervasive, with a rigidity that one Brazilian I spoke with compared to South Africa's. This factor is absolutely essential for understanding the gay scene in Rio. The middle class (not only the very rich) has servants, takes taxis, and, apparently without any special awareness of it, profits in day-to-day life from a class structure that provides inexhaustible supplies of cheap labor. Class mixes with race, as it does in the United States; Brazilian racism is far more subtle, far less violent and sexually obsessed than American racism, but in Brazil one finds fewer blacks on airplanes, at the opera, or in the more expensive restaurants, and blacks appear on television only as maids and chauffeurs. Even without that peculiarly Anglo-Saxon fear of miscegenation that helped fuel the worst excesses of American racism—a Ku Klux Klan would be laughable in Brazil—all sorts of subtle and constant pressures have preserved an almost perfect correlation between racial origin and class position.

Thus, more than in the First World, the gay scene here is stratified along class lines (though this is a matter of degree, not an absolute), and money, if more rarely love, is often an important means of crossing these lines. Indeed, the middle class gay-male scene of Copacabana and Ipanema resembles that of a large United States city ten years ago; if there are no backroom bars or S-and-M boutiques, there are bars (often outdoors), discos, saunas, gay couples, and the assorted problems of jealousy, infidelity, dealing with parents, and managing double lives.

The female gay scene is, as usual, all but invisible, and since Brazilian gay men are as chauvinist as their straight peers, there is not very much contact (although there do seem to be a number of marriages of convenience between gay women and men—not, of course, a phenomenon unknown elsewhere). As is the case with gay men, it is the lower class lesbians who are most visible, and they tend to play out butch/bitch roles in a way that is rapidly disappearing in the West. I was told of one lesbian softball match at which the teams were respectively butch and bitch, and I assume the latter had the good sense to be trounced.

Role-playing is crucial in Brazilian gay life and is similar to that found in Mediterranean countries like Italy or Greece, although, as Brazilians are fond of telling you, the Afro-Portuguese heritage has produced a unique culture. To put it very crudely, homosexuality seems widely accepted (for men) *provided* it conforms to the pattern of role-playing between men and

women; one can be either a macho or a bitch homosexual, at least in outward appearance. (Since some transvestite prostitutes claim to have fucked
their clients, the appearance can be deceptive.) Compared with the rest of
Latin America, which is both Spanish-speaking and far less African, Brazil
has a degree of openness about homosexuality that is striking.

In Rio, homosexuals cruise everywhere; unlike in North American
cities, where encounters are ritualized and surprisingly difficult outside the
ghetto, men in Rio look at each other continually, apparently with little of
the fear of violent rejection that haunts cruising outside in the American
ghettos. (My favorite example: being cruised on a bus by a man who
crossed himself devoutly when we drove past a church.) Despite what one
hears, such open cruising is not performed mainly by hustlers, though hustlers exist in profusion, especially in the center of the city and at certain
cafes in Copacabana. With a perennial summer climate—the beaches are
packed ten to eleven months of the year—and a Latin love of outdoor
"cafes" (really bars that don't even serve coffee), there is much less need
for specifically gay commercial ventures.

Of course, they exist anyway. There are discos which are just like
Parisian _boîtes_, if less unfriendly. There are saunas, which I didn't visit. (I
did see one in São Paulo; it resembled a small version of the old Everard
Baths in New York, far removed from the new luxury of late-seventies
saunas.) There is a whole list of cinemas where sexual contacts of a necessarily fleeting (and perhaps dangerous) kind occur. And there is a weekend
dance in a cinema in one of the older parts of downtown Rio.

The Cinema Iris at two in the morning was as close as I ever came to
the kind of exoticism that fires the imaginations of American queens as
they watch old Carmen Miranda movies on television in the midst of winter. It is a packed melange of disco, samba music (played by an eight-man
band), drag shows, and go-go boys on the balcony. One, dressed as Super-
man, may have been paid to exhibit himself but would probably have done
it for self-love. The clientele is far more mixed than elsewhere, at least
along the lines of class and race, but with few women, mainly gay. There is
the sort of exuberant sensuality one expects to find in Rio. Men kiss each
other on first sight—it is a myth that "macho" Brazilians do not kiss,
though they seem far less interested in cocksucking than most Americans—and there is much more instant contact than in New York discos,
where the object seems to be to look at nobody, except perhaps one's own
reflection.

Outside the Cinema, there are occasionally beggars (one emaciated
woman, clutching a sleeping child, stood patiently for hours, almost totally
ignored by all who entered) and often hustlers. There are two kinds of
hustlers: the "masculine" (though without any sort of _Midnight Cowboy_
drag—they often seem to be boys looking for an excuse to get off) and the
transvestites. Understanding the role of homosexual transvestites (and
Brazilians deny that there are any others) is crucial in understanding gay
life in Brazil. For reasons no one seems able to explain, the transvestite homosexual is accepted socially to a remarkable extent. Such men play an
important part in Carnival, in many religious cults, and in nightclub entertainment, and while the street queens of Rio look just like their counter-

parts in New York (many of whom are also Latins), they are accepted much more widely—and not just as freaks. Among the drag shows in Rio there is at least one theater where the performances are very decorous cabaret entertainments, with more talking than singing, and where most of the audience is at least ostensibly straight.

But here again, class seems all-important. As elsewhere, *bichas* are likely to come from lower-class families. Middle-class homosexuals, much less able to adopt this role (which, for all its caricature, is also a way of avowing one's sexuality) are more likely to assume the camouflage of respectability and lead double lives, accentuated by the very strong grip of family ties in Brazil. It seems not at all uncommon to find men in their forties and fifties living with their mothers, while perhaps maintaining an apartment for their tricks on the side.

I was told that only over the past two decades or so have there emerged in Brazil men who consider themselves homosexual without being *bichas;* that is, not only do they fuck with other men (which does not in itself create this identity), but they live rather like conservative middle-class gays in American cities before Stonewall and the Mineshaft. The embryonic Brazilian gay movement (more in evidence in São Paulo than in Rio) is recruited from this group.

The gay movement was in a sense launched by the newspaper *Lampiao,* which began in April 1978 under the control of a small group of Rio/São Paulo intellectuals and writers, several of whom are included in an anthology of Latin American writing just published by Gay Sunshine (*Now the Volcano,* edited by Winston Leyland). Despite intermittent police harassment—which in Brazil is something to be taken seriously—the paper continues to appear monthly and is distributed and read throughout the country. It is the first serious gay journal to appear anywhere outside the First World, and its content is reminiscent of that very good Italian paper, *Fuori.* Most important, *Lampiao* has moved toward a position of alliance with other "minority" groups in Brazil (two so-called minorities, blacks and women, may each constitute half the population). Recent issues have included a long interview with the charismatic union leader Lula (who expressed hostility toward feminism and ignorance of homosexuality—forging an alliance on the left is not easy for Brazilian gays); an interview with the black activist Abdias Nascimento, whose call for black assertion is heresy in a country that officially knows no racial distinctions; and a dossier on Indian tribes that in some cases are being exterminated for the sake of the Brazilian "economic miracle."

In São Paulo there has emerged a group known as Somos ("We Are") that is strangely reminiscent of early gay liberation groups in North America. If I were cynical, I would dismiss Somos as a group of overearnest middle-class white *Paulistas,* who sit around in endless meetings agonizing over why they are meeting, but this would ignore the very real problems of being gay in Brazil. For if, to reiterate, homosexual *sex* is widely available and acceptable, the only form of homosexual *identity* that is acceptable is that of the *bicha,* and outside certain prescribed contexts, even that is open to constant abuse and contempt.

Writing about his experiences in Brazil in 1973, Allen Young concluded that if gay activism were ever to come to Brazil, he was "quite certain that it will have a very radical political perspective, that it cannot fail to make the connection between gay oppression and imperialism." I'm less sure, although this has been the pattern in both Spain and Italy. The problems of organizing a gay movement in a country that straddles the First and Third worlds are immense, as the women's movement has found. (Does one invite one's maid to join the same consciousness-raising group?) How to become relevant in a society with such enormous and often bizarre socioeconomic divisions as Brazil is not self-evident, nor do the affluent First World countries offer much of a model.

The dominant attitude toward male homosexuals is a mixture of tolerance, amusement, and disgust. Attitudes toward female homosexuals are far less clear, as befits a machismo society; more than in most countries, lesbianism is not seen as a real possibility, even among feminist women. But then, female sexuality in general is badly understood and very much subordinated to male pleasure; feminists can recount stories of women who have been frequently raped without realizing that this was anything other than their natural lot. In a remarkable article on homosexuality in Latin America that appeared in the Summer/Fall 1979 issue of *Gay Sunshine* (and will therefore be largely neglected by academics), E. A. Lacey argued that the macho code makes "men the whole entity and women the incomplete one, whom it is man's duty (Latin Americans often conceive of their indiscriminate and promiscuous sexual activity as 'duty') to make complete.... But ... if the homosexual acts socially in public like a man, then he is a man and will be treated as such, whatever he may do sexually in private—that is his own business; similarly, if he acts socially like a woman (i.e., softly, effeminately, whatever he may do sexually) he is, and will be treated like, a woman."

What this means in terms of self-image, against which the *ententidos* of Somos are struggling, is characterized by the Argentinian homosexual Molina in Manuel Puig's novel *Kiss of the Spider Woman*, when he tells his cellmate Valentin:

> "... because a man ... what he wants is a woman."
> "And all homosexuals are that way?"
> "No, there's the other kind who fall in love with one another.
> But as for my friends and myself, we're a hundred percent female.
> We don't go in for those little games—that's strictly for homosexuals. We're normal women; we sleep with men."

In Brazil, the machismo tradition is perhaps softer, less confining than it is in the "southern cone" of Latin America, just as the Brazilian military is less repressive than its Argentinian or Chilean counterparts (not that it hasn't been perfectly willing, like them, to resort to widespread torture). It is very difficult to measure the various cultural factors at work, difficult to explain the relative importance of economic factors, of the Portuguese-Catholic background, of African-derived cults and the existence of slavery until 1888, of the lack of a firmly established democratic tradition. Discussion with academics and intellectuals, even those professionally interested in sexuality, tends to bog down in generalizations, often contradictory ones—for example, the Catholic Church is very important (it blocked divorce until several years ago), but no one takes much notice of its views on morality; the Portuguese were freer than the Spaniards; and so on.

The existence of the Latin macho tradition seems to preclude much imitation of the American gay-clone phenomenon that is currently sweeping northern Europe. The apparent absence of a leather or S-and-M scene can be partly explained in terms of economic and political factors, but one might also infer powerful psychological reasons. If, as I suspect, this vogue is in part a product of guilt and self-hatred, often at an unconscious level, and if it is a vogue rarely found in Latin countries (either in Europe or South America), this could mean that there is a real psychological difference between Catholic and Protestant guilt.

While the hypocrisy surrounding homosexuality is no more or less prevalent here than elsewhere, it is perhaps different. In Brazil it's quite OK to have homosexual sex, but much less OK to talk or write about it, whereas the opposite is more common in Anglo-Saxon countries. This may be because writing or talking about homosexuality is moving toward a *political* critique, which, in a country ruled by generals, is not encouraged.

The Brazilian military government, even before its present mood of "democratization," was on the whole not a particularly puritanical one compared with the governments in Argentina and Chile (although it has had its moments; in the sixties, sex education was forbidden in the schools with the marvelous justification that "flowers should not be opened by dirty hands"). The government's attacks on *Lampiao* are probably motivated more by politics than by moralism, although there are much more rigid restrictions on pornography in Brazil than in any First World country, except perhaps Ireland.

Gradually, the idea that sex is political has begun to infiltrate Brazil, along with democratization, American television programs, disco music, and translations of leftist books. If the present policy of *abertura* really succeeds in restoring democracy to Brazil, there could well be the same upsurge in gay and women's political activities that has accompanied liberalization in Spain. Meanwhile, gay life will continue in Rio with all the contrasts, contradictions, and anomalies that seem so much a part of all Brazilian life.

## Fado Lisboeta

*T*he Monsanto campsite a few miles from central Lisbon is reportedly the largest in Europe. Salazar built it for sturdy bourgeois tourists, the kind who would put everything they own on wheels and buy great quantities of beef in the camp's gourmet supermarket. The women could have their hair coiffed *à la française* at the resident beauty parlor, the men could chug beer or sip port around the pool or at one of the bars. When bored, they could file into buses to see, as the loud-speaker still advertises in five languages, "beautiful Lisboa" and eat a "typical Portuguese meal" and listen to traditional Portuguese music, called Fado—all for 100 francs or $23 or £8.

Now, two years after the revolution, half-empty buses still run into town promptly at five o'clock, although fares are sharply reduced to accommodate the smaller incomes of the French and Italian workers who have replaced the bourgeoisie and who buy hard cheese and Portuguese prosciutto. Some of the younger comrades are not averse to pinching a can of paté or bottles of tiny tasteless, but expensive, shrimp. This quasi-acceptable shoplifting (based on the rumor that the supermarket is still privately owned) is nothing compared to the rampant theft that afflicts thousands of tourists. Next to the large outdoor café every day one sees students or young workers whose money has been stolen asking for donations to get back to Milan or Bilbao. One young couple spoke of being robbed at knife-point by apparently sweet young hitchhikers. A young man told of having his gold chain ripped off his neck as he walked in the forest adjacent to the gay beach at Caprica, next door to a vast refugee camp.

At Monsanto, there are plenty of security guards. They were out in full force, joined by several dozen marines toting machine guns, on the night of the Portuguese-Italian Solidarity Rally. Hundreds of the Milanese and Romans at the camp came just for the rally, which began as a massive parade displaying farm machinery and other gifts from the Italian Communist party to their Portuguese comrades. The marchers were aided and often joined by the army—a collection of bearded and mustachioed young men who, true to the legends of Portuguese beauty, were astonishing to watch as they chanted, sang, and ripped off their shirts in the broiling Lisbon heat. Unlike their counterparts in France or the United States, these young men are outgoing and friendly, and it was through the offer of beer from a bearded, green-eyed corporal overseeing the crowd control contingent that I left Monsanto for nearly a week.

Pedro is from Evora, a poor but jewellike city in southern Portugal, and as soon as he was old enough to be a soldier he was sent off to fight guerrillas in Mozambique. There he met and later became lovers with a young native prisoner who was unusually sophisticated and who taught Pedro to write both French and Portuguese properly and to read everything from Lenin to Genet. The relationship was generally accepted by his comrades, which may seem astonishing to those who know how virulent European homophobia remains outside of Amsterdam or Copenhagen. In this respect Portugal is an anomaly not easily explained. There are no laws protecting homosexuals nor are there laws victimizing them. Except for a well-publicized gay march in Oporto nearly two years ago, there has been no gay movement in Portugal. After that march there was some discussion in the press and on radio in which gays had to defend themselves against traditional Communist homophobic polemics. But for reasons as obscure as the various political shifts over the last revolutionary months, the issue was dropped. Pedro claims that several very powerful military people who are gay simply decided that no discussion was necessary and that all military and police harassment of gays was to cease. The one thing curtailed was the rampant male prostitution in and around Edward VII Park at the head of Avenida Liberdade. On any evening during the old regime literally hundreds of men in uniform would roam this lovely expanse seeking to supplement their incomes through the use of their bodies. Now the only military people around are security police searching cars for explosives and whatnot.

However, some heterosexuals here have negative ideas about the gay issue. A young woman writing for one of the Trotskyite papers put it this way, "In Portugal, it is a man's society. As elsewhere in Latin Europe, women count for nothing. From the time they are young, men deal with men socially. They end up courting each other. Most men are not gay, but they may as well be, since their real loyalties and respect are to each other. But to us, nothing matters except the revolution."

Pedro, who smokes grass, is a sexual gymnast, and like many Portuguese men lacks the most overtly macho tendencies one finds too often in Spaniards and South Americans, concurred with the young woman's final sentiment, although he was at a loss to explain why he was attracted to men. "An American boy told me last year that you talk a lot about being gay and what it means. I guess we're not quite ready to deal with that. We have fascists and counterrevolutionaries to worry about."

After the rather tedious rally, we walked back toward the tiny flat Pedro shares with two army friends when he is off duty. Despite the late hour, the streets were jammed, and as usual in this truly revolutionary city, everyone was talking—young, old, men and women—all debating the revolution, which is remarkably short on violence but also short on agreed-upon solutions to the dismal state of the Portuguese economy. We sat for a while at a side-street café where several workers were discussing their formerly multinational company, which not only paid them a third of what similar workers get in France and Germany but which closed shop without paying their final month's salary. Such workers may or may not be Communists but they are united in their detestation of Mario Soares and his promise to bring foreign capital back to Portugal through the multinationals. Soares dreams of turning Portugal into another Holland, but he overlooks what is known by every Lisbonite who has worked in Amsterdam, which is that the Dutch subsidize their excellent social benefits partly through exploitation of foreign workers. The more fortunate workers are hired on year-long contracts, with no pensions or medical benefits. The majority must telephone daily to learn the mysterious pick-up points where they will be whisked away blindfolded to a factory and paid a pittance after long hours of labor. The bitter irony is that these workers still earn more than they ever could in Portugal and they rarely pump their incomes back into the Portuguese economy. Thus, the fervent urging of emigrant workers to come home is more touching than practical.

Further along on the way to Pedro's we passed a bank with a sign in the window proclaiming, "This Bank Is Now for the People." A block later the poster in a Bloomingdale's-type store gave notice: "We are having a final sale of our luxury goods. This store will now only sell clothes for the People." Just the tourist shops appear unchanged.

Pedro, as his apartment shows, has few material possessions and appears not to resent that. "I am a soldier of the Revolution," he would repeat during the week in tones ranging from anger to bemusement. He is still in a state of revolutionary euphoria, as is much of the country. His radio is constantly tuned to one of the many stations that play nonstop antibourgeois folk music. One song will be anticlerical, the next antibusiness, and so on. Despite the fact that he's heard these songs a hundred times, he roars at the satire. "You know they used to play Amalia Rodriguez all day. She was our Piaf, but she was also Salazar's favorite—so no more Amalia."

One of Pedro's roommates, João, isn't quite as progressive. His obsession with clothes surprised me. Out of uniform João looks every bit the Parisian—the look of the old regime, according to Pedro, who tells me that makes perfect sense for someone like João, who is addicted to the bars. When Pedro went out on night duty, he urged João to take me on a tour of his haunts. These turned out to be four bars, where one knocked to be admitted, Prohibition style. My memory of all of them is of chrome: chrome tables, chrome mirrors, chrome lighting fixtures. These four clubs appear to be anachronisms and seem to have a near monopoly on the pristine, ordered style one associates with Cherry Grove and Cannes and advertisements in the *New York Times Magazine*.

Pedro was pleased that I didn't warm to the plated atmosphere. The following night, we wandered downtown into a small restaurant on the Bairro Alto that is run by a famous longtime antifascist lesbian who looks every bit Gertrude Stein with a bun. The patrons, besides the radical chic of Lisbon, consist of a flaming international gay coterie that uses the fin de siècle decor of lovely Portuguese tile as a backdrop for a theater of campy jokes in four languages. The loudest diners are the Spaniards, who undoubtedly live in Lisbon to escape the severest homophobic system in Western Europe. In Spain one can be confined to a mental hospital for being gay.

The situation of lesbians here is analogous to that of women in general, and there is no bar or club where gay women can meet solely on their own. They share restaurants and bars with the men, which has made for close bonds between the sexes. At the gay beach at Caprica it is common to see mixed groups of gay men and women. One lesbian, a teacher, explained, "You know, outside Lisbon most women would want to slit our throats if they knew we were Saphique. There is no real women's movement. The *pédés* are the only ones who know our struggles."

A week later, Pedro decided I was bored and said, "Let's go to a rally." It was like saying, "Let's go to the movies," and like the movies, rallies in Lisbon come in all lengths and qualities. Since there can be three simultaneous rallies on any day, one must pick and choose carefully. Pedro wouldn't dream of attending any meetings but those supported by the Portuguese Communist party (PCP). And at least from the dramatic point of view, the PCP rallies are far and away the most exciting. The rally of the day was called the United Front Against the Reactionaries and Support for the MFA (the umbrella military group). For six hours the intensity remained at a pitch that can only be described as hyperhysterical. There was cheering for everyone—the visiting Italian and French comrades, various labor leaders, and speaker after speaker.

After the rally Pedro and I said farewell, since he had been reassigned to a city in the north. Groups of men and women walked past us singing the Party anthem, "Avanti, Comara, Avanti," with fervor and an upraised fist at every chorus. When the roar of a large motorcycle added to this din, I turned to see an Italian friend from Monsanto, Giancarlo, and hopped on his BMW to head back to camp, where the guards and marines were still standing as if they hadn't moved from their spots of a week before.

Giancarlo was unusual for a young Roman heterosexual. Three days after our initial café encounter he had apologized for not sleeping with me. "I know it would be, how do you say, politically just to make love with you, but I cannot. Still, I like you very much and want you as my friend." This expression of regret referred specifically to a 2 A.M. encounter at his tent on my instigation and led to a discussion of his recently overcoming five years of impotence. "I can now sleep only with women I like much, and I am afraid that if I sleep with men, I will be impotent again." Understanding this personal logic, I accepted his position and now, after Pedro, was rather glad to share the nooks and crannies of Lisbon with a fellow tourist.

Giancarlo sported a collection of perfectly worn jeans, work shirts, and a soft black leather jacket. He topped this off with an addiction to long dreadful cigars. This was not so much a radical chic stance as the practical outfit for someone whose friends were all left politicos of one sort or another. In Italy, one is not usually friends with one's political or class enemies. Thus, when Giancarlo's friend Theresa, a teacher in a Communist school and, like most Italians visiting Portugal, a supporter of the PCP, discovered that many of my friends were not even socialists, she viewed me with a certain suspicion. For her the class struggle comes first. "You Americans can never understand the class struggles in Italy and Portugal. I read that Kennedy says this and that against the government and then goes on vacation or to parties with the same people he is attacking. They are all part of the same capitalist oppression." She admitted to being confused about homosexuality, which she always referred to as if only men were involved. Her attitude was analogous to Pedro's—if homosexuals are on the correct side of the class struggle, fine; if not, they are the enemy.

The next day a busload of young Australians rolled into Monsanto. They were overjoyed to find someone else who spoke English, even though it was of the New York variety. When I asked them about their experience in Portugal, they said that they could barely tell one country from another and were surprised and titillated by my descriptions of the demonstrations and activity here. They had been completely unaware that anything was going on in Portugal. It was almost like being home again.

# DENNIS ALTMAN

# *Paris*

*P*aris occupies a special place in the homosexual imagination. It offers neither the tolerance of Amsterdam or San Francisco, nor the inexhaustible sensuality of New York. But we are reminded by such names as Proust, Gide, Cocteau, Colette, and Genet that Paris has certainly been a major center for homosexual culture and a refuge from more repressive cultures for homosexuals such as Oscar Wilde, Radclyffe Hall, Gertrude Stein, and James Baldwin (who set *Giovanni's Room* there).

More than in most cities, homosexuality in Paris was, until recently, the preserve of the chic and the rich. Not, of course, that homosexual behavior hasn't always been widely practiced among all classes. But to be a homosexual—to assume that as a particular identity—was an activity almost entirely confined to an intellectual and aristocratic elite.

This distinction has largely collapsed over the past decade, as it has elsewhere in the western world. The pivotal event in France was not the Stonewall riots, whose influence abroad was largely symbolic, but rather the events of May 1968, out of which emerged both the first radical homosexual movement and, more important, very real changes in self-perception and political attitudes among French homosexuals. May 1968 marked a turning point in French history; there is a post-1968 generation which impinges on every area of French society, and this is particularly true for homosexuals. The casual gay tourist, phrase book in one hand and Spartacus guide in the other, is unlikely to see this. He—less likely she—will go to the expensive bars and *boîtes* (clubs) around the rue Ste. Anne, be approached by a number of insouciant hustlers, who demand either 200 francs or 'a present,' and will flee Paris declaiming its rudeness, its expense, and its lack of friendliness.

There is more of a gap in Paris than in American cities between the commercial and the movement gay scenes; although there is a concentration of gay bars and restaurants in several areas, there is no ghetto here comparable to the West Village or Castro, and gay life is less centered around exclusively homosexual enterprises. Paris has gay porn shops, cinemas, saunas, and restaurants. But gay life here is more complex than an inventory of these would suggest.

A good example of this complexity is found along the Boulevard St. Germain, where, around the two cafes beloved of expatriate Americans, the Flore and the Deux Magots, and alongside the expensive clothing stores, one finds a constant parade of chic Paris. There is a steady flow of young men who may or may not be cruising but who are certainly not averse to being admired. St. Germain is chic, androgynous, and pan-sensual.

The Tuileries are less ambiguous. There, beginning around the entrance to the Orangerie and extending along the Seine, is the central cruising ground of Paris and, at night, a major trysting ground. The cruising is conducted in a typically French manner, rather the way models parade at a fashion show, and encounters seem rare. Ironically, on the streets, the metro, and the buses, encounters are likely to be more relaxed, friendly, and frequent.

At night, things change a little: the dancers go to rue Ste. Anne and pay $10 to enter minuscule *boîtes* where the object of the game seems to be to remain as unaware of anyone's interest in you for as long as possible. Frequently, there is an adrogynous chic to Paris *boîtes* that can be intimidating. In the provinces, gay clubs are much simpler; the Rocambole, located southeast of Paris at Villecresnes, is an old inn which has been converted to a restaurant-bar-disco where hundreds of *français moyens* of all ages and inclinations dance to some of the worst music of the sixties and throw streamers and balloons at each other. But provincial gay life remains very closeted; as for everyone else in France whose ambitions take them beyond the conventional, Paris remains the magnet for homosexuals.

The homosexual movement in France dates back to 1954—more recent than in Germany, Switzerland, or Holland but further back than most French homosexuals realize. In that year, the review and movement *Arcadie* were founded under the influence of Andre Baudry, who remains their dominant figure. Today, *Arcadie* claims fifty thousand subscribers (only 5 percent women) and has branches in most large centers in French-speaking Europe. Arcadie continues to epitomize the traditional homosexual organization. Baudry expresses only contempt for those who "march in the streets half-clad, wearing makeup and carrying obscene banners." Just as the generation that experienced Stonewall found the Mattachine Society or the Daughters of Bilitis unacceptably apologetic and overly concerned with respectability, so the young homosexuals, both women and men, who experienced May 1968 rejected Arcadie (if, indeed, they knew of its existence). A few desultory moves to organize homosexuals amidst the frenzy of that month (described in Dominique Fernandez's novel *L'Etoile Rose*) were followed a couple of years later by the emergence of FHAR (Front Homosexual d'Action Revolutionaire). The rise and decline of FHAR resembled those of gay liberation groups in America. Marked by theatricality, a fervent desire to flaunt homosexuality as positive, and a concern with demonstrating solidarity with other factions of the extreme (that is, non-Communist) Left, FHAR soon collapsed in a welter of recriminations and backbiting.

The last several years, however, have seen a recrudescence of gay militancy in France and the development of a large number of groups both in and outside Paris. There have been demonstrations, homosexual film festivals, gay candidates in elections, summer camps (including a "summer university" last year in Marseilles), and, most important, the emergence of a real gay press, which had previously consisted only of a number of semi-pornographic magazines with artistic pretensions and a number of Xeroxed movement bulletins.

Last year saw the birth of both a radical gay newspaper *Le Gai Pied* (B.P. 183, 75523 Paris, Cedex 11), and a magazine, *Masques* (c/o Librairie Anima, 3 rue Ravignan 75018 Paris). *Pied* is a word impossible to translate, but it carries connotations of pleasure, enjoyment, even orgasm. With intentions of being both a movement and a popular homosexual monthly somewhat modeled on *Liberation* (the ultraleft daily paper which was founded in the early seventies) and with the aim of being sold at every kiosk in France, *Le Gai Pied* represents a possible expansion of the radical gay movement outside small groups of marginal leftists. In its first year it published long interviews with people like Foucault, Burroughs, and Hockney and claimed a readership of thirty-five thousand.

Looking through the paper, one is struck by the lack of concrete movement activity compared to that in most Anglo-Saxon countries. There are GLH groups (Groupes de Liberation Homosexuelle) in most large cities, but they seem strangely inactive compared with the activities one finds in any large American city. Nor has the French gay movement been successful in nurturing alternatives to the expensive commercial gay scene. (For a while there was a gay community center near Montparnasse, but it collapsed.) Apart from occasional—and exciting—fund-raising dances and cabarets, the Arcadie club rooms remain the only real alternative to the commercial scene in Paris.

This absence of alternative institutions explains why one cannot speak of either a gay community or a gay ghetto in Paris. It explains also in part why the French regard the American gay movement with both awe and suspicion. French homosexuals consider America—above all New York—to be the center of liberated homosexuality where anything is possible. It is no accident that two of the backroom bars here (both harassed recently by the police) are called the Bronx and the Manhattan or that a new gay bar-cafe is called Le Village. The largest sauna in Paris is known as the Continental, in memory of a former New York landmark. The Continental, which extends some distance beneath the Grands Boulevardes, is a French version of an American sauna—and hence has only a mythological resemblance to one. To New Yorkers, accustomed to the functional efficiency of bathhouses, there is something overly elegant about the place: patrons lie on chaise longues around a kidney-shaped swimming pool, sunbathe in the fluorescent light, eat at a poolside restaurant, and can even have their hair cut between screws. There are other, less opulent saunas in Paris, including one Arab *hammam* reputedly frequented by some of Paris's better-known intellectuals, but the Continental is by far the largest.

In Paris, the United States is seen as a symbol of social change on a scale that can only be a dream in Europe. Thus, the third issue of *Gai Pied* was dedicated to the myth of Stonewall and its tenth anniversary, which was duly celebrated across Europe. But this vision of New York both excites and repels; an article in an earlier issue on the Mineshaft brought a hostile reaction to "the new homosexual: as functional, practical, and serious as a self-cleaning oven." One hears in France that Americans are very good at the *techniques* of sex.

It is a strange testament to American influence that the first *entirely* gay demonstration in France took place in 1977 to protest the activities of Anita Bryant. (The demonstration was successfully steered by the police into a distant working-class quarter.) Homosexuals had demonstrated before but usually as part of a broader left-wing activity, as on May Day. The May Day March remains important and large, and is firmly controlled by the Communist-dominated trade-union federation; the stalwarts of the Communist party (which, along with the Gaullist party of Jacques Chirac, is the most staunch defender of traditional morality) are not overjoyed by their new allies, and homosexual contingents are firmly relegated to the back of these marches, where their slogans against "work, the family, and the phallus" can presumably corrupt fewer workers.

The French Left (which means essentially the Communist and Socialist parties) has been at best indifferent to the homosexual movement; there exists neither the interest-group organization nor the libertarian ideology that has led a few American politicians to recognize and even court "the homosexual vote." Only on the extreme Left and among environmentalists has there been any hint of recognition of homosexuals, and there is no formal acceptance of a gay constituency as in the Italian Radical party. A few homosexual candidates ran in the 1978 legislative elections (and there was a homosexual ticket in the municipal elections in Aix), but the vote was derisory. The French gay movement has thus far failed to find ways either to build a large pressure group or to influence the major political parties.

But where are the lesbians? They are more invisible, it would seem, than in America. (One American woman I know complained bitterly that she could find no lesbians in Paris. The problem was one of recognition: the feminist lesbian who refuses to dress according to conventional standards is very rare in Paris.) The lesbian world in Paris seems both elegant and concealed (as it is described in Elula Perrin's *Women Prefer Women* [Bantam, 1979]), and the relative reticence of French feminism has meant a correspondingly small number of women who have come to terms with their (homo)sexuality.

Women participated in both FHAR and GLH, but they were always a minority and, as elsewhere, tended to drop out to work within the women's movement. (One friend remarked that she had heard all the rhetoric five years ago in Australia. Indeed, the French have generally been much less involved in sexual discussion over the past decade than have Anglo-Saxons.) Thus, for lesbians in France the discovery of political dimensions of their sexuality accompanies the discovery of feminism, and the result is that separation is almost total.

Most notable over the last few years has been the emergence of a number of lesbian novelists in addition to those already known (for example, Colette, Violette Leduc, Monique Wittig). A lesbian journal appeared last summer under the name *Desormais* ("Henceforth"). But while in the Anglo-Saxon world there have at least been attempts to construct a dialogue between gay women and men, this is less obvious in France. Apart from Masques, in which women participate, the movement is completely male-oriented, and unlike in America, feminism is not important to the analysis that political (male) homosexuals make of their position.

The views that France and America have of each other are strangely distorted. If America is seen by Parisian gay men as *la baise permanente* (that is, sex without pause), then France in the eyes of Francophile Americans is a land of tenderness, romance, and dazzling intellectual discourse. It may well be true that at some level the French *are* more romantic (if less sentimental) than Americans, although one feels that they reserve real passion for money rather than love. It is true that intellectual life in Paris has a vigor unknown in Anglo-Saxon countries outside a few restricted circles, although if some of the cafes scintillate with discussion, this is at the expense of the universities, most of which are depressingly mediocre and conventional.

Yes, one does sometimes talk of Foucault and Levi-Strauss when cruising, and one does meet charming young men at the Centre Beaubourg who are equally at home with Haydn and punk rock. This phenomenon is by no means confined to Paris: I have discussed literature in the Ramrod and debated the merits of various recordings of the Verdi *Requiem* in a Sydney backroom bar. Nevertheless, intellectuals *are* important in France in a way that they are not in the Anglo-Saxon world, and on the whole it seems sensible to take more note of their views on politics than those of rock singers and film stars (although I would trust Jane Fonda's instincts over Louis Althusser's any day).

The Parisian intellectual milieu—at least since World War II—certainly has not demonstrated the homophobia found among the pseudo-intellectuals of New York, which even today has a surprising intensity. The recent avowals of their homosexuality by Barthes and Foucault only confirmed what was already widely known and accepted. French writing on homosexuality is likely to be widely discussed outside specifically gay publications.

Of the post-1968 gay writers, the most important is Guy Hocquenghem, whose *Homosexual Desire* (Allison and Busby, 1972) is in essence a reappraisal of homosexuality within the post-Freudian tradition developed by Deleuze and Guattari in their *Anti-Oedipus*. Hocquenghem has also written short stories, books on pederasty and politics, and, most recently, a critique of French complacency called *The Beauty of the Métis* (the half-cast). He is best known in the United States for the semidocumentary, semifantasy film *La Race d'Ep*, which he made with Lionel Soukaz.

Hocquenghem is the most important theorist of the gay movement produced in France and an excellent example of the post-1968 generation: scornful of all political parties, hostile to both the orthodox Left and the "new philosophers" (themselves a product of 1968), a teacher at the University of Vincennes and a journalist at *Liberation* (both quintessential products of 1968). His writing is best where it evokes the shadowy world of the nighttime homosexual, as in his story "The Bird of the Night," which is the basis of the last part of *La Race d'Ep.*

For Hocquenghem, gay life in Paris is both sad and snobbish, with neither the advantages of a proper ghetto (that is, a place where homosexuals live, not just spend money, together) nor the diffuse sexuality one finds in a Mediterranean city like Barcelona or Palermo. One might again note that this conflicts with the predominant Anglo-Saxon image of gay Paris. For us, France has always (if not as much as Italy) been the place where homosexuality could express itself freely. It is no accident that Oscar Wilde is buried under a huge and ugly mausoleum in the Père Lachaise cemetery (which, incidentally, must be included in every gay tour of Paris—Proust, Bellini, Sarah Bernhardt, Edith Piaf, and even Jim Morrison are buried there). But then, France is not really a Mediterranean country outside the coastal strip around Nice. France seems firmly anchored, through both temperament and prosperity, in northern Europe.

French gay life is by and large more like that of Germany or Britain than that of Spain or Italy, in that there are large numbers of men (if far fewer women) who identify themselves as homosexual, with a considerable commercial world that caters to them. Homophobia is quite widespread, but more subtle than in the United States; it is most often expressed through what Christopher Isherwood once called "annihilation by blandness." While there has been considerable police harassment in recent years, it has always been in the name of protecting public morals or defense of minors and never against homosexuality per se. With neither sodomy laws to protest nor any real tradition of legal protection of minority rights, it is not surprising that the French homosexual movement remains weak.

In truth, France seems to me the most resolutely heterosexual of all European countries, prepared to tolerate homosexuality as long as it remains invisible. One has only to remember the staple story of so many French movies: a romance between a young girl and a middle-aged man. It is no accident that this is the theme of the prototypical movie-within-the-movie in Truffaut's *Day for Night.* Homosexual characters appear rarely and then only as figures of fun. (The recent film *La Cage aux Folles* is in the genre of *Staircase,* but a decade later.) It is Italy, not France, where one finds important gay film directors, and London, not Paris, where a political gay theater has emerged. The famous Code Napoleon means little besides a particular conception of how to maintain the particular stigma against homosexuality. Paris may abound with homosexuals, but even along the

Boulevard St. Germain the only couples to be seen embracing are heterosexual. Even with the public "coming out" (the "franglais" phrase) of a
number of writers in recent years, homosexuality in France remains far
more discreet than in the United States—or, for that matter, in Germany,
Holland, or Britain. The idea that homosexuality is a private matter that
only concerns the authorities when it becomes a "public offense" has as its
corollary the fact that homosexuals here are less likely than in the United
States to think of themselves as part of a political and cultural minority.

While American (male) homosexuals seem obsessed with the matter
(and sometimes the techniques) of sadomasochism, the French are obsessed with pederasty. There is a flood of novels on the subject; the best
known are the books of Roger Peyrefitte and Tony Duvert. I remember
one militant telling me that he always came to Paris to cruise on Wednesday afternoons, which is a school half-holiday. I don't know whether the
practice of pederasty is more common here than elsewhere, although the
presence of Catholic boarding schools (now declining) has done much to
foster it. Certainly French homosexuals, and especially homosexual intellectuals, are more eager to discuss the subject than their American counterparts.

Does this predilection for pederasty tell us something about French
sexual hang-ups? Or perhaps, as Guy Hocquenghem suggests, this signifies a French homosexual urge to retain the Socratic model of an idealized
relationship between youthful sensuality and aging wisdom—a relationship impossible in the enclosed ghettos of the West Village or Castro,
where age is abhorred. Could one go on to argue that this is in turn related
to a continuing aristocratic and effete self-image that runs against the democratic athleticism found everywhere in American gay culture from Walt
Whitman to the Village People?

I suspect that in France there is less openness and experimentation in
matters sexual, that French puritanism is as crippling in its way as Anglo-
Saxon puritanism, and that more French homosexuals than American feel
themselves afflicted in some way and unable to live openly. At the same
time, there really seems less of a need to proclaim either one's masculinity
or one's sexuality, both of which are part of the code of the new macho homosexual. The French maintain that it is far easier to be a homosexual in
the United States than in France. I am less than convinced, and not just
because very few French gays have ever been to Dayton. The French respect for culture and intellect results in far less demand for the sort of masculine role-playing that places such a strain on the American homosexual.
(This also explains why the macho look of Christopher Street has relatively little following in France.) If Paris can boast neither a ghetto nor a
movement able to mobilize thousands for an annual march, it is nonetheless a city in which it is very pleasant to live as a homosexual.

# London Diary

*I*t has been two years since my last visit, an interval that has seen the defeat of the Labour party and the accession to power of Margaret Thatcher. During that same interval there has been a major shift in England's fortunes. The poverty and filth so apparent during my last visit, seeming to linger on from a Victorian novel, are no longer in evidence, and with them has gone the defeatism that has dominated England through the years since Suez.

I arrive two days after the British managed to successfully "raid" the occupied Iranian embassy, an extraordinary display of paramilitary power that was carried live on television and that redounds greatly to the credit of Mrs. Thatcher and her right-wing supporters.

My first evening, still not completely recovered from the effects of the flight (which makes dinner at one in the morning, *my* time), I have dinner at a friend's flat. One of the guests works for a major British publisher and is the lover of a well-known American expatriate writer. I mention my plans to visit London's gay bookshop, and he and I are soon locked in a heated discussion. Nikos can see no need for such a thing. England, he declares, has no need of liberation; it has always been liberated. That sort of thing—gay bookshops and the like—is typical of America. I am in for a long lecture on the evils of America and an attack on ghetto mentality.

I try to suggest that gay bookstores do not create the ghetto, that they perhaps respond to it and attempt to alleviate it. I remind him that W. H. Smith, England's mass-market bookseller with branches in virtually every train station in this land of trains, refuses to stock gay books or periodicals if they are aware that they are gay. But Nikos will have none of it. Literature is literature, he retorts; there is no such thing as gay literature. You can buy any book you want in any bookstore. He is convinced that Americans are the enemies of culture, exporting a political strategy that can have no relevance to enlightened societies like England.

It is a comment that I shall hear repeated often during my stay. Still, I remind myself that Nikos is Greek, despite his English manners and attitudes. His view of England is one that seems determined by his decision to become as English as he can, having grown up in a very unliberated society. His hatred of America probably also reflects some of his expatriate lover's ambivalences; I can only guess at what it means to be an American writer of French-Canadian origin who has chosen to be British, feeling himself in some sense to be following in the footsteps of Henry James. The English themselves do not hate America (they are more likely to be charmed and perhaps bemused); but those who have chosen to become

English against their own grain often see America, with its quest for self, in a diabolical guise.

The following night I see a somewhat more representative view of England: I go to a pub in the theater district (the West End). The Salisbury is one of the most famous of London's gay pubs, and it attracts dancers (the Coliseum is across the street), actors, stagehands, and tourists, as well as those Englishmen in search of them. The decor is what one expects of an English pub—pure Edwardiana: red plush, dark wood, and gilded light fixtures. The atmosphere is relaxed and sensual. Although this is a gay pub and probably 90 percent of the customers are gay, something of the neighborhood homeliness of every English pub is still present. People know each other and stop to chat; they look to see who the new arrivals are; they offer you a drink.

Because they are subject to the usual English licensing laws and must close by 11 P.M., even gay pubs in England lack the hysterical sexual drive of American bars. People drop in because they feel at home. They may meet someone attractive and interesting; then again, they may not. It doesn't really matter that much. They come to drink beer served at a palatable temperature and to talk in a room without loud music.

Yet one sees the signs of America, above all in dress. There is a sharp contrast between the Edwardian atmosphere and the leather jackets that are affected by many of the customers. The jackets were mostly purchased during a week's holiday in New York or California, and they don't seem to sit quite right on English shoulders. Many of the men I speak to tell me about their trips to North America, a place that continues to intrigue them and to provide a sexual mystique. But their American attributes remain superficial, a dash of spice that adds to their sophistication but which doesn't change their basic perception of America as a deeply foreign place.

Although pubs remain the center of English gay life, there are also gay discos, just as there have always been after-hours dancing clubs (members only, because of the laws, but membership is easily acquired). The most celebrated disco at the moment is Heaven, in the vaults of Charing Cross. My friends all urge a visit, assuring me that it's just like America. It's difficult to explain to them that I didn't come all this way to try a little bit of Americana (unlike the American tourist who heads straight for McDonald's). In any case, despite their claims for American authenticity and daring, it turns out that the excitement is limited to the light show and the dress of the customers. Sex on the spot? The question astounds them. The answer is evident.

Another evening I find out about a different kind of entertainment. I visit the bookshop that so annoyed my dinner companion a few nights earlier and have coffee in the coffee house at the rear of the shop. The coffee (or tea) is available whenever the shop is open (I met people who claimed they went there only because the coffee is so good: English coffee is rarely potable, let alone good), but Thursday evenings are a particular occasion: there is always a reading, a book-signing, or some other event accompanying the coffee. The bookstore, called (a bit cutely) Gay's The Word, is run by a charming and knowledgeable young man named John, who gave up a more conventional career as a banker to take over this active shop on

Marchmont Street, in the heart of Bloomsbury (one can almost hear Lytton Strachey's voice). It is beginning to attract a large and varied public, and the night that I'm there the relatively small premises are pleasantly full. There is an excellent choice of both new and used books and a good selection of periodicals. I am disappointed to notice that, among the new books, there is almost nothing that isn't also available in the States. John confirms my observation: all English gay books get picked up and reprinted in the United States. The reverse is not, alas, true. A great many successful gay titles are simply unavailable in the United Kingdom. The bookstore tries to compensate for this by ordering directly from the publishers, but it is a difficult and time-consuming process. It also frequently involves problems with Her Majesty's customs inspectors. *The Joy of Gay Sex*, for instance, has not been published in England and has difficulty getting into the country even on a direct-order basis.

After the bookstore closes, we go to the nearby flat of a friend. John is an American, the son of a Baptist preacher in Alabama, who came to life when he met the gay poet Jonathan Williams as a student at Wake Forest College and subsequently fled to civilization and a job in a London bookstore. He now does publicity for a group of American university presses and has little affection for the United States. It obsesses him, though, and he wants to talk at great length about being gay in America and about what America has done to him. I suspect it's more his Baptist-preacher father than "America," but I decide not to tell him that. Still, Daddy may have been more complex than I allow: John shows me a copy of Whitman's *Leaves of Grass*, his father's copy, which he recently received as a gift from his parents. He has discovered that someone (his father or mother) has underlined all the sexual passages!

The tiny flat (housing is a real problem in London) is pleasantly arranged, with a nice mix of taste and kitsch. The living room is dominated by a signed and dedicated David Hockney; another Hockney is in the lavatory. John lives here with his lover, Barry, who works at the University of London. They worry about sexual experiences outside their relationship (although John at least seems constantly aware of the charms of passing young men). Their close-couple relationship seems characteristic of London gay life. Most of the people I met at the bookshop were there with their lovers, and during the rest of my stay I met very few unattached men. This may in part be a function of age (if I were meeting eighteen-year-olds, I would presumably meet more single men), but it appears above all to be a function of English social life and the way in which it has integrated a certain kind of gay life. The gay couples I meet have adopted a life-style that would seem hopelessly cozy to New Yorkers; they are unashamedly domestic.

I remember the jibe "a nation of shopkeepers," and I think of the Queen Mum. Gay Londoners seem to have little of the adversary sense that seems increasingly to characterize gay life in North America. The English would argue that this difference is due to British society's ability to absorb gay intellectual and artistic life. British gays do not share the gay American fear that this assimilation necessarily leads to a diminution of the force of gay perspective; on the contrary, they believe that gays flourish in England precisely because they can become so much a part of upper-middle-class life. Even those close to the royal family who are widely believed to be gay—Lord Snowdon and Princess Margaret's current boyfriend, Roddy Llewellyn, for example—are tolerated to a degree that would not be possible in America.

Certainly there has long been a strong homosexual presence in English literature and particularly in English theater, still probably the greatest in the world, despite the commercial inroads made by American musical comedy. Several gay plays, or gay versions of plays, are now running. The most important of these is a splendid production of Christopher Marlowe's *Dr. Faustus* with an all-male cast. The play itself is difficult to stage, since it is so nearly a medieval morality play with its set allegorical pieces, but this version, brilliantly directed by Christopher Fettes, succeeds magnificently in transforming the text into a vivid battle for the soul of a tormented Faustus, who is drawn freely from Marlowe's own life. Never has the play seemed more erotic—or more baroque. Patrick Magee is an exceptionally strong Mephistophilis, and James Aubrey is a good Faustus. But the sensation of the evening is Simon Cutter, a young New Zealander, as Helen of Troy. A perfect androgynous beauty enables Cutter to carry off with ease and grace not merely the role of a woman, but that of the most beautiful woman in the world.

Also interesting is a new production of Sir Terence Rattigan's play *The Browning Version.* Rattigan's work was always subtly gay, but the allusions were kept discreet during his lifetime. It is possible to be somewhat more frank today. Another play which suggests more than it demonstrates is *The Dresser*, Ronald Harwood's study of the relationship between a well-known actor and his dresser. One is reminded of the Harold Pinter–Joseph Losey film *The Servant*, as well as of Hartley's *The Hireling:* in England, class and sex seem inextricably intertwined.

I have a taste of life among the upper orders over the weekend: I am invited to a country house in Sussex, on the south coast of England. Country-house weekends are a tradition among the English, of course, and although this one may not contain all the ceremony of those recorded by Mark Girouard in his splendid study *Life in the English Country House*, it nonetheless displays a sense of ordered ease that is far different from a weekend at even the nicest place in the Hamptons.

The house itself is an Edwardian curiosity, built to be a large and elegant version of an English cottage for a woman who had established herself in the village as a weaver, in the tradition of the Arts and Crafts Movement of William Morris. She left behind a wonderful drawing room, one part of which is covered by an imposing loggia, from which she received guests. Her outbuildings have been refashioned into comfortable summer rooms with great long corridors of bedrooms above them. I am shown to one of them—which has been disarmingly made to match the rest of the house, even to the wooden-latched doors—with a fine view of the garden. My host shares the house with his lover and several friends, none of whom is there very often. Dinner is one of those elegantly simple affairs that are always claimed to have been whipped up in fifteen minutes: cold poached chicken, a quiche (or flan, as the English call it) filled with herbs from the garden, delicious small tomatoes vinaigrette, a choice of English cheeses including a superb Stilton, and various homemade treats for the sweet course.

After dinner there is sloe gin *maison* in the drawing room, where we look at one of the housemate's albums of royal autographs. When I'm asked if I want to see these, I hesitate for a moment before realizing that no one is jesting. It's not solemn, but it is serious; that, it occurs to me, is true of a great deal in England.

Soon it's time to retire, each of us to his little room along the passage. My host carefully points out to me where his room is, for no apparent reason, and then assures me that he will pay me a nocturnal visit in an hour or two. He does indeed, although it is a visit that must be kept short enough to enable him to emerge from his own room in the morning. Since his lover is out of town and the other housemates have rooms at the other end of the house, I wonder about the need for all these arrangements and precautions. I decide, American that I am, that they represent undue caution, and I am ready to denounce a kind of closet spirit. But by the end of the long weekend, I have come to enjoy the excitement of these half-expected visits, their uncertainty and their danger. When I tell another friend about it, he reminds me that indeed it is art which makes life. Trysts at night in an English country house seem to symbolize the nature and extent of "high civilization" (Henry James), with all its power to create and destroy.

Here again I am struck by the way in which gay life has been woven into the English social fabric. Five gay men living together in a country house located near a tiny English village: can one imagine the equivalent arrangement in America? My friends take an active part in the life of the village: they support the parish church, entertain the vicar, attend the strawberry fete and the jumble sale, and even help out with the recital in the village hall. They never mention their gay life, but it is there, quite evident for anyone to see. Everyone must know, yet, apparently, they prefer that this knowledge remain understood and unspoken. Decorum is maintained, like the separate bedrooms at night, and beneath this outward obeisance to order, there is a willingness to accept what would be unthinkable in rural America.

Back in London the following week, I am reminded that not all English gay lives are quite so jolly. I have dinner with a well-known writer who was a friend of E.M. Forster and is the literary executor of Forster's good friend J. R. Ackerley. My host is still active in English literary life, where he moves quite freely as a gay man. He lives in a beautiful house in Kensington with his lover, a young actor. The house is filled with mementos of a life lived in the highest circles of gay literary and artistic England. We dine beneath a portrait of a nude boy by Duncan Grant, the last survivor of the Bloomsbury group and a onetime lover of Lytton Strachey, and we sit in the drawing room beneath a portrait by Henry S. Tuke, the most famous of the "boys bathing" school of English art, many of whose paintings are in the collection of the Royal Academy.

Much of our conversation concerns Ackerley, whose diary my host is now editing. The preceding week the BBC broadcast a very moving program about Ackerley's life. The show is quite honest about Ackerley's homosexuality and shows him in bed with several soldiers (a pound a night for a foot soldier, somewhat more for a horse guard). It also sensitively portrays the only fulfilling love of Ackerley's life, that for his dog Queenie. He acquired the dog after a boyfriend was sent to prison and his family was unable or unwilling to care for it; Ackerley found in the dog the fidelity and selfless love that he always sought and failed to find in his guardsmen. What is refreshing about the BBC show (which I hope will be picked up by PBS here) is that it is neither condemnatory nor apologetic. Ackerley was gay, and his homosexuality and the unhappiness it caused him affected much of his life; this had to be shown honestly, but the point of the show is to capture the nature of the man, not to attempt the sort of sociological exercise that seems to be the only treatment that gay people receive on American television. Still, if British television is far more sophisticated than American television, this is partly due to a difference in the audience. Anyone who attempted to broadcast the Ackerley program in America would probably be confronted by a demonstration because the film is not positive enough. There is little of that sort of "gay liberation" in England—and little desire for it.

A friend who knows Anthony Blunt speaks of his lover's apparent suicide attempt after Blunt had been publicly humiliated as a former spy. Although my friend has great sympathy for Blunt, who, he feels, was treated unfairly (the Queen is widely believed to have acted dishonorably by removing his knighthood, since she presumably knew he was a spy for many years), his "boyfriend," from a less privileged background, is angry at Blunt and very much anti-Soviet.

Although I have referred to the "special friends" of the men I know as their "lovers," I was informed that the latter term is not used in England: everyone here says "boyfriend." The term naturally implies a difference in age, and in fact the majority of the couples I meet do differ substantially in age as well as in class or education (which amounts to the same thing, these days), but it is used even if the lovers are the same age. The British preference for *boyfriend* over *lover* may reflect their love of ceremony and inclination toward euphemism, but it also seems to reflect the deep-seated Greek roots of English homosexuality.

Why is it that everyone in England tells me that there are no problems for English homosexuals? In part, this attitude stems from the fact that upper-middle-class England is the society that has come closest to recreating and incorporating the sexual ethos of classical Greece. Its most cherished institutions, the public schools, virtually enforce homosexuality among young boys. The system of "fagging" (which is probably the source of the modern use of the term) establishes a relationship between older and younger boys that is often situated at the boundary between power and eros. Learning from the past is one of the highest values of English civilization, and it therefore follows quite logically that the best love relationship encourages tradition, respect, and order. Young men see their lovers as moral teachers. At their best, these relationships embody the Platonic ideal of the fusion of the spiritual and the physical; at worst, of course, they instill a love of power and a docility before that power or a hopeless yearning for the blue-eyed, fair-haired beloved.

One young friend takes me to see his public school. As we pass through in the car, he briefly greets the headmaster, who is very busy watching his students at sports. Later on, I hear my friend's story: Several years earlier, when he was a pupil there, the headmaster (a mere master then) offered my friend a pound if he would let him cane him. My friend knew the master as a teacher, husband, and father, and the incident disturbed him. He spoke to the chaplain, who assured him that he had misunderstood the master's words. As headmaster of one of England's more prestigious public schools, that man can now indulge his taste all he wants—and no longer needs to pay a pound apiece for a nice young male bottom.

The price of civilization, perhaps, is hypocrisy. There is certainly plenty of both in England, and the hypocrisy may be less offensive than the Bible-thumping kind of the American heartland. It is certain, though, that my first night's dinner partner spoke out of an assurance that, although widespread, seems hard to justify fully. All is not well in England; it is merely muddling along, as it has always done. But it muddles along in its own way and seems determined to work out its own solutions without too much help from Americans. On that Nikos was right: the worst thing about Americans is our arrogant belief that we have the answers to everyone's problems. We are as naive as Isabel Archer ever was about the nature of experience, or about the world's desire to follow our lead down the yellow brick road. The new England that is emerging under Margaret Thatcher is very much an old England and, as such, seems less likely than ever to throw it all over for (as it were) a night at the Mineshaft. Everyone wants to hear about such places, many even want to visit, but in the end they'll curl up with a good book and some old port, as the dogs sleep on the lawn.

# JEAN LE BITOUX
## AND GILLES BARBEDETTE

❖❖❖❖❖❖❖❖❖❖❖❖❖❖❖❖

## *Jean-Paul Sartre: The Final Interview*

### Translated by George Stambolian

*April 19, 1980: four days after Sartre's death, the crowd attending his burial at Montparnasse Cemetery was so great that Simone de Beauvoir, who was seated precariously near the grave, seemed on the verge of being crushed. At that moment, an anonymous voice cried out to reassure her: "Don't be afraid of anything, Madame, we are Sartre's people!"*

*And so they were. The French Left was there in all its otherwise warring factions, from Socialists to Maoists. Present also were those whom society had exploited or dominated or scorned—proletarians, blacks, Jews, women, homosexuals. One commentator proudly called them "the International of Marginal People." By his writings and actions, Sartre had fought for these and other groups. To all he had given the same fundamental message—not simply that every human being has a right to be free, but that one can act to create that freedom, to create oneself as a free individual.*

*Many homosexuals remembered that in 1945 it was Sartre, together with Jean Cocteau, who had successfully petitioned the president of the French Republic to obtain Jean Genet's release from life imprisonment; that, in 1971, it was Sartre who, as editor in chief of the leftist review* Tout, *had published the manifesto of the Front Homosexuel d'Action Revolutionnaire (FHAR), the first radical public statement by a homosexual group in France. The review was condemned for this "affront to public morality," and Sartre was fined. They remembered that, as a novelist and playwright, Sartre had created a number of important homosexual characters, such as the pederastic Self-Taught Man in* Nausea *(1938), the powerfully articulate lesbian Ines Serrano in* No Exit *(1944), and the collaborator Daniel Sereno in the unfinished novel cycle* Roads to Freedom *(1945–49). They also knew that he had explored the sexual ambiguities in the lives of Baudelaire (1947) and Flaubert (Idiot of the Family, 1971–72), and that this group of biographical studies included Sartre's most important work on homosexuality and one that he considered among the finest achievements of his career—*Saint Genet: Actor and Martyr *(1952).*

*Yet what probably recurred most often in the thoughts of lesbians and gay men that day was the knowledge that on February 28, less than three weeks before his hospitalization, Sartre had agreed for the first time to be questioned on homosexuality by homosexuals. The interview had just been published in the first-anniversary April issue of France's leading gay newspaper,* Le Gai Pied. *Now, with Sartre's death, his remarks had acquired a special significance, for they had suddenly become his last published words on this or any other subject.*

*What follows is the complete text of this* Gai Pied *interview conducted by Jean Le Bitoux and Gilles Barbedette. Several excerpts from Sartre's works have been provided in order to give a broader context for his remarks, which, as always, have created controversy. "In this interview, Gilles and I tried to shed some light on a mystery," said Jean. "For a long time, we had noticed a secret thread running through Sartre's novels, plays, and biographical studies—the whole complex question of homosexuality. We had also noticed that there was little or nothing on this subject in the enormous number of critical studies and analyses devoted to his work. In granting us this interview, it was as if Sartre wanted to prevent any effort to 'normalize' his work or to gloss over this aspect of it." "When we got to his apartment," Gilles recalls, "Sartre greeted us with simplicity and warmth. Being blind himself, he asked if we had enough light. He listened to our questions very carefully and took time to think about them. When he answered, the words came slowly in that famous scratchy voice. His interest never wavered. He told us from the beginning, 'I have a passion for understanding men.' "*

*Certain male characters in your novels, such as Mathieu in* Roads to Freedom *and Roquentin in* Nausea, *are not very sure of their masculinity and constantly question themselves about their relationships with women and with men. Why?*

Because that corresponds more or less to my personality, to what I ask myself.

*In line with Flaubert's remark, "Madame Bovary is me," could one say that Roquentin in* Nausea *and other male characters in your novels are, to a certain extent, women disguised as men?*

No, it would be an exaggeration to go that far. No, they are men who have sexual relations with women but who are not sure of their masculinity and who don't think that being masculine is an essential quality to have.

*In your studies of Flaubert and Baudelaire, you emphasize the difficulties they had situating themselves sexually. You even see in Flaubert's style of writing and in Baudelaire's dress and conduct as a dandy a painful component of "femininity"—that is, a certain feminine quality. Do you think this femininity is important and even essential to an understanding of these writers? Without this component of femininity, would there have been a Baudelaire, a Flaubert, a Mallarmé?*

Mallarmé's femininity, in any case, was of a different kind. It would be better to say that he was totally free of machismo. As for Flaubert and Baudelaire, it is possible and even quite probable that they had homosexual experiences. It seems certain in Baudelaire's case, and one could say that for many years Flaubert was in love with his friend Maxime [du Camp]. So there was something feminine in both of them.

*In your study on Baudelaire, you seem to affirm that a writer takes on a certain femininity because he doesn't make his living working among men. Is the act of writing above all a feminine act?*

No, not above all. But I recognize that it's becoming more and more feminine.

*Is it this feminine component of the writer that makes you prefer the company of women to that of men, which you have said you find boring?*

That's possible, because I don't like to talk about my job, which, of course, is hardly a job at all. And I like to talk about subjects that are less constrained and more gratuitous, perhaps. It's quite possible that it's a certain kind of femininity in me that makes me prefer women, because that preference—although I also love women from an erotic point of view—has absolutely nothing sexual in its origin. It's a preference for their conversation.

*You've said that for Genet there was only one way to escape from the indecent conditions of his life, a way he followed fully, in fact—writing. Do you see a parallel between the writing that saved Genet from those conditions and your own writing, which, according to your autobiography,* The Words, *saved you from your childhood?*

I haven't thought about it. Let's say that the escape was harder and more beneficial for Genet. Genet, who was in some ways a foundling, was consigned to peasants and later put in prison for a series of thefts. Going through prison like that amounts to a truly tragic childhood for a kid on public welfare. Still, he loved those peasants he lived with; he was rather happy. But all the same, it was a tragic childhood. I did not have a tragic childhood, and I tore myself away from it because it was too soft, too protected. Writing was solitude. But despite all that, there is a connection between my writing and Genet's, even though our ways of writing and the circumstances out of which they came are very different.

*When one feels called on to write, is it because one foresees a destiny that one also wants to escape? Does one sense danger and begin to write at that moment?*

Perhaps, as long as you understand that one doesn't know what the danger is. One tries to escape something without knowing what it is. It's a kind of vague feeling.

*When you wrote in* Saint Genet *that "writing is an erotic medium," do you mean to suggest that writing is also a form of seduction because it utilizes and produces fantasies?*

Yes, it can be. It can come from the writer's own capacity to be seduced and his relationship to eros in general. That's what creates the erotic aspect of writing.

*You've also been interested in works in which you have quickly discovered a "dark and magic power": Flaubert, Sade, Mallarmé, and, above all, Genet. Why this interest, when in your own work you always seem concerned with convincing the reader by means of solid dialectical reasoning?*

I think that I have in fact been interested in the literature of hidden and secret things and inevitably that literature is essentially erotic, except in periods of social constraint when there is political literature that is equally hidden. But when we look closely, we see that the great secret works are erotic. And I think that one cannot understand literature if one does not also know these works, if this dark half of literature is not accessible. Those who know only Pascal, Saint-Simon, and Boileau have a very incomplete view of literature.

*But did Rimbaud and Mallarmé care about dialectical precision?*

They had a sense of precision, and that's very important. For the dark half of literature, precision is as essential and even more essential than for the literature of daylight. There's a precision in Baudelaire's poems that is very particular, very sensitive. There's precision when Genet talks about his life through the myths he invents and all the images he forges. He expresses ideas, and literature is certainly for him—as it is for so many others—and for me a precise construction that can have the ambiguity, remoteness, and scope of the sublime but that is always precise and tries to define a situation. It's in that aspect of Sade as well as of the dark writers of the nineteenth century, although in different degrees, that I encountered a kind of dark rationality.

*In your recently edited* Writings, *there is a previously unpublished passage from* Saint Genet *in which you say that "literature, like homosexuality, represents a potential solution that one invents in certain situations and that in other situations is not even considered because it would be of no use." Why do you make that comparison?*

That was in reference to Genet, of course. And then I thought that the way Genet assumed his condition when he was a prisoner in order to really turn it into homosexuality was like a man who is trapped, completely mixed up, and lost in relation to others and who invents literature—that is, who invents the act of writing—in order to find a solution, a way out. In short, I'm talking about Genet's decision in favor of homosexuality, his will to become completely a homosexual and to accept the violence he sometimes endured at the hands of his fellow inmates at Mettray. And he wanted to accept this violence, to ask for it, so that by this very act it would cease to be violence. A writer tries to think out in freedom the relationships that exist among people and the various acts of violence they inflict on each other. In this way, one attains a kind of gratuity, acceptance, and willpower.

*In* Saint Genet, *there is this sentence: "One is not born homosexual or normal; each person becomes one or the other according to the accidents in his life and his own reaction to these accidents." You also affirm: "It's a way out a child discovers at the moment of suffocation." By saying that, don't you make the homosexual the best example of your existential views?*

Of course, because when I made the decision to write *Saint Genet,* I took the homosexual that Genet was as the very model of the man who creates himself in a situation. Finally, Genet is homosexual both because he is an orphan and because he is a thief, because he committed thefts. So homosexuality was a kind of reprise of all that, and he became, as he says himself, *the* Thief. The Thief is at the same time *the* Homosexual.

*Why?*

Well, I explained that in *Saint Genet.* Naturally, Genet is a particular case. One can't say those things about just any homosexual, nor can one say that every homosexual is a thief—that wouldn't have any meaning. But it is true in Genet's case. He found that he was a thief, that he was mistreated by adults and thrown into prison. And it was in prison that he finally found kids who were thieves like himself but who treated him sexually as a victim. He could no longer escape from this situation. He was caught; he was in the hands of the other kids and was their victim—unless, in order to escape, he wanted in fact to be the victim. He did want it. Actually, he explains later on that there are other types of homosexuality than passive homosexuality. So he gave himself in order to become the boy who wants to be sodomized, and that became one of the essential components of his personality. Therefore, he transformed a kind of defeat, a capture, into a victory, and one that he will continue to desire.

*And if one isn't a homosexual, is it for lack of circumstances?*

No, because one can become a poet without experiencing homosexuality. Or one can experience it—it depends on the circumstances. For example, I think the only way out for Genet was to become homosexual. But one can imagine equally constraining circumstances that would not lead to that way out, to that sexual solution.

*You've also said about Genet: "I admire this child who has willed his own existence." Why such fascination for this precocious choice in favor of marginal existence?*

Because it was a choice, and a precocious choice. Obviously, the choice of a ten-year-old child, if it has depth, can only be that of marginality. He can't follow the same road as everyone else, because that wouldn't be a choice any more; it would be the force of everyone else imposing itself. And consequently, this personal choice, profound and rigorously individual, and with a single goal, is truly an act of formidable willpower on the part of a child.

*There are repeated connections made in your work between the fascination for military order, the rejection of violence, and the homosexual's search for symbols of male power. For example, the homosexual character Daniel in* Roads to Freedom *applauds the arrival of German troops in Paris. We find this adhesion to male order again in Genet. Does that mean that in the political world the homosexual is a potential traitor?*

It's possible. I didn't say it because, in a sense, it ceased to concern me directly. I wasn't a homosexual, so I couldn't say it. But I would have tried to think about treason or to think about something equivalent to it if I had been homosexual. And I do think that the homosexual is a potential traitor, *but we must understand clearly what that means.* The traitor is the dark side of the thing, but the bright side, the shining side, is that the homosexual tries to be a deep reality, very deep. He tries to find a depth of being that heterosexuals don't have. But that very thing, that depth that he tries to have with simplicity, with clarity, can be taken over again by the other dark side. In the homosexual, there is a dark aspect that defines him, that reveals itself to him but not necessarily to others.

*Hitler had the SA massacred in 1934 by claiming that homosexuality was dangerous to the social order. Stalin had just launched similar raids. Isn't homosexuality the inevitable scapegoat that is used every time a political regime tries to consolidate its power?*

I'm not sure that it happens every time. In any case, homosexuality is certainly one scapegoat that is used. Generally, a fascist regime is against homosexuals. Only don't forget that in Hitler's regime the opposite was also true. The Hitler Jugend were very often homosexuals or in any case leaned toward homosexuality. So there were these two aspects. The same ambiguity exists in all examples of fascism, every time the masses are controlled, unified, or given to military exercise. In all these cases, there's a tendency toward homosexuality because men are together all the time—sleeping together, living together, having more or less intimate relations with each other. Therefore, there is a threat of homosexuality. I say "threat" because the fascist leaders not only know that there is some homosexuality born with fascism, but wanting at the same time to be macho, they are also against this homosexuality. That proves that the two aspects exist and creates the profound contradiction within fascist or dictatorial regimes.

*But that was also true in Stalin's case.*

Yes.

*Why isn't there a word in your political writings on the extermination of homosexuals by Stalin and Hitler?*

It's because I didn't know the exact nature of these massacres. I didn't know if they were systematic or how many people they affected. I wasn't sure. So I could reproach these dictators about hundreds of things, but I couldn't reproach them about these things, because I didn't know about them.

*To what do you attribute the fact that you didn't know about these historical facts?*

Historians talk about it very little. Your newspaper is designed to discuss facts of this kind. You should do analyses of these matters from time to time.

*In your short story, "The Childhood of a Leader," published in* The Wall, *you present the character Lucien Fleurier, who, like the hero of Moravia's* The Conformist, *refuses to accept his homosexuality by taking refuge in the fascistic order. Do you think that's also true of many homosexuals who are looking for a solid hierarchical frame of reference?*

I don't know. Lucien Fleurier's case clearly indicates that what he rejected was rather disorder. He felt that the homosexual was related not to order but to disorder. And in fact, Lucien Fleurier is not a homosexual. He is tempted by it, but he is essentially a heterosexual, although he has homosexual tendencies. In any case, this desire for order doesn't seem to come from homosexuality; he's had it for a long time.

*In your novels and plays, certain characters make sodomy the act of domination par excellence, because it allows one man to force another into submission. Frantz, in your play* The Condemned of Altona, *declares: "Once you have two leaders, they either have to kill each other or one has to become a woman for the other." Why do you see passive sodomy as a form of execution?*

It's sort of an impression that I had and that I developed out of my conversations with Genet. When I was writing my book on him, I had the chance to speak with him, and I would make hypotheses and then submit them to him. Sometimes, despite his objections, I would keep my hypotheses, but occasionally he was the one who was right. And then again, it's because I did see it that way. I didn't claim that in all circumstances it had to be seen that way, but in Frantz's situation—being thrown into the army by the Germans, his leaders—I saw that as an execution. He had to repeatedly execute their orders, and finally it was a real execution because he was subjected to it. I'm talking to you here about a possible fate that awaits the homosexual. Heterosexual society dominates him and leads him more or less cunningly to execution.

*Don't you think that what's missing is a thorough analysis of the latent homosexuality that exists in torture, sports, and all institutions where men are together?*

I think indeed that that should be analyzed and that it certainly exists.

*Isn't the sole origin of this general taboo against homosexuality the fear of passive sodomy?*

It's possible; it's even probable.

*The passive homosexual offers himself and gives himself. For you he seems to lose all dignity. He becomes, as you have written, "an imaginary woman who takes pleasure in the absence of pleasure." Why do you show such lack of respect that seems to strike and encompass not only the passive homosexual but every woman who has had heterosexual relations?*

Read Genet; he's the one who gives that impression. He's the one who says that he doesn't experience pleasure. He looks for it but doesn't find it. And when he turns to the artificial role of the active homosexual, he has a little scorn for the passive homosexuals, although he nevertheless considers passive homosexuality to be the true homosexuality. He thinks that it's this homosexuality that counts and that the other is a developed homosexuality, where one becomes an active homosexual after having really been a passive homosexual. So in this respect I trusted Genet, since I was talking about him.

*Do you really think that passive sodomy always creates an absence of pleasure?*

No, there's no reason for that. But it is certain that Genet does not seem to have gotten much pleasure from it.

*In 1980, what do you think of the social status of homosexuals? Can this minority be fully integrated into society by means of a hypocritical liberalization of social and sexual mores?*

No. I think that for the moment the homosexual minority is obliged to remain rather isolated, to be a group in this prudish society, a group which is separated from it and which cannot blend into this society. I think that it should reject this society and, to a certain extent, hate it. Homosexuals should reject this society, but the only thing that they can hope for at present in certain countries is a kind of free space, where they can come together among themselves, as in the United States, for example.

# IV

RECOVERING
THE PAST

# ROBERT K. MARTIN

## Reclaiming Our Lives

*A* leading American art magazine recently devoted a special section to the work of poet-painter Marsden Hartley (1877–1943). Many pages and authors traced in detail the events of Hartley's life: his friendship with Gertrude Stein, his years in Germany, the influence of Kandinsky, his collaboration with Steiglitz, his eventual return to America and his native Maine. But nowhere did the bright young academic authors find it necessary to even mention that Hartley was gay or that important aspects of his work were influenced by this fact. One article, on the "hidden symbolism" of Hartley's Berlin paintings, at least gives the name of Hartley's German lover who was killed in World War I: Lieutenant Karl von Freyburg. This is indeed a small concession when one considers the fact that the paintings were done as a tribute to von Freyburg and that all of the "hidden symbols" refer to him and to Hartley's occult belief that they would be reunited in another spiritual existence. The author attributes Hartley's denial that the paintings contained any such symbols (von Freyburg's age, the name of his regiment, pieces of his uniform, and mystic symbols of transcendence) to the prevalence of postwar anti-Germanism. Her explanation does not hold up, of course, since the paintings appear much more "pro-German" and politically suspect if one ignores the personal significance of the symbols than if one recognizes the paintings as icons of personal love (I use the term *icon* deliberately, since Hartley frequently borrowed from the iconography of Byzantine painting, Bavarian folk art, and even American Indian adaptations of Christian art).

The belated attention that Hartley is now receiving is largely due to the Whitney Museum's major show which opened in March. The show itself is long overdue; Hartley is, after all, the only German expressionist that America ever produced. The Whitney catalogue (New York University Press, 1980) identifies Hartley as a homosexual and refers to his "spiritual marriage" (his term) to von Freyburg. But according to the author, Barbara Haskell, homosexuality did not play any major role in the development of Hartley's life and art. Ms. Haskell prefers the "broader notion" of Hartley's paintings as depictions of the idea of a German officer rather than the particular officer whom Hartley loved. The catalogue's approach is in line with almost all the critics and biographers currently writing about "our" lives. Sexual liberation has made it possible—even necessary—to acknowledge the sexuality of an artist; but most writers are themselves embarrassed by the subject and hope to move quickly on to somewhat safer ground.

Being gay is still not considered an integral part of an artist's life or work. Since most criticism is intended at least partially to praise the artist in question, it has been important to suppress, or at least diminish, any element of homosexuality. Whereas it was once assumed that an artist, if gay, could not be great (because of the prevalent theory that homosexuality represented a serious personality disorder, which would necessarily be reflected in a flawed creation), it is now generally assumed that homosexuality is irrelevant. This is the result of the liberal defense of homosexuals during the fifties and sixties. Faced with social oppression, gays and their defenders often claimed that homosexuality was a private matter of taste, like preferring chocolate to vanilla ice cream, which would in no way detract from the quality of a work of art. There were obvious political and legal advantages at stake in this strategy, which helped to eliminate some of the more obvious forms of discrimination. But if homosexuality is really "private," then it can have nothing to do with our social selves, nor can it be seen as a part of any art we create.

Hartley's life and work comprise an excellent argument against the theory of homosexuality's irrelevance in the life and work of an artist. Karl von Freyburg was woven inextricably into the paintings that memorialize him. To ignore the fact that these paintings present an abstracted vision of the beloved is to misread them. After Freyburg's death, all that remained for the painter were the objects transformed by their association with Freyburg. Their permanence in art guaranteed a victory over time and mortality. As Hartley wrote in a very moving "letter-never-sent" to Freyburg, "I have the few souvenirs of your departure still—your silver shoulder straps with glittering copper buttons of the now defunct regime—as brilliant as the day you wore them in your youth." Hartley's symbolism is deeply personal, not political, and the apparent obscurity of some of his paintings is best understood not as a protective device against American anti-German feeling but as a screen against the revelation of Hartley's homosexuality.

At the same time, it is crucial to understand that this screen is, by design, less than totally opaque. At the center of most gay art, there is, I suspect, a desire both to reveal and to conceal. The need for concealment is a social one; the need for revelation is a personal urge, with its source in the desire for community. There are many examples of the same process occurring in other artists. Whitman, whom we think of as a poet without symbols, turned to such figures as the "calamus" and such concepts as "adhesiveness" precisely in order to make homosexuality an important part of his poetry while *at the same time* concealing it from readers who might disapprove. Hartley's friend Hart Crane developed a poetic style that may owe a good deal of its apparent obscurity to this "reveal-conceal" impulse. As an example, one need only read these lines from Crane's suite of love poems, *Voyages:*

> And so, admitted through black swollen gates
> That must arrest all distance otherwise,—
> Past whirling pillars and lithe pediments,
> Light wrestling there incessantly with light,
> Star kissing star through wave on wave unto
> Your body rocking!

The lines are a brilliant depiction of two men making love, but Crane's visionary language has withheld this image from his (straight) critics.

Part of the problem is, of course, the failure of the straight imagination. It always requires at least some effort to imagine that which is beyond the range of our personal experience. As gay people, however, we are required to do this every day. The culture which we inhabit and share has been shaped mostly by a heterosexual imagination, and we have been trained since childhood to understand its terms even when they have no meaning in our personal lives. We see heterosexually because we have been taught to and because our survival depends upon it. (There is an obvious analogy with the situation of blacks, who must learn the signals of a white community without expecting whites to learn even the most elementary black semiotics.) From childhood, gay people must be able to move back and forth skillfully between two worlds, while learning to communicate homosexually within the boundaries of a heterosexual world. Body language (use of the eyes, hips, wrists—even the little finger) and verbal cues (back when *gay* meant *happy* to most people, it meant *queer* to us) are used in a complex manner in order to establish bonds and convey information while shielding us from exposure. Under such circumstances, the tendency was always to raise the stakes, to increase the openness of one's allusions in order to see how far one could go without being detected. It was a way of flaunting one's subversiveness behind enemy lines; daring them to know was a way of showing oneself how little indeed they did know, even as they asserted that they could spot a homosexual anywhere. When Oscar Wilde "feasted with panthers," he was not, as some have suggested, seeking his own destruction; he was testing the limits of his own disguise.

The end of modernism (or, more accurately, its entry into history) has been marked by the turn from criticism to biography. Manifestations of this shift may be found everywhere, in *People* magazine and in the pages of scholarly journals. Even the Hartley essays mentioned earlier are part of this movement; it would have been inconceivable a few years ago to even mention Hartley's "friend," let alone to provide his name. Analysis was purely formal, rendered in terms of color, shape, and line. And Hartley's reputation suffered under this formalism, because he, although an expressionist, was clearly a representational expressionist, not an abstract expressionist.

In literary criticism too, an enormous shift in taste has occurred. Leon Edel's five-volume biography of Henry James (Lippincott) seems a perfect document of the transition. James himself was a critic whose views on art seem closely linked to a classicized or formalist aesthetic, and Edel treated James as a subject for a kind of biographical criticism which suggests that the nature and subject matter of James's art might be traced back to his life. Edel successfully demonstrates that the work of even the most "impersonal" of artists has its origins in the personality and experience of the artist. Edel's biography of James, his study of Willa Cather, his book *Literary Biography* (Indiana University Press), and his recent talk at the National Portrait Gallery in Washington are only the most evident signs of a new critical direction. We can expect a lot of lives to be reexamined in the next few years.

It may be possible to reconcile a formalist-structuralist aesthetic with a gay analysis through, for instance, the study of recurring image patterns or through the analysis of style. Many are skeptical about the success of such endeavors, however, and even more predict that the attempts to reinvigorate formalist analysis are doomed. We seem to have entered the age of the biography. If formalism has often managed, by accident or design, to suppress gay lives, what can we expect from biography? The record is not encouraging. It has been utterly impossible for most biographers to imagine being gay at any period or place. The lives of most gays, as they are written, revolve around a central void. The biographers, believing that they are simply eliminating the sex from the life, have eliminated the heart. Biographers of heterosexuals frequently devote long, purple passages to courtship, marriage, and family. If necessary, extramarital sexual affairs are recounted in detail, and some attention is paid to the effect such affairs had on the life under discussion. But the homosexual is presented in biographies as a solitary figure, cut off from almost all human contact. Some gays have lived—and continue to live—in appalling isolation. In most cases, however, that isolation is the product of the individual's inability to express his or her sexuality in an open manner within society.

There are few documents sadder than William Carlos Williams's account in his *Autobiography* of a visit to Marsden Hartley's studio. "I felt sorry for him, growing old. That was the moment he took for his approaches. I, too, had to reject him. Everyone rejected him. I was no better than the others." Hartley's failed "pass" at Williams confirms (in Williams's eyes, at least) Hartley's loneliness and isolation, and Williams feels a twinge of guilt mixed with condescension. Unfortunately, we do not have the other side of the story. One would like to know how Hartley would have told it. Inevitably, pain is a part of the story of most gay lives, but that pain can give rise to anger, not pity.

We have been deprived of the lives of our greatest talents, in part by omission, in part by distortion. The many biographers' treatments of Walt Whitman provide the clearest examples. In the case of Whitman, homosexuality has been denied, a heterosexual mistress was invented, and, finally, when those strategies no longer sufficed, homosexuality was simply dismissed as insignificant. This is certainly an odd fate for the man who wrote, in the *Calamus* poems, "Publish my name and hang up my picture as that of the tenderest lover."

Although Whitman's most important biographer, Gay Wilson Allen (who wrote to the *New York Times* to complain about the misuse of his good name!), bragged in his preface that he had written "a more complete, more exhaustive, and therefore a *truer* life of Whitman than anyone else [had] yet achieved," he managed in a very large volume (*The Solitary Singer*, New York University Press) to ignore completely Whitman's homosexuality or the part it played in his work. Allen declared, "The important fact is not his affection for men like Lewis Brown, Thomas Sawyer, and Peter Doyle, but his struggle for self-control and self-understanding." Not affection, but "struggle and self-control"; not love, but repression. A new biography of Whitman is now being written by Justin Kaplan. There are indications that it will reveal to us a far different figure from the one enshrined in literary history. Kaplan said recently, "What is at stake is . . .

the biographer's obligation to give Whitman himself the freedom he never had to pursue his recognition that love, of whatever sort it may be, was the root of roots in his life and poetry."

Biographers of other artists have treated homosexuality more openly but with equally damaging results. Hart Crane is a good example of a poet who has had precisely this sort of "honest" biography: *Voyager: A Life of Hart Crane*, by John Unterecker (Farrar, Straus and Giroux, 1969). The first page of this biography acknowledges Crane's "homosexual adventures with sailors in hallways and bums in public parks," although the book tries very hard to offset this with Crane's "normality": he "found—like most men—real joy in painting a door or in planting a garden." Crane may have been queer, but he wasn't a queen, we are reassured. Unterecker also strains to make us "understand" Crane's love for Emil Opffer. He evokes the *Phaedrus* and "that open, generous, affection we call Platonic love." He reports that Crane told his friend Waldo Frank that his relationship with Opffer "was founded not so much on sex as on a 'purity of joy.'" In fact, Crane said nothing of the kind to Frank or to anyone else; he said that "sex was beaten out," implying a passion which moved beyond sexuality by passing *through* it, not denying it. (Since that same "beating out" is characteristic of Crane's poetry, one wonders if Unterecker is any more responsive to Crane's art than he is to his life.) Still, Unterecker did reveal much more about Crane's life than earlier biographers, and he was willing, for the first time, to reveal the name of Crane's lover.

The refusal to name names has been a part of a process of distancing, a way of making a writer's gay love affairs seem anonymous and dirty. The edition of Crane's letters, for instance, refers to Emil Opffer as "E———." It is possible that the publishers were concerned about libel (although they don't seem to have asked Opffer, who is still alive), but the effect is to make the affair seem shady and covert when in fact Crane told his family and friends about Opffer and included him in his life. Throughout the biography, Opffer is referred to as a "young sailor," despite the fact that Crane called him a "ship's writer," that he was twenty-seven when he met the twenty-four-year-old Crane, and that he was an active participant in the intellectual and artistic community of New York, where he published a Danish-language newspaper and where his brother was an artist whose work appeared in the *Dial*. Perhaps these are mere oversights, but they are nonetheless significant factors in conveying the complete image of Crane's sexuality. Indeed, Crane was tormented at times, but at other times he was filled with joy and creative energy. Almost all of his wonderfully campy letters to his friend Wilbur Underwood were omitted in the published *Letters*. Consider this passage, for instance, from an unpublished letter of 1922: "Saturday night I at last was taken into the arms of love again! Seldom have I had such affection offered me. An athlete—very strong—20 only—dark-haired—distantly Bohemian. I hope it will last a while—I deserve a little kindness and he *was* so kind!" Crane's straight friends, who provided the interviews and letters on which the biographies have been based, were unacquainted with this side of Crane or were unable to understand it except insofar as it was a "neurosis" which interfered with his poetry. No biographer has been willing to find out what it was like to be a gay poet growing up in Ohio in the first years of this century or living in New York in the 1920s. No one has wondered about the loneliness that resulted from Crane's friends' inability or unwillingness to accept his homosexuality as anything other than neurosis. No one has explored the kinds of gay community that Crane strove to create in his life and in his art.

It would be easy to extend the list of gay lives that have been misappropriated and rewritten, from Sappho to Willa Cather, from Socrates to Herman Melville. It is time to reclaim some of these lives. One need not argue from the perspective of gay liberation; simple honesty demands that the biographer tell all he or she knows about the life in question. The problem remains that biographers do not know all, because they cannot see the meaning of all the facts which confront them. Leon Edel, for instance, has recently acknowledged that if he were to rewrite the biography of Henry James, he would treat some aspects differently. When Edel was writing, he either did not know that throughout James's life some of his most important friends were gay or he didn't see any significance in the fact. But since James was regularly at the center of a gay coterie (which overlapped with Edith Wharton's circle), perhaps we should see his work in a different light. Surely James's passionate letters to young men were more than expressions of Victorian "conventions of friendship" (that refrain has been heard before, from Shakespeare to Tennyson). Biographers must steep themselves in the period fully to understand the context in which their subjects lived. But it is time for biographers to supply the sexual context as an important part of the whole subject. As we are asked to understand straight lives, we must ask straight biographers to understand gay lives.

What will this entail? First of all, biographers must be willing to explore the sexuality of the life being examined *in its own terms*. This requires, once and for all, the abandonment of Freudian and Eriksonian "understandings" of our lives. Let us have no more falsifying biographies centered on the Oedipus complex, or adolescent arrestment, or oral fixation. All such paradigms operate on the assumption that the only successful arrangement is what Erikson calls "heterosexual mutuality." It is time to accept the multiple sexualities of our lives as equally satisfying and complete; it is time that we stopped judging.

Second, lives need to be shown within all of the appropriate contexts; for a gay life, this means finding out what it was like to be gay then and there. We assume that it is of some consequence in the life of an artist if he or she was black, Jewish, Protestant, rich, or poor. Surely it is time to be told about the ways in which being gay affected the life and work of an artist. As Richard Whelan recently indicated in these pages, Michelangelo is only the most obvious example of an artist whose life has been consistently altered to suit the needs of heterosexual readers, the result of what John Addington Symonds called "a pious fraud" by Michelangelo's grandnephew. If letters are to be published, they must be published in as complete a form as possible; any editing must be performed in the spirit of scholarship, not of partisan argumentation. Archives should be open for anyone to verify the accuracy of transcriptions. It takes very little effort, after all, to see *she* where *he* was written.

Finally, we must ask the straight biographer to make a leap of the imagination. Gay lives cannot be examined through straight spectacles. This is not to say, of course, that one must be gay in order to write a gay life, but it does mean that our lives must be treated with the same respect that we are called upon to give theirs. Every biographer must at some point become his or her subject; it is precisely at that point of sympathy and identification that biographies of gays have failed, because their authors have not been willing to imagine a gay life from within.

They have taken away our lives, and we have paid for the loss. We have had to see ourselves as radically alone, without historic figures to whom we could turn and who might let us know that to be gay was not merely to be the dirty old man in the park or the women's gym teacher. We have always been there, but we have been invisible. Our American history texts have told a story that utterly ignores Indians, Spaniards, blacks, and women (even recent texts have tended to present heavily laundered and idealized versions); similarly, biographies have presented lives as either heterosexual or empty. Look at our family album, at our bachelor cousins and spinster aunts. Where have their lives gone? They have been lost, not because they weren't there, but because we didn't know how to see them. It was, after all, a *family* album. It is time we reclaimed them, for their sake and for our own.

## WALLACE HAMILTON

## The Secret Life of Horatio Alger

Horatio Alger was one of the great American myth-makers. In over one hundred novels that he wrote between 1868 and the year of his death, 1899, Alger shared his personal fantasies with an estimated 50 million readers and was to imprint his name in the American language. The "Alger hero" is a street urchin who, by pluck and luck, goes from rags to riches.

Alger himself summarized the story in a bit of doggerel:

> That John Smith, plebian, who forty years since
> Walked Broadway barefooted, now rides as a prince;
> Having managed, though not overburdened with wit,
> But rather by chance and a fortunate hit,
> To take a high place in Society's rounds.

The key element in an Alger story is "a fortunate hit": an older man who somehow meets up with the plucky kid and offers him a job or some other means to help him get ahead in the world. Without that chance meeting with a generous older patron, the Alger hero, no matter how plucky and righteous he might be, would presumably spend his life among the wage-slaving proletariat.

The "fortunate hit" was the fantasy of every nineteenth-century farm boy who longed to come to the city to make a name for himself, and Alger stories kept enhancing that dream for those out there in the haylofts. But I can't help wondering how many men also read Alger's books to enhance *their* dream of finding some ragged boy to take care of, educate, and send on his way to success. Surely that was Alger's personal dream, and in his life he made it come true a hundred times over.

Alger was the bard of the pedophilic relationship between man and boy. The evidence strongly suggests that his writing was rooted in an intense emotional and sexual involvement with boys, and that his pederasty was the basis for personal, courageous actions for the public good that have significance to this day. The bottom-line Alger hero is Alger himself. He peddled success, but he lived integrity.

The wonder of the Victorian age was that Alger was conceived as a pillar of conventional morality, and honored accordingly with addlepated adulation, while the secret of his strength—"the abominable and revolting crime of unnatural familiarity with boys"—remained locked in a bank vault on Cape Cod for a century.

And yet, God knows, Alger did not make it all that much of a secret. Like Walt Whitman, he simply assumed, and rightly so, that Victorians would deny the existence of something staring them right in the face. But unlike Whitman, Alger didn't even bother to protest his "innocence": he just went about his pedophilic business as if it were the most natural thing in the world, and what happened in his private room at the Newsboys' Lodging House in New York was nobody's business but his own. And it worked! The bank vault on Cape Cod remained secure, and Alger died an honored man . . . for most of the wrong reasons.

He was not the worst writer in nineteenth-century America. But compared to Whitman, Twain, Henry James, Bret Harte, even Louisa May Alcott, he was a literary Lilliputian, and he knew it. He longed to write "serious" adult fiction and even made a few feeble attempts, but he always returned to his central theme of man and boy, and he turned the books out at the rate of three or four a year, year after year. His reading public bought and read them insatiably. If the plots wandered, the characters were flat, and the situations stretched coincidence to the breaking point, no matter. Alger could spin a rattling good story that any farm boy—or middle-aged merchant—could understand. He wrote fantasies that could be shared. "Alger's heroes never slew dragons," wrote Herbert Mayes, his first biographer, "but they lifted mortgages." And the nineteenth century understood mortgages. Those who did not owe their soul to the company store owed it to the bank, and the bank could foreclose whenever it wished.

Until about 1970, biographers found it difficult to explain this curious but amazingly successful little man. Just what did he *do* with those street boys he so obviously adored? And what creative powers did he draw from them? What gave him the courage to expose the padrone system of indentured slavery which was smoothly run by an 1870 version of the Sicilian Mafia? Strange doings for a puritanical Unitarian minister with a Phi Beta Kappa from Harvard! A man like that is supposed to sermonize virtue in respectable surroundings and not collect a bunch of throwaway slum kids and do something about it. But Horatio did a lot.

His life began conventionally enough. He was born in 1832 of impeccable Yankee stock. His father was a Unitarian minister who served for a time as member of the Massachusetts state legislature. As a child, Horatio was unimpressive, a stutterer, and an asthmatic. He entered college at his full height of five feet, two inches, weighing about 130 pounds. A graduation daguerreotype shows him with a wistful, observant expression and a Hapsburg jaw, subsequently counteracted by a resplendent mustache. (In his later years, he grew amiably rotund, and his hair became a surrey-fringe around his head. But the observant, patient eyes were always there.)

Alger wanted to be a writer—a real, serious, no-nonsense writer. He went to Europe to savor the thinning airs of Parnassus. In the time of Poe, Whitman, Melville, and Thoreau, it was nonetheless generally believed in Europe that the American colonies were incapable of producing serious writers. Aspirants therefore went to Europe. Alger returned to America to produce a volume of twenty stories and poems called *Bertha's Christmas Vision* and several other books of limited success. Alger ruefully concluded (as have many others before and since) that it is very tough to earn a living by writing books. He buckled, went to Harvard Divinity School, and followed his father's footsteps into the ministry.

Who is to say what guardian angels stand over a man to inflict those redeeming disasters through which he can fulfill himself and his destiny? Those angels struck Horatio Alger at Brewster on Cape Cod. The crucial time was March 1866.

Pre-1970 biographers were ambivalent. John Tebbel put what he knew most succinctly. "He began to regard the ministry as a dead end. He could not bring himself to think of ending his career in such blameless and obscure piety. In March 1866, he resigned his pastorate and moved to New York."

Sometime after Tebbel wrote his curious apologia, however, one Richard M. Huber pried the gory truths out of that bank vault in Brewster, and published them in his book *The American Idea of Success* (McGraw-Hill, 1971). Alger, it appeared, was run out of town for sodomizing the sons of his parishioners—with at least their consent, if not their enthusiastic concurrence.

Jonathan Katz, with his customary industry, pounced on this finding and published it in his *Gay American History* (T. Y. Crowell, 1976). Another biographer, Edwin Palmer Hoyt, also recounted it in 1974 with bewildered awe.

Alger stood revealed! But as what?

The congregation at Brewster in 1866 certainly had no doubts. Cornholing boys in the pine flats around Brewster, an activity reasonably familiar to a goodly segment of the Godly, was described as a deed "too revolting to relate"; wifely innocence was thereby protected from errant male peccadillos behind the barn: "Whereupon the committee sent for Alger and to him specified the charges and evidence of his guilt (the testimony of two boys), which he neither denied nor attempted to extenuate but received it with apparent calmness of an old offender—and hastily left town on the very next train for parts unknown."

Interesting choice of words here: "He neither denied nor attempted to extenuate." The outraged citizenry of Brewster saw Alger as a sodomite. But another reading of the text might show that Alger was a remarkably honest man who, by not contending the charge, was protecting the young witnesses against him from any further bedevilment by the community. That characteristic of pedophiles, carried out at great sacrifice to themselves, is known in court proceedings to this day.

When life hands you a lemon, the saying goes, make lemonade. After 1866, as a writer in New York, Alger made gallons of it. What might have destroyed another man served to inspire Alger. Within two years after the incident at Brewster, he produced his first best seller—*Ragged Dick*. The books that followed counted as the sands of the sea. Literature they were not, but, for better or for worse, they helped shape twentieth-century America and enshrined subliminal pedophilia in the national psyche, where it remains despite all efforts to root it out. Adult males still help boys for other than spiritual reasons and, worse yet, feel good about it. Perhaps nature, without consultation with the Divinity, planned it that way. (If so, I'm rather grateful to nature: as a young man I needed the arrangement. Among other things, it got me my first trip to Europe!)

But the wondrous thing about Alger is that he continued neither to deny nor to attempt any extenuation: he just went right on with his pedophilic ways which were to center, after the publication of *Ragged Dick*, around the Newsboys' Lodging House, first located at Fulton and Nassau in downtown Manhattan and later at William Street.

In those first years in New York, there was tension between the Yankee puritan and the maturing pedophile in Alger. He expressed it in a flowery poem, entitled "Friar Anselmo," published in 1872, and quoted by Hoyt. The friar labors under the weight of some "deadly sin," but an angel comes to him as he is on the verge of suicide and says: "Courage, Anselmo, though thy sin is great,/ God grants thee life that thou may'st expiate." The puritan in Alger wanted to expiate. The pedophile wanted the boys. Somehow Alger managed to fulfill both those desires. Amazing, those Victorians!

Boys. There were fifty thousand of them adrift in New York City in the 1850s: runaways, throwaways, flotsam of the industrial revolution and the increasing urbanization of America. By the end of the Civil War, the number was increased by the demobilization of drummer-boys mustered out of the Union Army. As Tebbel notes: "They ranged in age from twelve up to sixteen or seventeen, and were making a precarious living as bootblacks, delivery boys, and newsboys."

The Lodging House had been established by the founder of the Children's Aid Society, Charles Loring Brace, and by the time Alger took up residence there in the late 1860s, the superintendent was Charles O'Conner. Tebbel, writing gingerly in the 1960s, has this to say: "Alger appeared to be living a kind of existence which was homosexual in nature, if not in fact. He had renounced women and the conventional patterns of sex. As far as anyone knows, he had no women friends. All his time was spent either with O'Conner or the young boys who surrounded them."

Tebbel apparently did not know about that bank vault in Brewster. He therefore handled Alger's pedophilia with the same squeamishness that early biographers handled Walt Whitman's further-ranging homosexuality. In effect, "Well, you know, he may have been a little queer, but surely he never *did* anything about it!"

No knowledgeable gay person could possibly believe such nonsense about anyone other than well-known monuments of asexuality, like Ed Koch and Andy Warhol. Jonathan Katz took considerable glee in printing Walt Whitman's diary of his pickups in Brooklyn. But Alger must have been a soulful and heartfelt boy lover; his love affair with a bereft little Chinese kid named Wing, described by Tebbel, brought tears to my eyes.

Now, admittedly, we must examine anything written about Alger with caution. Mayes, his original biographer, was apparently given to considerable embellishment of Alger's diaries, and since later biographers relied on Mayes, it will take considerable scholarship with the primary sources to separate fact from fiction. But the story of Wing has a ring of truth about it. There was romance in Alger as well as puritanism.

Alger found Wing on a winter evening in Chatham Square, in the heart of Manhattan's Chinatown, as he was being set upon by a gang of young thugs who were intent on burying him in the snow. Alger, all five-feet, two inches of him, waded into the melee, rescued the boy, and carried him back to the Newsboy's Lodging House, where he dried him out, fed him, and put him to bed. The year was 1873, shortly after Alger had written his poem about "expiation."

What may have begun as expiation soon turned into something much deeper. Plainly, Alger fell in love with the kid, and for nearly four years thereafter he lavished attention on him. Wing became a resident of the Lodging House, and Alger paid for his upkeep. He taught the boy English and paid a neighborhood patrolman to keep track of him when he went out, lest he be attacked by gangs of whites who considered any Chinese person fair game. Wing grew up to be a bright boy, returning the devotion that Alger had given him. Alger was a happy man.

One afternoon in August 1877, Alger sent Wing on a neighborhood errand. Wing did not return. As evening came, Alger grew frantic. The next day, the patrolman and the entire corps of newsboys joined Alger in the search for Wing. The news came late that evening. Wing had been trampled to death by a runaway horse on Broadway, near Spring.

"Overnight, Alger was a changed man," Tebbel writes with perhaps just a touch of hyperbole. "What hair he had remaining turned white, and a flood tide of bitterness washed out most of what religion remained in him." The puritan was puritan no longer; his faith was the pedophilic dream. He wrote it, and he lived it.

For limited periods of time, indentured servitude was a commonplace part of American immigration right through to the end of the nineteenth century. Young people in Europe were contracted by American families needing servants or by employers needing workers. For a prescribed length of time—perhaps five years—they would "work off" the cost of their transportation to the New World, and thereafter they would be citizens free to make their own way.

Usually it was a contract agreeable to both sides, and if it was exploitative for a time, the time was limited and opportunity was foreseeable. But the Mafia put a vicious twist on this practice. They bought young peasant boys from parents in southern Italy and Sicily, transported them to America, taught them to play some musical instrument, and sent them out to beg in the city streets. If they came back with less than $2 for a day's panhandling (all of which the padrone took), they were beaten and sent to bed hungry. On a regimen like that, few could be expected to live to maturity.

The padrone system was a form of peonage more destructive, if possible, than slavery in the South, where the slave-owner had at least some self-interest in the longevity of the slave as property. The boys in the padrone system were useless as income generators once they passed the time of youthful appeal that could bring in the pennies, nickels, and dimes.

Familiar with the street urchins in general, Alger must have known something of the padrone system in the early 1870s, but it took the goading of a Newark merchant named George Nelson Maverick to get Alger interested in the subject. Once Alger had made some investigations, the shy little man became a flaming crusader.

He and Maverick organized public meetings of protest all over Manhattan, castigating not only the padrones, but the police and city government for allowing the system to flourish in New York. Alger, with pulpit experience behind him, became quite an orator. "The next time you hear a violin playing, look out your window and gaze hard at the boy who is playing it. See the paleness on his face. See the rags he calls clothes. Get close and you will find more bones than flesh. And happiness! Try and see a glimmer of it anywhere in him."

The Mafia was not happy with Alger's crusade. They assaulted him on the streets, invaded his room on Seventeenth Street, and beat him into unconsciousness. He carried a pistol to protect himself, and before one of his investigative forays into the Lower East Side, he left his notes with a journalist friend to publish if he did not come back alive.

Finally, he wrote a book exposing the padrone system, *Phil the Fiddler*, which caused a furor of public outrage, and was one of the factors that led to the passage by the New York state legislature of the first statute ever enacted anywhere for the prevention of cruelty to children. It was the legal instrument through which the Society for the Prevention of Cruelty to Children was able to wipe out the padrone system in New York.

Embedded in the story of Alger's life are a transcendent irony and a comment on the public attitudes toward pedophilia that still exist. The good people of Brewster, Massachusetts, were reduced to speechless horror at the thought that their sons were having sex with the minister. Quite possibly, if Alger had stayed in Brewster and attempted to defend himself, he would have been lynched.

But when Alger went on his crusade to save the very lives of a horde of nameless little Italian kids at the risk of his own life, the early response was tepid at best. He appealed to his father, one of the pillars of New England Unitarianism, but Alger senior considered it a police problem, having nothing to do with religion, and felt that Unitarians would only be laughed at for their concern over immigrants who should not have been permitted to come to America in the first place.

And who was to care if Alger or anyone else had sex with them? They were not, after all, nice little Unitarian boys from Brewster. They were only penniless immigrants who should be expected to fend for themselves as best they could and find whatever affection and security was available without disturbing professed public morals.

If Alger was nearly lynched in Brewster for his pedophilia, he was acclaimed in New York while he lived the same life. The only difference seems to have been that no one really cared what happened to those street urchins in New York City . . . except Horatio Alger.

MARTIN DUBERMAN

# The Therapy of C. M. Otis: *1911*

*M*ost of the great manuscript libraries scattered around the country are woefully understaffed. Some of their richest collections are uncatalogued—still crated. Many archivists lament this condition as much as scholars do. But not all. Some—by temperament and training—prefer acquisition to information. A few are downright hoarders, guarding their treasures like ferocious stone lions fronting on some fabled monarch's tomb. When such archivists receive an inquiry from someone lacking "proper credentials," they dismiss it with hauteur. Should a "genuine" scholar—one with the "correct" number and kind of degrees, publications, and academic appointments—knock at the door, their reaction is fright. An invader has appeared, a potential enemy—someone who might disseminate and thus dilute the unique value of their "holdings" (that revealing term!).

I exaggerate, of course. But not by much. As I think Jonathan Katz, for one, will attest. As an independent scholar unaffiliated with any academic institution, Katz often met with overt hostility—when polite evasion failed—as he gathered material for his anthology *Gay American History*. Of course, anyone looking for historical documents on sexual behavior, including the heterosexual variety, must be prepared for a substantial amount of resistance; even as someone with traditional credentials, I've run up against a fair share of it in my research travels around the country. But whereas all of us attempting to do research in this field face the double obstacle of puritanism and homophobia, Katz had to parry sheer academic snobbery as well. His book has been rightly hailed (in the gay press, at least) as a milestone, but it's not been sufficiently recognized that Katz had to struggle—and did so valiantly—against the stupefying self-importance of academia.

All of which is to describe the worst side of trying to locate and gain access to unpublished sources on sexual behavior. There's a brighter, perhaps more characteristic side, too, typified by my recent experience at the Countway Library of Medicine in Boston, one of the country's great manuscript depositories. Its chief archivist, Richard J. Wolfe, is a man whose goodwill is matched by enormous energy. I had barely arrived at the Countway when Wolfe filled the table in front of me with cartons of documents—many of recent acquisition, never before researched. Torn between euphoria and incipient numbness (at the days of digging that lay ahead), I apprehensively mentioned that the feminist scholar, Barbara Sicherman, had suggested I also have a look at the L. Eugene Emerson papers. Wolfe's eyes lit up and off he raced. He was back within minutes. "Marvelous tip!" he said, dumping eleven more cartons in front of me. "Emerson was one of the first psychotherapists in Boston, worked at the Psychopathic Hospital, should be lots of stuff in there for you, nobody's ever really gone through it."

Many days later, I got around to the Emerson papers. The tip had indeed been marvelous. Among other items, the collection contained hundreds of pages of handwritten notes the doctor had taken down while listening to his patients talk. For the pre–World War I period, this kind of documentation, nearly stenographic, is extremely rare. And—as it proved—extremely difficult to decipher. I battled for weeks with the Xerox copies of Emerson's notes that I carted home with me from the Countway, and I'm not entirely sure even now that I've accurately decoded all of his elliptical, abbreviated scrawl. Clearly he had written at top speed, trying to get down verbatim what the patient was saying. Thus, the special value of the material.

But also its special limitations. Emerson had scant time (perhaps inclination as well) to record his own reactions. His notes contain only a few parenthetical remarks, the barest hints, of what he himself had thought, felt—and prescribed. Time and again, I longed to know how this thirty-eight-year-old New England therapist, during those tumultuous early days of the Freudian movement, had responded to the personal intimacies revealed to him.

That curiosity will never be satisfied. But at least we do have the case histories. Many are fragmentary, lacking the needed detail for reconstructing personalities and events. (One exception—which I'm preparing for publication—is extraordinary: 150 pages of notes, plus correspondence, about a "masochist" woman Emerson "treated" over a period of several years.) One reason for the brevity of most of the histories is that therapists at the turn of the century typically didn't see their patients for the long stretches of time that have since become commonplace. Even those few whom Emerson (in his words) "intensively studied and analyzed" were discharged after several months. And *not*—it should be added—with glib claims of "cure." In a summary Emerson wrote up on December 9, 1912, he conscientiously recorded that of the sixteen patients that year with whom he had attempted "psychoanalytic treatment for therapeutic purposes," seven had been "without much success."

Case No. 15 of the preceding year (1911) would surely have fallen into the "without much success" category. The "case" was a thirty-three-year-old man named C. M. Otis, a patient at the Psychopathic Hospital with whom Emerson held a total of six therapy sessions between April and August. He took thirty-three pages of notes on Otis—one of the fuller histories.

The initial session took place on April 26, 1911. Here are the very first words Emerson jotted down on his note pad (which doesn't necessarily mean, of course, the first words Otis spoke):

Reading a farm paper, about horse breeding, saw a picture of stallion, & had an erection—Abt. [About] 13 [years old].

"Mmm," I thought, gliding into a slow canter in my chair at the Countway, "at last—a male Catharine the Great!" Wrong. But it took several more pages before C. M. Otis came into better focus. Switching into the third person (as they often do), Emerson's notes continue:

Remembers before he came to Michigan ... had a girl. . . . Never touched her—just adored her from afar. . . .

Mother died when he was 10.

Played very intimately with brother.

Can't remember that he was especially loving towards his mother.

Never has had sexual intercourse.

First time masturbated abt. 17—Saw[?] a boy, they were lying on the ground[?], he took his penis out & showed how it was done—When he masturbated it gave him a very agreeable sensation ... has masturbated off & on ever since. Stopped when he was abt. 30 and joined the Church (Congregationalist)—2½ yrs—When he was traveling in the south [as a salesman] for D. M. Ferry he got discouraged, location was so bad, roads so bad, was late & company called him down for being so slow. . . . Then he began to masturbate

again. . . . Saturday night would report the week's work—supper
time till 12—Would feel . . . tension inside & a dread of starting the
work, & before starting this report would masturbate.

At this point in his notes Emerson suddenly indents and inscribes a single
word in the middle of the page, as if entitling an essay. *I* hadn't yet gotten
the message, but Dr. Emerson had. The single word? *Boys.* (The notes
shift back into the first person:)

> The first experience that I had, didn't know anything abt. it
> then, had a class of boys [Otis was teaching Sunday School], it was
> when I joined the church. . . . There was a boy . . . I used to like to
> have him come & go out walking. . . . After I quit my work in the
> bank, this boy & my brother, wanted to go camping, so I arranged
> it. This chap & I slept together. Then this thing happened. I don't
> know why or how it happened. I used to sleep with my arm around
> him, & I awoke one night & instead of finding my hand where it
> ought to be, it was down on his private parts. He awoke. . . . I took
> him aside & said I wouldn't want to do anything to you that [would
> harm you?]. Had him come out to see me at the farm but never
> touched him again.

The next paragraph is all but illegible. But the few words that can be
deciphered give us some sense of Otis's subsequent experience: "Has slept
with other boys, in the south—touched two . . . erections frequently . . .
those two boys also had erections. . . ."

Otis then started talking about his brother. The two often read poetry
together: "Oliver Wendell Holmes, etc., we had our window open, it was
cold, so we cuddled together." He hastened to add that "my brother never
learned anything from me." It had simply been a matter of finding it cold
when they got up, "so we'd hop back into bed and cuddle up close together
naked."

Otis next touched briefly (at least Emerson's notes are brief) on several
subjects—that he had once met "a nice young fellow" while traveling to
Battle Creek one day "who came to sit beside me—he was musical & we
talked abt. music"; that he feared the "men patients in the Psychopathic
Hospital know," and was apprehensive that they would persecute him;
that his mother had been an invalid for two years ("She was one of the
most nervous persons . . ."); that in 1905 he had attended a dental college
for a year, but "when it came to examinations, I couldn't satisfy . . . my
professors." Emerson's notes on the first session conclude with Otis's
painful statement that he "dreads to see a boy with his hands in his
pockets, hates to see pictures of boys in papers, in fact I wish the boys
would get off the earth (laughs), or else I would."

In the second session, held the following day (April 27, 1911), Otis
talked about his hopes, when younger, of becoming a market gardener. But
his family "jumped up & down & said it was impractical . . . just because I
couldn't plough . . . they were dead against me." Having no money of his
own, he had put aside his dream of becoming a farmer and in the interven-

ing years had shuttled among a variety of unsatisfying jobs: ferryboat operator, bank clerk, salesman, gas-meter reader. He was worried, he told Emerson, about how his family would react to his hospitalization, formulating his concern in a revealing analogy. "Suppose nothing is done for me here. . . . Suppose I'd committed a crime & had been sent to a state institution, they would have looked for some change when I came out—Well, they will look for some change now."

From there, Otis began to speculate about what had caused his "peculiar trouble." It "had been brought on," he thought, "by masturbation," and also by the reading he'd done. In 1895, at age 17, he had followed the newspaper accounts of Oscar [Emerson spelled it "Oskar"] Wilde's trial: "Reading that case of Oskar Wilde, didn't help my case a bit." He felt he had been further harmed by consulting "medical dictionaries abt. the habit I had, how it came abt."—that material apparently having been suggested by a "medical doctor at the asylum" in Pontiac, Michigan, with whom Otis had once talked. "All this homosexuality," Otis told Emerson at one point—momentarily shifting the blame off masturbation—"took its start in [my] study of abnormal psychology." He may have meant—I'm guessing here—that the readings had simultaneously stimulated his desires and convinced him "that he could not change them." What seems certain is that they enhanced his sense of persecution: while reading one day in the public library in Battle Creek, "I heard the telephone ring & after the librarian answered it, she couldn't keep her eyes off [me]—a degenerate abroad! . . . the police called her up."

Otis came back to the theme of persecution often during the remaining sessions. At one point he blamed his "notoriety" on having mistakenly confided in a dentist for whom he briefly worked; Otis was "positive" he had been overheard—"& now it is all over there, that I am what I am." At another point, Otis blamed the boy he had touched while on the camping trip: "He talked abt. it—& they watched to see if I was all right—He wouldn't talk abt. it would he? I think he would, & I think he did." Otis's fear of discovery and harassment sometimes became acute. During the fifth session (May 11, 1911), he told Emerson that there was an organized effort—"like the nightriders"—to "do him harm." He was "afraid to leave & go to work . . . feels safe in the hospital." At another session, he confessed that he'd thought of suicide a good deal—how some people blew their brains out, others took chloroform.

Emerson was not the first doctor Otis had seen. Earlier he had consulted two of the most famous medical figures of the day—Dr. John Duncan Quackenbos of Columbia University and Dr. Isador Coriat, twice (1924, 1937) elected to the presidency of the American Psychoanalytic Association. Coriat remained all his life a highly respected orthodox Freudian, but Quackenbos (so destined by his name?) was more on the fringes of respectability. Nathan G. Hale, Jr., in his invaluable book *Freud and the Americans*, recounts Quackenbos's widely publicized use of hypnosis in "curing" everything from "neurasthenic insanity" to "erotomania" to tea and coffee drinking. Hale describes the "nattily dressed, gorgeously moustached" doctor hypnotizing his patients "with a red carnelian [a variety of quartz] or a diamond mounted on the end of a gold pencil." Jonathan Katz, in *Gay American History*, has republished an 1899 paper by Quackenbos entitled "Hypnotic Suggestion in the Treatment of Sexual Perversions and Moral Anaesthesia," in which the doctor records his successful treatment (in two visits) of "a gentleman of twenty-five." The "line of suggestion" Dr. Q. used was simplicity itself: he told the man to resist his "abnormal feeling" and acquire "a natural desire for the opposite sex properly directed and controlled." For good measure, Quackenbos depicted—doubtless while flashing that red carnelian—the "moral, mental, and financial ruin" consequent upon "indulging the unnatural lust." The patient at once responded with "exaltation of the will power and an acquired ability to resist."

Otis's consultation with Dr. Q. took quite a different turn when he started to tell the doctor about his fears of "being watched." Quackenbos quickly "pooh-poohed the idea" (later, Dr. Coriat did "the same") and showed him to the door. Otis told Emerson that he thought Quackenbos had "preconceived notions of how a neurasthenic ought to behave." Perhaps he had had to tell Quackenbos so at the time. More likely, because he did not "weep with mortification" (as had the "gentleman of twenty-five"); nor did he have that gentleman's financial resources (the anonymous earlier patient had held "a position of trust in the office of one of our great life-insurance companies"). Whatever the reason, Otis had "never had the chance to talk this thing out." He was therefore grateful to Dr. Emerson for at least listening to him—for the "thing" had "got [him] down."

The future concerned him especially. He had no job. He had no confidence that he could "change" (from age sixteen, "I can say that I seem to have noticed certain attractive younger boys much as others will have noticed girls"). He continued to dream of suicide. He continued to fear exposure and persecution. He wondered if his "symptoms" might signify some "serious mental trouble like paralysis or softening of the brain." He could conjure up only a plaintive vision of what lay ahead: "... if I can get my position [job], if I have the physical vigor to do the work, & I can get it, & everything else falls into line, I can work out my own salvation, I think, I don't know." Plaintive—yet not without a touch of dignity and self-reliance.

After five sessions spanning little more than two weeks (April 26–May 11, 1911), Dr. Emerson apparently terminated the "therapy." The last time he recorded in his notes for the final May 11 session seems, on its face, stern and bleak: Otis "shows no adequate emotional reaction to my suggestions." When I first read that sentence, it surprised me. Up to that point I'd gotten the impression that Emerson felt considerable compassion for Otis—although I could only defend it through negative evidence: nothing in Emerson's notes had suggested the self-congratulatory posturing of a Dr. Quackenbos or the rigid conformity of a Dr. Coriat. Perhaps Emerson's final note of May 11, I thought, had erupted out of his sense of helplessness in the face of misery. Abruptness—particularly in New Englanders—can sometimes substitute for concern.

That interpretation is tentatively confirmed in the additional two pages of notes Emerson appended some three months later. On August 4, he made this entry (recorded here almost in its entirety):

> When I came home this afternoon, a little after 4, I found Otis waiting for me at the corner. He came back to the house with me & we sat a while in the piazza.
>
> The reason he came to me was because I had not condemned him & he wanted some advice—I gave him some & think he will take it. He said I had helped him a good deal.
>
> I told him of Leonardo da Vinci. . . .
>
> He has been on a farm helping the man who has charge of the baths. [?] at Hospital.

We don't know what "advice" Emerson gave. That he mentioned Leonardo suggests some effort at comfort and support—at the least, an effort to be nonjudgmental. Otis apparently thought so, since he had made the special trip to Emerson's house to thank him for "not condemning [me]"—although the oppressed are not always able to distinguish condescension from acceptance.

Thus stands our knowledge of Case No. 15. It is all we are ever likely to know of C. M. Otis—his fears and hopes, his experiences, his subsequent fate. The little we do know is the result of the chance preservation of a few dozen pages of notes. Only through that accident are we able to give a name and the bare outline of a personal history to one of millions of our anonymous predecessors who have suffered through time because of their attraction to the "wrong" sex.

## SIMON KARLINSKY

# Sergei Diaghilev: Public and Private

The name of Sergei Diaghilev is invariably linked with ballet in most people's minds. In just what capacity is not always clear. When Diaghilev died in Venice in August 1929, people at newsstands in London and New York were heard to remark, "What a pity, I never saw him dance." Of course, those better informed have long known that the bulky, heavyset Diaghilev was neither a dancer nor a choreographer. In 1951, a young art student named Jacqueline Bouvier (better

known today as Jackie Onassis) won a contest sponsored by *Vogue* magazine with an essay in which she described Diaghilev as "an alchemist
unique in art history," whose specialty was achieving an interaction of the
arts and an interaction of the cultures of East and West. The same essay
cited Diaghilev's ability to get the best out of his composers, designers, and
dancers, and to incorporate it into "a unified yet transient ballet masterpiece."

This view is not wrong. But it is incomplete, because it only takes into
account Diaghilev's activities from the time he became involved with ballet
fulltime, that is, after 1909, when he was thirty-seven years old. This usual
Western view omits his major impact on the arts in Russia between 1899
and 1909, a time when Diaghilev and a group of his friends altered the
course of their native culture with their educational activities. In the Russian context, Diaghilev is a major figure in the history of literature, of
painting, of philosophy, of music, and of all the other arts; it is not giving
him full credit to restrict his significance to ballet (where he is admittedly
very important) as the two recent books published in this country have
done. [Richard Buckle, *Diaghilev*, Atheneum, New York, 1979; John Percival, *The World of Diaghilev*, Harmony Books, New York, 1979.]

Diaghilev's story begins in 1890 when, at eighteen, he came from his
home in the provinces to St. Petersburg hoping to become either a singer or
a composer. He settled at the home of his aunt, a remarkable woman named
Anna Filosofova, widely known at the time as a civic leader and prominent
feminist. Friend to a number of important writers, including Tolstoy,
Anna Filosofova was the sister of Diaghilev's father. Liberal, and in some
ways even radical, in her politics, she was married to a public prosecutor
noted for his zealous persecution of political dissidents and revolutionaries.
Somehow their ideological differences did not prevent this oddly matched
couple from bringing four children into the world and giving them a warm
domestic environment that was the envy of their classmates. Their youngest son, the tall, blond, and spectacularly handsome Dmitry, usually called
Dima, was the same age as Diaghilev. He had just graduated from high
school, where he was the center of an intellectual coterie of young boys
that later became the nucleus of the World of Art movement and of the
journal of the same name that Diaghilev edited.

Late in 1890, Diaghilev and Dima Filosofov traveled to Italy together.
During that trip, they became lovers, a relationship that was to endure for
the next ten years. It was his cousin and lover Dima and Dima's circle of
school friends who stimulated Diaghilev's intellectual development and
helped form his views on art and his artistic tastes. Dima's classmates included two of Diaghilev's future stage designers, Alexander Benois and
Leon Bakst; the dilettante-musician Walter Nouvel, who was later to be
closely associated with Diaghilev in his ballet enterprises; and Konstantin
Somov, who became a famous painter in Russia in the early twentieth century (he emigrated to America after the Revolution and was active in this
country as a portrait painter in the 1920s and 1930s).

Like Dima Filosofov, Somov and Nouvel had been gay since their
teens. According to the memoirs of Alexander Benois, Dima and Konstantin Somov had had a passionate love affair in high school, which was well-

known to their classmates. Walter Nouvel carried a torch for the handsome Dima Filosofov for the rest of his life. While he never got to be his lover, Nouvel did remain a lifelong friend of both Filosofov and Diaghilev. Other members of this group, such as Benois and Bakst, were straight. What bonded together these young men of diverse sexual orientation from the age of about seventeen or eighteen on was their shared interest in the arts and their dissatisfaction with the way the arts were perceived and written about at that time.

At the end of the 1880s and in the early 1890s, cultural life in Russia was politically polarized and artistically provincialized. On the one hand, there was academic stagnation: a taste for patriotic, storytelling painting; conventional, well-made plays with a bourgeois moral; Victorian novels. On the other hand, criticism was dominated by a school of critics who are now called revolutionary democrats in the Soviet Union but whom it is more meaningful to call radical utilitarians. Forerunners of present-day socialist realism, the influential Russian critics of the end of the nineteenth century demanded that all art be socially relevant, address itself to current problems, be patriotic and strictly realistic in form. Their criteria entirely overlooked such values as originality or profundity. They preferred that the didactic message, which they saw as the aim of all art, be couched in familiar and accessible terms. Their insistence on topical relevance precluded any serious interest in the arts of earlier periods or of other cultures.

The young men around Diaghilev and Filosofov in the World of Art group saw both of those approaches to art—official academic and counter-cultural revolutionary—as equally limiting, provincial, and philistine. The aim of their association was mutual education and expansion of their cultural horizons. They quickly discovered whole areas of important art the critics of their time were ignoring: the Russian icons, church frescoes, and church architecture of the earlier centuries, which the art critics of that time thought backward and superstitious, not beautiful; in painting, the eighteenth-century and early nineteenth-century Romanticism, which were both held in contempt for supposedly lacking realism and social significance; and some recent Western phenomena, such as the Pre-Raphaelites in England, the music of Wagner and his followers, and, after some hesitation—it took them a while to recognize them—the French impressionist painters such as Degas and Monet. In the field of literature, the World of Art group was among the first to realize that the great Russian writers of the nineteenth century—Gogol, Turgenev, Tolstoy, Dostoevsky—were important not only as topical social commentators or indicters of the inequities of czarist Russia but also as magnificent and original literary artists each of whom had his own idiosyncratic vision of life that could not be fully explained by the catchall term *realism.*

By twenty-five, Sergei Diaghilev had come to realize he had no future as a musician. He had a pleasant singing voice but not of a caliber for a concert or operatic career. He tried studying musical composition with Rimsky-Korsakov and Liadov, but both told him he had no talent as a composer. Something of an apprentice to his lover, Dima, and Dima's friends when he first joined the World of Art group, within a few years Diaghilev discovered his organizational talent, which made him the group's undisputed leader. In the second half of the 1890s, members of the group made a few disjointed attempts to bring the universalist aesthetic of the World of Art group to public attention. Dima Filosofov published some literary criticism, Alexander Benois designed the sets and costumes for Wagner's *Die Götterdämmerung* for the Maryinsky Theater, and Diaghilev edited the yearbook of the Russian imperial theaters, which turned out to be a triumph of typographical art. One of Diaghilev's often overlooked contributions was to the visual side of books and journals, a fact that is very much recognized in the history of typography in Russia.

In 1898, Diaghilev put his considerable fund-raising abilities (which were to serve him so well during his later years as ballet impresario) to good use and persuaded two wealthy individuals to finance his pathbreaking journal, *The World of Art*, which he edited jointly with Dima Filoso-fov and with the participation of other members of the World of Art group as art critics, music critics, designers of typographical layout, and illus-trators. The journal was published for only five years, but historians of Russian literature, art, and culture—at least those in the West—see its ap-pearance as triggering a major turning point in Russian cultural attitudes. D. S. Mirsky, the most authoritative historian of Russian literature, points out that between the 1860s and 1890s, literature and the arts were valued in Russia only if they expressed ideas that were considered currently rele-vant. This explains, for example, why such a major literary figure as Anton Chekhov had difficulty getting recognition. The reigning radical ideo-logues thought Chekhov lacked topical relevance and therefore judged him politically harmful. However, by the end of the first decade of the twen-tieth century, Mirsky argues, Russian society was aesthetically one of the most sophisticated in Europe. He gives the main credit for this to Sergei Diaghilev.

This two-pronged offensive against academism and conformity, on the one side, and the supposedly revolutionary insistence on the propagandis-tic and didactic aspects of art to the exclusion of everything else, on the other, caused an enormous stir when *The World of Art* began publication. Attacks came from diverse quarters, right and left alike. The most usual accusation was that the journal was decadent, but it was also called sick, immoral, and antipatriotic. In the West, one often hears that Diaghilev was an art-for-art's-sake aesthete, a view repeated in the two recent books on Diaghilev by the English dance critics Richard Buckle and John Percival. This is totally erroneous. The debate between art for art's sake and socially engaged art had been argued in Russia and settled back in the 1860s. By Diaghilev's time, it was a question of freedom to enjoy the great art of the past and to create a new art of the future without the restraint of simplistic party lines promulgated by narrow-minded and ignorant critics.

*The World of Art* and several other remarkable journals patterned on it between the end of the nineteenth century and the 1917 Revolution served as rallying points for the finest Russian modernist painters, poets, critics, and musicians of the early twentieth century. The literary section was edited by Dima Filosofov, and it was through his literary contacts that his relationship with Diaghilev came to an end. Among the prominent literary contributors to *The World of Art* was the important and innovative woman poet Zinaida Gippius (or Hippius), a key figure in twentieth-century Russian poetry, and a poet whose work influenced just about every other twentieth-century Russian poet. The first few issues of *The World of Art* serialized her travel account called "On the Shores of the Ionian Sea." One of the chapters described her visit during the previous summer to the all-male gay colony in the town of Taormina in Sicily, centered around the pioneering photographer of male nudes Baron Wilhelm von Gloeden (his work has been rediscovered recently, and there has been much writing about him and reproduction in the gay press of his photographs of young Sicilian boys).

Zinaida Gippius and her husband came to be good friends with von Gloeden—she even describes an all-male dance she attended in his studio. As we know from her published diaries, that summer in Taormina was a pivotal juncture in her life. Since she was twenty, she had been married to the prominent novelist and critic Merezhkovsky, but it was a platonic, never-consummated marriage. She had romantic involvements with some other men and women, all of which broke off inconclusively because she could assume neither a male nor female sexual role. In most of her poetry, she writes of herself in the masculine gender, and according to some memoirists, she may have been physically a hermaphrodite, with sexual characteristics of both sexes. Yet in outward appearance she was a very pretty and elegant young woman. Her summer with the all-gay male crowd around von Gloeden convinced Gippius that she was an androgyne—that is, a man intellectually and emotionally but with a woman's body. When she returned to St. Petersburg, she began searching for a male androgyne with the exact reversal of her traits as her ideal lover. Her choice fell on Dima Filosofov. With the willing assistance of her husband, she set out to break up the relationship between Diaghilev and Filosofov.

By the turn of the century, that love relationship must have been under some strain. Filosofov was getting more and more involved in religion and mysticism and also in the revolutionary ferment that was to culminate in the 1905 Revolution, which gave Russia a parliament and some shaky constitutional guarantees. Gippius and Merezhkovsky were also interested in mysticism and politics and used these shared interests to alienate Filosofov from Diaghilev. To keep Filosofov more securely within their orbit they joined some other literary figures in organizing the Religious-Philosophical Society, a series of meetings that ended the decades-old estrangement between the Russian liberal intellectuals and the Orthodox clergy. Several books have recently been written about this phenomenon, because the outcome was a new religious strain in Russian symbolist poetry and philosophy, a religious sensibility that affected Russian literature for the rest of the twentieth century, all the way to Pasternak's *Dr. Zhivago* and Solzhenitsyn's *August 1914*. In this area as well, Diaghilev had his impact, albeit a negative one, since the entire phenomenon of the Religious-Philosophical Society was organized in order to break up his affair with Filosofov.

Zinaida Gippius was mistaken in thinking that Dima was her ideal male androgyne. He was and remained a homosexual man. It is not likely that any woman, no matter how attractive, could have seduced him away from Diaghilev. But Gippius offered a package deal: not only herself, but her husband Merezhkovsky, to whom Filosofov was very much attracted, as well as a new kind of mystical and revolutionary church that the three of them were to organize to replace the existing Orthodox church. After a tug of war over Filosofov that lasted for several years and culminated in a physical fight (when Diaghilev caught Dima having dinner with Gippius at the most elegant French restaurant in St. Petersburg, the Donon, and tried to beat him up until the waiters pulled him away), Zinaida Gippius got her way. Filosofov moved in with her and Merezhkovsky. He stayed with them from 1904 to 1919, when he deserted them in order to fight the Bolshevik government with a group of Russian anarchists based in Poland.

As we now know from correspondence that has been made public, they all ended up losers. Instead of her ideal androgynous soul-mate, Gippius found herself loving a gay man who, after a brief erotic fling with her, confessed that it nauseated him to be physically near her. Filosofov, who was hoping for a ménage à trois in order to win Merezhkovsky, learned that Merezhkovsky was unable to respond sexually to other men (or, apparently, to anyone). Diaghilev lost what was probably the greatest, most formative, and longest-lasting love of his life.

The breakup of this ten-year relationship led to a drastic change in Diaghilev's career and sphere of interests. There now seemed no purpose in publishing the journal he and his lover had jointly founded. In any case, it was then that *The World of Art* lost its financial backing. And there seemed no point in continuing to live in St. Petersburg, where Diaghilev ran the constant risk of encountering the man he had loved and lost in the company of the two people—Gippius and Merezhkovsky—who won him away. It was partly to be away from St. Petersburg that Diaghilev turned his attention to acquainting Western Europe with Russian art and music. In the years between 1906 and 1909, he organized a succession of exhibits in Paris of Russian art of all periods, as well as concerts of Russian music and performances of Russian opera. By 1908, Diaghilev and his other associates from *The World of Art* were planning a Russian ballet season in Paris, intended to highlight the choreography of Michel Fokine, the reformer of Russian ballet, whose work blended traditional ballet with modern dance as practiced by Isadora Duncan. At this point, Diaghilev met the man who was to become his next great love, and it was this encounter that sealed his commitment to ballet for the rest of his days.

That man was, of course, Vaslav Nijinsky. At the time of his first meeting with Diaghilev, Nijinsky was a promising young dancer at the Imperial Ballet, noted primarily for his elevation—the ability to perform high leaps. In his private life, Nijinsky was kept by a wealthy aristocrat, Prince Pavel Lvov, who paid his bills, bought his clothes, and was known to lend him overnight to influential elderly friends. This was something Nijinsky hated but went along with because he loved Prince Lvov and was willing to do anything for him. For Lvov, Nijinsky was only one of a series of kept lovers, and he was looking for a pretext to get rid of him when Diaghilev conveniently appeared on the scene.

If Nijinsky was no more than an expensive toy for Prince Lvov, his love relationship with Diaghilev exemplified the finest features of the ancient Greek love between a teacher and his disciple. In their five years together

Diaghilev developed a promising, little-known young dancer into the greatest male dancer the world has ever seen, a dancing actor of amazing depth and power, and an innovative choreographer who collaborated as an equal with the most important artists and composers of the age, among them Claude Debussy, Richard Strauss, and Igor Stravinsky. Diaghilev placed Nijinsky in the very center of the fabulous artistic projects he devised, had him participate in the creation of such durable masterpieces as Stravinsky's *Petrushka* and *Rite of Spring*, Debussy's *Afternoon of a Faun*, and Ravel's *Daphnis and Chloë*, and had him dance as the partner of the greatest ballerinas of that time: Kchessinska, Pavlova, Karsavina.

They shared their life for five years, which were also the years of their shared artistic triumphs. Then, finding himself away from Diaghilev during an ocean crossing to South America, Nijinsky suddenly proposed marriage to a young Hungarian woman he hardly knew and with whom he had exchanged no more than a few sentences. There was a bisexual side to Nijinsky, which was bottled up during his years with Diaghilev but which now came to the surface. Diaghilev felt betrayed when he got the news of Nijinsky's marriage. It was the Filosofov experience all over, with a woman stepping in once more and taking his lover away from him. But he still loved Nijinsky and still valued him as dancer and choreographer. Two years later they had a reunion in New York. Nijinsky arrived with his wife and daughter. Diaghilev was there to meet them with flowers.

Diaghilev had by then found a new lover in the person of Leonide Massine; he was willing to let bygones be bygones and wanted Nijinsky to dance for his company. But he had not reckoned with Romola Nijinsky. Always inept in practical matters, Nijinsky let his wife manage his career. Her idea of managing was to sue Diaghilev for back pay for the five years when Nijinsky and Diaghilev were lovers and shared their finances, or to threaten to call off a ballet performance unless Nijinsky's fee for that evening was raised. The situation soon became intolerable, and it was made worse by the presence in the company of two Tolstoyan religious fanatics who kept assuring Nijinsky that his earlier relationship with Diaghilev was a sin and a crime against God. It was too much for a man of Nijinsky's sensitivity, and he lost his mind soon after.

In looking over Nijinsky's oft-described career, one realizes that there would not have been a Nijinsky without his relationship with Diaghilev. The popular legend of a Nijinsky exploited by Diaghilev, of a Svengali-like Diaghilev holding sway over the great dancer owes its origin to the entries in Nijinsky's diary, made when he was going insane, and to the vindictive writings of Romola Nijinsky, who bore Diaghilev bitter hatred. The legend owes its acceptance to a combination of homophobia and a popular taste for melodrama. Instead of the reality of a brilliant man shaping and developing his lover's genius for the sake of the art they both loved, people find it more satisfactory to believe the version reflected, for example, in the famous 1940s film *The Red Shoes*, where the Nijinsky figure was changed into a woman (played by Moira Shearer) and the character based on Diaghilev was played as an irrationally possessive tyrant.

Leonide Massine was a sixteen-year-old dance student when Diaghilev discovered him. Unlike Filosofov, who was gay, or Nijinsky, who was bisexual, Massine was totally heterosexual. But he was willing to become Diaghilev's lover for the sake of his career and for the artistic education he knew he would derive from the relationship. He had no cause to regret his decision. An unknown teenager when he met Diaghilev, Massine was one of the best-known choreographers in Europe when he ran away from Diaghilev with a pretty English dancer seven years later. It is remarkable how little the three women who took Diaghilev's most important lovers away from him got for their pains. Zinaida Gippius got Filosofov, only to end up with a man who saw himself her prisoner and could not bear to touch her. Romola Pulszka got Nijinsky, only to end up with a human vegetable on her hands, for whom she had to care for the rest of her days. Vera Clarke, the English dancer who seduced Massine away from Diaghilev, found herself abandoned two years later and faded into obscurity.

During the last decade of his life, when he was in his fifties, Diaghilev had nonexclusive, nonpossessive love relationships with three remarkably handsome young men, affairs that overlapped in time and did not end in loss, as did the three great loves of his younger days. All three of these men were unknown and unformed artistically when they came to him and all of them had long and productive careers in the arts, lasting, as it happens, to this very day. The English dancer Patrick Healey Kay, better known by the stage name Diaghilev devised for him, Anton Dolin, appeared in some of Diaghilev's last ballets and was a soloist with various ballet companies after Diaghilev's death (including the American Ballet Theater in the 1940s). Dolin is still active in London theater life. Serge Lifar, a Russian who became a naturalized Frenchman, went on to a career as the premier danseur and choreographer of the Paris Opera, and he also wrote one of the first and still one of the best biographies of Diaghilev. Igor Markevich, Diaghilev's last love, is today one of the best-known orchestra conductors in the world.

Of course, Sergei Diaghilev served as mentor or patron or formative influence to many artists who were not his lovers or were not gay—straight men like Stravinsky or Balanchine, gifted women dancers, women choreographers, and even women stage designers. But as Igor Stravinsky was to complain somewhat puritanically in his old age to Robert Craft, the backstage atmosphere at all Diaghilev enterprises was unabashedly homosexual. Everyone who worked with him had to accept this openly gay presence. A symbiosis between homosexuality and art was something Diaghilev took for granted. As a very young man, he sought out Tchaikovsky a few weeks before the great composer's death and established a friendship with him on the basis of their shared sexual orientation. Somewhat similarly, he met Oscar Wilde in Paris in 1898, just before launching *The World of Art*, in part to obtain some Aubrey Beardsley drawings from him.

But it is his personal involvements with the men he loved that can be said to be memorialized in much of his achievement. When histories of Russian literature and culture tell us that *The World of Art* changed the whole Russian cultural outlook in the first decade of this century, that fact stands as a monument to the love affair between two gay cousins, Dima Filosofov and Sergei Diaghilev, who created that journal and jointly formulated its aesthetic principles. If we look at the brilliant age of Diaghilev ballets just before World War I—the dazzling scenery and costumes that set the Western art world on its ear, the great ballerinas, the memorable music—we can see how it was all centered by Diaghilev around his lover Nijinsky. In the post-Nijinsky period, the remarkable collaborations—the Satie-Picasso-Massine ballet *Parade*, recently revived by the Joffrey ballet, the de Falla-Picasso-Massine *Three-Cornered Hat*, the Rossini-Respighi-Derain-Massine *Boutique Fantasque*—were all created to highlight the talents of Massine both as dancer and choreographer. And the Balanchine ballets of Diaghilev's final years, some of which are still greatly in evidence, such as the Stravinsky-Balanchine *Apollo* or the Prokofiev-Rouault-Balanchine *The Prodigal Son*, which Baryshnikov danced recently on public television, were originally vehicles for Diaghilev's young lovers Serge Lifar or Anton Dolin.

Diaghilev is very much around these days. There are new biographies, there are exhibits of Diaghilev-inspired designs every few years, ballet companies from the Joffrey to the Oakland Ballet are arranging programs of homage to Diaghilev. It is impossible to turn on the radio without hearing Stravinsky's *Firebird* or de Falla's *Three-Cornered Hat* or Ravel's *Daphnis and Chloë* or Poulenc's *Les Biches* or some other ballet Diaghilev commissioned or inspired or helped create. What is not always remembered is that while he was helping to give the world all this great music and dance and art, Sergei Diaghilev was also expressing his gay love for the men in his life.

# R ICHARD PLAN T

# *Nazis and Gays*

Over the last few years enough evidence has been accumulated to prove that the Third Reich exterminated countless gays throughout Europe. Numerous documents have finally come to light proving that many gays, arrested and indicted, but without a trial, were put into concentration camps and forced to wear a pink triangle (the homosexual equivalent to the Jews' yellow star) on shirt sleeves and pants; within the camps, gays were often beaten, tortured, or killed. The persecution started around 1935 and in many ways ran parallel to that of the Jews. Now, some forty years later, we possess countless eyewitness testimonies to the Jewish holocaust; we can study detailed chronicles dealing with different countries; we can even watch films taken by the Nazis themselves. The Eichmann trial, thoroughly explored by Hannah Arendt, alerted even larger segments of the American public to the fate of the European Jews. But the gay minority has no Hannah Arendt. The books, the documents we have, most of them written in German, are sparse, and no film exists of the sufferings inflicted upon those men with the pink triangle.

I was a witness to the happenings in Germany, although fortunately from a privileged position at the border of the Third Reich. In February 1933, while a freshman at Frankfurt University, I realized I had to get out if I wanted to stay alive. My father, a liberal, a Jew, and the co-founder of the League of Socialist Physicians, had been arrested when Hitler took power. Some time later the authorities released him: he had served as a front-physician in World War I. They set him free but he did not survive the Crystal Night (November 9, 1938), when the Nazis destroyed over two hundred synagogues and burned down the houses of Jews, Socialists, and other "treacherous elements." I immediately registered at the University of Basel (Switzerland), a city ten minutes away from the German border. There I began to collect everything available about the antiminorities campaigns undertaken by the Nazis. Several of the trends that later surfaced in Germany I had experienced myself as a member of the Wandervögel ("Birds of Passage"), one of the many youth movements in Germany similar to the Boy Scouts, whose leaders were elected without adult supervision. Although there existed unequivocally homoerotic relationships among some of the young males, the leaders preached an antisexual credo, some praising abstinence, some promoting health foods, some denouncing the "bourgeois" Weimar Republic and, occasionally, the Jews. The Wandervögel, together with the other youth groups, most of them religious, such as the Evangelical and Catholic youth groups, were slowly coerced by the Nazis into surrendering their independence: they were channeled into the Hitler Youth. The Catholic movements, however, were more resilient than the others, so the Secret Police, under directives from Himmler, started to trump up charges against the leaders—either embezzlement (money to be shipped to Rome) or homosexual acts with their young charges.

One of my earliest playmates, Ferdi, left the Wandervögel when I did, although for different reasons. A bit older than I, blond, stocky, sexually experienced, very much an extrovert, he worked at the pharmacy that supplied my father's office. He didn't hold it against me that he had to scrounge for a living—his father, a drunkard, hated him and gave him no help—while I was "the Red doctor's boy" who would go on to the university. Ferdi joined the SA, which soon got him a better job. When he showed up in his dull-brown uniform, I cursed him. But Ferdi continued to be friendly with me, even though things got tougher. When my father was taken to jail, it was Ferdi who persuaded me to leave Frankfurt right away. He discovered my passport was not valid and managed to get me to the passport office, at the top floor of police headquarters, before it officially opened. He bribed another gay working there, and I got on the train to Basel with a passport valid for five years. Without it, I wouldn't have been able to survive in Switzerland and migrate to the United States some years later.

To understand the particular virulence of Himmler's antigay campaign, we have to go back to the Roehm affair. At the start of Hitler's career in the twenties, he met Ernst Roehm, a short, plump, scarred mercenary, deliberately vulgar, a "butch" lover of handsome boys. He knew he was notorious; he flaunted it because he also knew he was indispensable. Roehm built up Hitler's first squadrons, the SA, from a tiny collection of dropouts and malcontents into a tough, paramilitary troop numbering one hundred thousand by 1931. Soon he became so powerful he threatened the positions of Hitler's star-centurions, Goering, Goebbels, and Himmler. He also made a big mistake. Around 1934, shortly after Hitler took office, Roehm campaigned to incorporate his troopers into the official German army, the Reichswehr. Hitler needed the Reichswehr to stay in power, and although many of the old-fashioned generals loathed him, they loathed Roehm even more. The leaders of big industry whom Hitler was courting for funds also despised Roehm, and they feared his proletarian brownshirts, some of whom were ex-Communists. Big industry preferred the Himmler competition, the black-shirted SS, which was considered an "elite order." Roehm was aware that many SA men felt cheated: the so-called revolution had brought them a measly bounty, while the SS maneuvered into the rewarding positions. Roehm started talking about a "second revolution." This proved to be fatal.

Himmler, his SS leaders, the industrial captains, and the Reichswehr urged Hitler to get rid of Roehm. In June 1934, after a long meeting with the Führer, Roehm sent his SA on a vacation. Together with several of his closest lieutenants he went to Wiessee, a small resort near Munich. By then Goering and Himmler had persuaded the vacillating Hitler to eliminate Roehm once and for all. Numerous SS units were secretly mobilized and converged on the Pension Hanselbauer in Wiessee, where Roehm's group was staying. A few SS bullies stormed into the hotel in the early morning hours, broke down the doors, arresting everyone. SA General Edmund Heines, Roehm's ally, was allegedly found in bed with a young SA man. Neither Roehm nor any of the SA men knew why they were arrested and put into prison. Heines and a few others were machine-gunned right away; Roehm, invited to shoot himself, refused and was killed a few days later by a special extermination squad.

Meanwhile, the SA was rounded up in all major cities—but not only the SA. Himmler had drafted an "enemies list," enumerating the names of men in all areas of government, among them Catholic dignitaries, liberal journalists, and Reichswehr generals. The infamous Night of the Long Knives had started. On June 28, 1935, over two thousand people were eliminated. Meanwhile, Goebbels had concocted a cover story: Not only had Roehm schemed up a "putsch" to overthrow the Führer, but his moral conduct had become unacceptable to true Swastika standards. Therefore, Hitler himself had stormed into the rooms of Roehm and Heines, disarmed and arrested them single-handedly. Hitler was so shocked by the depraved scene he uncovered, he ordered "the ruthless extermination of this pestilent tumor." Since the putsch story didn't go over well—how could the SA have planned it when most of them were on a vacation—Goebbels stressed the "homosexual horrors."

Quickly, the famous Paragraph 175 concerning sexual acts between males was changed to 175A. While the old 175 had not included mutual masturbation but only acts of penetration, now any contact between males of any age that could be construed as sexual would be severely punished. Even having your name listed in a suspect gay's address book could lead to incarceration. This new law was made public on June 28, 1935, as a directive for "the ruthless persecution of sexual vagrants," and the date referred directly to Ernst Roehm.

If sufficient pretexts to prosecute a political enemy could not be found, he could always be accused of having proposed "unnatural acts," and the Gestapo regularly provided some youngster, released from jail and well rehearsed, to swear to that. In October 1936, Himmler demanded the "elimination of all degenerates." He proceeded without legal procedure to move those already arrested—numbering thousands by now—into the camps. By November 1941, Himmler, now in total command of all internal security operations, proposed castration for minor offenses, death for major ones.

The man who relentlessly persecuted gays, even when every man was needed for the munitions factories, the architect of the Final Solution for the Gays, has remained to this day an enigmatic and colorless personality. Himmler's early years show him to be a dedicated file clerk, a worshipper of all things military who was rejected by one military organization after another; a bourgeois déclassé, in fear of his father, a director of a Munich high school who believed he belonged to the upper strata of society but who was wiped out by the inflation of the twenties. Himmler's mania for meddling appeared early, as did his obsession with minutiae: he listed every letter and postcard received and mailed. Brought up to respect the old German virtues of thrift, obedience, and neatness, he was also taught to be a good Catholic and attended mass and confession. He lost his faith during the "lawless years of the Weimar Republic." When he met Hitler, he found his new lord and liege, and his new faith.

The SS was Himmler's creation, an outgrowth not only of his anti-Semitism but also of his aversion to all "contragenics." I have coined this expression to characterize any group that doesn't fit into the framework of society—here anything non-Germanic, anything nonstandard: the Jews, the gays, the gypsies, the crippled, the handicapped, the feeble-minded, the Jehovah's Witnesses. Strangely enough, Himmler showed no interest in lesbianism. When lesbian incidents were reported in Ravensbrück, a camp reserved for women that supplied prostitutes to the all-male camps, he reacted with indifference.

By 1941, Himmler ruled over twelve separate SS fiefdoms, keeping a tight rein on each, playing one against the other, his agents infiltrating every level of society. The SS established its own courts of justice; the regular judiciary had caved in shortly after 1935–36. By then Himmler had organized the first concentration camps, although the extermination camps—most of them in eastern Europe—did not start their activities before 1942. Himmler could order the "definitive resettlement" of thousands without a moment's hesitation, but he collapsed when witnessing an execution. He was totally removed from reality—the only sentiments he mustered while speeding the annihilation of contragenics, was pity for the "brave SS elite" troops who had to carry out these orders.

While in Basel during 1933–34, I learned that almost all the members of my liberal student group had either been arrested or fled to a foreign country—most to Czechoslovakia or France—where they were caught later. Then after June 1935, I received an unsigned note postmarked Frankfurt am Main. It was from Ferdi, my early companion, and it hinted that he would try to get out to Holland. He also mentioned a few other gays we knew had disappeared—and I noticed even then what could be called a "conspiracy of silence." Neither the Swiss nor the French papers I read mentioned the arrest or disappearance of any gays in the Third Reich. Of course, in those days we didn't hear much about concentration camps. Only in the forties, mostly through the efforts of Jewish organizations, did we learn what had been happening there. Furthermore, the gays who managed to escape always declared themselves to be political refugees; if they were Jewish, they didn't need to furnish any explanations.

We also learned much later that at the height of the extermination campaign, around 1943–44, Himmler added something new for men who wore pink triangles. Those who agreed to castration would be discharged from the camps. A few really believed this; they were castrated but not freed. Instead, the authorities transferred them to the feared Penal Division Dirlewanger, which consisted of former criminals. Dirlewanger, one of the most hated leaders of World War II, specialized in liquidating partisans but also had his own men shot from the back if he didn't trust them. It is no wonder that almost none of the castrated men survived.

The following accounts are taken from the writings and much later from the interviews of those who did survive, not only Dirlewanger's camp, but Sachsenhausen, Natzweiler, Sonnenburg, Dachau, Gross-Rosen, Mauthausen, Ravensbrück, Neuengamme, Flossenbürg—almost all Level 3 camps, death mills for Jews, homosexuals, and other contragenics.

Dr. L. D. von Classen-Neudegg, a physician from Sachsenhausen, published several accounts in a small magazine during the fifties:

> After roll call on the evening of June 20, 1942, an order was suddenly given: "All prisoners with the pink triangle will remain standing at attention." We stood at the desolate broad square and from somewhere a summer breeze carried the sweet fragrance of resin from the regions of freedom, but we couldn't taste it because our throats were dry from fear. Then the guardhouse door of the command tower opened and an SS officer and some of his lackeys strode toward us. Our detail commander barked: "Three hundred criminal deviants present as ordered." . . . We learned we were to be isolated in an intensified penal colony and would be transferred as a unit the next morning to the Klinker brickworks. We shuddered, for these human death mills were more than feared. . . .
>
> Forced to drag along twenty corpses, the rest of us encrusted

with blood, we entered the Klinker works. . . . We had been there for almost two months but it seemed like endless years to us. At the time of our "transfer" here, we had numbered around three hundred men. Whips were used more frequently each morning when we were forced down into the clay pits under the wailing of the camp sirens. "Only fifty are still alive," whispered the man next to me.

The witness gives three to four more pages of the deadly work in the clay pits. Among the victims: an elderly reverend who committed suicide, several youngsters, a gay Jew. He had to wear both the pink triangle and the yellow star. He had managed to get part of his money into Switzerland, and an intelligent Swiss lawyer would hand over the money only if he signed for it in person. The SS block warden knew this and tried to force him to leave part of the money to him. The witness was forced to strip in the snow, he had to do pushups in below-zero temperature, he was tortured so often that they thought he was dead. Finally, someone took him away, and he managed to get to Switzerland, but the Nazis got the major part of his money.

Another survivor witnessed several of the sadistic games the SS organized when ordered to "liquidate vigorously the 'derailed deviants' " to make room for the newly arrested gays from the occupied territories. One game: The prisoners worked in a quarry surrounded by a high-voltage fence. If they stepped within five feet of the fence, they were shot. The SS would throw a prisoner's cap against the fence and order him to retrieve it. He would be electrocuted if he touched the cap, or he was shot for disobedience if he refused to go after the cap.

Later on, as the situation worsened, as the cities were bombed and food was getting scarce, as more prisoners crowded the camps, the SS invented other methods. They picked an inmate they didn't like, either one with a pink triangle or one with a yellow star (by now more and more Jews were brought in). Two guards threw him on the floor; a third put a metal bucket over his head. The first two men then started drumming on the bucket. After a while the victim began to lose control, to thrash around, to shout in terror. When the bucket was suddenly removed, they pushed him in the direction of the high-voltage fence. Half unconscious, he would stumble against it and be electrocuted; if he didn't touch it, then they would shoot him for disobeying orders.

With handcarts we had to bring earth and clay in order to build a hill for catching the bullets from the range. The hill was to be quite high. At the start things went quietly. But soon groups of SS men began to practice shooting while we had to empty the carts behind the range. When we stopped unloading because we would be hit easily, they used their whips and threatened us with torture unless we continued unloading the earth. The SS kept on shooting; a number of my co-workers were wounded, several were killed. We had become living targets. More of us than any other group died on the shooting range.

The witness had to endure this for a few weeks; then he was rescued by one of the Kapos [inmates acting as guards] who got him a safer job. This enabled him to survive in a position of statistician-clerk. However, he had to watch the tortures of his friends.

I returned to Germany for the first time after the war in 1954 to search for a few missing friends. In Frankfurt am Main, my home town, I found several gay groups, among which was one which was nicknamed the "Farinellis," after a famous eighteenth-century castrato. This was a group of older castrated men who liked younger men. Of the bars they went to, called "Onkelchen Bars" ("uncle bars"), the most popular was Willi's. The bartender, after I told him what I was interested in, shook his head and told me to forget it: there were a few Farinellis among his customers, but they never talked about their experiences. I had already learned that most survivors had isolated their experiences in some time-proof capsule and were loath to bring back the past. Furthermore, at that time the laws against homosexuality were still on the books in West Germany, and the survivors had little interest in revealing themselves to strangers.

Why these castrated men frequented the gay bars, although they could only be partially interested in sexual contacts, later became clear to me: like members of any minority in an alien territory, they liked to be with their group. "Misery likes company," the bartender repeated. But finally, after many tries, I gained the confidence of a man I'll call Herbert.

Herbert was corpulent but not much more so than many of the older regulars. His voice was high-pitched but not exactly feminine. It possessed, however, a certain flat quality that made listening sometimes painful.

The order of events Herbert related wasn't always logical. But then, neither were Himmler's theories nor was the way they were put into practice. In any case, I pieced together the following chronicle.

Herbert was a bakery apprentice when he met Franz, a Jewish medical student. It must have been around 1934—Herbert remained vague on this because he didn't want me to know his exact age. Neither Herbert nor Franz had any inkling of what risks they were taking. Then, because the university wouldn't let him finish his medical studies, Franz was forced to leave; he went to England, planning for Herbert to follow as soon as he was halfway settled.

By that time the new antigay laws were in force (1935). Herbert's father, an admirer of Hitler, found out about his son's affair with a Jewish student and forced him to leave home; he was also let go by his employer. Franz didn't have the means to bring Herbert to England, so Herbert quickly found a job with an older, more sympathetic baker and stayed with friends, leading a quiet life. He wasn't drafted because he had a weak heart. In 1941, he was arrested by the Special Police and put into jail. He had little memory of his trial—it was a mockery and he was forced to sign a confession. Transferral to Camp Oberhausen came after weeks in prison.

At this point Herbert faltered. It seems that several physicians experimented with drugs on the prisoners. Various medicines were prescribed, causing him to vomit for hours; he was exposed to poisonous gases; and there were other experiments he wouldn't or couldn't recall.

Toward 1943 Himmler introduced a new ruse. Since the camps began to be overcrowded with prisoners from occupied countries, since the bombed factories needed more and more workers, gays would be "rehabilitated" and sent as laborers to essential industries. "Rehabilitation" meant that the guards would take those gays they thought were only "corrupted" to prostitutes who at this time were brought into the camps to bolster the morale of the guards and selected inmates. If the gays could "perform" properly with one of them, they were declared cured and usually—but not always—shipped to factories where they were saddled with the lowest jobs.

Others with the pink triangle who agreed to castration were shipped to the factories, and this happened to Herbert. I didn't press Herbert as to what actually had taken place, but he repeated that he had been "one of the lucky ones," because the SS often reneged and the castrated gays died in camp or were shipped to a penal brigade.

When Herbert was transported to a munitions factory in south Germany, his train was bombed a few times. He and the other prisoners then realized that all those "defeatist" rumors about Allied attacks had been right, that Germany might be beaten, and this somehow gave them the strength to survive the inhuman labor conditions in the factory, the lack of food, the primitive living quarters. In 1945, at the end of the war, Herbert managed to hike back to Frankfurt. He never looked up his father—his mother had died some time before—but he encountered an old friend in the suburb of Rödelheim, with whom he stayed.

I didn't meet the man with whom Herbert is living in Frankfurt. He was suspicious of anyone trying to come close, and he worried that somebody might write an anonymous letter to his present employer, another baker, who then would surely fire him. He admitted that he shouldn't go to Willi's if he was afraid of being discovered but explained that so many of the old crowd were dead and he needed new friends. Perhaps I would have been given more information, but during our last talk his reserve broke.

He blamed the Allies for having bombed civilian targets such as Dresden and Frankfurt and for not having bombed the camps, or for having done so much too late. He pointed out that in many camps the SS quarters and the factories were located outside the electric barbed-wire fence that enclosed the barracks of the inmates. "You could have spot-bombed those factories, the SS villas with their greenhouses and dog kennels, without hitting the prisoners. As a matter of fact, the British and you did some bombing. Why did you wait until the end, until 1944?" When I fumbled for something to say, he went on, "Yes, I know during the August 1944 raid on Buchenwald a few inmates got killed. But the camp was happy because many SS guards were hit. The electric fence and the underground munitions factory were destroyed. And what's more, the SS got scared— the big shots in their villas and the barrack guards with their whips. They knew Germany had lost for good. And you know what they did? They stopped beatings, they gave out bigger rations, they made deals with the prisoners. You could have spot-bombed every camp, and you should have done it systematically, from 1942 on." I found no answer to this in 1954. I don't have one now.

\* \* \*

In 1969, a compromise law was pushed through in West Germany that abolished all of Hitler's 175A and most of 175. But while those who had worn the yellow star in camp or the red triangle (political) were often granted some form of restitution, the courts ruled that gays imprisoned and/or tortured were not to be considered political, but criminal, inmates. Those forced to wear the pink triangle were essentially to be treated like the Kapos with the green triangle. West Germany, like East Germany before it, has abolished the worst features of the antigay legislation, but it apparently still considers the killings of the men with the pink triangle legally justified.

# NED ROREM

## An Auden

My friend Frank O'Hara once recalled showing his verse to Wystan Auden. Said the master: "You've got to be an Auden to get away with lines like that." An Auden! the younger poet marveled, taking in the prunelike lips dribbling vodka onto a sweater unchanged for weeks, the tobacco-stained thumbs and the urine-stained pants, the seedy carpet slippers (which because of chronic corns Auden wore everywhere, to the drugstore as to the opera), the whole pontifical form slumped like a mummy in a gutted sofa whose dust beclouded a setting no less gorgeous than the Collier brothers'. This portrait of the artist as an old mentor, corroborated by all who met him, is but the rough side of the canvas, for Auden was the most disciplined, the smoothest, and maybe the greatest English-language poet of our time; O'Hara had seen him as he saw others: ". . . I imagine you before my eyes/ Flushed with the wine I order and my wit."

A product of industrial England—he was born in York in 1907—one might nonetheless place him intellectually somewhere between Jean Cocteau, eighteen years his senior from a country he avoided, and Paul Goodman, five years his junior from a country he adopted.

Like Goodman, Auden was a clearheaded formalist in a distressingly unhygienic body, a rude bully who was monetarily kind, profoundly homosexual but a champion of the family as stabilizing unit. (When Cyril Connolly learned that Auden, who adored anagrams, had turned T. S. Eliot into "toilets," Connolly turned Wystan Auden into "a nasty unwed." Yet Auden's wedding in 1935 to Thomas Mann's daughter was legal and lifelong, although of strictly political convenience—they never lived together. But his thirty-year union with Chester Kallman was, at least on Auden's side, modeled on bourgeois values. After Erika Mann died in 1970, and Chester was far away, Auden proposed to other women, including Hannah Arendt, to her purported embarrassment. Both Auden and Goodman reveled in music but played the piano thumpingly, confusing love for ability; expert at hearing others, they couldn't hear themselves. Both were professional and caring teachers, periodically looked upon as arbiters, wielding no less influence through sociological belief (Auden liberal-conservative, Goodman regimented-anarchist) than through verse forms. Yet both were finally forsaken by the young; while planning to live until eighty, each died in his sixties of overwork and disenchantment at having evolved into the obsolete species of Educated Poet.

Like Cocteau, Auden was an aphorist who monopolized conversation with quips that brooked no argument. Cocteau too, vastly "official" in his waning years, had been spurned by the very generations whose style he had shaped, and he died, successful and sad, in a mist of self-quotation. When Auden had become a monument, he welcomed the interviewers he had shunned for years but spoke to them solely in epigrammatic non sequiturs. ("As a poet, my only duty is to defend the language from corruption. . . . History would be no different if literature had never existed; nothing I wrote against Hitler prevented one Jew from being killed. . . . I live by my watch. I wouldn't know to be hungry if I didn't have my watch. . . . Italian is the most beautiful language to write in, but terribly hard for writers because you can't tell when you've written nonsense. In English you know right away. . . . I don't go along with the generation gap. We're all contemporaries, anyone walking the earth at this moment. There's a certain difference in memories, that's all. . . . Art is our chief means of breaking bread with the dead—you can still enjoy the *Iliad*. . . . I like to fancy that, had I taken the Anglican holy orders, I might now be a Bishop.") Like Cocteau, Auden was a Jack-of-all-trades, authoring not only haikus but very long poems, plays, librettos, screen scenarios, translations from many a language popular and obscure, and the most original essays of our century on subjects far from his "specialty." Like Cocteau, Auden was also a professional actor and a social star, but while both were wildly candid in the parlor, they were circumspect in print: when their respective forays into so-called pornography, *Le livre blanc* and *The Platonic Blow*, were stolen and published, they were nervous. Because Cocteau's musicality was less proprietary (music was the one art he did not presume to practice), his collaboration with musicians was more expert: he did not, as did Goodman and Auden, concoct "settable lyrics" but left musical decisions to the composers. Nor did he fall into the fatal trap of the others who, during later years, revised early poems, making changes for change's sake, always to the disadvantage of the original. To Cocteau revision was a moral error; the old poet is not the same person as the young poet, although they bear the same name.

Auden's thoughts on Goodman are not recorded. But as early as 1929 he asked himself, "Do I want poetry in a play, or is Cocteau right: 'There is a poetry in the theater, but not of it'?" Neither he nor Goodman ever created for the stage with the inborn panache of Jean Cocteau, probably because, too literarily convinced of what theater *ought* to be, they grew hamstrung before the fact. Auden did translate two plays by Cocteau, of whom he wrote, "The lasting feeling that his work leaves is one of happiness; not, of course, in the sense that it excludes suffering, but because, in it, nothing is rejected, resented, or regretted." That is the only good word he ever had for any Frenchman of any period. He loathed France, the French, and, as he termed it, Frog culture.

The foregoing play of comparisons could seem extravagant but for the lingering influence of Humphrey Carpenter's definitive thesis (*W. H. Auden, A Biography*, Houghton Mifflin Company, 1981), of which each contagious page echoes the games of the protagonist, forever sizing up society and art through contrast and metaphor, and emphasizing that the best reviews are made from quotes. The very fact of the new book is itself an exercise in contradiction, Auden having claimed that "the biography of an artist, if his life as a man was sufficiently interesting, is permissible, provided that the biographer and his readers realize that such an account throws no light whatsoever upon the artist's work." He did add that "more often than most people realize, his works may throw light upon his life"— this, despite earlier admonitions that his letters be burned. Such admonitions, of course, always mean "Don't burn my letters." So he had his cake—for posterity to eat. Now Carpenter has made an elaborate icing to Charles Osborne's memoir of 1979 (most of the anecdotes are identical, but the tone is less chatty, the narrative more thorough), serving also as complement to Edward Mendelson's historical interpretation of the poet's work up to 1939 (*Early Auden*, Random House, 1981).

The youngest of three sons, Auden grew up in a secure and musical milieu, behaving ever afterward like a precocious favored child. His lapse at fifteen from the Anglican Church ("People only love God when no one else will love them") coincided with a growing homosexual awareness, which in turn concurred with his emergence as a poet. The emergence came in a flash, fired by the offhand question of a chum at Gresham's boarding school:

> Kicking a little stone, he turned to me
> And said, 'Tell me, do you write poetry?'
> I never had, and said so, but I knew
> That very moment what I wished to do.

Until "that very moment" he was pondering a future as a mining engineer, and until he died, he remained less drawn to the Mediterranean decor that was his eventual home than to the northern melancholy of factory neighborhoods which shaded so much of his work. As to the stylistic landscape, he underwent the necessary influences—Frost, Hardy, Dickinson, Owen, De la Mare, Riding, Eliot—but achieved his own mature voice quite early. "An incurable classic" he labeled himself, and like a true classic—Ravel, for example—he can't be relocated by "periods": he sprang full-blown from the head of his muse, his coolly intelligent timbre altering little with the decades. Since the French are nothing if not also coolly intelligent (what did he think of Ravel?), Auden's Francophobia seems to have stemmed mainly from revolt against the Francophilic generation immediately preceding his. But he was also anti-Romantic, notwithstanding an abiding attraction to Freud (nothing if not Romantic), and given to psychoanalytic quips, both toward his own guilt about feeling guilty ("And that Miss Number in the corner/ Playing hard to get:/ Oh I'm happy I'm not happy. / Make me good Lord, but not yet") and toward the psychosexuality of others—for example, "Ackerly did not belong to either of the two commonest classes of homosexuals, neither to the 'orals' [among whom Auden placed himself], who play son-and/or-mother, nor to the anals, who play wife-and/or-husband." Indeed, in the interests of high camp he often replaced *I* with *Mother*, either to set matters straight (from the audience to a lecturer on Debussy: "Take it from Mother, *Pelléas* is shit!"), or to jar an oversolemn subjectivity ("Mother wandered lonely as a cloud").

At Oxford, despite doing badly on exams ("There is nothing a would-be poet knows he has to know"), he was already the famous leader of a gang that included Isherwood and Spender. To the latter he wrote: "My dominant faculties are intellect and intuition, my weak ones feeling and sensation. This means I have to approach life via the former: I must have knowledge and a great deal of it before I can feel anything."

"Feelings" began to turn up, along with a knack for suppressing them, in Berlin, where the newly graduated Auden plowed the terrain before Isherwood made it notorious. There the poet became dazzled by one John Layard, a sort of precursor to J. D. Laing, and by his own notions of psychosomatism, which seemed to cover anything. "Rheumatism is simply a refusal to bend the joints and therefore an indication of excessive obstinacy. Abnormal tallness such as Stephen Spender's is an attempt to reach heaven. Cancer and homosexuality are caused by the frustration of the wish to have a child."

Returning from Germany to Larchfield Academy in Scotland, later to Downs School at Colwall, he was, in the guise of a schoolmaster, about to spend the most contented five years of his life. As eccentric ham and practical joker, as one who talked to all people on his own terms and not theirs, he was a born instructor. Like Kenneth Koch today, Auden showed schoolchildren that "poetry" was no more and no less than "memorable speech. We shall do poetry a great disservice if we confine it only to the major experiences of life. . . . Poetry is no better and no worse than human nature." Teaching also afforded him the leisure for book reviewing and essay writing ("It's awfully important that writers aren't afraid to write badly. . . . The moment you're afraid of writing badly . . . then you'll never write anything good"), for he hadn't previously developed a prose style. As for poems, his first collection was published in 1930 by T. S. Eliot at Faber and Faber, which remained his English outlet until the end.

By 1932 his Communist sympathies allowed him to declare that "unless the Christian denies the value of any Government whatsoever, he must admit . . . the necessity for violence, and judge the means by the end," a viewpoint he would refute. Later he would refer to "the intellectual Communism" of his youth as "old-fashioned social climbing," although he was never embarrassed that his poems of the earlier period preached ideas to which he did not really subscribe, for in poetry "all facts and beliefs cease to be true or false and become interesting possibilities."

In 1935 he switched careers dramatically, becoming scenarist for government documentary films in which he collaborated regularly with Benjamin Britten, his first real work with a musician. Yet he was always a bit lofty about movies and interrupted the work to co-write three plays with Isherwood and to travel in Iceland, land of his forefathers, from where the news about Spain brought him back to the "real" world.

Before leaving for Spain, where he felt duty called, he wrote the best known and last of the lyrics whose subject is no longer specifically homosexual but is on the impermanence of all interpersonal rapports: "Lay your sleeping head, my love/ Human on my faithless arm." The Barcelona of 1937, with its open Communism, elated him less than the closed churches depressed him; how could his "side" stop people from doing what they liked, "even if it is something silly like going to church?"

The next year he traveled with Isherwood to China as professional correspondent and, as with Isherwood, made a book from it, *Journey to a War*. The two men returned to London by way of America, where they were wined on red carpets, provided with "blond boys," and offered high fees (by British standards) for their writings. Neither of them put it immediately into words, but each one planned in his heart to emigrate, which they accordingly did the following January on the eve of World War II. The poet Richard Eberhart announced prophetically, "Auden's coming to America may prove as significant as Eliot's leaving it."

So much for the first half of the poet's life.

America offered Glory and Great Love. Glory, of course, had strings attached. "One makes more money by lecturing on poetry than by writing it." And there is evidence that had he bent to the Swedish Academy's demand that he retract remarks to the effect that Dag Hammarskjöld took himself for God, he would not have had to say stoically in 1964 and every year thereafter, "Well, there goes the Nobel Prize." It might be argued too that there was a decline in the energy, the *necessity*, of the later poems. Auden did have a trump card denied most poets: his prose, which increasingly and dazzlingly took over.

The Great Love also had drawbacks. Chester Kallman, a quickminded student ("far cleverer than I"), a poet, very blond, son of an immigrant Latvian Jewish dentist ("It is in you, a Jew, that I, a Gentile, inheriting an O-so-genteel anti-Semitism, have found my happiness"), age eighteen, appeared at a time when Auden, at thirty-two, was fed up with one-night stands. If the older man enjoyed the Socratic role, he in turn learned from Chester, who was a marvelous cook (though sloppy to a fault), a connoisseur of camp (everyone was "Miss this" or "Miss that"), and, most importantly, a devotee of bel canto, which Auden adopted completely ("No gentleman can fail to admire Bellini") along with Chester's aversion to Brahms. Chester meanwhile took on Auden's most dubious points, but his loud, drunkish opinions lacked authority because he lacked Auden's supporting gifts. Arrogance without talent is galling, but when certain friends recoiled from Chester—among them the gentle Britten and even Auden's father—Auden credited their dislike to anti-Semitism and dropped them. Chester was cavalier with Auden as well, calling him "Miss Master" and, more gravely, halting permanently their sexual relationship while flaunting his own promiscuity. Their "marriage" was ultimately founded on the sympathy of mutual work which they accomplished while cohabiting, for better or worse, for three decades. One cannot know to what extent Auden's librettos, assuming he would have written any, might have been different had he worked them out with someone else—with Isherwood, for instance, who is unmusical and so would not have let his text adapt an untheatrical preciosity due to "musical considerations." Nor can one know to what extent the librettos themselves might not be largely the work of Chester. Auden had answered Stravinsky's invitation to write the book for *The Rake's Progress* with: "I need hardly say that the chance of working with you is the greatest honour of my life." The work itself, while surely honorable, is hardly the greatest effort of either man (though it's Stravinsky's longest by far); but the real collaboration was between Chester and Auden, which Stravinsky used as a *fait accompli.* The fact remains that innumerable operatic adaptations of classics, plus four major operas— one by Stravinsky, two by Henze, one by Nabokov (none of whom had English as a mother tongue)—would never have existed, whatever their worth, were it not for the Kallman-Auden union. When Auden died, Chester survived him by little more than a year, stating that "my criterion is gone."

The remaining chronology in Humphrey Carpenter's biography is divided among six subjects:

*Conversion.* In 1940, aghast at what he perceived, in the Allies as in the Axis, to be "this denial of every humanistic value," he returned to the church. Long after the war when Auden, declaring himself to be an "old hand at this sort of thing," agreed to write a text for Stravinsky's elegy to [President John F.] Kennedy's memory, the composer said to Robert Craft: "Wystan is wholly indifferent to J.F.K.: what he cares about is form. And it is the same with his religion. What his intellect and gifts require of Christianity is its form—even, to go further, its uniform." Another musician, Marc Blitzstein, remarked, "Wystan doesn't love God, he's just attracted to him." Such bon mots in retrospect seem more glib than the poet. Auden had immersed himself in Kierkegaard ("the individual must either abandon himself to despair or throw himself on the mercy of God"), who influenced his epic *New Year Letter* ("versified metaphysical argument is very difficult"). In the face of England's annoyance with his defection in time of war—Harold Nicolson called him "a disgrace to poetry"—Auden felt that "aloneness is man's real condition. . . . At least I know what I am trying to do, which most American writers do not, which is to live deliberately without roots." Those "American writers" with whom he lived, literally under one roof on Middagh Street in Brooklyn, were Gypsy Rose Lee and Golo Mann, Paul Bowles and Jane Bowles, Carson McCullers and

George Davis, and also his countrymen, Benjamin Britten and Peter Pears. Auden played Mother Superior to the motley household, presiding at meals and ordering punctuality, but kept private his weekly excursions to the Episcopalian Mass.

*Crisis.* Another motive for the return to God was his breakdown at discovering that Chester had taken another lover, a person whom he seriously planned to murder. The situation was aggravated when Chester's affair withered into a series of casual adventures which were to endure forever after. "His promiscuity is harder to take," Auden confided, "because it fills one with jealousy and anxiety for his spiritual welfare while a genuine love fills one with jealousy and respect":

"If equal affection cannot be, / Let the more loving one be me." . . . and he survived, as he always had and would, through routine: "The surest way to discipline passion is to discipline time."

*Teacher again.* Routine, no matter how innovative his curriculum, is the teacher's sine qua non, and Auden relished his 1941–42 stint at Ann Arbor. He refused courses in so-called creative writing and modern poetry—"Poets who teach should keep as far as possible from their own field of work"—launching instead a syllabus ranging from Aeschylus to librettos and forbidding his class to take notes, since "one person cannot really communicate anything specific to another." As usual, he arose each dawn to pursue work on *A Christmas Oratorio* as a memorial to his mother, the only work in which he used Christianity as a direct subject, for "Culture is one of Caesar's things." In 1943–44 he taught at Swarthmore; in 1945 returned to Germany as a bombing research analyst; in 1946 became at last an American citizen, went briefly to Bennington, had an affair with his secretary (female), spent a long session on Fire Island (". . . where nothing is wicked / But to be sorry or sick"), visited Tanglewood to hear Britten's *Peter Grimes,* which left him lukewarm, and with whose composer he had a permanent falling out due partly to the failure of their operetta, *Paul Bunyan;* then moved back to Manhattan, living this time at 7 Cornelia Street, where, when Spender once tried to let in some daylight, the curtains fell down ("You idiot! In any case there's no daylight in New York."). In 1947, *The Age of Anxiety* won the Pulitzer Prize. Auden was indifferent to the Bernstein-Robbins ballet composed on this long poem but was overwhelmed when Stravinsky, this same year, approached him for a libretto. Thus began a permanent change of inventive focus, and the first of his long chain of co-billings with Chester.

*Ischia.* The 1950s saw Auden ever less in the United States. The decade began with *The Rake's Progress*'s Venetian premiere. Despite its success, Stravinsky never worked with Auden again (possibly because Auden announced far and wide that Britten, who had seen the score, liked everything except the music). Auden and Chester summered at Ischia now and commuted to their new and final American apartment on St. Mark's Place. The Latin sunshine, some say, contributed to Auden's premature and bizarre wrinkling ("My face looks like a wedding cake left out in the rain."). After a residency at Oxford, he finally removed his summer abode, in 1957, to Kirchstetten. To live within reach of the Austrian opera houses attracted both Chester and Auden, who also relished the prospect of a

German-speaking community. Yet Auden—and here is a paradox among great artists with an "eye" for words—had scant talent for either talking or writing foreign tongues. He was deeply moved at finally owning a home of his own ("what I dared not hope for / is, in my fifties, mine"), and although he never regretted quitting the Italian island, he wrote: ". . . though one cannot always./ Remember exactly why one has been happy / There is no forgetting that one was."

*"A minor Atlantic Goethe."* While working on translations of Goethe, Auden came to think of the German poet as a "dishonest old hypocrite," and yet "Great Mr. G" grew into an image of what he himself hoped to achieve at this period of his life. His enduring prolificity and fame led Chester, now middle-aged and balding, to vanish for periods into Greece to lead his own life. Auden was lonely, drank, was obsessed about money, returned to Iceland and otherwise traveled widely as lecturer, revised his old works and worked unstintingly on new ones. He and Chester continued to work together on musical projects. But by the 1960s the world saw Auden as an unquestioned Absolute, a sort of Anglo-American Aschenbach as well as a deteriorating specimen on whom liquor, cigarettes, and the airless years had taken their toll.

*Return to England.* He remained listed in the Manhattan phone book. When an anonymous caller announced, "First we will castrate you, then we will kill you," Auden was delighted by his quick reflex: "I'm afraid you have the wrong number." Yet he was increasingly unnerved by American violence. Although far from senile, he seemed incapable of give-and-take conversation; though far from self-pitying, he feared a coronary which might leave him dead and unapprehended on the bathroom floor. He arranged, for his own safety and for reasons of nostalgia, to become writer-in-residence at his Alma Mater, to which he moved in 1972. The move was a mistake; the old Oxford days were gone. As irony would have it, the dreaded heart attack occurred not in Oxford but in a Viennese hotel room. By further irony, however, it was not a chambermaid but Chester himself who found the body. The body is buried in his beloved Kirchstetten, and the lane where he lived is now named Audenstrasse. On the memorial marble in Westminster Abbey are engraved these lines from his elegy on Yeats: "In the prison of his days / Teach the free man how to praise."

Anyone who uses the phrase Great Artist must surely thus qualify Wystan Auden. Not only is his verse as strong, original, and influential as any in English since Eliot, his work has a breadth generally linked to the notion of Great. As a man of the flesh Auden was a Master, insofar as the term obtains to those Romantic creators whose personae were no less viable than God or State: he was for half a century an intimidating and coercive leader, a well-trained organizer of the intellect, and, not incidentally, a maker of Masterpieces. Two shortcomings, however, denied him the wreath of what the French call Sacred Monster. First, his sense of frivolity: the public of the Great frowns upon Charm. Second, he was just too young: the period of the Masterpiece, which ran roughly from Beethoven to Proust, could in a pinch be stretched to Mann or Picasso or Stravinsky, but ours is no longer an age of worshipping individuals, when even rock superstars are promoted as being like you and me.

Humphrey Carpenter's survey is a model of scholarship. It is virtually without editorializing, and almost willfully without style, a wise choice—if indeed choice is involved—since to write with style about style is to becloud the issue. If the book lacks the color and compassion of Millicent Dillon's concurrent biography of Jane Bowles (yes, the same Jane Bowles who in that famous house on Middagh Street served briefly as Auden's stenographer), that is because Auden was not a walking wound; he kept his wound at a distance as something to write a letter to (his chronic anal fissure became the object, not the subject, of a lengthy piece—"you are taking up more of my life every day"). If on the face of it Auden seemed invulnerable, it is that like many an artist with an iron will, he could hold his vulnerability in abeyance, check it at the studio door.

Carpenter's book, considering its great length, has only the minimum of redundancies, mistakes in French, and juxtapositions of chronology which disorient the reader. If the book errs—and I am of mixed feelings about this—it is that Auden's ongoing libidinous history threads the pages as prominently as does his poetry. Are documents of heterosexual poets—of Wallace Stevens, say, or William Carlos Williams, or even the rakish Dylan Thomas—as prone to detailing not only each gloomy romance but every casual pickup? When Carpenter goes beyond this, he has a knack for entering that studio door without calling attention to himself and of collecting what he finds on the other side. The result is a treatise that appears all that will ever be needed on the remarkable subject.

# DAVID JACKSON

# *Three Pictures of W. H. Auden*

1965   W.H.A. is arriving from Austria to visit Chester Kallman. I go off to meet his plane. Auden hasn't been in Greece since the early thirties, and it's *changed*. We start up Syngrou Avenue, which runs from the Sea to the columns of the Temple of Zeus, near City Center. Now, instead of country, ugly car salesrooms and various pseudomodern office buildings line this street. "My dear! What a pity! It was all quite open before. All the way from the Sea one had an unobstructed view of . . ." (a break in the buildings, the Acropolis appears) "Oh, my God, there it *is!*"

1972   Auden is back. This time it is the Greece of the Junta. Chester had problems with these colonels who, like all military tyrants, feel free by torture to indulge their S-and-M fantasies while taking an utterly pure line on public morals—the area where Chester has had his run-in. On Wystan's arrival we rally the press: Leading Poet of English Letters Visits Local Resident and Longtime Friend. A great party, literati, society, old pals, journalists. (Absent are Chester's numerous friends in uniform or out of it—never less than three or four hulking mustached proprietary figures coming and going in the flat; W.H.A.: "Like so many schoolgirls, my dear, fighting over who gets the hockey mistress." Wystan on a couch, rather more dressed than usual, although still in carpet slippers, is saying to an intent young reporter: "Yes, we too, in England, have known repressive puritanical regimes. Obviously, Cromwell in his day . . ." and on, setting the record straight for another hundred words, until interrupted by the journalist looking perplexedly up, "How write this Kromhouel?" And such a look comes over the poet's face.

1973   In Auden's New York apartment on St. Mark's Place, shared for nearly two decades with Chester. I've arrived for supper before taking Chester on to a New Year's Eve party in Harlem. The possible dangers lurking in Harlem preoccupy Wystan: "My dear, does Jimmy [Merrill] know you're going up there?" I try to distract him by describing the elaborate flat of the musician, David Fontaine, where we've gone to other parties, met people like Mae Barnes and Arthur Mitchell, but see that he is still leery and agree to call my host: "David, uh, I'm driving up there with Chester and Tom Victor, uh, is there a place to park near you?" A pause while David cleverly takes in my question, then: "Oh, yes, I'm sure you can squeeze your little car in among those Cadillacs outside." Chester remarks, "I might have known, just another Uptown party!"

Meanwhile, one looks around. No self-respecting Welfare Recipient would spend a night in this flat. A sad scene of sagging bookshelves, sprung-seat overstuffed chairs, a dusty and scarred "cozy-corner" and everywhere litter, piles of paper and magazines, this morning's crusted dish of egg. I go to the toilet—not looking long into the kitchen—and switch on the light, they've *flocked* the walls! Then these move, a vertical nation of cockroaches shifting about uneasily. One of Chester's lesser dinners is set down on the dining room table. This, covered in glass, has a great crumb-filled crack running through it. We chat. "Wystan, aren't you sad to be leaving New York?" Between spoonfuls he thinks; at last he answers—the tone, is it the poet's, the lover's fond oblivion to the work of time? There is a touch of a sigh. "Yes, yes, particularly now that we've fixed the place up."

## The Fifties

The fifties began, in my personal mythology, when Parker Tyler and I gave a champagne dinner party for Marius Bewley and Garry MacKenzie to celebrate the jubilant victory of all that was true and good and noble in the American liberal political tradition—the election of Adlai Stevenson as president of the United States. We had the good sense not to turn on the radio to listen to the election returns until after dinner. We wanted to avoid any disagreeable suspense that the ambiguity of early returns might generate. We planned to concentrate on the exhilarating air of victory. Adlai was our hero. Hadn't the New York *Daily News* called his voice "fruity"? And did he not secretly represent for us the first gay candidate for president? This was sheer wish fulfillment, but somehow it seemed to be what the election was really about. The snide attacks on Stevenson's masculinity were blue-collar locker-room talk, but they had surfaced on the pages of a major newspaper with an immense circulation. Of course, Adlai was not the first gay (or, as we said in those days, Athenian) candidate for president and we knew it, but it was an irresistible fantasy. And if it had been true would not the election have been very much the way it was? Or so, in our innocence, we believed.

The election had a deep effect on one of our guests. Marius Bewley had not yet written *The Complex Fate* and *The Eccentric Design*, in which he isolates and examines the uniquely American essence of the adjective *American* placed before the noun *Literature,* particularly as it is manifest in the books of Hawthorne and Henry James. The defeat of Adlai Stevenson did much to shape his sense of the complexity of the American fate and the eccentricity of the American design. Adlai Stevenson appeared like one of James's heroes of the earlier fiction, who, we feel, will be a winner. And, in addition, the Democrats had not lost a presidential election in a generation. We dreamers sentimentally believed that liberalism was about to expand into new areas of human freedom presided over by a "fruity" voiced president.

Marius was euphoric. His Cantabrigian tenor soared in laughter over the conversation. Yet I do not remember anything specific that Marius or Parker or Garry said. As with many mythological dramas it was the choral odes that mattered. Our grand chorus of victory was chanted with the accompaniment of champagne, chicken in wine and herbs, and cherries jubilee. Then the fifties began: a telephone call, the first returns, Stevenson losing. It was time for the grand chorus of lamentation. Hyperbole is not misplaced here because the liberal thrust *was* thwarted; the growth of freedom *was* delayed. And somewhere along the way the imitation of Stevenson's voice by Senator Joseph McCarthy represented the ugly nadir of repression. The unrepression of the repressed was to occur later with the bounce of beer cans. And predictions of one's Trotskyite friends were to be proven true after all.

The Age of Eisenhower meant nothing, but that does not mean that the fifties did not see innovative art movements, radical Supreme Court decisions, and other significant advances. Yet, just because it was the Age of Eisenhower, memory is tinged with its grayness relieved by bursts of color. One such burst happened in July of 1952, just before the gray descended. It was a party given by Alice de la Mar for the departure of Pavel Tchelitchew from America. Interesting people are always coming and going, but in the fifties the accent of significance seemed to fall on the going—going to Europe, going to Africa, going to Mexico, going anywhere (to quote Baudelaire) out of this world. Of course, they were not fleeing Eisenhower, but it seemed that way even though they came back. Tchelitchew did not come back. And his farewell party was like a theme whose modulations continued over the decade. There was chic—Ruth Ford dressed as Man Ray (Ruth, Roses, and Revolvers), Kevin McCarthy dressed in his young skin and a few Dionysian leaves, Marie Menken dressed as the Statue of Liberty and/or Isadora Duncan. There was subversion—Philip Lamantia giving himself a fix in the parking lot, Willard Maas servicing the parking lot attendants. And there was Tchelitchew, arriving late and leaving early, in a velvet smoking jacket calmly saying goodbye, goodbye.... And enjoying the party more than anyone—Charles Henri Ford: greeting friends, relishing the fireworks and dancing to the music of Mary Lou Williams.

The end of the decade is marked for me by an event that prefigured the sixties. Stan Brackhage had just had the premiere of WINDOW / WATER / BABY / MOVING, his film about the birth of his first child. It is an extraordinary film, flowing from a hand-held camera like a river of light celebrating eroticism, color and birth—the double birth of his child and this film. In the lobby of the Living Theater at Seventh Avenue and Fourteenth Street after the performance Maya Deren denounced Stan Brackhage for having "violated the women's mysteries." This was no small transgression for the woman who was the artistic leader of the experimental-film movement and an initiated Vodoun priestess as well. For me it is the mythological and classic prototype of women's liberation meeting men's liberation head-on. Nor do I believe there is even now a clear resolution of the conflict. But true to the fifties, a great deal was started that is still unresolved, still in progress.

# V

## CULTURAL POLITICS

# DENNIS ALTMAN

<><><><><><><><><><><>

## Interview with Gore Vidal

$T$his interview was recorded at Gore Vidal's house at Ravello, on the Italian Coast, in August 1977.

*You've said that the word* homosexual *should be used as an adjective and never as a noun. Yet, the homosexual movement is based on the assumption that there are homosexuals, that there is a homosexual identity. Do you agree?*

If there is such a thing as a homosexual identity, you must then admit that there is such a thing as a heterosexual identity. You must find a significant likeness between the late Bertrand Russell and the late Lyndon Johnson, two men who had absolutely nothing in common except that they both liked to go to bed with women. And death, of course. They're both "into" that now. Since I don't recognize such a thing as a heterosexual personality, how can I define or detect a homosexual personality? *Homosexual* is just an adjective that describes a sexual act between two members of the same sex, an act as normal, whatever that may mean, or natural—clearer meaning—as that between two members of the opposite sex. Nothing more. If there is such a thing as "gay sensibility," then why not a "realtor's sensibility" or a "White Plains, New York, sensibility"? My mind tends to move in political directions. The United States is a nation founded by lawyers in order to enrich lawyers, and the law is to us what religion was to other societies. It is the law that perverts sexual relationships. Law can only be changed by political action. I think those of us who favor removing victimless crimes from the statutes should organize something on the order of the Anti-Defamation League or the NAACP—some overall organization that would work to remove the law from the private lives of the citizens. There are constitutional precedents that could be usefully served.

*But the ADL or NAACP were basically organized by those who identified as Jews or blacks, and it was this identification that gave them the incentive to organize. If you deny that there are such people as homosexuals, who is going to organize such a movement?*

I'm thinking of something larger and more important than just trying to change laws and attitudes which make life difficult for full-time homosexualists—there's a noun, at last, but a clumsy one. How, by the way, is one to make a noun out of that idiotic adjective *gay? A gayist? A sprite? Pollyanna?* Anyway, I'd include other "criminals"—gamblers, prostitutes of both sexes, etc. . . . In other words, I'm for a much larger coalition, one that could affect almost everybody. The late Dr. [Alfred] Kinsey said that if all the sex laws in the United States were put into effect, something like

90 percent of the male population would be in prison. The repeal of all these laws is most important. Obviously, full-time practicing homosexualists have the greater motive to join. But don't be exclusive.

*The basic problem is that homosexuals are either too scared to do anything—and this sort of activity means that, to some extent at least, you have to come out—or they believe things are pretty good anyway, so why rock the boat. How are you going to get enough to involve themselves in this sort of movement? Surely the success of the movements you referred to was due to the willingness of blacks and Jews to participate.*

I'm not so sure—for instance, the NAACP had many white members. I used to belong to it. I can remember a good deal of complaint from black leaders about apathy among those they worked to serve and defend. The point is, you must get together as many people as you can whose attitudes toward sex are post-Mosaic, post-Pauline. Then, go to the courts, the legislators, and go to the polls. From the beginning, both blacks and Jews tried to get allies from both whites and gentiles. Once you start sounding exclusive or superior, then you are ringing a change on that "black is beautiful" line of the sixties, which no one really bought, including the blacks. After all, if blacks are beautiful, then whites are ugly, and though this may or may not be true in individual cases, you can't generalize. In a way, the Anita Bryant thing has been useful. This essentially fascist caper convinced a lot of homosexualists (who thought they were having a pretty good time, since no one was hassling them at the moment) that they should act. But how? That's when organization is needed. Bryant and the Far Right are organized and rich. They are touching what is known in politics as the "hot buttons"—fags, drugs, Panama Canal—well, let us do likewise. Let's press the cool buttons of the Golden Rule, "Do unto others, etc. . . ." Of course, the current Nixon Supreme Court is hostile to personal freedom—as opposed to granting any corporation or police department any license it wants to rip off consumers or to terrorize citizens. Even so, I would keep on in the courts. There must be enough homosexualist lawyers willing to give a little free time to this.

*You're talking along the lines used in Britain in the sixties when there were very respectable people pushing for reform. The Law Reform Society . . .*

Including my cousin, Lord Arran, many times removed from me by blood but close in spirit.

*. . . was not basically homosexual, and lots of its members who were, went to great lengths to hide it. It's debatable, I think, whether changing the law made any real difference for most homosexuals in Britain and also whether this sort of strategy does anything about the enormous feelings of guilt and self-hatred and self-loathing most homosexuals still feel.*

Now you're moving into something else. You have to go step by step. Whether each step is as broad as you might like is something else again. The Wolfenden Report was necessary; the laws that went through Parliament were necessary. The fact that the British police are occasionally inclined to persecute is a fact. After all, the average male in the Anglo-American world is hysterical on the subject of homosexuality. It is in the culture, a vestige of Judeo-Christianity, now in its terminal stage. Everyone knows he has homosexual instincts; and since everyone has been told from birth that if he gives way to such instincts, he is sick and evil and, in most American states, a criminal, fag-bashing is bound to be very popular for a long time. Religio-social attitudes change slowly. That's why I'm interested in what the TV commercials call "faster action." Change the laws. Scare the police. Take California. They have got fairly liberal laws on victimless crimes, but the Los Angeles police are still busy entrapping homosexualists because the police chief in Los Angeles is very antifag. He is a member of the Far Right and homophobia is the hottest button he's got to push. So he uses police as decoys—illegal. Now there's a very easy way of stopping this, and I may devote some time to it this winter. Operation Set Up the Police: Wire someone for sound; put him on Selma Avenue. From a distance, train a camera on him. Plainclothesman approaches our decoy. Plainclothesman makes the first move, does the soliciting. Then, as is the merry custom in those parts, a second plainclothesman helps the first to make the arrest, often indulging in a little nonconsenting S and M. Now on tape and film we have the evidence that the police entrapped our decoy, preferably a man: a man with two children and a membership in the Rotary Club. When the plainclothesmen lie in court, as they always do, produce the film and send them to jail. As Thomas Jefferson would say, arrests of this kind would have "a very wholesome effect" on police departments everywhere.

*A number of people have argued that what really changed in the homosexual world in the past ten years in countries like the United States is that the ghetto has come out; most homosexuals still live the sort of life they've always lived but the ghetto is much larger, much more commercial than it ever was. Would you agree?*

I think that's probably true in the major cities. I certainly noticed it in Los Angeles when I was living there last winter. Since I have never lived in a ghetto of any kind, I'm fairly sensitive to in-bred groups, New York literary life, Bel-Air movie-makers, homosexual enclaves anywhere. I think it stunting to live only one kind of life with like-minded people. But then, heteros are as likely to cling to their own kind—I mean socially, economically, ethnically, rather than sexually—as homos. Anyway, at worst, homosexualists tend to mirror heterosexual society, and that the heterosexual society is deeply ill is of more concern to me than that god-awful phrase "life-style." The women's role has changed and with it the role of the family. This is a phenomenon of greater cultural interest than the problems of the homosexualist; it is also related. Between the collapse of Judeo-Christianity and overpopulation-cum-insufficient-energy, there is no great premium on having children—rather, the reverse. Yet everyone's brought up to behave as if the United States were a sparsely populated agrarian society that needs lots more babies. These attitudes are not easily changed.

*Isn't there a contradiction between traditional legalistic procedures, on the one hand, and arguing, on the other, that homosexuals—which I agree with—should become part of a much broader political movement concerned with the great questions?*

I think you have to operate on three, four, five different levels at once. When I'm out speaking to a women's group in Parkersburg, West Virginia,

I'm going to speak in certain terms that I wouldn't use, say, when I'm writing for the *New York Review of Books*. You have to get through as best you can. Means differ. Ends are fairly constant. You must also be prepared to learn from others. Few public figures have this gift. I think that I do—the result of not being a specialist but a generalist. You point to the fact that once the law is changed, you still haven't altered attitudes. Of course you haven't. But one step at a time. Do what you can do. In a country created by lawyers, that means using the law to good ends. Don't worry about being loved or respected or that "gay sensibility" is not recorded as the highest state man has yet achieved.

*I sometimes think the gay movement would be much better off if it said, "Yes, we do harm society and it's a good thing."*

Well, it's a society that should be harmed—that is, altered. Certainly, Judeo-Christianity should be smashed to bits. Except for Christianity, there is no religion more deeply depressing and antilife than the Jewish. But then, Christianity is a Jewish heresy. The hatred of women in the Old Testament is pathological. St. Paul is no improvement. Worse, Christianity is based on murder and torture . . . study the lives of our blessed saints and martyrs . . . that one result of all this emphasis on blood and pain should be S and M is hardly surprising. Which other major religion is based on the godhead incarnate being whipped, tacked to a cross, stabbed? Only the Marquis de Sade could have made up a sicker religion. It's no wonder that those brought up in such a culture hate life and enjoy inflicting pain. All societies are sick, but some are sicker than others. Christian societies are certainly among the sickest. As for the Eastern European paradises . . . well, an Archbishop of Canterbury once called Communism a Christian heresy. We mirror each other.

*Which puts you in conflict with the fastest growing section of the gay movement, the gay churches.*

I'm perfectly willing to accept the gay churches as a tactic. It may be a good idea to get in with the Jesus Christers. When you run with the wolves, said St. Lenin (Eastern rite orthodox), you must howl with the wolves.

*I don't think gay Christians are any less earnest about their Christianity than anyone else.*

If so, they're in trouble, for their religion does not smile upon their practices. But then there were Nazis who were Jews, and in the early days of the movement they would not believe that Hitler really planned to put good National Socialists into concentration camps.

*I suspect the gay churches will be successful in legitimizing homosexual marriages just when heterosexual marriage ceases to exist as a major institution.*

My impression is that the only people interested in marriage are Catholic priests and homosexualists. Most enlightened heterosexuals now avoid marriage in much the same way as Count Dracula steers clear of garlic.

*Is that a form of homosexual self-hatred—it's all right to be homosexual provided you live according to the most rigid tenets of heterosexual society?*

I think society is essentially a whole with many fractured elements within it. Years ago I noticed in so-called enlightened Amsterdam that the faggot arrangements were exactly like the heterosexual arrangements. Everybody was solemn and solid and married—exactly like mummy and daddy or brother and sister-in-law. Nothing wrong with that, of course. But it is not the world of Plato's *Symposium*, where my imagination has its being.

*It's often said that the American literary establishment—you might argue whether there is such a thing—is relentlessly antigay.*

I think that's quite true, at least during the thirty-odd years that I've been writing. Much of this reflects the general ethos of the country. Then there are special problems. The *New York Times* is essentially a Jewish newspaper. Until recently, the editors were a sort of rabbinate upholding Mosaic values. Fag-baiting was routine there. The fifties was a very bad time, in general. But then for most American men—yesterday and now—the only thing worse than being a woman is to be a man who wants to be a woman. The fact that 99.9 percent of homosexualists haven't the slightest desire to be women, nor do they think of themselves as women, is still unknown out there in the wild American dark, and I can't think why. Old Testament canards, I suppose. The fact that all the so-called he-man occupations (warriors, sailors, athletes) are heavily populated by homosexualists is simply denied even though anyone who has served in an army knows otherwise.

*How far have you suffered in terms of reviews, etc., from being known, in your phrase, as a "homosexualist"?*

Contrary to legend, I have never discussed my private life in my work or in public—except once. As a result of something my old friend Jack Kerouac wrote about the two of us in *The Subterraneans*, I responded in *Two Sisters*. By temperament not a self-revealer, on the other hand I've been an activist when it comes to changing laws and so on, and I'd say the reactions to that were pretty venomous. After two highly praised books, I published *The City and the Pillar*. Half the newspapers wouldn't review it, and the *New York Times* would not take advertising for it. Orville Prescott (the daily reviewer for the *Times* and the most powerful bookchat writer in the country) said that not only would he not review that book, but he would never again review a book by me. So my next five novels were not reviewed in the daily *Times*. Silence is a great destroyer. That was how John Horne Burns was, in a sense, murdered by our literary homophobes. But I am not easily destroyed.

*In the study of gay literature that's going on now in the United States you've been classed along with Williams and Capote and Burroughs as one of the important postwar American gay novelists. Do you reject that definition?*

Yes. I deal in other subjects. Politics, history, theology. As a novelist I have dealt with The Subject on occasion. And, prematurely—1948 is a long time ago. But isn't *The City and the Pillar* really about sexual obsession? Admittedly, I show a fair spectrum of a world unknown to the fiction of that day, but the theme was the same as *Lolita*'s with the difference that Nabokov was a middle-aged man when he wrote his masterpiece and I was a twenty-one-year-old ex-soldier when I wrote my ... observations on the middle depths.

But, of course, the heterosexual dictatorship not only recognizes its en-

emies but defines them in its own terms. In the last few months, I have
been singled out not only as the National Fag but as the creator of a new
order that means to destroy The Family, The American Empire, Capitalism, and Warm Mature Heterosexual Relationships. This shit is being dispensed, variously, by Norman Podhoretz in *Harper's* magazine, Joseph
Epstein in *Commentary,* Alfred Kazin in *Esquire,* and what I take to be a
Tel Aviv hotel named the Hilton Kramer in *Partisan Review.* All these
fag-baiters are Jews who have swung to the right, to join Anita Bryant and
the Jesus Christers, who, officially, want us to prepare for that military
showdown with international Communism that will mean (as far as their
American-Jewish allies go) security and victory for Israel. Of course, it
will mean only death for all. But these people are fools and dangerous.
More to the point, they don't realize to what extent they themselves—the
Jews—are hated out there in Goy-Land. If they had any sense, they would
ally themselves with us. But they don't, so. . . .

*You're also regarded as very cynical about romantic love, and since the
gay movement is, by and large, a great believer in romantic love, you've
come in for a certain amount of criticism on that.*

I should hope so. But my lips are sealed on that subject. Since those
who believe in romantic love suffer so much anyway, I would not dream of
adding to their sufferings.

TIM DLUGOS

# A Cruel God: The Gay Challenge to the Catholic Church

*B*ob Hummel spent the evening of
Monday, March 6, alone in his small suite at Georgetown University. For
Hummel, a graduate student and dormitory director, weeknights were
often a quiet time, passed in reading and working on his dissertation in
medical ethics. But this particular evening he was especially grateful for
the solitude.

The previous morning, in an interview in the *Washington Star,* Hummel had admitted that he was a homosexual. In a city with as large and

visible a gay population as Washington, such an admission would not be newsworthy at all except for one significant fact: Bob Hummel is a Roman Catholic priest.

Toward eleven the phone rang. The call was from a friend in Richmond, Virginia, the seat of Hummel's home diocese.

"You're all over the papers down here," said the friend. "Were you surprised?"

"By the publicity? A little," replied Hummel.

"The publicity?" Hummel's friend paused. "Don't tell me you haven't heard."

"Heard what?"

"Bob, the bishop's told the papers down here that he's suspended you from the priesthood."

That was how Bob Hummel learned that he had been officially forbidden to "offer Mass, hear confessions, and preach the Gospel"—forbidden, that is, to exercise the ministry to which he had solemnly professed his life. The prohibition came not as a result of what Bob Hummel did or did not *do* but because of who he *is*——an openly gay member of that most respected of clubs, the Catholic clergy, with the temerity to believe that his religious commitment and his sexual identity are not mutually exclusive.

The flurry in the papers over Hummel's suspension was just the first in a series of confrontations between Catholic officials and proponents of gay rights that kept religious reporters hopping from Washington to Boston to Mount Rainier, Maryland, to New York all spring. At times, the situation must have seemed to America's bishops like a summer in Southern California, when smoke drifts from a dozen brush fires into a deceptively peaceful sky. Conflagration (read "bad press" or "controversy") is what these custodians in the Repository of Faith worry most about. But gay Catholics with torches have only begun to struggle for what they see as their rightful place in a church that condemns their love lives when it does not deny their existence.

This article is about the Catholic men and women helping with that struggle: laity, sisters, brothers, priests, and even an occasional bishop. Some are homosexual; some are not. Some have asked me to conceal their identities; their requests bear witness to the actual practice of an institution that, in theory, defines authority as "freedom to serve." In writing this article I have learned once more that the struggle I describe is my own. For years I called myself a "Catholic with a sense of paradox": an ex-Catholic religious, an ex-Catholic Resister, an off-and-on ex-Catholic. My experience as a writer and gay man living in New York coexisted uneasily with my loyalty to orthodox religious formulations ("There is no God and Mary is His mother," as Santayana quipped in a different context).

That dilemma is shared by thousands of gay Catholics who are unwilling to throw out the baby with the baptismal water—unwilling, that is, to abandon the message of Christian love and the sacramental presence of their Lord because of the oppression perpetuated by some of his current earthly representatives. However painful, however frustrating, gay Catholics are discovering that the tension between episcopal pronouncement and grass-roots practice can be an important source of creativity. What is more, it is part of a great Judeo-Christian tradition that dates back as far as the Old Testament bickering between priests (the codifiers of the Law) and prophets (who break through to find new applications). And, as Edmund White has pointed out, the existence of "gay people" as a self-defined group is historically a new phenomenon.

In exploring how gay Catholics create their identity, I have become aware of unresolved tensions in myself (I am as nervous about coming out as a Roman to certain friends in Manhattan as I was about coming out as gay to Catholic friends and relatives). I've also rediscovered a large capacity for anger. But, for better or worse, I am once again grappling with my religious roots.

*Religion*, as every first-year seminarian knows, means literally "to bind back." Gay Catholics might take heart from that most paradoxical of observers, Jesus Christ, who insisted that, in the process of returning to our common source, the cords that bind are cut and we are finally home free.

I

I visited Georgetown University on a wet and warm spring morning, the kind of weather that heightens one's impression of Washington as a city upholstered in green. In contrast to late-winter Manhattan, the tentative foliage, blooming forsythia, and new grass between the simple markers in the Jesuit cemetery made Georgetown look positively lush. On an athletic field in the distance a lacrosse squad counted off their exercises, mock-military style, in the soft drizzle: "One-two-three-*one*. One-two-three-*two*." There was no other sound. Georgetown bore no outward sign of the battle over gay rights that had polarized it for nearly a year. The most prominent casualty of that battle was waiting for me in his office on the ground floor of Harbin Hall, a contemporary dormitory tower cleverly situated at the bottom of a hill so as not to dwarf the school's trademark gray battlements.

At first meeting, Bob Hummel conveys contrasting impressions—friendly yet distant, stocky yet trim—that somehow resolve themselves after a few minutes of conversation. He had a press packet ready (reporters had been falling in for interviews at an amazing rate), which contained his correspondence with Bishop Walter Sullivan. Hummel settled back in his desk chair and talked with considerable alacrity—and not a trace of regret.

"I grew up in Brooklyn, though my grandparents are from Virginia," he began. His first stab at a religious vocation was as a Trinitarian, an order whose original members had vowed to ransom Christians from the Turks by becoming slaves themselves if necessary. The priesthood, he says, offered "a very protective environment, literally a way to salvation." But community life "proved a little stifling for me, so I joined the Richmond diocese in 1968."

Hummel studied theology at St. Mary's Seminary on Paca Street in Baltimore. In the year before his ordination, he served as a counseling intern in a hospital, beginning a highly effective career as a chaplain and counselor to the sick and dying. One year after his ordination, while sitting in Mary's, a Baltimore gay bar, Hummel saw a friend—another priest—enter the bar.

"He didn't recognize me, but I saw him," recalled Hummel in an interview in the *Star* that was picked up by the Associated Press. "He was drunk and obviously in a great deal of pain. I was shocked to see another priest there. I guess I was pretty innocent and naive, because I thought I was the only gay priest in the world."

Back in Richmond, Hummel continued his hospital ministry, conducting therapy sessions for teenagers and counseling the dying, children, and surgical patients. His specialty was working with families and patients in emergency rooms and intensive care. Gradually, Hummel established a pastoral-care department at St. Mary's hospital; in a short time he had hired six other counselors to work with him. Two years ago he received permission to study for a doctorate in medical ethics at Georgetown.

Hummel's professional growth paralleled what he calls "grappling with the authenticity of my own life."

"I'd known I was gay since I was fourteen, but I'd never dealt with it because of guilt and fear. (The Catholic church is an expert at guilt and fear.) Gradually, I started seeing that being gay wasn't bad, it was good. And that older priest in the bar, obviously alcoholic . . . I've seen a lot more since then."

(The implication that there may be hordes of gay priests "out there" may well be the most threatening element of Bob Hummel's disclosure as far as the church is concerned. Combined with the theme of priestly alcoholism—a staple of best-selling fiction from Edwin O'Connor's *The Edge of Sadness* to Mary Gordon's *Final Payments*—the charge gains additional drama and a kind of credence by association. In a church still touchy about the allegations of *Maria Monk*—a virulent nineteenth-century anti-Catholic tract—and other such propaganda, one begins to understand why Hummel's bishop would punish him for "causing much public harm and consternation." According to Bishop Sullivan's letter of suspension, Hummel's offense was one of scandal, not sex. Interestingly, the bishop's press release reads exactly the opposite.)

At Georgetown, Hummel got a job as a dorm director. He also became the campus's leading champion of a group of gay students who were trying to win official university recognition for their organization. By the summer of 1978 Hummel decided it was time to take a public stand. He announced that he was gay to his friends, his family, and his bishop, who was widely regarded as one of America's most socially progressive churchmen.

"I told the bishop that I was gay, that I was going to continue to work with the gay students' group, and that I didn't know where this would take me," recalls Hummel. "I'd seen the kind of oppression the gay students and faculty faced at Georgetown, and this was something I had to do."

The bishop's reaction?

"He was very supportive. He told me that if things got out of hand he might have to do something, but that he'd let me know if that were the case and we could discuss it. He didn't even bring up the possibility of suspending my faculties. And he knew I was gay long before the *Star* story."

Was the question of Bob's priestly vow of celibacy raised?

"I kept it on a theoretical level," he says. "Of course, the celibacy issue is always raised to undermine credibility. But I don't think it's pertinent to the issue of *being* gay. After all, it's never asked of heterosexual priests."

As pressure for university recognition of the gay group mounted, Bob was interviewed in the *Hoya*, Georgetown's campus newspaper. Asked if he was gay himself, he answered yes. The interview ran in September 1978, with no reaction from Bishop Sullivan.

"There hasn't been one issue of the student newspaper this year that didn't deal with the gay group," notes Hummel. "I think it resulted in a certain growth of acceptance and understanding." Reflecting that acceptance, the Student Senate voted 11 to 2 last winter to recognize the gay students as an official university organization. At the same meeting they rejected a bid for a campus Right to Life chapter. The next day, the university administration overturned both decisions and created a campuswide crisis.

At that point the University Forum (a student club) asked Hummel to debate Andre Hellegers on the issue of gay rights. (Hellegers, who died last May, was director of the university's Kennedy Institute for Ethics.) The debate took place at the 1789, a pub popular among the students, and drew a standing-room crowd inside—and four uniformed American Nazi pickets outside, brandishing antigay placards. It was the Nazis who finally captured the attention of Washington's major dailies (swastikas sell papers).

The *Star* called Hummel for a followup interview the next week. But the interview about the rights of gay students turned out to be a profile of an openly gay priest. Bob Hummel found himself a national celebrity.

"The biggest disappointment," says Hummel sadly, "is the way gay priests have been cowered into a hypocritical stance, and then try to justify their hypocrisy. Being gay is a good thing. I can use it for my own growth and to help others grow. I think there is no justification for anyone to be in the closet, especially a gay priest.

"There's such a primitive level of discourse about the issue. You can't even discuss the theological implications of what celibacy means in a gay context. But I can go to any gay bar in Washington and point out one or two priests. I know a lot of gay priests, and I've noticed a real pulling back from me since this hit. I have the feeling that not too many people want to be identified with me—it's a natural reaction to living in the closet. I understand it but I don't agree with it.

"What I've had to do as a person is to tear up a lot of old value systems. I can't compromise with who I am—that's schizophrenic and hypocritical. The main responsibility for any gay Christian is to live as authentically as possible. For survival, we have to realize that the institution is bigoted. We have to reach a point of ethical self-actualization," he concludes, the jargon of his academic discipline creeping into his speech.

Hummel seems as undaunted by his bishop's actions as he was by the harassment that followed him around campus (an office window broken, the taunts of students, "lots of uncreatively obscene phone calls"). He will stay on at Georgetown and get his degree; the university has renewed his contract as dorm director for another year. With the Jesuits' traditional independence from diocesan politics, the school views Hummel's suspension as "a private matter between my bishop and myself."

What will he do after he obtains his doctorate?

"I did a lot of thinking after Harvey Milk was killed," says Hummel. "I'll probably go into politics eventually, in D.C."

Bob Hummel is no longer trying to defend himself to his diocese. ("The church isn't open to that," he says simply.) Instead, he is making some demands of his own. In a letter to Bishop Sullivan, written two weeks after his suspension, Hummel asked the bishop for a statement of full acceptance of openly gay people in the ministry and a fully supported ministry to gay people. "It is only with these," he wrote, "that there can be any hope in conquering the social and cultural prejudice from which we suffer. . . . If there is the possibility of such an official statement, then I would be more than willing to meet with you at your convenience. If this possibility does not exist, then I will view my suspension, for the present time at least, as a witness to the alienation which all gay Catholics must continue to suffer." Addressing the charge of scandal, Hummel declared pithily, "To advocate that an individual keep silence in the face of oppression seems to me to be the ultimate scandal."

"I've seen thousands of people die and lots of regrets," said Hummel in a low voice, looking out the window at the spring rain. "Even if I were to die tomorrow, I'd feel comfortable with what I've done. That's a unique experience. I've used the gifts I have to make a positive statement about being gay, being who I am and being Catholic. It's brought a sense of freedom I'd like to communicate to everyone."

Bob Hummel suggested that I contact Jim Ryan, the president of Georgetown's gay student organization, for another perspective on gay rights on a Catholic campus. When I met Jim for lunch the next afternoon, my first experience was an overwhelming sense of déja vu.

Partly, it was because we met in Mr. Henry's. As a novice in a Catholic brotherhood ten years ago, I would occasionally slip out of the novitiate in Maryland and drive to Georgetown (into "the world," as we half-jokingly referred to all nonconsecrated ground) to hoist beers with high-school friends at Mr. Henry's. In 1973, when I moved back to Washington after abandoning college and Catholicism for the (largely imaginary) glamour of life as a poet, I sat in the same bar with friends from Georgetown, listening to them plot strategies to obtain university recognition of . . . yes, a gay student group. Listening to Jim Ryan, whose voice and manner uncannily resemble those of the first Georgetown gay group's first president, I recognized whole sentences of argument. Through his story of coming out ran a religious thread peculiar to Catholic men (although most Catholic gay men may never express it). I began to realize, from the quiet determination in the way Jim Ryan spoke, that this time around the gay students at Georgetown may win their fight.

Jim Ryan is a Georgetown classic: neatly trimmed dark hair, stylish glasses, slim frame sheathed in a Lacoste shirt and neatly pressed jeans, de rigeur Top-Siders. His face is a paradigm of the Good Catholic Student: his eyes lively, his expression meditative. He is slow to speak and a good listener; his humor is quiet, his sincerity disarming. He is what they call *priestly*, I realized with a start. Like so many other gay Catholic men, that is what Jim once thought he was, too.

"In high school," explained Jim, "I'd seriously considered the priest-hood, for all the wrong reasons. The first person I ever told that I was gay was a priest. He advised me to leave home and do some thinking on my own."

So instead of going to Fordham (near his home in the Bronx), Jim went to the State University of New York in Albany for two years, where "I did a lot of walking around and being depressed." He remembers it as a lonely time; it was largely because of that loneliness that he transferred to Georgetown for his junior year ("from a liberal school in a conservative town to a conservative school in a liberal town," he smiles).

On his summer vacations in New York, Jim had attended Masses sponsored by Dignity, an organization for gay Catholics. In Washington, Dignity's weekly mass is celebrated on the Georgetown campus (no parish has been given official approval to say the masses, and the Archdiocese of Washington has spread the unofficial word that they will turn down any formal requests). Through Dignity/D.C., Jim discovered the gay student movement. He went to a meeting in the spring, which turned out to be the group's annual election. As one of two people present who were not gradu-ating seniors, Ryan suddenly found himself the group's president—and the most visible homosexual at Georgetown.

"I got phone calls telling me how easily my kneecaps could be broken with a crowbar," he remembers. "Born-again Christians followed me around campus, telling me they were praying for me. Some of the Jesuits were sympathetic—they told me their doors were always open if I wanted to discuss my illness."

For all that, Jim is resolute in his affirmation that, "If there's any place that needs a gay student group, it's a Catholic school."

"I remember the guilt trip I had to deal with in coming out," he says. "A lot of people at Georgetown are dealing with that right now. To be that lonely and that afraid and not to be able to share it with anyone else is really hell.

"There are no university services for gay people at Georgetown. Gay students have been told by Jesuit counselors, 'Don't worry, you don't look gay' or 'You just haven't met the right woman yet.' " (This lack of sensitiv-ity extends to the women who now study at the formerly all-male school. Last year Georgetown's Student Health Service refused to hire a gynecolo-gist because they had determined that the only purpose for such a specialist would be to promote abortion and contraception.)

"At a conference on sexuality that the university sponsored," continued Jim, "a Jesuit told me, 'I feel sorry for you, you haven't developed prop-erly.' Scientific evidence to the contrary is discounted. It's hard to deal with dogmatism."

The group Jim Ryan heads is in the process of appealing the univer-sity's decision not to recognize them, a process that could take months, de-pending on how long each administrator tries to stall his answer. After they receive the final no—which the group fully expects—the next step will be a class action suit against the university. Several Washington law-yers are willing to take the case pro bono.

"I feel good about what's happening at Georgetown," concludes Jim.

"We've gotten the subject out of the closet. But it's frustrating, like hitting your head against a rather well-built wall."

As a Catholic, Ryan says that he has "had to draw distinctions between the message and spirit of the Bible and the narrow interpretations of people who are antigay. Whoever Christ was, the university has used the *symbol* of Christ to justify hatred and oppression. And that's unconscionable.

"In a lot of ways," says Ryan, "straight priests in the Georgetown administration aren't our problem. It's the gay priests, who want to protect their positions, who are totally opposed to us. I know of at least five or six gay priests who are still in the closet. I've seen them in bars and other places haunted by gays. Dignity has fifteen chaplains, but not one of them has given a bit of support to Bob Hummel."

"Bob Hummel sold Sullivan down the drain when Sullivan was trying to be understanding," said Don Fredey emphatically.

We were in the sitting-room half of his small suite in a Catholic rectory in suburban Washington. The suite was decorated with a loving precision I remember from my days as a brother, when each community member's room was a carefully stuffed cubbyhole of warmth and color, in contrast to the bland institutional air that hung over the "common rooms" (refectory, library, lounge). A Hummel music box—an ironic touch—lay open on a table underneath framed pages of the *Missale Romanum*. A tank of tropical fish burbled on the bookcase. In one corner was a makeshift scripture stand, a table covered with a white cloth and a Jerusalem Bible open to Psalm I. We were drinking bourbon.

I have known Don Fredey since just after his ordination. He coached a rival debate team when I was in high school; years later, a mutual friend ran into him at the Lost & Found (D.C.'s most popular gay disco), and our social circles intersected again. One year, Don came to a Christmas party at my apartment. A month later, my lover and I found ourselves the only nonclerics at a mammoth gay New Year's party in his rectory (the pastor was out of town). I recall one distinguished seminary rector talking that night about his fear that the young gardener he had been forced to fire would blab about their affair. It sounded like a bad French novel, until I realized that each of the men in the room—and there were at least seventy, from seminarians to retired *monsignori*—could face the same kind of threat to their careers and reputations any day. They moved in a world as clandestine as those of gay diplomats and gay Hollywood stars. Don Fredey is not publicly homosexual and does "not admire" Bob Hummel's public stand.

"Bob went down to Sullivan and Sullivan was very fair. He said, 'As long as you're discreet about it, you can come out on campus.' Sullivan's not antigay. He's appointed two priests as chaplains to Dignity/Richmond and he's celebrated mass for them himself. But when Bob came out in the papers, Sullivan felt betrayed. And the apostolic delegate [the Vatican's representative in the United States] called Sullivan to complain. . . . He couldn't let that pass by."

Don is forthright in private about his own homosexuality and says that his vocation as a priest is in no way compromised by his sex life. "Occasionally there is a little interference," he admits with a smile. "For instance, the guy I'm seeing yelled 'Jesus Christ!' at an ecstatic moment and later apologized for using the Lord's name in vain." As an actively gay priest, Don can "be comfortable in the sight of God, but I know I couldn't make a good case to my bishop."

Hasn't Don taken a vow of celibacy?

"Originally celibacy was an expedient law to prevent church property from passing to a priest's children," he explains. "It wasn't required of diocesan priests until early in the ninth century. It had to do with preventing families, not with preventing sex. I can see maintaining celibacy—that is, having no sex at all—in a religious order. It can be divisive in a community for people to be sleeping with each other. Some religious houses in Washington have sizable gay minorities that go to the bars. That's bad. But for a diocesan priest like myself, I think celibacy basically means not having a marital, or an exclusive, relationship with anyone."

I asked Don if he was worried about pretending to be something he was not.

"The only word to use is hypocrisy," he replied. "I feel terribly compromised by the whole thing. It's important for me not to lie—though some people may see me as living a lie." He paused. "But if I were in Bob Hummel's place, if I went public, I'd have to leave this area and start from scratch again, somewhere far away. It would absolutely destroy my effectiveness as a minister."

Is Don's ministry effective now?

"Well, not to our gay parishioners. We pretend they don't exist. We have a homophobic pastor, but our parish really isn't a traditional 'family' parish. We have the elderly, young singles, young marrieds without children, gays, Spanish people, Vietnamese—and we have special programs for all of the other minorities, but not for the gays."

Several years ago, while getting a doctorate in another state, Don was a Dignity chaplain. But word filtered back to his home archdiocese that he was working in the gay ministry, and as a result Don eventually stopped working with Dignity. He suspects the informant was a priest he knows who "does tearooms and rest areas and hasn't really accepted himself as a gay person or resolved that with his priesthood. Some of the worst homophobes are guys in the clergy and hierarchy who are gay," he explains.

Just how many gay priests are there?

"In my own archdiocese, I'd say 10 percent are gay, not all of them functioning [his word for having sex]. Some would consider it 'falling.' Others occasionally function. There's only one priest in the archdiocese I know of who goes to bars. I know of three who have lovers or ongoing affairs. But I don't *want* to know gay priests in my own archdiocese."

Despite the rather predictable percentage of homosexuals he has discovered among his fellow priests, Don avers that the *issue* of homosexuality permeates a priest's life from seminary on. "We had a saying in the seminary," he relates, "that if you weren't queer when you came in, you certainly gave it a second thought after all the emphasis everyone put on it."

There are situations Don would feel uncomfortable in; for instance, if a teacher in the local Catholic high school were exposed as gay. "I'm not sure what I'd do, but I'd probably recommend that he be fired," he says slowly. "The parents shouldn't be asked to accept that. They send their kids to us to protect them." In other situations, Don is more comfortable, such as when he is counseling gay people who do not know that he is gay himself. "In counseling, you try to get the person to make up their own mind, and then affirm them," he explains. "I'm a good counselor." He is telling the truth. I remember kids I knew ten years ago whose lives he helped straighten out.

What would Don say to a gay Catholic who felt rejected by the church?

"The church is the People of God," Don replies quickly. "No one can really tell you if you belong or not. A gay person has to have the strength of character to say, 'I am part of this body. You can't throw me out. I'm family.' That's what people in Dignity are doing. I see progress in the official church about that. I wouldn't be surprised to see [Rev. John] McNeill's point about the natural law including homosexuality adopted in twenty years. But the church often operates on expediency. When the general public accepts gays more, the church will go along.

"When it comes to change, there are two ways to go. The Catholic Church says to move slowly and keep as many as you can in the fold. Some of the smaller Protestant churches are able to say, 'Move fast and let those who want to, follow.' The church will never come out and say, 'You don't belong.' But the bishops will have their fingers in the wind long after the Unitarians and small Protestant sects have said, 'Gays can be full followers of the church.' It's hard to move people in a direction they don't want to move in."

Two Sundays after its interview with Father Robert Hummel, the *Washington Star* printed two letters commenting on the controversy, one supportive of the priest, the other opposing him. Here is the text of the supportive letter:

> When I read of the cruel actions of some Georgetown University students who taunted Father Robert F. Hummel, the self-acknowledged homosexual priest pursuing his studies at Georgetown, I was both angry and disgusted. Instead of studying economics, history, etc., these students should take a course in "how to be more human."
>
> They remind me of the mob of people who on Palm Sunday were proclaiming Jesus as their King yet on the following Friday helped to crucify him. I am not in agreement with the life-style of homosexuals, but I believe Christ loves every one of us, be we sinners or otherwise. He forgave and showed compassion to Mary Magdalene and the woman at the well.
>
> Shame, shame on these students! They are little people. Perhaps they should look at their own life-styles before they judge others'.
>
> Did not Christ say, "He who is without sin, let him cast the first stone"? Also I believe the Richmond bishop and the clergy should look within themselves and show more understanding and compassion.

The letter did not come from a priest, a member of Dignity, or even a gay Catholic. It was signed Mary C. Dlugos—my mother. I was flabbergasted (one of my mother's words) to see it. My mother's devout loyalty to the church and its teachings defines and completes the genre "Irish Catholic." She had told nobody, including me, that she had written a letter in support of Bob Hummel.

The evening the *Star* printed the letter, my mother received an anonymous phone call.

"Do you believe what you wrote?" asked a male voice.

"Of course," replied my mother.

"Well, young lady, you're very naive. If I ever see that so-called priest, I'll take a shotgun and blow his head off."

"Thank you for your expression of opinion," said my mother in her most deadpan talk-show-host imitation. Then she hung up.

## II

Paul Shanley is a new kind of Catholic priest. I don't mean he's part of that so-called new breed of committed and engaging young clerics disgorged by major seminaries at regular intervals, about whom the only new thing is their charming enthusiasm for work. They are the contemporary equivalents of the popular young priests of my childhood—crew-cut, idealistic, doctrinally pristine big brothers who played basketball with high-school jocks on Saturday morning, then bawled them out in the confessional later that day for masturbating.

Shanley's youthful enthusiasm belies his twenty-plus years as a priest. He can be almost overwhelmingly engaging. These surface qualities, however, are not what makes his role new. Shanley is one of a handful of priests (Dan Berrigan is another) who have come under attack from the Catholic hierarchy and large parts of the Catholic community for the oddest of reasons—because their ministries have been so successful. They are just too good for comfort. Shanley, after a traditional start as a chaplain to cops and juvenile delinquents, managed to work his way into two of the most controversial apostolates around.

As Boston's nationally famous "Street Priest" in the sixties, Shanley worked among the multitudes of disaffected young who had flocked to that city looking for an East Coast version of the Haight. It never quite materialized, but Shanley became one of the best-known features of Boston's near-miss Love Culture (along with the music of the Ultimate Spinach and the thrill of dropping acid while riding in a Swan Boat in the Public Garden). Although he had been appointed special chaplain to runaways by Cardinal Cushing himself, Shanley drew conservative fire for his long hair and love beads, as well as for such shocking statements as his observation that smoking pot does not necessarily lead to heroin addiction. But those criticisms were mild compared to the flak he received in his next post as the only Catholic priest in the world engaged in a full-time ministry to sexual minorities.

Shanley was assigned to that post in 1970 by Cardinal Humberto Madeiros, who had replaced Cushing as Boston's archbishop. "He told me,

'Go with my blessings,' " remembers Shanley. " 'They'll hate you, but they already hate me because I'm Portuguese.' " Over the next eight years, however, the cardinal came to regret his endorsement of Shanley's new ministry. As in his work with the children of the streets, Shanley discovered that Catholicism's myths about gay life did not fit the facts—and he did not hesitate to share his findings with anyone who would listen.

"The cardinal hoped that I'd get homosexuals to shrinks, forgive their sins, and keep them from sinning again," says Shanley. "I found that they weren't sick, they weren't sinful, and that Jesus had gotten there long before Shanley and the Catholic church."

Such observations, as well as the assertion that "it is homophobia, the fear of homosexuals, which properly belongs on the couch and in the confessional," made Shanley one of the country's most popular and provocative lecturers in pastoral techniques and gave him enormous credibility among his widely scattered flock—except in Boston, where issues of sexual morality seem to carry even more weight (if such were possible) than in the rest of the American church. For instance, Cardinal Madeiros refused the sacrament of baptism to an infant whose parents supported a woman's right to an abortion, then arranged the expulsion from the Jesuits of a priest who defied his ban. It was almost inevitable that Paul Shanley would find his work on an ecclesiastical hit list.

The ax fell last March. Shanley was removed from his free-lance ministry and assigned to an upper-middle-class parish in the Boston suburbs. There was no longer any need for a special ministry to sexual minorities, the cardinal declared; it was a tribute to Shanley's success that now any priest in the archdiocese could deal with homosexuals in the confessional.

"In the *confessional*!" The sarcasm in Shanley's voice is only slightly mitigated by the deep humor in his eyes (eyes that actually smile, as in the famous song). He uncrosses his legs, then crosses them again. In the airy parlor of the rectory where he now lives, his nervous energy seems as out of place as the subject under discussion.

"I'm not concerned with gays in the *confessional*. Most of the gays I worked with don't go to confession. They've left the Catholic church—and I'd say rightfully so—to maintain their sanity. They didn't leave God or spirituality, of course. They left the homophobia of the institution. But even if every priest *were* capable of dealing with gays, how about the other sexual minorities? What happens to them?" (Shanley has identified thirty-one of these groups besides homosexuals; he will not list them, though, saying that to do so would be less useful than sensationalistic.)

Shanley has used scientific information-gathering techniques, in addition to his counseling skills, to make his work with sexual minorities more effective. Nevertheless, he claims, "My expertise is narrow. I'm supposed to be knowledgeable about the prediction and prevention of juvenile problems. In the early sixties, I saw that the big problem coming down the road would be drugs. In the early seventies, I realized it would be sexual confusion." Toward the end of his ministry to street youth, Shanley says, more than half of the runaways with whom he worked were homosexual. Today, youth counselors tell him the figure approaches 80 percent. Often they are youngsters from Catholic families, who have been disowned for being gay.

"It's a cultural prejudice," observes Shanley, "but it's been justified by religion. They think it's their theology that makes them hate gays, but it's their culture." In an interview in the *Boston Globe* (Shanley sometimes seems to get as much press exposure in Boston as all other archdiocesan phenomena combined), he went further: "It's incredible the ease with which parents can destroy one of the strongest bonds in humanity. I remember twenty years ago, Catholics throwing their children out if they married a Protestant. I remember ten years ago, parents disowning their children as cowards because they were conscientious objectors. Today, many parents will put their children out because they happen to be homosexual."

After receiving the cardinal's permission for his ministry to sexual minorities, Shanley tried to visit every gay gathering place in Boston at least once a month.

"When I first timidly came into the gay scene I was scared. But the only time I was shocked was when I went into a gay bar and saw five hundred men in one room dancing with each other. I had never seen a man *touching* another man, never mind dancing with one. I sat down, quickly downed my drink, and ordered a second—and haven't been shocked since."

Shanley ran into many gay priests and seminarians in his forays into Boston's gay world. "There was one section of the dance floor in the 1270 which was jokingly referred to as 'Catholic Corner,' " he recalls. "In one night, I met twelve seminarians from one order alone. And of course, there's a high number of ex-seminarians in the gay community.

"I've been told that 80 percent of all applicants to the priesthood are gay. But that shouldn't shock anyone. It's obvious why. If you're eighteen, gay, and Catholic, what's in store for you? You're told that God is going to hate you, society's going to hate you, the church is going to hate you. Your own mother will hate you if she finds out. But if you become a priest, you don't have to get married. God will love you, society will love you, the church will love you. And of course, your mother will love you. If Catholics knew what we know about gay priests and seminarians, the church would be decimated," asserts Shanley. "But then," he adds with a sardonic half-smile, "it's already been decimated."

Shanley is puzzled by the lack of official reasons behind his removal from his ministry to gays. (Interestingly, he clings to notions of due process and reasoned judgment in an institution that is not required to give a reason for anything it does—a literal definition of "irresponsibility.")

"Madeiros said he'd had three letters complaining about my latest tape cassette," explains Shanley, whose work has generated a number of commercially sold educational tapes on the subjects of youth, religion, and sexuality. The tape in question is a debate between Shanley and Professor Richard Lovelace, author of the United Presbyterian church's 1978 report recommending that homosexuals be barred from ordination. "But the cardinal wouldn't show me the letters or tell me what they contained. In fact, he hadn't even listened to the tape."

A long pastoral letter issued four months after Shanley's dismissal made Madeiros's official position on a gay ministry public, if not exactly clear.

"He says that no one priest will be assigned as a minister to sexual minorities," comments Shanley, "that all priests should do it. The letter contains the necessary things—love homosexuals, try to help them—then becomes a thirteenth-century supertraditional diatribe, almost, against gays. He says that he will authorize no priest to celebrate mass for gay people, whatever that means—no priest has to have his authorization to say a mass—and that homosexuals shouldn't congregate together. On page one of his letter, he tells us that homosexuals should be celibate. Then, on page thirteen, we learn that homosexuals won't be allowed in the seminary because they can't be celibate. He says he consulted with people before he wrote the letter. I want to know who they were—not any gay groups I know of."

In fact, the cardinal has told Shanley that he will not meet with any " 'homosexuals as homosexuals,' whatever that means." (A week after the pastoral letter from Cardinal Madeiros denied the need for a gay ministry in Boston, the Diocese of Trenton appointed college chaplain Rev. Vincent Inghilterra to do precisely that work.)

Shanley sees Cardinal Madeiros's refusal to perceive the special dilemma of gay Catholics as a form of blindness. "He tells me that gays are welcome at any Catholic church in the world. I told him I would send a letter to every parish in Boston saying, 'Dear Monsignor or Father: Because the cardinal tells us the church's doors are open to gay people, I and one hundred homosexuals will visit your parish for Mass next Sunday.' He knows as well as I do that blood would run in the streets if that ever happened."

Does Shanley believe that gay Catholics should remain in the church and fight for change?

"Well," he observes, "part of what precipitated my extremity is the fact that so many liberal and radical Catholics have dropped out, ceding the church to the conservatives. Who pays the bills calls the shots. Things won't change as long as the reactionary element is in the driver's seat. Sometimes I feel like I'm presiding at a requiem. Madeiros is burying the church in this diocese. On the other hand, I realize the constant emotional drain that fighting has been for so many people, and I understand why they leave. My ministry wasn't exclusively to gay Catholics, though. The people I care about stopped caring about what Humberto Madeiros thinks long ago."

When asked why he has not left the church himself, Shanley thinks a long time before replying. "If you look at the world in general, I think you'll see the church is doing more good than harm," he says slowly. "Vis-à-vis sexual minorities, it's doing more harm than good—I mean, the present conservators of the church are. But I guess I'm still here because it's my church."

One positive effect of Shanley's reassignment is that now he can speak openly about the particularly touchy subjects he was forbidden to discuss while working directly with gay people.

"The cardinal forbade me to do four things in my ministry to gays: to say mass for homosexuals; to start a gay parish; to encourage gay unions; and to give my opinion on the morality of homosexual acts."

Is Shanley in favor of special parishes for gays who want to stay in the church?

"It's up to gay people to decide what they want," he replies. "Personally I'm not in favor of a gay parish, but I'd defend the right of people to have one. I'm not in favor of parochial schools either, but if people want them and can support them, then it's up to them."

Would he encourage gay unions?

"I certainly would," Shanley quickly announces. "I don't mean marriage in the sacramental sense. We haven't gotten that far yet, though I wouldn't preclude it as a possibility in the future. But for constitutional, irreversible homosexuals—gays whose histories have given evidence that promiscuity is the only other avenue open to them—I think a union is the only choice. The whole Catholic position requiring homosexuals to be celibate implies that gays are more intelligent or morally stronger than straight people. It's poor pastoral theology. No potent heterosexual has ever been asked to be celibate. Yet we ask it of 20 million gays.

"The church thinks of celibacy as a charism, a special gift of the Holy Spirit. People who enter religious life are supposed to possess that charism. With all the spiritual, institutional, and cultural support they get, ten thousand priests have left the church because of celibacy. How impossible it must be for gay people, who have none of that support! To *require* celibacy of them impoverishes the charism as well. A God who would give a gay person all the equipment, all the sexual needs, all the sexual desires—a whole sexuality like everyone else has—and then thumb his nose and say, 'You can never use it, alone or with others'—that would be a cruel God."

Shanley sees a gradual acceptance of his position on gay unions among the predominantly Catholic audiences who attend his lectures on the subject of counseling gays. "I put it to them as a question," he says. "When a fourteen-year-old asks you what his life choices will be if he's gay, what do you tell him? Then I list the alternatives. He can marry the opposite sex. He can enter a gay union. He can be promiscuous. He can enter religious life, though the cardinal claims there is no bishop in the country who will knowingly ordain an avowed homosexual. He can be celibate. Or he can commit suicide. Those are the alternatives. There aren't any others. Five years ago, many people in my audiences would have told the fourteen-year-old to get ready for a lifetime of celibacy. Now they don't object to the notion of gay unions."

The change in attitude doesn't seem to touch the church's hierarchy. ("Bishops don't listen," quips Shanley, "bishops teach.") When the subject under discussion is a change in the sexual mores to which the church devotes so much time and energy, a receptive ear is especially hard to find. "The Catholic mind is prurient," observes Shanley. "It goes right to the bed."

The most ominous overtone of Shanley's reassignment is that it seems to have made Catholic audiences chary about inviting him to speak. Within a month after his ouster hit the papers, four speaking engagements were cancelled. One of those speeches was to be made before the New England Congress of Religious Education, a group Shanley has addressed in previous years. According to Father William McCaffrey, the president of the new group that holds the congress, the publicity about Shanley was a factor in rescinding the invitation.

"The congress is sponsored by New England's bishops and managed by the diocesan directors of religious education," explained McCaffrey. "We had previously had some difficulty with controversial speakers. William Loeb objected to one of our guests a few years back." (Loeb was the ultraconservative publisher of the Manchester, New Hampshire, *Union-Leader*.) "We had approved Paul as a speaker a year ago. At our executive committee meeting in January his name was brought up, not by his own diocese but by a diocese outside of Massachusetts. We decided to check to see if he had the support of his own diocesan director of religious education and of the local bishop. That support was not forthcoming.

"It was a corporate decision not to invite him," concluded McCaffrey. "One of the goals of our congress is to maintain the support of the bishop."

After visiting Paul Shanley, I drove west along the Massachusetts Turnpike toward my next stop. The highway passed within miles of the places where I had been formed as a Catholic. The familiar road signs near Springfield filled me with a sense of connection to those places that I have not felt in years. "East Longmeadow" meant St. Michael's parish, where I first served Mass, where I dreaded benediction because I was so awkward with the censer ("Love your drag, but your purse is on fire" is the classic gay punch line about the ceremony) and where I made many Miraculous Medal novenas. "Springfield—Liberty Street" meant Sacred Heart School, where the St. Dominic Savio Classroom Club elected me "Savio of the Year" in 1963. (St. Dominic died in 1852 at age fourteen; his motto was "Death But Not Sin." I remember being impressed that he had a motto.) "West Springfield" meant the Passionist Monastery, where I went to meetings of the CVC (Catholic Vocation Club, Connecticut Valley Chapter) on Saturdays, where we made many visits to the chapel and had long discussions about the relative merits of minor seminary and Boston College Prep.

I had forgotten that my destination, near Albany, also contained a childhood memory, until I pulled into the long driveway of the seminary in the hills, saw the low granite building, and realized I had been there before, on an altar boys' outing seventeen or eighteen years ago. I remembered best the enormous pool and the chapel, where dozens of cassock-clad men had knelt for evening prayer.

The population of Our Lady of the Berkshires Seminary (as I will call it) has diminished considerably; the outward trappings of religious formations have changed. The three seminarians who welcomed me were dressed in secular clothes. One of them, my good friend Terry, would be ordained a priest two weeks after my visit. Lou and Gary are a year behind Terry; they became deacons this summer. All of them are from different East Coast dioceses. Although their attitudes toward their future ministries range from the conventional to the radical, they share the common secret of homosexuality. They were reluctant to be interviewed on campus, so we retired to a nearby creperie to discuss the influence of that secret on their lives as clerics.

"The seminary is a macho place," remarks Terry, "really awful on that level. Those of us who *are*"—his caution about gay references sometimes carries over into private conversation—"have to be careful. We have so much to lose."

Would they be expelled if seminary authorities found out?

"Probably."

I volunteer that it seems like a terrible way to live.

"None of us has a vocation to the *seminary*, Tim," responds Terry impatiently. "It's just something you have to pass through on the way to priesthood."

Terry, Lou, and Gary believe that they have been called by God to serve Him as priests. On the strength of that belief, they lied on the psychological tests they took before entering the seminary: when asked if they were homosexual, they said no. They were not going to let the current prejudice of an institution get in the way of their vocation to serve in that institution. As Terry says, quoting from *A Man for All Seasons:* "God made the angels to show Him splendor. He made the flowers to show Him beauty. But He made man to serve Him in the tangle of his wits."

Do they feel a special responsibility to work on behalf of gay Catholics?

Terry and Lou both say yes; Gary's response is a puzzled no. Terry plans to work with Dignity after his ordination, although it will be a sideline to his official parish assignment. Lou transferred out of the Archdiocese of New York because of its virulent homophobia and is now sponsored by a diocese whose bishop, he feels, is more open to dialogue with gay Catholics. Gary sees his vocation in the most traditional terms, although he has chosen to work in a diocese within driving distance of New York so he can get into the city now and then.

I look at the three seminarians—gay men who cannot talk freely in their school, who will not be able to talk freely in their rectories, whose capacity for a special kind of love may always remain a secret—and my reportorial sense evaporates. All I feel is recognition of their alternatives, admiration for their courage, and pain at the probable consequences of their choice. I tell them that it seems to me they are part of a long line of idealistic young priests who, for all their good intentions, end up being devoured by an oppressive machine.

### III

Jeannine Gramick takes a sip of iced tea. "Since 1971," she says, "we've seen a lot of changes in the church's attitude toward gay people that others haven't seen. I think that people in the church are getting ready to deal with it."

It is a hot afternoon. But Gramick is getting used to heat. She and her colleague, Robert Nugent, have taken a lot of it this year—from the Vatican's Sacred Congregation for Religious, from the Archdiocese of Washington, and from Catholic newspapers around the country. Gramick is a School Sister of Notre Dame; Nugent is a Salvatorian priest whose faculties to say Mass in the Washington area have been suspended. Together they are New Ways Ministry, a self-described "ministry of reconciliation and social justice for Catholic gay persons, other sexual minorities, their families, friends, and the larger Catholic community."

The apartment where they work, in Mount Rainier, Maryland, is part of a dusty collection of low-rises just across the D.C. line from Catholic University, an area riddled with dozens of communities of sisters, priests, and brothers. (As a novice in the Christian Brothers, I passed through the neighborhood every morning on my way to theology class at my order's now-defunct Washington house of studies.) Their working space is small but cheery: two old wooden desks next to the living-room window; a portable typrwriter; a framed poster of Picasso's *Don Quixote* on the wall; dried flowers in a Blue Nun bottle on a shelf behind the front door.

Jeannine Gramick has been a sister since 1960, but her work with gay Catholics did not start until 1971 when, as a graduate student at the University of Pennsylvania, she met a gay person at a "home liturgy." (Such experimental living-room Masses were especially popular in Philadelphia, which was—and still is—among the most conservative archdioceses in the American church.)

"We started having home liturgies for gay people in his apartment," Gramick remembers. "The *Philadelphia Bulletin* ran an article about the masses, and Bob read it and wrote me a letter."

Nugent was then a diocesan priest working in a parish in Levittown, north of Philadelphia. Gradually he became a regular celebrant of the home liturgies, began to counsel gay people, and read all he could find about homosexuality. When Gramick was graduated from Penn, she was assigned to teach math at her order's college in Baltimore—safely out of reach of the Philadelphia church, which had begun to look askance at her work. Nugent remained in the City of Brotherly Love and later testified before the city council in favor of a gay-rights ordinance, in direct contradiction of the official archdiocesan position. (That bill and subsequent versions of it have been killed, largely due to church pressure; ironically, the archdiocese's official spokesman against gay rights was arrested early this year in New Orleans for making a homosexual advance to an undercover cop in a porno bookstore.)

In 1975, Nugent broke with the archdiocese and joined the Salvatorians, a religious order whose special interest is working for social justice. (Early in the seventies, the order's Task Force on Gay Rights wrote the first description of a possible Catholic ministry to gays.) The next year, he and Gramick moved to the Washington area to work on the staff of Quixote Center, a Catholic activist organization that lists gay rights among its many priorities for social change. Gramick and Nugent founded the New Ways Ministry last year.

"We both wanted to devote our full time to the gay issue," says Gramick. "We perceive a lot of hope and openness to what we're doing, in religious communities and in peace and justice groups. We did a workshop last summer in Los Angeles, and the Priests' Senate, the official organization of priests in the area, recommended that their members attend. Lots of them did, too."

New Ways also claims the sympathy, if not the outright support, of some Catholic bishops. "At least fifteen bishops could be called sympathetic to the need for a gay ministry," reports Gramick. "We received a financial contribution and a statement of support from one auxiliary bishop in New England, and a bishop in California told us that he supported our work, though he couldn't say so publicly." Neither bishop wanted his name mentioned by New Ways. Both Gramick and Nugent say that the priests and religious most interested in opening the church to gays are not gay themselves. "Gay clergy are far more homophobic than straight clergy," observes Gramick, "and it's the straight women religious who are speaking out on behalf of the gay women religious."

New Ways Ministry has been in hot water with various ecclesiastical authorities almost since its inception. One of the reasons Jeannine Gramick and Bob Nugent seem able to persevere in their work is an uncanny ability to find silver linings in the most ominous clouds. Last December, for instance, a retreat that they were to conduct for Dignity/St. Louis almost did not take place. A crudely mimeographed, anonymous letter from "The Catholic Laymen's League of St. Michael the Archangel and St. Maria Goretti" was mailed to convents, parishes, and religious orders in St. Louis, denouncing the retreat as "Satanic." The circular made the archdiocese unhappy; after "consultation" with Cardinal Carberry of St. Louis, the Sisters of St. Joseph, who had offered a facility to New Ways for the weekend, withdrew their offer. The retreat did come off but in an abbreviated one-day version at the Catholic Worker Movement's local house of hospitality.

Despite the sabotage, Gramick and Nugent printed a list of the good effects of the St. Louis experience in the next issue of their newsletter:

> From the painful experience came ... a dialogue between Dignity and the sisters who are interested in pursuing gay ministry; a dialogue between the sisters and Cardinal Carberry who acknowledges a need to do something more about ministry to gay Catholics; a reception for New Ways following the retreat that attracted more than a dozen area seminarians, brothers, sisters, and priests, including a provincial leader, a generalate staff member, and social justice coordinators ... some positive publicity for Dignity/St. Louis ... and a public acknowledgment of the Dignity retreat in an introduction of Jeannine and Bob to the worshipping community at College Church, St. Louis University, where Bob celebrated Sunday liturgy in the church of the famous "St. Louis Jesuits."

Such experiences as the Dignity retreat were just skirmishes, however, compared to other trouble in store for Gramick and Nugent. Their major problems began when New Ways received a $38,000 grant from the National Institutes of Health for a two-year sociological study of "the coming-out processes and coping strategies" of gay women. The study is ground-breaking, according to a New Ways press release, because it "assumes that being gay is a valid expression of a person's life-style, involving more than the simple notion of sexual preference."

When the *Washington Star* (which seems to have been more than generous in its coverage of the gay Catholic issues) changed the word "gay" to "practicing homosexual" in a story about the study, the Washington archdiocese was quick to respond. An editorial in its official newspaper, the *Catholic Standard*, lambasted New Ways: "Homosexuals deserve justice, compassion, and every help in changing their way of life. But to try to legitimize homosexual activity is a disservice to homosexuals and a clear violation of the teachings of Christ and His Church."

A month after the editorial appeared, another New Ways project engaged the archdiocese's interest, a project that would eventually involve the heads of Gramick's and Nugent's religious orders and the Vatican itself: a weekend retreat for gay nuns.

"There are groups of gay religious in touch with each other all over the country," explains Nugent. (Gramick has been forbidden by her religious superiors to discuss the retreat and will not say a word about it.) "Some of these groups have been meeting informally for recollection and prayer. A couple of the sisters involved asked us to coordinate and sponsor a weekend retreat. We weren't asked to take part in it, just to plan and schedule it."

New Ways sent out a mailing to women's communities throughout the country, announcing the retreat as "an historic event in the American Catholic Church." The letter also said, "While we are planning to give the event the widest possible publicity in the Catholic community and especially among communities of women religious, we are also sensitive to the need for respecting the privacy of the individual retreatants."

"Talking about 'the widest possible publicity' was a mistake," Nugent now admits. The letter leaked to the secular press. When a story about the proposed retreat appeared in the *Washington Post*, all hell broke loose.

Gramick's provincial superior, Sister Ruth Marie May, circulated a letter to everyone who had received the New Ways mailing. "Publicity which uses such terminology as 'gay women religious,'" she wrote, "I see not only as offensive and misleading, but ultimately detrimental to the present image and role of celibate women in a faith community.... While we do not deny that this orientation exists, we are nowhere near the time when we or the general public are equipped or integrated enough to handle the suspicion that this publicity evokes.... It would be well," she concluded, "to cancel the retreat."

The archdiocese of Washington was next to act. Its chancellor sent a terse statement to every Catholic bishop and religious provincial in the country, informing them that Gramick and Nugent "have not received permission or authorization to engage in any ministry within the archdiocese of Washington."

"Two years before," recalls Nugent, "we'd had members of the Priest's Senate of Washington and the priests' personnel board coming to our workshops. All of a sudden, without ever contacting us or asking what our work was about, the archdiocese decides we're unauthorized."

The chancellor's letter was followed by the removal of Nugent's faculties to say mass anywhere in Washington. Since New Ways was not an approved ministry, the logic ran, Nugent should not be allowed to promote that work by dispensing the sacraments as part of it. No other priest in

Washington whose work lacked local church sanction has ever been thus disciplined, including such priests as Congressman Robert Drinan, S.J., and HUD Undersecretary Geno Baroni, who carry on unauthorized ministries as officials in the federal government.

Finally, the Vatican itself stepped into the controversy. "My order's superior general in Rome got the word from the Sacred Congregation of Religious that I was to cancel the retreat," says Nugent. But when the directive came down through channels to Nugent's immediate superior, Salvatorian provincial Myron Wagner, Wagner balked. Rome placed Wagner under "canonical obedience"—the little-used ecclesiastical equivalent of the army's "direct order"—to quash the retreat. Subsequently Robert Nugent was solemnly forbidden to organize the weekend. New Ways withdrew its sponsorship.

The retreat of gay sisters *did* take place—at an undisclosed location in the East, under Jeannine Gramick's sponsorship "as a person, not as a sister or part of New Ways." Nugent will not say how many sisters attended, but there were undoubtedly fewer than would have shown up had the fracas not occurred.

What is next for New Ways? Gramick and Nugent spent the summer in England and the Netherlands, meeting with people engaged in gay ministries in those countries. They have scheduled two retreats for Catholic lesbians this fall. And they are planning a course called "Recycling Gay Catholics," for gay people who left the church before the Vatican Council and want to come back now. "It's not the same church they left," comments Nugent, despite his recent experiences.

One of New Ways Ministry's most ambitious and successful projects has been to organize the Catholic Coalition for Gay Civil Rights, whose members "urge all Catholics to support sound [gay] civil rights legislation on both federal and local levels." Over one thousand Catholic groups and individuals have endorsed the statement, including the National Coalition of American Nuns, the National Assembly of Religious Brothers, and many leading Catholic theologians and writers. The Catholic Coalition has not drawn the kind of attention New Ways' controversial retreats have, but it may be their most significant work—a gathering of America's leading Catholic thinkers that gives the lie to the spurious theology behind attacks on gay rights by church authorities in such cities as New York and Philadelphia.

I asked Jeannine Gramick if she could put me in touch with a gay nun who would be willing to talk about her experience. She promised to give my telephone number to the sister who had moderated the retreat for gay women religious. Two weeks later, "Sister Benedicta" called me.

Sister Benedicta (unlike most American nuns, she has not changed her religious name back to her family name) has a voice instantly recognizable to anyone who has ever attended Catholic elementary school. It is Sister's Voice—kind, sincere, and well-modulated, with an undercurrent of energy and a total absence of irony. I was surprised to find myself a bit flustered when that familiar voice started to describe her coming out.

"I'm not out publicly," said Sister Benedicta, "but I have come out to my reverend mother and some of the other sisters. Coming out was a long process for me. It took a couple of years. I was going to a priest for counseling. He told me that just because I felt attracted to other women didn't mean I was gay. Then a friend of mine, a brother, started to work with Dignity and I got involved too.

"My first reaction to dealing with my sexuality was one of struggling to become more knowledgeable about myself. I wanted to run. I wouldn't let anyone else know. But gradually I came to accept it.

"I've done a little experimentation and have come to the conclusion that I must live celibate—that is, without genital sex. I know that there are others in religious life who choose a different way. There are people for whom celibacy means don't get involved with one person. There are others for whom sex is an expression of friendship and deep sharing.

"Right now, I have no tension with my vocation. Everything I've done, my reverend mother knows about. Of course, I wouldn't want it to get back to Rome."

Sister Benedicta entered religious life in 1950, a year after she graduated from high school. She describes herself as coming "from a very conservative family background." Her order, a small missionary community, has been "very accepting of me; they don't seem frightened by my being gay."

She refuses to discuss the retreat she moderated. "I think if anything else comes out about it, we'll have the bloodhounds on us," she says. "Right now, the important thing to do is help people. Every major superior is confronted with the issue. We just have to be careful about getting the issue out in the open without crucifying individuals.

"Some people challenge me," says Sister Benedicta. "They say, 'If you really believe in what you're saying, then stand up and shout about it.' But that's really not an option for me."

Sister Benedicta is one of hundreds of gay religious who, without shouting, are exploring the meaning of their sexual orientation in the life they have chosen to lead. So far there is one national newsletter in which gay sisters, brothers, and priests can share the fruits of that exploration. It is a measure of the loneliness and risk involved in that effort that every person I asked about the newsletter urged me not to publish its name, the city where it is edited, or the identities of its editors (who only use their first names, in any case).

I will not break that confidence. But I will mention the newsletter's subtitle: "A dialogue on the relationship between personal sexuality and ministry for the purpose of building community among gay clergy and religious." The publication is written by gay religious from around the country, and while the writing lacks polish, it bears moving testimony to a process of reflection that, much more than a specific function like "teaching" or "saying mass," defines what Catholic religious life is all about. The following lines from a priest in the Midwest capture some of the pain and hopefulness of that process:

When I entered religious life, I was certain that religion was my only bid for a life of human dignity and morality. Homosexuality

was a curse to be escaped. Later on, I felt it was a cross, gratuitously
given, to be nobly born [*sic*]. Then I began to discover that my sexuality was the source of most of my personality traits that I valued
and found effective in ministry. Now it is clear to me that my gayness is a key for growth and health and relationship.

A friend of mine once quipped . . . that he was a practicing homosexual and intended to continue practicing until he was good at
it. I feel the need, with great insistence, to integrate and perfect my
gayness, to practice until I am good at it. What that means really in
the context of celibate life, I do not yet know. . . . I do know for certain that I must find a way of replacing the cycle of repression and
depression that I have inflicted on myself as a way of "reconciling"
my sexuality and my vows with some as yet undiscovered pattern
of expression and celebration.

I entered the Christian Brothers as a postulant in 1968, one week out of
high school, and left them three years later, a month after coming out. I
used to say that being a brother was the most formative experience of my
life. Now I know that is not true, although recently I have begun to redis-
cover its significance in my personal history.

There were thirteen postulants in my class; eight of us have turned out
to be gay.

Ted and Matt were lovers in the novitiate, a daring arrangement presenting serious logistical problems. I have lost track of Ted. After a number of years with a male lover, Matt married a woman and returned to his
family home near Syracuse, New York.

After leaving the brothers, Keith taught at a school for emotionally disturbed boys. He adopted one of his charges, and they now live with Keith's
parents in Erie, Pennsylvania, where Keith works in a home for crippled
children. He joined the Episcopal Church early this year.

Patrick left the brothers in a huff after college, when the provincial refused to let him accept a fellowship at a midwestern university. The last
time I saw him he was part of the Philadelphia collective that published the
*Gay Alternative.* (I remember a very funny parody Patrick wrote, called
"Changing Heterosexuality in the Male.")

Dan was my "particular friend" in the novitiate, the person who stayed
up with me during many long nights of insomnia and waves of anxiety.
Particular friendships are frowned upon in religious communities, where
they are seen as the first step to homosexual relationships. Dan left the
order halfway through the novitiate; in a letter shortly afterward he told
me he was gay. I do not know where he is or what he is doing now.

Andrew was the most secretive about his homosexuality. I only found
out about it by accident—a good friend of mine dated his ex-lover. After I
became known as gay (in one year I went from brother-in-formation to
president of Gay Lib at my order's Philadelphia college), Andrew and I
did not have a lot to say to each other any more.

If Andrew was the most closeted gay man in my class, Mario was the
most visible. He holds the distinction of having been asked to leave the
brothers twice: once in novitiate for his unpredictable, irrepressible high

spirits ("false hilarity," the authorities called it); and again three years later when, as a scholastic, he was in the habit of bringing gay friends from Philadelphia's bars to the community for mass and dinner. After college, he spent summers working at Lyle's lunch counter, an institution on New York Avenue in Atlantic City's gay ghetto. In the years that followed, Mario balanced a promising career as a copywriter with a near-legendary status as a "good-time" person in Philadelphia's gay social whirl.

I had heard that Mario was serious about Catholicism again. I phoned him this spring after a mutual friend told me that Mario had reapplied to become a brother, this time in a different order.

"I really feel like a man without a country," Mario told me, his usual laugh not quite hiding the seriousness in his voice. "I'm not a het-er-o-*sex*-yew-ell, but I'm not part of the gay community any more, either. That's just not *me*, my dear." Another laugh.

Mario worked with the missionary order to which he applied for admission in Guatemala two summers ago. He has no doubts that he is called to that work, but he admitted being worried about whether the order would accept him. "I didn't lie on the psychological test. They asked whether I had strong attractions to men and I said yes. I guess if they don't accept me I'll feel a lot of bitterness. But if the Lord wants me to do this, then I'll get in."

Mario got in. I phoned him two weeks later to see how he was taking the news. He sounded as delightfully giddy as he had been ten years before.

"I'm so grateful they accepted me, Tim, I'll kneel before them like Mary Magdalene and rub soothing unguents into their feet with my hair. I guess I'll have to grow my hair *very* long. . . ."

Toward the end of our conversation, Mario told me not to write about him in this article. "I'm not gay, Tim. Gay is a subculture. I'm a person with the capacity to love men as well as women."

I blew up. "I don't care if you ever went to a gay bar in your life. I'm talking about a way of loving too. Everything we heard about grace and the presence of God in the novitiate—well, I didn't know what those words meant until I came out. Being gay was the next logical step to being in the brothers. It was an extension of my religious vocation, not a contradiction of it." By this time I was shouting. "So don't try to tell me that being gay is just one little part of your life. Don't isolate it like that. Because if there was ever a key to your religious life, to your ability to love, it's being gay. Do you know what I'm saying?"

Mario didn't miss a beat.

"Of *course*," he drawled.

This time, his laughter was full of recognition.

IV

Brian McNaught, America's most prominent gay Catholic layman, used to be one of Catholic journalism's brightest young men. Handsome, articulate, still in his midtwenties, his social conscience stirred and sometimes dismayed readers of his regular column in the *Michigan Catholic*, the newspaper of the Detroit archdiocese. But in mid-1974 McNaught's social conscience strayed a bit too far for the archdiocese's comfort. First, he devoted a column to the subject of gay love. Two months later, he came out in an interview in the *Detroit News*. The next working day, he was fired.

Unlike other church employees who have been dismissed from their jobs, McNaught decided to fight back. His action was consistent with what he now calls "my desire to put my name and reputation on the line for the Gospel." He went on a water fast, to protest the sins of the church against gay people.

McNaught's fast was a Detroit media sensation, covered by every television station and both local newspapers. (It also proved acutely embarrassing for McNaught's father, the public relations director at General Motors.) Twenty-four days after he began his fast, the archdiocese agreed to McNaught's demands and issued a statement affirming the need for justice and compassion for gay Catholics. In the years since then McNaught has made a living as a free-lance writer and editor. His column appears in five gay papers around the country, and he has edited religious publications too, mostly for the Episcopal Church. Today, he lives outside Boston. He sees the plight of gay Catholics as mirroring the problems most Catholics face with the church's teachings on sexuality.

"The majority of people born and raised in the Roman Catholic Church are on the edges today," he asserts. "The Vatican's declarations on sexual ethics have put an enormous chunk of the church outside looking in. There are gay people, of course. Then there are the clergy involved in homosexual and heterosexual relationships, the clergy who've left over celibacy, all the couples who use artificial methods of contraception, everyone who masturbates. . . . When you add them up, you're talking about the vasy majority of Catholics."

McNaught believes that the church's rigidity on the issue of gay rights is a manifestation of two long-time problems. "It was always perceived by non-Catholics that nuns and priests were homosexual," he says. "The church is very touchy about that. And there is a large amount of homosexual activity in monasteries and seminaries. Secondly, for people who find sexuality itself threatening, homosexuality is a convenient target on which to focus their guilt and fear about sex in general. I had a hell of a lot of guilt about sex as a teenager. In high school we were told that if you masturbated, you were too immature to marry."

By his senior year of college, McNaught had admitted his homosexuality to himself, but tried to divorce it from the rest of his life. "I swore when I had sex, I'd never do it with anyone I knew," he recalls. "The first three people I went to bed with turned out to be priests and seminarians."

McNaught still considers himself a Roman Catholic. "When I came out," he says, "I was intensely religious for a while. In the last year or so, I've been through a dry period. I've been angry and frustrated by the church. What [Thomas] Merton and [Daniel] Berrigan talked about—a combination of action for social justice and spirituality—still has great appeal to me. Some of the most dynamic witnesses to those values are Catholic lay people, sisters, brothers, and priests who live radically and are a constant thorn in the side of the hierarchy.

"Roman Catholics can talk for hours about the church and laugh at it and love it," McNaught says wistfully. "I don't want to give that up. I don't see why I have to give it up."

Brian McNaught used to be National Director of Social Action for Dignity, but he is no longer active in the organization. I asked him why. "Dignity seems to me most successful in the spiritual realm," says McNaught. "That aspect was important to me, but I was more concerned with mobilizing people in social action. There was a lot of resistance to that. I think I'm able to accomplish more working on my own."

Dignity is the vehicle through which thousands of gay Catholics manage to hang on to their religious affiliation. It has four functions. First, it is an instrument through which gay people can experience a spiritual life, where they can attend mass and be helped out of the guilt induced by poor theology. Second, it serves an educational purpose, especially for the clergy. Third, it is involved in social action for gay rights. Fourth, it fills a social need. Founded on the West Coast in 1970 (both the Los Angeles and San Diego chapters claim to be the oldest), Dignity now has 81 chapters, most of which meet regularly for mass. Eleven new chapters are in the process of formation.

The place of Dignity in the institutional church is even more problematical than the places of individual gay people. Like the "underground church" of the sixties, Dignity provides a congenial and stimulating alternative to the frequently abysmal spiritual life of traditional parishes. But while gay Catholics certainly owe no loyalty to an anemic parish structure that so badly serves their needs, "gay Masses" do tend to perpetuate a ghetto, as well as keep the heat off local pastors who would otherwise have to start responding to gay parishioners. The genius of Catholicism is, after all, its catholicity. Nevertheless, in the real world, where Catholicism is overwhelmingly hostile to its gay devotees, Dignity services are the only palatable kind for many of its members.

In New York, Dignity meets at St. Francis Xavier Church, a Jesuit parish in Chelsea. To celebrate its masses in a Catholic church is a new experience for Dignity/New York; they could not find a parish to welcome them until early this year. Ironically, St. Francis Xavier used to be the residence of gay deacon Tom Sweetin, who complained to the *New York Times* in 1977 when the Jesuits refused to ordain him. Sweetin has since left the order.

I visited a midweek Dignity Mass one hot night last summer. Built in the nineteenth century, the cavernous church works hard at being a baroque fantasy, but with little success. St. Francis himself stands atop the portico out front, brandishing a cross that he seems ready to fling down at the noisy preteens who hang out on the sidewalk below. Nearly one hundred people—largely white, largely male, largely not young—had shown up for the mass. The priest who celebrated it was very young and spoke with a soft Irish brogue.

"Our mission as gay Catholics is vital to the church and the world," he declared in his homily, "but for so long we have remained silent in our oppression." We must meet and find God, he told his congregation, in the bars and baths as well as in the more usual places. "We follow a man who fulfilled the Law by living outside it," he concluded. It was not the kind of sermon that would go over on a Sunday in a large suburban parish. Yet it reminded me how often gay Catholics are subjected to lectures on the joys of marriage and parenthood. There is something to be said for special-interest homilies.

At the Offertory, we gathered around the altar. At the Lord's Prayer, everyone joined hands. At the Kiss of Peace, some big wet smooches were exchanged, in addition to the conventional handshakes. At Communion, bread and wine were passed from worshipper to worshipper, gay people administering the sacrament to each other.

I had seen such trendy liturgical variations dozens of times in small masses. But the fact that the people with whom I shared in this most ancient of Christian rituals were all gay, too—proudly, unabashedly gay—moved me far more deeply than I expected. If the church is not yet willing to integrate its gay members into the full life of a parish community, Dignity's masses give a taste of the deep affirmation that will come when gay Catholics can manifest their special gifts in the presence of their coreligionists. The danger is that the urgency of that quest for full integration will dissipate in the beauty, and the Dignity, of the ghetto.

New York's Dignity chapter has been called the "most controversial" in the country by *Insight*, Dignity's own journal. That is in no small part due to the work of Andy Humm, the New York chapter's dynamic social action coordinator. Talking to Humm can resemble talking to a speeding train. The heat of battle is in his voice and in his eyes when he talks about his run-ins with the Archdiocese of New York.

Headed by Terence Cardinal Cooke, New York is the wealthiest and most influential archdiocese in the United States. It is also one of the most unremittingly antigay. Church pressure has been the primary reason gay rights bills have been defeated in the New York City Countil time after time. The archdiocese's official statement on the issue is pathetically ill-reasoned, pitting "the basic human right to protect children from immoral influences, as their parents so determine" against "the right of another person (e.g., a homosexual) to specific housing or employment," and giving priority to the former. The statement also raises the specter of Affirmative Action or, as the church puts it, "hiring goals and timetables for the sexually disoriented." In a city as tolerant as New York, the church's stand against gay civil rights is particularly vexing. It reinforces the view that Catholic concerns are either oppressive or trivial (as in a new archdiocesan guide to the morality of TV shows). And if rumors (repeated in print by Gore Vidal) about the late Cardinal Spellman's secret homosexual life are true, the New York church's antigay position becomes actually ludicrous.

The night before the Gay Pride Parade up Fifth Avenue last June, Humm and his Social Action Committee organized an all-night vigil for gay rights on the steps of St. Patrick's Cathedral. I arrived at 2 A.M. The night was cool and windy. As usual, Humm carried the conversation.

"The archdiocese is *proud* of leading the fight against gay rights," he declared. "They even formed front groups to help. There was something called the Committee for Family Life, which was organized through the Archdiocesan Office of Communications. I was told by a source in the

Chancery that they were willing to spend $2 million to fight gay rights if it went to a referendum. What's happening is that money for hospitals and the poor gets put into these campaigns on issues like gay rights and abortion.

"The last time the gay rights bill was up, the church tried hard to influence some key votes. Mary Codd [a council member from Staten Island and sister of New York's ex–police commissioner] announced she'd vote to free the bill from the committee, where it was tied up. Well, the church called her into the Chancery. There were nine men at the meeting. Some were from the Knights of Columbus; some were her political enemies. They raked her over the coals. She came out of that meeting saying that if it weren't for the good priests she knew, she'd have lost her faith."

In 1978, archdiocesan representatives met with Dignity board members. The meeting, says Humm, was unproductive.

"Gene Clark [Msgr. Eugene Clark, director of communications for the archdiocese] told us that we shouldn't call ourselves Catholics," says Humm. "He said that the sinfulness of homosexuality is an authentic teaching of the church and that we should be doing penance. The only reason I pushed for the meeting at all was so the board could know exactly where we stood, so we don't have any investment in bothering with the archdiocese. Though we didn't think we'd change any of their minds, we asked if they'd help us conduct meetings with pastors in areas where there are lots of gay people."

The archdiocese's response?

"They said Dignity would be the last group they'd let do that, because to arrange that kind of meeting would be to show approval of us."

Humm says that many Dignity members work for the archdiocese as teachers and social workers, although "they'd lose their jobs if they ever came out." That threat applies to diocesan priests, too. One Manhattan pastor sent a letter to the city council supporting the gay rights bill but refused to testify publicly because he said he would lose his parish if he did.

By this time it was 3 A.M. Muttering imprecations, a teenager high on something walked back and forth in front of the dozen or so demonstrators. I asked a gray-haired woman wearing a large cross around her neck why she was at the sit-in. "I'm here," she replied, "because I am a sister who feels we should have a commitment to working against oppression even when it comes from our own church."

Sister Mary Lou Steele, who was baptized at St. Patrick's, taught school for nineteen years before resigning to work at Clergy and Laity Concerned in New York. She has been involved in Dignity for four years but deplores the lack of women in the organization. "There are many lesbians of Catholic background who have been turned off by the church as *women,*" she declares. Nevertheless, she believes that women—"especially religious women"—are in a good position to change society's attitudes.

"So many people blame their hang-ups on the religious who taught them," she reflects. "Now we have the power to release people from their hang-ups, their homophobia. I wouldn't be surprised if homophobia is a fear of sexuality itself."

(Sister Steele's commitment is shared by others in her community. Sister Winifred Sweeney, another Sister of Charity, works for gay rights as part of the Intercommunity Center for Justice and Peace, a social-action consortium of twenty-one religious orders in the New York area. In light of the archdiocese's bigotry, it is heartening to know that so many communities of sisters, brothers, and priests promote gay rights through the center's work.)

Sister Steele is more hopeful than Andy Humm is about the possibility of change within the hierarchy. "The archbishop of Atlanta celebrated mass last winter for Dignity," she told me. "Dignity members prayed and fasted for a week before they met with him. He not only agreed to say mass for them, he gave them a church to meet in. Now they're working in the parish where they meet, so people find out they're normal and compassionate. Then the archbishop said they were free to meet with any pastor in Atlanta. People hate the church, but it's not monolithic. You see, the archbishop of Atlanta is from New York. His name is Thomas Donnellan, and he used to work right here, in the Chancery. I find such a sign of hope in that."

The morning after I finished writing this article, I got an 8 A.M. phone call from Jean Proulx (a pseudonym), who was traveling through the city. I had heard of Proulx for years from a mutual friend of ours.

As a philosophy student in England in the fifties, Proulx had decided that there were four defensible philosophical choices for his life: he could become a Communist; he could become a Catholic; he could become a Buddhist; or he could commit suicide. At twenty-four, he converted to Catholicism. At thirty-one, he was ordained a priest. Today, he is a high-ranking monsignor in Rome, equally comfortable with the intrigue of Vatican politics and the fine points of moral theology.

Proulx, who is gay himself, had heard that I was writing about gay Catholics and suggested that we get together for a chat. That afternoon, I met him and his traveling companion, a student from Milan named Luchino, in Greenwich Village for a late lunch.

"The problem is not just with homosexuality," Proulx observed. "It's with divorce, contraception, and every part of the theology of sexuality. Homosexuality is just a small part of the whole problem. But sometimes, it may be better that the church remain silent, that she not be forced to take a stand. Pope Paul VI didn't want to issue his encyclical against contraception; he was pressured into it by people who demanded an answer. Then some of them didn't like the answer they got."

What, he wanted to know, distressed me most about the church's stand on homosexuality?

"The hypocrisy," I answered, "their concern for public relations first and justice second."

"But not telling people something isn't hypocritical," said Proulx. "It can even be an act of charity to refrain from telling someone something that would scandalize or overly disturb them."

We talked about John McNeill's book *The Church and the Homosexual.* "Not very good scholarship," commented Proulx. "Arrupe [the Jesuits' superior general] was reprimanded for allowing it to be published."

"I'm not really concerned with good theology," I told him. "I'm concerned about the kids who don't know about theological disputation, but who grow up being told by the church that it's evil to be gay."

"You're right, of course," said Proulx. "But I don't know how much waving it as a flag will accomplish."

"Sometimes," said Luchino, "you have to wave a flag."

They walked me to the subway. As we neared West Fourth Street, Jean whispered, "You're still a Catholic?"

"Yes," I answered and was filled with the warmth that comes from sharing an important secret. "I'm still a Catholic."

Jean beamed. "It's really the only thing to be, don't you think?"

We kissed goodbye on the crowded street, and I ran to catch my train.

# R OB BAKE R

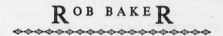

# *A Time for Schizophrenia: Reflections on the Transvestite Threat to the (Gay) Macho Mystique*

## Incidents

If you're going to open a can of worms, the first thing you have to do is open the can:

(1) In a recent short-lived Broadway comedy called *Checking Out*, a young black actor portrays a male nurse. The characterization is outrageously overdone: simpering, flouncing, posing, eye-rolling, lisping, the works—every stereotypical image of the swish queen that the stage has ever known. The second-night, largely heterosexual audience cackled and roared at each mince, encouraging the actor to even greater depths of self-conscious camp. Earlier this year the same actor was used by playwright Rosalyn Drexler to portray the half-witted faggot-villain brother of her quasi-feminist protagonist, Hatshepsut, the cross-dressing queen of Egypt. There, too, the gay male image was presented in cardboard silhouette, and there, too, the overwhelming negativity of jokes being directed *at* the char-

acter was complicated and strained even further by the fact that the character is black as well as gay.

(2) In a play called *Greta Garbo on 42nd Street* at New York's Spanish-speaking INTAR Theater, a young, Cuban-born actor does for Off-Off-Broadway what the black actor above did for Broadway. Portraying a male nurse (again?) who picks up a young hunk in the rain outside Port Authority, the actor uses his wrists and hips to punctuate each line and pose. His apartment is a shrine to Greta Garbo; he drinks like a fish when not snorting poppers or chain-smoking cigarettes and grass; he teeters about in gold-lamé, platform-heeled bedroom slippers. The trick turns out not to be a hustler after all, but just a humpy innocent fresh off the boat from the Dominican Republic. He is at last seduced by the evil queen, plays trade and pops pills for two acts, then goes home to Santo Domingo in defeat. Again I wondered why the whole thing seemed so offensive to me until the friend I was with (who was born and raised in Argentina) pointed out the obvious: there are only two images of homosexuality the Latin mind will accept: the screaming queen, who is so outrageous (and *funny*) that he is no threat to general Latino machismo, or the straight man who occasionally lets himself be blown, with no real compromise to his "masculinity" involved.

(3) Broadway's *Chicago* is a musical based on the real-life incident of a young woman reporter who writes a series of newspaper stories about an accused love-tryst murderess in Chicago in the twenties—and succeeds in winning "Roxy Hart" her freedom. When Gwen Verdon and her husband, director Bob Fosse, started trying to get the rights to the plot a few years back (a nonmusical play and movie had been done in the forties), the real-life reporter (who had written the original play as well) balked. Only after her death did *Chicago*, the musical, become a reality. In the musical, the character of the reporter is turned into an abrasive, unladylike woman who, in the end, is revealed to be (titter, titter) a transvestite. Some joke.

(4) One night a few months back in Boots and Saddle, a Village bar of the semileather persuasion, one of Christopher Street's better-known transvestites (generally fond of attending gala openings in full red beard and assorted glitter drag) was holding court. Even out of a dress, his affectations lingered, along with his brash loudness, his calculated disruptiveness. The bartenders were polite, but customers began to drift away. It's not exactly your typical Boots and Saddle scene—a definite turn-off, in fact, like when those gaggles of screamers trounce into your favorite backroom bar or truck-tryst, giggling and chattering, and spoil things for everyone else, then swish on.

## Visibility

Homosexuality has made the media at last. The taboos are down. Mary Hartman tries to convert the gay next door—and fails miserably. Elton John tells *Rolling Stone* he's bi. Hollywood reveals that the real mystery behind Billy Joe's ode is you-know-what. Marcello Mastroianni and Jean-Louis Trintignant play lovers on the screen. A New York punk rock group (whose manager should know better) delights its listeners with a little ditty about a "Fifty-third and Third" hustler who takes a razor to his john. This is progress?

Visibility is not acceptance. Visibility can, on occasion, even preclude, complicate, postpone acceptance. The whole question of media exposure hinges on the delicate question of who's really being exposed—and in whose interest.

Important inroads are being made: the Thames television imports from England shown here recently; the fact that a leading mystery magazine (a field that reeks of conservatism and antigay sentiments) is about to publish a nonsensational gay murder story in which even the private eye appears to be gay; the positive portrayals of everyday gays on prime-time coast-to-coast television (especially Norman Lear's shows) and in mainstream movies like Paul Mazursky's *Next Stop Greenwich Village* (proof positive that the characterization of an effeminate black can be done sensitively and effectively in drama).

But at the same time we're left with the above examples and incidents, several of which may be doing a lot more harm than good to the gay image, among both gays themselves and the general public. Media presentation of gay stereotypes only reinforces those stereotypical patterns, making them self-fulfilling prophecies in the lives of more and more young gays (especially outside of urban areas like New York). Being a queen, a camp, a performing bear for the straight world becomes the easy way out, the path of least resistance for these gays, a bit like being a Stepin Fetchit black.

All gay men (and presumably straight men too, although that doesn't particularly interest me) need to come to terms with the feminine side of their nature, with their ability to respond, to handle softness and feeling. The "effeminacy" entailed in the above incidents is not what bothers me. It's the use of a superficial pose of effeminacy to escape real identity, real self-confrontation.

I once wrote a letter to the *New York Times* objecting to an article in the Arts and Leisure section (about gay themes in the movies and onstage) entitled "Why Can't We Have Happy Endings, Too?" What I objected to (and still do) was the attitude that gay art should have more (or less) "happy endings" than any other art. We don't need artificial Hollywood climaxes to our stories, just as we don't need anyone telling us that we have to have only "positive" images of gays on the stage, screen, or jukebox. Art should reflect life, in all its wonderful contradictory convolutions and complications. But we don't need gays as a chic object of ridicule either. Gays who play the fool—instead of playing themselves—for "liberated" straights are embarrassing the hell out of some of the rest of us.

## Dragon's Head

In astrological symbolism there's a complicated mathematical factor called the nodes of the moon, which relates the angle the moon's axis makes with the path of the earth around the sun to certain areas of a person's life, which must be watched with great care. Danger spots.

The northern node is commonly known as the Dragon's Head, and the main thing to remember when you're fighting dragons (or opening cans of

worms) is that you don't pussyfoot around; you aim right for the head. Get
the bastard right between the eyes. Much so-called Transvestite Theater of
Off-Off-Broadway in the late sixties and early seventies did exactly that,
hitting right on target. There were the early works of Charles Ludlam and
John Vaccaro and personae on the scene (social and theatrical) like Jackie
Curtis and Holly Woodlawn and Candy Darling, the two troupes of all-
male ballerinas, Ekathrina Sobechanskaya and Her Trockadero Gloxinia
Ballet and the more comedy-oriented Ballets Trockadero de Monte Carlo.

What each of these performers did was trash stereotypes, trash preconceptions of sex roles and role-playing in general. Nothing was sacred to
Ludlam and Vaccaro (or Tom Eyen and Ronald Tavel and Harry Kou-
toukas), and their outrageousness broke down the barriers that kept
American theater moribund for so long. Likewise Larry Ree (Ekathrina
Sobechanskaya) and others in the Trockadero groups (particularly Tony
Bassae and Peter Anastos) dared to question the centuries-old tradition of
sacrosanct classical ballet, a tradition infuriatingly grounded in the sexist
patterns of role-playing and (especially) keeping women in their place by
putting them on a virginal pedestal as swans and wilis and other personal-
ityless untouchables.

Cabaret performers like Curtis and Woodlawn also dared to skirt the
no-man's-land of sexual fantasy, exploring consciously the homosexual
fantasy of the supergoddess mystique (which was not all that different
from the ballerina syndrome). Bette Midler did the same, getting accused
in the process (quite accurately I now realize, although I objected violently
at the time) by one gay writer as "imitating a he imitating a she." Anyway,
what was reflected onstage in Curtis, Midler and Vaccaro found its way to
the streets (or vice versa) in the Stonewall street-queens, in Rollerina,
Ruth Truth, Marsha P. Johnston and the rest; culminating, in part, in a
street-politics-based theater company called Hot Peaches.

Transvestism was no longer little boys dressing up in their mothers'
clothes. Onstage and off, it was radical politics, perhaps the most radical
sexual politics of all.

## Steven

All this was pre-Steven in my life, which is to say pretty much precon-
sciousness of the whole question of feminism. The love thing didn't work
out for us, for a lot of reasons, I guess, but I'll never be able to look at anything about being gay, being a man, being a person, quite the same way
again.

We met in Julius's on my birthday, almost three years ago. Steven had
already been through Marxism, SDS-type radical politics and gay liberation, and by the time I met him he was into feminism (or as he called it,
"effeminism"—men couldn't be feminists, only a kind of fellow travelers),
and almost everything we discussed related back to problems of sexism, of
male dominance (in both the gay and straight worlds), of the sins of the
patriarchy.

Our first real fight was about Ekathrina Sobechanskaya. Steven found
the whole idea of transvestism appalling, oppressive and insulting to
women in that it was a cheap imitation of them—their dress, their posture

and gestures, their vocal patterns, to say nothing of their sexuality and sensitivity. Moreover, transvestites—the whole queen syndrome (and I think Steven would object rather violently to the term *queen* on similar grounds)—was glorifying, glamorizing the very things about feminine roles that contemporary women in the movement were rejecting: fashion, makeup, being soft and delicate and pretty and "feminine."

By calling himself an effeminist, Steven not only aligned himself with the positive energies of the women's movement but established an identity outside the patriarchal system of masculine role models. He dressed, acted, moved as himself, without affectation of masculinity or femininity. It made—makes—him one of the most complete persons I've ever known.

Weakly, I would keep insisting the things I believed about transvestites making a radical political statement. Steven would have none of it. I would go back to see the performers who had seemed so relevant to me before and the magic was gone, the outrage was shallow. And I was appalled at the cheap, vicious jokes transvestites made about women. Whoever got the idea that to be progay you had to be antiwoman? Men calling each other "bitch" and "cunt" onstage and getting a thunderous round of applause for each put-down of the very role models they were aping. What kind of liberation is that?

## Dragon's Tail

Suddenly everything got twisted from trashing stereotypes to stereotyping trash. The southern node of the moon is the Dragon's Tail, which is a lot more dangerous than the head. Only a fool stabs a dragon in the tail. Dane Rudhyar calls it the path of least resistance, the easy way out.

I go back to Boots and Saddle or down Christopher Street or up to the bars, and everyone I see seems to be caught in their Dragon's Tail phase, cross-dressing into look-alike levis or leathers, sporting matching inhalers and cokespoons to waft them to the latest, chicest escapist high, merging visual-psychic identities into the latest self-fulfilling, self-defeating stereotype. Charles Pierce, one of the old-guard drag entertainers, tells four full houses at the cavernous Beacon Theatre uptown for the Cecil B. Demented Broken Blossoms Revue and Ballet Company, "We're stereotypes because we like it like that." I feel a flicker of the old thrill, the old radical flaunting of the conventions—Pierce is on our side for a change, instead of playing down to the straights. But it's all gotten confused. I have breakfast with Lucina, a wonderfully strong, righteously stubborn Taurus woman who describes marching in the Gay Pride Parade in Chicago with a large black lesbian sister, a fat black queen and a skinny little Spanish queen (the words are not wrong on Lucina's lips), helping them hold up the banner. I tingle at that. Somewhere, under all the rhetoric, something still holds.

## Letter from a Peach

To close the can of worms, here, virtually verbatim, a letter from Hot Peaches founder Jimmy Centola in London. Because it substantiates, confuses, negates and explains all of the above. Hopefully.

Dear Robb—

Hi. How goes all over there. The same, I suppose, as ever. Wow, there are times when New York is on my mind with a vengeance. Never mind, we will return in about six or seven months, I suppose.

Well, you'll be happy to hear that, professionally, things have been popping for us. We've been all kinds of lucky and the people here have been real good to us.

Our first show was at the Oval House Theatre—south of the river, i.e., the revolutionaries, the real people, GLF-ers, etc., came while the trendy queens, the establishment, etc., stayed away. Well, needless to say, that was just our cup of tea—if you'll excuse the expression.

The theater manager who was running a very unsuccessful summer festival "fitted us in" to a late-night slot (10 P.M. is late here—are you ready!). Well, we turned it out. We had our type people in a small theatre, and it was packed every night while the shows downstairs played to four and five per show. Well, Miss Thing, although all the other performers gave us a lot of attitude when we arrived, they now became very friendly. And we all had a ball. They held us over, and we still filled the place—the unventilated place—right through a heat wave. We were all very high off that.

While this was all happening, we found ourselves an old Victorian mansion in Hampstead and moved in. It is a squat. That means it was derelict until some people moved in and fixed it up. Now we all live here—rent free. And it's a trip, full of stained glass windows and garden and sun roof and all sorts of English kids—we also built a bar-b-que pit in the back—our bicentennial contribution to the house.

After the first show—we did *The Divas of Sheridan Square*—we did a few one-nighters. One for a GLF getting together in Brighton, a very poor but very energetic area. We're all writing poetry now. I am Hellas, even Sister Tui. So we strung our poems together in a little story and performed on gay day. It was great.

Then they had another gay day here, but a week after ours. So we did another show for Che—England's answer to Mattachine. And it was a trip. Five hundred screaming queens and dykes and it was like being home. Funny how the gay vibe is the same in England as it is at home. From all this we've been offered a tour—a gay tour—for the month of December, and Ian is presently negotiating terms, because the tour is through England and we are leaving for Amsterdam quite soon.

The last big show we did in London got us jobs in Amsterdam and Germany. We did *Divas* at the ICA (Institute of Contemporary Arts) and it was no problem at all. Because even though it was the center of town—which meant establishment straights and West End queens—our reputation from the Oval and the Che shows paved the way. We had crowds all week and the last night about 350–400 people showed up and the management said it was the biggest crowd they'd ever had. And dar-ling, that crowd was glorious.

Our final crowd was 95 percent gay. They came from all over, Birmingham, Bristol, South End, West End, East End—everywhere. In glorious costume—men in bathing suits and boas, women in fedoras, ties and vests, high boots and beads and painted down. It was *el glorioso*. All those gay people under one roof—what a night.

Now we're getting on and going to Amsterdam. And that means dope. I can't wait. The English and dope don't mix well at all. Also it means stoned audiences, and well, you know. We'll be doing dates there for the month of September and then, all going well, somebody in Germany is fixing up a tour of that country for us.

There is also a new Peach. Miss Bette. Well, darling, Miss Bette is an English queen of some maturity, and really he's just too much. Excellent on stage and *très* together off. Much costume, *à la Rocky Horror Show*, but that will grow into something "grander," to use Bette's word. He's terribly terribly and oh so very—real. Can't wait til you meet him.

So that's the news from abroad. Will write again from Amsterdam and let you know what's what—in the meanwhile . . .

> *Have you seen all the divas of Sheridan Square?*
> *Kroozin down to the river by Morton St. Pier.*
> *Some are tall tough and taki*
> *But some are flawlessly fair*
> *And we ain't dishin'*
>    *just wishin.*
>    *We could be standing there.*

Love
Jimmy
&
The Hot Peaches

# CHARLES ORTLEB

## *The Context of* Cruising

> *. . . the camera's rendering of*
> *reality must always hide more*
> *than it discloses.*
> —Susan Sontag, *On Photography*

New York has become a city where directions can be given based on remembered violence against gays. "Meet me at the restaurant where the cops threatened to beat us up and then gave us a summons for 'jaywalking.' " "I'll see you later, on the corner where Tim was attacked with rocks by kids shouting 'Fag!' " "Let's go for a walk in the park, where those guys with baseball bats attacked gays." "Let's have a drink at the bar where the bouncer beat Doug up for handing out leaflets about *Cruising.*"

Everyone thinks his or her incident is isolated. But at an ad hoc town meeting to protest the filming of *Cruising* in the gay community this summer, the crowd of several hundred gay people was asked who among them had been assaulted or personally knew someone who had been assaulted recently because he or she was gay. Over half the people present raised their hands.

That is the New York in which William Friedkin set about filming a gay murder mystery.

> *It's 1941. Let's make a murder mystery in Germany with Jewish bankers for local color. Don't tell me about the camps, about the isolated incidences of violence against Jews. My film is about something else.*

> The camera is a kind of passport that annihilates moral boundaries and social inhibitions, freeing the photographer from any responsibility toward the people photographed.
> —Susan Sontag, *On Photography*

## Gays as Local Color

They come from New Jersey and Long Island. Actually, they come from all over. They walk down Christopher Street hand in hand, a little nervously but still in a bemused mood. Sometimes they stop to kiss each other, flinging their heterosexuality like acid into the faces of gay men passing on the streets. They shake their heads disapprovingly when they see two male or female hands touch. They don't stop to buy drugs because they're too busy shooting up superiority.

They have come into the city from the doubt of the suburbs to smirk and to slum. They need to see our neighborhoods as zoos in order to maintain certain notions about the "civilization" of their own.

> There is an aggression implicit in every use of the camera.
> —Susan Sontag, *On Photography*

## Setting Yourself Up as an Exception

When *Cruising* comes out in theaters you may find yourself having to explain (like pre-Holocaust Jews) that you are "respectable," that *you* aren't an uncouth ghetto homosexual, that you are *an exception.* In her essay "We Refugees" Hannah Arendt describes certain tendencies among Jews in the death camps "to interpret the whole accident as personal and individual bad luck." You may find yourself having to make mystical statements about antigay violence when it happens to you. You may be forced to view history as a matter of fate. You may or may not be one of the lucky homosexuals who escapes. Statistically, you are safe. Everyone cannot be attacked on the same night.

The demonstrations this summer were *politically important:* The protest created a counterimage of *connectedness* in the gay community.

> Through photographs, each family constructs a portrait chronicle of itself—a portable kit of images that bears witness to its connectedness."
>
> —Susan Sontag, *On Photography*

## The New Political Stereotype: The Affable Homosexual

Harmlessness has become a part of gay urban charm. At a time when neoconservatives want to make harmfulness the gay urban image, we are seeing the emergence of a new political stereotype: the affable homosexual.

During a confused political period, like our mini-outbreak of history this summer in Greenwich Village, the affable are the most confused and try to turn their confusion into a kind of charm. The affable choose to make clever personal comments during times of trenchant political protest. The affable worry constantly about the motivations of the nonaffable. During the protests against *Cruising* some of the affable wanted to know if the demonstrators had jobs (or were these more uncouth ghetto homosexuals?). The protesters disturbed the comity of the affable homosexuals' image.

One affable homosexual talent agent said to me in an elevator, "Do you realize that they'll make this movie a hit?" The affable seemed to see the whole *Cruising* affair in terms of budgets, overages, and Al Pacino's career prospects. Many of the affable are never attacked on the streets. They take cabs.

Harmlessness draws the fury of the oppressor. Gay disinterest in gay power is a communal suicide note. (Hannah Arendt about the Jews in a similar political situation: "The Jews without knowledge of or interest in power, never thought of exercising more than mild pressure for minor purposes of self-defense.")

## The Emergence of the Performing Homosexual

> Whenever the enemy seeks control he makes a point of using some oppressed element of the population as his lackeys and henchmen, rewarding them with special privileges, as a kind of sop.
>
> —Hannah Arendt, "The Jew as Pariah"

William Friedkin's Performing Homosexuals acted like small grateful puppies at the master's table. The master didn't say, "Bark"; he said, "Cruise." The master didn't say, "Roll over"; he said, "Fist-fuck." The master didn't say, "Fetch"; he said, "Fellatio." Sometimes the master didn't say anything at all. The puppies knew what to do.

Kevin McCarthy, one of the *Cruising* extras, in an article in the *SoHo Weekly News*, called what the master told them to do "acts of fellowship and union and love." Another individual suggested that homosexuals will do anything to be in a movie. We now know their price. They will perform homosexual local color for $60 a day. During the shooting on the Lower East Side, some of these Performing Homosexuals called the protesters "radical fairies." Joe McCarthy gave us a good example of the kind of person Arendt describes as one who "begs from those he ought to fight."

The *Cruising* extras were either too drugged or too ignorant to see that Weintraub and Friedkin were on the set with a sexual ideology that held them in implicit contempt.

> To take a picture is to have an interest in things as they are, in the status quo remaining unchanged (at least for as long as it takes to get a "good" picture), to be in complicity with whatever makes a subject interesting, worth photographing—including, when that is the interest, another person's pain or misfortune.
> ... using a camera is not a very good way of getting at someone sexually.
> —Susan Sontag, *On Photography*

### The Gay Love Affair with the First Amendment

Many of us who were born into the gay movement at colleges had our first political experiences defending our First Amendment right to form campus gay organizations. This continues to be a problem on many campuses across the country. We were using the First Amendment to stop gay oppression long before Friedkin and Weintraub utilized it to initiate gay suffering.

Homophobic liberal columnists who tried to disassociate us from our support of the First Amendment were engaging in a familiar pre-Holocaust tactic: denying a people their history—indeed, mocking our history.

### The Superstructure Strategy

> To photograph is to appropriate the thing photographed. It means putting oneself into a certain relation to the world that feels like knowledge—and, therefore, like power.
> —Susan Sontag, *On Photography*

One year it was born-again Christians. Now it's a sleazy Hollywood film project. Next year it will be the born-again Nazis. The Superstructure Strategy is to exhaust the gay community. Demagogic filmmaking, like demagogic politics, intends to sap the community's strength.

In an essay in a new collection called *Hannah Arendt: The Recovery of the Public World* (St. Martin's Press), Bernard Crick discusses Arendt's understanding that before you exterminate a people you must "degrade" them—break their wills and create hopeless resignation. The first goal is to trick the community out of thinking of itself as a community.

How clever to send the cameras into the ghetto. Make them pose in one-sided images of uncouthness, then utilize that partial picture to make them feel that they have somehow *asked* for anything that happens to them as a result of it.

Just as the camera is a sublimation of the gun, to photograph someone is a sublimated murder—a soft murder, appropriate to a sad, frightened time.

—Susan Sontag, *On Photography*

In his essay on Arendt, Crick writes that "Minorities, like the Jews, at first thought it enough to be emancipated from formal restraints; it took them long to realize that, as it were, the price of freedom-from-restraint is not just vigilance but constant activity."

I think the coming together of the Village gay community on this issue was in part a way of telling the Jewish survivors of the Holocaust, "We too have learned from your history. Your lessons have transcended your people." As Arendt said at the end of "The Jew as Pariah," "Only within the framework of a people can a man live as a man among men, without exhausting himself."

While William Friedkin and Jerry Weintraub ran around the city this summer trying to humiliate the gay community, I could have sworn I saw the framework of a people more clearly than ever.

# LAWRENCE MASS, M.D.

## The New Narcissism and Homosexuality: The Psychiatric Connection

> *Long before Dreyfus's days, the homosexual was already one of psychiatry's favorite scapegoats. American psychiatry's true feeling about homosexuals showed in all its ugliness once more in the trial of Dan White. Let us hope that the White affair will arouse the sense of justice in the gay community and in the hearts of all those who sympathize with such victimization; and that the result will be the long-overdue expulsion of the psychiatric liars from the courtroom—whether they come to pervert justice by imprisoning the innocent or by exculpating the guilty.*
>
> —Thomas Szasz *Inquiry* Magazine (August 1979)

### The New Narcissism

Many psychiatric terms have entered our everyday conversation. *Projection, denial, sublimation, regression, depression, neurosis, masochism*—these words are used so commonly to describe such regular features of so many that their medicolegal ferocity and their ability to stigmatize have been substantially defused.

Or eliminated. *Neurosis*, for example, used to intimidate by suggesting a severe psychiatric condition. It is now, however, recognized as so universal a phenomenon that its characterization as such no longer appears in the American Psychiatric Association's *Diagnostic and Statistical Manual of Mental Disorders*. As was the case when *homosexuality* was deleted, millions of people were suddenly "cured" of their "mental disorder."

A newer term to the public, *narcissism*, may be just the latest pop psychology stigma to wend its way into the American household. Like *neurosis*, it may eventually be defused or replaced. (In fact, this process may have already begun. In the Woody Allen film, *Manhattan*, the protagonist twice confesses, "My analyst thinks I'm a narcissist.") In the meantime, "narcissism," like "homosexuality," is certain to become the newest source of psychiatric stereotyping, oppression, and abuse. Its principal victims, incidentally, will once again be homosexuals.

That which inspired Woody Allen's sense of humor inspired in Christopher Lasch an apocalyptic vision. The theoretical foundation of his much-touted, best-selling doomsday book *The Culture of Narcissism* (Norton, 1978) is in fact our newest psychiatric classification of character pathology: "narcissistic personality disorder." Lasch's keynote address on this subject at the 1978 American Psychiatric Association convention in Atlanta received a standing ovation. (At a neighboring hotel, standing ovations were also accorded Anita Bryant and President Carter for their invocations at the Southern Baptist Convention. In the midst of these events, "The Dick Cavett Show" featured a two-evening debate on homosexuality. Cavett's panelists included only one psychiatrist: Dr. Charles Socarides. A flauntingly orthodox psychoanalyst, Socarides had just published a "new" text, *Homosexuality* [Jason Aronson, 1978], a desperate face-lift of his earlier work *The Overt Homosexual* [Grune and Stratton, 1968]. Socarides had also just been appointed consulting psychiatrist for the Department of Defense.)

Following Lasch's talk at the convention, narcissism was illustrated by a full-length presentation of *Sunset Boulevard*, popular among film buffs as a Hollywood genre classic but sometimes derogated for its camp appeal to "the homosexual."

The post-Freudian psychoanalytic conception of "pathological narcissism" was developed by Columbia University Medical Center's Dr. Otto Kernberg, in some conflict with the similar observations of Dr. Heinz Kohut at the University of Chicago. The clinical syndromes of narcissism are described with the most arcane (for the lay reader) analytic liturgy in Kernberg's book *Borderline Conditions and Pathological Narcissism* (Jason Aronson, 1975). This information concerns the layman, however, since she, whether feminist, atheist, communist, single, or—especially— homosexual is precisely the antisocial deviant who will be most victimized by this new classification's vagueness and potential for political abuse.

The work of Kernberg and Kohut responded to the changing symptoms of patients in analytic therapy. According to one psychiatrist quoted by Lasch, "You used to see people coming in with handwashing compulsions, phobias, and familiar neuroses. Now you see mostly narcissists." According to Kernberg, the narcissist is summarily characterized by an inability "to accept the fact that a younger generation now possesses many of the previously cherished gratifications of beauty, wealth, power and, particularly, creativity. To be able to enjoy life in a process involving growing identification with other people's happiness and achievements is tragically beyond the capacity of narcissistic personalities."

In an interview for *Psychology Today* (June 1978), Dr. Kernberg observed that narcissists are often highly intelligent, creative, and productive individuals. "And, of course, narcissistic personalities can be found as leaders in political life, or in industry or academia, or as outstanding performers in the theater or the arts." In the next breath, however, he cautions that "careful observation of their productivity over a long period of time will give evidence of superficiality and flightiness in their work, of a lack of depth which reveals emptiness behind the glitter. Quite frequently, narcissists are the 'promising' geniuses who then surprise other people by never fulfilling the promise of their talents, whose development ultimately proves to be banal."

In fairness, the psychoanalysts are the first to admit that their work on narcissism is embryonic. Kernberg's text actually concludes with an apologia: "As our clinical and theoretical understanding of narcissism progresses, some of the confusing terminological issues and discrepancies between metapsychological formulations and clinical observations may be resolved into a more sharpened, circumscribed, and clinically relevant usage of the term narcissism." As if it weren't difficult enough to circumscribe and sharpen a concept like "narcissism" in the lab, Lasch has exploited this concept to characterize an entire culture.

As beheld by the professor of *Narcissism*, today's culture is without beauty. It is a venereal eyesore, a concubinage of vanity and cowardice in the outskirts of hell. Lasch exposes the culture of narcissism, beneath its costumes of self-improvement, for what he sees it to be—coy, castrating, and thoroughly corrupt: "In the Seventies, a harsher time, it appears that the prostitute, not the salesman, best exemplifies the qualities indispensable to success in American society. . . . She craves admiration but scorns those who provide it and thus derives little gratification from her social successes. . . . She remains a loner depending on others only as a hawk depends on chickens." In a word, the culture of narcissism is feminine, and patriarchal order is threatened by it.

The children of narcissism are also belligerent. In scornful transgression of authority, they wander in aimless search of the paternal discipline they never knew. Narcissistic expectations have the ring of "boundless optimism," but pierce with dissonant undertones of suppressed rage. In Lasch's ears, the hopes of today's generations become the selfish cries of unruly brats. Narcissists unconsciously seek the loving punishments that would set them straight. In the Law of the Father, in the guiding strength of his right hand, lies the narcissist's only true hope for salvation: "The moral discipline formerly associated with the work ethic still retains a value independent of the role it once played in the defense of property rights. That discipline—indispensable to the task of building a new order—endures most of all in those who knew the old order only as a broken promise, yet who took the promise more seriously than those who merely took it for granted." These trumpets of rectitude have already been dismissed by many critics as the familiar racket of reactionary backlash. But many critics have ignored—or perhaps not heard—its invocation of psychoanalytic psychiatry, of America's most subtly reverberant organ of patriarchal authority.

*The Culture of Narcissism* is difficult to read. Its prose is rhetorical, condescending, and as completely devoid of humor as it is of hope. The sensibility of moral outrage is sustained; a clear sense of direction, however, is not. In an early chapter, Lasch explains that "for the narcissist, the world is a mirror, whereas the rugged individualist saw it as an empty wilderness to be shaped to his own design." The ensuing chapters of *Nar-*

*cissism* wander aimlessly in reflections of psychoanalysis. Accusations of narcissistic decadence are zigzaggingly leveled at life-styles, ideologies, technologies, and bureaucracies; beyond that there is no unifying design, no sense of destination, no real shape.

Lasch is fixated in the present, rarely projecting, except in his despair, to the future. When his gaze finally does lift from its downward cast, it does so reluctantly, as if it were too late to anticipate anything but doom. That "the struggle against bureaucracy . . . requires a struggle against capitalism itself" comes too late in the last chapter to be anything but conspicuous. Two sentences later, Lasch's gaze has shifted abruptly from left to right: "Only then will the productive capacities of modern capitalism, together with the scientific knowledge that now serves it, come to serve the interests of humanity instead." Lasch's ambivalence here better characterizes the narcissist than the "rugged individualist" of his allusions.

Lasch's indictments are sometimes obscured by intimidating psychoanalytic imagery. More often, his use of the language of psychoanalysis sounds pretentious and archaic: "Chronically bored, restlessly in search of instantaneous intimacy—of emotional titillation without involvement and dependence—the narcissist is promiscuous and often pansexual as well, since the fusion of pregenital and Oedipal impulses in the service of aggression encourages polymorphous perversity."

An allegedly typical defense mechanism of clinical narcissism is "pseudo self-insight," a capacity for superficial self-reflection and criticism. An instance of this mechanism occurs in *Narcissism* when Lasch tries to mitigate the contradictions that may become apparent to the reader: "Theoretical precision about narcissism is important not only because the idea is so readily susceptible to moralistic inflation but because the practice of equating narcissism with everything selfish and disagreeable mitigates against historical specificity. Men have always been selfish, groups have always been ethnocentric; nothing is gained by giving these qualities a psychiatric label."

That said, Lasch resumes his otherwise nonstop fire-and-brimstone denunciation of every conceivable social vicissitude, from "The Apotheosis of Individualism" to "The Eclipse of Achievement," from "The Sexual 'Revolution' " to "The Socialization of Reproduction and the Collapse of Authority," from "Narcissism, Schizophrenia and the Family" to "Feminism and the Intensification of Sexual Warfare"—all are seen as the "narcissistic lesions" of Oedipal disease.

When they are mentioned at all, any positive aspirations or achievements of today's culture are dismissed as characteristically superficial. Lasch seems utterly unable "to accept the fact that a younger generation now possesses many of the previously cherished gratifications of beauty, wealth, power and, particularly, creativity."

Lasch repeatedly asserts hopelessly unsubstantiated psychoanalytic biases as if they were the proven formulas of major empirical scientists. But Lasch sees no inconsistency in reducing the scrupulously documented findings of preeminent sex researchers Masters and Johnson to one completely false and astonishingly arrogant quip: "The famous Masters-Johnson report on female sexuality added to anxieties by depicting women as sexually insatiable, inexhaustible in their capacity to experience orgasm after orgasm."

There is no mention here of *The Crisis of Psychoanalysis* (Fawcett), as Erich Fromm described it in 1970, or of *The Death of Psychiatry* (Penguin), which E. Fuller Torrey predicted in 1975. Lasch also neglects to counter Martin Gross's devastating critique of psychoanalytic theory and practice within the American psychiatric industry, *The Psychological Society* (Random House, 1978), and he barely mentions Thomas Szasz, perhaps the most articulate critic of psychoanalysis. Lasch skirts the fact that his indictments are based on the Freudian and post-Freudian assumptions, which have been superseded at most levels of theory and practice within the profession itself.

For Lasch, reduction and extrapolation are the dominating principles of criticism. Since psychoanalytic theory also accounts for psychosis, Lasch is quite comfortable in suggesting that mass murderers are the predictable result of Oedipal malnurture: "The criminal who murders or kidnaps a celebrity takes on the glamor of his victim. The Manson gang with their murder of Sharon Tate and her friends, the Symbionese Liberation Army with its abduction of Patty Hearst, share with the presidential and would-be assassins of recent years a similar psychology." Thus, Charles Manson is a narcissist. Are all narcissists potential Charles Mansons? "The contemporary psychoanalytic position," Lasch posits, is that "schizophrenia is above all a narcissistic disorder. It is not surprising, therefore, that studies of the family background of schizophrenic patients point to a number of features also associated with narcissistic families." The implicit relationship between narcissism and psychosis here gains special credibility by the discreet omission of what is apparently for Lasch a minor detail: that the evidence for physiological anomaly as the basis of most true schizophrenia has never been stronger. But even before these discoveries, the psychoanalytic theories of origin were already being discredited for lack of empirical data. As Gross concludes in *The Psychological Society*, "Events move quickly in the psychiatric world, but one fact is indisputable. As scientific advance continues in finding the cause of schizophrenia and the affective psychoses, and new treatments are developed to cure these scourges, the primitive cultist views of the Freudian revolution will recede as effectively as did the centuries-old theory of 'humors' causing sickness within the human body."

## The Connection to Homosexuality

Neither Kernberg nor Lasch talks much about an important historical correlate of narcissism: homosexuality. Since narcissism ("retarded adolescence," "arrested psychosexual development") is for most analysts the very definition of homosexuality, the relative absence of homosexuality from both books is both conspicuous and suspicious. While Kernberg briefly discusses what many analysts still call "sexual inversion," his few remarks leave no doubt that he holds the thoroughly discredited (even *officially*, within his own profession) orthodox psychoanalytic view that *all* homosexuality is pathologic and *always* narcissistically so. "We may classify male homosexuality along a continuum that differentiates the degree of severity of pathology of internalized object relations."

It is unclear what and whom Lasch is referring to when he discusses narcissists who are not necessarily more numerous than in the past, just more "conspicuous." According to Lasch, "radical lesbians ... carry the logic of separation to its ultimate futility." Yet male homosexuality is not mentioned directly—not once, even though "the" male homosexual is clearly Lasch's archetype of narcissistic decay.

Is Lasch subliminally courting homophobia? Is *The Culture of Narcissism*, despite its costume of social criticism, actually a gigantic subliminal attack on homosexuality?

Before determining the tactical advantages of playing down the psychoanalytic connections between narcissism and homosexuality, the substance of these connections must be examined. *Are* homosexuals narcissistic? Are they sociopathic? Are they paranoid? Are they (sado)masochistic? Is there indeed some truth to what Kernberg, Socarides, Bieber, Hatterer, Bergler say, to what an entire psychiatric and psychoanalytic tradition has been saying about homosexuality for more than fifty years?

Yes—the same kind of truth that labels blacks as sociopathic and of inferior intelligence because of their higher crime, unemployment, and illiteracy rates. Many homosexuals are obligatory narcissists. Deprived of role models, of social structuring, of identity, constantly ridiculed, threatened, punished, and endangered for natural sexual instincts, homosexuals have been completely excluded (not unlike women) from honest participation in the patriarchal societies they have lived in for almost two milleniums. The "narcissistic" self-absorption that so many homosexuals exhibit may actually be among the most extraordinary examples of human adaptability in the face of adversity, in the absence of alternatives, that nature has ever demonstrated.

What of the homosexual's "envy," his "barely suppressed antisocial rage"? Many homosexuals may envy most heterosexuals' incomparably greater freedom to love, to be openly proud of socially approved and rewarded sexual identities, to be their true selves. When a heterosexual male gives his girlfriend a public kiss in Omaha, he does not risk scandal, arrest, or even death.

As for the "rage," there may be a great deal of "antisocial hostility," even "heterophobia" among gays—a normal, sympathetic, and circumstantial reaction to the far greater preexisting homophobia (replete with legal persecutions and sociocultural proscriptions) of the sexually repressed, erotophobic Judeo-Christian middle class. (According to Masters and Johnson, one out of every two marriages in the United States is "a sexual disaster area.") It's entirely comparable to what blacks and Jews (with homosexuals) feel toward WASP chauvinism, to what Jews (with homosexuals) feel toward Nazis.

Paranoia? Some homosexuals may indeed feel paranoid. Oppressed, harassed, and endangered people, like Jews in the Third Reich, often become so. (On Sixth Avenue in Manhattan, someone actually stamped "narcissistic rage" over a series of posters advertising the "1979 International *Blueboy* Man of the Year Contest.")

Beyond all this lies the psychoanalytic piece de resistance: "distorted object relations." Homosexuals are allegedly incapable of establishing fully committed, "mature" relationships. Their sexual communications are said to be based entirely in fantasy. Worse, these fantasies are described as universally infantile and sadomasochistic. This line of reasoning can be similarly dissected. Homosexual coupling in patriarchal cultures has always been so fraught with guilt, with taboo, with serious, sometimes mortal danger that some homosexuals (like some heterosexuals with comparably repressive backgrounds) have been conditioned to include those elements in their lovemaking. For most homosexuals, as for most human beings, the instinct to love must be gratified even where risk or pain is conditionally involved. If that risk has been sufficiently augmented by sociocultural mores (the orthodox, patriarchal religions and their related political structures), these individuals may have "sadomasochistic" difficulties in expressing their warmest emotions. ("There's no question about it. Absolutely, unequivocally, religious orthodoxy, whether Jewish, Catholic, or Protestant, is responsible for a significant degree of sexual dysfunction" [Masters and Johnson].) If the resultant conditioning is sufficiently aversive, some of those same individuals may indeed have repeated difficulty in establishing close attachments, even in situations where risk has been lessened. If these people are thus narcissistic and sadomasochistic, they have been made so. Even today, prevailing social circumstances discourage most homosexuals and many heterosexuals from achieving sexual health and happiness.

What would be the advantage to Lasch and to Kernberg of so conspicuously understating and avoiding the psychoanalytic connection between narcissism and homosexuality? Simply this. The orthodox psychoanalysts and their intellectual converts are not unaware of the scientific fragility of their hypotheses. If the new narcissism were to be immediately assaulted on the basis of disreputable theories of homosexuality, its credibility would be seriously—perhaps mortally—undermined. By *subliminally* rather than overtly suggesting the connection, they minimize the risk of adverse publicity from gay protest.

Paranoid? Lasch has recently attended advisory sessions and a special White House dinner with President and Mrs. Carter. The reason? *The Culture of Narcissism* has been generously cited in presidential press interviews and on prime-time television as one of the most important influences on the president's political thinking.

Paranoid? A major goal of psychoanalytic pathologists of homosexuality has long been to find some way of publicly exposing the "true nature" of homosexuality. In the italicized words with which Dr. Edmund Bergler concluded his most inquisitionally homophobic book, *Homosexuality: Disease or Way of Life?* (Hill and Wang, 1956):

> *The only effective way of fighting and counteracting homosexuality would be the wide dissemination of the knowledge that there is nothing glamorous about suffering from the disease known as homosexuality, that the disease can be cured, and that this apparently*

*sexual disorder is invariably coupled with severe unconscious self-damage that will inevitably show up outside the sexual sphere as well, because it embraces the entire personality.*

*This triad of countermeasures could be effective—in the long run.*

With *The Culture of Narcissism*, that "way" has been found.

(Incidentally, Bernardo Bertolucci's film *Luna* could have been written by Bergler. It is the most recent example of the intellectual Left's discovery of the *new* narcissism. Here, Irving Bieber's Close-Binding-Intimate [CBI] Mother unconsciously encourages the "polymorphous perversity" of her heroin-addicted son in an incestuous minestrone of indigestible Freudian leftovers, served on stock Marxist platitudes. In *Luna*, homosexuality is oh-so-daringly unmasked as Mom-induced narcissism. If we were to eliminate capitalism and restore Dad to his rightful place in the nuclear family, psychoanalyst Bertolucci deduces, narcissistic pathologies like CBI-Mom and homosexuals would disappear [along with property, class, disharmony, and evil]. The picture could not be more clear: the *new* Left has discovered neo-Freud.)

The Bergler quotation highlights another important similarity between the new narcissism and homosexuality: the disastrous results of treating either conditions with what is allegedly the only hope for "cure"—psychoanalysis. The unbreakable strength of the narcissist's (and of the homosexual's) defenses is said to render "the narcissistic lesion" refractory to successful therapeutic intervention. Recidivism in therapy is consequently great.

So the patient most frequently encountered by today's psychoanalyst is "the narcissist." Narcissists are male and female, heterosexual and homosexual. But not all males, females, and heterosexuals are narcissists. *All* homosexuals, however, are. All suffer from pathology (smothering, sadistic mothers and absent, weak fathers). All narcissists (all homosexuals) could be treated, cured, with psychoanalysis. But because of their narcissistic belligerence, they in fact do poorly. Specifically, if they don't drop out early, they exhibit an extraordinary, often unassailable resistance to insight and change, depending on the character and extent of their pathology.

So the death of psychoanalytic credibility is not due to the empirical dismantling of psychoanalytic theories, not due to the $60,000 cost of a five-year, five-days-a-week analysis, not due to the analysts' disgraceful 33 percent "success rate" for treating these "disorders" (or anything else, for that matter), not due to the fact that a patient has a better prognosis for symptomatic improvement by *not* undergoing therapy, and not due to the fact that analytic institutes are now attracting few candidates. No: we are to believe that the failures of psychoanalysis are due to a recalcitrant, sociopathic therapeutic population for which there appears to be scant prognostic hope, for they are the culture of narcissism.

This is where nearly a century of (orthodox) psychoanalytic theorizing has brought us—back, full circle, to the nuclear family; back to "morality," to "discipline"; back to religious orthodoxy, to sexual repression, to homophobia; back, in other words, to patriarchy. We have returned to the civilization that engendered our need for psychoanalysis in the first place, returned to the "civilization" of our most wintery and profound discontents, born, yet again, of prejudice, of fear, of superstition, and of ignorance.

# SIMON KARLINSKY

# Decadence

The most popular dessert currently offered at the better Berkeley restaurants is a concoction called chocolate decadence. It consists of an excessively rich and sweet chocolate cake topped with an even more cloyingly sugared raspberry puree. Having tried it once, I thought the word *decadence*, with its connotations of the redundant, the overripe, and the degenerate, appropriate. Combined together, the two flavors all but canceled each other out and what was left was sugar, sugar, and more sugar. Why do so many discerning people like it, I wonder. Could it be the modish name? After all, the idea of decadence is now enjoying as great a vogue as it did in the last decades of the nineteenth century. Then, as now, it was bandied about as a negative epithet by those who felt their society was going through a moral and artistic decline. Then, as now, it was enthusiastically appropriated by a minority who believed they were the bearers of new social and aesthetic values appropriate for a world in a state of decay.

Personally, I was never happy with the use of the words *decadent* and *decadence* to describe either societal processes or developments in the arts. Neither those who revel in the idea of decadence nor those who revile it are ever clear about what the term means. Dictionary definitions are of no help. In literature, the word was first applied as a term of approval to the poetry of Charles Baudelaire and some of his successors, such as Mallarmé and Verlaine. But if *decadence* means decay or decline, how do we reconcile this with the fact that the poetry of Baudelaire (probably the greatest poet France ever produced), Mallarmé, and Verlaine is so obviously superior to that of their nondecadent predecessors, such as Victor Hugo or Lamartine?

In 1857, the year the French judiciary found nothing better to do with its time than to charge with corrupting public morals the greatest French novel of the nineteenth century, Flaubert's *Madame Bovary*, and the same century's finest collection of verse, Baudelaire's *The Flowers of Evil*, the conservative Catholic writer Montalembert thundered in a widely publicized speech that the younger generation of the time had gone decadent and abandoned "good taste and morality, reason and honor, conscience and faith" due to the encroachments of realism in literature, art, and philosophy. The magistrates at the trial of Baudelaire's book, having read Montalembert's speech in their morning papers, demanded that the poet remove from his collection six poems "conducive to the arousal of the senses by virtue of a coarse realism offensive to modesty." Two of the six offensively realistic poems they banned dealt with the theme of lesbianism, including "Lesbos," surely the most amazing affirmation of the value and beauty of lesbian love ever penned by a heterosexual male poet.

In 1899, the aged Leo Tolstoy sought to expose the decadence and corruption of czarist Russia in his novel *Resurrection* and his philosophical treatise *What Is Art?* As evidence he cited such, to his mind, self-evidently decadent new phenomena as the appreciation of French impressionist painters and the operas of Richard Wagner, trials of criminal cases by juries of the defendants' peers, and tolerant treatment of homosexuals by the police and society at large. Realism in literature? Trials by jury? It can be seen that, in historic perspective, the term *decadence* has been used with such a wide array of meanings as to virtually defy the possibility of precise definition. But I did not suspect just how imprecise it was until reading Richard Gilman's fascinating book-length essay, *Decadence: The Strange Life of an Epithet* (Farrar, Straus & Giroux, 1979). By the time Gilman is done with his investigation, there is not a shred of meaning left that one could logically claim for the word *decadence* other than as a senseless term of opprobrium or of equally senseless modish self-glorification. But the concepts that account for the term's survival and its recent new lease on life are exposed to our scrutiny, and they are anything but meaningless.

The essay begins and ends with understandably irritated enumerations of some of the uses to which the word is currently put by film critics, politicians, TV announcers, and *Women's Wear Daily*. The episodes of "The Forsyte Saga" are to be rerun in "one decadent 24-hour marathon showing." The dress designer Claude (Gilman means Karl) Lagerfeld is termed the "baron of decadence" because of the shape of some trench coats he designed. The Chinese press considers the present-day Soviet Union to be decadent. The critic Kenneth Tynan is quoted to the effect that life in Germany under the Weimar Republic (of which more presently) "was about as decadent as it's humanly possible to be," but adds that it was also fairly democratic and "seemed to be moving toward socialism." But another celebrated critic, Pauline Kael, regularly links decadence with fascism—that is, with the regime that destroyed the Weimar Republic and was its very opposite. Senator Jacob Javits speaks of the "systematic decadence" of Nixon's presidency, while a talk-show host thinks Hugh Hefner and *Playboy* are decadent, but adds that their decadence is of "a benevolent kind."

Now, clearly, all these people think they know what they mean by decadence. Yet how could life in Germany have been decadent under both the Weimar Republic and the Nazis? What do Nixon, Hefner, the Soviet Union as seen from China, and Lagerfeld's trench coats have in common? The body of Gilman's essay establishes the two perpetual myths that underlie all this diverse rhetoric: the myth of the Golden Age that has led people of all periods and cultures to assume blindly that the past has always been better than the present; and the pseudoanalogy between the birth, growth, and aging of the human organism and the inception and decline of human societies.

To quote Alexander Pushkin (one of the few great writers Gilman *does not* get around to citing in his essay): "The idea of the Golden Age is inherent in all nations. All it proves is that people are never satisfied with their present and, taught by experience to place little hope in the future, tend to adorn the irretrievable past with all the flowers of their imagination." While the word *decadence* did not gain currency until the Middle Ages, the idea that everything has declined in comparison with the past has been expressed again and again since the beginning of recorded history. Hesiod at the dawn of Greek civilization, Plato in *The Republic*, Horace, Lucretius, various church fathers of early Christianity, Voltaire in the eighteenth century, and the nineteenth-century French socialist Proudhon were all convinced that they lived at a time when taste and morals had declined, the arts had degenerated, and people were enjoying life less than their parents and grandparents did. The recent trend to idealize life in America during the confused, wartorn 1940s and the dull, repressive 1950s, as reflected in retro-fashions, films such as *Yanks* and musicals such as *Grease*, simply continues the same age-old error.

As to the concomitant notion that there are young and old societies and cultures, with the old ones becoming decadent through age, Gilman shows that this is a handy metaphor with little actual reality behind it. Societies mutate into their next phase. They may flourish or decline in importance. Or they might be physically exterminated. All this may offer some valid parallels with animal species, but not with individual human or animal organisms, which is presupposed in the idea of the decadence of a society. A declining species, yes, but can one seriously speak of a middle-aged or decadent species?

What, then, of those individual artists of the late nineteenth century who considered themselves to be, and were acclaimed by their admirers as, decadent? Gilman offers extended close-ups of Baudelaire, who, as he says, embodies the serious aspects of the popular idea of decadence, and of Oscar Wilde, who embodies its frivolous aspects. In both of these instances, a close examination of what is traditionally regarded as their decadence reveals it as two divergent examples of specialized dandyism, a pose consciously assumed by the artist as protective camouflage in order to survive in a philistine and puritanical age. In the case of Baudelaire, his self-degradation was initially motivated by a desire to shock his military-officer stepfather. This was his revenge for being prevented from squandering his inheritance (besides being a poet of genius, Baudelaire was also one of the worst examples in history of a pathologically compulsive spender). Eventually, his journey into the lower depths led Baudelaire to discover new, permanently valid forms of beauty in what was previously regarded as merely sordid. As for Wilde, Gilman sees his pose of dandy and dilettante as a "means of safeguarding from an uncomprehending and therefore intolerant public the immensely vulnerable seriousness of his worship [of beauty]."

Gilman is less convincing when he denies that Wilde's "masks and ruses" were intended as a cover-up for his homosexuality, on the grounds that "he never practiced as a homosexual nor showed any carnal leanings toward men until long after his reputation as an aesthete and dandy had been established." One would not think it necessary to point out in this day and age that acting out previously repressed homosexual desires is not what makes a person a homosexual. In fact, everything that Gilman writes about both Baudelaire and Wilde convinces me that their art and their decadent pose were closely interconnected with their respective sexuality—Wilde's lifelong homosexuality, whether acted out or not, and Baudelaire's lifelong masochism, expressed in his need to be rejected or humiliated by the women who attracted him (which also accounts in part for his fascination with lesbianism).

Another pertinent case from the Victorian age, not mentioned by Gilman, is Lautréamont. This was the pen name of Isidore Ducasse, who died at the age of twenty-four in 1870 and who wrote *The Songs of Maldoror*. A unique blend of a penny-awful horror novel and transcendent surrealistic poetry, the book is full of scenes of erotic violence that anticipate everything that recent punk rock has managed to devise. Ignored in his day, Lautréamont was rediscovered in the 1920s by the surrealists, who found his imagery congenial and who correctly perceived that his shock tactics were a form of protest against Victorian prudery and hypocrisy. But the surrealists themselves were guilty of prudery when they passed over in silence the fact that the sexuality of the protagonist of *The Songs of Maldoror* was not only sadomasochistic, but distinctly homosexual. As Alex de Jonge has pointed out in his study of Lautréamont, *Nightmare Culture* (St. Martin's, 1974), the only female being to whom the protagonist relates sexually is a giant female shark. Otherwise, the objects of his desire and of his erotic violence are invariably young men.

The Sixth Canto of *The Songs of Maldoror* is a parody, both hilarious and horrifying, of the seduction of a sheltered and innocent Victorian maiden by a cynical foreign libertine bent on destroying her. The hackneyed situation, all too familiar from the trashy novels and melodrama of the nineteenth century, sparkles with ironic new meanings through Lautréamont's stratagem (reminiscent of the musical comedy *Boy Meets Boy*) of making both the evil seducer and his eager victim homosexual males. Of course it would be simplistic to reduce the "decadent" postures of Baudelaire, Lautréamont, or Wilde to mere camouflage of aberrant sexuality. But it is also inescapable that their challenge to society contained a strong bid for liberating their sexual selves from incomprehending moralistic restrictions.

Richard Gilman covers the topic he selected—the uses of the term *decadence* as an epithet shown in historical perspective—so thoroughly that it makes little sense to chide him, as the critic Frank Kermode did in his hostile review (*New York Review of Books*, June 28, 1979), for not branching out into some tangential areas and writing a different book altogether. But it so happened that I read Gilman's book just before reading Alex de Jonge's book on Lautréamont and the very remarkable *Permissive Britain: Social Change in the Sixties and Seventies*, by Christie Davies (Pitman Publishing, 1975), the latter kindly brought to my attention by Louis Crompton. The three books in conjunction gave rise to some additional thoughts about decadence that I would like to share with the reader.

Among the places and periods associated with the idea of decadence in the popular mind, Gilman lists "Paris of the Belle Epoque, London of the Yellow Nineties [that is, prior to Oscar Wilde's trial], Istanbul, Berlin in the twenties, Hollywood, Fire Island." The grouping may be based on superficial stereotypes, as Gilman rightly complains. Yet there is a striking common denominator to all these places and periods: a thinly veiled or totally overt homosexual presence. Had modern Russian history been more generally known in the West, we would probably also find St. Petersburg between the end of the Russo-Japanese war of 1904–06 and the October Revolution of 1917 in this Baedeker of decadence. And, of course, the United States today is regarded as profoundly decadent not only by fundamentalists of various persuasions ranging from the Ayatollah Khomeini to Fidel Castro but also by many openly gay women and men who have not sorted out in their minds the difference between *decadence* and *liberation*.

Reading *Permissive Britain*, which contains a chapter examining the social and political conditions conducive to the emergence of an openly gay presence, with examples from British and German history, has confirmed for me that gay liberation in the America of the 1970s had its historical precedents in some periods which in subsequent, less permissive times have been branded "decadent." The instances I am most familiar with, besides today's America, are Russia during the decade before the Revolution and the Weimar Republic in Germany. In all three cases, the overt presence of homosexuality (in literature and the arts in Russia and in social and political life in Germany and America) became manifest after the respective country lost an unpopular war: the war with Japan in Russia, World War I in Germany, and Vietnam in America. For all three countries, the loss of the war meant the abandoning of all imperialist ambitions, a decline in the admiration of the army and the military, and a weakening of the dominant religions and ideologies. To those of a conservative turn of mind, this could only spell decadence.

But to continue the parallels: in all three cases the new permissive atmosphere also resulted in a tremendous increase of the freedom of expression for all strata of the population. Censorship was either curtailed or abolished. Hitherto silent minorities were heard from, more-just solutions to economic inequalities were sought (but not necessarily found), and widespread criticism of perceived abuses was not only expected but even encouraged. Literature and the arts went through a period of lively experiment and solid achievement. And homosexuals could stop hiding and pretending. They could be themselves.

Yet, in all three countries, the increase in freedom of expression and social concern was met with cynicism or with denials that it had happened. As in today's America, both the conservative elements and the countercultural dissidents of prerevolutionary Russia and of Germany of the twenties often regarded their time as corrupt and decadent. The more liberated each society became, the more generally it was perceived as being oppressive on an unprecedented scale. The totalitarians of the Right (the reactionary Black Hundreds in Russia, with their chauvinism and pogroms against the Jews, the Nazis in the Weimar Republic, and the New Right in today's America) and of the Left did their best to discredit the very idea of personal rights or democratic freedoms as illusory, fraudulent, and serving only the interests of plutocratic elites.

The persistent reputation of the Weimar Republic as the epitome of decadence is an especially striking instance of such historical astigmatism. The very name cannot be uttered these days without the compulsory adjective *decadent*. The managing editor of *Opera News*, Stephen Wadsworth, referred to that period as "a dark and cynical hour" in connection with the Met's recent production of the Brecht-Weill *Mahagonny* (that this piece of simpleminded agitprop can be taken so seriously today shows how close our mental climate is to that of the Weimar Republic). In a disgustingly homophobic essay in *Time* (December 3, 1979), reminiscent in tone of the notorious Jew-baiting tract *Protocols of the Elders of Zion*, Malcolm Muggeridge equated homosexuality with perfidy and treason, and wrote: "Such scenes [of homosexual destructive attitudes] can be best conveyed by the use of the word *decadence,* whose reality I first encountered in Weimar Germany, and which so easily turned into Hitler's Third Reich."

There you have it: homosexuality equals decadence equals fascism. This might be expected from an uninformed homophobe like Muggeridge. But how could Luchino Visconti build his entire film *The Damned* (called *Die Götterdämmerung* in Europe) around this very same notion? By suggesting that Hitler's advent to power was brought about by transvestites, child molesters, and the SA soldiers who liked wearing drag (he treats them all as if they were the same phenomenon), Visconti not only falsified history but let off the hook the millions of ordinary, respectable German shopkeepers, workers, and housewives who actually voted Hitler into power. Nor can I understand the enthusiasm of so many gay friends for the Liza Minnelli film *Cabaret*, where behind the amusing prattle about "divine decadence" and green fingernails, a strong implication was sounded that sexual permissiveness and widespread homosexuality are what brought the Nazis into power—an idea that was not even hinted at in Christopher Isherwood's original *Goodbye to Berlin* stories.

Once the Bolsheviks took over there were no more gay novels published or gay plays staged in Russia, as there had been between 1906 and 1917. (Gay poetry went on being published for a few more years.) After the Revolution, the entire permissive prerevolutionary decade was dubbed "decadent" by Soviet commentators. Hitler and Goebbels also regarded the time that preceded the Nazi regime as flabby and decadent. By Lenin's or Hitler's standards, we live in a decadent period today. As Richard Gilman's book shows, many of us complacently agree with their judgment.

Our own emerging Brecht, the playwright Albert Innaurato, writes play after play that shows our life and society as rotten to the core and obviously doomed. Numerous recent films spell out the same message. And, indeed, doesn't the fate of Russia in 1917 and Germany in 1933 indicate that we, too, are irrevocably fated to end up under a New Right fascist dictatorship or a Marxist-Leninist one?

Alexander Solzhenitsyn once outlined a theory of lost war as a blessing in disguise. At the very beginning of the eighteenth century there was a bloody war between Russia, then ruled by Peter the Great, and Sweden, ruled by Charles XII. After Russia won, Peter reinforced the system of serfdom, increased taxes, and embarked on a policy of militaristic expansion that imposed incalculable hardships on his subjects. Sweden, after losing the war, curtailed its military ambitions and concentrated on internal improvements that eventually gave its citizens one of the highest standards of living in Europe, centuries of prosperity, and a freedom of expression that was remarkable for its time. To some people's way of thinking, Sweden had become decadent.

It could just be that the loss of the Vietnam War handed the same kind of opportunity to the cause of human rights in America in general and to America's homosexuals in particular. Today's poets can shout from the rooftops what Oscar Wilde had to convey by hint and innuendo. Those who are into S and M, whether gay or straight, can enact their secret desires beyond the wildest imaginings of Baudelaire. But all too many people find this much freedom, for themselves or for others, unbearable. There are those who actually gag on it. Some idealize the Eisenhower 1950s. Some seek refuge in various cults. Others look longingly to countries like Cuba, a certifiably nondecadent society with a macho warrior-priest firmly in charge, with feared and respected troops who regularly engage in wars of imperialist conquest in Africa and elsewhere for the greater glory of the dominant ideological faith, and with the homosexuals cringing in fear where they cannot be seen—the same place they have been for so much of human history.

If we manage to use our post-Vietnam opportunity constructively, as, according to Solzhenitsyn, Sweden did in its equivalent period in the early eighteenth century (and so far we have—beautifully), we might convince ourselves and others that personal liberation that allows for each human being's individuality is not really decadent after all. If we waste this opportunity, it does not matter who comes to rule us: a new Dwight Eisenhower, an American Lenin, a Reverend Moon, or a fundamentalist American Khomeini. There will be no more gay parties or parades or baths or newspapers and no decadence—divine, chocolate, or otherwise. And when that happens, a few people here and there will come to understand that *decadence* was all along just a dirty word for "individual freedom."

## Interview with Guy Hocquenghem

*Let's begin by talking a bit about the history of the French gay movement, your involvement in it, and the differences between the French and American gay communities.*

The first thing to keep in mind is that we don't have a gay community in France. That is, we have a gay movement—with several organizations actively working for political rights, as in all the Western countries—but people do not feel part of a *community*, nor do they live together in certain parts of the city, as they do here in New York City or in San Francisco, for example. And this is the most important difference and the most significant aspect of gay life in the United States: not only having a "movement," but having a sense of community—even if it takes the form of "ghettos"—because it is the basis for anything else. Of course, unlike the United States, in France consensual sexual acts between adults have been legal since the French Revolution. So we don't carry with us the religious legacy of committing "unnatural acts"—at least as far as the state is concerned—as you must in the United States. You still haven't achieved separation of church and state, and paradoxically, this fact has been a basis for the gay movement.

*While retaining this distinction between a political movement and the existence of a gay community or a gay culture, the French gay movement has its roots in the Left and the events following May 1968. Would you briefly trace its development?*

Well, its roots were certainly not in traditional organizations of the Left—that is, the Communist or Socialist parties. Even among the student revolutionaries after 1968—and the issue was never raised in 1968—homosexuality and the idea of gay liberation was very controversial, because it was feared that we would alienate the working class. Furthermore, the Left in France was influenced ideologically in matters of sexuality by the idea of "sexual freedom"—meaning heterosexual freedom—of Wilhelm Reich, who was strongly homophobic. In fact, we had a little contingent at each First of May parade [the annual political march for the Left in Paris, including trade unionists, students, Communist Party members, activists], and with our gay-liberation banners and occasional drag queens we were continually harassed and even beaten up by the rest of the crowd—usually led by the Communists. It was very much like the situation of the pederasts of the North American Man-Boy Love Association (NAMBLA) at gay marches here in the United States. However, acceptance by the Left is increasing, and we are receiving a lot of support from the intellectual establishment in France. You know, most of its leading members—Roland Barthes, Michel Foucault, Louis Althusser, Jean Genet—are queens, with the exception of Sartre, who, incidentally, was the first to popularize Genet and who was an early supporter of gay rights.

Anyway, in 1971, after Stonewall, a group of us founded FHAR (Front Homosexuel d'Action Révolutionnaire) to work from within the Left and generally increase our visibility. And I must admit that considering the string of gay organizations which succeeded it, the first one was the best, as the first of anything—having sex, coming out, whatever—is always better than what follows it. We were all close friends, often living together, and our meetings were more like wild consciousness-raising sessions, and not like the strategy sessions and the vituperative polemical exchanges which followed in later organizations. FHAR eventually burst out of love (and sex, since it was these two elements which seemed to hold it together), into GLH (Groupe de Libération Homosexuelle), a network of twenty groups throughout France. It is, in fact, attempting to create a gay community by focusing upon activities like movies, shows, newspapers, and dances on the local level. It was as though FHAR, with both its foolishness and revolutionary self-confidence, constituted our act of coming out and proclaiming our difference from the rest of society, while the later groups seem concerned, in a more serious way, with the kinds of problems we face in our everyday existence as "out" gay people. This includes lobbying against the two remaining antigay laws in France: one which prohibits homosexual relationships with or among individuals under the age of consent and one which prohibits sex in public places such as parks, restrooms, parked cars, and so forth.

*Your film is entitled* Race d'Ep. Ep *is a derogatory colloquialism for* pédéraste, *like* faggot. *What is the word for* gay *in French?*

We don't have one; we don't have a word because we don't have the thing itself. You know, I think the name is the most important aspect of the thing it names. I think what we call "coming out" for gay people is saying, "I am gay." Nobody knows that you are gay until you say it—even if you are effeminate or show some outward signs that you are gay. It's not the same for, say, blacks, and the case is clearer here than it is for Jews: nobody will know that you are gay—perhaps not even yourself—unless you say it. The word *gay* is very useful because at the same time it is a very "positive" word, but it is not a sexual or a medical word. In France we have the problem of lacking the vocabulary with which to come out. The word *gai* has been tried without much success because nobody knows what it means, and anyway, it's an American word, and it makes people think of American imperialism. The problem of the *name*, of what we call ourselves or of what we are called, has always been one of our greatest problems. Every word that is used to describe homosexuality refers to a different social or historical being, to a different psychological status. So the terms *gay*, *sodomite*, *homosexual*, and *Uranian* do not all refer to the same thing, like the same character in different plays. That's why it's so important, as we show in the film, to keep in mind when the term *homosexual* was invented in the nineteenth century and when the term *gay*, albeit with its roots in Whitman, was invented in the twentieth—in fact, only ten years ago.

*Well, following this notion of the significance of* naming, *giving something a being or an identity in the world, what historical or psychological forces are represented in our use of the word* gay *to describe ourselves? It is crucial, it seems to me, that in this case the name was chosen by the people to whom it refers and not, as with psychiatric or medical or religious nomenclature, imposed by others.*

You are absolutely right. The word we use to represent ourselves—to signify the way we are *supposed* to be—contains two ideas. The first is the sense of joy for being who we are and the end of self-hatred. The second is the assertion that gay people are at the same time cultural troublemakers—as in Whitman's sense of *gay*—and a positive solution to the modern crisis, that we will build a world of love and joy and poetry. We and the ways in which we live our lives are, in a sense, models for everybody and not just for gays in the strict sense. But the most important point is this *way* in which we are creating our identity: by choosing our name and saying it. For us, the most important fact in our lives—psychologically, socially, or politically—is not having sex, because even heterosexuals have homosexual sex, but rather *saying our name,* saying "I am." It is this self-conscious effort to gain an identity that distinguishes us from all other social minorities as well as from homosexuals in any other historical period. We are not like a minority to which people can point because they all have the same skin color or because they are all the same race and can be given a name. This is absolutely not the way we came into being, because our effort has been to create an identity which didn't exist before. Feminists claim that women have never had an identity, but they have always had one, even if it was male-created and oppressive: there has always been a "culture of the female," as manifested by certain female writers and certain ideas upon which it is based, matters of daily life surrounding the household, emotional intimacy, and the like. And there is nothing in history that approaches the existence of a "homosexual consciousness" such as we have now. I don't agree with the idea of a homosexual history beginning in classical Greece and continuing into the present. Homosexuality in Greece was mainly pederastic and was linked with an idea of erotic education to integrate young boys into the society; it had nothing to do with what we now call "gay consciousness" or even with homosexuality itself. In fact, most homosexuality before the end of the eighteenth century was mainly either pederastic or libertine—that is, concerned with the deliberate breaking of divine or natural law, as we find in Sade and in some atheist and sacrilegious attitudes, unrelated to a particular kind of sexuality or to a distinct subculture with a corresponding individual and social identity. In fact, it constituted more of a negative identity. The emergence of a specific homosexual subculture occurred only in the mid-nineteenth century, with particular ways of dressing, specific places for cruising, and characteristic behaviors which are shown in the police records of the time for London, Paris, and Berlin. So we must say that homosexuality in the modern sense of the term is an invention of the Western urban way of life in the nineteenth century and has a more or less continuous history up to the 1930s—then a gap of virtually complete suppression until the late sixties and the Stonewall rebellion.

*Yes, there is a historical silence during the thirty-year period beginning when the Nazis came into power and including the Soviet suppression of gays. What is shocking is that most gay men and lesbians, I believe, don't realize how total this silence was. We seem to lack the historical sense which other social groups have attempted to cultivate—often, as in the case of blacks and women, despite an oppressive "history" already written by others.*

It's a very strange fact. In 1969 here and in 1971 in France, we were absolutely sure that we were the first to be involved in anything like a gay-rights movement—which is simply wrong. Even now, there are only two or three books on gay history, and only one film—ours! Perhaps it's related to the fact that we don't have children, that we have to reconstitute our world in each generation. If you don't have a direct and very obvious, visible way of transmitting the gay idea, it just stops. An isolated person is *not* a gay person. An isolated black person is always black, that's obvious. But someone perfectly alone as a gay person is not gay; he isn't acting as a gay, he isn't even having homosexual sex, except perhaps cautiously, the way many heterosexuals do. He thinks that he is the only person who might be gay, and he probably wouldn't even be thinking *that*—since being the *only* one would mean that he is a monster—so he doesn't have any kind of social identity.

*And this was the historical fact for the period from 1933 or 1934 up to the 1950s; even into the 1960s there were only very rare and weak exceptions, like the Mattachine Society or the Daughters of Bilitis.*

You know, there was a gay community in Germany before the Nazi period which had all the characteristics of the community we have now—including community centers, balls, newspapers, a scientific research institute—everything. I am struck by the ignorance among gay people about the past—no, more even than ignorance: the "will to forget" the German gay holocaust. That we forgot about these hundreds of thousands of people and about the fact that out of one hundred years of gay life, in thirty of them we had a virtual vacuum—that we forgot in such a *radical* way is, I think, something of a warning. This has happened to no other minority. Even the Armenian genocide was remembered, at least by the Armenians. But *we* aren't even the only ones who remember—*we don't remember!* So we find ourselves beginning at zero in each generation. Our lesson from history, then, is that we can't be sure we won't be suppressed.

*And also that we secretly know that and don't want to be reminded of it.*

The fact that we can be totally suppressed is very special to our situation. A sexual minority—and we are the only sexual minority—is much easier to suppress than, say, women, who are not a minority anyway and whose suppression would result in the end of society. Homosexuals are far easier to suppress than any political or racial minority—which, historically, has never been completely successful or has been so for only a limited time.

*We know from experience that it is possible to completely destroy a sexual minority: it is not even a question of being hidden, but of continuing to exist. When we become invisible and act just like heterosexuals, we cease to exist: we lose any historical significance as well as any real expression in the daily life of society.*

As long as gay genocide is not officially acknowledged, it *could* happen again. This is not to say that it *will* happen but that somehow the political forces against us can keep it in mind. Perhaps I sound like a doom-sayer. But if you put these two ideas together—gays having become "visible" in American society without having acquired any significant political protection or status, and this new role of "scapegoat," in which gays seem to have replaced the traditional scapegoat, the Jews—you can't be unaware of a dangerous trend. If there really is a social crisis beginning, gays are in a position similar to that of the Jews in pre-Nazi society. They are suspected of being a powerful and secret "conspiracy," supposedly rich—or at least luxury consumers—and the most advanced innovators of the capitalist economy. Just the right image to make us scapegoats both for public immorality and for inflation.

*Why do you say we are the only sexual minority?*

Everybody talks about sexual minorities, by which they seem to mean the feminist movement and the homosexual movement. But women are not a minority, and they don't constitute a movement based upon sexuality. Gay people, despite their diversity, comprise a single sexual minority. This idea of a sexual minority is a very modern one and is related to the idea that sex itself has a real social significance. That is, in previous centuries, people did not look at sex or employ the notion of sexuality as an important way to understand social life. Rather, they spoke of sin, marriage, childrearing practices, pleasure, lust, and so forth in their discourse about the nature of society. Thus, sexuality is a very modern category in this regard and is connected with the development of medical science and psychoanalysis in the nineteenth century. It has been invested with such social significance that sexual oppression is coming to be viewed as comparable to, for example, workers' oppression. So the idea of a sexual minority—that is, people who are defined by the fact that they are "different from the others" sexually and that they are marginal in society and who, as a result, become a distinct social group with its own culture and self-identity—this is something very new. Gays are the only group of this kind. Of course, history could have placed people in this category by virtue of the fact that they engaged in some other activity, like having sex with animals, but it didn't happen that way. The historical task of being the idea of a sexual minority personified was performed under the label of "homosexual."

*What are your observations on the gay community here in the United States?*

Well, there are several. Here, everyone seems to think that because we are a significant social movement—which is true—that we are also an organized minority group in the political arena just like any other group. I think there are some important differences, though. We are always overestimating our real strength on the official level. I am struck by the fact that after years of gay marches with hundreds of thousands of people and with millions of people living in gay ghettos, there have been no significant successes on the legislative level—you have an antisodomy law here in New York and could all be put in jail tomorrow. Also, you have no directly elected, openly gay officials; you have some political appointees and some officials working behind the scenes to provide a gay voice in the everyday workings of government, but with the exception of Harvey Milk—and a very unusual exception he was—you have no gay politicians. This is obviously different from other minorities—there are black and women politicians who are elected in large part because they are representatives of these groups. Not only do you not have ordinary politicians who have let it be known that they are gay, you don't even have gay officials who see themselves—as do those of other minority groups—as representing the gay community with respect to any given issue. Other minority politicians would never get away with this. Instead, you have politicians who defend themselves against the idea that being openly gay is decisive in relation to the kinds of policies they seek to promote. The gay community puts up with this because, I think, many of us feel the same way as these politicians about our gayness—"If things go too far, I will just retreat and return to my closet." I don't think this is possible, but this sentiment does seem to be just below the surface in the gay community.

At the same time, we are always *underrepresented* and *overestimating* our strength. There is something like a misunderstanding between society and us: we think we have the right to be represented, and we *are* represented, whether by gay or sympathetic straight officials, while society (including most of its politicians) thinks that we are not represented and doesn't even recognize us as a legitimate minority. This illusion of the gay community is reinforced by the vicious ambiguity of many of your politicians. This occurs, for example, in the kind of artificial support which you receive from some of them, as when Marion Barry, the mayor of Washington, sent a message of support for gay rights to the March on Washington, but refused to present it himself, as though this would give him the opportunity to deny it someday. It occurs when certain politicians, like your mayor here in New York, exploit what is perceived within the gay community as the ambiguity of their sexual preference, so that straights think that this politician is straight while gays think he or she is gay. Of course, it is our fault for believing that this person is gay and is working for us but cannot come out for fear of public opinion and losing his or her effectiveness. It's as though we try to imagine them, since we don't have any real gay leaders—and you in America have nothing like a Martin Luther King for the gay movement. So the gay community has the illusion of political power when in fact it has none, and this is the result of the kind of action we have tried to take politically—always indirect, through lobbying for civil rights at the level of the aides to those who actually have power. And my condemnation of this approach is not a moral one, it's a practical one: this approach has not worked.

These discussions in the States about "gay capitalism" remind me of those during the Vietnam War, as though we should compare this segment of the gay community to a "national bourgeoisie" or to a "comprador bourgeoisie." Of course, the gay movement has been moving dangerously far to the Right since its early days, but it is ironic that we are all worried about the implications of the growth of this thing we call "gay capitalism"—whether we should endorse its growth and work with gay capitalists as a political strategy—and yet we aren't gaining any of the bourgeois benefits of its alleged growth.

*Don't you agree that the texture of daily life for the average gay person has changed for the better over the past ten years and that to a large extent this has been accomplished necessarily within the framework of "gay capitalism"—of gay-owned businesses which provide services and opportunities to members of the gay community which were never before available, as well as financial support for the political initiatives of the gay community? It is an irony that "gay capitalism" has been a principal vehicle for building a gay community.*

You are right, but I wouldn't call what you've described "gay capitalism," or if it is, it's gay capitalism at a very primitive level. The idea of gay capitalism implies a very strong economic power which can be used for political lobbying and in the marketplace against other powerful capitalist interests. We tend to confuse gay capitalism and simple aspects of gay life itself—an association of bar owners, of gay businessmen, even of the gay media, which are nationwide—all these seem very powerful to us on the *inside*, because they represent such a large chunk of our daily lives. However, viewed from the *outside*, two things become apparent: first, it is a very weak economic power in relation to others in this society; and second, it is a masochistic one, because it wants to deny the very basis of its own growth—that is, once these capitalists have reached a certain point in their development, they become reactionary, claiming that political militancy among gays will only bring down the wrath of others on us, that all we need is a good friend in the government to protect us, and that while it's all right to be open about our sexuality inside the ghetto, we should hide ourselves from the outside world. No, what we call gay capitalism is really akin to a consumer movement. What is important to a capitalist society is the gay market and the colonization of sexual needs as a solution, on some level, to the capitalist economic crisis.

*I see your point. And since consumerist self-help associations constitute a decentralized network, unlike the centralized power which corporations can use to influence political decisions, I can understand your distaste for lobbying. We are the perfect consumers, at least in theory, for a variety of reasons, and we are rather affluent for a stigmatized minority. Doesn't the existence of a "gay market" give us the basis for a certain kind of political power, through, for example, a boycott?*

Yes, I think we are closer than ever before to becoming an economic power. The economic power of gay people is based on the fact that they spend a lot of money and that they are very sensitive about *what* they buy, a sensitivity which is connected with the consciousness about *fashion* among gays. So, a gay person might say, "I just won't use this product any more, it isn't chic," or, "I just can't feel those Village People any more, they've lost something for me." It is as if your tastes about what you buy are related to your situation as a gay person, but you don't know *how* it is related. And because this decision is not necessarily a consciously ideological one, it results in a form of boycott which is not "political" in the conventional sense, but is more of a life-style boycott. Of course, I'm not saying that the orange-juice boycott caused sales to collapse; it didn't have to do that to create a lot of problems for the orange-juice producers.

*Yes, here we have a very decentralized economic power, yet a commu-*

*nity that is in touch with itself through the "gay grapevine" with fashion as its code, and the result is a very spontaneous form of action.*

It is spontaneous, yet potentially very strong and very efficient.

*What do you think has created the gap between women and men in the gay community—the separation in our social lives, our differing political views, the mutual distrust that many gay men and lesbians feel toward each other? Do you think there is any basis for cooperation among us?*

Perhaps we should ask: by what abberation is the women's movement linked to the homosexual male's movement? That is a paradox in itself. In the domain of sex itself, what women call sex and what gay men call sex is incommensurable. All you have to do is read feminist literature on the nature of the orgasm and the way women are feeling; it's something related to maternal feelings, secure and warm, to something profound, often using the image of the sea. I don't know if they really have these feelings or only want to, but it is in these terms that they express themselves. To understand their difference from men, we need only go to the West Village and see all those people trying desperately to be fucked no less than ten times a night. It's quite the contrary from women and is related to speed, variety, superficiality. Of course, it's also related to the male potency fantasy—the impossible search for the "hard cock" which will never let us down. Women don't have this problem—they have the problem of frigidity, but it's very different. Unlike men, they have nothing to "prove." Naturally, I don't think masculine values are any more progressive than feminine ones; I'm not making a moral judgment. I'm only describing the way we have pleasure and the way women have pleasure.

There is also the very important problem of the age at which you can begin to describe a person as sexual. Sexuality begins as something *responsible* in women, as they themselves say; it begins later than in boys, and it comes with experience; it's not the obsession that it is with young boys. Women are not ex-male teenagers, and this is the main reason they have not supported a lowering of the age of consent. They cannot understand the real crucifixion of young males who are denied sex. A twelve-year-old boy, for example, is just a little sexual animal—it's a fact that a little boy is obsessed with his own cock. We are built that way, and I think the cruelest thing that can be done to a human male is to prevent him from having sex.

*I think many feminists would claim that your conception of the difference between male and female sexuality is not a "natural" one but rather a consequence of socialization into a patriarchal society.*

But *I* didn't decide that these characteristics were natural or not; I was quoting the women themselves. *They* decided that it was important to represent certain characteristics as naturally feminine. It is as if—just as in gay consciousness—the "coming out" of women involves a conscious decision to say that they are linked to a certain number of values which are specifically feminine. I don't know if they're right or not, but I think that it is perhaps the most vicious way of repressing sex—suggesting that asexuality is the only paradise and the solution to war and all the world's problems, like a dream of complete security.

Of course, we gay men are living lives of "hard sex," and gay life is becoming harder and harder here in New York. A lot of this is very theatrical, but it's difficult to know when the comedy ends and when real life begins. People are becoming less and less concerned with human rights, and in the erotic sphere—cruising, picking someone up, leaving him afterward—relationships are becoming more and more dehumanized.

*Sex itself has been banalized; it has become a minor event, like going to the bathroom. But is this necessarily a negative development, considering the exaggerated romanticism and profound guilt with which we tended to endow it before? However, it is dehumanizing when we objectify others so that they become mere machines for our gratification.*

Yes, but the traditional way of objectifying was very different. It used to describe, for example, violence as the expression of a specific emotional need, but in a very sensational sense, like the murder of Pasolini or mass murder for pleasure. What is happening now is obviously not that, but rather a very subtle, soft, nonaggressive form of dehumanization. What is new is that we have banalized sex without feeling guilty about it. Of course, we had this kind of sex before, but always felt guilty about it; not any longer. And this—very banal, simple dehumanization, not at all romantic or tragic—constitutes the art of what you call the "clone." And we can even call *ourselves* "clones" without any fear, which is at least paradoxical, because we see ourselves as simple sex machines with similar habits and feelings in common. Just don't worry about what all these women do—always having sentiments and crying after you. I think it's related to the general concern with virility among males in the United States, combining the softness of sexuality with the hard power of an obsession with the sex act itself.

Anyway, the third point of conflict between women and gay men concerns education and rests on the simple fact that motherhood has always been in conflict with gay male sensuality; within the family, this constitutes the fundamental problem in childhood. Naturally, we are talking about the women of patriarchal society whose role is to raise children. It's very strange, because although the "new woman" is not supposed to have her life defined by the raising of children, she is now standing up and saying, "I want my children back." And she is saying it in a very political way, by having rallies against pornography, demonstrations against kiddie porno—this is the beginning of something which is simply antigay. What they are actually saying is, "We don't want our children taken by pederasts or becoming *gay.*" You know, if there was to be a new moral campaign in the United States, it would be very efficient to use feminist ideology or simply women against gay people. Nobody wants to believe it when some old Baptist minister rants against gays, but when women, especially feminists who consider themselves the leading edge of the sexual revolution, appear on television speaking out against obscenity and pornography, it has a very powerful effect. And who are the main offenders here? It is mainly—almost as if these were code words for—gay men. Not just pederasts, either, but also those into S and M and drag queens—who are supposed to be parodies of women.

*It's as though the image of women leading these campaigns is the only way to reach something deep in the consciousness of Middle America, to*

*break through its ideology of "do your own thing" by claiming that fun-*
*damental and irreparable moral damage will result if this position is taken*
*with respect to gays.*

Yes. It seems as though consensual homosexual acts between adults are
something that Middle America is beginning to accept. But they won't accept the possibility that this might continue into the next generation. It's as
though they have a conscious or subconscious agreement with themselves:
they can't put all the gays alive to death now because so many of them have
come out, there have been so many human testimonies about them, and so
forth. But they *can* try to prevent the same thing from happening in the
*next* generation. So this is the significance of education, because it is the
only way to suppress homosexuality. And it is for the same reason that I
think gay child-custody cases will, in the future, be one of the fiercest battles we'll have to fight. I think there will be more and more public trials
surrounding the attempt of gay people who had children before they came
out to gain and retain custody of them. It's a good thing that the March on
Washington articulated this as one of its demands.

*I can understand, now, why you believe that ending the prohibition*
*against pederasty and lowering the age of sexual consent is so crucial for*
*gay people.*

I think that childhood is a central problem of our era, for the simple
reason that we know so little about it. You know, except for the nobility,
people in ancient times weren't that concerned about their families, and
even the nobles were concerned only for the transmission of their names.
The family itself did not have any great social significance, nor was it a
matter of concern for the individual consciousness. There are many historical works which have been written about this, like those of Foucault, Don-
zelot, and Aries. With the emergence of the modern family, two new ideas
become both the greatest social problems as well as the central ideals of
human happiness: raising children and having sex. All major political
struggles are like storms hovering over these problems. This modern social
concern is growing in a very imperialistic way, as people in Africa and Asia
are also beginning to create families in the Western sense. But within the
new family, it was the women who were placed in complete charge of the
children, and, in the last century, patriarchal society made this appear as
natural law. As Edmund Shorter has shown in his book on the history of
the family, there was a complete disinterest in young children before
Rousseau, and it took a hundred years after that to develop enough of a
concern for raising children to turn it into a subject for social science. So
women were, so to speak, professionally built by society to be child-raisers.
Thus, women came to see themselves as in charge of children affectively
and, therefore, the only ones who are really able to *love* children—which,
obviously, is the best way to instill an education, because it's like black-
mailing someone. Before the child can say or think anything, you declare,
"I am the only one who really loves you." Well, I'm really afraid that this
position between women and men is reaching a contradiction, and I'm very
sad about it because I like women very much.

*I'm glad you said that because many of your comments on these issues*
*of sexuality and education could be interpreted as being against women*
*per se and as advocating, for example, gay male separatism.*

Not at all. I'm absolutely against this kind of monstrous racism we find in the West Village which makes it scandalous to have any female friends. Are we in the Middle Ages? However, this doesn't mean that I think women have the right to proclaim themselves the "leading class" of the sexual struggle by virtue of being the most oppressed class in a sexist society—just as Marx proclaimed the proletariat to be the most oppressed class in the struggle against capitalism. We are all oppressed in a sexist society, and I think there's nothing more dangerous than when one group claims to have a monopoly on truth or moral righteousness in this kind of a struggle. Up to now, lesbians have taken mainly retrogressive positions on the new issues of the gay movement, which mainly include pedophilia. Also, it seems to me that many gay men are ashamed to discuss certain aspects of their daily lives with lesbians, and it shouldn't be this way. The best lesbians, to my way of thinking, are the ones who don't care what gay men do in the privacy of their own homes.

*It sounds, again, as though you don't think there is much of a basis for political cooperation between gay men and lesbians.*

If we want to continue in an activist struggle common to women and men, we must take this contradiction into account—that is, the contradiction between gay men and lesbians in relation to who can care for, and love, children. I don't think the gap between our respective ways of experiencing sex constitutes a contradiction—only the fact that we live in different sexual universes. But we must acknowledge this as well. We can't just put some lesbians in the front of a march or rally, like little angels, and never speak about sex or the problems which divide us. The March on Washington, which was very positive and successful, made people feel very proud but, I think, at the same time deceived them. There is a kind of political hypocrisy in the gay movement which tries to cover up the differences between, for example, gay men and lesbians, between white and black gay men—who tend to suffer more harassment than whites, from other blacks. Let me put it this way: there are many new conflictive situations in the gay movement now, and there will be more in the future. I think we must discuss these problems in an open and honest way. I don't agree with those who say that since we are in a political movement, we should postpone discussion until sometime in the future, "after the revolution."

*Earlier, you spoke of the lack of any real leaders in the gay community. Could you elaborate on this assertion?*

Until now, we have not had a sufficiently strong political identity to have a leader; we're not sure that we want a leader, because we feel that if things start going badly for us, we will just go back into our closets. And I think people are afraid to be leaders for this reason too, which is not a bad situation, because it makes the movement more democratic—even though the resulting collective leadership is composed of people who are much more politically moderate. It's related to our self-identity, which is not necessarily the positive assertion we usually think it is: "I am proud to be gay, and I think everyone else should be too." There is something fanatical and frail in this self-identity, as though people feel that they have to make the best of their time and energies in these few days before the return of some horrible repression.

*As though gay liberation of the past ten years is a dream from which we will soon awaken. Underlying our professed self-confidence, there is a deep feeling of frailty—that we are living on borrowed time. Perhaps it is symptomatic of the acceleration of our lives due to a movement which in ten years has accomplished what wasn't accomplished in forty years in Germany—or by any other minority, for that matter—and this fact must be acknowledged. Nevertheless, you can imagine what kind of panic would occur if ten gay activists were arrested tomorrow. Don't you think it's significant that gays are speaking to millions of people on television about their sexuality?*

Where they are boring everybody by telling them about the dignity they have. They *certainly* don't speak about their sexuality. I sat for two hours in front of the television and not once did they speak about fucking. It's incredible—they're there because they're supposed to be the sexual part of our society, but any advertisement is more sexual than they are.

*I think we don't want to be completely out, as you suggested earlier in relation to gay capitalism, where it sounded like a criticism. But I think it's related to something very deep in our psyches. You know, we certainly don't conceive of ourselves as a political party, and I'm sure neither you nor I think of ourselves as only political beings.*

Besides, people are afraid of being shot if they are in such a leadership position, and I can empathize with them. It's one thing being murdered for *pleasure;* it's quite another . . . to be murdered for *that.*

*Did you have fun at the Mineshaft last night?*

I think the bar area at the Mineshaft is the most human place in New York. And I love all the drag leather queens there. Beyond that, the "non-speaking area" begins: the S-and-M back room. I must admit that I can't have sex without speaking. And I am rather confused about S and M and have been for ten years. It has become the most successful gay sex scene—discos are the *fun* scene, and poppers, back rooms, fistfucking, and leather are the *sex* scene. *Specialization.* And as far as we gays think of ourselves mainly as sexual beings, S and M has become our main ideological problem.

At the same time, it's a very idealistic scene—acting or creating the theater of sex, rather than simply "doing it"—and a very imperialist one as well: every gay person is supposed to be deeply, unconsciously perhaps, secretly at least, involved in "heavy sex." If some don't do it, it's just because they are self-repressed. S and M is *the* sex: the kind we always desired from the time we became homosexuals, a sex game between real tough men—the theater of what male heterosexuals would be doing between themselves if they had sex together. It is also a very *fragile* theater, which is why it's a nonspeaking area: no critics allowed, actors perform only for a participating public.

I don't want to enter into a discussion of the various psychological explanations of this, like those which attempt to understand us through the sadomasochistic implications of anal intercourse or through the idea of narcissism. Let me only say that we gays are doing everything we can to accredit these theories—which would perhaps be a better way of getting at the root issue here. We have always, in pre-Nazi and Hirschfeld's Germany as now, acted as symptoms or *proofs* of what the latest theory about us was. We enjoy that. Rather than expressing guilt—for breaking society's taboo against homosexuality—the S-and-M sex code expresses the "sophisticated" pleasure of being a complete cliche, destroying oppressive social imagery of us by caricaturing it ourselves—perversion as the negation of neurosis, or the pleasure of punition subverting the moral code of painful guilt. But at the same time, don't be too optimistic. Many of us are dealing with what used to be conceived—in Sade, for example—as an aristocratic subversion in a very direct way, by taking S and M beyond mere theater. John Rechy, in his book *Rushes*, stressed this very simple point: S and M is the theater of the real violence that imposes itself on gays, and we should note that the growth of the "new" homophobia and of S-and-M sex are occurring at the same time. Whether the explanation is a *political* one, as the reflection of violence directed against us from outside our own community, or *feminist*, as the macho dream beginning to express itself shamelessly in places forbidden to women, or even *Marxist*, as a new consumerization and commercialization of gay sex in the form of a complete S-and-M sex package—all these explanations are missing something. I think it is more simple than that.

*A transformation in the conception of sex itself seems to have occurred, which is in evidence among those at the Mineshaft. Sex is no longer simply "doing it." It has essentially become more of a voyeuristic and exhibitionistic activity.*

Yes, I was struck by this incredible transformation, a paradoxical one which I can't completely enjoy. Most Mineshaft consumers don't do anything "sexual," in the old sense. They show, they look at. Exhibitionism seems to be the real new perversion, playing upon the boundary between private and public. The real aim of this new sex is to become a solution to the oldest unsolved problem of male sexuality: impotence. Curiously enough, the "hard cock" becomes, in the leather scene, a pure and simple figure of rhetoric most of the time. Rare, very rare, are the hard cocks at the Mineshaft: drugs and alcohol have destroyed simply "sexual" energy. But nobody cares: fist replaces cock, piss replaces sperm, showing and looking replace doing. Have slaves or masters instead of lovers; submit instead of being fucked. Of course, you will *also* be fucked—sometimes, in the morning usually, but not so often, and even then, only because your master is still an old-fashioned homosexual in leather drag. Be a man, a real one, without being afraid of a possible treason by your unreliable penis. Just buy a whip and a jockstrap.

# Goodbye to Sally Gerhart

*T*he issue of pornography can be boiled down to a very sharp dichotomy:

To women: The experience and fear of unleashed male sexuality in the form of rape is the most naked expression of women's domination by men. Freedom from rape is the first, necessary step toward women's liberation. Anything that glorifies, encourages, or forgives rape—actually or symbolically—is intolerable. To women, pornography is precisely such a symbolic act of rape.

To gay men: The fear of one's own sexuality, especially in the form of internalized self-hatred and self-disgust, is the most pernicious expression of sexism in our society. The first step toward personal and communal liberation is unlearning those lessons of socialization which made our cocks and asses dirty. The acceptance of our bodies, the unhindered celebration of our sexuality, and the act of loving other men spiritually, romantically, *and physically* is the necessary first step toward liberation. Anything that helps to free our repressed selves—including pornography—has a positive value.

Those two statements contain a profound basis for opposition. But the recent feminist turn toward a stance of puritanical guardianship of sexual morality has short-circuited any possible explorations of the important implications of this opposition for both the gay and women's movements.

There is less and less doubt that the women's movement is perfectly willing to bully gay men over issues of male sexual expression. Recent conferences, including the last National Organization for Women (NOW) national convention, have laid down the law: you gay men must be respectable if you want to stand with us. That message provokes an automatic negative response in gay men. Just as rape is a "tape" for women, just as it produces intolerably painful associations with their sense of powerlessness, so does any injunction to be respectable activate insufferably painful tapes for us. The specific association involves the haunting memories of the desperate hope that gay men would be accepted if only ... if only you get rid of the drag queens ... if only you wouldn't flaunt your sexuality ... if only you wouldn't talk about *it* so much ... if only you wore decent clothes ... if only we didn't know what you did ... *then* we would accept you. The problem is that if we did do all those things and excluded all those people, we would no longer be gay.

NOW and its sister organizations have simply escalated the "if onlys." If only gay men wouldn't indulge in promiscuous sex, would give up explorations of sadomasochism, would cease any exploration of intergenerational sex, then we would be okay.

But men who define themselves as members of the gay community don't seem willing to give in to these demands any longer. For one thing, the source of liberation is increasingly seen as coming from *within* our own community. Relationships with the rest of society are based less often on a search for acceptance by others and more often assumed to be contentious. This, really, is the primary reason for the ghettos of gay America and the ascendance of the clone, probably the most unfairly demeaned political activist in the short history of the gay movement. It is the clone and his personal decision to wear the uniform of the ghetto that are finally quantifying gay existence to an unimagined degree. No matter how much scorn and ridicule are heaped on him, it is the clone who will spontaneously erupt in rage in San Francisco, march on Washington without his leaders telling him to do so, memorialize murder victims in New York, and call them brother.

The clone—the gay everyman—is vitally concerned with sexual expression. He does not discuss the power issues of sadomasochism in workshops; he experiences it as an often positive force which can break through his inhibitions. He is not a pedophile in the classic sense of the word, but he is certainly attracted to situations in which an age discrepancy heightens erotic appeal between men whom he sees as peers. He very probably does seek emotional attachments and worries greatly about his and other men's abilities to construct meaningful relations, but sex for him is play. Heterosexual marriage and its assumed mandate for monogamy are not only *not* accepted as models; they are undesirable. He has also produced a remarkable cultural revolution. The very uniform he wears—be it denim, leather, or Lacoste—is the externalization of a total redirection of gay sexual attraction. Theorists can search forever for its roots in the traditional American images of masculinity, but the reality is that the clone is *not* going after some longed-for heterosexual image. The uniform is a signal which announces a gay man's attraction to, identification with, and desire for other *gay* men. That often maligned look—the flannel shirts in Manhattan, the leather jackets in California, the collegiate style in Chicago—are the first widespread, visible signals that gay men exist in great numbers. They're not attempts to idolize straight men; they're announcements of *gayness*, perfectly obvious to both the wearer and the onlooker.

People who attempt to direct the gay political movement without taking into account the revolution of the clone are doomed to lead a soldierless army. The hope of overcoming divisiveness between gay men and lesbians must be rejected if the only basis upon which the breach can be mended is the acquiescence of gay men to the antimale sexual demands of feminists.

The power of the clone ghetto, however, is very limited. Even where it exists in its most mature forms in New York and San Francisco and in resort communities such as Provincetown and Key West, it exists under constant threat of very real physical violence. Only the most foolish gay man believes himself free from the danger of assault by bigots. Gay men who live outside larger ghettos are all the more open to assault—physically and politically—and are all the more aware of the danger they are in.

Gay men *are* remarkably vulnerable. It is actually quite amazing that such large numbers have risked career, family, and privilege for the sake of the exploration that is involved in being gay today. Some women's organizations have evidently perceived the vincibility of the rights and dignity of gay men. When it becomes apparent that gay men are not all united in blind obedience to a mythical, feminist truth or when it becomes apparent that a feminist goal can be most easily achieved by overriding gay concerns, there are few groups that won't take advantage of the situation.

It is almost a truism that we live in an antisexual society. The very presence of gay men and our acknowledged erotic nature is judged an ipso facto obscenity by the majority of the nation. But there is another point here: homosexuality is, after all, the most complete expression of male sexuality possible. It is very clear that the *maleness* of gay men presents an image that many feminists find repulsive. It also should be very clear to gay men that we cannot afford to give up the victory which is the celebration of that maleness. This unwillingness to accede to the feminist prohibition against male sexuality is cited by many women as an example of the gay man's powerful privilege. Gay men cannot make that illogical connection.

One of the great myths of the women's movement is the absolute law that any man is more powerful than any woman. It follows, then, in a perverse form of Aristotelian logic that any gay man must be more powerful than any woman. With increasing frequency, certain feminists are using this tight progression of reasoning to pronounce gay men the enemy. The reaction from most gay men, though, is utter incredulity. Gay men have almost no sense of power. We have all too vivid perceptions, in fact, of our own powerlessness. Nowhere is the discrepancy between self-concept and feminist accusation more apparent than in the current battle over pornography. Gay men are actively denounced for lechery, sexual self-indulgence, promiscuity, and love of erotica. Gay men's response is a great confusion.

After all, we are accustomed to prompt agreement with feminist mandates. But with this issue, there is an instinctual reaction of protest. They are wrong this time, and we know it. Yet that response is accompanied by another: gay men feel betrayed by women.

No other single group of men in this society has been willing to do so much with the women's movement as gays. None. Gay periodicals, for the most part, reflexively used nonsexist terminology as soon as it was promoted as a tool of equality. Those gay organizations which have not given up the hope of gender coalition are by far the most willing of all political groups in this country to have women in positions of key leadership; they have traditionally opted for equal gender representation on boards, committees, speakers' platforms, and the like. Countless gay organizations have paralyzed themselves when they heard the shout "Sexist." Nowhere—nowhere at all—has there been as much feminist consciousness-raising among men as in the gay men's community, both inside and outside the organizations. But now gay men are the enemy. Without doubt, one reason is that we are perceived as the easiest target. It is always easy to attack male homosexuals. Anita Bryant knew that; her sisters in the movement have learned her lessons well.

Sally Gerhart's infamous election letter condemning gay male lifestyles in San Francisco and calling for the dissociation of gay male and feminist political groups is noteworthy in this context because of its honesty. The ways in which women's organizations have been willing to trade on fag-hating are seldom so forthright.

Take Back the Night (TBTN) is one of the most visible feminist organizations here in Portland, Maine. It is self-described as a coalition, a confederation of women's groups brought together to combat sexism in general and pornography and sexual harassment in particular. TBTN shares many qualities with other feminist organizations. For one thing, it has remarkable access to the media. Portland's television, radio, and print news offices do not differ from their counterparts elsewhere. The women's movement is news. Female reporters are emerging in dramatically increasing numbers—as well they should be. They and their male co-workers automatically cover whatever events women activists announce as important.

But TBTN does not passively count on such spontaneous reactions. Its leadership has proven itself virtuoso in providing that special dramatic touch that gives the media their payoff: when TBTN holds an action, it is careful to make sure that the activity justifies front-page, lead-story coverage.

The most recent TBTN event was a tour of Portland's adult bookstores. Women were given guided expeditions through the half-dozen or so sexual emporiums that exist in this city, whose metropolitan population of 200,000 makes it the largest urban area in the tristate northern New England region. Certainly similar tours have been conducted in New York, Boston, and other much larger cities. But still, the timing of this particular event was suspect, to say the least.

Adult bookstores in Portland are a joke by big-city standards. Even such relatively tame publications as the *Advocate* are stapled shut or wrapped in cellophane. Until recently, the stores were limited to Congress Street, the main thoroughfare of the downtown area. Almost all of them, in fact, were in the same two-block stretch as the city's two "adult" movie theaters. This neighborhood, Portland's red-light district, is so inconspicuous in comparison to its peers that most New Yorkers would walk right through it without recognizing its function. Most Bostonians would prefer it to untold numbers of retail blocks in their city. There are a few drunks, a bit of prostitution, and even a little hustling, and it does justify the city's concern for it as a center of what crime does exist here, but believe me, it's not Times Square, and it's no combat zone.

While adult bookstores were limited to this area, TBTN made some protests, but nothing like the current campaign of headlines, tours, speeches, and calls for eradication. The change in attitude cannot be isolated from another event: the opening of Portland's first *gay* adult book-store.

The existence of homosexually oriented erotica was not new. But the shop, the Blueboy, broke two rules when it opened its doors. For one, it stocked *only* homoerotic material. Second, it was located in the Old Port, the city's gentrified residential and retail shopping area. While the site certainly produced some honestly motivated objections from residents who simply did not want any adult bookstores in their neighborhood, it is perfectly clear that the vast majority of complaints were not similarly motivated. The people who were making the most noise did not give a damn about the Blueboy's Old Port address. They just did not want faggots to be visible anywhere. TBTN must have loved it.

The issue was actually fairly humorous at first. Hysterical debates on the true function of glory-holes between the coin-operated movie booths took place in one of the daily newspapers. "For ventilation," insisted the proprietor. "If you don't know, I won't say," insisted the chief of police. Actually, the city council and the owner settled the dispute fairly quickly. The shop was licensed, *sans* glory-holes. There the matter might have died. But the issue of pornography in Portland was now hot, heated by its equation with homosexuality in the public mind.

One reason feminists have focused on the issue of pornography is because it is apparently the issue of radical concern that strikes the most responsive chord in the general community. While abortion, affirmative action, and lesbian concerns all seem to carry the threat of backlash because of the repugnance of some religious and ethnic groups, pornography is safe. It is a sanitary rallying point. Like most other excursions into moral politics, however, it produces some strange alliances.

A Baptist minister recently threatened a referendum drive to close all the adult sex enterprises in Portland. The goals of the referendum were strikingly similar to those of TBTN, and there was press speculation that the fundamentalists would form an alliance with the feminists. I don't know whether or not that would have happened. Qualifying a referendum for the ballot here is a formidable task. (Voters must sign petitions at City Hall between the hours of nine and five weekdays; the petitions cannot be circulated freely.) In any event, the petition drive failed. But I see no reason to believe that the women's organizations would not have supported that vote. The closure of the adult bookstores has become a well-advertised priority on their political agenda. In any event, none of them publicly spoke about the one area in which TBTN and the local quasi–Moral Majority differed: the proposed referendum not only called for the end of sales of adult erotica; it would also have closed the only gay bars that operate on a year-round basis in the entire state.

In this context, the idea that women, when they are compared to gay men, are a powerless group is an absurdity. TBTN is only one of a growing number of women's organizations in Portland. While it is clear that women have had a bitterly difficult struggle promoting their cause, it is also true that they have constructed a power base incomparably greater than gay men's. They have access to the media, where they are almost always treated with respect. They have to fight for academic appointments, but they do get them. Politics have opened to them in ways that gay men can only dream about. (Portland recently joined those American cities headed by a woman mayor.) And, with obvious, painful difficulties and not without harsh infighting and an onerous burden of needing to determine personal priorities, lesbians have been able to take advantage of this situation and assume positions of influence and leadership. Gay men have no comparable situation in their lives.

Even with the heavy economic stake in Ogunquit and the much less visible (though certainly significant) economic investment in the Old Port, gay men exist here without any discernible power. That powerlessness is not abstract. Omnipresent vulnerability to physical attack on the beaches of a gay resort like Ogunquit does not need any sophisticated analysis to be labeled as impotence.

What gay rights exist in Maine exist at the sufferance of a few liberal groups. A pattern of police harassment in Portland was broken by the Maine Civil Liberties Union a few years ago. (No one, though, has moved against an even more severe pattern in Orono, site of the University of Maine campus. A single bar in that town becomes a "private club" one day a week. Gays from the university and from neighboring Bangor, the second-largest city in the state, are routinely stopped, identified, and questioned by local police as they leave the club's parking lot.) Such liberal alliances are well known for their lack of commitment to any profound sense of gay liberation. When I recently surveyed the candidates for election to the Maine Civil Liberties Union (MCLU) Board of Directors, asking why gay issues were not mentioned as a priority in any of their position statements, I received only a single reply, from the editor of the "liberal" weekly *Maine Times*, who affirmed that gay rights was not a cause that the organization should take on as a priority. He asserted that the MCLU should act on the rights of gay people only insofar as they involved rights of privacy.

But credit where credit is due: it is amazing that Maine came closer than any other state to enacting a gay rights bill. The bill to add gays to the already-existing civil rights legislation was defeated by a narrow 16–13 vote in the senate after a strong campaign by Democratic Majority Leader Gerard Conley, a prominent Roman Catholic layman whose activities should be the model for our expectations of elected officials. His attitude toward issues of "validating gay life-styles" or "passing approval on homosexuality" is especially noteworthy. When I asked him how he dealt with those objections, he gruffly responded: "When these people have jobs, can rent apartments, and can walk the streets of their hometowns without fear of being attacked by hoodlums, then I'll indulge in the luxury of commenting on the morality of their private lives. Until then, this is simply, purely, and absolutely a pressing, unjust denial of civil rights in our state. That lack of rights is the only issue I will allow myself to address."

The men who testified in favor of the gay rights bill in the hearings in Augusta, the state capital, were not middle-class professionals seeking memberships in elite organizations or media mavens seeking stardom. They were mill workers who had lost minimum-wage jobs so desperately vital for survival in this, one of the poorest of the United States. They were not men who found an abstract oppression in the news priorities of the national television networks. One man spoke of leaving his machinist position in a shoe factory—the only employer in his small town. Other workers had expressed their rage at the fact of his very existence among them by continually sabotaging the machinery with which he worked. Going to his job began to mean risking his life.

When any people of privilege made public announcements of gayness during the Augusta hearings, they were women holding managerial positions in women's organizations.

Still, even in Maine, gay men have been supportive of women's organizations. The only active, year-round gay group in the state is the Gay People's Alliance (GPA) headquartered on the Portland campus of the University of Southern Maine. (Another group exists during the academic year in Orono; there is a Dignity chapter with a Lewiston address; a primarily social organization exists in the bilingual northern extreme of the state, Northern Lambda Nord.) The GPA is a gender-mixed group with little contact with the year-round community of Portland and even less with the summer colony of Ogunquit, the two centers of gay life in Maine. It is not surprising that GPA members are the most active group of men attached to a male auxiliary to TBTN. They report little problem with total support for the women's position on rape. They understand fully the impact of sexual harassment on the job and in public places, as well they should, since such torment is not a hypothetical issue for gay men either, it's a question of sincere importance; especially for those men who understand that verbal abuse can easily escalate to fag-bashing. (Fag-bashing is a real problem in Maine, most severely in Ogunquit, where many incidents have been reported during the last few summers. Only a dullard would fail to make the connection between those beatings and the fact that when seniors in Wells High School—the regional secondary school for Ogunquit and other neighboring communities—were asked to name in their yearbook the things they hated most, the plurality wrote, "Faggots.") But the GPA men do have a problem with the issue of pornography. It is not an easy issue for them to resolve. Feminists are not responsive to the depth of the dilemmas posed by this issue for gay men.

The issues of the Blueboy bookstore and the exploitation of its infamy were not ignored by other members of the Portland gay community. While GPA members share with other gay organizations an exasperation over the seeming unwillingness of gay men to join in their activities, in reality, I witnessed a number of conversations between men which shared a common theme, a theme whose importance would be recognized by the clone if not the politico: Is this where we have to do something? Were the city, the police, the media coming down so hard on the Blueboy that it had become an issue of self-defense to support it? The final consensus was no. A primary interference was the fact that the Blueboy was owned by a straight man. That so many businesses directed toward gay men are so often owned by nongays is itself an oft repeated symbol of gay impotence.

Why, then, would an unorganized population of men consisting of Portland's own version of clones have even considered defending an adult bookstore against the forces of police, mayor, and media—and later the intrusive tours of TBTN?

Without question, the adult bookstores in small-city America are the only conduits for national gay media. The *Advocate* and *Christopher Street* are not available for retail sale anywhere else in the entire city of Portland. Not one bookstore has a gay section (all have women's sections). No matter how lacking in desirability these places are, they—and especially the Blueboy—served a real communication function. (There is also no reason to deny that many of us use erotica as a masturbatory aid or as a source of pleasure in and of itself.)

Gay men do not find delight in discovering a need to defend others for homosexual activities in public places. We do not delight in needing to go to sleazy bookstores to purchase our reading matter. We do not delight in the knowledge that most often our social contacts with one another must be made in substandard bars. But we know that this is the reality we must begin to work with, and we know that even if we individually do not indulge in what others call promiscuous sex, we are just as vulnerable to attack by a population that will always identify us with those men who do so indulge. One amazing lack of perception by feminists as they look at the entire issue of pornography retail stores has been their inability or unwillingness to deal with one of the functions of such operations: they are places of homosexual assignation.

There is a fairly universal pattern to the extraordinary gay male process of coming out. Life begins in a heterosexual family, sexual identity is self-discovered, it is hidden, some level of self-acceptance is attempted, an integration of sexuality and social existence is formulated.

This last step—the integration of sexuality and social existence—takes many forms. Often the time and place of coming out determine major elements of the result. (It should not be a surprise, for instance, that there appear to be many more gay fathers in Maine than in New York City; the rural setting provides pressures for a much earlier marriage than the urban.)

It is easy to lose touch with the enormousness of the gay revolution, which has created the clone, the ghetto, the movement, and the literature that combine to offer so many options for gay men today. Only ten years ago—certainly twenty years ago—the majority of men whose counterparts are contemporary clones chose a closeted life, mutually oppressed with those heterosexual women who often became their wives. There was a time, not so long past, when men who did take this option were considered traitors by the rest of us. Now they are pitied. They have lost out, not able to take advantage of the excitement that the rest of us now consider part of being gay. Few of those men have been able to survive without a homosexual outlet. There are no baths in a city like Portland; the bars are the turf of the clones here. Deering Oaks Park and the adult bookstores and movie houses—certainly not only the Blueboy—are the only outlets open to those left behind, those men living in need of homosexuality without the joy of gayness.

Feminists insist on perceiving adult bookstores as pandering to the most sexist, base, dangerous men. Their stock is considered fodder for the fire that will flame into violent rape. Gay men see those same bookstores as the territory of the walking wounded, those men (who once upon a time included ourselves) now cut off from communal support and identification.

So, in the end, the gay men here in Portland see the incursions into the adult stores as cruel, unfair assaults on a delicate and even poignant space for men whom we see less and less as enemies and more and more as victims. Their assailants are bullies, difficult to differentiate from the adolescents who beat up strays on the beach of Ogunquit or on the paths of Deering Oaks Park. Here, in this populist estrangement from women, is the specific example of the repercussions of feminist attempts at intimidation.

One major effect of that estrangement is contempt for the cowardice of it all. I know of no better example of that pusillanimity than the outrageous assault upon Giovanni's Room, a gay and lesbian bookstore in Philadelphia, that took place about two years ago. Certainly there were ways in which Giovanni's Room fell short of the purity that radicals of all persuasions demand of their organizations. For instance, the store, a privately owned, for-profit operation, solicited volunteer labor from the community. But the real point of contention came over the stocking of a single book: the heterosexually sadomasochistic novel *The Story of O.*

The novel, one of the first above-ground explorations of S and M, was sought by many gays as a source. But a coalition of women's groups demanded that the book be removed from the store. The owners—a gay man and a lesbian—declined. In the ensuing brouhaha picket lines were formed, editorials were written, there was even a televised debate on the entire issue, which was actually more of an ambush of the owners by their opponents. Giovanni's Room stuck to what it deemed a question of principle in resisting censorship. The store has actually prospered and now claims to be the largest mail-order retailer of gay and lesbian books in the country. The real point is, what kind of perverse, poltroonish priorities would lead to such a massive assault against what was then a marginal operation, when nothing close to the magnitude of dissent has ever been addressed to the B. Dalton and Waldenbooks chains, whose *daily* sales of overtly sexist—and homophobic—books are measured in multiples of the *annual* revenues of even the largest gay bookstores? Why are adult bookstores in Portland, Maine, the target of a coalition as powerful as TBTN?

*Cowardice.*

Women seem unwilling to wage any battle that they are going to lose hands down. To gay men, who so seldom have an honest expectation of success in their continuing battles against the government, the churches, the media, and other centers of true power in our society, the choices of some women's priorities are not just questions of bad judgment, but often proof of malice. Rather than deal with the hard core that is so willing to counterattack, women have all too often chosen to feed off the vulnerable residues of guilt and the sincere desire for sexual equality that exist in gay men. How much easier it is to righteously attack us for purchasing *Drummer* than it is to tell the A&P to stop selling *Playboy.*

Another part of that cowardice is an apparent insistence that we gay men should divest ourselves of any hint of power in situations in which women perceive themselves to be less privileged than they say we are. Recently in Portland, an absurd situation developed that demonstrated this demand that gay men express a depraved solidarity with lesbians. As in most small cities, Portland's bars cater to both genders. Apparently, the lesbian community cannot support its own bars. Women in the gay nightspots demanded—and, for a brief moment this summer, won—an injunction against men taking off their shirts on the dance floor. If lesbians could not bare their breasts, then neither should gay men display their pectorals.

But the issue really was not the right of women to take off their blouses. The cowardice that is often displayed by women organizationally very often covers a more fundamental contempt for gay men than they are willing to own up to. The preposterous situation described here carries with it a rudimentary point which gay men simply can no longer overlook. The issue was clearly not just a quid pro quo insistence on equality of mistreatment. That was a transparent rationalization for the real function of the protest: women hated seeing male-mating divested of any of its disguises.

The expression of gay male sexuality is evidently experienced by women as the expression of the same male sexuality which leads to rape. *That misconception is not our problem.* If women cannot distinguish among the elemental components of gay male sexuality—a force attempting to make men equals, a process dependent upon consent, a celebration of the male body which is not dependent upon the denigration of the female body—*it is their perception that is at fault, not our behavior.* If the viewing of gay male lust—the manifestation of a primary form of gay liberation—is repulsive to women because they cannot separate it from the lust of heterosexual males whose goal is the subjugation of women, *it is not our responsibility to erase that view; it is women's responsibility to deal with the fears that entrap them.*

The goal of gay men is to release ourselves from the closet and to become pro-active forces in our own lives. *It is an intolerable expectation to think that gay men will resume the most dreaded forms of behavior for the sake of women's sensibility.*

The most important repercussion for gay men has been the deflection of our own focus as we have been reactive to the increasingly divergent priorities of feminists and ourselves. The clone has actually served a purpose here by his insistence that the actions of sexual liberation be addressed. His uniform, his willingness to spend time and money in his pursuit of sexual fulfillment, and his anxious investigation of different forms of sexuality and relationship forces us to pay attention to those areas in which he demonstrates such interest. Witness the number of articles on promiscuity and sadomasochism that have appeared in *Christopher Street* and the *Advocate* in the last year—even in such a righteously correct political publication as Boston's *Gay Community News.*

Yet too often these investigations have only been elite attempts to understand what the populace is thinking. Seldom—very seldom indeed— have they been expressions of the participants' experiences, rather they tend to be interviews with others or commentaries on another tribe's behavior. Lost in all this has been any serious pro-active investigation of what role pornography does—or can—perform in gay men's lives.

It is clear that erotic writings and photographs are very dear to gay men. Whenever a company has printed an attempt at a serious magazine and also a consciously sexual magazine, the sexually oriented publication has outsold its partner, regardless of promotion or organizational expectation. Thus, *Honcho* outsells *Mandate; Numbers* overshadows *Blueboy; Drummer* must provide the funds to support the *Alternate.* No one involved in any of these projects expected that outcome. It is simply true that the supposedly limited market for erotica is greater than anticipated and that the expected market for what is self-defined by publishers as "quality" nonfiction and fiction falls short of its goal.

Even the pretensions of the *Advocate* are not exempt. Years ago, when I was editor, we had planned to drop those nasty classifieds to make the paper more acceptable to large national advertisers and, we thought, to attract more bourgeois subscribers. The slightest bit of market research proved that any such move would have been a disaster. Too many people of every class and level of sophistication were buying the *Advocate only* for that nastiness. The segregation of sexual ads into a "pink section" was the compromise. At least some people could throw away that section—which just happens to generate the richest advertising revenues in gay publishing.

Marketing is not the only factor here. Many of the men regarded as the best gay writers also turn their talents toward exploring sexuality and relationships in ways that are most compatible with the editorial requirements of sexual magazines. Artists whose work can be seen in the better New York galleries seem to have little personal or professional problem in selling their work to publications like *Honcho.* These writers and artists are following an honorable tradition in American gay life. People who have published their work in erotic magazines have played many important roles in our liberation.

A seemingly universal and persistent oppression among gay men is the feeling we had when we first came out: that we existed alone, without friends, without anyone who was like us. During my own initiation into gay life in the sixties, I learned not only that I was a member of a group— potentially a community—by reading the gay periodicals that were sold only in adult bookstores, I learned much more. I read about the importance of integrity in gay life in Joseph Hansen's pseudonymous novels. Samuel Steward was the writer who, in his Phil Andros books, let me know how utterly fascinating my future was going to be. Tom of Finland's drawings promised me that that future was going to be *fun.* It was not a radical who instructed me about the political facts of my life; it was Jim French who used the name Rip Colt when he drew the first poster that would electrify me with the phrase "Gay Power."

The reality is that the erotic is recognized as an important area for gay men to explore. At first, I thought my own excursions into writing pornography were only a way to earn money. Two events changed that. First, after I had produced a certain body of work, I found consistent, nearly subconscious themes being exposed, themes of personal liberation through sexual liberation. Other chords sounded warnings about sexual danger.

Here I unknowingly wandered into the tradition of Phil Andros by marking boundaries and limits of trust, realistic expectation, and danger in gay life. But second, I was forced to acknowledge that even the least impressive, least well written stories were having a tremendous impact on readers. Pornography, be it vanilla in *Mandate* or S and M in *Drummer*, is not read only by sad, lonely old men who sleep alone in hotel rooms. It is carefully read, sincerely analyzed by the clone.

We do a great disservice to ourselves and to any hope of community if we dismiss the sincerity of this gay everyman. At one time, I was certainly guilty of doing this by throwing away early opportunities to communicate with him through my fiction. I learned quickly how much he still wanted to learn about himself and his personal options by reading about others' experiences. But pornography is the vehicle that is accessible to him, not quasi-scientific articles or distanced interviews with people who do not resonate as being his peers.

Those readers are not the sexually obsessed, unconscious mass that many gay leaders insist their nonfollowers are. They were not blind to issues of liberation that were presented to them in forms that related realistically to their lives. Above all, the message of gay pornography is the affirmation of the male's love for other men. It is the most pure elevation of male beauty and male sensuality. It is for this reason that the women's movement has so much trouble accepting it. But what is male homosexuality if not the love of men? Are we supposed to deny it?

There are important parallels to this process of "cleansing" negation in gay community organizing and political activity. The purpose of leadership is not to educate the constituency on points that the constituency cannot readily identify as important so much as it is to enunciate the constituency's priorities and to identify ways to achieve them with maximal integrity.

The usual impulse of gay leadership has been one of astonishing elitism. We accepted an ideology based on feminism, attempted to synthesize it with a passive conception of homosexuality, and insisted that people buy this ideology as a revealed truth, as holy as that of the women's movement. Membership in gay organizations has been treated as a reward bestowed only on those who sign a pledge. Members have not been expected to influence the platform, they have been expected to wholeheartedly subscribe to it.

It has been as easy for gay leadership to dismiss the Nautilus-bodied man on Christopher Street or the leather bedecked stud on Folsom Street as it was for me to dismiss readers of *Blueboy*. The point is that neither group deserves such treatment. When they receive it, they react against it. More profoundly, we indulge in a self-destructive self-deception whenever we attempt to disassociate ourselves from those who are, after all, our fellows. I may want to think of myself with certain labels: writer, New Englander, intellectual. But I place myself in mortal danger if I forget for one moment the essential fact of my homosexuality. I may try to ignore the truth that I am a clone, but this society and its nascent forces of repression will never forget it.

Here lies the tragic fault of the lesbians in the women's movement as the clone sees it: they believe they have the power to alter their identification with us. They expect the general population will eliminate its own equation of male and female homosexuality. They have been seduced into believing that feminism equates an absence of homophobia. Gay men listen to Andrea Dworkin and wonder how she cannot be mortally terrified of Betty Friedan.

Is the clone really so apolitical? Is he really so trapped in bourgeois hedonism that it is a foregone conclusion that he will never be active in a gay movement?

To dismiss the clone, to devalue his experience, or to judge his life-style as frivolous is to ignore the central fact of gay liberation: to publicly acknowledge oneself as homosexual in this society is an act of profound political import.

The clone has not made his decision to advertise his existence lightly. It is a decision with conscious repercussions. The Portland GPA wonders why it has so few members while the men in the city's bars articulate their real concern that they may have to take a stand, alone, against the combined forces of political power in this city. The synthetic, abstract lambda was decreed the symbol of the gay movement, but the clone who converges on New York and San Francisco for an annual march of resistance wears the pink triangle of the Nazi concentration camp. To deprecate the inherent defiance which is the elemental engagement of the clone's life is to devalue the very essence of what it means to be gay in America.

It is not the rarefied theorist who is the fundamental building block of our movement, it is the gay everyman. When our aspiring leaders go to him to organize, to attempt a true understanding of our present and future, they will have to be prepared to do so through praxis, not habitus, and they will have to grasp how this population views the recent activities of the women's movement.

Women's organizations have covertly—and, in some instances, overtly—allied themselves with forces of moral repression whose priorities are not a hypothetical threat, but an integral part of the social and political forces which would actually eliminate gay men. Women's organizations are calling for the gay everyman to return to a time when he saw himself as filthy, perverse, and undesirable. But the lifework of every gay man has been the transformation of the loathed into the loved. He is not likely to give up this magic. Gay leadership—be it political, literary, or community-based—must begin its work not by pledging itself to an increasingly irrelevant feminist ideology but by making a covenant with its population that is based not only on what we might become but that also celebrates who we already are. What is homophobia if it isn't the insistence on seeing filth in the fact of homosexuality? What is gay liberation for men if it isn't an affirmation of the beauty of men?

## The New Separatism

One year ago, in June 1980, a half-dozen gay activists paced a corridor outside a basement meeting room in Washington's Mayflower Hotel. Inside the room, Kennedy and Carter forces were battling out the shape of the 1980 Democratic platform. In response to gay requests, Kennedy representatives were pushing for a gay rights plank that detailed steps to eradicate discrimination, including a presidential executive order. Carter representatives wanted a more generally worded plank but were split on the issue as a result of intense gay lobbying.

As the night grew on, some of the Kennedy team left for other commitments. Finally, enough had left that, even including the defection from the Carter side, the strongly worded version of the plank would fail. The vote was taken, and Marty Franks, Carter's point man in the session, stepped out into the corridor, smiled, and told the waiting gays, "We're going to teach you to count yet."

The Franks lesson—to count votes, not pledges—is only one of many that gays are having a difficult time learning. It later emerged that Franks should have added another: learning how to read. Completely unnoticed was the fact that, while defeating a stronger gay rights plank, Carter had, for the first time, put gay rights in with other minority rights and had taken it out of the realm of privacy rights, the next section in the party platform.

That shift should have registered as an earthquake in the progress of gay politics. It was an acknowledgment not only that gays have a right to be free of discrimination but also a claim to acceptance as a community in a pluralistic nation. This did not register in gay consciousness, however, and that it failed to do so says more about our failures than our successes.

In this case, we did indeed snatch defeat from the jaws of victory. Gay Democratic clubs, for example, endorsed Carter, but too late in the campaign to be of much use. Gay politicos such as Bill Kraus, co-chair of the Lesbian and Gay Caucus of the Democratic Party, and Mel Boozer, nominated at the convention as vice-president of the caucus, sat on their hands during the entire campaign and, in Boozer's case, publicly argued against a Carter endorsement. As late as six months after Reagan's inauguration, gay San Francisco supervisor Harry Britt told reporters that Reagan serves gay interests better than Carter's reelection would have.

Britt, Boozer, and Kraus are heirs to a tradition in gay politics born a decade ago, representing an approach that demands failure in order to politicize gays. That we are still at this stage, ten years later, is perhaps the greatest failure of all.

It is not difficult to find the roots of this approach or to understand its continuing appeal. It is unpleasant to do so because it forces some painful reexamination and discards some comforting assumptions.

In the aftermath of Stonewall, an unprecedented number of gays began participating in confrontational politics. The boundaries placed around our lives became the only issue, and political action became synonymous with planned skirmishes along a front of resistance designed to activate ever-increasing numbers of gays in a full-fledged war at that border.

This was an approach that would work only as long as the resistance to our pleas for responsive government was nearly total. When the first door was opened, the result was an internal debate among gays about how to form an agenda. That debate was at its most acrimonious in the early 1970s, and as it turned out, it was a debate with no resolution. Instead, gay activists learned that specific agendas were the quickest way to alienate some of their politicized followers, and the objective of an agenda was pitted against the objective of mobilizing as many gay people as possible.

In retrospect, the result was to sidestep the question of an agenda altogether. This was accomplished either by trivializing any political opening made in response to gay concerns or by pressuring straight politicians and government agencies to join the gay bandwagon. City gay rights ordinances became less tools to actively eliminate discrimination than weapons to intimidate the next level of politician to in turn join up. We developed a movement with the sole purpose of choosing up sides in a game in which we had no other rules; whoever had the biggest team at the end won.

Today, the costs of this approach are considerable. We are in danger of cheapening the value of the very laws we seek, abusing our political supporters, and, having misused the political system, becoming vulnerable to the misuse of that system against us as our enemies follow exactly the path we pioneered. These are dangers that we need not face, and that may prevent us from making—or recognizing—the actual progress we are capable of.

To date, both our successes and our failures stand out as examples of an undefined agenda, a movement whose purpose is merely to become a movement. The four years since 1977 provide vivid examples.

When Jimmy Carter took over the White House in January 1977, gays had their first opportunity to discuss their concerns at the federal level. There were some immediate results; some agencies reversed their policies, and others opened up to more direct contact through White House pressure. By the end of 1977, however, that dialogue came to a virtual standstill as gay leaders, notably the National Gay Task Force, deserted the field for other areas.

The two most important aspects of that hiatus were overlooked in the 1980 campaign. One was that it was gays, and not the White House, that stepped out of the dialogue. In point of fact, the White House and the federal government continued, unprompted by any gay organization, to remedy federal discrimination policy. The second element was that the gay leaders who set those discussions aside did so on grounds not directly related to the gay concerns they were advocating. Jean O'Leary, the co-executive director of the National Gay Task Force, resigned from a presidential commission because of her support for dissatisfied feminists; gay issues did not enter her decision at all. At that particular time, the Task Force was issuing press releases about its White House efforts that indicated its work was nearly universally successful.

It is only now that we can know precisely what gays walked away from when they let O'Leary defer to feminist standard-bearers. What follows is a partial list, including steps that were taken later in the administration but initiated at that time.

• An offer to review employment policy of all federal contractors and, if private negotiations with discriminatory employers were ineffectual, to issue an executive order banning discrimination by federal contractors. This action was contingent only on gays making a formal request in writing with an endorsement from one nongay organization; there was no gay response.

• An offer of official United States support for an amendment to the United Nations Bill of Rights to include gays. The offer was contingent only on gays providing some case examples of discrimination and persecution of gays in other nations, information that had already been unofficially compiled at the State Department. There was no gay response.

• An offer to review gay proposals for additions to the federal budget to benefit gays through increased grants to community centers, research programs, etc. There was no gay response.

• Repeated offers to name gays to presidential commissions in which gays had a strong interest. No nominations were made by gay organizations, aside from support for women's commissions.

• An offer from the United States Civil Rights Commission to discuss using gay religious groups as the basis for expanding civil rights protection to gays based on religious beliefs. No response was made to the offer of a meeting.

• An offer to review model federal sex education materials submitted by gays as guidelines for school districts throughout the country. No submissions were made.

• A revision of federal civil service law, the first in a hundred years, that was officially interpreted to ban discrimination against gays. The congressional revision took place without any gay participation.

• An official policy banning discrimination in employment and services in ACTION, the federal program of volunteers for the Peace Corps, Foster Grandparents, etc. The agency, which is not covered by the civil service, was not prompted by any gay organization to make this change. An official policy banning employment discrimination was also issued at the Agency for International Development (also not covered by civil service law). The change came following a gay employee's dismissal and his challenge but was not officially supported by any gay organization.

• A review of the employment practices at the General Accounting Office, the investigative arm of Congress with over five thousand employees. Its policies were to be brought into conformance with new civil service regulations, but no gay organization contacted the office to ensure that gay protections were specifically included.

• Granting charitable and educational gay groups IRS status for tax-exempt and tax-deductible purposes. The change, resisted during the Ford administration, came after gay leaders met at the White House and directly benefited the leading gay organizations.

• Permission for gay religious groups to minister to prisoners in federal prisons and for gay publications to be admitted. The change, which required considerable arm-twisting by the White House, will now have little substantive meaning; the Metropolitan Community Church, which led this effort, has just announced that it will discontinue its prison ministry program.

• Formal endorsement of a change in immigration law, the first endorsement of legislation proposed by gays by any president, and a change officially endorsed in Congress by less than 25 of the 435 members and not endorsed by the chairman of any of the appropriate congressional committees.

• Pressure, following the 1980 Democratic Convention inclusion of the gay rights plank, to have the Texas Democratic Party follow suit, and orders to other state Democratic parties to reach out to gay voters for the first time.

• Offers of patronage jobs to gays during the 1980 census. No response was made by gay organizations other than to announce the offer to the gay press.

• Private meetings between the White House senior staff and top Pentagon and CIA managers about their discriminatory policies. The meetings took place without the knowledge of gay leaders.

• Promulgation of a new model federal adoption code for consideration by state agencies that would have permitted gay couples to adopt children. The model code was prepared without gay participation and was not pushed by gays at any state level.

• Reversal of the United States Surgeon General's position that gays could be certified for immigration exclusion. The change followed lawsuits brought by gays and gay organizations but was also strongly encouraged at top White House levels.

• At least three major occasions when the president directly and personally acknowledged gays and their rights. The first came in the official statement of sympathy following the murder of gay San Francisco supervisor Harvey Milk, which was not carried in a single gay newspaper in the country. The second came when the president addressed the White House Conference on Families, where the appropriateness of gay concerns was sharply challenged; Carter called for an end to government interference "in our bedrooms." The third came during the 1980 campaign itself, when militant Christians attacked Carter in a Memphis, Tennessee, stopover for seeking gay support, and he responded by challenging their assertion that a "religious test" belonged in politics.

• Upgrading the discharges of gays in the military, making them eligible for all benefits they had earned while in military service. This decision was challenged in a congressional committee, and an effort was made to overturn it through an appropriations bill.

• Strong defense of gay participation in such programs as CETA, legal services, research, and humanities grants to gay groups, all challenged in and out of Congress.

This list could actually continue by reaching down into the lower levels of the administration where support was forthcoming, but it makes an important point. Why, in the final summation, were all these steps ignored by so many gay people? If this was not what we wanted when we asked for an open-door administration, then what was the agenda?

The answer one heard constantly during the campaign was "an executive order." That, and nothing else, was what it would take. Given this priority, and the notion that it could overcome any other accomplishment, it is worth noting that this request was complete nonsense. That gays should demand it without having the slightest idea of what it would or could do represents the crassest type of manipulation. How, then, did it come to play such a role in our politics?

To begin with, an executive order can be overturned by Congress. In fact, a number of President Carter's executive orders, just like those of presidents before him, were overturned by Congress. This political reality, particularly in light of congressional approval of antigay measures, never entered the discussion at all.

To add another reality, the only area in employment that would be covered by such an order would be the military and intelligence/foreign service areas. The Pentagon has the strongest lobby of any group in the country, and it is indisputable that the testimony from merely one general opposing such an order would have killed it in Congress then and there. For those who believe that a president can order the Pentagon to do what he wants, keep in mind the debate when Congress learned that Carter was simply lobbying his generals on the Salt II agreements.

Beyond that, gays had no design of what an executive order should contain. At the meeting in the White House's Roosevelt Room a year before Carter left office, representatives of more than twenty gay organizations sat around a table with top White House officials to discuss an executive order. Not one of them had brought so much as a draft of a proposed order. There were not even copies of executive orders signed by the governors of Pennsylvania and California for comparison. In the dark days of McCarthy, President Eisenhower did sign an executive order barring gays from security-related jobs. No one had a copy of that order, nor was its existence even mentioned.

The only conclusion to be drawn from this is that an executive order was never sought as a serious remedy for existing discrimination. It was, instead, the ultimate step in a politics that views laws and policies as emblematic of our successes rather than a purposeful accomplishment. All other considerations were forced to give way before this demand that we be given tokens of the esteem in which we are held.

This is a perspective that infuses gay politics today, and one that may destroy us. It is fair to say that nondiscrimination ordinances, for example, now serve the same purpose for us that sodomy statutes serve for those who oppose us. Neither are meant to be taken seriously, enforced vigorously, or even to give substance to the views that each represents. They are our rites of passage. There is no effort to monitor whether they achieve their objective beyond insuring status as a symbol.

This is a serious mistake. Discrimination does not end because it is illegal. Making it illegal only ends our status as outcasts. If that is all we are seeking, if all we want is an emblematic success, then our efforts are better directed elsewhere. We would be as well off if the criteria of success were declarations of Gay Pride Week.

This, obviously, does not have to be the case, but we are the ones who have made it so. In doing this, the gauntlet has been thrown down before those who correctly see that all we are asking for is acceptance. There is nothing wrong with a conflict over that issue (it is inevitable), but we are using the wrong chips to ante up in the game. We are throwing away important protections because we, like them, ultimately see these protections only as symbols of our acceptance.

Consider the differing gay rights ordinances in San Francisco and Washington, D.C. The Washington version, enacted before San Francisco's, is actually broader and stronger. Presently, gays in both cities are challenging local Catholic universities that are discriminating against gay groups. The San Francisco case, however, is being postponed until the Washington case is argued, in hopes that its precedent will bolster San Francisco's argument. In this instance, as in nearly all other enactments of city ordinances, prior victories are cited for their political and not legal value, and the result is widely disparate versions of gay rights ordinances. Such ordinances are being touted as tests of acceptability, and not as serious legal remedies for discrimination.

One must again fall back on the fact that gay politics still rely on the dynamic of failure, still count on being rebuked as a means to mobilize the great unwashed apathetic folk who merely need the right incentive to get involved. Behind this is a fantasy that one day gays, charged by some apocalyptic defeat, will march by the millions, shoulder to shoulder, through the streets of the nation. It is time to point out that this has nothing to do with politics.

Gays were saved, during the past four years, from facing this painful fact by Anita Bryant and her spawn, Jerry Falwell. There were battles to be fought, and the fact that we lost most of these was easily dismissed. Bryant saw that we use these ordinances as emblems and tokens, and she wanted them taken away. Amazingly, in fighting back, it occurred to some that laws should not be used as tokens. It was an argument, however, that we had started ourselves, and we were destined to lose on those grounds.

Much has been made of the fact that California and Seattle were supposed to have halted this antigay rights bandwagon. Unfortunately, three other California jurisdictions subsequently defeated gay rights proposals, and this seems to have been overlooked. Even worse, it does not seem to concern many that these efforts, once confined to the local level, now appear headed for Congress, and the bets are on their side. Already, this Congress has overwhelmingly approved the most restrictive amendment against gays in recent years. A rider on the Legal Services Corporation bill prohibits gays from turning to that agency for help if they lose a job or an apartment in cases where their homosexuality is alleged to be an issue. Only the fact that Legal Services does not handle criminal cases kept this restriction from being extended to cover those as well.

This amendment was not passed without a fairly lengthy debate on the issue, also a first in the House of Representatives. The members who argued against the restriction knew that they would lose; in conversations with a number of them afterward, it was clear that they hoped to cut off even worse bills by staking out some ground now.

Such bills will be considered, and some of them may pass. Christian Voice, one of the antigay lobbies, concedes that it is considering a measure which, in effect, would be a national Briggs Initiative. Any school district in the country which hired an "avowed homosexual" would be denied federal funds. The antigay lobby says that it knows such a measure would never pass through a committee; instead, they hope to bring it directly to the floor, where it can be turned into a quick and dirty emotional issue that members dare not vote against.

The Family Protection Act is also back with us again this year and will doubtlessly get a better hearing than it did in the last Congress. Among its provisions is one barring federal aid to anyone who espouses gay rights, a provision that the Congressional Research Service says could be interpreted to deny even Social Security to gay activists. The measure would also deny federal funds to any organization, corporation, or other group which suggests that gays are acceptable, and when it was pointed out to Senator Paul Laxalt, Reagan's close friend and the bill's chief sponsor, that this could include the Democratic Party, he responded by saying that that would be fine with him.

Britt, in the same interview in which he suggested gays would eventually be better off with Reagan than Carter because Reagan offers a target of resistance, also asserted that he is not worried about the Family Protection Act: he does not think it will pass. This ignores the fact that the Legal Services restriction was part of last year's Family Protection Act and has already been passed separately. But Harry Britt has yet to get the name of the bill right. He was a force in getting the San Francisco Board of Supervisors to condemn "S. 1808" last April; there is no such bill. That is the designation of last year's bill. As it turned out, the San Francisco resolution was passed around congressional offices for the laugh of the day.

There are obviously remedies to many of these problems, and for the most part, we have already created the tools we need to get the job done. We have, for example, done a fairly impressive job of impressing upon the nation that some protections are needed for gay people. In the period between August 1980 and May 1981, when the Moral Majority and others used gay rights as a campaign issue, NBC polls found that Americans became *more* supportive of gay rights. Previous polls showed a 44–41 percent split in favor of gay rights. By last May it was 48–38 percent, and the increased gap from 3 percent to 10 percent in our favor is significant. It is just that we are putting these tools to the wrong use at the present time, and in one important respect, we have yet to ask the right question of the gay political movement that claims to have an answer to our problem. It is the basic question of precisely what we expect our politics to do for us. In the larger context, it is also a question of what it is we think the gay community *is*.

The second, larger part of that question deserves some serious attention. Luckily, it is getting that attention in a number of places. One place to begin, however, might be to ask why, if there is a gay community, did it

not respond to the federal initiatives of the past four years. Quite apart
from what gay politicos were telling us, why was there no constituency for
programs designed specifically to serve a community? Why did we not
hear stronger voices from the gay health clinics, the gay churches, the gay
educational groups—the whole list that we traditionally cite when we
claim that we are a community?

Perhaps the answer is that, as the failure of our response indicates, we
are not in fact a community. We may, at best, be a network. At the national
level, we would be fortunate if we could lay claim to being a committee.
There are reasons to believe that the model the gay community is based on
is a feudal society, in which each group declares itself a principality, negotiating treaties of nonaggression with one another, but rarely alliances. If
the federal acceptance of gays during the Carter years told us anything, it
should have awakened us to how we have become trapped in our own
hype.

On the more narrow issue of an agenda for gay politics, there also needs
to be a careful reexamination. There are differences, for example, in seeking
to end discrimination through privacy arguments and through nondiscrimination statutes. With privacy arguments, the claim is that homosexuality
is an irrelevant factor in employment, housing, and so forth. No consideration need be given to it; it is, in fact, an improper area of inquiry. This does
not mean, as gay rights opponents argue, that privacy is necessarily a euphemism for invisibility. One may well be aware that another is gay, just
as one is aware that another is married with children, but it does not enter
into legal consideration.

There is no question that this has an appeal to all but the most ardent
antigay forces. Its lack of appeal for many gay leaders may well be that,
while it offers some protection, it does not offer recognition of a community in the same way that nondiscrimination laws can be manipulated to
do. Those laws, for all practical purposes, place gays in a recognized minority status, suggesting that protections are being extended because the
government recognizes a class of people.

One aspect that has not been given much consideration in this is that
we can still be a community and be recognized as such through either
route. We must merely accept the particular uses and limits of each approach, and not confuse them. In the scenario in which gays are protected
by privacy arguments, there is absolutely nothing to prevent us from using
that space to connect with each other, discover what it is that we share,
and build institutions and associations that become a community. The
privacy argument only suggests that this is a responsibility we bear to
ourselves and that labeling us as a minority does not somehow make us a
community.

One lesson that needs to be learned from the debate of a decade ago is
that making these choices in defining an agenda is not an effort that can
produce results if we are sidetracked into the agendas of others. The space
we require for this effort is a separate one intimidated neither by the phil-
osophies that others try to graft onto gays nor by those who would merely
use gays as a means to other objectives. For too long we have made obligatory obeisance to questionable propositions. One may well believe that the

gay struggle is part of the oppression of all groups, but one does not have to drop gay objectives every time one is guilt-tripped by the oppression of others. Not only have we done this, we have institutionalized it.

The National Gay Task Force board of directors, for example, is not composed of individuals who bring some expertise in designing education, media, or citizenship programs that will alleviate discrimination. Instead, it is composed of individuals selected according to a careful formula of quotas representing various elements of oppressed groups. Half are mandated to be women (a firm principle until the women on the board felt they had more qualified candidates than the men did, and asked that the formula be removed), a portion must be Third World, another portion must be rural, and so on and so on. As a leading New York politician once noted, this approach always leaves out Swedish dwarves.

Nor have we limited ourselves to simply building such banalities into our structures. One of the reasons a gay philosophy has remained unarticulated is that we have allowed the dialogue to be manipulated by other approaches. We are equally guilty of confusing the need to eliminate discrimination with the need to accept Marxist analyses of oppression or feminist theories on patriarchy. On one occasion, this led the D.C. Area Feminist Alliance, the largest lesbian-dominated group in the city, to march in support of Ayatollah Khomeini at a time when gays were being executed in Iran under his orders. The excuses offered on behalf of Castro, in the face of the most thoroughly documented discrimination against gays we have yet seen, beggar description. One commentary actually suggested that Cuban concentration camps were really no different from the closeted lives of gays in many American states. One suspects that in fact we are seeing ideologies in pursuit of recruits no matter where they may be found; given the level of seriousness of our discussion at this point, one may think of it as Avon ladies barnstorming a Tupperware party because it offers people in a buying mood.

The time has come for us to recognize that such positions conflict with our own major concerns. It may well turn out that we will be unable to identify our concerns until we focus directly on those and those alone and reject the emotional blackmail that accompanies the insistence that we incorporate disparate agendas. Lesbian feminists, for example, would do well to talk more about their oppression as homosexuals in their discussions with gay men or even in their discussions among themselves. It is nothing short of astonishing that lesbians have failed to feel involved by the immigration ban, for example, when its most concrete expression has been to deny lesbians the right to cross the Canadian border to the annual women's music festival. Those cases far outnumber the problems that gay men face in entering America.

There is a great deal going on that convinces one that the separate space we require in order to develop our agenda is being created. Gay historians such as Alan Berube in San Francisco are delving into the history of gay culture as well as the lives of past gay individuals. Gay writers are examining portions of gay life from which we may develop a better understanding of the whole of gay experience. If there is a gay consciousness and a gay community, one suspects that it will come from just such sources and not from gay politics.

Jorge Luis Borges has described Argentinians as "patriots without countrymen." Patriots, of course, are needed for wars; countrymen are required to build communities and nations.

# RANDY SHILTS

## The Life and Death of Harvey Milk

### Prologue: The Death of a Man

November 27, 1978. 11 A.M. A huddle of disbelieving reporters masses around a small locked door. Just a few feet away, down a narrow hallway and behind another closed door, the long lanky body of Supervisor Harvey B. Milk sprawls face down in a spreading pool of blood.

The outer door is opened and closed by police and fellow supervisors; the reporters knock elbows to get a fleeting glimpse of any tangible details. They don't know what they're looking for, but it's their job to look anyway. Milk's young aides fall into one another's arms weeping, their eyes dazed with confusion.

Harvey had always told them it would end this way. But only when they see the black rubber bag, covered with a creased hospital sheet and rolled to the waiting ambulance, does Harvey's prophecy become the painfully palpable stuff of which bad dreams and bold headlines are made.

Within hours, forty thousand tiny flames quiver in the night breezes as candle-bearing mourners trudge somberly to City Hall. Clad in three-piece suits, black leather jackets, blue jeans, and neatly pressed dresses, they gather under cloudy autumnal skies to remember the gangly ward politician with the funny name, the big nose, the thick black hair, and the heavy New York Jewish accent.

The speakers apologize for talking less about the loss of the powerful mayor than about the murder of the supervisor who had only served eleven months in elected office. The focus surprises few in the largely homosexual crowd. The mayor had given them leadership, but Harvey Milk had given them a dream. The shivering mourners remember Harvey's prodding exhortation: "You're not given power, you have to take it"—which is exactly what *he* had done, rising from repeated political defeat to a final rousing victory that to many in the crowd represented nothing short of the fulfillment of an improbable dream. With his death, the shadow of Harvey Milk's dream gains far greater proportions than Milk himself could have engineered in life. Already some speak of a Harvey Milk legend.

At midnight, the crowd ebbs quietly from the Civic Center, setting their flickering candles on the bronze statue of Abraham Lincoln that sits in front of City Hall, leaving them behind to cast curious shadows of tribute. Slowly they file out onto Market Street, back toward the supervisorial district Milk represented, spreading throughout the city on their way home. Most, however, trek the two miles back to the Fifth District's showcase neighborhood around Castro Street—the paragon of gay political and economic muscle that Harvey Milk had helped to build.

It makes sense for this night of mourning to end here. This is where Harvey Milk's story began.

## The Mayor of Castro Street

An hour before midnight, some years earlier. A single light burns in the Victorian storefront of Castro Camera. Harvey Milk—in his usual outfit of sneakers, Levi's, and worn-out corduroy jacket—slumps over the counter, industriously thumbing through the photos he has just picked up from the lab. Other shops along Castro Street closed hours ago; outside, handsome young troopers in fleece-collared bomber jackets are making their first sorties of the evening. But an elderly Irish widow in the neighborhood has relatives visiting from Sacramento, and she has asked Harvey if he could, please, get the pictures back extra fast? So he has spent two hours getting the rush job done and will later drop off the photos himself at the widow's home.

"It's part of the job," Milk explains matter-of-factly—and he isn't talking about the camera business. "No matter what office I run for from now on, I'll always have her vote, and her son's vote, and her daughter-in-law's vote." After ticking off these reasons for being a good Samaritan on his fingers, Milk smiles, pondering the sweetness of statewide office, and adds, "Then, if I ever need votes in Sacramento. . . ."

That's how his Castro neighbors remember Harvey Milk, not out cruising the strip but stooped over his desk, spending two hours to get three votes, or stomping into a commission hearing to angrily oppose a street widening that might put a handful of small shopkeepers out of business.

People came to Harvey with their problems—and he usually knew what to do, or he found out fast. Harvey knew who to call in the Police Department when investigators seemed sluggish in sleuthing a local burglary. He knew how to hustle a new stop sign for a busy corner near the local Catholic grade school. If political cajoling failed, Harvey knew which reporter would listen to his story of moral outrage.

A martyr in death, in life Harvey Milk acted more the role of an Irish ward politician, playing politics by the time-tested rules of the game. He attended hundreds of candidates' nights, shook thousands of hands, and spent years building name recognition. For all his political acumen, however, Milk had a streak of unabashed idealism. "All the forces in the world are not so powerful as an idea whose time has come," read the hand-lettered motto from Victor Hugo that Milk displayed on his wall—and Milk devoted his political career to the notion that acceptance of homosexuality was just such an idea. But a ward politician needs a ward, and the story of Harvey Milk the Politician is largely the story of the Castro.

Harvey had a hunch that Castro Street, a run-down stretch of an old Irish neighborhood gone to seed, might one day become America's gay Main Street. He was among the first merchants to open a store there. While Milk's hunch proved a wise business move, it did not take a visionary to see the Castro's potential. The neighborhood's climate, its antique architecture, and its convenient location at the geographical center of San Francisco made it an inviting refuge from the start. The rows of 1880s Queen Anne–style Victorians could be had for a pittance. Landlords would lease the deserted storefronts at some of the cheapest rents in the city, just to get some return on the deteriorating facades.

During the late 1960s a trickle of gay businesses opened in the area. Gay bars started drawing crowds around 1967. The inexpensive housing attracted counterculture gays from the nearby Haight-Ashbury, where the do-your-own-thing scene had set the psychological groundwork for them to thumb their noses at society.

In 1973, Milk hung his wooden, handcarved shingle in the century-old storefront that became Castro Camera. Although at forty-two Milk seemed nearly elderly for this hippie world, he clearly prized his image of an iconoclastic radical and sported a thick black mustache. His only nod to respectability was to keep his shoulder-length locks tied back in a ponytail. "I'm your basic left-winger, a street person," said Milk, and the self-description was to stick with him long after he traded in his sneakers for wing tips.

Milk occupied a perpetually disheveled apartment above his store. A few left-wing posters and an odd collection of sculpted metal insects adorned the walls. Stacks of papers, growing ever higher, buried the table tops; boxes of odds and ends filled the corners. It was several years before people stopped asking Harvey if he had just moved in. Although Milk sometimes shared the flat with a lover, the small bit of private life he allowed himself took a back seat to his constant politicking.

"Some people call me the Unofficial Mayor of Castro Street," Milk began telling reporters within months of moving into the old storefront. Nobody was sure who "some people" were, or if they even existed, but it made good copy, so nobody groused.

Soon Castro Camera became less a business establishment than a vest-pocket City Hall from which Milk held court. The store's large picture windows displayed announcements of upcoming demonstrations, environmental protests, neighborhood meetings, or commission hearings on Castro-area issues. Petitions for a host of causes—from whale-saving to gay rights—cluttered the beat-up office desk that served as the shop's makeshift counter. Milk devoted only the barest minimum of space to the business of cameras. Most of the shop lay behind tattered room dividers, where Harvey sat on a frumpy, overstuffed maroon couch to talk politics and troubleshoot for his neighbors.

As the trickle of gay émigrés became a visible wave, Milk's "mayoral" duties multiplied. The gay influx startled many of the working-class ethnics who had remained in the neighborhood. Gays frequently fell victim to beatings, in which San Francisco's heavily Irish police force seemed reluctant to intervene. Meanwhile, old-line Castro merchants weren't about to be displaced by this "invasion" without a fight. They shut the new gay businesses out of their invitation-only neighborhood merchants meetings.

The early battle over Castro Street gave Harvey Milk the chance to coin his first slogan: "Gay For Gay"—with "Gay Buy Gay" becoming the economic offshoot. "If those businessmen are so against us being in the neighborhood," fumed Milk, "then they just don't have to take our money."

Milk took to mustering the two most potent weapons of capitalist democracy—money and votes. Over pitchers of beer in the back room of the Sausage Factory, a Castro pizza parlor owned by a friendly Italian family, Milk and a number of other fledgling gay merchants decided they would start their own group—the Castro Village Merchants Association.

The new group signed up a handful of members, then plotted to gain credibility and clout by picking up members from mainstream Castro businesses. They invited the Castro branch of the Hibernia Bank, one of San Francisco's leading financial institutions, to become a member. The bank refused. The association then circulated a letter urging the bank to join, to the bottom of which members affixed their Hibernia deposit stamps. The bank got the hint and signed on.

The "Gay Buy Gay" slogan easily converted to "Gay Vote Gay," which in 1973 meant voting for Harvey Milk. The first campaign set the style for all of Milk's later races for the Board of Supervisors—the eleven-member council that runs San Francisco's city-county consolidated government—as well as for his state assembly race.

Milk immediately assumed the outsider's role. "At Last *You* Have a Candidate for Supervisor" read the flier Milk tirelessly handed out on street corners, at grocery stores, and at bus stops. The "humanistic" candidate who would favor the little over the big, Milk campaigned against big freeways, big high-rises, big business's control of the board, big industry's pollution, and big government's nosing into citizens' sex lives via vice squads.

Milk cut an anomalous figure. He cherished his role as the hippie candidate, attending candidates' nights in his ponytail, mustache, Levi's, and Pendleton plaid shirt, railing against marijuana laws—while rarely using marijuana, alcohol, or even tobacco himself. And, while his notoriety stemmed chiefly from his open homosexuality—he referred to himself as "a queen"—he was also a disorganized, absentminded schlep.

This disparity between Milk's image and his reality stemmed from the essential act with which he defined himself—rebellion. The campaign bi-

ography that emerged from his early media interviews reads like the blueprint for a maverick.

Born in Woodmere, New York, Milk took to cruising the gay tract of
Central Park in his early teens. At fourteen he was among a group of gay
men rounded up by the police because they had removed their shirts.
When the police did nothing about a group of equally shirtless heterosexual men they passed, Milk got his first inkling that there might be something inequitable in society's treatment of gays.

A high achiever, Milk skipped two grades in high school and attended
college in Albany, where he earned a degree in education. A decorated
deep-sea rescue diver, his stint in the navy ended in 1956 when, after a
vague "incident," he was dishonorably discharged on grounds of homosexuality.

With the discharge permanently blocking his entry into teaching, Milk
became a Wall Street financial analyst. At one point he entered show business, producing, directing, and even acting in off-Broadway and Broadway
shows. In 1969 he moved to San Francisco and went back to work as a securities analyst. But it was a brief curtain call. Milk became so disenchanted with the establishment after the American invasion of Cambodia
in 1971 that he dropped out of securities for good, started being open about
his homosexuality, and entered politics.

These liberal doses of oppression, conscience, and rebellion were
enough to perk any journalist's pen—especially reporters eager to get a
fresh angle on an otherwise boring supervisorial election. Milk learned rapidly to compact his outsider's image into a two-sentence newspaper paragraph or a fifteen-second television quote.

Milk added one more key element to his old-fashioned combination of
showmanship and ward politics: hope. "I'm running to show that gay people no longer have to hide, that they can be who they are and make it,"
Harvey said again and again to interviewers, slowly and patiently so they
could understand. "All over the United States there are young gay people
who think they're going to fail *because* they're gay. I want to show them
they can succeed—that they can have hope." It was one of the few statements he ever made without smirking or cracking a joke. In later races Milk
would hone "young gay people" into a single hypothetical teenager from
Dayton or Des Moines. Later still he would claim to have actually found a
real model for this vision. Harvey's "hope speech" became the most familiar element of his political campaign. Naturally—it made good copy.

The rush of Milk stories in the press overshadowed many of his candidacy's weaknesses. The gay political establishment, which had worked for
years to cultivate "friends" in liberal Democratic circles, snubbed Milk as a
rabble-rousing Johnny-come-lately. His only major support came from a
beer truckdrivers' local—Milk had advocated a boycott of the antiunionist
Coors company—and from a radical newspaper that liked his neighbor-
hood-oriented politics. Political analysts tended to view Milk as an experimental aspirant rather than as a serious contender.

"Everybody watched him because nobody had any idea whether a gay
vote really existed and, if it did, whether it would support a gay candidate," recalls Rollin Post, a twenty-year veteran of local political reporting.

Milk surprised these observers by polling a hefty seventeen thousand votes in the 1973 election, placing him eleventh in a field of thirty-two candidates. The results did not put him anywhere near winning one of the five at-large seats in the at-large election, but they ensured that politicians would take this "hippie" seriously in the future. Moreover, the precinct-by-precinct returns revealed that Milk's voter concentrations centered around Castro, Polk, and Folsom streets—a veritable tour guide of San Francisco's gay enclaves. Clearly, if given the chance gays would vote gay.

Meanwhile, back in the Castro the makings of a bona fide boom were under way. By 1974 gays made up a large but uncounted percentage of the area's twenty-five thousand residents. The long-neglected Victorians, refurbished by single men who did not have to spend their time financing dependent spouses and 2.2 children apiece, burst forth in polychromatic splendor. The wholesale renovations upped real-estate values dramatically; housing prices doubled within six months—and went up another 50 percent six months after that.

Business along the two-block Castro shopping strip soared. Antique stores, gift boutiques, and clothing shops replaced the bakeries, butcher shops, candy stores, and five-and-dime emporiums of decades past, reflecting the changing priorities of the new high-disposable-income populace. On a sunny day in August 1974 over five thousand people attended the first Castro Street Fair sponsored by the Castro Village Merchants Association. A year later the area's reputation drew fifty thousand people, making the fair the largest in San Francisco. With the expanding influence came politicians who stalked the neighborhood's gay bars, shaking hands with an enthusiasm once reserved for union halls and Chamber of Commerce luncheons.

Harvey's hunch had paid off. Gays had clustered in defined neighborhoods of major cities for decades, but this was different. "This isn't some cruisy street in Greenwich Village," Milk insisted exuberantly. "For the first time, we've bought up an entire neighborhood—its stores, everything."

By the summer of 1975 Harvey was again running for the Board of Supervisors. This time he thought he could win. The gay vested interest in the Castro was too great to be entrusted to friendly liberal politicians. He cut his hair, shaved off his mustache, and started wearing nondescript two-piece suits that even his own aides called "downright ugly." With his hippie habit and the shock value of his homosexuality behind him, Milk emerged as a far more palatable candidate to many San Franciscans. Ironically, Milk's appearance and demeanor became so devastatingly average that he sometimes had to fend off allegations that he was actually heterosexual. "If I were," he told one reporter, "there sure would be a lot of surprised men walking around San Francisco."

For all his new-found respectability, Milk's hellfire-and-brimstone populism remained undiminished. While this kept him an anathema to the more sedate gay political establishment, he rolled up endorsements from environmental, women's, and neighborhood organizations, as well as from the Teamsters and the highly politicized Firefighters Union.

Once again, Milk's theatrics helped him draw heavy media coverage as he persevered with his old-fashioned meet-the-people campaign. "His days of campaigning were like performances," recalls Jim Rivaldo, who comprised half of Milk's two-man volunteer staff for the shoestring-budget campaigns. Weary commuters from downtown sometimes found themselves greeted by a long, grinning-and-waving human billboard of volunteers holding Milk posters. Harvey had stolen the idea from Cesar Chavez's farm workers, but no matter. It was great copy.

Milk's showing in 1975 even startled many of his adherents. He placed seventh in a field of twenty-seven candidates, just a notch short of grabbing one of the six seats at stake in the election—polling over 53,000 votes, more than triple what he had won in 1973. Once more, the votes came from the city's burgeoning gay neighborhoods. In the Castro alone, between 60 percent and 70 percent of the vote went to Milk. He also received substantial support from straight voters. Hip progressives from the Haight-Ashbury area showed that they could be as iconoclastic as the next guy, giving Milk a high proportion of their votes. Milk also did well in the affluent Pacific Heights area, where straight socialites got the chance to exorcise their liberal guilt by backing an increasingly fashionable commodity. As Rivaldo put it, "We got the hippie, McGovern, and fruit voters."

The city's liberal politicians took note. Many of their own votes came from the same precincts where Milk had grabbed his best tallies. In fact, some colleagues of Mayor-elect George Moscone credited *his* narrow three-thousand-vote victory to gays' fears of Moscone's ultraconservative opponent, John Barbagelatta. The gay vote would not be taken lightly in San Francisco again.

Moscone appointed Milk to the powerful Board of Permit Appeals, the commission that reviews every contested permit in the city and county of San Francisco—not bad for a ward politician. The appointment marked the first time anyone openly gay had served on a San Francisco commission.

Milk's future seemed clearly mapped. All Harvey had to do was play ball with the big boys for the next two years, after which, for the first time, he would have the tacit support of the insiders in the 1977 supervisorial contests. The only problem was that Harvey Milk didn't want to play ball.

## Harvey Milk vs. The Machine

"I'll tell you why I can't stand Harvey Milk," stormed David Goodstein, the editor and publisher of the *Advocate*, America's largest, and only national, gay tabloid. "He's goddamned crazy, that's why. He can't be trusted."

Goodstein was not alone in his estimation of Harvey Milk. Although Milk's 1973 and 1975 supervisorial campaigns had gained him growing support among liberals, established gay leaders regarded him as an abrasive upstart. Milk's campaigns established him as the city's best-known, but not its most powerful, gay politico. A gay-rights movement had been growing in San Francisco since the 1950s. The first openly gay candidacy had preceded Milk by twelve years. In 1961 the drag queen Empress Jose I ran for the Board of Supervisors to protest police harassment of gay bars. In the 1960s, however, political organizing tended to take a less flamboyant, more behind-the-scenes, work-within-the-system tack, with gay activists adopting the Clean-for-Gene techniques of the McCarthy volunteers to show local politicians that gays could be as respectable and upstanding as the best of them.

The strategy worked. By 1969 liberal politicians began cautiously seeking gay endorsements. Raids on gay bars diminished. The city loosened up. Politicians took gay political power more seriously as gay politicos courted "Our Friends"—the liberal politicians whom gays would put into office and who, in turn, would help out gays.

Three key figures emerged: David Goodstein, who courted Democrats with large campaign contributions; Rick Stokes, an affluent attorney and bathhouse owner who developed legal strategies for gays; and Jim Foster, a sometime Goodstein employee who delivered a prime-time television address on gay rights at the 1972 Democratic National Convention and who had earned his credentials when he engineered a gay-bar petition effort that qualified George McGovern for the top spot on the California primary ballot. These leaders gained the confidence of straight politicians after years of doling out hefty campaign contributions and tedious nights of sitting through long candidate interviews. Once inside they claimed to be the gay community's only "Responsible Gay Leaders," assuring Our Friends that they, not the feisty gay radicals who marched in the streets, represented the great silent majority of gays—who would vote as the RGLs advised them to.

To be sure, Our Friends still had to be reassured that homosexuals were just the same as everybody else, that, above all, homosexuals posed no threat. Rather, homosexuality was merely a matter of personal preference in the bedroom, nothing more. Although Our Friends remained fidgety, in 1975 the state legislature decriminalized gay sex between consenting adults, largely on the privacy argument. It would not, however, do for an RGL to try something so brash as to seek major office. In fact, by 1973 the most prestigious post any RGL had sought was a slot on the Community College Board.

These seasoned activists perceived Harvey Milk as something of a joke when he first set out to gain public office in 1973. Years later, Jim Foster would laughingly tell one reporter how a ponytailed Milk had come to him for an endorsement:

"Why should I endorse you, Harvey?" Foster asked.

"Because I'm gay and a lifelong Democrat," replied Milk.

"You know, Harvey," countered Foster, "we're like the Catholic church—we take converts, but we don't make them pope the same day."

Milk had to seek elsewhere for his political base. From then on the battle lines between Milk and the RGLs began to take shape.

The RGLs' fears went beyond Milk's appearance. Milk confronted instead of conciliated. Worse, he was militant, always imploring gays to "come out," consequences be damned. That might be easy for a hippie camera-shop owner but not for Responsible Gays in high positions, who were uninclined toward melodramatic political statements and who, to be sure, had more to lose by publicly coming out. Add to these stylistic differences Milk's rough edges, which even his supporters found irritating. At times Harvey exhibited a deep persecution complex which may have been rooted in his Jewish background. He seemed to analogize every vaguely antigay action with Hitler's genocide. If a cop failed to arrest a gay-beater, the police were part of a Hitleresque political conspiracy to wipe out gays.

Milk's obvious passion for the limelight also left RGLs wondering whether Harvey was just a glory seeker out to ride the gay cause for personal aggrandizement. Where, they asked, had he been during the long, tedious hours of canvassing, voter registration, and candidates' meetings?

"At different meetings," answered Milk, operating in the less stolid sphere of neighborhood ward politics. He had, after all, come from the rough-and-tumble antiwar movement, which had little use for the RGLs' pin-striped suits and *Roberts*-ruled meetings.

Milk regarded the RGLs' distrust for street people as the classism of an elite who wanted to keep other gays out of the system. Moreover, he considered their cautious approach of soothing Our Friends to be Uncle Tomism. ("You're not given power; you have to take it.")

It was only a matter of time before the adversaries met head-on.

The feud erupted into a major battle in 1976. Milk challenged Art Agnos—the aide of Assembly Speaker Leo McCarthy, whose political power in California ranked below only that of the governor—for a vacant state assembly seat in the Sixteenth District, an area that swept the southeast corner of San Francisco, with its heaviest concentration of voters in the Castro.

The challenge stunned the city's liberal political establishment. Agnos had the support of every important Democrat in the city. They had all agreed that Agnos would take the seat. To Commissioner Milk this "understanding" represented nothing less than the foisting of an unknown candidate upon a district by a Chicago-style Democratic machine. "They just want us to be happy little gays who vote for the people they want us to vote for while we keep our seats at the back of the bus," Milk said bitterly, maintaining that the city's politicians didn't want gays to have the kind of real power that would come with having gay office holders.

Milk's moral outrage was also fueled by his ambition and political pragmatism. He thought he could win the seat and champion the little guy once again, this time against the big political bosses. The neatly color-coded maps from the 1975 supervisorial race showed that Milk's heaviest support had come from the gay and hip neighborhoods that comprised a substantial portion of the Sixteenth District. Since the Democratic nomination all but insured election, Milk had merely to beat this Art Somebody in the primary and bypass the small-time sandbox of city politics in favor of the big-time arena of the state legislature.

Milk's closest advisors argued against his entry into the race. He was still in debt from his 1975 campaign and would, by running for the assembly, risk blowing his sure shot for a supervisorial seat in 1977. Moreover, the almost immediate reentry into campaigning, just months after the 1975 race, would leave Milk vulnerable to critics' charges that he was a megalomaniac out to gain political glory at all costs.

None of the arguments worked. In late April 1976 Milk filed candidacy papers—and started learning about big-time hardball and the internecine world of gay politics.

Mayor Moscone, who had spent much of his last term as state senator running for mayor, immediately booted Milk out of his prized commissioner's seat, saying he could not effectively serve on the commission and run for office at the same time. This act of political retribution resulted in a newspaper headline that Milk turned into his campaign slogan: "Harvey Milk vs. The Machine."

The RGLs saw their chance to throw Milk his third strike and pulled out all stops against him. They imported Representative Elaine Noble, a gay state legislator from Massachusetts, to endorse Agnos and convince San Francisco gays that they didn't need a gay state legislator in California. Noble needed the California RGLs' help to raise funds for her own planned bid for the United States Senate in 1978. And, sniped Milk's allies, another openly gay legislator might dilute Noble's publicity value.

Milk, meanwhile, relished the symbolism of his battling the Goliath of both the liberal and the gay political establishments. "This just isn't a campaign to get me elected," he pontificated, giving his hope speech a new twist. "This is to show that in a democracy the people should decide who their leaders are, not a bunch of old-boy politicians in a back room." He dug his two-piece suits out of the closet and reestablished his 6 A.M. campaign regimen, making the now-familiar rounds of bus stops, street fairs, community meetings, and informal coffees.

Agnos outspent Milk two to one, drawing large contributions from special-interest committees who wanted to curry favor with Speaker McCarthy. (Agnos spent more on postage for a sophisticated direct-mail effort than Milk spent on his entire campaign.) When the final days had the race still looking like a squeaker, Governor Jerry Brown—then riding high on his presidential bid—broke his promise of neutrality and issued an endorsement of Agnos that was mailed to every Democrat in the district.

Milk's street-corner politicking couldn't overcome these odds. Within two hours of the closing of the polls, Milk's tearful aides were reading returns that would eventually show a 45–55 percent loss for Milk. Milk himself was near tears when he climbed onto the stage of the hippie restaurant (with a bustling marijuana trade upstairs) in which his supporters had gathered.

"We gave them a good fight," he said. "We showed them that they can't take us for granted, that we're always going to have some say." Harvey's voice was cracking. "Maybe not this time. But remember that every election we get closer. And you've got to keep working, getting people to vote, because if you do there's no way they can stop you."

Harvey's hope speech again. But this time *he* needed hope more than anybody else.

"Two defeats for the price of one," a reporter called Milk's loss of both the election and his commissioner's seat. The RGLs cheerfully dubbed Milk "a gay Harold Stassen" and breathed easier. Rick Stokes replaced Milk on the Board of Permit Appeals, setting the most conservative voting record of any member. Now he, Foster, and Goodstein were the undisputed "ins"—and any gay-related affairs involving City Hall had to go strictly through them.

Even as the RGLs counted their blessings, however, Milk was campaigning in the general election for the passage of Proposition T, a measure that would end the citywide election of supervisors and set up eleven smaller supervisorial districts. Sensitive to the gay vote, the framers of the measure consolidated the Castro and surrounding areas into one district—a gay district. The proposition passed in November, drawing overwhelming margins in the Castro.

The maroon couch at Castro Camera was never more tattered than at the end of 1976. The shop's wall had a new, carefully color-coded map of election returns from the 1976 assembly race. Milk drew a line around the newly created Fifth District, showing that he had carried that area against Agnos with about 60 percent of the votes. "That map says it all," Milk would state confidently when asked about his chances of carrying the district in the 1977 supervisorial election. "You tell *me* who's going to win."

The ward politician finally had his own ward.

## Showdown in District Five

The San Francisco gay community entered 1977 with a sense of homophile manifest destiny. Gay émigrés flocked to the nation's one liberated gay zone, convinced that San Francisco was fated to become gay from sea to shining bay. Media estimates numbered the gay population at between 75,000 and 125,000 out of San Francisco's 660,000 inhabitants.

Castro Street became less a gay neighborhood than a sociological phenomenon, with its own cruising rituals and dress code. Denizens adopted such rigidly structured male images—cowboys, bikers, jocks, lumberjacks—that they were dubbed Castroids. Were these ultrabutch clones of the Marlboro Man the end result of a decade of gay liberation? Maybe not, but the Castro Street gay scene of the 1970s was as much a cultural watershed for San Francisco as North Beach's Beat Generation had been in the 1950s and Haight-Ashbury's hippies had been in the 1960s. Gays from around the world called the Castro Mecca.

All of this was good for business. Milk estimated that at the end of 1976 "the shops on these two blocks of Castro alone had to net at least $30 million, and that's at least $10 million more than they did last year." As old leases expired, landlords tripled and even quadrupled the rents on the now-valuable storefronts. Milk himself had to move from his Castro Street location when his lease expired and his rent spiraled, leaving Harvey a victim of the economic miracle he had helped to pioneer. With characteristic aplomb, Milk branded the real-estate speculators "bloodsuckers."

The rampant speculation pushed housing and rental prices so high that many counterculture gays were forced to establish new gay enclaves deep inside the black and Latin neighborhoods adjacent to the Castro. In their place came successful young professionals—doctors, lawyers, admen—who crowded the Castro's bus stops every morning in their three-piece suits.

Even as Castro Street gained full-scale respectability, 1977 rapidly unfolded as the year of the street people—who set a militant tenor for the city's gays in a series of demonstrations unmatched by anything since the student protests of the 1960s. The new militance was largely sparked by the repeal of the Dade County gay-rights ordinance in June. Within hours after the returns came in from Florida, thousands of angry gays assembled on Castro Street to march through the city, shouting "Civil Rights or Civil War!" At one point the march almost erupted into a riot, but Milk—one of the few leaders the radicals would listen to—prevailed upon the marchers to keep the demonstration nonviolent.

The Miami loss—and the announcement that an antigay initiative was planned for the California ballot—left San Francisco gays feeling painfully vulnerable. They reviewed the rewards of their highly touted political clout and found them wanting. The mayor whom they had helped to elect had given them three commission appointments—only one of which had any power—as compared to the dozens of plums routinely doled out by City Hall to other minority groups. San Francisco still had no comprehensive gay-rights law banning discrimination in employment and housing—the RGLs did not want to threaten Our Friends by rocking the boat with such a legislative demand. Clearly, press coverage, social cachet, and "friends" did not necessarily add up to political power.

This realization created an intense frustration in the gay community, which finally overflowed just a few days after the Dade County defeat at a Democratic party rally in Golden Gate Park. Ironically, Vice-President Walter Mondale had come to speak on human rights. As Mondale rose to address the group, gay protesters started shouting at him to make a statement on the Bryant campaign—confusing the state's Democratic leaders, who turned to Jim Foster. Why couldn't he keep this rabble in line? Weren't they *his* people? Foster, who had spent so long insulating the Democrats from such radicals, was powerless. Mondale cut short his speech and slipped out the back door, spoiling the fund-raiser.

The Democrats were furious. They pointed to the recently announced initiative sponsored by State Senator John Briggs and warned gays of an impending backlash. Dan White—a thirty-year-old ex-cop, ex-fireman, ex-paratrooper, and all-American boy then running for supervisor in a working-class neighborhood—tried to make political hay out of the gay colonization of the city by announcing, "I am not going to be forced out of San Francisco by splinter groups of radicals, social deviates, and incorrigibles. You must realize there are thousands upon thousands of frustrated angry people such as yourselves waiting to unleash a fury that can and will eradicate the malignancies which blight our beautiful city." White's slogan: "Stand Up and Fight for Dan White."

At about the same time, three Latino youths attacked and killed a gay gardener outside his San Francisco home. Early reports said one youth shouted, "Faggot, faggot, faggot!" as he stabbed the gardener repeatedly in the face. The gardener's friends went to Harvey. Milk fed the story to the press, blaming the murder on the antigay activities of Anita Bryant and John Briggs. Days later, over 250,000 people filled the streets for the annual Gay Freedom Day Parade, marching in a solemn funeral procession for the gardener that was also the largest assemblage of people in San Francisco in nearly a decade. Still, most of the city's prominent politicians feared that the march would erupt into violence and avoided it, leaving many gays to feel abandoned during their time of crisis.

Against this uneasy backdrop, the 1977 supervisorial race in District Five turned into a showdown between the RGLs and the radicals led by Harvey Milk. The RGLs, with attorney Rick Stokes as their standard-bearer, dubbed Milk a loudmouthed, perennial loser who would make the gay community the laughingstock of the city. "Harvey will embarrass the shit out of us," warned David Goodstein.

"They embarrass *me*," retorted Milk—and returned to campaigning in the only way he knew how, making the rounds of bus stops, shaking hands, passing out wordy fliers, and giving his hope speech to any crowd that would listen.

Milk gathered a wide array of incongruous endorsements, from supporters of marijuana legalization to the Teamsters, the Firefighters Union, and the Building Trades and Construction Council, from radical neighborhood groups to the *San Francisco Chronicle*. Faced with what seemed like a Milk juggernaut, Rick Stokes took a vacation from the campaign and reportedly toyed with the idea of withdrawing, only to be prodded back into the race by Assemblyman Agnos. Real estate interests, fearing Milk's outspoken support of speculation control, filled Stokes's campaign chest, giving him nearly $60,000—the third highest budget of the more than one hundred supervisorial candidates running for election in the entire city, and an astronomical three-to-one spending edge over Milk.

But the strategy of Stokes's key supporters was shifting. They were not so much trying to get Stokes *in* as they were working to keep Milk *out*. According to one of Stokes's aides at the time, Stokes even approached the leading heterosexual candidate to make a deal. The two candidates would sponsor a private poll of the district. Whoever made the weaker showing would withdraw in favor of the stronger candidate—even if it meant keeping a gay off the board. The straight candidate refused the deal.

Once again it was "Harvey Milk vs. the Machine." Milk maintained that City Hall liberals were lending tacit support to Stokes in an effort to divide the gay vote and keep gays from gaining any real political power. "They'll do anything to keep me out, because I won't cut deals," said Milk. "My first commitment is to the voters, not the machine."

"It's a red-herring approach," countered Stokes in a magazine interview. "Harvey's born to be a martyr."

Milk claimed victory within an hour after the polls closed, drawing over 30 percent of the vote in the seventeen-way race for the seat—more than double the votes won by Stokes or the nearest runner-up. The next day he made the front pages again when his campaign manager, Anne Kronenberg, dressed in full leather gear, drove Milk on the back of her motorcycle from City Hall to his Castro Street victory party. "I didn't win; *you* won," Milk told the screaming crowd between gulps of champagne. "Don't ever let anyone tell you that you can't make it, that you don't have the power because you're gay—or because you're anything. We've showed that you *can* do it."

Days later, Milk added the finishing touches to his hope speech when he emerged with a vaguely apocryphal tale of a sixteen-year-old boy from

Altoona, Pennsylvania, who had called to thank Milk for giving him hope that he could make something of his life. No more talk of Dayton or Des Moines. For the rest of his career, Milk's basic hope speech mentioned a teenage boy from Altoona. But even as the public Milk waxed eloquent about Altoona and hope, the private Milk got to work playing political hardball.

Soon after his election, Milk met with Mayor Moscone and demanded that he be consulted on every gay appointment in the city and any issue related to gays. "I'm the number-one queen in town now," he later claimed to have said. "I start running for reelection tomorrow, and if you guys oppose me again, then just be ready to lose."

Ten days after his election, Milk stayed late in his camera shop to tape record his political and personal will. He had received a death threat. The tapes were to be left with three separate friends, to be played for the mayor only if Milk were indeed assassinated. At the time, Milk's aides considered the tapes to be merely a particularly melodramatic manifestation of Harvey's persecution complex—spiced, perhaps, with a dash of megalomania. But Milk seemed to be caught up in the symbolic drama of his assassination. "Let the bullets that rip through my brain smash through every closet door in the nation," his voice uttered from one tape.

Meanwhile, unaware of either the threat or the tapes, David Goodstein made a belated attempt to get into Milk's good graces by throwing a series of inauguration-night parties for Milk at gay discos. Noting the irony of this situation, reporter Francis Moriarty recalls how Goodstein, an admirer of Machiavelli, kissed Milk's hand as they parted company after the long night, saying "Goodnight, sweet Prince"—Horatio's famous farewell to the slain Hamlet. The line comes just after Hamlet, with his dying breath, endorses Fortinbras in the coming struggle for power. Goodstein was not to know for nearly a year that his parting line followed Milk's own secret, taped nominations of his successor—nominations intended to freeze out Goodstein's closest allies, Rick Stokes and Jim Foster.

It was as if Milk knew—even as Stokes had claimed during the campaign—that he was indeed born to be a martyr.

## Supervisor Harvey Milk

I can't believe it," sputtered an aide to another San Francisco supervisor, tossing his morning *Chronicle* on a table in the City Hall lunchroom. "Every time you pick up the paper, there's Harvey doing something new. How in hell does that guy do it?"

Harvey's long cultivation of reporters paid off handsomely during his year as supervisor; he soon became one of the city's best-publicized politicians. Milk had a fresh, newsworthy slant on just about everything. When Proposition 13 budget cuts threatened to eat into city social-service programs, Milk proposed legalized gambling in San Francisco—an idea that never had a chance of getting off the ground but that made the front pages.

Milk maneuvered a minor proposal on disposal of dog droppings into a major media event—perhaps the most memorable of all his stunts. He gave televised demonstrations—using ersatz turds—of how his proposed "pooper scooper" bags worked, concluding the news segments by stepping into some of the real stuff himself. Milk walked away from the shootings with dirty feet, but his picture made the Associated Press wires.

Even the routine rotation of the city's acting mayorship among supervisors when Moscone went on vacation became a front-page media event for Milk, who posed for photographers behind Moscone's massive desk and gave a quickie version of his hope speech about how some day a homosexual could hope to sit at a mayor's desk. (Once the public pontification was completed, Milk spent much of the rest of the day privately speculating on the merits of the desk as a seduction site for any of a number of handsome young City Hall bureaucrats.)

The most significant front-page photo appeared in April 1978 and showed Milk handing Mayor Moscone a lavender pen with which to sign San Francisco's first comprehensive gay-civil-rights bill into law. The measure—opposed only by Supervisor Dan White, because of his "Catholic constituency"—showcased the dramatic moves forward gays were making with their new supervisor. Backed by the prestige of his office, Milk cajoled the city into allocating more money to gay groups and even jawboned the United Way into making its first contribution to a gay organization.

"You'd never get those things by just having one of Our Friends in office," sneered Milk. "It only happens when you've got power yourself and the big boys are scared shitless of you."

Milk himself was making more than token concessions to respectability. Even his most hardened enemies admitted that he was not the disaster they had predicted he would be. Milk was rarely seen in public without his best RGL suit and tie. He reined in the once-galloping pace of his speech to a reasonable canter. The formerly frenzied waving of arms gave way to a calmer, more confident gesture of one arm, index finger extended—which photographed better.

Milk's outspokenness and zeal for the limelight thrust him into the role of leading liberal on the board—and he started building a broad-based coalition of support among other minorities. He helped lead the fight to get Gordon Lau, the new Chinese supervisor, elected board president, even voting for Lau after Lau had withdrawn in favor of the obvious winner, Dianne Feinstein. Milk sponsored a resolution asking South Africa to abandon its San Francisco consulate. He was the sole sponsor of a long list of proposals to improve working conditions for city employees. And Milk pushed tirelessly for an ordinance to discourage "bloodsucker" real estate speculators—gay and straight—from pricing the poor out of the city.

A bane to big businessmen, a gadfly to staid moderates, a godsend to the Left, Milk soon appeared to be an invincible candidate in future supervisorial elections—and a potential standard-bearer for the city's liberals after Mayor Moscone completed his expected second term in 1983.

Despite Milk's rosy political future, his year as California's openly gay officeholder was marked by thorny problems and by personal tragedy. Throughout early 1978, the national gay-rights movement suffered a series of devastating setbacks. Prodded by local cadres of fundamentalist Christians, voters in St. Paul, Minnesota; Wichita, Kansas; and Eugene, Oregon, repealed gay-rights ordinances they had formerly passed. After each defeat, crowds gathered on Castro Street to march through downtown San Francisco—shouting, singing, and sometimes crying. After the Wichita defeat, they once again swept past City Hall shouting, "Civil Rights or Civil War!"

Harvey was there as usual, shuffling along the edges in his worn-out corduroy jacket, Levi's, and sneakers. He was worried. You could tell by the calm quiet of his tone. "Listen to them," he said. "You can only shove people up against the wall so much and then—*bam!*" Milk slugged his fist against his hand. "They're going to fight back."

The street radical in Milk clearly enjoyed speculating on the riot potential of the situation. "It could just be the start of another ten years of destruction and violence," he said. "We'll just keep going through it again and again until people learn." But he had become media-wise enough to be concerned about how gay riots would play in Peoria.

The apocalypse neared California when the Briggs Initiative qualified for the November 1978 general-election ballot as Proposition 6. Proposition 6 mandated the firing of any public school teacher who was gay or who advocated homosexuality as a normal way of life—thus legislating discrimination if it passed. The measure was taken as a personal affront by many California gays, most notably Milk's Latino lover, Jack Lira.

Lira had lived with Milk for some time, performing the household chores, but had kept far in the background of Milk's public life. In fact, many people did not know that Milk *had* a lover until the day of his inauguration, when Harvey introduced Lira to the crowd. Milk's reticence may have been motivated by more than a need for personal privacy. The twenty-six-year-old Lira was having a hard time coming to grips with his homosexuality. He was unable to hold down a job. When Milk offered to finance schooling for him—anything to get him to work—Lira withdrew instead. The relationship was reportedly disintegrating.

Ordinarily prone to depressions and tantrums, Lira grew despondent and morose after seeing the television movie *Holocaust.* Several weeks passed. One summer afternoon, Milk walked home from City Hall and discovered the body of his lover hanging beneath a paperback version of *Holocaust* Lira had nailed to a doorframe in their apartment. Harvey made the front pages again.

Other events, however, soon shoved this personal tragedy out of the limelight. Milk was in demand throughout California as a speaker on Proposition 6. In a series of debates with Senator Briggs, Milk had Briggs imploring him to "Stop calling me 'Hitler.' " Even more galling to Briggs was the humor Milk employed to counter the tight-lipped senator. At one point Briggs cited statistics showing that the average male homosexual has over five hundred sexual contacts—to which Milk responded, "I wish." These speaking engagements often drew Milk into the most hostile territory of southern California. He was frightened of what might happen to him, but he would hear nothing of it when his aides encouraged him to hire bodyguards. "If they can shoot a president of the United States," he argued, "they can get some lowly supervisor."

But no serious incidents occurred during Milk's travels, and on Election Day, Proposition 6 suffered a landslide defeat. In San Francisco, 75 percent of the voters said no to the Briggs Initiative.

"Let these results go out tonight to all over the United States," Milk shouted to a cheering crowd on election night. "Let the New Right know that they can no longer draw this country apart with their hatred, their lies, their bigotry.

"It is also up to us to go into the homes of the people who voted yes—to go in and show them we are not who they think we are. It's up to each of us to come out and do that—because there's lots of education that needs to be done."

Only four of the city's nine-hundred-plus precincts voted yes on Proposition 6—all of them in the district of Supervisor Dan White.

On November 10, three days after the defeat of Proposition 6, White abruptly announced his resignation from the board, saying that he couldn't afford to staff his fast-food business and support his wife and newborn child on his $800-a-month supervisor's salary. Milk understood White's problem. He had been forced to close his camera shop that week because he didn't have time to keep it up. On November 14, however, White changed his mind and wanted his seat back. Mayor Moscone agreed to reappoint him.

But legal complications prolonged the process. And, while the city attorney prepared an opinion on the correct course to follow, liberals began privately to urge Moscone *not* to reappoint the board's most conservative member. Then Milk jumped into the fray, becoming one of the few liberals outside White's district to publicly argue against the supervisor's reappointment. Milk reminded Moscone that he would be up for reelection in 1979 and that the mayor stood to lose his gay support if he reappointed the board's most antigay member. Moscone accepted the validity of Milk's analysis of the situation and started sifting through other candidates more amenable to liberals.

Milk got to work organizing his own 1979 reelection campaign. Viewed as a virtual shoo-in, he began lining up endorsements. Milk also encouraged rumors that he might run for mayor in 1983. But even as he cut political deals for the next election, a preternatural calm settled into Milk's personal life. Nobody's sure why, but Harvey spent much of late November settling his financial affairs, arranging for a $3,000 loan to meet some outstanding bills. He returned his leased car and consolidated his debts.

On Thanksgiving weekend, Milk met with Jim Rivaldo to discuss politics. When Rivaldo suggested that they talk about the mayoral campaign, Milk looked at him quizzically—as though Rivaldo should know better—and said, "I won't be around for that. Let's just talk about tomorrow."

A layer of thick, dark clouds gathered over San Francisco's City Hall as Harvey Milk entered it the morning of November 27. He was going to pick up his loan. Across the rotunda, Mayor Moscone was preparing for a press conference at which he would announce Dan White's replacement. Downstairs, in the basement of the building, an engineer heard a tap at a window.

Dan White had lost his keys. He apologized to the engineer and came through the window, evading the metal detectors at the main entrances to the building. He slipped unannounced into the mayor's office.

An aide rose to greet White; the mayor emerged from his private office.

Moscone waved off the aide's request to sit in on any meeting with White. An argument developed between White and Moscone; the pair went into the mayor's private office to have a drink.

A series of loud noises came from the mayor's inner office. Minutes later, Moscone's aides walked in to discover the mayor lying face down in a pool of blood.

"Can I talk to you for a minute, Harvey?" asked Dan White, appearing at Milk's door. Milk was in the process of thanking a friend for the $3,000 loan he had just received. Milk accompanied White into White's former office.

Three loud pops. "No, no!" shouted Milk. Then, two more pops. White rushed from the office.

According to the coroner's report, Milk had been shot in the chest three times. Two more shots, fired into his brain with cool, execution-style precision after he collapsed to the floor, killed Harvey Milk instantly.

## Epilogue: The Birth of a Legend?

The *EXTRA* editions sold out almost immediately. Within an hour of the shootings, knots of gays huddled on Castro Street, reading the newspaper headlines over one another's shoulders. The normally bustling bars along the street draped their doors in black, closing early that evening. Thousands of mourners converged along the strip to walk the same two miles to City Hall that Harvey and his lover Jack had walked, arm in arm, eleven months before. Nobody chanted or shouted now. They just walked silently, candles in hand, dazed.

The dual murders of Harvey Milk and George Moscone numbed a city already stunned from the bizarre end of the People's Temple cult in Guyana. A week of emotional services for George and Harvey followed. The two men, sometimes at odds in life, became inextricably linked in death. Lesbian separatists leaned to touch the casket of the handsome Italian family man, while Catholic crones genuflected in front of the casket of the gay Jew. Unified in a way few could have imagined a week earlier, everyone in the city plugged into the tragedies in his or her own way.

Gays had a martyr now—and with this they attained a respectability that would forever seal them into the mainstream of the city's political life. They had also acquired a bogeyman whose memory would make any anti-gay politician in San Francisco immediately suspect.

Throughout it all, the dark clouds hung relentlessly over the city.

Like many gays, Harvey seemed to have had no past before he moved to San Francisco. Now revelations of his early life added unimagined dimensions to the slain leader.

Two days after the shootings, a short, portly man with a prominent nose, thick dark hair, and a heavy New York Jewish accent stepped off a plane. Robert Milk had come to say goodbye to his younger brother. He had thought Harvey was a minor county officeholder until he turned on his television and saw the thousands of mourners standing in the chilly midnight air holding candles.

Robert Milk remembered a stubborn, determined boy who had spent his childhood entering raffles at the local matinee house because he liked going up on stage when he won. "When Harvey told us he was going into politics five years ago," Milk recalled, "we just thought, 'There's Harvey being Harvey again.' We never thought he would win."

Now Robert Milk, a Long Island stock salesman, was being consoled by a governor, a lieutenant governor, a United States senator, a state chief justice, big-city mayors, and a presidential representative. He was the guest of a state senator. One black judge came up to him to say, "You should be proud that Harvey was born to do what he did."

Harvey's brother remembered how Harvey had warned him that it would end this way—with an assassination. His eyes grew vacant. He told of how their mother had died exactly sixteen years to the day before Harvey and how, the night before Harvey's death, he had lit a twenty-four-hour ceremonial candle to commemorate her passing. But the candle kept burning for hours after it should have gone out.

The final memorial service for Harvey was held in the ornate beaux arts San Francisco Opera House. Thousands of mourners overflowed into the surrounding courtyards of the opera house to hear the final tributes to Milk. They talked of a legend. "People are already recounting things Harvey said, or never said, or might have said," announced Supervisor Carol Ruth Silver, Milk's closest ally on the board.

After the service, organizers urged the mourners to take the flowers from the wreaths that filled the stage: "Nothing should be left to die here." Many later passed out the extra flowers on city buses as they went home.

Saturday, December 2, 1978. Finally, the clouds lift from the city. A group of Harvey's closest friends board the sixty-two-foot schooner *Lady Frei.* One of them carries a brown Safeway shopping bag under his arm. On board, Harvey's friends drink wine, smoke marijuana, and make approving comments about the teenage boys perched above them adjusting the sails.

Once properly out to sea, somebody pulls a box, wrapped in *Doonesbury* comics, out of the bag. The box is wrapped in funny papers because—after all—Harvey would not want to be seen in plastic. It contains Harvey's ashes. Across one side of the box, spelled out in neat rows of rhinestones, are the letters *R.I.P.*

Harvey's friends pose for pictures, holding the box reverently to their chests. Four of Harvey's former boyfriends pose with the package for a traditional widow's portrait. Then everyone assembles on deck while another friend fires a single shot from the boat's miniature cannon.

Silently one mourner tears open two packages of pastel powder. Another removes the comics, revealing the simple plastic box with the label "Cremated Remains of Harvey B. Milk." They scatter the ashes and the powder off the end of the boat.

Harvey is gone, leaving behind only a memory. And, on the glittering, cold Pacific Ocean, a small patch of lavender.

# MICHAEL DENNENY

<><><><><><><><><><><><><><><><><><>

## Gay Politics: Sixteen Propositions

> crackers are born with the right to be
> alive
> i'm making ours up right here in yr face
> —Ntozake Shange

*P*olitical reflection must begin with and remain loyal to our primary experience of ourselves and the world or it degenerates into nonsense, the making of idle theory of which there is no end (and consequently, no seriousness). These thoughts begin with the fact—somewhat startling when I think about it—that I find my identity as a gay man as basic as any other identity I can lay to claim to. Being gay is a more elemental aspect of who I am than my profession, my class, or my race. This is new but not unheard of. It corresponds to what Isherwood was getting at in *Christopher and His Kind*, when he frankly confesses his loyalty to his "tribe" in contrast to his desertion of his class and his troubling realization that he had less in common with his countrymen than with his German lover who had been drafted to fight against them in the Second World War. Obviously being gay was not Isherwood's sole claim to identity. Nor is it mine, but it *is* of enormous significance to how I find and feel myself in the world. Those who do not find this to be the case with themselves will probably find these reflections pointless. And since they are based on the experiences of a gay man, it is unclear how much of this discussion would be relevant to lesbians, if indeed any.

### Proposition 1
Homosexuality and gay are not
the same thing; gay is when you
decide to make an issue of it.

*Homosexual* is properly an adjective; it describes something you do. *Gay* is a noun; it names something you are. Gore Vidal, who prefers the adjectively intensified word *homosexualist*, insists on this distinction tirelessly; one assumes he is right in his own case. For him, being homosexual is not a central part of his identity; it merely describes some of his behavior, in which case the adjective homosexualist is probably more precise, if inelegant.

Whether or not being gay is a central part of one's identity—one's felt sense of self in everyday life, who I am—*is not a theoretical question*. It is a fact and can be ascertained by fairly elemental self-reflection. There are

Jews for whom that fact is an accident of birth and nothing more; blacks for whom the most monstrous aspect of racism is its bewildering irrelevance to who they are. But there are also gays, Jews, and blacks who know themselves as this particular gay man, this particular Jew, this particular black. Such people experience their humanness *through* being gay, Jewish, or black; they do not experience their humanity apart from its concrete manifestation in the world. The following analogy can illustrate, not prove, this position: one can be an athlete *through* being a pole-vaulter, football player, or swimmer; one cannot be simply an athlete without taking part in some sport.

One can argue about whether one *should* gain a significant part of one's identity in this way; whether one actually *does*, however, is a *fact*. Facts, of course, can change. Eight years ago I did not experience myself *primarily* as a gay man; today, if I spend more than four days in a totally straight environment, I feel like climbing the walls. I experience myself as a fish out of water, as a "homosexual alien," in the words of the Immigration Service.

## Proposition 2

> Gays insofar as they are gay are ipso facto
> *different* from straights.

Merle Miller entitled his courageous pamphlet *On Being Different*, which was both accurate and apt. The liberal line that gays are no different from anyone else is less to the point than Richard Goldstein's observation that gays are different from other people in every way *except* in bed. Liberals assert that we are *essentially* the same as them and therefore our oppression is unjust. This passes for tolerance. However, tolerance can only be tolerance of real diversity and difference. The liberal position is not really tolerant—although it is subtle—because it denies that we are different, which at bottom is another way of denying that we exist *as gays*. This position is absurd—if we are not different, why all this fuss in the first place?

By relegating homosexuality to the realm of privacy—that which is not spoken about or seen and is therefore unimportant politically (consequently "no different")—liberal "tolerance" becomes a perfect example of what Herbert Marcuse called "repressive tolerance" (a concept that seemed to me idiotic as applied in the sixties). The way liberals have of not noticing that one is gay or, if forced to notice, of not wanting to hear about it or, if forced to hear about it, of asserting that "that's your private life and no concern of mine or of anyone else" is an extremely insidious tactic that in practice boils down to "let's all act straight and what you do in the bedroom is your own business."

This is the source of the liberals' famous lament: why *must* you flaunt your homosexuality? (Flaunt is the antigay buzzword as *shrill* and *strident* were the antifeminist buzzwords.) This position is identical to that of Anita Bryant, who repeatedly made it clear that she was no dummy, she knew that many of those "bachelors" and "spinsters" in the schools were gay, and she was not advocating a McCarthy-like witch hunt to have them rooted out and fired; all she wanted was that gay teachers not hold hands and kiss in public, that gay adults not "recruit" impressionable youngsters for the "gay life-style." In other words, get back in the closet and we won't bother you. Anita Bryant was not your traditional bigot; she was something new, a direct response to the emergence of gay liberation. As such, we can expect more of her ilk.

When you point out that this is also the essence of the liberals' position, for all its tolerance, they sometimes get infuriated. They have an odd animus against the very idea of gay oppression. People who are otherwise perfectly sensible get uncomfortable and sometimes hostile when you suggest that even *they* might have internalized some of the pervasive antigay hostility and prejudice of the larger society. It is hard to know how to respond when they act like you have insulted their honor, but I suspect the best answer is Curtis Thornton's simple observation about white people: "I understand why they don't want us to think they are prejudiced. But if most of them were not prejudiced, it wouldn't be a prejudiced country" (in John Gwaltney's marvelous book *Drylongso*).

Liberals in general tend to get upset if one tries to make an issue of being gay or if one says that being gay is an important and central part of one's life and identity. One feels like asking them whether their own heterosexuality is not an important part of *their* lives. But, of course, they do not talk about heterosexuality, they talk about sexuality. Which is the whole point.

## Proposition 3
The central issue of gay politics is sexuality.

It is sexuality that makes us homosexuals; it is the affirmation of ourselves as homosexuals that makes us gay. Sexuality is not the same as love. Homosexuality is not the same as "men loving men," though it sounds good as a slogan to make us respectable in the eyes of the straight world. Even at our most chauvinistic it is absurd to imply that the straight world is unfamiliar with or unfriendly to the concept of men loving men. They have developed a multiplicity of forms for male bonding, some of which they even regard as noble, some of which even we can regard as noble. What drives them nuts is not love between men but sex between men. It is one of the many virtues of Martin Sherman's play *Bent* that he keeps this steadily in mind. In the face of the implacable hostility of society and the deeply insidious homophobia we have internalized, even most gay authors falter and sublimate homosexuality into homosentimentality. Sherman is unusual in being aware of the quite obvious fact that the Nazis did not throw men into concentration camps for *loving* other men but for *fucking* with other men. The theatrically and theoretically brilliant climax of the play is not the noble expression of yet another doomed love but the simultaneous orgasm of the two lovers as they face the audience—a moment that truly shocks the public, including gays.

If the central issue of homosexuality is sexuality, by definition—theirs *and* ours—it should come as no surprise that we are obsessed with sex. Indeed we are and rightly so. What else would we be obsessed by? Straights throw this at us as an accusation. What they would like—at least the liberals among them—are homosexuals not "obsessed" with sex, i.e., self-denying, repressed, closeted homosexuals, whom they have always been willing to put up with (except for a few real nut cases like Irving Bieber). The only thing wrong with being obsessed with sex is that this obsession sometimes leads to the paltry results we see in too many gay bars. There is nothing wrong with gay bars, but there is a lot wrong with bad gay bars.

*Proposition 4*

>Society does not hate us because
>we hate ourselves; we hate
>ourselves because we grew up
>and live in a society that hates us.

"The problem is not so much homosexual desire as the fear of homosexuality," as Guy Hocquenghem states in the first sentence of his book *Homosexual Desire*.

Many straights—and unfortunately even some gays—have the irritating habit of pointing to one of the more bizarre, extreme, confused, or self-lacerating (but rarely self-destructive) manifestations of homosexuality as the reason for their general repugnance and intolerance. But they have it ass-backward. These evasions of self, confusions of sex, and manifestations of despair are the *result* of the implacable hostility of society—"the havoc wrought in the souls of people who aren't supposed to exist" (Ntozake Shange). There is a savage hypocrisy here that reminds one of Bieber's assertion that homosexuals were neurotic because they were, among other things, "injustice collectors."

Internalized self-hatred is deep and pervasive in the gay world and the havoc it can work should not be underestimated, but to compound it by assuming guilt for the sometimes deplorable effects of society's hostility toward us is foolish and self-defeating. It leads to a miasma of depression when what is called for is anger.

The relative absence of clearly directed and cleansing anger in the gay world is surprising and worthy of note; it is probably a bad sign.

*Proposition 5*

>The appalling violence—
>physical, psychological, social,
>and intellectual—unleashed
>against gays by Western society
>in modern times is a clear attempt
>at cultural genocide.

Most gay men I know will feel uncomfortable with this assertion, which is nevertheless an unavoidable conclusion. The implied parallel with the suffering of American blacks, the Jews, the Vietnamese, and other colonized or persecuted peoples makes us sharply aware of the peculiarities of our own situation, which include the unusual opportunity for wealth, influence, and a tenuous security that have historically been our options. But the point is not to claim an equality of suffering—pain, physical or psychological, is almost impossible to measure in any case, and attempts to compute or compare it reek of vulgarity—still less to assume that a preoccupation with one's own hurt somehow slights or diminishes someone else's. The point is to establish precisely what has been done and to delineate the peculiarities of our own oppression, which are grounded in the peculiarities of our situation.

American racists have inflicted extraordinary suffering on American blacks but they have not tried to pretend that the black hero, Crispus Attucks, the first casualty of the American Revolutionary War, was white. The Nazi lunatics sought to systematically exterminate Jews, yet opened perverse "museums" of "decadent" Jewish art (which, ironically, were very popular). The astonishingly systematic yet spontaneous attempts to *expunge* our very existence from the historical record—through silence, deliberate distortion, and mendacious interpretation—have very few precise parallels: one thinks of some of Stalin's more bizarre attempts at rewriting history or the nearly successful extermination of the Albigensians, even in memory. Even the cynical will be startled by the catalogue of lies briefly reviewed by John Boswell in his brilliant and seminal work, *Christianity, Social Tolerance and Homosexuality*. To quote one of the more amusing instances: "Sometimes their anxiety to reinterpret or disguise accounts of homosexuality has induced translators to inject wholly new concepts into texts, as when the translators of a Hittite law apparently regulating homosexual marriage insert words which completely alter its meaning or when Graves 'translates' a nonexistent clause in Suetonius to suggest that a law prohibits homosexual acts."

When one reflects that the Stalinist scholars worked under the threat of totalitarian terror, that the Albigensian Crusades were fueled by a wave of popular hysteria that was transitory, if devastating, and contrasts these to the calm, systematic, uncoerced, uncoordinated, utterly pervasive, enduring, and relentless attempt to destroy, falsify, and denigrate gay history, paranoia seems a sane response. What are we to do with people who will go to such lengths as to doctor the records of a Hittite civilization that flourished three-and-a-half thousand years ago?

The attempt to reclaim gay history, so ably argued and exemplified by Robert K. Martin (on Hart Crane) and Simon Karlinsky (on Diaghilev) recently in the pages of *Christopher Street*, will be accomplished only in the teeth of intense resistance by the straight scholarly establishment. Any ground won will be bitterly contested; we can expect them to get truly vicious as inroads are made. This struggle to get our history back is enormously important, for the past brings us possibility, and possibility gives us the psychological space that can prevent our suffocation in the present oppression.

In this regard it is important to note that violence *can* destroy the past along with the spirit. Force *can* destroy culture, as Simone Weil pointed out. The past can be distorted, even obliterated; it has no force of its own to preserve itself. The truth will not out in any automatic way. It is foolish in the extreme to believe that gay liberation will *inevitably* triumph.

*Proposition 6*

> All gays are born into a
> straight world and socialized
> to be straight; consequently,
> we have internalized the enemy,
> and all political struggle must be
> simultaneously a self-criticism
> and self-invention.

*Corollary:*

> *Self*-criticism does not mean criticism by gays of other gays
> who are perceived to be different, as Steve Wolf seemed to
> assume in a recent *Christopher Street* Guestward called
> "The New Gay Party Line."

The controversy kicked up by *Bent* over whether in fact the Nazis assigned the Jews or the gays to a lower circle of hell was mostly beside the point. It would be important to know exactly how the Nazis treated gays and how this compared and contrasted with the treatment of other groups—although it is morally tacky for any group to try to lay claims to preeminence in suffering in the face of the Holocaust. Sherman's dramatic point was quite different: all gays had been raised as straights; in terms of the play, every queer had internalized a Nazi within and therefore had a spiritual fifth column that could become a collaborator. When Max denies his gay self, denies his "friend" Rudy, fucks the dead twelve-year-old girl to prove he's straight, he has collaborated with the Nazis in his own spiritual extermination, the point Horst eventually teaches him. For Horst, spiritual extermination is worse than physical extermination.

To the Jew the Nazi is other, an external, if insanely malevolent, agent of destruction. To the "bent" the straight can never be so totally external.

*Proposition 7*

> The elemental gay emotional
> experience is the question:
> "Am I the only one?"
> The feeling of being "different,"
> and our response to it,
> dominates our inner lives.

The gradual or sudden but always unnerving awareness that one is "different" leads to the fear of being the only one. Gays emerge *as gay* in this trauma. One suspects that it haunts gay life in countless subtle ways that we have not begun to trace. One wonders if the extraordinary fear of rejection that dominates the social interactions in gay bars—and that appears so senseless, since we have all been rejected many times and know from experience that it is certainly not devastating—is nothing more than a replay of adolescent psychological scenarios, when natural sexual desire threatened to expose one as "different" and invited the devastating possibility of total rejection, even *and especially* by those "best friends" to whom one was most attracted. This undermining of sexual and affectional preference, putting into question what one *knows* with immediacy and certainty, traumatizes a person's integrity to the point of making one feel that one's very being is somehow "wrong."

This assault on the integrity of the self, which every gay experiences, should never be underestimated. It is the basic tactic our weirdly homophobic culture uses to destroy us—first isolate, then terrorize, then make disappear by *self*-denial.

As our archetypal emotional donnybrook, it also helps to explain many things in the gay world—gay pornography, for instance, is by and large a positive fantasy fulfillment that counteracts the nightmarish fears of our adolescent years and, as such, is politically progressive.

*Proposition 8*

"Only within the framework
of a people can a man
live as a man without exhausting
himself." (Hannah Arendt)

If society tries to destroy us by first isolating us, it follows that what is necessary to fight back is not only defiance but the acknowledgment of a community and the construction of a world. Individual defiance may lead to heroism—as we can see in the cases of Quentin Crisp and Jean Genet—but, while we should honor our heroes, the cost is too high. Few individuals have the integrity or the energy to sustain the violence to the soul and the consequent psychological deformations that heroism entails.

The further construction and consolidation of the gay ghetto is an immediate and necessary political objective. The singularity of the gay situation makes this "ghetto" unique, generating perplexities we have barely begun to address and rendering parallels to the experience of other groups dubious at best. But this should not obscure the fact that *ghetto* is another word for *world* and that *coming out* means asserting our right to appear in the world as who we are. As Walter Lippmann observed (if not practiced): "Man must be at peace with the sources of his life. If he is ashamed of them, if he is at war with them, they will haunt him forever. They will rob him of the basis of assurance, will leave him an interloper in the world."

From the blacks and the colonized we can learn much about the pain of being interlopers in the world, "invisible men," but we should also learn that if we want to live in the world and not in the closet, we must create that world ourselves on every level. It will not be handed to us on a silver platter. We need to create networks of friendships, love relationships, public places and institutions, neighborhoods, art, and literature. A gay culture is a political necessity for our survival.

*Proposition 9*

Gay politics (using politics in
its narrow meaning) is a
politics of pure principle.

For us there is no "social question." We are not asking for a bigger slice of the pie but for justice. We do not require social programs, jobs, day-care centers, educational and professional quotas, or any of the other legitimate demands of previously exploited minority groups. Our demands will not cost the body politic one cent. We demand only the freedom to be who we are. The fact that this demand, which takes away nothing from anyone else, is met with such obstinate resistance is a noteworthy indication of how deep-seated is the hostility against us.

On the other hand, we could expect that gay politics has its best chance in countries that are constitutional republics, where the belief that justice is the ultimate source of authority and legitimacy for the government gives us a powerful lever against the prejudice of society. It seems to me no accident that gay politics and gay culture have arisen first and most strongly in the United States. This is the only "nation" I know of that was brought into being by dissidents; whatever revisionist history may teach us are the facts of the case, the enormous authority the image of the Pilgrims and the Founding Fathers has for this country should not be underestimated. It often seems that non-American observers simply cannot understand our feeling that *as Americans* it is our *right* to be faggots if we choose—or as historian and lesbian novelist Noretta Koertge puts it: "Being American means being able to paint my mailbox purple if I want." Invoking the ultimate principles—if not realities—of this country is one of our most promising tactics, and should be explored and emphasized.

*Proposition 10*
> We have *no natural allies*
> and therefore cannot rely on
> the assistance of any group.

We have only tactical allies—people who do not want barbarous things done to us because they fear the same things may someday be done to them. Tactical allies come into being when there is a perceived convergence of self-interest between two groups. One can accomplish much in politics with tactical allies, as witness the long alliance between blacks and Jews, but there are limits that emerge when the group-interests diverge, as witness the split between blacks and Jews over school decentralization in New York City.

A natural ally would be someone who is happy we are here, rather than someone who is unhappy at the way we are being treated. It would seem that the most we can expect, at least in the immediate future, is a tolerance based on decency. No one, no matter how decent, seems glad that gays exist, even when they may be enjoying works inspired by our sensibility. As far as I can see, even our best straight friends will never be thankful that we are gay in the way we ourselves (in our better moments) are thankful we are gay. This is nothing to get maudlin over. It does, however, sometimes seem to limit communication—the sharing that is the essence of friendship—with straights. It is a rare straight friend to whom one can say, "I'm so glad I'm gay because otherwise I never would have gotten the chance to love Ernie," and not draw a blank, if not bewildered and uncomfortable, reaction. It is understandable that they do not see it as something to celebrate—but we should.

On the personal level, it is generally unlikely that one's straight family or friends will easily learn genuine acceptance; luckily it would appear that they can, notwithstanding, often learn love. For our part, the paranoia that this situation tends naturally to generate should be rigorously controlled.

*Proposition 11*
> Our political enemies are
> of two kinds:
> those who want us not to exist
> and those who want us not to appear.

Those who want us not to exist are the well-known, old-fashioned bigots, who would stamp us out, apply shock therapy or terroristic behavior modification, cordon us off and separate us from society, and ultimately try to kill us as the Nazis did. Fortunately these bigots are also a threat to many other segments of society and a number of tactical allies can be mobilized in the fight against them. Bigots are essentially bullies, and this bullying impulse seems to be exacerbated to the point of massacre by the lack of resistance. This suggests that the best response to them is probably a violent one: unchecked aggression seems to feed on itself and simply pick up velocity, like one of Lear's rages. I suspect that when epithets are hurled at one in the street, it is best to shout epithets back; trying to ignore them with dignity or responding with overt fear seems only to intensify the hostility. Although I am open to correction on this, I have the feeling that the *safest* response to physical assault is fighting back; the bruises one may incur seem to me preferable to the corrosive rage that follows from helplessness, and I suspect they might avoid a truly dangerous stomping. In short, bullies become worse bullies when they are unchecked and the cost of resistance is probably worth it in the long run.

Those who want us not to appear are more subtle and probably more dangerous, since it is harder to mobilize tactical allies against them. This seemed to me the most significant aspect of the Anita Bryant phenomenon. By carefully explaining that she was only against overt gay behavior—the "flaunting" of our life-style and the consequent "recruitment"—she managed to seem reasonable to a large segment of the public; by disavowing any McCarthy-type witch hunt, she managed to avoid tripping the wire that would have sent large parts of the Jewish community of Miami onto red alert. The difficulty of countering these people successfully is rooted in the fact that we *can* pass, a characteristic that distinguishes us from other minority groups, and is further compounded by the fact that when you come right down to it *everyone* would be more comfortable if we remained in the closet except ourselves.

These matters require much more consideration than we have yet given them. We cannot rely forever on the stupidity of our opponents—for instance, in the overreaching language of the Briggs Initiative in California, which led to its rejection for First Amendment reasons that were so obvious they even penetrated the mind of the public. It is urgent to give tactical and strategic thought to these matters—always keeping in mind the fact that in their heart of hearts the overwhelming majority of the American people would prefer us back in the closet. Our only hope is to make it clear that that would be so costly that they will not be willing to pay the price.

*Proposition 12*
> "The only remedy
> for powerlessness is power"
> (Charles Ortleb).

Economic exploitation, one of the great nineteenth-century themes of political discourse, has largely been replaced in our own day by the discussion of oppression. Exploitation means basically that someone is stealing from you; oppression is essentially a matter of invisibility, of feeling weightless and insubstantial, without voice or impact in the world. Blacks, the colonized, women, and gays all share this experience of being a ghost in their own country, the disorienting alienation of feeling they are not actually there. This psychological experience is the subjective correlate to the objective fact of powerlessness.

It is odd that the desire for power has for many an unpleasant aura about it, for powerlessness is a true crime against the human spirit and undercuts the possibility of justice among people. In his *Inquiry Concerning the Principles of Morals*, David Hume lays this out quite clearly, albeit without being aware of it, when he speculates that "were there a species intermingled with men which, though rational, were possessed of such inferior strength, both of body and mind, that they were incapable of all resistance and could never, upon the highest provocation, make us feel the effects of their resentment, the necessary consequence, I think, is that we . . . should not, properly speaking, lie under any restraint of justice with regard to them. . . . Our intercourse with them could not be called society, which supposes a degree of equality, but absolute command on the one side, and servile obedience on the other. . . . Our permission is the only tenure by which they hold their possessions, our compassion and kindness the only check by which they [sic] curb our lawless will . . . the restraints of justice . . . would never have place in so unequal a confederacy."

Well, we know there are such "creatures intermingled with men"— women first of all, and the colonized races, as well as homosexuals, Jews, and mental patients. It is truly strange that this philosopher, who seems to think he is idly speculating, was quite clearly laying out the premises of the power structure that at that very moment was subjugating so many groups of people. And with two centuries of hindsight, it should be clear to all of us just how effective their "compassion and kindness" is as a check against their "lawless will." If we have to rely on "the laws of humanity" to convince them "to give gentle usage to these creatures," we will stay precisely where we have been, under their heel being stomped on.

I do not pretend to understand the origin and mechanics of this strange social system in which we live. But it seems to me it should be abundantly clear to even the dimmest wit that without power you will not get justice. How anybody could rely on "compassion and kindness" after looking around at the world we live in is beyond me. "Moderate" gays who think we can achieve tolerance by respectability seem to me willfully ignorant of our own history, as well as the history of other oppressed groups. They are the court Jews of our time, however good their subjective intentions.

Straights who object to our daily increasing visibility are basically objecting to the assertion of power implicit in that phenomenon. They would prefer that we continue to rely on their "compassion and kindness" and correctly sense that our refusal to do so directly insults them. With their record on the matter it is hard to imagine why they are surprised. In fact, our extraordinary explosion into visibility, the spontaneous and visible assertion of our sexual identity that constitutes the clone look is politically valuable. Not only are we more visible to each other, we are more visible to them. Of course, one would naturally expect a backlash at this point; it is virtually unknown in history for any group to give up power over any other without a struggle.

*Proposition 13*
>Gay life is an issue *only for gays;*
>whenever straights address the
>question, they are attacking us.

The quality of gay life is obviously an issue for us. There are many aspects of the gay world, many peculiarities of gay life that are disturbing; we should face them and, keeping an open mind, try to understand and evaluate them as possibilities for ourselves. (This does not mean attacking gays who choose to live differently than we do; it means deciding how *we* want to live, not how other people should.) But this discussion is totally off limits to straights.

Whenever straights, usually posing as friendly but concerned liberals, address the "issue" of gay life, they are actually raising the question of whether we should exist. Curiously enough, the answer is *inevitably* no. This question is not raised about blacks and Jews, at least not in polite company, because its murderous implications are at once evident. For instance, in Midge Decter's recent hilarious attack on us in *Commentary* ("The Boys on the Beach," September 1980), one finds the following: "*Know them as a group.* No doubt this will in itself seem to many of the uninitiated a bigoted formulation. Yet one cannot even begin to get at the *truth about homosexuals* [my italics] without this kind of generalization." To see what is being said here, simply substitute "the truth about Jews" or "the truth about blacks" and reread.

Straights who raise homosexuality *as an issue* are attacking us—about this we should not be confused. From Joseph Epstein's infamous article in *Harper's*—in which this man, a father himself, decides that he would rather see his son *dead* than homosexual—to Paul Cowan's shamefully bigoted review of *States of Desire* in the *New York Times Sunday Book Review*, the position is always the same. Straights who earn their living as cultural commentators, who try to set out terms for public discussion, display an unholy fear of being peripheralized by us. Perhaps more clearly (not more basically) than any other minority group or culture gays threaten their cultural power, which is based on preserving and policing a cultural uniformity. To acknowledge diversity or plurality seems to threaten the very existence of their own values. This is sick. We may be bent, but these people are truly twisted. Nevertheless they are dangerous; they control the organs of cultural definition in this country, and they have the power to confuse us with their disguised fanaticism.

*Proposition 14*

> It is absurd to believe that
> after coming out we are no longer
> conditioned by the virulent hatred
> of gays apparently endemic
> to this culture. Homophobia is an
> ever-present threat and pressure,
> both externally and internally.

I suspect that by now I will have lost many readers who will feel that these comments are too militant, overblown, or emotional. One of the problems peculiar to this subject matter is that it is often hard actually to believe in the reality of gay oppression. The hatred of gays makes so little *sense* to us, seems so uncalled for and pointless, so extremely neurotic *and* so easily avoided (by "passing") that we tend to dismiss it from our perception of reality. How very dangerous this can be is apparent to any student of Nazism. In the thirties most Germans *and* Jews refused to take seriously Hitler's quite explicit and well-known intentions toward the Jews because it was too much of an outrage to common sense. "It's only rhetoric, no one could be that mad." Even during the war, Bruno Bettelheim and other survivors have reported people refusing to believe their first-hand accounts of the concentration camps, to the point where they themselves doubted the reality of the experiences they had so harrowingly survived.

Something similar happens when one steps back to reflect on the clearly documented evidence of homophobia—let us not take the melodramatic examples of shock treatment and forcible sexual reprogramming but the purely prosaic refusal of the City Council of New York, one of the country's liberal strongholds, repeatedly, year after year, to vote civil rights for gays. I suggest that not to give this simple fact its due weight is willfully to blind ourselves to the reality of the situation in which we live.

It is even more painful when this happens in our immediate private life. Often a chance remark or a passingly uncomfortable comment by a good friend turns out to have such devastating implications that we prefer not to think about it. And if we do think it through, the results are so harsh we do not know what to do with them. To dwell on it seems willfully fanatic, slightly hysterical, or "oversensitive," as straight friends are fond of saying. It is less painful to let it go, to go along, to accommodate ourselves to these people in spite of their quirks because we value their company and friendship.

The willing suspension of belief in the reality of gay oppression, however, has serious and destructive consequences. Chief among them is the widespread predisposition to believe that once we have accomplished the psychological ordeal known as coming out, we are suddenly and magically free of the negative conditioning of our homophobic society. This is obviously absurd. Nevertheless we tend to consider our problems—from alcoholism and unfulfilling sexual obsession to workaholism, inability to handle emotional intimacy, cynicism, the self-destructive negativism of attitude, and on and on—as simply our own fault. At most, we will trace them to our inability "to accept ourselves." The point of the matter is *no one starts off with an inability to accept himself*; this emerges *only* after we find other people unable or unwilling to accept us. The conditioning of our homophobic society runs deep and is not easily eradicated; unless explicitly acknowledged and dealt with, it will continue to distort our psyches and our lives. We urgently need to understand the ways these destructive influences continue to pervade our immediate existence, to trace their impact on our behavior in bars and in baths, in the office and in bed, carefully and *without preconceptions* distinguishing what is useful for survival, if not admirable in an ideal society, from what can only demoralize us further. In this connection, I suspect we have, by and large, seriously underestimated the help gay novelists have offered us in books like *Dancer from the Dance*, *Faggots*, and *Rushes*.


*Proposition 15*
> The cultural, legal, and
> psychological assault on gays
> so weirdly characteristic of our
> society has not ceased, and there
> is no reason to believe it will cease
> in the immediate future.

Theoretical analyses have absolutely no impact on any social reality. Even the understanding of our concrete situation in the world that they hopefully engender will not of itself change the situation.

A black friend of mine said recently, "If writing a book exposing racism would end it, we would have ended it ourselves a long time ago." All the understanding of homophobia in the world will not make it disappear. We are not omnipotent; neither as individuals nor as a group do we control reality, which is something we share with all those with whom we share the globe. No psychological, interpersonal, intellectual, or spiritual achievements on our part alone will eradicate homophobia, for the problem does not rest only with us—"the problem is not so much homosexual desire as the fear of homosexuality."

What we *can* do is face up to the reality of the situation and begin to change it in our own case. In the sixties there was much talk of "making the revolution"; many people seemed to think that somehow this one apocalyptic event would result in the transfiguration of human society. But the revolution never came. The gay "revolution"—if that term should ever be used—can only be made in the daily lives of each one of us. What could gay liberation possibly be but a change in the quality of our actual lives? For better or worse, we create the face of gay liberation in every sexual encounter and love affair we have. With every circle of loyal gay friends established we are manifesting the gay world (the achievements we have been making in this area are documented in Ed White's *States of Desire: Travels in Gay America*). As we individually come to terms with our straight friends and help them to come to terms with us, we help to dissolve homophobia. While this prospect is not as dramatic or as emotionally satisfying as a "revolution," it does have the enormous advantage of being realistic. We are *already* in the midst of changing our lives and our world, but it will not happen automatically or without our individual participation.

*Proposition 16*

> "We gay people are the alchemists,
> the magicians, of our time.
> We take the toxins of a poisonous
> age, the nihilism that is given us,
> and turn it into a balm that heals.
> We heal ourselves and in that
>  we are an object-lesson
> for the others"
> (declared by a lesbian divinity student).

In the modern tradition, radical political theory has always assumed that society would be transformed by some group within that society which "carried" the revolutionary impulse. When Archimedes discovered the mathematical laws of leverage, he boasted that given a place to stand, he could move the entire earth. When modern political theorists thought they had discovered the laws of society, they assumed that with the proper lever the world could be transformed. The most persuasive scenario asserted that the proletariat, a class totally alienated—that is, outside the society—with "nothing to lose but its chains," would be the lever that would move the earth. But this theory forgot what Archimedes knew, that there was no such "Archimedian point" on which to stand; the voting of war credits by the German Social Democratic party in 1914 proved once and for all that the proletariat did not stand outside society; they were as jingoistic as any other group. The truly great vision of political transformation that had animated the West since the French Revolution died with that act.

But as always the debris of broken dreams lived on to confuse the minds of men. There is a constant tendency on the part of people involved in the struggle of their own group for liberation—blacks, feminists, the colonized, gays—to assume that their group is marked by history to be the liberators of all humanity, the class that carries the revolutionary impulse. It is an understandable error: since no group can be liberated unless the entire society is liberated (because of the simple fact that it is always the *others* who oppress the oppressed, therefore oppression will not cease until the oppressors cease being oppressive), it is easy enough to reserve the argument and say that the liberation of the oppressed group will liberate society. Unfortunately reality does not make such logical errors. Bertrand Russell's witty explanation of Bolshevism—since the proletariat has throughout history always been oppressed by other classes, it is only fair that they now have the chance to oppress everyone else—seems more to the point, as we can see in the unpleasant instance of the Vietnamese actions in Cambodia.

At this point in time, it would be silly and tedious for gays to make the same erroneous assertions. Gay liberation has no chance in hell of liberating society sexually. (The reverse argument is, of course, valid, if tautological; the sexual liberation of society would indeed entail the liberation of gays. The problem is only: what will cause the sexual liberation of society, who will bring this about? You see how one could fall into thinking about the agent or carrier of historical change.) Gay liberation will not be the carrier of the revolutionary idea if for no other reason than the fact that by "revolutionary idea" is meant the revaluation of all values, and values are not "things" that can be "carried" like shoulder bags or diseases. A discussion of the nature of value, however, would take us too far afield.

If gay liberation is not going to liberate society, has it any meaning beyond that of promoting the self-interests of the individuals who make up this particular group? (I hasten to add that defending and promoting the self-interest of any oppressed group is in itself totally justifiable.) I think the answer is affirmative, if somewhat speculative at this point.

It has been known for well over a century now that something is drastically wrong with our culture; our values seem to be working in reverse. Western civilization looks more and more like the sorcerer's apprentice: it has unleashed powers that threaten to overwhelm it. Nihilism is the name usually applied to this phenomenon. Our values have turned against us and threaten devastation if not extinction. This sounds rhetorical. It is not. It is a simple description of the current state of affairs, as a moment's uncomfortable reflection on the Holocaust, the threat of nuclear annihilation, the consequences of pollution and irreversible ecological intervention, genetic engineering, or a dozen other phenomena reported daily in the papers, makes quite clear. We need a revaluation of all our values, but how can this be accomplished if there is no Archimedian point on which to stand? If the salt has lost its savor, wherewith shall it be salted?

I suggest that the complex, subtle, everyday transformation of values that we gays have been engaged in for the last ten years, the self-renewal that constitutes gay liberation, is a creative response to the viciously negative values of our culture. As such, it would be *a part* of that urgently necessary revaluation of all values and could serve not as a historical catalyst that will save anybody else but as an example of what is necessary and as a welcome ally to those already engaged by this challenge. In the struggle for gay liberation we come home to ourselves and our world and take our place among the ranks of decent and responsible people everywhere who stand together at this decisive moment in humanity's career on the planet.

No doubt other propositions regarding the contemporary gay situation might be added to the sixteen I have sketched. My purpose, however, is not to be exhaustive but to give examples of the type of matters we must think about if we are to grasp the dynamics of our own lives. These are things which directly affect all gay men; what may seem at times overly theoretical or abstract is nonetheless an attempt to come to grips with the dilemmas that structure our sexual experience, shape our patterns of socializing, and all too often distort our psyches and blight our loves while simultaneously bringing us a reckless joy at being alive. These are matters that our writers and artists think about, as well as philosophers and gays on the street—whether they know it or not. They are important. For if we do not measure up to the unprecedented novelty of our current situation, we will piss away our lives in the confusion and evasions of a darkened epoch.

# ABOUT THE AUTHORS

DENNIS ALTMAN is the author of *The Homosexualization of America; The Americanization of the Homosexual, Coming Out in the Seventies* and *Homosexual: Oppression and Liberation.*

ROB BAKER is the author of *Bette Midler* and a former editor and critic for the *Soho News, Dance Magazine,* the *Chicago Tribune,* and the *New York Daily News.*

GILLES BARBEDETTE is a French journalist and the coauthor of *Paris Gay, 1925.*

ARTHUR BELL is the author of *Dancing the Gay Lib Blues* and *Kings Don't Mean a Thing,* a columnist for the *Village Voice,* and a widely published magazine writer.

MARK BLASIUS has taught at Princeton University, New York University, and the City University of New York. He is currently completing a study in political philosophy.

CHARLES BOULTENHOUSE has been published in *Poetry, The Nation, Art News Annual, Film Culture, Kulchur,* and other periodicals.

LARRY BUSH writes from Washington, D.C. on gay politics and national affairs: he has been published in the *New York Times,* the *Washington Star,* the *Village Voice,* and *Christopher Street* and is a regular contributor to the *New York Native* and the *Advocate.*

MICHAEL DENNENY is the author of *Lovers: The Story of Two Men,* and an editor at St. Martin's Press. One of the founders of *Christopher Street* magazine, he is an associate editor of *Christopher Street* and the *New York Native.*

TIM DLUGOS is the author of *Entre Nous* (a collection of poems); his articles and reviews have appeared in the *Washington Post Book World, Soho News,* and many other publications.

T.P.N. DODGE is the one-time-use pen name of Rick Fiala, currently art director of *Skiing* magazine.

MARTIN DUBERMAN, Distinguished Professor of History at City University of New York, is the author of nine books, winner of the Bancroft Prize, a finalist for the National Book Award, and was awarded a prize by the National Academy for "contributions to literature."

AARON FRICKE made national news when he took a gay date to his high school prom. His full story is told in his book *Reflections of a Rock Lobster.*

''G'' is the pseudonym of a writer who lives in New York City.

JOHNNY GREENE is associate editor of *Inquiry Magazine* and previously worked for *Harper's.*

WALLACE HAMILTON is the author of *Kevin, David at Olivet,* and *Coming Out.* He has written many plays, the most recent being *Friend of the Family* and *Invitation to a Bear Baiting.*

GUY HOCQUENGHEM was one of the founders of the French Gay Liberation movement, the author of *Homosexual Desire* and the recent, widely acclaimed novel *L'Amour en Relief.* He has made a film, *Race d'Ep,* about the history of homosexuality, and writes for the Parisian daily *Liberation.*

ANDREW HOLLERAN is the author of *Dancer from the Dance* and a frequent contributor to *Christopher Street* and the *New York Native.*

DAVID JACKSON, who lives most of the year in Athens, is the author of *The Day Roosevelt Died, Two Odds and an End,* and the O. Henry Prize–winning story "The English Gardens." He has been published in the *Partisan Review* and the *New York Times Book Review,* and was a friend of Auden's for over twenty years.

SIMON KARLINSKY is the author of *The Sexual Labyrinth of Nikolai Gogol* and *Marina Tvetaeva,* and the editor of *Chekhov's Life and Thought* and *The Nabokov-Wilson Letters.*

GREGG KILDAY is a journalist specializing in Hollywood and the movie industry.

SEYMOUR KLEINBERG is the author of *Alienated Affections: Being Gay in America* and the editor of *The Other Persuasion.*

JEAN LE BITOUX lives in France.

NEIL ALAN MARKS is a regular contributor to *Christopher Street* and the *New York Native.*

ROBERT K. MARTIN is the author of *The Homosexual Tradition in American Poetry* and coeditor of *E. M. Forster: Centenary Reevaluations;* he lives in Montreal and teaches at Concordia University.

LAWRENCE MASS is a primary care physician in New York City, and a contributing editor to *Christopher Street* and the *New York Native;* he has served as newsletter editor of the Gay Caucus of Members of the American Psychiatric Association.

CHARLES ORTLEB, founder and publisher of *Christopher Street* and the *New York Native,* is a writer and poet. He is the author of six books of cartoons (including three collections of gay cartoons: *And God Bless Uncle Harry, Relax This Book Is Only a Phase You're Going Through,* and *Le Gay Ghetto*), and has recently turned to song writing—his lyrics, set to music by Tom Steele, the editor of *Christopher Street,* have been performed by the irrepressible Mr. Steele in several cabarets around Manhattan.

FELICE PICANO is the author of *An Asian Minor, The Lure, Late in the Season, Eyes, The Deformity Lover and Other Poems;* editor of *A True Likeness: Lesbian and Gay Writing Today;* founder and publisher of The Sea Horse Press; and book editor of the *New York Native.*

RICHARD PLANT is the author of the forthcoming *The Other Solution,* a study of gays in the Third Reich, and of many essays on film and Germany. He was born in Frankfurt, Germany, studied film under Kracauer, and received a Ph.D. in history and literature from Basel University.

JOHN PRESTON is the author of *Frannie: The Queen of Provincetown,* former editor of the *Advocate* and a member of the National Book Critics Circle. He lives in Portland, Maine, where he is a correspondent for the *Portland Chronicle,* and he is a contributing editor for the *New York Native.*

NED ROREM, a composer, won the Pulitzer Prize for music in 1976. He is the author of eight books, including *The Paris Diary,* and *Pure Contraption. Setting the Tone,* his ninth, will be published in 1983.

RANDY SHILTS is the author of *The Mayor of Castro Street: The Life and Times of Harvey Milk.* A reporter for the *San Francisco Chronicle,* he has covered San Francisco city hall and the gay community since 1975 as a newspaper reporter and as a television correspondent for stations KQED and KTVU.

GEORGE STAMBOLIAN is a contributing editor to *Christopher Street* and the *New York Native.*

GORE VIDAL, author of *Creation* and *Myra Breckenridge,* lives in Italy and the United States.

EDMUND WHITE is the author of *Forgetting Elena, Nocturnes for the King of Naples,* and *States of Desire: Travels in Gay America,* in which both pieces contained herein appeared in slightly different form. His most recent novel is *A Boy's Own Story.*